The shift to a four-day public school week to save money cannot be academically
justified, argues the editorial board of the *USA Today* newspaper. Not so, responds
Gregory A. Schmidt, a school superintendent who defends four-day modified
schedules now adopted in eighteen states.

11 Description 323

Not only did Mom throw a mean fastball in her younger days, but at almost eighty
she continues to achieve new goals with determination and spirit, as described by
her son Cliff Schneider in this charming tribute.

Eighth Edition

Steps to Writing Well

with Additional Readings

Jean Wyrick

Professor Emerita
Colorado State University

WADSWORTH
CENGAGE Learning™

Australia • Brazil • Japan • Korea • Mexico • Singapore • Spain • United Kingdom • United States

WADSWORTH
CENGAGE Learning™

Steps to Writing Well with Additional Readings, Eighth Edition

Jean Wyrick

Publisher: Monica Eckman

Acquistions Editor: Margaret Leslie

Development Editor: Laurie Dobson

Assistant Editor: Amy Haines

Editorial Assistant: Elizabeth Ramsey

Media Editor: Amy Gibbons

Marketing Manager: Jennifer Zourdos

Marketing Coordinator: Ryan Ahern

Marketing Communications Manager: Stacey Purviance

Content Project Managers: Corinna Dibble and Aimee Chevrette Bear

Art Director: Jill Ort

Print Buyer: Susan Spencer

Permissions Editor: Katie Huha

Photo Manager: Leitha Etheridge-Sims

Production Service: Lachina Publishing Services

Compositor: Lachina Publishing Services

© 2011, 2007, 2004 Wadsworth, Cengage Learning

ALL RIGHTS RESERVED. No part of this work covered by the copyright herein may be reproduced, transmitted, stored, or used in any form or by any means graphic, electronic, or mechanical, including but not limited to photocopying, recording, scanning, digitizing, taping, Web distribution, information networks, or information storage and retrieval systems, except as permitted under Section 107 or 108 of the 1976 United States Copyright Act, without the prior written permission of the publisher.

For product information and technology assistance, contact us at **Cengage Learning Customer & Sales Support, 1-800-354-9706**

For permission to use material from this text or product, submit all requests online at **www.cengage.com/permissions** Further permissions questions can be e-mailed to **permissionrequest@cengage.com**

Library of Congress Control Number: 2009934770

ISBN-13: 978-0-495-90150-1
ISBN-10: 0-495-90150-4

Wadsworth
20 Channel Center Street
Boston, MA 02210
USA

Cengage Learning is a leading provider of customized learning solutions with office locations around the globe, including Singapore, the United Kingdom, Australia, Mexico, Brazil, and Japan. Locate your local office at **international.cengage.com/region**

Cengage Learning products are represented in Canada by Nelson Education, Ltd.

For your course and learning solutions, visit **www.cengage.com**

Purchase any of our products at your local college store or at our preferred online store **www.ichapters.com**

WITHDRAWN

Printed in the United States of America
1 2 3 4 5 6 7 12 11 10 09

CONTENTS

Part One The Basics of the Short Essay 1

1 Prewriting 3

2 The Thesis Statement 31

WS 2274782 6

808.
042
WYR

032012

5 Drafting and Revising: Creative Thinking, Critical Thinking 95

6 Effective Sentences 125

17 Writing about Visual Arts 485

18 Writing about Film 505

LIST OF ARTWORKS

LIST OF ADVERTISEMENTS

TO THE TEACHER

The eighth edition of *Steps to Writing Well with Additional Readings* has been written for teachers of composition who have had trouble finding a textbook that students can easily understand. Too many books on today's market, these teachers rightfully complain, are still unnecessarily complex, dry, or massive for the majority of students. Written simply, in an informal style and addressed to the student, this textbook offers a step-by-step guide to writing a variety of 500-to-800-word essays. The combination of concise, practical advice, a number of student and professional samples, and a brief handbook should provide more than enough helpful information for students enrolled in a one-semester course, without intimidating them.

This edition continues the tradition of plentiful new artwork throughout the chapters, including over fifty paintings and photographs, many used as exercises and writing prompts for today's visually oriented students. Two other features new to this edition also appear throughout the text. Because current research suggests that many students may improve their writing skills by working with classmates in **NEW** small groups or pairs, this edition now offers over two dozen collaborative classroom activities and assignments, presented in every chapter of Parts One through **NEW** Four. A new discussion of collaboration, with guidelines for small-group work, has been added to Chapter 5's advice on peer editing workshops, to help students participate effectively in a larger variety of exercises. Both teachers and students **NEW** may appreciate this edition's helpful new design feature, a diamond-shaped cross-reference symbol [◆] that will alert readers to related information (or additional practices) in other parts of the text.

Although many parts of the book have been revised or expanded for this edition, its organization remains essentially the same. Part One offers advice on "The Basics of the Short Essay"; Part Two discusses "Purposes, Modes, and Strategies"; Part Three focuses on "Special Assignments"; and Part Four presents "A Concise Handbook." Part Five contains thirty-four additional readings. This textbook still begins with the essay "To the Student," which not only argues that students can learn to write better with practice and dedication but also gives them a number of practical reasons why they *should* learn to write better.

Part One, containing eight chapters, guides students through the process of writing the short essay. Chapter 1, on prewriting, stresses finding the proper attitude ("the desire to communicate") and presents helpful suggestions for selecting a subject. This chapter then offers students ten methods for finding a significant purpose and focus for their essays. In addition, a section on using the journal explains more than a dozen ways that students may improve their skills by writing a variety of nonthreatening—and even playful—assignments. The section on audience, including an exercise addressing the appeals of advertising, should also help student writers identify their particular readers and communicate more effectively with them. After finding a topic and identifying their audience, students are ready for Chapter 2, devoted almost entirely to a discussion of the thesis statement. This

chapter first explains the role of the "working thesis" in early drafts and then clearly outlines what a good thesis is and isn't by presenting a host of examples to illustrate the advice. Also included in this chapter is an explanation of the "essay map," an organizational tool that can help students structure their essays and plan their body paragraphs.

Chapter 3 discusses in detail the requirements of good body paragraphs: topic sentences, unity, order and coherence, adequate development, use of specific detail, and logical sequence. Over forty paragraphs illustrate both strengths and weaknesses of student writing. These paragraphs are not complex literary or professional excerpts but rather well-designed, precise examples of the principles under examination, written on subjects students can understand and appreciate. This chapter twice provides the opportunity for students to see how a topic may progress from a working thesis statement to an informal essay outline, which in turn helps produce well-developed paragraphs in the body of an essay. To complete the overview of the short essay, Chapter 4 explains, through numerous samples, the creation of good introductions, conclusions, and titles.

Chapter 5, "Drafting and Revising: Creative Thinking, Critical Thinking," focuses on the revision process. Because too many students still think of revision as merely proofreading their essays rather than as an essential, recursive activity, this chapter emphasizes the importance of revision in all good writing. These pages offer a system for revising drafts in stages, including discussions of drafting and revising by hand and on a computer. A section on critical thinking shows students how to analyze and evaluate their ideas and those of others and stresses the role of critical thinking skills in the selection of evidence for all writing assignments. A student essay annotated to illustrate a revision process is included, and, **NEW** in response to teachers' requests, this edition also expands the chapter's exercises with additional editing and proofreading practice.

NEW Shaped by current composition research, a new section in Chapter 5 on collaborative activities begins by explaining those types most commonly found in college writing classes, and why they might be helpful. Teachers may find it useful, for instance, to assign small-group exercises, peer editing, or team-writing to foster discussion, suggest new viewpoints, encourage audience awareness, teach critical thinking, promote revision, and polish editing skills, as well as offering practice in co-authored writing often required in the workplace. To complement the list of steps for effective participation in peer workshops, this chapter now con- **NEW** tains advice for students working in small groups. (Additional advice for teachers organizing workshop activities may be found in the updated Instructor's Manual.) The chapter ends with a popular section on beating Writer's Block.

Chapter 6, on effective sentences, emphasizes the importance of clarity, conciseness, and vividness, with nearly one hundred fifty sample sentences illustrat- **EXPANDED** ing the chapter's advice. An expanded section on fused sentences, comma splices, and fragments offers help resolving these common problems. Chapter 7, on word choice, presents practical suggestions for selecting accurate, appropriate words that are specific, memorable, and persuasive. This chapter also contains sec- **NEW** tions on avoiding sexist language and "bureaucratese," as well as a new discussion underscoring the importance of understanding appropriate audiences for texting abbreviations and Internet language.

Chapter 8, "The Reading-Writing Connection," maintains that by learning to read analytically, students can improve their own writing skills. The chapter contains step-by-step directions for reading and annotating essays and suggests many ways students may profit from studying the rhetorical choices of other writers. A professional essay, annotated according to these steps, is included, as well as guidance for writing summaries of reading selections. Another section offers students suggestions for effective participation in class discussions, with advice for improving comprehension and note-taking skills. Teachers may wish to assign this chapter before asking students to read the professional essays that appear throughout this textbook.

Each chapter in Part One contains samples and exercises, many new to this edition. As in the previous editions, the "Practicing What You've Learned" exercises follow each major section in each chapter so that both teacher and students may quickly discover if particular material needs additional attention. Moreover, by conquering small steps in the writing process, one at a time, students should feel more confident and should learn more rapidly. The Practices and the Assignments, which also follow each major section in these chapters, suggest class activities and frequently employ "peer teaching." Activities called "Applying What You've Learned to *Your* Writing" follow the exercises and assignments. Each of these activities encourages students to "follow through" by incorporating into a current draft the skill they have just read about and practiced. By following a three-step procedure—reading the advice in the text, practicing the advice through the exercises, and then applying the advice directly to their own prose—students should improve their writing processes. In addition, each of the chapters in Part One concludes with a summary, designed to help students review the important points in the material under study.

Part Two presents discussion of the kinds of essays students are most often asked to write. Chapter 9, on exposition, is divided into separate discussions of the expository strategies: example, process, comparison/contrast, definition, division and classification, and causal analysis. Discussions in Chapter 9 and the chapters on argument, description, and narration follow a similar format by offering the students (a) a clear definition of the mode (or strategy), explained with familiar examples; (b) practical advice on developing each essay; (c) warnings about common problems; (d) suggested essay topics; (e) a topic proposal sheet; (f) sample student essay(s) with marginal notes; (g) professional essay(s) followed by questions on content, structure, and style, writing suggestions, and a vocabulary list; (h) a revision worksheet to guide student writers through their rough drafts; and (i) a progress report. In the lists of suggested essay topics, each #20 offers one or more of the pictures in this book as a writing prompt. Teachers may choose from a new

NEW selection of paintings, photographs, and advertisements to encourage thoughtful essays organized in a variety of ways. (For quick reference, a complete list of the artworks and advertisements appears at the end of the Table of Contents.)

The seventeen student essays in this text should encourage student writers by showing them that others in their situation have indeed composed organized, well-developed essays. The student essays that appear here are not perfect; consequently, teachers may use them in class to generate suggestions for still more revision. The twenty-two professional readings in Parts Two and Three were also selected to spur class discussion and to illustrate the rhetorical principles presented throughout the text. (The process analysis and comparison/contrast sections of Chapter 9 contain two professional essays so that students may see examples of two commonly used methods of organization; both division and classification are also illustrated by professional writing.) Those professional readings in Parts Two and Three most popular with the users of the last edition have been retained; six selections are new to this edition.

NEW
NEW

Chapter 10 discusses the argumentative essay, presenting a new pair of professional essays with opposing views and new advertisements, selected to help students analyze rhetorical appeals and supporting evidence. Chapters 11 and 12, on writing description and narration, may be assigned prior to the expository strategies or may be used as supplementary material for any kind of writing incorporating descriptive language or extended example. Chapter 11 presents essays that illustrate description of a person, place, or thing. Both chapters contain visual art designed to help students understand the importance of vivid details in support of a dominant effect.

Although this text shows students how to master individual rhetorical strategies, one essay at a time, experienced writers often choose a combination, or blending, of strategies to best accomplish their purpose. "Writing Essays Using Multiple Strategies," Chapter 13, concludes Part Two by offering advice to writers who are ready to address more complex topics and essay organization. This chapter also contains both student and professional essays to illustrate clear use of multiple strategies to accomplish the writer's purpose.

Part Three, called "Special Assignments," allows instructors to design their composition courses in a variety of ways, perhaps by adding a research paper, a literary analysis, an in-class essay, a review of an artwork or movie, or a business writing assignment. Chapter 14, "Writing a Paper Using Research," has been extensively

NEW

revised for this edition. Illustrating a new research process by following a student from her topic selection to final essay, this chapter shows students how they may focus a subject, search for information in a variety of ways, choose and evaluate evidence, avoid plagiarism, and effectively incorporate and cite source material

UPDATED

in their essays. These pages contain updated discussions of electronic sources and present the very latest guidelines for both MLA and APA documentation formats, drawn from the organizations' recently revised (2009) style manuals. This chapter also explains primary research and includes practical advice for collecting material through interviews and questionnaires. In response to teachers' requests, the

NEW

chapter concludes with a student essay presented in its entirety in two forms, illustrating both current MLA and APA citations and references.

Chapter 15, "Writing in Class: Exams and 'Response' Essays," is designed to help students respond quickly and accurately to a variety of in-class assignments by understanding their task's purpose and by recognizing key directional words. Advice for successfully organizing and completing timed writing should also help decrease students' anxiety. Because so many composition courses today include some variation of the "summary-and-response" assignment (used not only as an in- or out-of-class essay but also as a placement or exit test), this chapter also addresses that kind of writing and offers a sample student essay.

"Writing about Literature," Chapter 16, discusses multiple ways literary selections may be used in the composition class, either as prompts for personal essays or for papers of literary analysis. Students are offered a series of suggestions for close reading of both poetry and short fiction. The chapter contains an annotated poem, an annotated short story, and two student essays analyzing those works. Additional poems and stories, without marginal notes, have been included for classroom discussion or assignment.

Chapter 17, "Writing about Visual Arts," encourages critical thinking and good writing practice in discussions of paintings, photographs, and sculpture. To illustrate the guidelines for analysis, this chapter includes a student's prewriting notes and subsequent essay on Edward Hopper's popular painting *Nighthawks*. Composition students may choose their own subject matter from more than twenty artworks reproduced in this chapter and others throughout the text. Artists such as Vincent van Gogh, Frida Kahlo, Jacob Lawrence, Claude Monet, Dorothea Lange, Edvard Munch, Ansel Adams, Francisco Goya, Salvador Dali, and many others offer a variety of styles from social realism to abstract expressionism. Teachers may also wish to use the art in this edition as prompts for other kinds of assignments, such as descriptive paragraphs or comparison/contrast essays.

NEW Chapter 18, "Writing about Film," offers an opportunity for students to practice good writing skills in essays using movies as subject matter in a variety of ways. Suggestions for critical thinking and writing about films and a glossary of cinematic terms are included, as well as a student essay and a new movie review that may be critiqued in class. Chapter 19, "Writing in the World of Work," allows students to practice composing business letters, office memos, electronic mail, and résumés. With the increasing use of technology in the workplace, students may also profit from a section discussing "netiquette" that encourages writers to cultivate a sense of civility and professionalism, as well as clarity, in their electronic communications.

NEW

EXPANDED Part Four presents a concise handbook with accessible explanations and examples showing how to correct the most common errors in grammar, punctuation, and mechanics. To satisfy requests from teachers, two new sections, on the parts of speech and on sentence components and classifications, preface the chapters to help clarify the Handbook's advice. Additional editing practice is also included in this edition.

NEW Part Five gives instructors the opportunity to choose among thirty-four additional professional readings. These selections—some serious, some humorous, some familiar, ten new to this edition—offer a variety of ideas, structures, and styles to consider. Studying the professional selections presented in Part Five should help novice writers as they make their own rhetorical choices.

Once again, readers of this edition may note an occasional attempt at humor. The lighthearted tone of some samples and exercises is the result of the author's firm belief that while learning to write is serious business, solemn composition classrooms are not always the most beneficial environments for anxious beginning writers. The author takes full responsibility (and all of the blame) for the bad jokes and even worse puns.

Finally, a complimentary Instructor's Manual, updated for this edition, is available, containing suggestions for teaching and answers to exercises and essay questions. Contact your Wadsworth/Cengage Learning sales representative for more information.

Although a new edition of this textbook has allowed its author to make a number of changes and additions, the book's purpose remains as stated in the original preface: "While there are many methods of teaching composition, *Steps to Writing Well* tries to help inexperienced writers by offering a clearly defined sequential approach to writing the short essay. By presenting simple, practical advice directly to the students, this text is intended to make the demanding jobs of teaching and learning the basic principles of composition easier and more enjoyable for everyone."

Acknowledgments

I am indebted more than I can say to so many people at Cengage Learning for their help with this new edition. Many thanks to senior publisher Lyn Uhl for her continuing support of the book and its author. Margaret Leslie could not have been a better acquisitions editor; her strong commitment to a quality publication and her thoughtful responsiveness made working with her a pleasure. Loud cheers and long applause go to Laurie Dobson, my development editor *par excellence*, without whom I simply couldn't have finished this project. Thank you, Laurie, for all the hard work from the surveys to the last page proof—for your expertise and thoughtful supervision, for your dedication and patience, for your understanding and encouragement. Special thanks also to Scott Douglass, at Chattanooga State Community College, who successfully accomplished the enormously challenging task of updating and expanding Chapter 14 on Research with attention to detail and delightful good humor. We are greatly indebted to Julie Schoelles, who provided research and valuable new material for portions of that chapter, and to Barbara Armentrout, for her meticulous editing.

Much appreciation is due Corinna Dibble and Aimee Bear, content project managers, for their excellent work guiding the book throughout the production process. Another huge round of thanks to resourceful and efficient Karyn Morrison, who once again patiently scoured the world for the text's many literary permissions. Cheri Throop again did a fine job of locating and negotiating the complex array of artworks, photographs, and advertisements that make the book unique. I'm grateful to project manager Nicole Petel of Lachina Publishing Services for the easiest trip through production I have had in years and to Amy Schneider for her conscientious copyediting and thoughtful inquiries. Both Scott Douglass and David Hall improved the book with their thorough proofreading and beneficial suggestions. Thanks to Austin Hall, office assistant, for tackling a variety of chores that come with revising a textbook.

As always, I extend my ongoing gratitude to the students at Colorado State University and at other colleges who allowed me to reprint their words, from prewriting to completed essays, and to Christi Conti, who updated the complimentary Instructor's Manual.

I continue to be assisted by colleagues around the country whose helpful feedback informed many parts of this new edition:

Emory Abbott, *Georgia Perimeter College*
Wanda Addison, *National University*
Holly Bailey-Hofmann, *West Los Angeles College*
Craig Barrette, *Brescia University*
Amy Beaudry, *Mount Wachusett Community College*
Debbie Borchers, *Pueblo Community College*
Angela Chilton, *Tarrant County College*
David W. Chobar, *Morningside College*
Sujata Chohan, *Heald College*
Carol Coffin, *Mt. San Jacinto Community College*
Ronda Cox, *Northwestern Technical College*
Sandra Cusak, *Heald College*
Luke DeKoster, *Dordt College*
Josh Dickinson, *Jefferson Community College*
Sandra Douglass, *College of Marin*
Mark Dreisonstok, *Stratford University*
Amber Dyer, *LeTourneau University*
Marie Eckstrom, *Rio Hondo Community College*
Kevin Ferns, *Woodland Community College*
Julie Gamberg, *Glendale Community College*
Paul Gelinas, *Oakland University*
Andrea Glebe, *Victor Valley College*
Russell Gordon, *Pacific Baptist College*
Jacqueline Gray, *St. Charles Community College*
Robin Hanson, *Minnesota State Community and Technical College*
Mary Holley, *Mississippi Gulf Coast Community College*
Christian Holst, *Cosumnes River College*
Frances Ilnicky, *Texas State Technical College*
Katharine Ings, *Manchester College*
Paula Irwin, *Muhlenberg College*
Joanna Jackson, *Fitchburg State College*
Shawna Jackson, *Front Range Community College*
Suzanne Kaylor, *Craven Community College*
Mickey Kessler, *Washington State Community College*
Linda Koffman, *College of Marin*
Amy Kubista, *Minnesota School of Business*
Denise Kruizenga-Muro, *Riverside Community College*
Timothy LaFountaine, *Quinsigamond Community College*

Matthew Landrus, *Lake Land College*
Linda Lawliss, *College of the Desert*
Leon Linfield, *Chaffey College*
Anita Lorentzen, *University of Nebraska at Kearney*
Meredith Love-Steinmetz, *Francis Marion University*
Anna Maheshwari, *Schoolcraft College*
Larry Martin, *Hinds Community College*
William E. McCloskey, *Monroe County Community College*
Karen S. McKinney, *Georgia Perimeter College*
Elaina Meiners, *Columbia Basin College*
Donna Monahan, *College of Marin*
Luis Nazario, *Pueblo Community College*
Mary Newell, *Centenary College*
Tamara O'Hearn, *Manchester College*
John Orr, *Fullerton College*
Diane Plumlee, *Akron Institute*
Cris Robins, *Ranken Technical College*
Brent Robinson, *Indian Hills Community College*
Sheila Roe-Boston, *Westwood College*
Paul Rottenberg, *Broward College*
Rosalinda M. Ruiz, *Fullerton College*
James Ruppert, *University of Alaska at Fairbanks*
Kim Russell, *West Kentucky Community and Technical College*
Debra Ryals, *Pensacola Junior College*
Diane Ryan, *Tidewater Community College*
Marilyn Sargent, *Riverside Community College*
Arvis Scott, *McLennan Community College*
Chris Semansky, *Excelsior College*
Mark Spalding, *Manchester College*
Legatha Spelbring, *West Kentucky Community and Technical College*
Jennifer W. Sternhagen, *Minnesota School of Business*
Lawrence Tjernell, *College of Marin*
Rachel Van Horn, *Georgia Southern*
Tony Vannella, *San Antonio College*
Marla Wiley, *Hinds Community College*
Regina Zull, *Everett Community College*

Finally, no acknowledgment section is complete without mentioning my family—David, Sarah, Kate, and Austin—to whom this book has always been dedicated.

TO THE STUDENT

Finding the Right Attitude

If you agree with one or more of the following statements, we have some serious myth-killing to do before you begin this book:

1. I'm no good in English—never have been, never will be.

2. Only people with natural talent for writing can succeed in composition class.

3. My composition teacher is a picky, comma-hunting old fogey/radical, who will insist I write just like him or her.

4. I write for myself, not for anyone else, so I don't need this class or this book.

5. Composition classes are designed to put my creativity in a straitjacket.

The notion that good writers are born, not made, is a widespread myth that may make you feel defeated before you start. But the simple truth is that good writers *are* made—simply because *effective writing is a skill that can be learned.* Despite any feelings of insecurity you may have about composition, you should realize that you already know many of the basic rules of good writing; after all, you've been writing since you were six years old. What you need now is some practical advice on composition, some coaching to sharpen your skills, and a strong dose of determination to practice those skills until you can consistently produce the results you want. Talent, as the French writer Flaubert once said, is nothing more than long patience.

Think about learning to write well as you might consider your tennis game. No one is born a tennis star. You first learn the basic rules and movements and then go out on the court to practice. And practice. No one's tennis will improve if he or she stays off the court; similarly, you must write regularly and receive feedback to improve your composition skills. Try to see your teacher not as Dr. Frankenstein determined to reproduce his or her style of writing in you, but rather as your coach, your loyal trainer who wants you to do the very best you can. Like any good coach, your teacher will point out your strengths and weaknesses; she or he will often send you to this text for practical suggestions for improvement. And while there are no quick, magic solutions for learning to write well, the most important point to remember is this: with this text, your own common sense, and determination, *you can improve your writing.*

Why Write?

"OK," you say, "so I can improve if I try—but why should I bother? Why should I write well? I'm not going to be a professional writer."

In the first place, writing helps us explore our own thoughts and feelings. Writing forces us to articulate our ideas, to discover what we really think about an issue. For example, let's suppose you're faced with a difficult decision and that the arguments pro and con are jumbled in your head. You begin to write down all the pertinent facts and feelings, and suddenly, you begin to see that you do, indeed, have stronger arguments for one side of the question than the other. Once you "see" what you are thinking, you may then scrutinize your opinions for any logical flaws or weaknesses and revise your argument accordingly. In other words, writing lays out our ideas for examination, analysis, and thoughtful reaction. Thus when we write, we (and the world at large) see who we are, and what we stand for, much more clearly. Moreover, writing can provide a record of our thoughts that we may study and evaluate in a way that conversation cannot. In short, writing well enables us to see and know ourselves—our feelings, ideas, and opinions—better.

On a more practical level, we need to write effectively to communicate with others. While some of our writing may be done solely for ourselves, the majority of it is created for others to share. In this world, it is almost impossible to claim that we write only for ourselves. We are constantly asked to put our feelings, ideas, and knowledge in writing for others to read. During your college years, no matter what your major, you will be repeatedly required to write essays, tests, reports, and exercises (and possibly e-mail or letters home). Later, you may need to write formal letters of application for jobs or graduate training; your writing may make that important first impression. At work you may have to write numerous kinds of reports, proposals, analyses, and requisitions. To be successful in any field, you must make your correspondence with business associates and co-workers clearly understood; remember that enormous amounts of time, energy, and profit have been lost because of a single unclear office memo.

There's still a third—more cynical—reason for studying writing techniques. Once you begin to improve your ability to use language, you will become more aware of the ways others write and speak. Through today's mass media and electronic highways, we are continually bombarded with words from politicians, advertisers, scientists, preachers, teachers, and self-appointed "authorities." We need to understand and evaluate what we are hearing, not only for our benefit but also for self-protection. Language is frequently manipulated to manipulate us. For example, the CIA has long referred to the "neutralization" of enemies, and the Bush-Cheney administration authorized "enhanced interrogation techniques" on suspects, which others saw as torture. On occasion, Pentagon officials have carefully avoided discussion of times when misdirected "physics packages" (bombs) fell on "soft targets" (civilians). (One year not so long ago, the National Council of Teachers of English gave their Doublespeak Award to the U.S. officers who, after accidentally shooting down a plane of civilians, reported that the plane didn't crash—rather, it had "uncontrolled contact with the ground.") Some members of Congress have seen no recessions, just "meaningful downturns in aggregate output," so they have treated themselves to a "pay equalization concept," rather than a raise. Advertisers frequently try to disguise their pitches through "infomercials" and "advertorials"; realtors may promote dumps as "designer-ready" houses; the television networks treat us to "encore presentations" that are the same old summer reruns. And "fenestration engineers" are still window cleaners; "environmental superintendents" are still janitors; "drain surgeons" are still plumbers.

By becoming better writers ourselves, we can learn to recognize and reject the irresponsible, cloudy, or dishonest language of others before we become victims of their exploitation.

A Good Place to Start

If improving writing skills is not only possible but important, it is also something else: hard work. H. L. Mencken, American critic and writer, once remarked that "for every difficult and complex problem, there is an obvious solution that is simple, easy and wrong." No composition textbook can promise easy formulas guaranteed to improve your writing overnight. Nor is writing always fun for everyone. But this text can make the learning process easier, less painful, and more enjoyable than you might anticipate. Written in plain, straightforward language addressed to you, the student, this book will suggest a variety of practical ways for you to organize and write clear, concise prose. Because each of your writing tasks will be different, this textbook cannot provide a single, simple blueprint that will apply in all instances. Later chapters, however, will discuss some of the most common methods of organizing essays, such as development by example, definition, classification, causal analysis, comparison/contrast, and argument. As you become more familiar with, and begin to master, these patterns of writing, you will find yourself increasingly able to assess, organize, and explain the thoughts you have about the people, events, and situations in your own life. And while it may be true that in learning to write well there is no free ride, this book, along with your own willingness to work and improve, can start you down the road with a good sense of direction.

PART 1

The Basics
of the Short Essay

The first section of this text is designed to move you through the writing process as you compose a short essay, the kind you are most likely to encounter in composition class and in other college courses. Chapters 1 and 2, on prewriting and the thesis statement, will help you find a topic, purpose, and focus for your essay. Chapter 3, on paragraphs, will show you how to plan, organize, and develop your ideas; Chapter 4 will help you complete your essay. Chapter 5 offers suggestions for revising your writing and for participating effectively in collaborative classroom activities and peer-editing workshops. Chapters 6 and 7 present additional advice on composing your sentences and selecting the best words. Chapter 8 explains the important reading-writing connection and shows how learning to read analytically can sharpen your writing skills.

Prewriting

Getting Started (or Soup-Can Labels Can Be Fascinating)

For many writers, getting started is the hardest part. You may have noticed that when it is time to begin a writing assignment, you suddenly develop an enormous desire to straighten your books, water your plants, or sharpen your pencils for the fifth time. If this situation sounds familiar, you may find it reassuring to know that many professionals undergo these same strange compulsions before they begin writing. Jean Kerr, author of *Please Don't Eat the Daisies*, admitted that she often found herself in the kitchen reading soup-can labels—or anything—to prolong the moments before taking pen in hand. John C. Calhoun, vice president under Andrew Jackson, insisted he had to plow his fields before he could write, and Joseph Conrad, author of *Lord Jim* and other novels, is said to have cried on occasion from the sheer dread of sitting down to compose his stories.

© Roger Allyn Lee/SuperStock

To spare you as much hand-wringing as possible, this chapter presents some practical suggestions on how to begin writing your short essay. Although all writers must find the methods that work best for them, you may find some of the following ideas helpful.

But no matter how you actually begin putting words on paper, it is absolutely essential to maintain two basic ideas concerning your writing task. Before you write a single sentence, you should always remind yourself that

1. You have some valuable ideas to tell your reader, and

2. More than anything, you want to communicate those ideas to your reader.

These reminders may seem obvious to you, but without a solid commitment to your own opinions as well as to your reader, your prose will be lifeless and boring. If *you* don't care about your subject, you can't very well expect anyone else to. Have confidence that your ideas are worthwhile and that your reader genuinely wants, or needs, to know what you think.

Equally important, you must also have a strong desire to tell others what you are thinking. One of the most common mistakes inexperienced writers make is failing to move past early stages in the writing process in which they are writing for—or writing to—themselves only. In the first stages of composing an essay, writers frequently "talk" on paper to themselves, exploring thoughts, discovering new insights, making connections, selecting examples, and so on. The ultimate goal of a finished essay, however, is to communicate your opinions to *others* clearly and persuasively. Whether you wish to inform your readers, change their minds, or stir them to action, you cannot accomplish your purpose by writing so that only you understand what you mean. The burden of communicating your thoughts falls on *you*, not the reader, who is under no obligation to struggle through unclear prose, paragraphs that begin and end for no apparent reason, or sentences that come one after another with no more logic than lemmings following one another to the sea.

Therefore, as you move through the drafting and revising stages of your writing process, commit yourself to becoming increasingly aware of your reader's reactions to your prose. Ask yourself as you revise your drafts, "Am I moving beyond writing just to myself? Am I making myself clear to others who might not know what I mean?" Much of your success as a writer depends on an unflagging determination to communicate clearly with your readers.

Selecting a Subject

Once you have decided that communicating clearly with others is your ultimate goal, you are ready to select the subject of your essay. Here are some suggestions on how to begin:

Start early. Writing teachers since the earth's crust cooled have been pushing this advice—and for good reason. It's not because teachers are egoists competing for the dubious honor of having the most time-consuming course; it is because few writers, even experienced ones, can do a good job when rushed. You need time to mull over ideas, organize your thoughts, revise and polish your prose. Rule of thumb: Always give yourself twice as much time as you think you'll need to avoid the 2:00-A.M.-why-did-I-come-to-college panic.

Find your best space. Develop some successful writing habits by thinking about your very own writing process. When and where do you usually do your best composing? Some people write best early in the morning; others think better later in the day. What time of day seems to produce your best efforts? Where are you working? At a desk? In your room or in a library? Do you start drafting ideas on a computer, or do you begin with paper or a yellow pad? With a certain pen or sharpened pencil? Most writers avoid noise and interruptions (TV, telephone, friends, etc.), although some swear by music in the background. If you can identify a previously successful writing experience, try duplicating its location, time, and tools to help you calmly address your new writing task. Or consider trying new combinations of time and place if your previous choices weren't as productive as you would have liked. Recognition and repeated use of your most comfortable writing "spot" may shorten your hesitation to begin composing; your subconscious may recognize the pattern ("Hey, it's time to write!") and help you start in a positive frame of mind. (Remember that it's not just writers who repeat such rituals—think of the athletes you've heard about who won't begin a game without wearing their lucky socks. If it works for them, it can work for you!)

Select something in which you currently have a strong interest. If the essay subject is left to you, think of something fun, fascinating, or frightening you've done or seen lately, perhaps something you've already told a friend about. The subject might be the pleasure of a new hobby, the challenge of a recent book or movie, or even the harassment of registration—anything in which you are personally involved. If you aren't enthusiastic enough about your subject to want to spread the word, pick something else. Bored writers write boring essays.

Don't feel you have nothing from which to choose your subject. Your days are full of activities, people, joys, and irritations. Essays do not have to be written on lofty intellectual or poetic subjects—in fact, some of the world's best essays have been written on such subjects as china teacups, roast pig, and chimney sweeps. Think: what have you been talking or thinking about lately? What have you been doing that you're excited about? Or what about your past? Reflect a few moments on some of your most vivid memories; special people, vacations, holidays, childhood hideaways, your first job or first date—all are possibilities.

Still searching? Make a list of all the subjects on which you are an expert. None, you say? Think again. Most of us have an array of talents we hardly acknowledge. Perhaps you play the guitar or make a mean pot of chili or know how to repair a sports car. You've trained a dog or become a first-class house sitter or gardener. You know more about computers or old baseball cards than any of your friends. You play soccer or volleyball or Ping-Pong. In other words, take a fresh, close look at your life. You know things that others don't . . . now is your chance to enlighten them!

If a search of your immediate or past personal experience doesn't turn up anything inspiring, try looking in your local or campus newspaper for stories that arouse your strong feelings; don't skip the editorials or "Letters to the Editor" column. What are the current topics of controversy on your campus? How do you feel about a particular graduation requirement? Speakers or special-interest groups on campus? Financial aid applications? Registration procedures? Parking restrictions? Consider the material you are studying in your other classes: reading *The Jungle* in a literature class might spark an investigative essay on the hot dog industry today, or studying previous immigration laws in your history class might lead you to an argument for or against current immigration practices. Current news magazines or Web sites might suggest timely essay topics on national or international affairs that affect your life. In addition, there are, according to the search engine Technorati, over 112 million online blogs, personal web logs that offer diverse—and often controversial—opinions on almost every subject, from politics to entertainment, hobbies, health, and home. Any one of these print or online sources might present an idea or argument that invites your thoughtful response.

In other words, when you're stuck for an essay topic, take a closer look at your environment: your own life—past, present, and future; your hometown; your campus and college town; your state; your country; and your world. You'll probably discover more than enough subjects to satisfy the assignments in your writing class.

Narrow a large subject. Once you've selected a general subject to write on, you may find that it is too broad for effective treatment in a short essay; therefore, you may need to narrow it somewhat. Suppose, for instance, you like to work with plants and have decided to make them the subject of your essay. The subject of "plants," however, is far too large and unwieldy for a short essay, perhaps even for a short book. Consequently, you must make your subject less general. "Houseplants" is more specific, but, again, there's too much to say. "Minimum-care houseplants" is better, but you still need to pare this large, complex subject further so that you can treat it in depth in your short essay. After all, there are many houseplants that require little attention. After several more tries, you might arrive at more specific, manageable topics, such as "houseplants that thrive in dark areas" or "the easy-care Devil's Ivy."

Then again, let's assume you are interested in sports. A 500-to-800-word essay on "sports" would obviously be superficial because the subject covers so much ground. Instead, you might divide the subject into categories such as "sports heroes," "my years on the high school tennis team," "women in gymnastics," "my love of running," and so forth. Perhaps several of your categories would make good short essays, but after looking at your list, you might decide that your real interest at this time is running and that it will be the topic of your essay.

Finding Your Essay's Purpose and Focus

Even after you've narrowed your large subject to a more manageable topic, you still must find a specific *purpose* for your essay. Why are you writing about this topic? Do your readers need to be informed, persuaded, entertained? What do you want your writing to accomplish?

In addition to knowing your purpose, you must also find a clear *focus* or direction for your essay. You cannot, for example, inform your readers about every aspect of running. Instead, you must decide on a particular part of the sport and then determine the main point you want to make. If it helps, think of a camera: you see a sweeping landscape you'd like to photograph, but you know you can't get it all into one picture, so you pick out a particularly interesting part of the scene. Focus in an essay works in the same way; you zoom in, so to speak, on a particular part of your topic and make that the focus of your paper.

Sometimes part of your problem may be solved by your assignment; your teacher may choose the focus of your essay for you by asking for certain specific information or by prescribing the method of development you should use (compare running to aerobics, explain the process of running properly, analyze the effects of daily running, and so forth). But if the purpose and focus of your essay are decisions you must make, you should always allow your interest and knowledge to guide you. Often a direction or focus for your essay will surface as you narrow your subject, but don't become frustrated if you have to discard several ideas before you hit the one that's right. For instance, you might first consider writing on how to select running shoes and then realize that you know too little about the shoe market, or you might find that there's just too little of importance to say about running paths to make an interesting 500-word essay.

Let's suppose for a moment that you have thought of a subject that interests you—but now you're stuck. Deciding on something to write about this subject suddenly looks as easy as nailing Jell-O to your kitchen wall. What should you say? What would be the purpose of your essay? What would be interesting for you to write about and for readers to hear about?

At this point, you may profit from trying more than one prewriting exercise, designed to help you generate some ideas about your topic. The exercises described next are, in a sense, "pump primers" that will get your creative juices flowing again. Because all writers compose differently, not all of these exercises will work for you—in fact, some of them may lead you nowhere. Nevertheless, try all of them at least once or twice; you may be surprised to discover that some pump-primer techniques work better with some subjects than with others.

Pump-Primer Techniques

1. Listing

Try jotting down all the ideas that pop into your head about your topic. Free-associate; don't hold back anything. Try to brainstorm for at least ten minutes.

A quick list on running might look like this:

fun	training for races
healthy	both sexes
relieves tension	any age group
no expensive equipment	running with friend or spouse
shoes	too much competition
poor shoes won't last	great expectations
shin splints	good for lungs
fresh air	improves circulation
good for heart	firming
jogging paths vs. streets	no weight loss
hard surfaces	warm-ups before run
muscle cramps	cool-downs after
going too far	getting discouraged
going too fast	hitting the wall
sense of accomplishment	marathons

As you read over the list, look for connections between ideas or one large idea that encompasses several small ones. In this list, you might first notice that many of the ideas focus on improving health (heart, lungs, circulation), but you discard that subject because a "running improves health" essay is too obvious; it's a topic that's been done too many times to say anything new. A closer look at your list, however, turns up a number of ideas that concern how *not* to run or reasons why someone might become discouraged and quit a running program. You begin to think of friends who might have stuck with running as you have if only they'd warmed up properly beforehand, chosen the right places to run, paced themselves more realistically, and so on. You decide, therefore, to write an essay telling first-time runners how to start a successful program, how to avoid a number of problems, from shoes to track surfaces, that might otherwise defeat their efforts before they've given the sport a chance.

2. Freewriting

Some people simply need to start writing to find a focus. Take out several sheets of blank paper, give yourself at least ten to fifteen minutes, and begin writing whatever comes to mind on your subject. Don't worry about spelling, punctuation, or even complete sentences. Don't change, correct, or delete anything. If you run out of things to say, write "I can't think of anything to say" until you can find a new thought. At the end of the time period you may discover that by continuously writing you will have written yourself into an interesting topic.

   Here are examples of freewriting from students who were given ten minutes to write on the general topic of "nature."

Student 1:

I'm really not the outdoorsy type. I'd rather be inside somewhere than out in Nature tromping through the bushes. I don't like bugs and snakes and stuff like that. Lots of my friends like to go hiking around or camping but I don't. Secretly, I think maybe one of the big reasons I really don't like being out in Nature is because I'm deathly afraid of bees. When I was a kid I was out in the woods and ran into a swarm of bees and got stung about a million times, well, it felt like a million times. I had to go to the hospital for a few days. Now every time I'm outside somewhere and something, anything, flies by me I'm terrified. Totally paranoid. Everyone kids me because I immediately cover my head. I keep hearing about killer bees heading this way, my worst nightmare come true. . . .

Student 2:

We're not going to have any Nature left if people don't do something about the environment. Despite all the media attention to recycling, we're still trashing the planet left and right. People talk big about "saving the environment" but then do such stupid things all the time. Like smokers who flip their cigarette butts out their car windows. Do they think those filters are just going to disappear overnight? The parking lot by this building is full of butts this morning where someone dumped their car ashtray. This campus is full of pop cans, I can see at least three empties under desks in this classroom right now. . . .

These two students reacted quite differently to the same general subject. The first student responded personally, thinking about her own relationship to "nature" (defined as being out in the woods), whereas the second student obviously associated nature with environmental concerns. More freewriting might lead student 1 to a humorous essay on her bee phobia or even to an inquiry about those dreaded killer bees; student 2 might write an interesting paper suggesting ways college students could clean up their campus or easily recycle their aluminum cans.

Often freewriting will not be as coherent as these two samples; sometimes freewriting goes nowhere or in circles. But it's a technique worth trying. By allowing our minds to roam freely over a subject, without worrying about "correctness" or organization, we may remember or discover topics we want to write about or investigate, topics we feel strongly about and wish to introduce to others.

3. Looping*

Looping is a variation on freewriting that works amazingly well for many people, including those who are frustrated rather than helped by freewriting.

Let's assume you've been assigned that old standby, "My Summer Vacation." Obviously, you must find a focus, something specific and important to say. Again, take out several sheets of blank paper and begin to freewrite, as described previously. Write for at least ten minutes. At the end of this period, read over what you've written and try to identify a central idea that has emerged. This idea might be an important thought that occurred to you in the middle or at the end of your writing, or perhaps it was the idea you liked best for whatever reason. It might be the idea that was pulling you onward when time ran out. In other words, look for the thought that stands out, that seems to indicate the direction of your thinking. Put this thought or idea into one sentence called the "center-of-gravity sentence." You have now completed loop 1.

To begin loop 2, use your center-of-gravity sentence as a jumping-off point for another ten minutes of freewriting. Stop, read what you've written, and complete loop 2 by composing another center-of-gravity sentence. Use this second sentence to start loop 3. You should write at least three loops and three center-of-gravity sentences. At the end of three loops, you may find that you have focused on a specific topic that might lead to a good essay. If you're not satisfied with your topic at this point, by all means try two or three more loops until your subject is sufficiently narrowed and focused.

---

* This technique is suggested by Peter Elbow in *Writing Without Teachers* (New York: Oxford University Press, 1975).

Here's an example of one student's looping exercise:

Summer Vacation

Loop 1

I think summer vacations are very important aspects of living. They symbolize getting away from daily routines, discovering places and people that are different. When I think of vacations I think mostly of traveling somewhere too far to go, say, for a weekend. It is a chance to get away and relax and not think about most responsibilities. Just have a good time and enjoy yourself. Vacations can also be a time of gathering with family and friends.

Center-of-gravity sentence

Vacations are meant to be used for traveling.

Loop 2

Vacations are meant for traveling. Last summer my family and I drove to Yellowstone National Park. I didn't want to go at first. I thought looking at geysers would be dumb and boring. I was really obnoxious all the way up there and made lots of smart remarks about getting eaten by bears. Luckily, my parents ignored me and I'm glad they did, because Yellowstone turned out to be wonderful. It's not just Old Faithful— there's lots more to see and learn about, like these colorful boiling pools and boiling patches of mud. I got interested in the thermodynamics of the pools and how new ones are surfacing all the time, and how algae make the pools different colors.

Center-of-gravity sentence

Once I got interested in Yellowstone's amazing pools, my vacation turned out great.

Loop 3

Once I got interested in the pools, I had a good time, mainly because I felt I was seeing something really unusual. I knew I'd never see anything like this again unless I went to Iceland or New Zealand (highly unlikely!). I felt like I was learning a lot, too. I liked the idea of learning a lot about the inside of the earth without having to go to class and study books. I really hated to leave—Mom and Dad kidded me on the way back about how much I'd griped about going on the trip in the first place. I felt pretty dumb. But I was really glad I'd given the Park a closer look instead of holding on to my view of it as a boring bunch of water fountains. I would have had a terrible time, but now I hope to go back someday. I think the experience made me more open-minded about trying new places.

Center-of-gravity sentence

My vacation this summer was special because I was willing to put aside my expectations of boredom and learn some new ideas about the strange environment at Yellowstone.

At the end of three loops, this student has moved from the general subject of "summer vacation" to the more focused idea that her willingness to learn about a new place played an important part in the enjoyment of her vacation. Although her last center-of-gravity sentence still contains some vague words ("special," "new ideas," "strange environment"), the thought stated here may eventually lead to an essay that not only will say something about this student's vacation but may also persuade readers to reconsider their attitude toward taking trips to new places.

4. The Boomerang

Still another variation on freewriting is the technique called the "boomerang," named appropriately because, like the Australian stick, it invites your mind to travel over a subject from opposite directions to produce new ideas.

Suppose, for example, members of your class have been asked to write about their major field of study, which in your case is Liberal Arts. Begin by writing a statement that comes into your mind about majoring in the Liberal Arts, and then freewrite on that statement for five minutes. Then write a second statement that approaches the subject from an opposing point of view, and freewrite again for five minutes. Continue this pattern several times. Boomeranging, like looping, can help writers see their subject in a new way and consequently help them find an idea to write about.

Here's an abbreviated sample of boomeranging:

1. Majoring in the Liberal Arts is impractical in today's world.
   [Freewrite for five minutes.]
2. Majoring in the Liberal Arts is practical in today's world.
   [Freewrite for five minutes.]
3. Liberal Arts is a particularly enjoyable major for me.
   [Freewrite for five minutes.]
4. Liberal Arts is not always an enjoyable major for me.
   [Freewrite for five minutes.]

And so on.

By continuing to "throw the boomerang" across your subject, you may not only find your focus but also gain insight into other people's views of your topic, which can be especially valuable if your paper will address a controversial issue or one that you feel is often misunderstood.

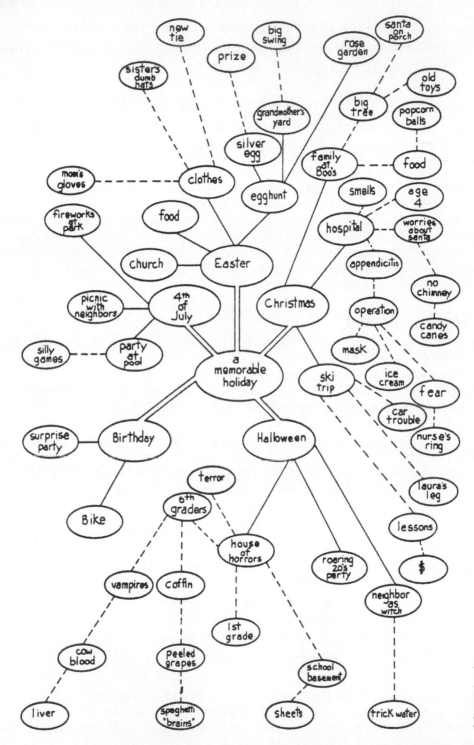

© Cengage Learning

5. Clustering

Another excellent technique is clustering (sometimes called "mapping"). Place your general subject in a circle in the middle of a blank sheet of paper and begin to draw other lines and circles that radiate from the original subject. Cluster those ideas that seem to fall together. At the end of ten minutes, see if a topic emerges from any of your groups of ideas.

Ten minutes of clustering on the subject of "A Memorable Holiday" might look like the drawing on page 12.

This student may wish to brainstorm further on the Christmas he spent in the hospital with a case of appendicitis or perhaps on the Halloween he first experienced a house of horrors. By using clustering, he has recollected some important details about a number of holidays that may help him focus on an occasion he wants to describe in his paper.

6. Cubing

Still another way to generate ideas is cubing. Imagine a six-sided cube that looks something like the figure below.

Mentally, roll your subject around the cube and freewrite the answers to the questions that follow. Write whatever comes to mind for ten or fifteen minutes; don't concern yourself with the "correctness" of what you write.

a. *Describe it:* What does your subject look like? What size, colors, textures does it have? Does it have any special features worth noting?

b. *Compare or contrast it:* What is your subject similar to? What is your subject different from? In what ways?

c. *Free-associate it:* What does this subject remind you of? What does it call to mind? What memories does it conjure up?

d. *Analyze it:* How does it work? How are the parts connected? What is its significance?

e. *Argue for or against it:* What arguments can you make for or against your subject? What advantages or disadvantages does it have? What changes or improvements should be made?

f. *Apply it:* What are the uses of your subject? What can you do with it?

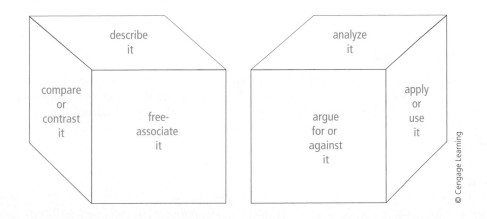

© Cengage Learning

A student who had recently volunteered at a homeless shelter wrote the following responses about her experience:

   a. *Describe it:* I and five other members of my campus organization volunteered three Saturdays to work at the shelter here in town. We mainly helped in the kitchen, preparing, serving, and cleaning up after meals. At the dinners we served about forty homeless people, mostly men but also some families with small children and babies.

   b. *Compare or contrast it:* I had never done anything like this before so it's hard to compare or contrast it to anything. It was different though from what I expected. I hadn't really thought much about the people who would be there—or to be honest I think I thought they would be pretty weird or sad and I was kind of dreading going there after I volunteered. But the people were just regular normal people. And they were very, very polite to us.

   c. *Free-associate it:* Some of the people there reminded me of some of my relatives! John, the kitchen manager, said most of the people were just temporarily "down on their luck" and that reminded me of my aunt and uncle who came to stay with us for a while when I was in high school after my uncle lost his job.

   d. *Analyze it:* I feel like I got a lot out of my experience. I think I had some wrong ideas about "the homeless" and working there made me think more about them as real people, not just a faceless group.

   e. *Argue for or against it:* I would encourage others to volunteer there. The work isn't hard and it isn't scary. It makes you appreciate what you've got and also makes you think about what you or your family might do if things went wrong for a while. It also makes you feel good to do something for people you don't even know.

   f. *Apply it:* I feel like I am more knowledgeable when I hear people talk about the poor or the homeless in this town, especially those people who criticize those who use the shelter.

After you've written your responses, see if any one or more of them give you an idea for a paper. The student who wrote the preceding responses decided she wanted to write an article for her campus newspaper encouraging people to volunteer at the shelter not only to provide much-needed help but also to challenge their own preconceived notions about the homeless in her college town. Cubing helped her realize she had something valuable to say about her experience and gave her a purpose for writing.

7. Interviewing

Another way to find a direction for your paper is through interviewing. Ask a classmate or friend to discuss your subject with you. Let your thoughts range over your subject as your friend asks you questions that arise naturally in the conversation. Or your friend might try asking what are called "reporter's questions" as she or he "interviews" you on your subject:

Who?	When?
What?	Why?
Where?	How?

Listen to what you have to say about your subject. What were you most interested in talking about? What did your friend want to know? Why? By talking about your subject, you may find that you have talked your way into an interesting focus for your paper. If, after the interview, you are still stumped, question your friend: if he or she had to publish an essay based on the information from your interview, what would that essay focus on? Why?

8. The Cross-Examination

If a classmate isn't available for an interview, try interviewing, or cross-examining, yourself. Ask yourself questions about your general subject, just as a lawyer might if you were on the witness stand. Consider using the five categories described below and on the next page, which are adapted from those suggested by Aristotle centuries ago to the orators of his day. Ask yourself as many questions in each category as you can think of, and then go on to the next category. Jot down brief notes to yourself as you answer.

Here are the five categories, plus six sample questions for each to illustrate the possibilities:

1. Definition
   a. How does the dictionary or encyclopedia define or explain this subject?
   b. How do most people define or explain it?
   c. How do I define or explain it?
   d. What do its parts look like?
   e. What is its history or origin?
   f. What are some examples of it?

2. Comparison and Contrast
   a. What is it similar to?
   b. What does it differ from?
   c. What does it parallel?
   d. What is its opposite?
   e. What is it better than?
   f. What is it worse than?

3. Relationship
   a. What causes it?
   b. What are the effects of it?
   c. What larger group or category is it a part of?
   d. What larger group or category is it in opposition to?
   e. What are its values or goals?
   f. What contradictions does it contain?

4. Circumstance
   a. Is it possible?
   b. Is it impossible?

   c. When has it happened before?

   d. What might prevent it from happening?

   e. Why might it happen again?

   f. Who has been or might be associated with it?

5. Testimony

   a. What do people say about it?

   b. What has been written about it?

   c. What authorities exist on the subject?

   d. Are there any relevant statistics?

   e. What research has been done?

   f. Have I had any direct experience with it?

Some of the questions suggested here, or ones you think of, may not be relevant to or useful for your subject. But some may lead you to ideas you wish to explore in more depth, either in a discovery draft or by using another prewriting technique described in this chapter, such as looping or mapping.

9. Sketching

Sometimes when you have found or been assigned a general subject, the words to explain or describe it just won't come. Although listing or freewriting or one of the other methods suggested here works well for some people, other writers find these techniques intimidating or unproductive. Some of these writers are visual learners—that is, they respond better to pictorial representations of material than they do to written descriptions or explanations. If, on occasion, you are stuck for words, try drawing or sketching or even cartooning the pictures in your mind.

You may be surprised at the details that you remember once you start sketching. For example, you might have been asked to write about a favorite place or a special person in your life or to compare or contrast two places you have lived in or visited. See how many details you can conjure up by drawing the scenes or the people; then look at your details to see if some dominant impression or common theme has emerged. Your Aunt Sophie's insistence on wearing two pounds of costume jewelry might become the focus of a paragraph on her sparkling personality, or the many details you recalled about your grandfather's barn might lead you to a paper on the hardships of farm life. For some writers, a picture can be worth a thousand words—especially if that picture helps them begin putting those words on paper.

10. Dramatizing the Subject

Some writers find it helpful to visualize their subject as if it were a drama or play unfolding in their minds. Kenneth Burke, a thoughtful writer himself, suggests that writers might think about human action in dramatists' terms and then see what sorts of new insights arise as the "drama" unfolds. Burke's dramatists' terms might be adapted for our use and pictured this way:

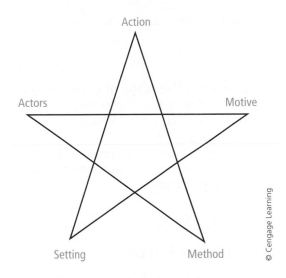

Just as you did in the cubing exercise, try mentally rolling your subject around the star and explore the possibilities that emerge. For example, suppose you want to write about your recent decision to return to college after a long period of working, but you don't know what you want to say about your decision. Start thinking about this decision as a drama and jot down brief answers to such questions as these:

Action: What happened?
               What were the results?
               What is going to happen?

Actors: Who was involved in the action?
               Who was affected by the action?
               Who caused the action?
               Who was for it and who was opposed?

Motive: What were the reasons behind the action?
               What forces motivated the actors to perform as they did?

Method: How did the action occur?
               By what means did the actors accomplish the action?

Setting: What were the time and place of the action?
               What did the place look like?
               What positive or negative feelings are associated with this time or place?

These are only a few of the dozens of questions you might ask yourself about your "drama." (If it helps, think of your "drama" as a murder mystery and answer the questions the police detective might ask: what happened here? to whom? who did it? why? with what? when? where? and so on.)

You may find that you have a great deal to write about the combination of actor and motive but very little to say in response to the questions on setting or method. That's fine—simply use the "dramatists' approach" to help you find a specific topic or idea you want to write about.

> ◆If at any point in this stage of the writing process you are experiencing *Writer's Block*, you might turn to the suggestions for overcoming this common affliction that appear on pages 121–123 in Chapter 5. You might also find it helpful to read the section *Keeping a Journal*, pages 26–28, because writing in a relaxed mood on a regular basis may be the best long-term cure for your writing anxiety.

After You've Found Your Focus

Once you think you've found the focus of your essay, you may be ready to compose a *working thesis statement*, an important part of your essay discussed in great detail in the next chapter. If you've used one of the prewriting exercises outlined in this chapter, by all means hang on to it. The details and observations you generated as you focused your topic may be useful to you as you begin to organize and develop your body paragraphs.

© Canstock Images, Inc./
Index Stock Imagery

PRACTICING WHAT YOU'VE LEARNED

A. Some of the subjects listed below are too broad for a 500-to-800-word essay. Identify those topics that might be treated in short papers and those that still need to be narrowed.

1. The role of the modern university

2. My first (and last) experience with skateboarding

3. The characters of William Shakespeare

4. Solar energy

5. Collecting baseball cards

6. Gun-control laws

7. Down with throwaway bottles

8. Computers

9. The best teacher I've ever had

10. Selecting the right bicycle

B. Select two of the large subjects that follow and, through looping or listing details or another prewriting technique, find focused topics that would be appropriate for essays of three to five pages.

1. Music
2. Cars
3. Education
4. Jobs
5. Television commercials
6. Politics
7. Animals
8. Childhood
9. Cell phones
10. Athletics

Discovering Your Audience

Once you have a focused topic and perhaps some ideas about developing your essay, you need to pause a moment to consider your *audience*. Before you can decide what information needs to go into your essay and what should be omitted, you must know who will be reading your paper and why. Knowing your audience will also help you determine what *voice* you should use to achieve the proper tone in your essay.

Suppose, for example, you are attending a college organized on the quarter system, and you decide to write an essay arguing for a switch to the semester system. If your audience is composed of classmates, your essay will probably focus on the advantages to the student body, such as better opportunities for in-depth study in one's major, the ease of making better grades, and the benefits of longer midwinter and summer vacations. However, if you are addressing the Board of Regents, you might emphasize the power of the semester system to attract more students, cut registration costs, and use professors more efficiently. If your audience is composed of townspeople who know little about either system, you will have to devote more time to explaining the logistics of each one and then discuss the semester plan's advantages to the local merchants, real estate agents, restaurateurs, and so on. *In other words, such factors as the age, education, profession, and interests of your audience can make a difference in determining which points of your argument to stress or omit, which ideas need additional explanation, and what kind of language to adopt.*

How to Identify Your Readers

To help you analyze your audience before you begin writing your working thesis statement and rough drafts, here are some steps you may wish to follow:

1. First, see if your writing assignment specifies a particular audience (editors of a journal in your field or the Better Business Bureau of your town, for example) or a general audience of your peers (your classmates or readers of the local newspaper, for instance). Even if your assignment does not mention an intended audience, try to imagine one anyway. Imagining specific readers will help you stick to your goal of communicating clearly, in engaging detail.

2. If a specific audience is designated, ask yourself some questions about their motivation or *reasons for reading* your essay.

   • What do these readers want to learn?

   • What do they hope to gain?

   • Do they need your information to make a decision? Formulate a new plan? Design a new project?

   • What action do you want them to take?

The answers to such questions will help you find both your essay's purpose and its content. If, for example, you're trying to persuade an employer to hire you for a particular job, you certainly would write your application in a way that stresses the skills and training the company is searching for. You may have a fine hobby or a wonderful family, but if your prospective employer-reader doesn't need to hear about that particular part of your life, toss it out of this piece of writing.

3. Next, try to discover what *knowledge* your audience has of your subject.

   • What, if anything, can you assume that your readers already know about your topic?

   • What background information might they need to know to understand a current situation clearly?

   • What facts, explanations, or examples will best present your ideas? How detailed should you be?

   • What terms need to be defined? Equipment explained?

Questions like these should guide you as you collect and discard information for your paper. An essay written to your colleagues in electrical engineering, for instance, need not explain commonly used technical instruments; to do so might even insult your readers. But the same report read by your composition classmates would probably need more detailed explanation for you to make yourself understood. Always put yourself in your readers' place and then ask: what else do they need to know to understand this point completely?

4. Once you have decided what information is necessary for your audience, dig a little deeper into your readers' identities. Pose some questions about their *attitudes* and emotional states.

   • Are your readers already biased for or against your ideas in some way?

   • Do they have positive or negative associations with your subject?

   • Are they fearful or anxious, reluctant or bored?

   • Do they have radically different expectations or interests?

It helps enormously to know the emotional attitudes of your readers toward your subject. Let's suppose you are arguing for the admission of a young child with AIDS into a local school system, and your audience is the parent-teacher organization. Some of your readers might be frightened or even hostile; knowing this, you would wisely begin your argument with a disarming array of information showing that no cases of AIDS have developed from the casual contact of schoolchildren. In other words, the more you know about your audience's attitudes before you begin writing, the more convincing your prose, because you will make the best choices about both content and organization.

5. Last, think of any *special qualities* that might set your audience apart from any other.

- Are they older or younger than your peers?
- Do they share similar educational experiences or training?
- Are they from a particular part of the world or country that might affect their perspective? Urban or rural?
- Are they in positions of authority?

Knowing special facts about your audience makes a difference, often in your choice of words and tone. You wouldn't, after all, use the same level of vocabulary addressing a group of fifth-graders as you would writing to the children's teacher or principal. Similarly, your tone and word choice probably wouldn't be as formal in a letter to a friend as in a letter to the telephone company protesting your most recent bill.

Without question, analyzing your specific audience is an important step to take before you begin to shape your rough drafts. And before you move on to writing a working thesis, here are a few tips to keep in mind about *all* audiences, no matter who your readers are or what their reasons for reading your writing.

1. Readers don't like to be bored. Grab your readers' attention and fight to keep it. Remember the last dull movie you squirmed—or slept—through? How much you resented wasting not only your money but your valuable time as well? How you turned it off mentally and drifted away to someplace more exciting? As you write and revise your drafts, keep imagining readers who are as intelligent—and busy—as you are. Put yourself in their place: would you find this piece of writing stimulating enough to keep reading?

2. Readers hate confusion and disorder. Can you recall a time when you tried to find your way to a party, only to discover that a friend's directions were so muddled you wound up hours later, out of gas, cursing in a cornfield? Or the afternoon you spent trying to follow a friend's notes for setting up a chemistry experiment, with explanations that twisted and turned as often as a wandering stray cat? Try to relive such moments of intense frustration as you struggle to make *your* writing clear and direct.

3. Readers want to think and learn (whether they realize it or not). Every time you write, you strike a bargain of sorts with your readers: in return for their time and attention, you promise to inform and interest them, to tell them something new or show them something familiar in a different light. You may enlighten them or amuse them or even try to frighten them—but they must feel, in the end, that they've gotten a fair trade. As you plan, write, and revise, ask yourself, "What are my readers learning?" If the honest answer is "nothing important," you may be writing only for yourself. (If you yourself are bored rereading your drafts, you're probably not writing for anybody at all.)

4. Readers want to see what you see, feel what you feel. Writing that is vague keeps your readers from fully sharing the information or experience you are trying to communicate. Clear, precise language—full of concrete details and specific examples—lets your readers know that you understand your subject and that you want them to understand it, too. Even a potentially dull topic such as tuning up a car can become engaging to a reader if the right details are provided in the right places: your terror as blue sparks leap under your nose when the wrong wire is touched, the depressing sight of the screwdriver squirming from your greasy fingers and disappearing into the oil pan, the sudden shooting pain when the wrench slips and turns your knuckles to raw hamburger. Get your readers involved and interested—and they'll listen to what you have to say. (Details also persuade your reader that you're an authority on your subject; after all, no reader likes to waste time listening to someone whose tentative, vague prose style announces, "I only sort of know what I'm talking about here.")

5. Readers are turned off by writers with pretentious, phony voices. Too often, inexperienced writers feel they must sound especially scholarly, scientific, or sophisticated for their essays to be convincing. In fact, the contrary is true. When you assume a voice that is not yours, when you pretend to be someone you're not, you don't sound believable at all—you sound phony. Your readers want to hear what *you* have to say, and the best way to communicate with them is in a natural voice. You may also believe that to write a good essay it is necessary to use a host of unfamiliar, unpronounceable, polysyllabic words gleaned from the pages of your thesaurus. Again, the opposite is true. Our best writers agree with Mark Twain, who once said, "Never use a twenty-five-cent word when a ten-cent word will do." In other words, avoid pretension in your writing just as you do in everyday conversation. Select simple, direct words you know and use frequently; keep your voice natural, sincere, and reasonable. (◆ For additional help choosing the appropriate words and the level of your diction, see Chapter 7.)

> ### Don't Ever Forget Your Readers!
> Thinking about them as you write will help you choose your ideas, organize your information effectively, and select the best words.

PRACTICING WHAT YOU'VE LEARNED

A. Practice identifying intended audiences by analyzing, first, the Geico insurance advertisement that appears on the next page and then at least two additional advertisements reprinted in other pages of this text, such as "Gas Heat Makes Me Nervous" (page 314) or "PETA Anti-Fur" (page 320). (A list of the ads in this text follows the Table of Contents.)

© Canstock Images, Inc./ Index Stock Imagery

In each case, first determine the purpose of the ad and then describe the ad's target audience, explaining your reasons for your response. You may find it helpful to consider some of the following questions:

1. What age group does the ad target? Does it appeal primarily to males, females, or both? Is the intended audience of a particular social or economic class?

2. What concerns or strong interests might this audience have?

3. What kinds of arguments are used in the ad to persuade its intended audience?

4. What specific words or phrases are chosen to appeal to this particular audience?

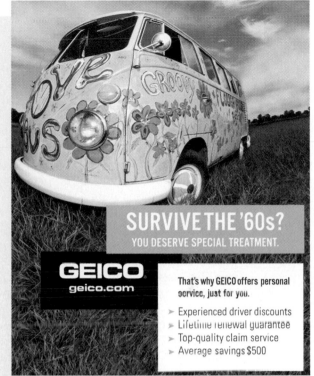

SURVIVE THE '60s?
YOU DESERVE SPECIAL TREATMENT.

GEICO.
geico.com

That's why GEICO offers personal service, just for you.

➤ Experienced driver discounts
➤ Lifetime renewal guarantee
➤ Top-quality claim service
➤ Average savings $500

Courtesy of Geico, Inc. Photo © Bettmann/CORBIS

B. Select an essay or feature story from a magazine or journal of your choosing and identify the intended audience. Explain how you arrived at this conclusion by showing ways the writer effectively addresses his or her audience.

© CORBIS

ASSIGNMENT

A. The article that follows appeared in newspapers across the country some time ago. Read about the diet called "Breatharianism" and then write one or more of the assignments that follow the article.

The Ultimate in Diet Cults: Don't Eat Anything at All

1   CORTE MADERA, CALIF.—Among those seeking enlightenment through diet cults, Wiley Brooks seemed to have the ultimate answer—not eating at all. He called himself a "Breatharian" and claimed to live on air, supplemented only by occasional fluids taken to counteract the toxins of urban environments.

continued on next page

2   "Food is more addictive than heroin," the tall, gaunt man told hundreds of people who paid $500 each to attend five-day "intensives," at which he would stand before them in a camel velour sweatsuit and talk for hours without moving, his fingers meditatively touching at their tips.

3   Brooks, 46, became a celebrity on the New Age touring circuit. ABC-TV featured him in October, 1980, as a weight lifter; he allegedly hoisted 1,100 pounds, about 10 times his own weight. He has also been interviewed on radio and in newspapers.

4   Those who went to his sessions during the past six months on the West Coast and in Hawaii were not just food faddists, but also physicians and other professionals who—though not necessarily ready to believe—thought this man could be onto something important. Some were convinced enough by what they saw to begin limiting their own diets, taking the first steps toward Breatharianism.

5   In his intensives, Brooks did not recommend that people stop eating altogether. Rather, he suggested they "clean their blood" by starting with the "yellow diet"—24 food items including grapefruit, papaya, corn products, eggs, chicken, fish, goat's milk, millet, salsa piquante (Mexican hot sauce) and certain flavors of the Häagen Dazs brand ice cream, including "rum raisin." These foods, he said, have a less toxic effect because, among other things, "their vibrational quality is yellow."

6   Last week, however, aspirants toward Breatharianism were shocked by reports that Brooks had been eating—and what's more, eating things that to health food purists are the worst kind of junk.

7   Word spread that during an intensive in Vancouver, Brooks was seen emerging from a 7-Eleven store with a bag of groceries. The next morning there were allegedly room service trays outside his hotel room, while inside, the trash basket held empty containers of chicken pot pie, chili and biscuits.

8   Kendra Wagner, regional Breatharian coordinator, said she herself had seen Brooks drinking a Coke. "When I asked him about it he said, 'That's how dirty the air is here,'" she explained. "We (the coordinators) sat down with Wiley after the training and said, 'We want you to tell us the truth.' He denied everything. We felt tricked and deceived."

9   As the rumors grew, some Breatharians confronted their leader at a lecture in San Francisco. Brooks denied the story and said that the true message of Breatharianism did not depend on whether he ate or not, anyway.

10   The message in his promotional material reads that "modern man is the degenerate descendant of the Breatharian," and that "living on air alone leads to perfect health and perfect happiness." Though followers had the impression Brooks has not eaten for 18 years, his leaflets merely declare that "he does not eat, and seldom drinks any fluid. He sleeps less than seven hours a week and is healthier, more energetic and happier than he ever dreamed possible."

11   In a telephone interview, Brooks acknowledged that this assertion is not quite correct. "I'm sure I've taken some fruit, like an apple or an orange, but it's better in public to keep it simple." He again staunchly denied the 7-Eleven story.

12   Among those who have been on the yellow diet for months is Jime Collison, 24, who earlier tried "fruitarianism," fasting and other special regimens, and moved from Texas to the San Francisco Bay area just to be around the Breatharian movement. "Now I'm a basket case," he said. "My world revolved around Wiley's philosophy." He had thought Wiley "made the jump to where all of us health food fanatics were going," Collison said.

13   Other Brooks disciples, though disappointed, feel they nevertheless benefited from their experience. Said a physician who has been on the yellow diet for four months: "I feel very good. I still don't know what the truth is, but I do know that Wiley is a good salesman. So I'll be patient, keep an open mind and continue to observe."

14   "Breatharianism is the understanding of what the body really needs, not whether Wiley eats or doesn't," said James Wahler, 35, who teaches a self-development technique called "rebirthing," in Marin County. "I'm realizing that the less I eat the better I feel." He also suggested that Brooks may have lied for people's own good, to get them to listen.

15   "Everyone has benefited from what I'm saying," Brooks said. "There will be a food shortage and a lot of unhappy people when they realize that I was trying to save their lives."

Each of the assignments that follow is directed to a different audience, none of whom know much about Breatharianism. What information does each audience need to know? What kinds of details will be the most persuasive? What sort of organization will work best for each purpose and audience?

1. Write a single-page flyer advertising the five-day intensives. What appeals might persuade people to pay $500 each to attend a seminar to learn to eat air?

2. Assume you are a regional Breatharian coordinator. Write a letter to your city council petitioning for a parade permit that will allow members of your organization to parade down your main street in support of this diet and its lifestyle. What do council members need to know before they vote on such a permit?

3. You are a former Breatharian who is now unhappy with the diet and its unfulfilled promises. Write a report for the vice squad calling for an investigation into the organization. Convince the investigators that the organization is defrauding local citizens and should be stopped.

B. *Collaborative Activity:* In a small group of three or four classmates, exchange the assignments you have written. Which flyer, petition, and report does the group find most persuasive for its intended audience, and why? Present your group's analysis to the class.

Keeping a Journal (Talking to Yourself Does Help)

Many professional writers carry small notebooks with them so they can jot down ideas and impressions for future use. Other people keep daily logs, diaries, or blogs for years to record their thoughts. In your composition class, you may find it useful to keep a journal that will help you with your writing process, especially in the early stages of prewriting. Journals can also help you prepare for class discussions and remember important course material.

You may have kept a journal in another class. There, it may have been called a "daybook" or "learning log" or some other name. Although the journal has a variety of uses, it frequently is assigned to encourage you to record your responses to reading material or class discussions as well as your own thoughts and questions. Often, the journal is kept in a notebook you can carry with you (spiral is fine, although a prong or ring notebook allows you to add or remove pages when you wish); some writers prefer to collect their thoughts in designated computer files or web logs. Even if a journal is not assigned in your composition class, it is still a useful tool.

Writers who have found journal writing effective advise trying to write a minimum of three entries a week, with each entry at least a half page. To keep a carry-around notebook organized, start each entry on a new page and date each entry you write. You might also leave the backs of your notebook pages blank so that you can return and respond to an entry at a later date if you wish.

Uses of the Journal

Here are some suggested uses for your journal as you move through the writing process. You may want to experiment with a number of these suggestions to see which are the most productive for you.

1. Use the journal, especially in the first weeks of class, to confront your fears of writing, to conquer the blank page. Write anything you want to—thoughts, observations, notes to yourself, letters home, anything at all. Best your enemy by writing down that witty retort you thought of later and wished you had said. Write about your ideal job, vacation, car, or home. Write a self-portrait or make a list of all the subjects on which you are (or would like to become) an "authority." The more you write, the easier writing becomes—or at least, the easier it is to begin writing because, like a sword swallower, you know you have accomplished the act before and lived to tell about it.

2. Improve your powers of observation. Record interesting snippets of conversations you overhear or catalog noises you hear in a ten-minute period in a crowded place, such as your student center, a bookstore, or a mall. Eat something with multiple layers (a piece of fruit such as an orange) and list all the tastes, textures, and smells you discover. Look around your room and write down a list of everything that is yellow. By becoming sensitive to the sights, sounds, smells, and textures around you, you may find that your powers of description and explanation will expand, enabling you to help your reader "see" what you're talking about in your next essay.

3. Save your own brilliant ideas. Jot down those bright ideas that might turn into great essays. Or save those thoughts you have now for the essay you know is coming later in the semester so you won't forget them. Expand or elaborate on any ideas you have; you might be able to convert your early thoughts into a paragraph when it's time to start drafting.

4. Save other people's brilliant ideas. Record interesting quotations, facts, and figures from other writers and thinkers. You may find some of this information useful in one of your later essays. It's also helpful to look at the ways other writers make their words emphatic, moving, and arresting so you can try some of their techniques in your own prose. (Important: Don't forget to note the source of any material you record, so if you do quote any of it in a paper later, you will be able to document it properly.)

5. Be creative. Write a poem or song or story or joke. Parody the style of someone you've heard or read. Become an inanimate object and complain to the humans around you (for example, what would a soft-drink machine like to say to those folks constantly beating on its stomach?). Become a little green creature from Mars and convince a human to accompany you back to your planet as a specimen of Earthlings (or be the invited guest and explain to the creature why you are definitely not the person to go). The possibilities are endless, so go wild.

6. Prepare for class. If you've been given a reading assignment (an essay or article or pages from a text, for instance), try a split-page entry. Draw a line down the middle of a page in your journal, and on the left side of the page write a summary of what you've read or perhaps list the main points. Then on the right side of the same page, write your responses to the material. Your responses might be your personal reaction to the content (what struck you hardest? why?) or your agreement or disagreement with a particular point or two. Or the material might call up some long-forgotten idea or memory. By thinking about your class material both analytically and personally, you almost certainly will remember it for class discussion. You might also find that a good idea for an essay will arise as you think about the reading assignments in different ways.

7. Record responses to class discussions. A journal is a good place to jot down your reactions to what your teacher and your peers are saying in class. You can ask yourself questions ("What did Megan mean when she said . . .") or note any confusion ("I got mixed up when . . .") or record your own reactions ("I disagreed with Jamal when he argued that . . ."). Again, some of your reactions might become the basis of a good essay.

8. Focus on a problem. You can restate the problem or explore the problem or solve the problem. Writing about a problem often encourages the mind to flow over the information in ways that allow discoveries to happen. Sometimes, too, we don't know exactly what the problem is or how we feel about it until we write about it. Remember the encouraging words of the philosopher Voltaire: "No problem can withstand the assault of thinking." Writing *is* thinking.

9. Practice audience awareness. Write letters to different companies, praising or panning their product; then write advertising copy for each product. Become the third critic on a popular movie-review program and show the other two commentators why your review of your favorite movie is superior to theirs. Thinking about a specific audience when you write will help you plan the content, organization, and tone of each writing assignment.

10. Describe your own writing process. It's helpful sometimes to record how you go about writing your essays. How do you get started? How much time do you spend getting started? Do you write an "idea" draft or work from an outline? How do you revise? Do you write multiple drafts? These and many other questions may give you a clue to any problems you might have as you write your next essay. If, for example, you see that you're having trouble again and again with conclusions, you can turn to Chapter 4 for some extra help. Sometimes it's hard to see that there's a pattern in our writing process until we've described it several times.

11. Write a progress report. List all the skills you've mastered as the course progresses. You'll be surprised at how much you have learned. Read the list over if you're ever feeling frustrated or discouraged, and take pride in your growth.

12. Become sensitive to language. Keep a record of jokes and puns that play on words. Record people's weird-but-funny uses of language (overheard at the dorm cafeteria: "She was so skinny she was emancipated" and "I'm tired of being the escape goat"). Rewrite some of today's bureaucratic jargon or retread a cliché. Come up with new images of your own. Playing with language in fun or even silly ways can make writing tasks seem less threatening. (A newspaper recently came up with this language game: Change, add, or subtract one letter in a word and provide a new definition. Examples: intoxication/intaxication—the giddy feeling of getting a tax refund; graffiti/giraffiti— spray paint that appears on tall buildings; sarcasm/sarchasm—the gulf between the witty speaker and the listener who doesn't get it.)

13. Write your own textbook. Make notes on material that is important for you to remember. For instance, make your own grammar or punctuation handbook with only those rules you find yourself referring to often. Or keep a list of spelling rules that govern the words you misspell frequently. Writing out the rules in your own words and having a convenient place to refer to them may help you teach yourself quicker than studying any textbook (including this one).

These suggestions are some of the many uses you may find for your journal once you start writing in one on a regular basis. Obviously, not all the suggestions here will be appropriate for you, but some might be, so you might consider using a set of divider tabs to separate the different functions of your journal (one section for class responses, one section for your own thoughts, one for your own handbook, and so on).

You may find, as some students have, that the journal is especially useful during the first weeks of your writing course, when putting pen to paper is often hardest. Many students, however, continue to use the journal throughout the entire course, and others adapt their journals to record their thoughts and responses to their other college courses and experiences. Whether you continue using a journal beyond this course is up to you, but consider trying the journal for at least six weeks. You may find that it will improve your writing skills more than anything else you have tried before.

Chapter 1 Summary

Here is a brief summary of what you should know about the prewriting stage of your writing process:

1. Before you begin writing anything, remember that you have valuable ideas to tell your readers.

2. It's not enough that these valuable ideas are clear to you, the writer. Your single most important goal is to communicate those ideas clearly to your readers, who cannot know what's in your mind until you tell them.

3. Whenever possible, select a subject to write on that is of great interest to you, and always give yourself more time than you think you'll need to work on your essay.

4. Try a variety of prewriting techniques to help you find your essay's purpose and a narrowed, specific focus.

5. Review your audience's knowledge of and attitudes toward your topic before you begin your first draft; ask yourself questions such as "Who needs to know about this topic, and why?"

6. Consider keeping a journal to help you explore good ideas and possible topics for writing assignments in your composition class.

CHAPTER 2

The Thesis Statement

The famous American author Thomas Wolfe had a simple formula for beginning his writing: "Just put a sheet of paper in the typewriter and start bleeding." For some writers, the "bleeding" method works well. You may find that, indeed, you are one of those writers who must begin by freewriting or by writing an entire "discovery draft"* to find your purpose and focus—you must write yourself into your topic, so to speak. Other writers are more structured; they may prefer prewriting in lists, outlines, or cubes. Sometimes writers begin certain projects by composing one way, whereas other kinds of writing tasks profit from another method. There is no right or wrong way to find a topic or to begin writing; simply try to find the methods that work best for you.

Let's assume at this point that you have identified a topic you wish to write about—perhaps you found it by working through one of the prewriting activities mentioned in Chapter 1 or by writing in your journal. Perhaps you had an important idea you have been wanting to write about for some time, or perhaps the assignment in your class suggested the topic to you. Suppose that through one of these avenues you have focused on a topic and you have given some thought to a possible audience for your paper. You may now find it helpful to formulate a *working thesis.*

What Is a Thesis? What Does a "Working Thesis" Do?

The thesis statement declares the main point or controlling idea of your entire essay. Frequently located near the beginning of a short essay, the thesis answers these questions: "What is the subject of this essay?" "What is the writer's opinion on this subject?" "What is the writer's purpose in this essay?" (to explain something? to argue a position? to move people to action? to entertain?).

---

* ◆ If you do begin with a discovery draft, you may wish to turn at this point to the manuscript suggestions on pages 97–99 in Chapter 5.

Consider a "working thesis" a statement of your main point in its trial or rough-draft form. Allow it to "work" for you as you move from prewriting through drafts and revision. Your working thesis may begin as a very simple sentence. For example, one of the freewriting exercises on nature in Chapter 1 (pages 8–9) might lead to a working thesis such as "Our college needs an on-campus recycling center." Such a working thesis states an opinion about the subject (the need for a center) and suggests what the essay will do (give arguments for building such a center). Similarly, the prewriting list on running (page 7) might lead to a working thesis such as "Before beginning a successful program, novice runners must learn a series of warm-up and cool-down exercises." This statement not only tells the writer's opinion and purpose (the value of the exercises) but also indicates an audience (novice runners).

A working thesis statement can be your most valuable organizational tool. Once you have thought about your essay's main point and purpose, you can begin to draft your paper to accomplish your goals. *Everything in your essay should support your thesis.* Consequently, if you write your working thesis statement at the top of your first draft and refer to it often, your chances of drifting away from your purpose should be reduced.

Can a "Working Thesis" Change?

It's important for you to know at this point that there may be a difference between the working thesis that appears in your rough drafts and your final thesis. As you begin drafting, you may have one main idea in mind that surfaced from your prewriting activities. But as you write, you may discover that what you really want to write about is different. Perhaps you discover that one particular part of your essay is really what you want to concentrate on (instead of covering three or four problems you have with your current job, for instance, you decide you want to explore in depth only the difficulties with your boss), or perhaps in the course of writing you find another approach to your subject more satisfying or persuasive (explaining how employees may avoid problems with a particular kind of difficult boss instead of describing various kinds of difficult bosses in your field).

Changing directions is not uncommon: *writing is an act of discovery.* Frequently we don't know exactly what we think or what we want to say until we write it. A working thesis appears in your early drafts to help you focus and organize your essay; don't feel it's carved in stone.

A warning comes with this advice, however. If you do write yourself into another essay—that is, if you discover as you write that you are finding a better topic or main point to make—consider this piece of writing a "discovery draft," extended prewriting that has helped you find your real focus. Occasionally, your direction changes so slightly that you can rework or expand your thesis to accommodate your new ideas. But more frequently you may find that it's necessary to begin another draft with your newly discovered working thesis as the controlling idea. When this is the case, don't be discouraged—this kind of "reseeing" or revision of your topic is a common practice among experienced writers (◆ for more advice on revising as rethinking, see Chapter 5). Don't be tempted at this point to leave your original thesis in an essay that has clearly changed its point, purpose, or approach—in other words, don't try to pass off an old head on the body of a new statue! Remember that ultimately you want your thesis to guide your readers rather than confuse them by promising an essay they can't find as they read on.

Guidelines for Writing a Good Thesis

To help you draft your thesis statement, here is some advice:

A good thesis states the writer's clearly defined opinion on some subject. You must tell your reader what you think. Don't dodge the issue; present your opinion specifically and precisely. For example, if you were asked to write a thesis statement expressing your position on the national law that designates twenty-one as the legal minimum age to purchase or consume alcohol, the first three theses listed here would be confusing:

Poor	Many people have different opinions on whether people under twenty-one should be permitted to drink alcohol, and I agree with some of them. [The writer's opinion on the issue is not clear to the reader.]
Poor	The question of whether we need a national law governing the minimum age to drink alcohol is a controversial issue in many states. [This statement might introduce the thesis, but the writer has still avoided stating a clear opinion on the issue.]
Poor	I want to give my opinion on the national law that sets twenty-one as the legal age to drink alcohol and the reasons I feel this way. [What is the writer's opinion? The reader still doesn't know.]
Better	To reduce the number of highway fatalities, our country needs to enforce the national law that designates twenty-one as the legal minimum age to purchase and consume alcohol. [The writer clearly states an opinion that will be supported in the essay.]
Better	The legal minimum age for purchasing alcohol should be eighteen rather than twenty-one. [Again, the writer has asserted a clear position on the issue that will be argued in the essay.]

If you want to write about a personal experience but are finding it difficult to clearly define your thesis idea, try asking yourself questions about the topic's significance or value. (Examples: Why is this topic important to me? What was so valuable about my year on the newspaper staff? What was the most significant lesson I learned? What was an unexpected result of this experience?). Often the answer to one of your questions will show you the way to a working thesis. (Example: Writing for the school newspaper teaches time-management skills that are valuable both in and out of class).

A good thesis asserts one main idea. Many essays drift into confusion because the writer is trying to explain or argue two different, large issues in one essay. You can't effectively ride two horses at once; pick one main idea and explain or argue it in convincing detail.

Poor	The proposed no-smoking ordinance in our town will violate a number of our citizens' civil rights, and no one has proved that secondhand smoke is dangerous anyway. [This thesis contains two main assertions—the ordinance's

violation of rights and secondhand smoke's lack of danger—that require two different kinds of supporting evidence.]

Better   The proposed no-smoking ordinance in our town will violate our civil rights. [This essay will show the various ways the ordinance will infringe on personal liberties.]

Better   The most recent U.S. Health Department studies claiming that secondhand smoke is dangerous to nonsmokers are based on faulty research. [This essay will also focus on one issue: the validity of the studies on secondhand smoke danger.]

Poor   High school athletes shouldn't have to maintain a "B" or better grade-point average in all subjects to participate in school sports, and the value of sports for some students is often overlooked. [Again, this thesis moves in two different directions.]

Better   High school athletes shouldn't have to maintain a "B" or better grade-point average in all subjects to participate in school sports. [This essay will focus on one issue: reasons why a particular average shouldn't be required.]

Better   For some students, participation in sports may be more valuable than achieving a "B" grade-point average in all subjects. [This essay will argue that the benefits of sports sometimes outweigh those of elective classes.]

Incidentally, at this point you may recall from your high school days a rule about always expressing your thesis in one sentence. Writing teachers often insist on this rule to help you avoid the double-assertion problem just illustrated. Although not all essays have one-sentence theses, many do, and it's a good habit to strive for in this early stage of your writing.

A good thesis has something worthwhile to say. Although it's true that almost any subject can be made interesting with the right treatment, some subjects are more predictable and therefore more boring than others. Before you write your thesis, think hard about your subject: does your position lend itself to stale or overly obvious ideas? For example, most readers would find the following theses tiresome unless the writers had some original method of developing their essays:

Poor   Dogs have always been man's best friends. [This essay might be full of ho-hum clichés about dogs' faithfulness to their owners.]

Poor   Friendship is a wonderful thing. [Again, watch out for tired truisms that restate the obvious.]

Poor   The food in my dorm is horrible. [Although this essay might be enlivened by some vividly repulsive imagery, the subject itself is ancient.]

Frequently in composition classes you will be asked to write about yourself; after all, you are the world's authority on that subject, and you have many significant interests to talk about whose subject matter will naturally intrigue your readers. However, some topics you might consider writing about may not necessarily appeal to other readers because the material is simply too personal or restricted to be of general interest. In these cases, it often helps to *universalize* the essay's thesis so your readers can also identify with or learn something about the general subject, while learning something about you at the same time:

Poor   The four children in my family have completely different personalities. [This statement may be true, but would anyone other than the children's parents really be fascinated by this topic?]

Better   Birth order can influence children's personalities in startling ways. [The writer is wiser to offer this controversial statement, which is of more interest to readers than the preceding one because many readers have brothers and sisters of their own. The writer can then illustrate her claims with examples from her own family, and from other families, if she wishes.]

Poor   I don't like to take courses that are held in big lecture classes at this school. [Why should your reader care one way or another about your class preference?]

Better   Large lecture classes provide a poor environment for the student who learns best through interaction with both teachers and peers. [This thesis will allow the writer to present personal examples that the reader may identify with or challenge, without writing an essay that is exclusively personal.]

In other words, try to select a subject that will interest, amuse, challenge, persuade, or enlighten your readers. If your subject itself is commonplace, find a unique approach or an unusual, perhaps even controversial, point of view. If your subject is personal, ask yourself if the topic alone will be sufficiently interesting to readers; if not, think about universalizing the thesis to include your audience. Remember that a good thesis should encourage readers to read on with enthusiasm rather than invite groans of "Not this again" or shrugs of "So what?"

A good thesis is limited to fit the assignment. Your thesis should show that you've narrowed your subject matter to an appropriate size for your essay. Don't allow your thesis to promise more of a discussion than you can adequately deliver in a short essay. You want an in-depth treatment of your subject, not a superficial one. Certainly you may take on important issues in your essays; don't feel you must limit your topics to local or personal subjects. But one simply cannot refight the Vietnam War or effectively defend U.S. foreign policy in Central America in five to eight paragraphs. Focus your essay on an important part of a broader subject that interests you. (◆ For a review of ways to narrow and focus your subject, see pages 6–18.)

Poor   Nuclear power should be banned as an energy source in this country. [Can the writer give the broad subject of nuclear power a fair treatment in three to five pages?]

Better   Because of its poor safety record during the past two years, the Collin County nuclear power plant should be closed. [This writer could probably argue this focused thesis in a short essay.]

Poor   The parking permit system at this college should be completely revised. [An essay calling for the revision of the parking permit system would involve discussion of permits for various kinds of students, faculty, administrators, staff, visitors, delivery personnel, disabled people, and so forth. Therefore, the thesis is probably too broad for a short essay.]

Better   Because of the complicated application process, the parking permit system at this college penalizes disabled students. [This thesis is focused on a particular problem and could be argued in a short paper.]

Poor	African American artists have always contributed a lot to many kinds of American culture. ["African American artists," "many kinds," "a lot," and "culture" cover more ground than can be dealt with in one short essay.]
Better	Scott Joplin was a major influence in the development of the uniquely American music called ragtime. [This thesis is more specifically defined.]

A good thesis is clearly stated in specific terms. More than anything, a vague thesis reflects lack of clarity in the writer's mind and almost inevitably leads to an essay that talks around the subject but never makes a coherent point. Try to avoid words whose meanings are imprecise and those that depend largely on personal interpretation, such as "interesting," "good," and "bad."

Poor	The women's movement is good for our country. [What group does the writer refer to? How is it good? For whom?]
Better	The Colorado Women's Party is working to ensure the benefits of equal pay for equal work for both males and females in our state. [This tells who will benefit and how—clearly defining the thesis.]
Poor	Registration is a big hassle. [No clear idea is communicated here. How much trouble is a "hassle"?]
Better	Registration's alphabetical fee-paying system is inefficient. [The issue is specified.]
Poor	Living in an apartment for the first time can teach you many things about taking care of yourself. ["Things" and "taking care of yourself" are both too vague. What specific ideas does the writer want to discuss? And who is the "you" the writer has in mind?]
Better	By living in an apartment, a first-year student can learn valuable lessons in financial planning and time management. [The thesis is now clearly defined and directed.]

A good thesis is easily recognized as the main idea and is often located in the first or second paragraph. Many students are hesitant to spell out a thesis at the beginning of an essay. To quote one student, "I feel as if I'm giving everything away." Although you may feel uncomfortable "giving away" the main point so soon, the alternative of waiting until the last page to present your thesis can seriously weaken your essay.

Without an assertion of what you are trying to prove,

To avoid feeling swamped as you gather your prewriting thoughts, craft a working thesis to help steer you through your first draft.

Image copyright © The Metropolitan Museum of Art/Art Resource, NY

The Great Wave at Kanagawa, 1831, by Katsushika Hokusai

your reader does not know how to assess the supporting details your essay presents. For example, if your roommate comes home one afternoon and points out that the roof on your apartment leaks, the rent is too high, and the closet space is too small, you may agree but you may also be confused. Does your roommate want you to call the owner or is this merely a gripe session? How should you respond? On the other hand, if your roommate first announces that he wants the two of you to look for a new place, you can put the discussion of the roof, rent, and closets into its proper context and react accordingly. Similarly, you write an essay to have a specific effect on your readers. You will have a better chance of producing this effect if readers easily and quickly understand what you are trying to do.

Granted, some essays whose position is unmistakably obvious from the outset can get by with a strongly *implied thesis*, and it's true that some essays, often those written by professional writers, are organized to build dramatically to a climax. But if you are an inexperienced writer, the best choice at this point still may be a direct statement of your main idea. It is, after all, your responsibility to make your purpose clear, with as little expense of time and energy on the readers' part as possible. Readers should not be forced to puzzle out your essay's main point—it's your job to tell them.

Remember: An essay is not a detective story, so don't keep your readers in suspense until the last minute. Until you feel comfortable with more sophisticated patterns of organization, plan to put your clearly worded thesis statement near the beginning of your essay.

Avoiding Common Errors in Thesis Statements

Here are five mistakes to avoid when forming your thesis statements:

1. Don't make your thesis merely an announcement of your subject matter or a description of your intentions. State an attitude toward the subject.

Poor	The subject of this essay is my experience with a pet boa constrictor. [This is an announcement of the subject, not a thesis.]
Poor	I'm going to discuss boa constrictors as pets. [This represents a statement of intention but not a thesis.]
Better	Boa constrictors do not make healthy indoor pets. [The writer states an opinion that will be explained and defended in the essay.]
Better	My pet boa constrictor, Sir Pent, was a much better bodyguard than my dog, Fang. [The writer states an opinion that will be explained and illustrated in the essay.]

2. Don't clutter your thesis with such expressions as "in my opinion," "I believe," and "in this essay I'll argue that. . . ." These unnecessary phrases weaken your thesis statement because they often make you sound timid or uncertain. This is your essay; therefore, the opinions expressed are obviously yours. Be forceful: speak directly, with conviction.

Poor	My opinion is that the federal government should devote more money to solar energy research.
Poor	My thesis states that the federal government should devote more money to solar energy research.

Better	The federal government should devote more money to solar energy research.
Poor	In this essay I will present lots of reasons why horse racing should be abolished in Texas.
Better	Horse racing should be abolished in Texas.

3. Don't be unreasonable. Making irrational or oversimplified claims will not persuade your reader that you have a thorough understanding of the issue. Don't insult any reader; avoid irresponsible charges, name-calling, and profanity.

Poor	Radical religious fanatics across the nation are trying to impose their right-wing views by censoring high school library books. [Words such as "radical," "fanatics," "right-wing," and "censoring" will antagonize many readers immediately.]
Better	Only local school board members—not religious leaders or parents— should decide which books high school libraries should order.
Poor	Too many corrupt books in our high school libraries selected by liberal, atheistic educators are undermining the morals of our youth. [Again, some readers will be offended.]
Better	To ensure that high school libraries contain books that reflect community standards, parents should have a voice in selecting new titles.

4. Don't merely state a fact. A thesis is an assertion of opinion that leads to discussion. Don't select an idea that is self-evident or dead-ended.

Poor	Child abuse is a terrible problem. [Yes, of course, who wouldn't agree that child abuse is terrible?]
Better	Child-abuse laws in this state are too lenient for repeat offenders. [This thesis will lead to a discussion in which supporting arguments and evidence will be presented.]
Poor	Advertisers often use attractive models in their ads to sell products. [True, but rather obvious. How could this essay be turned into something more than a list describing one ad after another?]
Better	A number of liquor advertisers, well known for using pictures of attractive models to sell their products, are now using special graphics to send subliminal messages to their readers. [This claim is controversial and will require persuasive supporting evidence.]
Better	Although long criticized for its negative portrayal of women in television commercials, the auto industry is just as often guilty of stereotyping men as brainless idiots unable to make a decision. [This thesis makes a point that may lead to an interesting discussion.]

5. Don't express your thesis in the form of a question unless the answer is already obvious to the reader.

Poor	Why should every college student be required to take two years of foreign language?
Better	Chemistry majors should be exempt from the foreign-language requirement.

> REMEMBER: Many times writers "discover" a better thesis near the end of their first draft. That's fine—consider that draft a prewriting or focusing exercise and begin another draft, using the newly discovered thesis as a starting point.

PRACTICING WHAT YOU'VE LEARNED

A. Identify each of the following thesis statements as adequate or inadequate. If the thesis is weak or insufficient in some way, explain the problem.

1. I think *Schindler's List* is a really interesting movie that everyone should see.

2. Which cars are designed better, Japanese imports or those made in the United States?

3. Some people think that the state lottery is a bad way to raise money for parks.

4. My essay will tell you how to apply for a college loan with the least amount of trouble.

5. During the fall term, final examinations should be given before Winter Break, not after the holidays as they are now.

6. Raising the cost of tuition will be a terrible burden on the students and won't do anything to improve the quality of education at this school.

7. I can't stand to even look at people who are into body piercing, especially in their face.

8. The passage of the newly proposed health-care bill for the elderly will lead to socialized medicine in this country.

9. People over seventy-five should be required to renew their driver's licenses every year.

10. Having a close friend you can talk to is very important.

B. Rewrite the following sentences so that each one is a clear thesis statement. Be prepared to explain why you changed the sentences as you did.

1. Applying for a job can be a negative experience.

2. There are many advantages and disadvantages to the county's new voting machines.

continued on next page

3. Buying baseball tickets online is one big headache.

4. In this paper I will debate the pros and cons of the controversial motorcycle helmet law.

5. We need to do something about the billboard clutter on the main highway into town.

6. The insurance laws in this country need to be rewritten.

7. Bicycle riding is my favorite exercise because it's so good for me.

8. In my opinion, Santa Barbara is a fantastic place.

9. The Civil Rights Movement of the 1960s had a tremendous effect on this country.

10. All my friends like the band Thriving Ivory, and it's too bad they don't play more venues around here.

ASSIGNMENT

Narrow the subject and write one good thesis sentence for five of the following topics:

1. A political or social issue

2. College or high school

3. Family

4. A hobby or pastime

5. A recent book or movie

6. Vacations

7. An environmental issue

8. A current fad or fashion

9. A job or profession

10. A rule, law, or regulation

© CORBIS

Using the Essay Map*

Many thesis sentences will benefit from the addition of an *essay map*, a brief statement in the introductory paragraph introducing the major points to be discussed in the essay.

*I am indebted to Susan Wittig for this useful concept, introduced in *Steps to Structure: An Introduction to Composition and Rhetoric* (Cambridge, MA: Winthrop Publishers, 1975), pages 125–126.

Consider the analogy of beginning a trip by checking your map to see where you are headed. Similarly, an essay map allows the readers to know in advance where you, the writer, will be taking them in the essay.

Let's suppose you have been assigned the task of praising or criticizing some aspect of your campus. You decide that your thesis will be "The Study Skills Center is an excellent place for first-year students to receive help with basic courses." Although your thesis does take a stand ("excellent place"), your reader will not know why the Center is helpful or what points you will cover in your argument. With an essay map added, the reader will have a brief but specific idea where the essay is going and how it will be developed:

Thesis

Essay map
(underlined)

The Study Skills Center is an excellent place for first-year students to receive help with basic courses. <u>The Center's numerous free services, well-trained tutors, and variety of supplementary learning materials can often mean the difference between academic success and failure for many students.</u>

Thanks to the essay map, the reader knows that the essay will discuss the Center's free services, tutors, and learning materials.

Here's another example—this time let's assume you have been frustrated trying to read books your teacher has placed "on reserve" in your campus library, so you have decided to criticize your library's reserve facility:

Thesis
Essay map
(underlined)

The library's reserve facility is badly managed. <u>Its unpredictable hours, poor staffing, and inadequate space discourage even the most dedicated students.</u>

After reading the introductory paragraph, the reader knows the essay will discuss the reserve facility's problematic hours, staff, and space. In other words, the thesis statement defines the main purpose of your essay, and the essay map indicates the route you will take to accomplish that purpose.

The essay map often follows the thesis, but it can also appear before it. It is, in fact, frequently part of the thesis statement itself, as illustrated in the following examples:

Thesis with
underlined essay
map

<u>Because of its free services, well-trained tutors, and useful learning aids,</u> the Study Skills Center is an excellent place for students seeking academic help.

Thesis with
underlined essay
map

For those students who need extra help with their basic courses, the Study Skills Center is one of the best resources <u>because of its numerous free services, well-trained tutors, and variety of useful learning aids.</u>

Thesis with
underlined essay
map

<u>Unreasonable hours, poor staffing, and inadequate space</u> make the library reserve facility difficult to use.

In addition to suggesting the main points of the essay, the map provides two other benefits. It will provide a set of guidelines for organizing your essay, and it will help keep you from wandering off into areas only vaguely related to your thesis. A clearly written thesis statement and essay map provide a skeletal outline for the sequence of paragraphs in your essay, frequently with one body paragraph devoted to each main point mentioned in your map. (Chapter 3, on paragraphs, will explain in more detail the relationships among the thesis, the map, and the body of your essay.) Note that the number of points in the essay map may vary, although three or four may be the number found most often in 500-to-800-word essays. (◆ More than four main points in a short essay might result in underdeveloped paragraphs; see pages 59–63 for additional information.)

Some important advice: although essay maps can be helpful to both writers and readers, they can also sound too mechanical, repetitive, or obvious. If you choose to use a map, always strive to blend it with your thesis as smoothly as possible.

Poor	The Study Skills Center is a helpful place for three reasons. The reasons are its free services, good tutors, and lots of learning materials.
Better	Numerous free services, well-trained tutors, and a variety of useful learning aids make the Study Skills Center a valuable campus resource.

If you feel your essay map is too obvious or mechanical, try using it only in your rough drafts to help you organize your essay. Once you're sure it isn't necessary to clarify your thesis or to guide your reader, consider dropping it from your final draft.

© Canstock Images, Inc./
Index Stock Imagery

PRACTICING WHAT YOU'VE LEARNED

A. Identify the thesis and the essay map in the following sentences by underlining the map.

1. *Citizen Kane* deserves to appear on a list of "Top Movies of All Time" because of its excellent ensemble acting, its fast-paced script, and its innovative editing.

2. Our state should double the existing fines for first-offense drunk drivers. Such a move would lower the number of accidents, cut the costs of insurance, and increase the state revenues for highway maintenance.

3. To guarantee sound construction, lower costs, and personalized design, more people should consider building their own log cabin home.

4. Apartment living is preferable to dorm living because it's cheaper, quieter, and more luxurious.

5. Not everyone can become an astronaut. To qualify, a person must have intelligence, determination, and training.

6. Through unscrupulous uses of propaganda and secret assassination squads, Hitler was able to take control of an economically depressed Germany.

7. Because it builds muscles, increases circulation, and burns harmful fatty tissue, weightlifting is a sport that benefits the entire body.

8. The new tax bill will not radically reform the loophole-riddled revenue system: deductions on secondary residences will remain, real estate tax

shelters will be untouched, and nonprofit health organizations will be taxed.

9. Avocados make excellent plants for children. They're inexpensive to buy, easy to root, quick to sprout, and fun to grow.

10. His spirit of protest and clever phrasing blended into unusual musical arrangements have made Bob Dylan a recording giant for more than forty years.

B. Review the thesis statements you wrote for the Assignment on page 40. Write an essay map for each thesis statement. You may place the map before or after the thesis, or you may make it part of the thesis itself. Identify which part is the thesis and which is the essay map by underlining the map.

C. *Collaborative Activity:* Write a thesis sentence with an essay map for an essay you might write for this or another class. Exchange your work with that of a classmate and, drawing on the advice of this chapter, reconfirm strengths you see as well as offering suggestions for revision.

ASSIGNMENT

Use one of the following quotations to help you think of a subject for an essay of your own. Don't merely repeat the quotation itself as your thesis statement but, rather, allow the quotation to lead you to your subject and a main point of your own creation that is appropriately narrowed and focused. Don't forget to designate an audience for your essay, a group of readers who need or want to hear what you have to say.

1. "Opportunity is missed by most people because it is often dressed in overalls and looks like work."—Thomas Edison, inventor

2. "Sports do not build character. They reveal it."—Heywood Hale Broun, sportscaster

3. "The world is a book and those who don't travel read only a page."—St. Augustine, cleric

Jackie Robinson stealing home plate during the 1955 World Series

continued on next page

4. "It is never too late to be what one might have been."—George Eliot (Mary Ann Evans), writer

5. "Noncooperation with evil is as much a moral obligation as is cooperation with good."—Martin Luther King, Jr., statesman and civil-rights activist

6. "When a thing is funny, search it carefully for a hidden truth."—George Bernard Shaw, writer

7. "I am a great believer in luck, and I find the harder I work the more I have of it."—Stephen Leacock, economist and humorist

8. "It is never too late to give up your prejudices."—Henry Thoreau, writer and naturalist

9. "When an old person dies, a library burns to the ground."—African proverb

10. "In this world there are only two tragedies. One is not getting what one wants, and the other is getting it."—Oscar Wilde, writer

11. "Education is the most powerful weapon. You can use it to change the world."—Nelson Mandela, anti-apartheid activist and former President of South Africa

12. "The journey is the reward."—Taoist proverb

13. "You can discover more about a person in an hour of play than in a year of conversation."—Plato, philosopher

14. "Nobody can make you feel inferior without your consent."—Eleanor Roosevelt, stateswoman

15. "Never doubt that a small group of thoughtful, committed people can change the world. Indeed, it is the only thing that ever has."—Margaret Mead, anthropologist

16. "If you are patient in one moment of anger, you will escape a hundred days of sorrow."—Chinese proverb

17. "Let your hook be always cast; in the pool where you least expect it, there will be a fish."—Ovid, Roman poet

18. "Even if you are on the right track, you will get run over if you just sit there."—Will Rogers, humorist and writer

19. "No matter what accomplishments you make, somebody helps you." —Althea Gibson, tennis champion

20. "The rope of a lie is short."—Syrian proverb

21. "Pearls lie not on the seashore. If thou desirest one, thou must dive for it."—Chinese proverb

22. "I took the [road] less traveled by, and that has made all the difference." —from "The Road Not Taken" by Robert Frost, poet (◆ For the complete poem, see pages 481–482.)

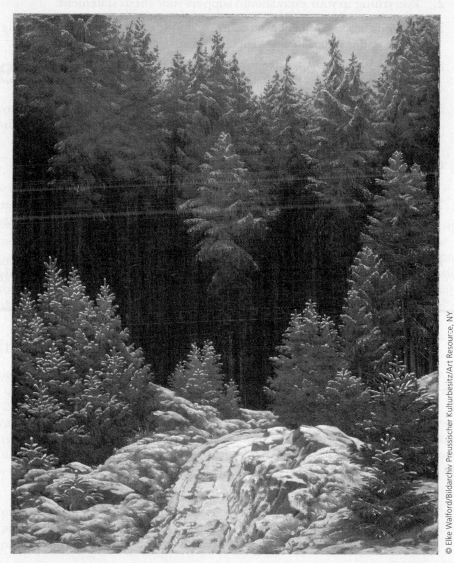

Early Snow, ca. 1827, by Caspar David Friedrich

© Elke Walford/Bildarchiv Preussischer Kulturbesitz/Art Resource, NY

When you are ready to begin drafting, read Chapter 5 for advice on composing and revising. ◆ Remember, too, that Chapter 5 contains suggestions for beating Writer's Block, should this condition arise while you are working on any part of your essay, as well as some specific hints on formatting your draft that may make revision easier (pages 97–101).

Composing the Body Paragraphs

There are many ways to organize and develop body paragraphs. Paragraphs developed by common patterns, such as example, comparison, and definition, will be discussed in specific chapters in Part Two; at this point, however, here are some comments about the general nature of all good body paragraphs that should help as you draft your essay.

> REMEMBER: Most of the body paragraphs in your essay will profit from a focused *topic sentence*. In addition, body paragraphs should have adequate *development*, *unity*, and *coherence*.

The Topic Sentence

Most body paragraphs present one main point in your discussion, expressed in a *topic sentence*. The topic sentence of a body paragraph has three important functions:

1. It supports the thesis by clearly stating a main point in the discussion.
2. It announces what the paragraph will be about.
3. It controls the subject matter of the paragraph. The entire discussion—the examples, details, and explanations—in a particular paragraph must directly relate to and support the topic sentence.

Think of a body paragraph (or a single paragraph) as a kind of mini-essay in itself. The topic sentence is, in a sense, a smaller thesis. It too asserts one main idea on a limited subject that the writer can explain or argue in the rest of the paragraph. Like the thesis, the topic sentence should be stated in as specific language as possible.

To see how a topic sentence works in a body paragraph, study this sample:

Essay Thesis: The Study Skills Center is an excellent place for students who need academic help.

Topic Sentence
1. The topic sentence supports the thesis by stating a main point (one reason the Center provides excellent academic help).

The Center offers students a variety of free services designed to improve basic skills. Those who discover their study habits are poor, for instance, may enroll in a six-week minicourse in study skills that offers advice on such topics as how to read a text, take notes, and organize material for review. Students whose math or writing skills are below par can sign up for free tutoring sessions held five days

2. The topic sentence announces the subject matter of the paragraph (a variety of free services that improve basic skills).

3. The topic sentence controls the subject matter (all the examples—the minicourse, the tutoring, the seminars, and the testing—support the claim of the topic sentence).

a week throughout each semester. In addition, the Center presents weekly seminars on special topics such as stress management and overcoming test anxiety for those students who are finding college more of a nerve-wracking experience than they expected; other students can attend evening seminars in such worthwhile endeavors as vocabulary building or spelling tips. Finally, the Center offers a series of tests to identify the presence of any learning disabilities, such as dyslexia, that might prevent a student from succeeding academically. With such a variety of free services, the Center can help almost any student.

© 2006 The Jacob and Gwendolyn Lawrence Foundation, Seattle/Artists Rights Society (ARS), New York; Smithsonian American Art Museum, Washington, DC/Art Resource, NY

The Library, 1960, by Jacob Lawrence

Here's another example from the essay on the library reserve facility:

Essay Thesis: The library's reserve facility is difficult for students to use.

Topic Sentence

1. The topic sentence supports the thesis by stating a main point (one reason the facility is difficult to use).

The library reserve facility's unpredictable hours frustrate even the most dedicated students. Instructors who place articles or books on reserve usually ask students to read them by a certain date. Too often, however, students arrive at the reserve desk only to find it closed. The facility's open hours change from week to week: students who used the room last week on Tuesday morning may discover that this week on Tuesday the desk is closed, which

2. The topic sentence announces the subject matter of the paragraph (the unpredictable hours).
3. The topic sentence controls the subject matter (all the examples—the changing hours, the sudden closures, the erratic holiday schedule—support the claim of the topic sentence).

means another trip. Perhaps even more frustrating are the facility's sudden, unannounced closures. Some of these closures allow staff members to have lunch or go on breaks, but, again, they occur without notice on no regular schedule. A student arrives, as I did two weeks ago, at the desk to find a "Be Back Soon" sign. In my case, I waited for nearly an hour. Another headache is the holiday schedule, which is difficult to figure out. For example, this year the reserve room was closed without advance notice on Presidents' Day but open on Easter; open during Winter Break but closed some days during Spring Break, a time many students use to catch up on their reserve assignments. Overall, the reserve facility would be much easier for students to use if it adopted a set schedule of operating hours, announced these times each semester, and maintained them.

Always be sure your topic sentences actually support the particular thesis of your essay. For example, the second topic sentence presented here doesn't belong in the essay promised by the thesis:

Thesis: Elk hunting should be permitted because it financially aids people in our state.

Topic Sentences

1. Fees for hunting licenses help pay for certain free, state-supported social services.

2. Hunting helps keep the elk population under control.

3. Elk hunting offers a means of obtaining free food for people with low incomes.

Although topic sentence 2 is about elk and may be true, it doesn't support the thesis's emphasis on financial aid and therefore should be tossed out of this essay.

Here's another example:

Thesis: During the past fifty years, movie stars have often tried to change the direction of America's politics.

Topic Sentences

1. During World War II, stars sold liberty bonds to support the country's war effort.

2. Many stars refused to cooperate with the blacklisting of their colleagues during the McCarthy Era in the 1950s.

3. Some stars were actively involved in protests against the Vietnam War.

4. More recently, stars have appeared in Congress criticizing the lack of legislative help for struggling farmers.

Topic sentences 2, 3, and 4 all show how stars have tried to effect a change. But topic sentence 1 says only that stars sold bonds to support, not *change*, the political direction of the nation. Although it does show stars involved in politics, it doesn't illustrate the claim of this particular thesis.

Sometimes a topic sentence needs only to be rewritten or slightly recast to fit:

Thesis: The recent tuition hike may discourage students from attending our college.

Topic Sentences

1. Students already pay more here than at other in-state schools.

2. Out-of-state students will have to pay an additional "penalty" to attend.

3. Tuition funds should be used for scholarships.

As written, topic sentence 3 doesn't show why students won't want to attend the school. However, a rewritten topic sentence does support the thesis:

3. Because the tuition money will not be used for scholarships, some students may not be able to afford this higher-priced school.

In other words, always check carefully to make sure that *all* your topic sentences clearly support your thesis's assertion.

Focusing Your Topic Sentence

A vague, fuzzy, or unfocused topic sentence most often leads to a paragraph that touches only on the surface of its subject or that wanders away from the writer's main idea. On the other hand, a topic sentence that is tightly focused and stated precisely not only will help the reader to understand the point of the paragraph but also will help you select, organize, and develop your supporting details.

Look, for example, at these unfocused topic sentences and their revisions:

Unfocused	Too many people treat animals badly in experiments. [What people? Badly how? What kinds of experiments?]
Focused	The cosmetic industry often harms animals in unnecessary experiments designed to test products.
Unfocused	Grades are an unfair pain in the neck. [Again, the focus is too broad. All grades? Unfair how?]
Focused	A course grade based on two multiple-choice exams doesn't accurately measure a student's knowledge of the subject.
Unfocused	Finding the right job is important and can lead to rewarding experiences. [Note both vague language and a double focus: "important" and "can lead to rewarding experiences."]
Focused	Finding the right job can lead to an improved sense of self-esteem.

◆ Before you practice writing focused topic sentences, you may wish to review pages 33–37, the advice on composing good thesis statements, as the same rules generally apply.

Placing Your Topic Sentence

Although the topic sentence most frequently occurs as the first sentence in the body paragraph, it also often appears as the second or last sentence. A topic sentence that directly follows the first sentence of a paragraph usually does so because the first sentence provides an introductory statement or some kind of "hook" to the preceding paragraph. A topic sentence frequently appears at the end of a paragraph that first presents particular details and then concludes with its central point. Here are two paragraphs in which the topic sentences do not appear first:

Introductory
sentence

Topic sentence

> Millions of Americans have watched the elaborate Rose Bowl Parade televised nationally each January from Pasadena, California. *Less well known, but growing in popularity, is Pasadena's Doo Dah Parade, an annual parody of the Rose Bowl spectacle, that specializes in wild-and-crazy participants.* Take this year's Doo Dah Precision Drill Team, for instance. Instead of marching in unison, the members cavorted down the avenue displaying—what else—a variety of precision electric drills. In heated competition with this group was the Synchronized Briefcase Drill Team, whose members wore gray pinstripe suits and performed a series of tunes by tapping on their briefcases. Another crowd-pleasing entry was the Citizens for the Right to Bare Arms, whose members sang while carrying aloft unclothed mannequin arms. The zany procession, led this year as always by the All-Time Doo Dah Parade Band, attracted more than 150,000 fans and is already preparing for its next celebration.

In the preceding paragraph, the first sentence serves as an introduction leading directly to the topic sentence. In the following example, the writer places the topic sentence last to sum up the information in the paragraph:

Topic sentence

> Rumors certainly fly around Washington's Capitol Building—but ghosts too? According to legend, the building was cursed in 1808 by construction superintendent John Lenthall, who was crushed by a falling ceiling following a feud with his architect over the wisdom of ceiling braces. Some workers in the building swear they have heard both the ghostly footsteps of James Garfield, who was assassinated after only four months as president, and the spooky last murmurings of John Quincy Adams, who died mid-speech on the House floor. Others claim to have seen a demon cat, so large and terrifying that it caused a guard to suffer a fatal heart attack. Perhaps the most cheerful ghosts appear on the night of a new president's swearing-in ceremony when the statues in Statuary Hall are said to leave their pedestals and dance at their own Inaugural Ball. *Whether these stories are true or merely the products of rich imaginations, the U.S. Capitol Building boasts the reputation as one of the most haunted buildings in America.*

As you can see, the position of topic sentences largely depends on what you are trying to do in your paragraph. And it's true that the purposes of some paragraphs are so obvious that no topic sentences are needed. However, if you are a beginning writer, you may want to practice putting your topic sentences first for a while to help you organize and unify your paragraphs.

Some paragraphs with a topic sentence near the beginning also contain a concluding sentence that makes a final general comment based on the supporting details. The last sentence of the following paragraph, for example, reemphasizes the main point.

Topic sentence

Of all nature's catastrophes, tornadoes may cause the most bizarre destruction. Whirling out of the sky at speeds up to 300 miles per hour, tornadoes have been known to drive broom handles through brick walls and straws into tree trunks. In one extreme case, a Kansas farmer reported that his prize rooster had been sucked into a two-gallon distilled-water bottle. More commonly, tornadoes lift autos and deposit them in fields miles away or uproot trees and drop them on lawns in neighboring towns. One tornado knocked down every wall in a house but one—luckily, the very wall shielding the terrified family. *Whenever a*

Concluding sentence *tornado touches the earth, spectacular headlines are sure to follow.*

Warning: Although topic sentences may appear in different places in a paragraph, there is one common error you should be careful to avoid. Do *not* put a topic sentence at the end of one body paragraph that belongs to the paragraph that follows it. For example, let's suppose you are writing an essay discussing a job you held recently, one that you enjoyed because of the responsibilities you were given, the training program you participated in, and the interaction you experienced with your coworkers. The body paragraph describing your responsibilities may end with its own topic sentence or with a concluding sentence about those responsibilities. However, that paragraph should not end with a sentence such as "Another excellent feature of this job was the training program for the next level of management." This "training program" sentence belongs in the *following* body paragraph as its topic sentence. Similarly, you would not end the paragraph on the training program with a topic sentence praising your experience with your coworkers.

If you feel that your paragraphs are ending too abruptly, consider using a concluding sentence, as described previously. Later in this chapter you will also learn some ways to smooth the flow from one paragraph to the next by using transitional devices and "idea hooks" (pages 77–78). For now, remember: Do *not* place a topic sentence that introduces and controls paragraph "B" at the end of paragraph "A." In other words, always place your topic sentence in the paragraph to which it belongs, to which it is topic-related, not at the end of the preceding paragraph.

© Canstock Images, Inc./
Index Stock Imagery

PRACTICING WHAT YOU'VE LEARNED

A. Point out the topic sentences in the following paragraphs; identify those paragraphs that also contain concluding sentences. Cross out any stray topic sentences that belong elsewhere.

Denim is one of America's most widely used fabrics. It was first introduced during Columbus's voyage, when the sails of the *Santa Maria* were made of the strong cloth. During our pioneer days, denim was used for tents, covered wagons, and the now-famous blue jeans. Cowboys found denim an ideal fabric for protection against sagebrush, cactus, and saddle sores. World War II also gave

continued on next page

denim a boost in popularity when sailors were issued jeans as part of their dress code. Today, denim continues to be in demand as more and more casual clothes are cut from the economical fabric. Because of its low cost and durability, manufacturers feel that denim will continue as one of America's most useful fabrics.

Adlai Stevenson, American statesman and twice an unsuccessful presidential candidate against Eisenhower, was well known for his intelligence and wit. Once on the campaign trail, after he had spoken eloquently and at length about several complex ideas, a woman in the audience was moved to stand and cheer, "That's great! Every thinking person in America will vote for you!" Stevenson immediately retorted, "That's not enough. I need a majority!" Frequently a reluctant candidate but never at a loss for words, Stevenson once defined a politician as a person who "approaches every question with an open mouth." Stevenson was also admired for his work as the Governor of Illinois and, later, as Ambassador to the United Nations.

Almost every wedding tradition has a symbolic meaning that originated centuries ago. For example, couples have been exchanging rings to symbolize unending love for over a thousand years. Most often, the rings are worn on the third finger of the left hand, which was thought to contain a vein that ran directly to the heart. The rings in ancient times were sometimes made of braided grass, rope, or leather, giving rise to the expression "tying the knot." Another tradition, the bridal veil, began when marriages were arranged by the families and the groom was not allowed to see his bride until the wedding. The tossing of rice at newlyweds has long signified fertility blessings, and the sweet smell of the bride's bouquet was intended to drive away evil spirits, who were also diverted by the surrounding bridal attendants. Weddings may vary enormously today, but many couples still include ancient traditions to signify their new life together.

You always think of the right answer five minutes after you hand in the test. You always hit the red light when you're already late for class. The one time you skip class is the day of the pop quiz. Back-to-back classes are always held in buildings at opposite ends of campus. The one course you need to graduate will not be offered your last semester. If any of these sound familiar, you've obviously been a victim of the "Murphy's Laws" that govern student life.

Want to win a sure bet? Then wager that your friends can't guess the most widely sold musical instrument in America today. Chances are they won't get the answer right—not even on the third try. In actuality, the most popular instrument in the country is neither the guitar nor the trumpet but the lowly kazoo. Last year alone, some three and one-half million kazoos were sold to music lovers of all ages. Part of the instrument's popularity arises from its availability, since kazoos are sold in variety stores and music centers nearly everywhere; another reason is its inexpensiveness—it ranges from the standard thirty-nine-cent model to the five-dollar gold-plated special. But perhaps the main reason for the kazoo's popularity is the ease with which it can be played by almost anyone—as can testify the members of the entire Swarthmore College marching band, who have now added a marching kazoo number to their repertoire. Louis Armstrong, move over!

It's a familiar scenario: Dad won't stop the car to ask directions, despite the fact that he's been hopelessly lost for over forty-five minutes. Mom keeps nagging Dad to slow down and finally blows up because your little sister suddenly remembers she's left her favorite doll, the one she can't sleep without, at the rest stop you left over an hour ago. Your legs are sweat-glued to the vinyl seats, you need desperately to go to the bathroom, and your big brother has just kindly acknowledged that he will relieve you of your front teeth if you allow any part of your body to extend over the imaginary line he has drawn down the backseat. The wonderful tradition known as the "family vacation" has begun.

B. Rewrite these topic sentences so that they are clear and focused rather than fuzzy or too broad.

1. My personality has changed a lot in the last year.

2. His date turned out to be really great.

3. The movie's special effects were incredible.

4. The Memorial Day celebration was more fun than ever before.

5. The evening with her parents was an unforgettable experience.

C. Add topic sentences to the following paragraphs:

Famous inventor Thomas Edison, for instance, did so poorly in his first years of school that his teachers warned his parents that he'd never be a success at anything. Henry Ford, the father of the auto industry, also had trouble in school with both reading and writing. But perhaps the best example is Albert Einstein, whose parents and teachers suspected that he was mentally disabled because he responded to questions so slowly and in a stuttering voice. Einstein's high school record was poor in everything but math, and he failed his college entrance exams the first time. Even out of school the man had trouble holding a job— until he announced the theory of relativity.

A 1950s felt skirt with Elvis's picture on it, for example, now sells for $150, and Elvis scarves go for as much as $300. Elvis handkerchiefs, originally 50 cents or less, fetch $150 in today's market; 1956 wallets imprinted with the singer's face have sold for over $400 each. Original posters from the Rock King's movies can sell for $750, and cards from the chewing gum series can run $30 apiece. Perhaps one of the most expensive collectors' items is the Emenee Elvis toy guitar that can cost a fan up to $1000, regardless of musical condition.

When successful playwright Jean Kerr once checked into a hospital, the receptionist asked her occupation and was told, "Writer." The receptionist said, "I'll just put down 'housewife.'" Similarly, when a British official asked W. H. Auden,

continued on next page

the award-winning poet and essayist, what he did for a living, Auden replied, "I'm a writer." The official jotted down "no occupation."

Cumberland College, for example, set the record back in 1916 for the biggest loss in college ball, having allowed Georgia Tech to run up 63 points in the first quarter and ultimately succumbing to them with a final score of 222 to nothing. In pro ball, the Washington Redskins are the biggest losers, going down in defeat 73 to 0 to the Chicago Bears in 1940. The award for the longest losing streak, however, goes to Northwestern University's team, who by 1981 had managed to lose 29 consecutive games. During that year, morale was so low that one disgruntled fan passing a local highway sign that read "Interstate 94" couldn't resist adding "Northwestern 0."

D. Write a focused topic sentence for five of the following subjects:

1. Job interviews
2. Friends
3. Food
4. Money
5. Selecting a major or occupation
6. Clothes
7. Music
8. Dreams
9. Housing
10. Childhood

ASSIGNMENT

Review the thesis statements with essay maps you wrote for the practice exercise on page 43. Choose two, and from each thesis create at least three topic sentences for possible body paragraphs.

© CORBIS

APPLYING WHAT YOU'VE LEARNED TO **YOUR** WRITING

If you currently have a working thesis statement you have written in response to an assignment in your composition class, try sketching out an outline or a plan for the major ideas you wish to include. After you write a draft, underline the topic sentences in your body paragraphs. Do your

© Keith Brofsky/
Photodisc/Getty Images

topic sentences directly support your thesis? If you find that they do not clearly support your thesis, you must decide if you need to revise your draft's organization or whether you have, in fact, discovered a new, and possibly better, subject to write about. If the latter is true, you'll need to redraft your essay so that your readers will not be confused by a paper that announces one subject but discusses another. (◆ See Chapter 5 for more information on revising your drafts.)

Paragraph Development

Possibly the most serious—and most common—weakness of all essays by novice writers is *the lack of effectively developed body paragraphs.* The information in each paragraph must adequately explain, exemplify, define, or in some other way support your topic sentence. Therefore, you must include *enough supporting information* or *evidence* in each paragraph to make your readers understand your topic sentence. Moreover, you must make the information in the paragraph clear and specific enough for the readers to accept your ideas.

The next paragraph is *underdeveloped.* Although the topic sentence promises a discussion of Jesse James as a Robin Hood figure, the paragraph does not provide enough specific supporting evidence (in this case, examples) to explain this unusual view of the gunfighter.

> Although he was an outlaw, Jesse James was considered a Robin Hood figure in my hometown in Missouri. He used to be generous to the poor, and he did many good deeds, not just robberies. In my hometown people still talk about how lots of the things James did weren't all bad.

Rewritten, the paragraph might read as follows:

> Although he was an outlaw, Jesse James was considered a Robin Hood figure in my hometown in Missouri. Jesse and his gang chose my hometown as a hiding place, and they set out immediately to make friends with the local people. Every Christmas for four years, the legend goes, he dumped bags of toys on the doorsteps of poor children. The parents knew the toys had been bought with money stolen from richer people, but they were grateful anyway. On three occasions, Jesse gave groceries to the dozen neediest families—he seemed to know when times were toughest—and once he supposedly held up a stage to pay for an old man's operation. In my hometown, some people still sing the praises of Jesse James, the outlaw who wasn't all bad.

The topic sentence promises a discussion of James's generosity and delivers just that by citing specific examples of his gifts to children, the poor, and the sick. The paragraph is therefore better developed.

The following paragraph offers reasons but no specific examples or details to support its claims:

> Living with my ex-roommate was unbearable. First, she thought everything she owned was the best. Second, she possessed numerous filthy habits. Finally, she constantly exhibited immature behavior.

The writer might provide more evidence this way:

> Living with my ex-roommate was unbearable. First, she thought everything she owned, from clothes to cosmetics, was the best. If someone complimented my pants, she'd point out that her designer jeans looked better and would last longer because they were made of better material. If she borrowed my shampoo, she'd let me know that it didn't get her hair as clean and shiny as hers did. My hand cream wasn't as smooth; my suntan lotion wasn't as protective; not even my wire clothes hangers were as good as her padded ones! But despite her pickiness about products, she had numerous filthy habits. Her dirty dishes remained in the sink for days before she felt the need to wash them. Piles of the "best" brand of tissues were regularly discarded from her upper bunk and strewn about the floor. Her desk and closets overflowed with heaps of dirty clothes, books, cosmetics, and whatever else she owned, and she rarely brushed her teeth (when she did brush, she left oozes of toothpaste in the sink). Finally, she constantly acted immaturely by throwing tantrums when things didn't go her way. A poor grade on an exam or paper, for example, meant books, shoes, or any other small object within her reach would hit the wall flying. Living with such a person taught me some valuable lessons about how not to win friends or keep roommates.

By adding more supporting evidence—specific examples and details—to this paragraph, the writer has a better chance of convincing the reader of the roommate's real character.

Where does evidence come from? Where do writers find their supporting information? Evidence comes from many sources. Personal experiences, memories, observations, hypothetical examples, reasoned arguments, facts, statistics, testimony from authorities, many kinds of studies and research—all these and more can help you make your points clear and persuasive. In the paragraph on Jesse James, for example, the writer relied on stories and memories from his hometown. The paragraph on the obnoxious roommate was supported by examples gained through the writer's personal observation. The kind of supporting evidence you choose for your paragraphs depends on your purpose and your audience; as the writer, you must decide what will work best to make your readers understand and accept each important point in your discussion. (◆ For advice on ways to think critically about evidence, see Chapter 5; for more information on incorporating research material into your essays, see Chapter 14.)

Having a well-developed paragraph is more than a matter of adding material or expanding length, however. The information in each paragraph must effectively explain or support your topic sentence. *Vague generalities or repetitious ideas are not convincing.* Look, for example, at the following paragraph, in which the writer offers only generalities:

> We ought to ban the use of cell phones in moving vehicles. Some people who have them think that's a really good idea, but a lot of us don't agree. Using a phone while driving causes too many dangerous accidents to happen, and even if there's no terrible accident, people using them have been known to do some really stupid things in traffic. Drivers using phones are constantly causing problems for other drivers; pedestrians are in big trouble from these people too. I think this is getting to be a really dangerous situation, and we ought to do something about it soon.

This paragraph is weak because it is composed of repetitious general statements using vague, unclear language. None of its general statements is supported with specific evidence. Why is car phone use not a "good" idea? How does it cause accidents? What are the "problems" and "trouble" the writer refers to? What exactly does "do something about it" mean? The writer obviously had some ideas in mind, but these ideas are not clear to the reader because they are not adequately developed with specific evidence and language.

By adding supporting examples and details, the writer might revise the paragraph this way:

> Although cell phones are a time-saving convenience for busy people, they are too distracting for use by drivers of moving vehicles, whose lack of full attention poses a serious threat to other drivers and to pedestrians. The simple act of dialing or answering a phone, for example, may take a driver's eyes away from traffic signals or other cars. Moreover, involvement in a complex or emotional conversation could slow down a driver's response time just when fast action is needed to avoid an accident. Last week I drove behind a man using his phone. As he drove and talked, I could see him gesturing wildly, obviously agitated with the other caller. His speed repeatedly slowed and then picked up, slowed and increased, and his car drifted more than once, on a street frequently crossed by schoolchildren. Because the man was clearly not in full, conscious control of his driving, he was dangerous. My experience is not isolated; a recent study by the Foundation for Traffic Safety maintains that using a cell phone is more distracting to drivers than listening to the radio or talking to a rider. With additional studies in progress, voters in our state should soon demand legislation to restrict phone use to passengers or to drivers when the vehicles are not in motion.

The reader now has a better idea why the writer feels such cell phone use is distracting and, consequently, dangerous. By using two hypothetical examples (looking away, slowed response time), one personal experience (observing the agitated man), and one reference to research (the safety study), the writer offers the reader three kinds of supporting evidence for the paragraph's claim.

After examining the following two paragraphs, decide which explains its point more effectively.

1   Competing in an Ironman triathlon is one of the most demanding feats known to amateur athletes. First, they have to swim many miles, and that takes a lot of endurance. Then they ride a bicycle a long way, which is also hard on their bodies. Last, they run a marathon, which can be difficult in itself but is especially hard after the first two events. Competing in the triathlon is really tough on the participants.

2   Competing in an Ironman triathlon is one of the most demanding feats known to amateur athletes. During the first stage of the triathlon, the competitors must swim 2.4 miles in the open ocean. They have to battle the constantly choppy ocean, the strong currents, and the frequent swells. The wind is often an adversary, and stinging jellyfish are a constant threat. Once they have completed the ocean swim, the triathletes must ride 112 miles on a bicycle. In addition to the strength needed to pedal that far, the bicyclists must use a variety of hand grips to ensure the continued circulation in their fingers and hands as well as to ease the strain on the neck and shoulder muscles. Moreover, the concentration necessary to steady the

bicycle as well as the attention to the inclines on the course and the consequent shifting of gears causes mental fatigue for the athletes. After completing these two grueling segments, the triathletes must then run 26.2 miles, the length of a regular marathon. Dehydration is a constant concern, as is the prospect of cramping. Even the pain and swelling of a friction blister can be enough to eliminate a contestant at this late stage of the event. Finally, disorientation and fatigue can set in and distort the athlete's judgment. Competing in an Ironman triathlon takes incredible physical and mental endurance.

The first paragraph contains, for the most part, repetitious generalities; it repeats the same idea (the triathlon is hard work) and gives few specific details to illustrate the point presented in the topic sentence. The second paragraph, however, does offer many specific examples and details—the exact mileage figures, the currents, jellyfish, inclines, grips, blisters, and so forth—that help the reader understand why the event is so demanding.

Joseph Conrad, the famous novelist, once remarked that a writer's purpose was to use "the power of the written word to make you hear, to make you feel . . . before all, to make you *see*. That—and no more, and it is everything." By using specific details instead of vague, general statements, you can write an interesting, convincing essay. Ask yourself as you revise your paragraphs, "Have I provided enough information, presented enough clear, precise details to make my readers see what I want them to?" In other words, a well-developed paragraph effectively makes its point with *an appropriate amount of specific supporting evidence*. (Remember that a paragraph in a handwritten rough draft will look much shorter when it is typed. Therefore, if you can't think of much to say about a particular idea, you should gather more information or consider dropping it as a major point in your essay.)

Paragraph Length

"How long is a good paragraph?" is a question novice writers often ask. Like a teacher's lecture or a preacher's sermon, paragraphs should be long enough to accomplish their purpose and short enough to be interesting. In truth, there is no set length, no prescribed number of lines or sentences, for any of your paragraphs. In a body paragraph, your topic sentence presents the main point, and the rest of the paragraph must give enough supporting evidence to convince the reader. Although unnecessary or repetitious detail is boring, too little discussion will leave the reader uninformed, unconvinced, or confused.

Although paragraph length varies, beginning writers should avoid the one- or two-sentence paragraphs frequently seen in newspapers or magazine articles. (Journalists have their own rules to follow; paragraphs are shorter in newspapers, for one reason, because large masses of print in narrow columns are difficult to read quickly.) Essay writers do occasionally use the one-sentence paragraph, most often to produce some special effect, when the statement is especially dramatic or significant and needs to call attention to itself or when an emphatic transition is needed. For now, however, you should concentrate on writing well-developed body paragraphs.

One more note on paragraph length: sometimes you may discover that a particular point in your essay is so complex that your paragraph is growing far too long—well over a typed page, for instance. If this problem occurs, look for a logical place to divide your information and start a new paragraph. For example, you might see a convenient dividing point in a series of actions you're describing or a break in the chronology of a narrative or between explanations of arguments or examples. Just make sure you begin your next paragraph with some sort of transitional phrase or key words to let the reader know that you are still discussing the same point as before ("Still another problem caused by the computer's faulty memory circuit is . . .").

PRACTICING WHAT YOU'VE LEARNED

A. Analyze the following paragraphs. Explain how you might improve the development of each one.

1. Professor Wilson is the best teacher I've ever had. His lectures are interesting, and he's very concerned about his students. He makes the class challenging but not too hard. On tests he doesn't expect more than one can give. I think he's a great teacher.

2. Newspaper advice columns are pretty silly. The problems are generally stupid or unrealistic, and the advice is out of touch with today's world. Too often the columnist just uses the letter to make a smart remark about some pet peeve. The columns could be put to some good uses, but no one tries very hard.

3. Driving tests do not adequately examine a person's driving ability. Usually the person being tested does not have to drive very far. The test does not require the skills that are used in everyday driving situations. Supervisors of driving tests tend to be very lenient.

4. Nursing homes are often sad places. They are frequently located in ugly old buildings unfit for anyone. The people there are lonely and bored. What's more, they're sometimes treated badly by the people who run the homes. It's a shame something better can't be done for the elderly.

5. There is a big difference between acquaintances and friends. Acquaintances are just people you know slightly, but friends give you some important qualities. For example, they can help you gain self-esteem and confidence just by being close to you. By sharing their friendship, they also help you feel happy about being alive.

B. Practice developing paragraphs by choosing two of the following three topics, fleshing out each paragraph with an example from your own experience or that of a close friend. Use vivid, specific details to make each paragraph clear and interesting. (If you cannot think of an appropriate example, you

continued on next page

© Canstock Images, Inc./ Index Stock Imagery

may rework the topic sentence; for instance, in the first paragraph, you might change the topic to a product or service that exceeded your expectations rather than one that disappointed you.)

1. Too many products today have expensive advertising campaigns but simply don't live up to their claims. For instance,

2. Sooner or later, almost everyone experiences that dreaded moment when he or she suddenly forgets something familiar. Someone forgets a friend's name in the middle of an introduction; someone else experiences memory loss standing in front of the ATM or just after volunteering to answer a question in class. I too have temporarily "gone blank," but eventually regained my composure. For example,

3. Unexpected help is a miracle that often comes just in time to prevent a disaster or foolish move. Such help can come from a variety of sources— from friends, family, or even strangers. For example,

© CORBIS

ASSIGNMENT

A. Find two well-developed paragraphs in an essay or book; explain why you think the paragraphs are successfully developed.

B. Select one of the paragraphs from Practice A (page 63) and rewrite it, adding enough specific details to make a well-developed paragraph.

C. *Collaborative Activity:* Exchange paragraphs with a classmate. Mark any weaknesses you see in the topic sentence or in the paragraph's development. Rewrite at least one problematic area so that the paragraph is stronger, with enough appropriate supporting detail. In a sentence or two, explain why you made the changes you did.

© Keith Brofsky/
Photodisc/Getty Images

APPLYING WHAT YOU'VE
LEARNED TO **YOUR** WRITING

If you are currently drafting an essay, look closely at your body paragraphs. Find the topic sentence in each paragraph, and circle the key words that most clearly communicate the main idea of the paragraph. Then ask yourself whether the information in each paragraph effectively supports, explains, or illustrates the main idea of the paragraph's topic sentence. Is there enough information? If you're not sure, try numbering your supporting details. Are there too few to be persuasive? Does the paragraph present clear, specific supporting material, or does it contain too many vague generalities to be convincing? Where could you add more details to help the reader understand your ideas better and to make each paragraph more interesting? (◆ For more help revising your paragraphs, see Chapter 5.)

Paragraph Unity

Every sentence in a body paragraph should relate directly to the main idea presented by the topic sentence. A paragraph must stick to its announced subject; it must not drift away into another discussion. In other words, a good paragraph has *unity*.

Examine the following unified paragraph; note that the topic sentence clearly states the paragraph's main point and that each sentence thereafter supports the topic sentence.

(1)Frank Lloyd Wright, America's leading architect of the first half of the twentieth century, believed that his houses should blend naturally with their building sites. (2) Consequently, he designed several "prairie houses," whose long, low lines echoed the flat earth plane. (3)Built of brick, stone, and natural wood, the houses shared a similar texture with their backgrounds. (4)Large windows were often used to blend the interior and exterior of the houses. (5)Wright also punctuated the lines and spaces of the houses with greenery in planters to further make the buildings look like part of nature.

The first sentence states the main idea, that Wright thought houses should blend with their location, and the other sentences support this assertion:

Topic Sentence: (1) Wright's houses blend with their natural locations

(2) long, low lines echo flat prairie

(3) brick, stone, wood provide same texture as location

(4) windows blend inside with outside

(5) greenery in planters imitates the natural surroundings

Now look at the next paragraph, in which the writer strays from his original purpose:

(1)Cigarette smoke is unhealthy even for people who don't have the nicotine habit themselves. (2)Secondhand smoke can cause asthmatics and sufferers of sinusitis serious

Frank Lloyd Wright's Fallingwater House in Bear Run, Pennsylvania

© Richard A. Cooke/CORBIS

problems. [3]Doctors regularly advise heart patients to avoid confined smoky areas because coronary attacks might be triggered by the lack of clean air. [4]Moreover, having the smell of smoke in one's hair and clothes is a real nuisance. [5]Even if a person is without any health problems, exhaled smoke doubles the amount of carbon monoxide in the air, a condition that may cause lung problems in the future.

Sentence 4 refers to smoke as a nuisance and therefore does not belong in a paragraph that discusses smoking as a health hazard to nonsmokers.

Sometimes a large portion of a paragraph will drift into another topic. In the following paragraph, did the writer wish to focus on her messiness or on the beneficial effects of her engagement?

> I have always been a very messy person. As a child, I was a pack rat, saving every little piece of insignificant paper that I thought might be important when I grew up. As a teenager, I filled my pockets with remnants of basketball tickets, hall passes, gum wrappers, and other important articles from my high school education. As a college student, I became a boxer—not a fighter, but someone who cannot throw anything away and therefore it winds up in a box in my closet. But my engagement has changed everything. I'm really pleased with the new stage of my life, and I owe it all to my fiancé. My overall outlook on life has changed because of his influence on me. I'm neater, much more cheerful, and I'm even getting places on time like I never did before. It's truly amazing what love can do.

Note shift from the topic of messiness

This writer may wish to discuss the changes her fiancé has inspired and then use her former messiness, tardiness, and other bad habits as examples illustrating those changes; however, as presented here, the paragraph is not unified around a central idea. On the contrary, it first seems to promise a discussion of her messiness but then wanders into comments on "what love can do."

Also beware a tendency to end your paragraph with a new idea. A new point calls for an entirely new paragraph. For example, the following paragraph focuses on the *origins* of Muzak; the last sentence, on Muzak's *effects* on workers, should be omitted or moved to a paragraph on Muzak's uses in the workplace.

> Muzak, the ever-present sound of music that pervades elevators, office buildings, and reception rooms, was created over seventy years ago by George Owen Squier, an army general. A graduate of West Point, Squier was also an inventor and scientist. During World War I he headed the Signal Corps, where he began experimenting with the notion of transmitting simultaneous messages over power lines. When he retired from the army in 1922, he founded Wired Radio, Inc., and later, in 1934, the first Muzak medley was heard in Cleveland, Ohio, for homeowners willing to pay the great sum of $1.50 a month. That year he struck upon the now-famous name, which combined the idea of music with the brand name of the country's most popular camera, Kodak. *Today, experiments show that workers get more done when they listen to Muzak.*

Breaks unity

In general, think of paragraph unity in terms of the following diagram:

The sentences in the paragraph support the paragraph's topic sentence; the paragraph, in turn, supports the thesis statement.

PRACTICING WHAT YOU'VE LEARNED

In each of the following examples, delete or rewrite any information that interferes with the unity of the paragraph or begins to drift off topic:

In the Great Depression of the 1930s, American painters suffered severely because few people had the money to spend on the luxury of owning art. To keep our artists from starving, the government ultimately set up the Federal Art Project, which paid then little-known painters such as Jackson Pollock, Arshile Gorky, and Willem de Kooning to paint murals in post offices, train stations, schools, housing projects, and other public places. During this period, songwriters were also affected by the Depression, and they produced such memorable songs as "Brother, Can You Spare a Dime?" The government-sponsored murals, usually depicting familiar American scenes and historical events, gave our young artists an opportunity to develop their skills and new techniques; in return, our country obtained thousands of elaborate works of art in over one thousand American cities. Sadly, many of these artworks were destroyed in later years as public buildings were torn down or remodeled.

After complaining in vain about the quality of food in the campus restaurant, University of Colorado students are having their revenge after all. The student body recently voted to rename the grill after Alferd Packer, the only American ever convicted of cannibalism. Packer was a Utah prospector trapped with an expedition of explorers in the southwest Colorado mountains during the winter of 1874; the sole survivor of the trip, he was later tried by a jury and sentenced to hang for dining on at least five of his companions. Colorado students are now holding an annual "Alferd Packer Day" and have installed a mural relating the prospector's story on the main wall of the restaurant. Some local wits

continued on next page

have also suggested a new motto for the bar and grill: "Serving our fellow man since 1874." Another well-known incident of cannibalism in the West occurred in the winter of 1846, when the Donner party, a wagon train of eighty-seven California-bound immigrants, became trapped by ice and snow in the Sierra Nevada mountain range.

Inventors of food products often name their new creations after real people. In 1896 Leo Hirshfield hand-rolled a chewy candy and named it after his daughter Clara, nicknamed Tootsie. In 1920 Otto Schnering gave the world the Baby Ruth candy bar, named after the daughter of former President Grover Cleveland. To publicize his new product, Schnering once dropped the candy tied to tiny parachutes from an airplane flying over Pittsburgh. One of our most popular soft drinks was named by a young suitor who sought to please his sweetheart's physician father, none other than old Dr. Pepper. Despite the honor, the girl's father never approved of the match, and the young man, Wade Morrison, married someone else.

States out West have often led the way in recognizing women's roles in politics. Wyoming, for example, was the first state to give women the right to vote and hold office, back in 1869 while the state was still a territory. Colorado was the second state to grant women's suffrage; Idaho, the third. Wyoming was also the first state to elect a woman as governor, Nellie Tayloe Ross, in 1924. Montana elected Jeannette Rankin as the nation's first congresswoman in 1916. Former U.S. Representative from Colorado Patricia Schroeder claims to be the first person to take the congressional oath of office while clutching a handbag full of diapers. Ms. Schroeder later received the National Motherhood Award.

Living in a college dorm is a good way to meet people. There are activities every weekend, such as game night and parties where one can get acquainted with all kinds of students. Even just sitting by someone in the cafeteria during a meal can start a friendship. Making new friends from foreign countries can teach students more about international relations. A girl on my dorm floor, for example, is from Peru, and I've learned a lot about the customs and culture in her country. She's also helping me with my study of Spanish. I hope to visit her in Peru some day.

APPLYING WHAT YOU'VE LEARNED TO **YOUR** WRITING

© Keith Brofsky/
Photodisc/Getty Images

If you have written a draft of an essay, underline the topic sentence in each body paragraph and circle the key words.
For example, if in an essay on America's growing health consciousness, one of your topic sentences reads "In an effort to improve their health, Americans have increased the number of vitamins they consume," you might circle "Americans,"

"increased," and "vitamins." Then look closely at your paragraph. All the information in that paragraph should support the idea expressed in your topic sentence; nothing should detract from the idea of showing that Americans have increased their vitamin consumption. Now study the paragraphs in your draft, one by one. Cross out any sentence or material that interferes with the ideas in your topic sentences. If one of your paragraphs begins to drift away from its topic-sentence idea, you will need to rethink the purpose of that paragraph and rewrite so that the reader will understand what the paragraph is about. (◆ For additional help revising your drafts, turn to Chapter 5.)

Paragraph Coherence

In addition to unity, *coherence* is essential to a good paragraph. Coherence means that all the sentences and ideas in your paragraph flow together to make a clear, logical point about your topic. Your paragraph should not be a confusing collection of ideas set down in random order. The readers should be able to follow what you have written and see easily and quickly how each sentence grows out of, or is related to, the preceding sentence. To achieve coherence, you should have a smooth connection or transition between the sentences in your paragraphs.

There are five important means of achieving coherence in your paragraphs:

1. A natural or easily recognized order
2. Transitional words and phrases
3. Repetition of key words
4. Substitution of pronouns for key nouns
5. Parallelism

These transitional devices are similar to the couplings between railroad cars; they enable the controlling engine to pull the train of thought along as a unit.

A Recognizable Ordering of Information

Without consciously thinking about the process, you may often organize paragraphs in easily recognized patterns that give the reader a sense of logical movement and order. Four common patterns of ordering sentences in a paragraph are discussed here.

The Order of Time

Some paragraphs are composed of details arranged in chronological order. You might, for example, explain the process of changing an oil filter on your car by beginning with the first step, draining the old oil, and concluding with the last step, installing the new filter. Here is a paragraph on black holes in which the writer chronologically orders the details:

A black hole in space, from all indications, is the result of the death of a star. Scientists speculate that stars were first formed from the gases floating in the universe at the beginning of time. In the first stage in the life of a star, the hot gas is drawn by the force of gravity into a burning sphere. In the middle stage—our own sun being a middle-aged star—the burning continues at a regular rate, giving off enormous amounts of heat and light. As it grows old, however, the star eventually explodes to become what is called a nova, a superstar. But gravity soon takes over again, and the exploded star falls back in on itself with such force that all the matter in the star is compacted into a mass no larger than a few miles in diameter. At this point, no heavenly body can be seen in that area of the sky, as the tremendous pull of gravity lets nothing escape, not even light. A black hole has thus been formed.

The Order of Space

When your subject is a physical object, you should select some orderly means of describing it: from left to right, top to bottom, inside to outside, and so forth. For example, you might describe a sculpture as you walk around it from front to back. In the following paragraph describing a cowboy, the writer has ordered the details of the description in a head-to-feet pattern:

> Big Dave was pure cowboy. He wore a black felt hat so big that it kept his face in perpetual shade. Around his neck was knotted a red bandana stained with sweat from long hot days in the saddle. An oversized blue denim shirt hung from his shoulders to give him plenty of arm freedom, and his faded jeans were held up by a broad leather belt with a huge silver buckle featuring a snorting bronc in full buck. His boots, old and dirt-colored, kicked up little dust storms as he sauntered across the corral.

Deductive Order

A paragraph ordered deductively moves from a generalization to particular details that explain or support the general statement. Perhaps the most common pattern of all paragraphs, the deductive paragraph begins with its topic sentence and proceeds to its supporting details, as illustrated in the following example:

> If a group of 111 ninth-graders is typical of today's teenagers, spelling and social science teachers may be in for trouble. In a recent experiment, not one of the students tested could write the Pledge of Allegiance correctly. In addition, the results showed that the students apparently had little understanding of the pledge's meaning. For example, several students described the United States as a "nation under guard" instead of "under God," and the phrase "to the Republic for which it stands" appeared in several responses as "of the richest stand" or "for Richard stand." Many students changed the word "indivisible" to the phrase "in the visible," and over 9 percent of the students, all of whom are Americans from varying racial and ethnic backgrounds, misspelled the word "America."

Inductive Order

An inductive paragraph begins with an examination of particular details and then concludes with a larger point or generalization about those details. Such a paragraph often ends with its topic sentence, as does the following paragraph on Little League baseball:

> At too many Little League baseball games, one or another adult creates a minor scene by yelling rudely at an umpire or a coach. Similarly, it is not uncommon to hear

adults whispering loudly with one another in the stands over which child should have caught a missed ball. Perhaps the most astounding spectacle of all, however, is an irate parent or coach yanking a child off the field after a bad play for a humiliating lecture in front of the whole team. Sadly, Little League baseball today often seems intended more for childish adults than for the children who actually play it.

Transitional Words and Phrases

Some paragraphs may need internal transitional words to help the reader move smoothly from one thought to the next so that the ideas do not appear disconnected or choppy.

Here is a list of common transitional words and phrases and their uses:

giving examples	for example, for instance, specifically, in particular, namely, another, other, in addition, to illustrate
comparison	similarly, not only . . . but also, in comparison
contrast	although, but, while, in contrast, however, though, on the other hand, nevertheless
sequence	first . . . second . . . third, finally, moreover, also, in addition, next, then, after, furthermore, and, previously
results	therefore, thus, consequently, as a result

Notice the difference the use of transitional words makes in the following paragraphs:

Working in the neighborhood grocery store as a checker was one of the worst jobs I've ever had. In the first place, I had to wear an ugly, scratchy uniform cut at least three inches too short. My schedule of working hours was another inconvenience; because my hours were changed each week, it was impossible to make plans in advance, and getting a day off was out of the question. In addition, the lack of working space bothered me. Except for a half-hour lunch break, I was restricted to three square feet of room behind the counter and consequently felt as if I were no more than a cog in the cash register.

The same paragraph rewritten without transitional words sounds choppy and childish:

Working in the neighborhood grocery store as a checker was one of the worst jobs I've ever had. I had to wear an ugly, scratchy uniform. It was cut at least three inches too short. My schedule of working hours was inconvenient. My hours changed each week. It was impossible to make plans in advance. Getting a day off was out of the question. The lack of working space bothered me. Except for a half-hour break, I was restricted to three square feet of room behind the counter. I felt like a cog in the cash register.

Although transitional words and phrases are useful in bridging the gaps between your ideas, don't overuse them. Not every sentence needs a transitional phrase, so use one only when the relationship between your thoughts needs clarification. It's also a mistake to place the transitional word in the same position in your sentence each time. Look at the paragraph that follows:

It's a shame that every high school student isn't required to take a course in first aid. *For example*, you might need to treat a friend or relative for drowning during a family picnic. Or, *for instance*, someone might break a bone or receive a snakebite on a camping trip. *Also*, you should always know what to do for a common cut or burn. *Moreover*, it's important to realize when someone is in shock. *However*, very few people take the time to learn the simple rules of first aid. *Thus*, many injured or sick people suffer more than they should. *Therefore*, everyone should take a first aid course in school or at the Red Cross center.

As you can see, a series of sentences each beginning with a transitional word quickly becomes repetitious and boring. To hold your reader's attention, use transitional words only when necessary to avoid choppiness, and vary their placement in your sentences.

Repetition of Key Words

Important words or phrases (and their synonyms) may be repeated throughout a paragraph to connect the thoughts into a coherent statement:

> One of the most common, yet most puzzling, phobias is the *fear* of *snakes*. It's only natural, of course, to be afraid of a poisonous *snake*, but many people are just as frightened of the harmless varieties. For such people, a tiny green grass *snake* is as terrifying as a cobra. Some researchers say this unreasonable *fear* of any and all *snakes* is a legacy left to us by our cave-dwelling ancestors, for whom these *reptiles* were a real and constant danger. Others maintain that the *fear* is a result of our associating the *snake* with the notion of evil, as in the Garden of Eden. Whatever the reason, the fact remains that for many otherwise normal people, the mere sight of a *snake* slithering through the countryside is enough to keep them city dwellers forever.

The repeated words "fear" and "snake" and the synonym "reptile" help tie one sentence to another so that the reader can follow the ideas easily.

Pronouns Substituted for Key Nouns

A pronoun is a word that stands for a noun. In your paragraph you might use a key noun in one sentence and then use a pronoun in its place in the following sentences. The pronoun "it" often replaces "shark" in the description that follows:

> [1]The great white shark is perhaps the best equipped of all the ocean's predators. [2]*It* can grow up to twenty-one feet and weigh three tons, with two-inch teeth that can replace themselves within twenty-four hours when damaged. [3]The shark's sense of smell is so acute that *it* can detect one ounce of fish blood in a million ounces of water. [4]In addition, *it* can sense vibrations from six hundred feet away.

Sentences 2, 3, and 4 are tied to the topic sentence by the use of the pronoun "it."

Parallelism

Parallelism in a paragraph means using the same grammatical structure in several sentences to establish coherence. The repeated use of similar phrasing helps tie the ideas and sentences together. Next, for example, is a paragraph predominantly unified by its use of grammatically parallel sentences:

(1)The weather of Texas offers something for everyone. (2)If you are the kind who likes to see snow drifting onto mountain peaks, a visit to the Big Bend area will satisfy your eye. (3)If, on the other hand, you demand a bright sun to bake your skin a golden brown, stop in the southern part of the state. (4)And for hardier souls, who ask from nature a show of force, the skies of the Panhandle regularly release ferocious springtime tornadoes. (5)Finally, if you are the fickle type, by all means come to central Texas, where the sun at any time may shine unashamed throughout the most torrential rainstorm.

The parallel structures of sentences 2, 3, and 5 ("if you" + verb) keep the paragraph flowing smoothly from one idea to the next.

Using a Variety of Transitional Devices

Most writers use a combination of transitional devices in their paragraphs. In the following example, three kinds of transitional devices are circled. See whether you can identify each one.

transitional words   repetition of pronouns   repetition of key words

© Cengage Learning

Avoiding Whiplash

The preceding example not only illustrates a variety of transitional devices but also makes an important point about their use—and their limitations. Transitional devices show connections between sentences, but they alone cannot create a logical flow of ideas if none exists. For example, notice in the following sample the "disconnect" between the first three sentences and sentence 4:

(1)Despite our growing dependency on computers, one of our most useful household tools is still the lowly pencil. (2)Cheap, efficient, and long-lasting, the pencil may be operated by children and adults alike, without the necessity of a user's manual or tech support. (3)According to the Incense Cedar Institute, today's pencil can draw a line 70 miles long, be sharpened 17 times, and write an average of 45,000 words. (4)Chinese factories don't have to follow as many environmental regulations, and their workers are paid less than their American counterparts. (5)Many pencils used in this country are still manufactured in China because of the cheaper cost.

Did you suffer "reader's whiplash" as your mind experienced the sudden jerk from the discussion of pencil use to "Chinese factories"? No addition of a simple transitional word will fix this problem; the writer needs to revise the paragraph's internal logic and flow or perhaps even consider a new paragraph on cost or production. In other words, don't rely on transitional devices when deep-structure revision for coherence is needed. Make your reader's trip through your prose an enjoyable one by avoiding sudden stops and starts in thought, and then smooth that ride with appropriate transitional devices when they are necessary.

© Canstock Images, Inc./Index Stock Imagery

PRACTICING WHAT YOU'VE LEARNED

A. Identify each of the following paragraphs as ordered by time, space, or parallelism:

My apartment is so small that it will no longer hold all my possessions. Every day when I come in the door, I am shocked by the clutter. The wall to my immediate left is completely obscured by art and movie posters that have become so numerous they often overlap, even hiding each other. Along the adjoining wall is my sound system: CDs are stacked several feet high on two long, low tables. The big couch that runs across the back of the room is always piled so high with schoolbooks and magazines that a guest usually ends up sitting on the floor. To my right is a large sliding glass door that opens onto a balcony—or at least it used to, before it was permanently blocked by my tennis gear, golf clubs, and ten-speed bike. Even the tiny closet next to the front door is bursting with clothes, both clean and dirty. I think the time has come for me to move.

Once-common acts of greeting may be finding renewed popularity after three centuries. According to one historian, kissing was at the height of its popularity as a greeting in seventeenth-century England, when ladies and gentlemen of the court often saluted each other in this affectionate manner. Then the country was visited by a strange plague, whose cause was unknown. Because no one knew how the plague was spread, people tried to avoid physical contact with others as much as possible. Both kissing and the handshake went out of fashion and were replaced by the bow and curtsy, so people could greet others without having to touch them. The bow and curtsy remained in vogue for over a hundred years, until the handshake—for men only—returned to popularity in the nineteenth century. Today, both men and women may shake hands upon meeting others, and kissing as a greeting is making a comeback—especially among the jet-setters and Hollywood stars.

Students have diverse ways of preparing for final exams. Some stay up the night before, trying to cram into their brains what they avoided all term. Others pace themselves, spending a little time each night going over the notes they took in class that day. Still others just cross their fingers, assuming they absorbed enough along the way from lectures and readings. In the end, though, everyone hopes the tests are easy.

B. Circle and identify the transitional devices in the following paragraphs:

Each year I follow a system when preparing firewood to use in my stove. First, I hike about a mile from my house with my bow saw in hand. I then select three good-size oak trees and mark them with orange ties. Next, I saw through the base of each tree about two feet from the ground. After I fell the trees, not only do I trim away the branches, but I also sort the scrap from the usable limbs. I find cutting the trees into manageable-length logs is too much for one day; however, I roll them off the ground so they will not begin to rot. The next day I cut the trees into eight-foot lengths, which allows me to handle them more easily. Once they are cut, I roll them along the fire lane to the edge of the road, where I stack them neatly but not too high. The next day I borrow my uncle's van, drive to the pile of logs, and load as many logs as I can, thus reducing the number of trips. When I finally have all the logs in my backyard, I begin sawing them into eighteen-inch lengths. I create large piles that consequently have to be split and finally stacked. The logs will age and dry until winter, when I will make daily trips to the woodpile.

Fans of professional baseball and football argue continually over which is America's favorite spectator sport. Though the figures on attendance for each vary with every new season, certain arguments remain the same, spelling out both the enduring appeals of each game and something about the people who love to watch. Football, for instance, is a quicker, more physical sport, and football fans enjoy the emotional involvement they feel while watching. Baseball, on the other hand, seems more mental, like chess, and attracts those fans who prefer a quieter, more complicated game. In addition, professional football teams play sixteen games a season, providing fans with a whole week between games to work themselves up to a pitch of excitement and expectation. Baseball teams, however, play almost every day for six months, so that the typical baseball fan is not so crushed by missing a game, knowing there will be many other chances to attend. Finally, football fans seem to love the halftime pageantry, the marching bands, the cheers, and the mascots, whereas baseball fans are often more content to concentrate on the game's finer details and spend the breaks between innings filling out their own private scorecards.

continued on next page

C. The following paragraph lacks common transitional devices. Fill in the blanks with appropriate transitional words or key words.

    Scientists continue to debate the cause of the dinosaurs' disappearance. One group claims the _____ vanished after an asteroid smashed into the Earth; dust and smoke _____ blocked the sun for a long time. _____ of no direct sunlight, the Earth underwent a lengthy "winter," far too cold for the huge _____ to survive. A University of California paleontologist, _____, disputes this claim. He argues that _____ we generally think of _____ living in swampy land, fossils found in Alaska show that _____ could live in cold climates _____ warm ones. _____ group claims that the _____ became extinct following an intense period of global volcanic activity. _____ to killing the _____ themselves, these scientists _____ believe the volcanic activity killed much of the plant life that the _____ ate and, _____, many of the great _____ who survived the volcanic eruptions starved to death. Still _____ groups of _____ claim the _____ were destroyed by acid rain, by a passing "death star," _____ even by viruses from outer space.

D. The sentences below are out of order. By noting the various transitional devices, arrange the sentences into a coherent paragraph.

How to Purchase a New Car

    a. If you're happy with the car's performance, find out about available financing arrangements.

    b. Later, at home, study your notes carefully to help you decide which car fits your needs.

    c. After you have discussed various loans and interest rates, you can negotiate the final price with the salesperson.

    d. A visit to the showroom also allows you to test-drive the car.

    e. Once you have agreed on the car's price, feel confident that you have made a well-chosen purchase.

    f. Next, a visit to a nearby showroom should help you select the color, options, and style of the car of your choice.

    g. First, take a trip to the library to read the current auto magazines and consumers' guides.

    h. As you read, take notes on models and prices.

E. *Collaborative Activity:* Rearrange a paragraph you have written so that your sentences are listed out of order, in similar fashion to those in the preceding exercise. Exchange your sentences with those of a classmate. If the original paragraphs were written with logical unity and enough transitional devices for a smooth flow, it should be easy for both of you to reassemble the sentences into their proper cohesive order. If you cannot solve your classmate's paragraph puzzle or if you experience "reader's whiplash," explain the problem, offering suggestions for revision.

Paragraph Sequence

The order in which you present your paragraphs is another decision you must make. In some essays, the subject matter itself will suggest its own order.* For instance, in an essay designed to instruct a beginning runner, you might want to discuss the necessary equipment—good running shoes, loose-fitting clothing, and a sweatband—before moving to a discussion of where to run and how to run. Other essay topics, however, may not suggest a natural order, in which case you must decide which order will most effectively reach and hold the attention of your audience. Frequently, writers withhold their strongest point until last. (Lawyers often use this technique; they first present the jury with the weakest arguments, then pull out the most incriminating evidence—the "smoking gun." Thus the jury members retire with the strongest argument freshest in their minds.) Sometimes, however, you'll find it necessary to present one particular point first so that the other points make good sense. Study your own major points, and decide which order will be the most logical, successful way of persuading your reader to accept your thesis.

Transitions between Paragraphs

As you already know, each paragraph usually signals a new major point in your discussion. These paragraphs should not appear as isolated blocks of thought but rather as parts of a unified, step-by-step progression. To avoid a choppy essay, link each paragraph to the one before it with *transitional devices.* Just as the sentences in your paragraphs are connected, so are the paragraphs themselves; ◆ therefore, you can use the same transitional devices suggested on pages 71–73.

The first sentence of most body paragraphs frequently contains the transitional device. To illustrate this point, here are some topic sentences lifted from the body paragraphs of a student essay criticizing a popular sports car, renamed the 'Gator to protect the guilty and to prevent lawsuits. The transitional devices are italicized.

Thesis: The *'Gator* is one of the worst cars on the market.

- When you buy a *'Gator,* you buy physical inconvenience. [repetition of key word from thesis]
- *Another* reason the *'Gator* is a bad buy is the cost of insurance. [transitional word, key word]

---

* ◆ For more information on easily recognized patterns of order, see pages 69–71.

- You might overlook the *inconvenient* size and exorbitant *insurance* rates if the *'Gator* were a strong, reliable car, *but* this automobile constantly needs repair. [key words from preceding paragraphs, transitional word]

- When you decide to sell this *car*, you face *still another* unpleasant surprise: the extremely low resale value. [key word, transitional phrase]

- The most serious drawback, *however*, is the *'Gator*'s safety record. [transitional word, key word]

Sometimes, instead of using transitional words or repetition of key words or their synonyms, you can use an *idea hook*. The last idea of one paragraph can lead you smoothly into your next paragraph. Instead of repeating a key word from the previous discussion, find a phrase that refers to the entire idea just expressed. If, for example, the previous paragraph discussed the highly complimentary advertising campaign for the 'Gator, the next paragraph might begin, "This view of the 'Gator as an economy car is ridiculous to anyone who has pumped a week's salary into this gas guzzler." The phrase "this view" connects the idea of the first paragraph with the one that follows. Idea hooks also work well with transitional words: "This view, however, is ridiculous. . . ."

If you do use transitional words, don't allow them to make your essay sound mechanical. For example, a long series of paragraphs beginning "First . . . Second . . . Third . . ." quickly becomes boring. Vary the type and position of your transitional devices so that your essay has a subtle but logical movement from point to point.

APPLYING WHAT YOU'VE LEARNED TO **YOUR** WRITING

If you are currently working on a draft of an essay, check each body paragraph for coherence, the smooth connection of ideas and sentences in a logical, easy-to-follow order. You might try placing brackets around key words, pronouns, and transitional words that carry the reader's attention from thought to thought and from sentence to sentence. Decide whether you have enough ordering devices, placed in appropriate places, or whether you need to add (or delete) others. (◆ For additional help revising your drafts, turn to Chapter 5.)

© Keith Brofsky/ Photodisc/Getty Images

Chapter 3 Summary

Here is a brief restatement of what you should know about the paragraphs in the body of your essay:

1. Each body paragraph usually contains one major point in the discussion promised by the thesis statement.

2. Each major point is presented in the topic sentence of a paragraph.

3. Each paragraph should be adequately developed with clear supporting detail.

4. Every sentence in the paragraph should support the topic sentence.

5. There should be an orderly, logical flow from sentence to sentence and from thought to thought.

6. The sequence of your essay's paragraphs should be logical and effective.

7. There should be a smooth flow from paragraph to paragraph.

8. The body paragraphs should successfully persuade your reader that the opinion expressed in your thesis is valid.

Beginnings and Endings

As you work on your rough drafts, you might think of your essay as a coherent, unified whole composed of three main parts: the introduction (lead-in, thesis, and essay map), the body (paragraphs with supporting evidence), and the conclusion (final address to the reader). These three parts should flow smoothly into one another, presenting the reader with an organized, logical discussion. The following pages will suggest ways to begin, end, and also name your essay effectively.

How to Write a Good Lead-In

The first few sentences of your essay are particularly important; first impressions, as you know, are often lasting ones. The beginning of your essay, then, must catch the readers' attention and make them want to keep reading. Recall the way you read a magazine: if you are like most people, you probably skim the magazine, reading a paragraph or two of each article that looks promising. If the first few paragraphs hold your interest, you read on. When you write your own introductory paragraph, assume that you have only a few sentences to attract your reader. Consequently, you must pay particular attention to making those first lines especially interesting and well written.

In some essays, your thesis statement alone may be controversial or striking enough to capture the readers. At other times, however, you will want to use the introductory device called a *lead-in*.* The lead-in (1) catches the readers' attention; (2) announces the subject matter and tone of your essay (humorous, satiric, serious, etc.); and (3) sets up, or leads into, the presentation of your thesis and essay map.

---

*Do note that for some writing assignments, such as certain kinds of technical reports, attention-grabbing lead-ins are not appropriate. Frequently, these reports are directed toward particular professional audiences and have their own designated format; they often begin, for example, with a statement of the problem under study or with a review of pertinent information or research.

Here are some suggestions for and examples of lead-ins:

1. A paradoxical or intriguing statement

"Eat two chocolate bars and call me in the morning," says the psychiatrist to the patient. Such advice sounds like a sugar fanatic's dream, but recent studies have indeed confirmed that chocolate positively affects depression and anxiety.

2. An arresting statistic or shocking statement

One of every nine women will develop breast cancer this year, according to a recent report prepared by the Health Information Service.

3. A question

What are more and more Americans doing these days to stay in touch with friends and family? Overwhelmingly, the answer is text messaging: a whopping 880 billion of them were sent last year alone, according to the most recent analysis by CL King & Associates. That's nearly eight texts a day for every man, woman, and child in the country, based on our estimated population of 306 million.

4. A quotation from a recognized authority, historical figure, or literary source

Confucius wisely noted that "our greatest glory is not in never falling, but in rising every time we fall." Despite a frustrating series of close losses, my soccer team faced every new game with optimism and determination. My teammates' never-give-up attitudes have shown me that the value of sport is not winning but learning how to face defeat and begin again.

Note too that sometimes writers may challenge the wisdom of authorities or use their words in humorous ways to introduce lighthearted essays:

When Einstein wrote that the "most beautiful thing we can experience is the mysterious," I don't believe he was thinking about the mystery smell coming from our attic last summer.

5. A relevant story, joke, or anecdote

Writer and witty critic Dorothy Parker was once assigned a remote, out-of-the-way office. According to the story, she became so lonely, so desperate for company, that she ultimately painted "Gentlemen" on the door. Although this university is large, no one on this campus needs to feel as isolated as Parker obviously did: our excellent Student Activity Office offers numerous clubs, programs, and volunteer groups to involve students of all interests.

6. A description, often used for emotional appeal

With one eye blackened, one arm in a cast, and third-degree burns on both her legs, the pretty, blond two-year-old seeks corners of rooms, refuses to speak, and shakes violently at the sound of loud noises. Tammy is not the victim of a war or a natural disaster; rather, she is the helpless victim of her parents, one of the thousands of children who suffer daily from America's hidden crime, child abuse.

7. A factual statement or a summary who-what-where-when-why lead-in

   Texas's first execution of a woman in twenty-three years occurred September 14, 2005, at the Huntsville Unit of the state's Department of Corrections, despite the protests of various human-rights groups around the country.

8. An analogy or comparison

   The Romans kept geese on their Capitol Hill to cackle alarm in the event of attack by night. Modern Americans, despite their technology, have hardly improved on that old system of protection. According to the latest Safety Council report, almost any door with a standard lock can be opened easily with a common plastic credit card.

9. A contrast or a before-and-after scenario

   I used to search for toast in the supermarket. I used to think "blackened"—as in blackened Cajun shrimp—referred to the way I cooked anything in a skillet. "Poached" could only have legal ramifications. But all that has changed! Attending a class in basic cooking this summer has transformed the way I purchase, prepare, and even talk about food.

10. A personal experience

    I realized times were changing for women when I overheard my six-year-old nephew speaking to my sister, a prominent New York lawyer. As we left her elaborate, luxurious office one evening, Tommy looked up at his mother and queried, "Mommy, can little boys grow up to be lawyers, too?"

11. A catalog of relevant examples or facts

    A two-hundred-pound teenager quit school because no desk would hold her. A three-hundred-pound chef who could no longer stand on his feet was fired. A three-hundred-fifty-pound truck driver broke furniture in his friends' houses. All these people are now living healthier, happier, and thinner lives, thanks to the remarkable intestinal bypass surgery first developed in 1967.

12. Statement of a problem or a popular misconception

    Some people believe that poetry is written only by aging beatniks or solemn, mournful men and women with suicidal tendencies. The Poetry in the Schools Program is working hard to correct that erroneous point of view.

13. Brief dialogue to introduce the topic

    "Be bold! You can do it!" said my roommate again and again during the weeks before choir tryouts, despite my whimpering cries of "I can't, I can't." For a shy person like me, the thought of singing in a public audition was agony. But thanks to the ABC Relaxation Method suggested by the Counseling Center, I performed so well I was chosen for a solo. The ABC method, incorporating visualization and proper breathing techniques, is a helpful process every shy person should practice regularly.

14. A proverb, maxim, or motto

"One falsehood spoils a thousand truths," says the African proverb. Caught in the biggest lie of his political career, once-popular local mayor Paul TerGhist is learning the meaning of this old saying the hard way, as his former friends and supporters are now deserting him.

15. A recognition, revelation, or insight

As someone who earned "A's" throughout my Spanish classes, I thought I had a good grasp of the language. However, immersion in the Tres Amigos Building Project in Monterrey, Mexico, over Spring Break this year showed me I had much to learn about conversational speech patterns.

© Image Source/CORBIS

16. An appeal to a common or imagined experience

Come on, you know you've done it . . . in your bedroom, bathroom, car, wherever you've listened to hard rock music. You played your air guitar—and you're good, but maybe not great. If you keep practicing, though, you might be able to join the best air-shredders in the country as they compete annually in front of sold-out crowds at the national Air Guitar Championships.

Thinking of a good lead-in is often difficult when you sit down to begin your essay. Many writers, in fact, skip the lead-in until the first draft is written. They compose their working thesis first and then write the body of the essay, saving the lead-in and conclusion for last. As you write the middle of your essay, you may discover an especially interesting piece of information you might want to save to use as your lead-in.

Avoiding Errors in Lead-Ins

In addition to the previous suggestions, here is some advice to help you avoid common lead-in errors:

Make sure your lead-in introduces your thesis. A frequent weakness in introductory paragraphs is an interesting lead-in but no smooth or clear transition to the thesis statement. To avoid a gap or awkward jump in thought in your introductory paragraph, you may need to add a connecting sentence or phrase between your lead-in and thesis. Study the following paragraph, which uses a comparison as its lead-in. The italicized transitional sentence takes the reader from a general comment about Americans who use wheelchairs to information about those in Smallville, smoothly preparing the reader for the thesis that follows.

Lead-in   In the 1950s African Americans demanded the right to sit anywhere they pleased on public buses. Today, Americans who use wheelchairs

Transitional   are fighting for the right to board those same buses. *Here in Smallville,*
sentence   *the lack of proper boarding facilities often denies disabled citizens basic*
transportation to jobs, grocery stores, and medical centers. To give

Thesis   people in wheelchairs the same opportunities as other residents, the City Council should allocate the funds necessary to convert the public transportation system.

Keep your lead-in brief. Long lead-ins in short essays often give the appearance of a tail wagging the dog. Use a brief, attention-catching hook to set up your thesis; don't make your introduction the biggest part of your essay.

Don't begin with an apology or complaint. Such statements as "It's difficult to find much information on this topic . . ." and "This controversy is hard to understand, but . . ." do nothing to entice your reader.

Don't assume your audience already knows your subject matter. Identify the pertinent facts even though you know your readers know the assignment. ("The biggest problem with the new college requirement. . . ." What requirement?) If you are writing about a particular piece of literature or art, identify the title of the work and its author or artist, using the full name in the first reference.

Stay clear of overused lead-ins. If composition teachers had a nickel for every essay that began with a dry dictionary definition, they could all retire to Bermuda. Leave Webster's alone and find a livelier way to begin. Asking a question as your lead-in is becoming overworked, too, so use it only when it is obviously the best choice for your opener.

PRACTICING WHAT YOU'VE LEARNED

Describe the lead-ins in the following paragraphs. Did any of the writers blend more than one kind of lead-in?

1. In the sixth century, Lao-Tzu, the father of Taoism, described the "good traveler" as someone who has "no fixed plans and is not intent on arriving." If that ancient Chinese philosopher is correct, then my aimless but eventful wanderings across the South last fall qualify me as a World-Class Traveler.

2. Ever wonder if those long hours hitting the books are worth it? Do grades really matter to employers? According to a survey by the National Association of Colleges and Employers, the answer is . . . yes. Strong grades and a go-getter attitude are the keys to securing a good job after college.

continued on next page

© Canstock Images, Inc./
Index Stock Imagery

6. A quotation from an authority or someone whose insight emphasizes the main point

Even though I didn't win the fiction contest, I learned so much about my own powers of creativity. I'm proud that I pushed myself in new directions. I know now I will always agree with Herman Melville, whose writing was unappreciated in his own time, that "it is better to struggle with originality than to succeed in imitation."

7. An anecdote or brief example that emphasizes or sums up the point of the essay

Bette Davis's role on and off the screen as the catty, wisecracking woman of steel helped make her an enduring star. After all, no audience, past or present, could ever resist a dame who drags on a cigarette and then mutters about a passing starlet, "There goes a good time that was had by all."

8. An image or description that lends finality to the essay

As the last of the Big Screen's giant ants are incinerated by the army scientist, one can almost hear the movie audiences of the 1950s breathing a collective sigh of relief, secure in the knowledge that once again the threat of nuclear radiation had been vanquished by the efforts of the U.S. military.

(◆ For another last image that captures the essence of an essay, see the "open house" scene that concludes "To Bid the World Farewell," page 222.)

9. A rhetorical question that makes the readers think about the essay's main point

No one wants to see hostages put in danger. But what nation can afford to let terrorists know they can get away with blackmail?

10. A forecast based on the essay's thesis

Soap operas will continue to be popular not only because they distract us from our daily chores but also because they present life as we want it to be: fast-paced, glamorous, and full of exciting characters.

11. An ironic twist, witticism, pun, or playful use of words (often more appropriate in lighthearted essays)

After analyzing and understanding the causes of my procrastination, I now feel better, more determined to change my behavior. In fact, I've decided that today is the day for decisive action! I will choose a major! Hmmmm . . . or maybe not. I need to think about it some more. I'll get back to you, okay? Tomorrow. Really.

12. Return to the technique used in your lead-in (answer a question you asked, circle back to a story, extend a quotation, etc.)

So was Dorothy right in *The Wizard of Oz*? After the tough summer I spent on our ranch in Wyoming, mending barbed-wire fences and wrestling angry calves, I could think of nothing else on the long bus ride back to school. As eager as I had been to leave, I couldn't wait to get back there. It wasn't Kansas, but Dorothy and I knew the truth: There's no place like home.

◆ **Hint:** After reading the preceding suggestions, if you are still struggling with your conclusion, turn back to the advice for writing lead-ins on pages 81–84. One of the suggestions there may trigger a useful idea for closing your essay. In fact, following a first draft, you may decide that the technique you chose to open your essay might be used more effectively to conclude it.

Avoiding Errors in Conclusions

Try to omit the following common errors in your concluding paragraphs:

© Jack Hollirgs.worth/COFBIS

Avoid a boring, mechanical ending. One of the most frequent weaknesses in student essays is the conclusion that merely restates the thesis, word for word. A brief essay of 500 to 750 words rarely requires a flat, point-by-point conclusion; in fact, such an ending often insults the readers' intelligence by implying that their attention spans are extremely short. Only after reading long essays do most readers need a precise recap of all the writer's main ideas. Instead of recopying your thesis and essay map, try finding an original, emphatic way to conclude your essay—or as a well-known newspaper columnist described it, a good ending should snap with grace and authority, like the close of an expensive sports car door.

Don't introduce new points or irrelevant material. Treat the major points of your essay in separate body paragraphs rather than in your exit. Stay focused on your essay's specific thesis and purpose; don't allow any unimportant or off-subject comments to drift into your concluding remarks.

Don't tack on a conclusion. There should be a smooth, logical flow of thought from your last body paragraph into your concluding statements.

Don't change your stance. Sometimes writers who have been critical of something throughout their essays will soften their stance or offer apologies in their last paragraph. For instance, someone complaining about the poor quality of a particular college course might abruptly conclude with statements that declare the class wasn't so bad after all, maybe she should have worked harder, or maybe she really did learn something after all. Such reneging may seem polite, but in actuality it undercuts the thesis and confuses the reader who has taken the writer's criticisms seriously. Instead of contradicting themselves, writers should stand their ground, forget about puffy clichés or "niceties," and find an emphatic way to conclude that is consistent with their thesis.

Avoid trite expressions. Don't begin your conclusion by declaring, "In conclusion," "In summary," or "As you can see, this essay proves my thesis that. . . ." End your essay so that the reader clearly senses completion; don't merely announce that you're finished.

Don't insult or anger your reader. No matter how right you feel you are, resist the temptation to set up an "either-or" conclusion in an argumentative essay: either you agree with me or you are an ignorant/wrong/selfish/immoral person. Don't exaggerate your claims or moralize excessively as you exit. Remember that your purpose is to inform and persuade your readers, not to annoy them to the point of rejecting your thesis out of sheer irritation. Conclude on a positive note, one that encourages readers to see matters your way.

© Canstock Images, Inc./
Index Stock Imagery

PRACTICING WHAT YOU'VE LEARNED

Identify the weaknesses you see in the following conclusions. How might these writers revise to create more satisfactory endings for their essays?

1. My thesis in this essay stated that I believe that having to change schools does not harm children for three reasons. Children at new schools learn how to make new friends. They learn how to get along with a variety of people. They also learn about different teaching styles. For these three reasons, I believe that having to change schools does not harm children.

2. "A journey of a thousand miles must begin with a single step" (Lao Tzu). As I discussed in this causal analysis essay, I would have never started painting again if I hadn't gone back to school. I'm the first to admit that it was a long, hard road to get my degree, and sometimes I really questioned the value of certain courses I had to take (like algebra, for example, which I think is a totally useless course for artists. The entire math requirement needs revision, in my opinion). But going back to school was the right choice for me and, who knows, maybe it would be for others.

3. In conclusion, as I have shown here, our country's forest conservation policies are just plain stupid. If you don't stand up and join the fight against them, I hope you will enjoy living in a tent because pretty soon there isn't going to be any lumber for houses left. After selling out to the tree-huggers, will you be able to look at yourself in the mirror?

© CORBIS

ASSIGNMENT

Find three good concluding paragraphs. Identify each kind of conclusion, and tell why you think it is an effective ending for the essay or article.

How to Write a Good Title

As in the case of lead-ins, your title may be written at any time, but many writers prefer to finish their essays before naming them. A good title is similar to a good newspaper headline in that it attracts the readers' interest and makes them want to investigate the essay. Like the lead-in, the title helps announce the tone of the essay. An informal or humorous essay, for instance, might have a catchy, funny title. Some titles show the writer's wit and love of wordplay; a survey of recent magazines revealed these titles: "Bittersweet News about Saccharin," "Coffee: New Grounds for Concern," and "The Scoop on the Best Ice Cream."

On the other hand, a serious, informative essay should have a more formal title that suggests its content as clearly and specifically as possible. Let's suppose, for example, that you are researching the meaning of color in dreams, and you see an article in a database list titled merely "Dreams." You don't know whether you should bother to read it. To avoid such confusion in your own essay and to encourage readers' interest, always use a specific title: "Interpreting Animal Imagery in Dreams," "Dream Research: An Aid to Diagnosing Depression," and so forth. Moreover, if your subject matter is controversial, let the reader know which side you're on (e.g., "The Advantages of Solar Power"). Never substitute a mere label, such as "Football Games" or "Euthanasia," for a meaningful title. And never, never label your essays "Theme One" or "Comparison and Contrast Essay." In all your writing, including the title, use your creativity to attract the readers' attention and to invite their interest in your ideas.

If you're unsure about how to present your title, here are three basic rules:

1. Your own title should not be underlined, italicized, or put in quotation marks. It should be written at the top of page one of your essay or on an appropriate cover sheet with no special marks of punctuation.

2. Capitalize the first, last, and important words of your title. Generally, do not capitalize such words as "an," "and," "a," or "the," or prepositions, unless they appear as the first or last words of the title or follow a colon within the title.

3. Sometimes writers craft a title that presents a word or phrase followed by a colon introducing a definition, a revealing image, a question, or some other kind of explanatory material to interest the reader.

Examples   "Stephen Crane: Daredevil Reporter"
"Memories Carved in Stone: Tennessee Pioneer Memorials"
"Intervention in Iran: A Recipe for Disaster"
"Yoga: Does Twisting Like a Pretzel Really Help?"

You may use such titles to clarify a work's scope or perhaps to set the appropriate tone for your reader, but be careful not to overuse this structure. (Note that the word after the colon is capitalized as if it were the first word of the title.)

PRACTICING WHAT YOU'VE LEARNED

Describe any weaknesses you see in the following titles. How might each one be revised to clarify its essay's content and to attract more reader interest?

1. Advice for College Freshmen

2. Essay Assignment #3: "Review of a Favorite Movie"

3. Learning to Play Texas Hold'em

4. A Comparison of Two Heroes

5. The Problem of Abandoned Pets and Its Solution

6. Steroids and Athletes Today

7. The Effects of Three Popular Diets

8. The Best Laptop on the Market

9. An Explanation of the Human Genome Project

10. My Interpretation of Auden's "The Unknown Citizen"

ASSIGNMENT

A. Read one of the student or professional essays in this text and evaluate the title. Explain why you think the title is or is not effective. Or, if you prefer, write a new title for one of the essays in this book. Why is your choice as effective as (or even better than) that of the original writer?

B. *Collaborative Activity:* Bring to class three titles or headlines from print or online articles. In a small group of classmates, compare all the samples. Which ones would encourage members of the group to read on? Which one is the least interesting or helpful? (If time permits, select one effective title to read to the class as a whole.) How might your choices influence your crafting of a title for your next essay?

© Keith Brofsky/
Photodisc/Getty Images

APPLYING WHAT YOU'VE LEARNED TO **YOUR** WRITING

Look at the draft of the essay you are currently working on, and ask yourself these questions:

- Does the opening of my essay make my reader want to continue reading? Does the lead-in smoothly set up my thesis, or do I need to add some sort of transition to help move the reader to my main idea? Is the lead-in appropriate in terms of the tone and length of my essay?

- Does the conclusion of my essay offer an emphatic ending, one that is consistent with my essay's purpose? Have I avoided a mechanical, trite, or tacked-on closing paragraph? Have I refrained from adding a new point in my conclusion that belongs in the body of my essay or in another essay?

- Does my title interest my reader? Are its content and tone appropriate for this particular essay?

If you have answered "no" to any of these questions, you should continue revising your essay. (◆ For more help revising your prose, turn to Chapter 5.)

Chapter 4 Summary

Here is a brief restatement of what you should remember about writing introductions, conclusions, and titles:

1. Many essays will profit from a lead-in, the first sentences of the introductory paragraph that attract the reader's attention and smoothly set up the thesis statement.

2. Essays should end convincingly, without being repetitious or trite, with thoughts that emphasize the writer's main purpose.

3. Titles should invite the reader's interest by indicating the general nature of the essay's content and its tone.

CHAPTER 5

Drafting and Revising: Creative Thinking, Critical Thinking

There is no good writing, only rewriting.
—**James Thurber**

When I say writing, O, believe me, it is rewriting that I have chiefly in mind.
—**Robert Louis Stevenson**

The absolute necessity of revision cannot be overemphasized. All good writers rethink, rearrange, and rewrite large portions of their prose. The French novelist Colette, for instance, wrote everything over and over. In fact, she often spent an entire morning working on a single page. Hemingway, to cite another example, rewrote the ending to *A Farewell to Arms* thirty-nine times "to get the words right." Although no one expects you to make thirty-nine drafts of each essay, the point is clear: writing well means revising. **All good writers revise their prose**.

What Is Revision?

Revision is a *thinking process* that occurs any time you are working on a writing project. It means looking at your writing with a "fresh eye"—that is, reseeing your writing in ways that will enable you to make more effective choices throughout your essay. Revision often entails rethinking what you have written and asking yourself questions about its effectiveness; it involves discovery as well as change. As you write, new ideas surface, prompting you to revise what you have planned or have just written. Or perhaps these new ideas will cause changes in earlier parts of your essay. In some cases, your new ideas will encourage you to begin an entirely new draft with a different focus or approach. Revision means making important decisions about the best ways to focus, organize, develop, clarify, and emphasize your ideas.

When Does Revision Occur?

Revision, as previously noted, occurs throughout your writing process. Early on, you are revising as you sort through ideas to write about, and you almost certainly revise as you define your purpose and audience and sharpen your thesis. Some revising may be done in your head, and some may be on paper or computer screen as you plan, sketch, or "discovery-write" your ideas. Later, during drafting, revision becomes more individualized and complex. Many writers find themselves sweeping back and forth over their papers, writing for a bit and then rereading what they wrote, making changes, and then moving ahead. Some writers like to revise "lumps," or pieces of writing, perhaps reviewing one major idea or paragraph at a time. Frequently, writers discover that a better idea is occurring almost at the very moment they are putting another thought on paper. And virtually all writers revise after "reseeing" a draft in its entirety.

Revision, then, occurs before drafting, during drafting, between parts of drafts, and at the ends of drafts. You can revise a word, a sentence, a paragraph, or an entire essay. If you are like most writers, you sometimes revise almost automatically as you write (deleting one word or line and quickly replacing it with another as you move on, for example), and at other times you revise very deliberately (concentrating on a conclusion you know is weak, for example). Revision is "rethinking," and that activity can happen any time, in many ways, in any part of your writing.

Myths about Revision

If revision is rethinking, what is it not? Three misconceptions about revision are addressed here.

1. Revision Is Not Autopsy

Revision is not an isolated stage of writing that occurs *only* after your last draft is written or right before your paper is due. Revising is not merely a postmortem procedure, to be performed only after your creative juices have ceased to flow. Good writing, as Thurber noted, *is* revision, and revision occurs throughout the writing process.

2. Revision Is Not Limited to Editing or Proofreading

Too many writers mistakenly equate revision with editing and proofreading. *Editing* means revising for "surface errors"—mistakes in spelling, grammar, punctuation, sentence sense, and word choice. Certainly, good writers comb their papers for such errors, and they edit their prose extensively for clarity, conciseness, and emphasis, too. *Proofreading* to search out and destroy errors and typos that distort meaning or distract the reader is also important. Without question, both editing and proofreading are essential to a polished paper.

But revision is not *limited* to such activities. It includes them but also encompasses those larger, global changes writers may make in purpose, focus, organization, and development. Writers who revise effectively not only change words and catch mechanical errors but also typically add, delete, rearrange, and rewrite large chunks of prose. In other words, revision is not cosmetic surgery on a body that may need major resuscitation.

3. Revision Is Not Punishment or Busywork

At one time or another, most of us have found ourselves guilty of racing too quickly through a particular job and then moving on. And perhaps just as often we have found ourselves redoing such jobs because the results were so disappointing. Some people may regard revising in a similar light—as the repeat performance of a job done poorly the first time. But that attitude isn't productive. Revising isn't punishment for failing to produce a perfect first draft. Rarely, if ever, does anyone—even our most admired professional writers—produce the results he or she wants without revising.* Remember that revising is not a tacked-on stage nor is it merely a quick touch-up; it's an integral part of the entire writing process itself. It's an ongoing opportunity to discover, remember, reshape, and refine your ideas.

If you've ever created something you now treasure—a piece of jewelry, furniture, painting, or music—recall the time you put into it. You probably thought about it from several angles, experimented with it, crafted it, worked it through expected and unexpected problems, and smoothed out its minor glitches, all to achieve the results you wanted. Similarly, with each revision you make, your paper becomes clearer, truer, more satisfying to you and to your readers. With practice, you will produce writing you are proud of—and you will discover that revising has become not only an essential but also a natural part of your writing process.

Can I Learn to Improve My Revision Skills?

Because revision is such a multifaceted and individual activity, no textbook can guide you through all the rethinking you may do as you move through each sentence of every writing project. But certainly you can learn to improve your ability to think creatively and critically about your prose. To sharpen your thinking and revision skills, this chapter will suggest a step-by-step method of self-questioning designed to help you achieve your writing goals.

Preparing to Draft: Some Time-Saving Hints

Before you begin drafting (either a "discovery" draft or a draft from your working thesis), remember this important piece of advice: no part of your draft is sacred or permanent.

---

*All of us have heard stories about famous essays or poems composed at one quick sitting. Bursts of creativity do happen. But it's highly likely that authors of such pieces revise extensively in their heads before they write. They rattle ideas around in their brains for such a prolonged period that the actual writing does in fact flow easily or may even seem "dictated" by an inner voice. This sort of lengthy internal "cooking" may work well at various times for you, too.

No matter what you write at this point, you can always change it. Drafting is discovering and recollecting as well as developing ideas from your earlier plans. Take the pressure off yourself: no one expects blue-ribbon prose in early drafts. (◆ If you can't seem to get going or if you do become stuck along the way, try turning to pages 121–123 of this chapter for suggestions to help you confront your case of Writer's Block.)

At this point, too, you might consider the actual format of your drafts. Because you will be making many changes in your writing, you may find revising less cumbersome and time-consuming if you prepare your manuscripts as described here.

1. If you are handwriting your first drafts, always write on one side of your paper only, in case you want to cut and tape together portions of drafts or you want to experiment with interchanging parts of a particular draft. (If you have written on both sides, you may have to recopy the parts of your essay you want to save; your time is better spent creating and revising.)

2. Leave big margins on *both* sides of any handwritten pages so you can add information later or jot down new ideas as they occur. (Some writers also skip lines for this reason. If you choose to write on every other line, however, do remember that you may not be getting a true picture of your paragraph development or essay length. A handwritten double-spaced body paragraph, for example, may appear skimpy in your typed final copy.)

3. Devise a system of symbols (circles, stars, checks, asterisks, etc.) that will remind you of changes you want to make later. For example, if you're in hot pursuit of a great idea but can't think of the exact word you want, put down a word that's close, circle it (or type three XXXs by it), and go on so that your thinking is not derailed. Similarly, a check in the margin might mean "return to this tangled sentence." A question mark might mean a fuzzy idea, and a star, a great idea that needs expanding. A system of symbols can save you from agonizing over every inch of your essay while you are still trying to discover and clarify your ideas.

4. If your ideas are flowing well but you realize you need more supporting evidence for some of your points, consider leaving some blank spots to fill in later. For example, let's say you are writing about the effects of television commercials on our presidential elections; your ideas are good, but in a particular body paragraph you decide some statistics on commercial frequency would be most convincing. Or perhaps you need to cite an example of a particular kind of advertisement, but you just can't think of a good one at that moment. Leave a spot for the piece of evidence with a key word or two to remind you of what's needed, and keep writing. Later, when you come back to that spot, you can add the appropriate support; if you can't find or think of the right supporting evidence to insert, you may decide to omit that point.

5. If you do decide to rewrite or omit something—a sentence or an entire passage—in a handwritten draft, mark a single "X" or line through it lightly. Don't scratch it out or destroy it completely; you may realize later that you want to reinsert the material there or move it to another, better place. If you are composing on a computer, italicize or put brackets around material you may want to use elsewhere. Or consider moving a larger chunk of prose to a "holding page" or to the end of the current draft so you can take another look at it later.

6. If you begin with a handwritten draft, do eventually work on a typed copy. The more compact spacing of typed prose allows you to see more clearly the relationship of the parts in your essay, making it easier for you to organize and develop your ideas. It is also far more likely that you will catch spelling and other mechanical errors in a printed draft.

7. Always keep your notes, outlines, drafts, and an extra copy of your final paper. Never burn your bridges—or your manuscripts! Sometimes essays change directions, and writers find they can return to prewriting or earlier drafts to recover ideas, once rejected, that now work well. Drafts also may contain ideas that didn't work in one paper but that look like great starts for another assignment. Tracking revisions from draft to draft can give writers a sense of accomplishment and insight into their composing processes. And drafts can be good insurance in case final copies of papers are lost or accidentally destroyed.

Writing with Computers

Most college students today are accustomed to using computers at school, home, or work, and feel quite comfortable drafting and revising at their keyboards. If this has been your experience, you probably already know how helpful computers can be in all stages of the writing process. You can, for example, compose and store your prewriting activities, journal entries, notes, or good ideas in various files until you need to recall certain information, and you can easily produce extra copies of your drafts or finished essays without having to search out a copy machine and correct change. Spell-checkers and dictionaries can help you correct many of your errors and typos.

© Rick Gomez/CORBIS

But the most important use of the computer to a writer may be what it can do as you draft and revise your prose. A word-processing program enables you to add, delete, or change words easily; it allows you to move words, sentences, and even paragraphs or larger pieces of your essay. On a computer, for example, you can play "what if" by dropping below what you have written and phrasing your idea in another way. With some programs, you can even compare drafts side by side or with special "windows" that help you see your choices more clearly. In other words, computers can help us as writers do the kind of deep-structure revision necessary to produce our best, most effective prose—the kind of major changes that, in the past, we may have been hesitant to make because of the time involved in recopying or retyping major portions of our drafts.

Although computers have made composing and revising easier and more effective for many writers, such technology provides its own special temptations and potential problems. Here, in addition to the hints in the previous section, are a few more suggestions for drafting and revising your essay on a computer:

1. To avoid the "agony of delete," always save what you have composed every ten minutes or so, and consider printing out your work (or copying it to a portable storage device) after each drafting session in case your system crashes or gobbles your pages. Remember that all sorts of events, from electrical storms to carpet cleaning, have caused the tiny leprechauns in computers to behave badly; having copies of your notes and latest revisions will help you reconstruct your work should disaster strike. If you have drafts in multiple files, add the date to each file name (Rafting 4-10); for multiple versions on the same date, add a letter (Rafting 4-10a, Rafting 4-10b). (Also, if you are working on multiple writing tasks, as most students are, or if you are just the forgetful type, develop the habit of noting on each print copy the name you have given the file. Doing so may save you from a frustrating search through your list of existing documents, especially if several days have elapsed between drafts.)

2. Do learn to use the editing tools that your word-processing program offers. In addition to allowing you to make changes and move text, most programs offer a dictionary to help you check the proper spelling, meaning, and use of your words; a thesaurus can help you expand your vocabulary, avoid repetition of words, or find just the right word to express the shade of meaning you want. Even the "word count" command can help writers who want to trim the fat from their essays.

One of the most prized tools the computer offers writers is the spell-checker. For poor spellers and bad typists, the invention of the spell-checker ranks right up there with penicillin as a boon to humankind. The spell-checker performs minor miracles as it asks writers to reconsider certain words as typed on the page. If you have one available, by all means run it! But be aware of its limitations: spell-checkers highlight only words whose order of assembled letters they do not recognize or whose capitalization they question. They do not recognize confused words (*its/it's, you're/your, their/there, to/too*), incorrect usage of words, or typos that are correctly spelled words. To underscore this point, here's a sample of writing that any spell-checker would happily pass over:

> Eye have a knew spell checker
> That tells me wrong from write;
> It marks four me miss steaks
> My ayes kin knot high light.
>
> I no its let her perfect,
> Sew why due I all ways get
> Re quests to proof reed bet her
> Win my checker says I'm set?

The message of this brilliantly crafted poem? Don't rely on your spell-checker to catch all the errors in your final draft! Learn to edit, question your word choice, and proofread carefully with your own eyes and brain. (The same advice holds true for grammar-check and "style" programs, too. Although such programs have improved over the past several years, they are still limited in their ability to catch errors and see distinctions among usage and punctuation choices. Such programs may help you take a second look at your grammar, punctuation, or word choice, but do not rely on *any* computer program to do your editing and proofreading work for you.)

3. Use the computer to help you double-check for your own common errors. By using the "search," "find," or similar command, writers can highlight words they know they frequently misuse. For example, on a final sweep of editing, you might take one last look at each highlighted "its" you wrote to determine whether the usage truly calls for the possessive pronoun "its" or rather should be the contraction for "it is" (it's). Or perhaps you have an ongoing struggle with the uses of "affect" and "effect" and know that you have used these words often in your essay of causal analysis. Reviewing your word-choice decisions in the proofreading stage could make an important difference to your readers, who wish to travel smoothly through the ideas in your essay without annoying errors flagging down their attention. Also consider searching for and replacing words that you know you overuse or those that are lazy or vague. For example, until you break yourself of the habit, highlight any use of the word "thing." In each case, are you really discussing an unknown quantity—or do you need to press yourself to find a more specific or vivid word to communicate what you mean?

4. Even if you are comfortable drafting on your computer, resist doing all your work there. It's a good idea from time to time to read your screen version in its printed form—the format your readers will most likely see. Many—if not most—writers move back and forth multiple times between the computer screen and printed copies of their drafts. Experiment to discover the best ways for you to revise. Remember that a neatly typed draft can look professional but still need much rethinking, restructuring, and polishing!

Writing Centers, Computer Classrooms, and Electronic Networks

Today many schools have professionally staffed writing centers and computer labs open to composition students. The writing center or laboratory computers may have a variety of software designed to help you brainstorm, focus your ideas, organize a working structure, compose your drafts, revise your essay, and proofread. These computers also can help you to research a topic by allowing you to check information available in your campus library as well as providing access to other libraries and sources on the Internet. Many writing centers have special tutors on hand to answer your questions about your drafts as well as to explain effective uses of the available computer programs. In addition, many schools now have labs and special classrooms in which the computers are part of a network, linked together so that a specific group of writers can communicate with each other and/or with their instructor. In such a lab or classroom, for example, students might read each other's drafts and make suggestions or post comments about a current reading assignment on an electronic bulletin board for their classmates to consider.

Whether the program you are using at home or at school is a series of simple commands or an elaborate instructional system, make a point of getting to know how to use the computer in the most effective ways. Study the advice that accompanies your word-processing program, and don't be afraid to ask your instructor or computer-lab tutor for assistance. The more you practice using your program to help you organize, develop, and revise your prose, the better your writing will be.

A Revision Process for Your Drafts

Let's assume at this point that you have completed a draft, using the first four chapters of this book as a guide. You feel you've chosen an interesting topic and collected some good ideas. Perhaps the ideas came quickly or perhaps you had to coax them. However your thoughts came, they're now in print—you have a draft with meaning and a general order, although it's probably much rougher in some spots than in others. Now it's time to "resee" this draft in a comprehensive way.

But wait. If possible, put a night's sleep or at least a few hours between this draft and the advice that appears on the next few pages. All writers become tired when they work on any project for too long at one sitting, and then they lose a sense of perspective. When you've looked at a piece of prose again and again, you may begin to read what's written in your head instead of what's on the page—that is, you may begin to "fill in" for yourself, reading into your prose what you meant to say rather than what your reader will actually see. Always try to start your writing process early enough to give yourself a few breaks from the action. You'll find that you will be better able to evaluate the strengths and weaknesses of your prose when you are fresh.

When you do return to your draft, *don't try to look at all the parts of your paper, from ideas to organization to mechanics, at the same time.* Trying to resee everything at once is rarely possible and will only overload and frustrate you. It may cause you to overlook some important part of your paper that needs your full attention. Overload can also block your creative ideas. Therefore, instead of trying to revise an entire draft in one swoop, break your revising process into a series of smaller, more manageable steps. Here is a suggested process:

I.	rethink	purpose, thesis, and audience
II.	rethink	ideas and evidence
III.	rethink	organization
IV.	rethink	clarity and style
V.	edit	grammar, punctuation, and spelling
VI.	proofread	entire essay

IMPORTANT: Please note that these steps are not necessarily distinct, nor must you always follow this suggested order. You certainly might, for instance, add details to a paragraph when you decide to move or reorder it. Or you might replace a vague word with a specific one after thinking about your audience and their needs. After strengthening a particular point, you might decide to offer it last, and therefore you rearrange the order of your paragraphs. In other words, the steps offered here are not part of a forced march—they are here simply to remind you to rethink and improve any part of your essay that needs work.

Now let's look at each of the steps in the revision process suggested here in more detail.

I. Revising for Purpose, Thesis, and Audience

To be effective, writers need a clear sense of purpose and audience. Their essays must present (or clearly imply) a main idea or thesis designed to fulfill that purpose and to inform their audience. As you reread your draft, ask yourself the following questions:

- Have I fulfilled the objectives of my assignment? (For example, if you were asked to analyze the causes of a problem, did you merely describe or summarize it instead?)

- Did I follow directions carefully? (If you were given a three-part assignment, did you treat all parts as requested?)

- Do I understand the purpose of my essay? Am I trying to inform, persuade, or amuse my readers? Spur them to action? Convince them to change their minds? Give them a new idea? Am I myself clear about my exact intent—what I want to do or say—in this essay?

- Does my essay reflect my clearly understood purpose by offering an appropriately narrowed and focused thesis? (After reading through your essay once, could a reader easily state its purpose and main point?)

- Do I have a clear picture of my audience—their character, knowledge, and expectations?

- Have I addressed both my purpose and my readers' needs by selecting appropriate strategies of development for my essay? (For example, would it be better to write an essay primarily developed with examples illustrating the community's need for a new hospital, or should you present a more formal argument that also rebuffs objections to the project? Should you narrate the story of your accident or analyze its effects on your family?)

If you feel that your draft needs work in any of these areas, make changes. ◆ You might find it helpful to review Chapters 1 and 2 of this text to guide you as you revise.

II. Revising for Ideas and Evidence

If you're satisfied that your purpose and thesis are clear to your readers, begin to look closely at the development of your essay's ideas.

You want your readers to accept your thesis. To achieve this goal, you must offer body paragraphs whose major points clearly support that main idea. As you examine the body of your essay, you might ask yourself questions such as these:

- Is there a clear relationship between my thesis and each of the major points presented in the body of my essay? That is, does each major point in my essay further my readers' understanding, and thus their acceptance, of my thesis's general claim?

- Did I write myself into a new or slightly different position as I drafted my essay? If so, do I need to begin another draft with a new working thesis?

- Have I included all the major points necessary to the readers' understanding of my subject or have I omitted pertinent ones? (On the other hand, have I included major ideas that aren't relevant or that actually belong in a different essay?)

- Are my major points located and stated clearly in specific language so that readers can easily see what position I am taking in each part of my discussion?

If you are happy with your choice and presentation of the major ideas in the body of your essay, it's time to look closely at the evidence you are offering to support those ideas (which, in turn, support the claim of your thesis). To choose the best supporting evidence for their major points, effective writers use *critical thinking skills*.

What Is Critical Thinking?

Critical thinking means the ability to analyze and evaluate our own ideas and those of others. Because we are constantly bombarded today with all kinds of information and differing points of view, we need skills to examine ideas carefully before we accept or reject them.

Here's a common situation in which critical thinking comes into play: two of your friends are arguing over the use of animals in medical research. Each friend has many points to offer; each is presenting statistics, case studies, the words of experts, and hypothetical situations that might arise. Many of the statistics and experts on one side of the argument seem to contradict directly the figures and authorities on the other side. Which side do you take? Why? Are there other points of view to consider? How can you know what to think?

Every day we are faced with just such decisions. We must be able to judge intelligently the merits of what we hear and read before we can feel confident about what we think of a particular issue. We must practice analyzing our beliefs and those held by others to evaluate the reasons for maintaining those views. To think critically about ideas doesn't mean being constantly hostile or negative; it simply means that we need to examine opinions closely and carefully before we accept them.

Thinking Critically as a Writer

As a writer, you will be thinking critically in two important ways. First, you will need to think critically about any information you may be collecting to use as evidence in your essay. You will, for example, need to be a critical reader as you consider information from books, journals, or electronic sources. You almost certainly will need to be a critical listener as you hear other people talk about their experiences and beliefs.

As you draft and revise your essay, you must become a critical thinker in a second way: you must become your own toughest reader-critic. To convince your readers that your essay has merit, you must stand back and assess objectively what you have written. Are your ideas clear not only to you but to your readers as well? Will readers find your opinions well developed, logical, and supported? In other words, to revise more effectively, try role-playing one of your own most thoughtful critical readers, someone who will be closely examining the ideas and evidence in your essay before agreeing with its position.

Here are six suggestions to help you think critically as you draft and revise:

1. Learn to distinguish fact from opinion. A *fact* is an accepted truth whose verification is not affected by its source. No matter who presents it, a fact remains true. We accept some statements as facts because we can test them personally (fire is hot) or because they have been verified frequently by others (penguins live in Antarctica). We accept as fact, for example, that President John F. Kennedy was killed on November 22,

1963, in Dallas, Texas, while riding in a motorcade. However, even though much investigation and debate have focused on the assassination, the question of who was responsible for the murder is for many people still a matter of *opinion*. Most people believe that Lee Harvey Oswald was the lone gunman, but others insist that there were two shooters; still others claim involvement by a foreign government, the Mafia, or even the CIA. Opinions, then, are often based on personal feelings or beliefs or on one's interpretation of information. As you think about your evidence, be careful that you don't present your opinions as facts accepted by everyone. Opinions are debatable, and therefore you must always support them before your readers will be convinced.

2. Support your opinions with evidence. To support your opinions, you must offer evidence of one or more kinds. You have a variety of options to choose from. You might support one idea by using personal experiences. Or you might describe the experiences of friends or family. In another place you might decide to offer detailed examples or to cite statistics or to quote an expert on your subject. You can also use hypothetical examples, researched material, vivid descriptions, reasoned arguments, revealing comparisons, case studies, or testimony of relevant participants, just to name a few other strategies. Consider your purpose and your audience, review the possibilities, and choose the most effective kind of support. The more convincing the support, the more likely your readers are to accept your opinions as true. (◆ If you need to review some sample paragraphs developed by various types of evidence, turn to pages 59–62 of Chapter 3.)

> IMPORTANT REMINDER: If you decide to use research to support your ideas, you must evaluate the evidence and cite the sources of your borrowed material carefully. ◆ For information on selecting and accurately documenting research data, such as studies, statistics, or the testimony of authorities, see Chapter 14 on the writing of the research paper. Remember that if you include the specific ideas of others in your paper, you must give proper credit, even if you do not directly quote the material. Learning to identify and document your sources correctly for your reader will prevent any unintentional plagiarizing of someone else's work.

3. Evaluate the strength and source of your evidence. As you choose your evidence, you should consider its value for the particular point it will support. Scrutinize the nature and source of your evidence carefully. If you are using examples, do they clearly illustrate your claim? Does this example or a different one (or both?) provide the best illustration of your particular point? Is description alone enough support here? Are your statistics or researched material from a reliable, current source? Was information from your research collected in a careful, professional way? Are your experts unbiased authorities in the field under discussion? Where did your experts obtain their information? (For example, are you claiming that certain crystals possess healing powers because a woman on a talk show said so and she sounded reasonable to you? Just how much do you know about the source of a particular Web site?) Asking yourself the kinds of questions posed here (and others suggested throughout Part Two of this textbook) will help you develop a critical eye for choosing the best evidence to support your opinions.

4. Use enough specific supporting evidence. Readers need to see strong, relevant supporting evidence throughout your essay. You must be sure, therefore, that you have enough clearly stated evidence for each of your major points. If you present, for instance, too few examples or only a vague reference to an event that supports one of your ideas, a reader may remain unconvinced or may even be confused. As you revise, ask yourself questions such as these: "Do I need to provide additional information here?" "Do I need more details to clarify my supporting evidence?" "Is any of my evidence clouded by vague or fuzzy language?" If you feel additional supporting evidence or details are needed, take another look at any prewriting you did or use one of the "pump-primer" techniques described in Chapter 1 now to discover some new creative thoughts. For some topics, you may need to do more research or interviewing to find the information you need. (Writers occasionally need to prune ideas too, especially if they're repetitious or off the topic. But, in general, most early drafts are thin or overly general and will profit from more, rather than less, specific supporting evidence.)

5. Watch for biases and strong emotions that may undermine evidence. As you think critically about evidence you are using, monitor any biases and emotional attitudes that may distort information you wish to incorporate into your essay. If you are using personal experiences, for example, have you calmed down enough from your anger over your landlord's actions to write about the clash in a rational, persuasive way? In an essay criticizing a particular product, are you so familiar with the frustrating item that you are making ambiguous claims? (If you write, "The new instructions for assembly are more confusing than ever," have you shown that they were confusing in the first place? Or why they are more so now?) Be sensitive to any racial, ethnic, cultural, religious, or gender-based assumptions you or your sources may have. Opinions based on generalizations and stereotypes ("Japanese cars are good buys because Asians are more efficient workers than Americans"; "Women should stay home because they are better with children than men") are not convincing to thinking readers.

6. Check your evidence for logical fallacies. Thinking critically about your drafts should help you support your ideas with reasonable, logical explanations and arguments. Logical fallacies are common errors in reasoning that good writers try to avoid. ◆ Those fallacies found most often today are explained on pages 296–299 of this text; reviewing them will enable you to identify problems in logic that might appear in the writing of others or in your own drafts.

Critical thinking is not, of course, limited to the six suggestions offered here. But by practicing this advice, you will begin to develop and sharpen analytical skills that should improve any writing project.

III. Revising for Organization

In reality, you have probably already made several changes in the order and organization of ideas in your draft. As noted before, it's likely that when you thought about your essay's meaning—its major points and their supporting evidence—you also thought about the arrangement of those ideas. As you take another look at your draft's organization, use these questions as a guide:

- Am I satisfied with the organizational strategy I selected for my purpose? (For example, would an essay developed primarily by comparison and contrast achieve your purpose better than a narrative approach?)

- Are my major points ordered in a logical, easy-to-follow pattern? Would readers understand my thinking better if certain paragraphs or major ideas were rearranged? Added? Divided? Omitted? Expanded?

- Are my major points presented in topic sentences that state each important idea clearly and specifically? (If any of your topic sentences are implied rather than stated, are you absolutely, 100 percent sure that your ideas cannot be overlooked or even slightly misunderstood by your readers?)

- Is there a smooth flow between my major ideas? Between paragraphs? Within paragraphs? Have I used enough transitional devices to guide the reader along?

- Are any parts of my essay out of proportion? Too long or too brief to do their job effectively?

- Do my title and lead-in draw readers into the essay and toward my thesis?

- Does my conclusion end my discussion thoughtfully? Emphatically or memorably?

Don't be afraid to restructure your drafts. Most good writers rearrange and recast large portions of their prose. ◆ Reviewing Chapters 3 and 4 may help you address questions about organization, beginnings, or endings.

IV. Revising for Clarity and Style

As you've revised for purpose, ideas, and organization, you have also taken steps to clarify your prose. Making a special point now of focusing on sentences and word choice will help ensure your readers' complete understanding of your thinking. Read through your draft, asking these kinds of questions:

- Is each of my sentences as clear and precise as it could be for readers who do not know what I know? Are there sentences that contain misplaced words or convoluted phrases that might cause confusion?

- Are there any sentences that are unnecessarily wordy? Is there deadwood that could be eliminated? (Remember that concise prose is more effective than wordy, "fat" prose because readers can more easily find and follow key ideas and terms. Nearly every writer has a wordiness problem that chokes communication, so now is the season to prune.)

- Do any sentences run on for too long to be fully understood? Can any repetitive or choppy sentences be combined to achieve clarity and a pleasing variation of sentence style? (To help you decide whether you need to combine sentences, you might try this experiment. Select a body paragraph and count the number of words it contains. Then count the number of sentences; divide the number of words by the number of sentences to discover the average number of words per sentence. If your score is less than 15–18, you might need to combine *some* sentences. Good prose offers a variety of sentence lengths and patterns.)

- Are all my words and their connotations accurate and appropriate?

- Can I clarify and energize my prose by adding "showing" details and by replacing bland, vague words with vivid, specific ones? By using active verbs rather than passive ones?

- Can I eliminate any pretentious or unnecessary jargon or language that's inappropriate for my audience? Replace clichés and trite expressions with fresh, original phrases?

- Is my voice authentic, or am I trying to sound like someone else? Is my tone reasonable, honest, and consistent?

◆ The issues raised by these questions—and many others—are discussed in detail in Chapters 6 and 7, on effective sentences and words, which offer more advice on clarifying language and improving style.

V. Editing for Errors

Writers who are proud of the choices they've made in content, organization, and style are, to use a baseball metaphor, rounding third base and heading for home. But there's more to be done. Shift from a baseball metaphor to car maintenance for a moment. All good essays are not only fine-tuned but also waxed and polished—they are edited and proofread repeatedly for errors until they shine. To help you polish your prose by correcting errors in punctuation, grammar, spelling, and diction, here are some hints for effective editing:

Read aloud. In addition to repeatedly reading your draft silently, reading your draft aloud is a good technique because it allows your ears to hear ungrammatical "clunks" or unintended gaps in sense or sound you may otherwise miss. (Reading aloud may also flag omitted words. If, for example, the mother had reread this note to her child's teacher, she might have noticed a missing word: "Please excuse Ian for being. It was his father's fault.")

Know your enemies. Learn to identify your particularly troublesome areas in punctuation and grammar, and then read through your draft for one of these problems at a time: once for fragments, once for comma splices, once for run-ons, and so on. (If you try to look for too many errors at each reading, you'll probably miss quite a few.)

Read backwards. Try reading your draft one sentence at a time starting at the *end* of your essay and working toward the beginning. Don't read each sentence word-for-word backwards—just read the essay one sentence at a time from back to front. When writers try to edit (or proofread) starting at the beginning of their essays, they tend to begin thinking about the ideas they're reading rather than concentrating on the task of editing for errors. By reading one sentence at a time from the back, you will find that the sentences will still make sense but that you are less likely to wander away from the job at hand.

Learn some tricks. There are special techniques for treating some punctuation and grammar problems. ◆ If you have trouble with comma splices, for example, turn to the FANBOYS hint on page 146. If fragments plague your writing, try the "It is true that" test explained on page 129. Consider designating a special part of your journal or class notebook to record in your own words these tricks and other useful pieces of advice so that you can refer to them easily and often.

Eliminate common irritants. Review your draft for those diction and mechanical errors many readers find especially annoying because they often reflect sheer careless-ness. For example, look at these frequently confused words: *it's/its, your/you're, there/their/ they're, who's/whose* (◆ other often-confused words are listed on page 154). Some readers are ready for a national march to protest the public's abandonment of the apostrophe, the Amelia Earhart of punctuation. (Apostrophes *can* change the meaning of sentences: "The teacher called the students names." Was the instructor being rude or just taking roll?) It's a grammatical jungle out there, so be sensitive to your weary readers.

Use your tools. Keep your dictionary handy to check the spelling, usage, and mean-ings of words in doubt. A thesaurus can also be useful if you can restrain any tendencies you might have for growing overly exotic prose. If you are using a computer spell-checker, by all means run it after your last revisions are completed. Do remember, as noted ear-lier in this chapter, that such programs only flag words whose spelling they don't rec-ognize; they will not alert you to omitted or confused words (*affect/effect*), nor will they signal when you've typed in a wrong, but correctly spelled, word (*form* for *from*).

◆ Use Part Four of this text to help resolve any questions you may have about gram-mar, mechanics, and spelling. Advice on untangling sentences and clarifying word choice in Chapters 6 and 7 may be useful, too.

VI. Proofreading

Proofread your final draft several times, putting as much time between the last two read-ings as possible. Fresh eyes catch more typographical or careless errors. Remember that typing errors—even the simple transposing of letters—can change the meaning of an entire thought and occasionally bring unintended humor to your prose. (Imagine, for example, the surprise of restaurant owners whose new lease instructed them to "Please sing the terms of the agreement." Or consider the ramifications of the newspaper ad offering "Great dames for sale" or the 1716 Bible whose advice "sin no more" was mis-printed as "sin on more.")

Make sure, too, that any hard-copy paper looks professional before you turn it in. You wouldn't, after all, expect to be taken seriously if you went to an executive job interview dressed in cutoffs. Turning in a paper with a coffee stain or ink smear on it has about the same effect as a blob of spinach in your teeth—it distracts folks from hearing what you have to say. If your final copy has typos or small blemishes, you may use correction fluid to conceal them; but if you've patched so frequently that your paper resembles the medicine-dotted face of a kindergartner with chicken pox, reprint or photocopy your pages for a fresh look.

Check to be sure you've formatted your paper exactly as your assignment requested. Some instructors ask for a title page; others want folders containing all your drafts and prewriting. Most teachers requiring print copy want essays with pages that are numbered, ordered correctly, and paper-clipped or stapled, with clean edges (no sheets violently ripped from a spiral notebook still dribbling angry confetti down one side; no pages mutilated at the corners by the useless "tear-and-fold-tab" technique). Putting your name on each page will identify your work if papers from a particular class are accidentally mixed up.

> As it's often been said, essays are never really done—only due. Take a last reading using the checklist that follows, make some notes on your progress as a writer and thinker, and congratulate yourself on your fine efforts and accomplishment.

A Final Checklist for Your Essay

If you have written an effective essay, you should be able to answer "yes" to the following questions:

1. Do I feel I have something important to say to my reader?
2. Am I sincerely committed to communicating with my reader and not just with myself?
3. Have I considered my audience's needs? (See Chapter 1.)
4. Do my title and lead-in attract the reader's attention and help set up my thesis? (See Chapter 4.)
5. Does my thesis statement assert one main, clearly focused idea? (See Chapter 2.)
6. Does my thesis and/or essay map give the reader an indication of what points the essay will cover? (See Chapter 2.)
7. Do my body paragraphs contain the essential points in the essay's discussion, and are those points expressed in clearly stated or implied topic sentences? (See Chapter 3.)
8. Is each major point in my essay well developed with enough detailed supporting evidence? (See Chapter 3.)
9. Does each body paragraph have unity and coherence? (See Chapter 3.)
10. Are all the paragraphs in my essay smoothly linked in a logical order? (See Chapter 3.)
11. Does my concluding paragraph provide a suitable ending for the essay? (See Chapter 4.)
12. Are all my sentences clear, concise, and coherent? (See Chapter 6.)

13. Are my words accurate, necessary, and meaningful? (See Chapter 7.)

14. Have I edited and proofread for errors in grammar, punctuation, spelling, and typing? (See Part Four.)

And most important:

15. Has my essay been effectively revised so that I am proud of this piece of writing?

PRACTICING WHAT YOU'VE LEARNED

A. The draft of the following student essay has been annotated by its own writer according to some—*but not all*—of the questions presented in this chapter's discussion of revision. As you read the draft and the writer's marginal comments, think of specific suggestions you might offer to help this writer improve her essay. What changes, in addition to the ones mentioned here, would you encourage this writer to make? What strengths do you see in this draft?

© Canstock Images, Inc./Index Stock Imagery

My title and lead-in are too bland to attract reader's attention.

Would my thesis be clearer if I said what I did find?

My supporting examples could use more "showing" details so the readers can really see the unfriendliness.

Contradicts my point

This paragraph has some specific details, but it rambles and repeats ideas. Needs tighter organization.

Dorm Life

Dorm life is not at all what I had expected it to be. I had anticipated meeting friendly people, quiet hours for studying, eating decent food, and having wild parties on weekends. My dreams, I soon found out, were simply illusions, erroneous perceptions of reality.

My roommate, Kathy, and I live in Holland Hall on the third floor. The people on our dorm floor are about as unfriendly as they can possibly be. I wonder whether or not they're just shy and afraid or if they are simply snobs. Some girls, for example, ignore my roommate and me when we say "hello." Occasionally, they stare straight ahead and act like we aren't even there. Other girls respond, but it's as if they do it out of a sense of duty rather than being just friendly. The guys seem nice, but some are just as afraid or snobby as the girls.

I remember signing up for "quiet hours" when I put in my application for a dorm room last December. Unfortunately, I was assigned to a floor that doesn't have any quiet hours at all. I am a person who requires peace and quiet when studying or reading. The girls in all the rooms around us love to stay up until early in the morning and yell and turn up their music full blast. They turn music on at about eight o'clock at night and turn it off early in the morning. There is

continued on next page

always at least one girl who has music playing at maximum volume. Now, I am very appreciative of music, but listening to hard rock until three in the morning isn't really my idea of what fun is. The girls right across from us usually play soft rock or country artists, and I enjoy them. On the other hand, though, the girls on either side of our room love to listen to growling punk bands into the wee hours of the morning. It is these girls who run up and down the hall, yell at each other, laugh obnoxiously, and try to attract attention. All this continuous racket makes it nearly impossible to study, read, or get any sleep. Kathy and I usually end up going to the library or student cafeteria to study. As far as sleep goes, it doesn't matter what time we go to bed, but rather it depends on how noisy it is and how late the music is on. Sometimes the noise gets so loud and goes on for so long that even when it stops, my ears are ringing and my stomach keeps churning. It is on nights like this that I never go to sleep. I wish the people here were a little more considerate of the people around them.

Contradicts my ¶'s point

Parties, on weekends, are supposedly the most important part of dorm life. Parties provide the opportunity to meet others and have a good time. Holland Hall has had two parties that are even worth mentioning. One of them was a Fifties dance held in the courtyard approximately three weeks ago. Unfortunately, all the other dormitories, the fraternities, and the sororities heard about it, and by eight o'clock at night there were masses of people. It was so packed that it was hard to move around. The other party, much to my dismay, turned out to be a luau party. I do not really care for roast pig, and my stomach turned from the scent of it when I entered the room. Our floor never has parties. Everyone leaves their doors open, turns up the music, and yells back and forth. I suppose that there will be more floor parties once everyone becomes adjusted to this life and begins to socialize.

This paragraph doesn't support my thesis claim—do I mean the dorm has no good parties or not enough parties? Rethink so my point is clear.

As stated, this topic sentence contradicts my thesis.

Dorm food is what I anticipated it would be, terrible, and I was right, it is awful. Breakfast is probably the hardest meal to digest. The bacon and sausage are cold, slightly uncooked, and very greasy. Sometimes, it's as though I am eating pure grease. The eggs look and taste like nothing I ever had before. They look like plastic and they are never hot. I had eggs once, and I vowed I would never have another one as long as I lived in Holland Hall. The most enjoyable part of breakfast is the orange juice. It's always cold and it seems to be fresh. No one can say dorm food is totally boring because

Some good examples—could I use even more descriptive language?

Unity?

the cooks break up the monotony of the same food by serving "mystery meat" at least once every two weeks. This puts
a little excitement in the student's day because everyone
cracks jokes and wonders just what's in this "mystery meat."
I think a lot of students are afraid to ask, fearful of the
answer, and simply make snide remarks and shovel it in.

Can I conclude emphatically without switching positions?

All in all, I believe dorm life isn't too great, even though
there are some good times. Even though I complain about
dorm food, the people, the parties, and everything else, I
am glad I am here. I am happy because I have learned a lot
about other people, responsibilities, consideration, and I've
even learned a lot about myself.

B. As you work on strengthening your own revision skills, you may find it easier
in the beginning to practice on the writing of others. Assume the writer of the
draft that follows is directing these comments to a group of high school students contemplating their college choices. By offering helpful marginal comments and questions, guide this writer to a revised draft with more effective
arguments, organization, and clarity.

Maybe You Shouldn't Go Away to College

Going away to college is not for everyone. There are good
reasons why a student might choose to live at home and
attend a local school. Money, finding stability while changes
are occurring, and accepting responsibility are three to
consider.

Money is likely to be most important. Not only is tuition
more expensive, but extra money is needed for room and
board. Whether room and board is a dorm or an apartment,
the expense is great.

Most students never stop to consider that the money that
could be saved from room and board may be better spent in
future years on graduate school, which is likely to be more
important in their careers.

Going to school is a time of many changes anyway, without adding the pressure of a new city or even a new state.
Finding stability will be hard enough, without going from
home to a dorm. Starting college could be an emotional time
for some, and the security of their home and family might
make everything easier.

When students decide to go away to school, sometimes
because their friends are going away, or maybe because the
school is their parents' alma mater, something that all need
to decide is whether or not they can accept the responsibility
of a completely new way of life.

continued on next page

Everyone feels as if they are ready for total independence when they decide to go away to college, but is breaking away when they are just beginning to set their futures a good idea?

Going away to school may be the right road for some, but those who feel that they are not ready might start looking to a future that is just around the corner.

C. Practice your editing and proofreading skills by correcting all the errors you see in the paragraph that follows. Look carefully for problems in grammar, punctuation, spelling, word confusion, and sentence sense, as well as typos. Some proofreaders find it useful to place a blank piece of paper or index card under each line to help them focus as they read.

One fo the most interesting books I've read lately is Bold Spirit, by Linda Lawrence Hunt. Its the true story of Hega Estby's 1896 walk across america, form Eastern Washingto to New york City; in order to win a $10,000 prize to save the family farm. Acompanied by her teen age daughter Clara the two sets out with only $5 dollars each and walked 3500 miles on foot in Victorian clothes. Despite alot bad wheather and dangerous encounter along the the way. Helga and her daughter did arrive safely, but, unfortunately they weren't never able too collect there prize money. Worse then that, tho, Helgas family afterwards r so embarrasssed about her walk thatthey burned her diary, her notes & newspaper clippings, her story only came to light recently be cause a daughter-inlaw had secretly saved and album of clippings from the fire

ASSIGNMENT

Select a body paragraph from "Dorm Life" (pages 111–113) or "Maybe You Shouldn't Go Away to College" (pages 113–114) and revise it, making effective changes in focus, development, organization, sentence construction, and word choice. (Feel free to elaborate on or delete any supporting details to improve the paragraph's content.)

© CORBIS

© Keith Brofsky/
Photodisc/Getty Images

APPLYING WHAT YOU'VE LEARNED TO **YOUR** WRITING

If you have completed a draft of an essay, you have already revised many parts of it, changing ideas, sentences, and words as you wrote. Now begin to revise by moving through the stages outlined in this chapter. Remember, you cannot revise for everything at once, so this process calls for multiple readings—and rewriting. After another look at your work, are you satisfied that it accomplishes your purpose, that it addresses the needs of your specific audience? Using your best critical thinking skills, strengthen any weak development of your ideas; then tackle questions of order and coherence. You may find that you need another draft at this point to accommodate new material or deep-structure changes.

Once you are happy with your essay's larger issues of content and organization, work on clarity by polishing rough sentences and substituting better words. Proofread your draft for surface errors at least twice! Until a revision process becomes second nature to you, use the checklist on pages 110–111 as a guide.

Collaborative Activities: Group Work, Peer Revision Workshops, and Team Projects

Writers in both the business and academic worlds often consult their colleagues for advice; they might, for example, ask for help with a difficult explanation, a complex description, or a twisted sentence. Sometimes they may write together as part of a task force or committee. Similarly, you may find that working on composing and revising strategies with your colleagues—your classmates—can be enormously helpful.

You may have already noticed a practice exercise or assignment earlier in this text identified as a Collaborative Activity. "Collaborative" simply means working together, and these assignments are designed so you and your classmates can help each other improve particular writing skills. By offering reactions, suggestions, and questions (not to mention moral support), your classroom colleagues may become some of your best writing teachers.

Collaborative activities in composition courses take many forms and may occur in any stage of the writing process. Here are three of the most common types:

1. **Group Work:** Frequently in writing classes an instructor will ask three to five students to form a discussion or activity group. For example, students might be asked to evaluate a writing sample or to respond to an exercise or to ask for feedback on their own drafts. The possibilities are numerous, and small-group discussions can be especially useful early on as writers brainstorm on and focus their topics, as well as later in the writing process when they are striving for well-developed content and clear organization.

2. **Peer Revision Workshops:** On some days instructors may ask students to respond to each other's drafts in writing. Sometimes teachers will give student-reviewers a list of tasks to perform ("Underline the thesis") or questions to answer ("How

© C. Devan/zefa/CORBIS

successful is the conclusion?"); at other times, the writers themselves will create the inquiries. Although many workshops are organized as one-on-one exchanges of papers in the classroom, an increasing number of schools today have the electronic means to post students' drafts on protected sites so that a variety of student-reviewers may comment on them both in and out of class. Structured in many effective ways, peer workshops allow writers to see their drafts from a reader's point of view.

3. **Team Projects:** Sometimes students will be asked to work together to produce a single piece of writing. Because many organizations today require a set of members or employees to prepare such projects as proposals, position papers, or grants, the practice of writing together as a committee or team can provide a valuable experience. A "blended" project might call for members of a team to write individually and then compare their efforts, selecting and revising the best ideas and prose as they craft the final piece together. A "composite" approach might ask students to assign each team member a different task (investigate a problem, research a study, conduct an interview, etc.) or a particular section to write, with the group responsible for smoothly meshing the parts into a whole. Panel discussions, debates, and oral presentations are often based on this sort of team project.

There are, of course, numerous other ways instructors may create collaborative activities, depending upon the lesson, goals, and logistics. In one format or another, working collaboratively can frequently help writers consider alternative ways of thinking and that, in turn, may encourage clearer, more effective prose.

Benefiting from Collaborative Activities

Collaborative activities can be extremely useful, but working with other writers may also present challenges. To receive the most benefit from interaction with your classmates, you'll need to develop both a sense of cooperation and good communication skills. The following section offers suggestions for gaining the most value from one-on-one revision workshops as well as some advice for successful participation in small-group discussions.

Guidelines for Peer Revision Workshops

Students taking part in revision workshops for the first time often have questions about the reviewing process. Some student-reviewers may feel uneasy about their role, wondering, "What if I can't think of any suggestions for the writer? How can I tell someone that the essay is really terrible? What if I sense something's wrong but I'm not sure what it is—or how to fix it?" Writers, too, may feel apprehensive or even occasionally defensive about receiving criticism of their papers. Because these concerns are genuine and widespread, here is some advice for you in the roles of both writer and reviewer.

When you are the **writer**:

1. Develop a constructive attitude. Admittedly, receiving criticism—especially on a creation that has required hard work—can sometimes be difficult, particularly if your self-image has become mixed up with your drafts. Try to realize that your reviewer is not criticizing you personally but rather is trying to help you by offering fresh insights. All drafts can be improved, and no writer need feel embarrassed about seeking or receiving advice. (Take comfort in the words of writer Somerset Maugham: "Only the mediocre person is always at his best.") See the workshop as a nonthreatening opportunity to reconsider your prose and improve your audience awareness.

2. Come prepared. If your workshop structure permits, tell your reviewer what sort of help you need at this point in your drafting or revising process. Ask for suggestions to fix a particularly troublesome area, or ask for feedback on a choice you've made but are feeling unsure of. Don't hesitate to ask your reviewer for assistance with any part of your essay.

3. Evaluate suggestions carefully. Writing isn't math; most of the time there are no absolutely right or wrong answers—just better or worse rhetorical choices. That is, there are many ways to communicate an idea to a set of readers. You, as the writer, must decide on an effective way, the way that best serves your purpose and your readers' needs. Sometimes your reviewer will suggest a change that is brilliant or one so obviously right you will wonder why in the world you didn't think of it yourself. At other times you may weigh your reviewer's suggestion and decide that your original choice is just as good or perhaps even better. Be open to suggestions, but learn to trust thyself as well.

4. Find the good in bad advice. Occasionally, you may have a reviewer who seems to miss a crucial point or misunderstands your purpose entirely, whose suggestions for revising your paper seem uniformly unproductive for one reason or another. You certainly shouldn't take bad advice—but do think about the issues it raises. Although it's helpful to receive a dynamite suggestion you can incorporate immediately, the real value of a revision workshop is its ability to encourage you to rethink your prose. Readers' responses (yes, even the bizarre ones) challenge writers to take still another look at their rhetorical choices and ask themselves, "Is this clear after all? Does this example really work here? Did something in my essay throw this reader off the track?" Revision workshops offer you benefits, even if you ultimately decide to reject many of your reviewer's suggestions.

When you are the **reviewer**:

1. Develop a constructive attitude. Sometimes it's hard to give honest criticism—most of us are uncomfortable when we think we might hurt someone's feelings—but remember that the writer has resolved to develop a professional attitude, too. The writer

Avoid Overpacking Your Sentences

Because our society is becoming increasingly specialized and highly technical, we tend to equate complexity with excellence and simplicity with simplemindedness. This assumption is unfortunate because it often leads to a preference for unnecessarily complicated and even contorted writing. In a recent survey, for example, a student chose a sample of bureaucratic hogwash over several well-written paragraphs, explaining his choice by saying that it must have been better because he didn't understand it.

Our best writers have always worked hard to present their ideas simply and specifically so that their readers could easily understand them. Mark Twain, for instance, once praised a young author this way: "I notice that you use plain simple language, short words, and brief sentences. This is the way to write English. It is the modern way and the best way. Stick to it." And when a critic asked Hemingway to define his theory of writing, he replied, "[I] put down what I see and what I feel in the best and simplest way I can tell it."

In your own writing, therefore, work for a simple, direct style. Avoid sentences that are overpacked (too many ideas or too much information at once) as in the following example on racquetball:

> John told Phil that to achieve more control over the ball, he should practice flicking or snapping his wrist, because this action is faster in the close shots and placing a shot requires only a slight change of the wrist's angle instead of an acute movement of the whole arm, which gives a player less reaction time.

To make the overpacked sentence easier to understand, try dividing the ideas into two or more sentences:

> John told Phil that to achieve more control over the ball, he should practice flicking or snapping his wrist, because this action is faster in the close shots. Placing a shot requires only a slight change of the wrist's angle instead of an acute movement of the whole arm, which gives a player less reaction time.

Don't ever run the risk of losing your reader in a sentence that says too much to comprehend in one bite. This confusing notice, for example, came from a well-known credit card company:

> The Minimum Payment Due each month shall be reduced by the amounts paid in excess of the Minimum Payment Due during the previous three months which have not already been so applied in determining the Minimum Payment Due in such earlier months, unless you have exceeded your line of credit or have paid the entire New Balance shown on your billing statement.

Or consider the confusion of soccer players whose coach warned them in this manner:

> It is also a dangerous feeling to consider that where we are in the league is of acceptable standard because standard is relevant to the standards we have set, which thereby may well indicate that we have not aspired to the standard which we set ourselves.

Try too for a straightforward construction. This sentence by Ronald Reagan early in his campaign for the presidency, for example, takes far too many twists and turns for anyone to follow it easily on the first reading:

> My goal is an America where something or anything that is done to or for anyone is done neither because of nor in spite of any difference between them, racially, religiously, or ethnic-origin-wise.

◆ If any sentences in your rough draft are overpacked or contorted, try rephrasing your meaning in shorter sentences and then combining thoughts where most appropriate. (Help with sentence variety may be found on pages 145–149 of this chapter.)

Fix Major Sentence Errors

Rather than creating overpacked sentences, some writers have the opposite problem. They write *sentence fragments*, dropping thoughts here or there without forming them into complete, comprehensible grammatical units. Such fragments are confusing to readers, who must struggle to fill in the connecting link between the writer's ideas.

A complete sentence has both a subject (the thing that performs the action or maintains the state of being) and a predicate (the verb and any modifiers or complements). A sentence fragment is often missing its subject, as shown in the following example.

Fragment	David bought a gopher ranch. *Hoping to strike it rich.*
Correct	David bought a gopher ranch, hoping to strike it rich.
Correct	David bought a gopher ranch. He hoped to strike it rich.

Other fragments have the essential sentence components but are considered fragments because they begin with a subordinating conjunction (such as "although," "if," or "when") or a relative pronoun (such as "who," "which," "whose," or "that").

Fragment	David bought a gopher ranch. *Although he knew nothing about rodents.*
Correct	David bought a gopher ranch, although he knew nothing about rodents.
Fragment	David bought a gopher ranch. *Which was for sale at a low price.*
Correct	David bought a gopher ranch, which was for sale at a low price.

If you are having problems recognizing whether a group of words is a fragment or a complete sentence, try the "It is true that" test. When you suspect a fragment, say, "It is true that" in front of the words in question. In most cases, a complete sentence will still make sense, but a fragment will not.*

- It is true that . . . David bought a gopher ranch. [Makes sense: complete sentence]
- It is true that . . . hoping to strike it rich. [No sense: fragment]
- It is true that . . . which was for sale at a low price. [No sense: fragment]

Although they can appear anywhere, fragments most often "belong" to the thought in front of them. To make a fragment fully meaningful, consider connecting it to the preceding or following sentence, as appropriate, or simply rewrite it as a complete sentence (for examples, see the first two "Correct" sentences in this section).

---

*The "It is true that" test does not work on questions, elliptical responses or exclamations (such as "Hello," "Yes," "Help!"), or commands ("Go to your room right now").

In some cases a writer will intentionally use a fragment for a particular purpose, often for emphasis or to create a specific tone ("She felt rotten. Worse than rotten. Miserable-rotten."). But unless you clearly know how to use a fragment for effect and are certain that the tone it creates is appropriate for your essay and audience, stick to writing complete sentences.

◆ For more help with fragments, see page 564 in the Handbook. See also pages 146–149 in this chapter, which will suggest ways to combine thoughts through coordination and subordination.

In addition to unintentional fragments, another construction that may confuse meaning for readers is called a *run-on* (or *fused*) sentence. Run-ons are most often two complete sentences joined together without any punctuation. Such sentences may be corrected by making separate sentences, by placing a semicolon between the complete thoughts, by using a comma plus a coordinating conjunction, or by subordinating one clause.

Run-on	The toy water gun was confiscated during algebra class it was a weapon of math disruption.
Corrected with semicolon	The toy water gun was confiscated during algebra class; it was a weapon of math disruption.
Corrected with subordination	The toy water gun was confiscated during algebra class because it was a weapon of math disruption.

Don't, however, correct a run-on sentence by merely inserting a comma without a coordinating conjunction between the two sentences; doing so will likely result in another major sentence error called a *comma splice*.

Comma splice	My economics professor says success is a great teacher, my yoga teacher says adversity may be an even greater one.
Corrected with a comma and a coordinating conjunction	My economics professor says success is a great teacher, but my yoga teacher says adversity may be an even greater one.

The common coordinating conjunctions are "and," "or," "but," "for," "so," "nor," and "yet." ◆ For more information on coordination, turn to pages 146–147 in this chapter. (For more help correcting the run-on sentence and the comma splice, see pages 566–568 in the Handbook.)

Pay Attention to Word Order

The correct word order is crucial for clarity. Always place a modifier (a word or group of words that affects the meaning of another word) near the word it modifies. The position of a modifier can completely change the meaning of your sentence; for example, each sentence presented here offers a different idea because of the placement of the modifier "only."

1. Eliza said she loves only me.
   [Eliza loves me and no one else.]

2. Only Eliza said she loves me.
   [No other person said she loves me.]

3. Eliza said only that she loves me.

[Eliza said she loves me, but said nothing other than that.]

4. Eliza said only she loves me.

[Eliza said no one else loves me.]

To avoid confusion, therefore, place your modifiers close to the words or phrases they describe.

A modifier that seems to modify the wrong part of a sentence is called "misplaced." Not only can misplaced modifiers change or distort the meaning of your sentence, they can also provide unintentional humor, as illustrated by the following excerpt from the 1929 Marx Brothers movie *The Cocoanuts*:

Woman: There's a man waiting outside to see you with a black mustache.
Groucho: Tell him I've already got one.

Of course, the woman didn't mean to imply that the man outside was waiting with (that is, accompanied by) a mustache; she meant to say, "There's a man with a black mustache who is waiting outside."

A poster advertising a lecture on campus provided this opportunity for humor: "Professor Elizabeth Sewell will discuss the latest appearance of Halley's Comet in room 104." Under the announcement a local wit had scribbled, "Shall we reserve room 105 for the tail?" Or take the case of this startling headline: "Calf Born to Rancher with Two Heads."

Here are some other examples of misplaced modifiers:

Misplaced   Dilapidated and almost an eyesore, Shirley bought the old house to restore it to its original beauty. [Did the writer mean that Shirley needed a beauty treatment?]

Revised   Shirley bought the old house, which was dilapidated and almost an eyesore, to restore it to its original beauty.

Misplaced   Because she is now thoroughly housebroken, Sarah can take the dog almost anywhere. [Did the writer mean that Sarah once had an embarrassing problem?]

Revised   Because the dog is now thoroughly housebroken, Sarah can take her almost anywhere.

Misplaced   Three family members were found bound and gagged by the grandmother. [Did the writer mean that the grandmother had taken up a life of crime?]

Revised   The grandmother found the three family members who had been bound and gagged.

Misplaced   The lost child was finally found wandering in a frozen farmer's field. [Did the writer mean to say that the farmer was that cold?]

Revised   The lost child was finally found wandering in a farmer's frozen field.

In each of the preceding examples the writer forgot to place the modifying phrase so that it modifies the correct word. In most cases, a sentence with a misplaced modifier can be corrected easily by moving the word or phrase closer to the word that should be modified.

In some sentences, however, the word being modified is missing entirely. Such a phrase is called a "dangling modifier." Think of these phrases as poor orphans, waiting out in the cold, without a parent to accompany them. Most of these errors can be corrected by adding the missing "parent"—the word(s) described by the phrase. Here are some examples followed by their revisions:

Dangling	Waving farewell, the plane began to roll down the runway. [Did the writer mean the plane was waving farewell?]
Revised	Waving farewell, <u>we</u> watched as the plane began to roll down the runway.
Dangling	After spending hours planting dozens of strawberry plants, the gophers came back to the garden and ate every one of them. [Did the writer mean that the gophers had a good meal after putting in such hard work?]
Revised	After spending hours planting dozens of strawberry plants, <u>Ralph</u> realized that the gophers had come back to the garden and eaten every one of them.
Dangling	While telling a joke to my roommate, a cockroach walked across my soufflé. [Did the writer mean that the cockroach was a comedian?]
Revised	While telling a joke to my roommate, <u>I</u> noticed a cockroach walking across my soufflé.
Dangling	Having tucked the children into bed, the cat was put out for the night. [Did the writer mean that the family pet had taken up nanny duties?]
Revised	Having tucked the children into bed, <u>Mom and Dad</u> put the cat out for the night.

Misplaced and dangling modifiers (and many other kinds of sentence errors) often occur as you write your first "idea" drafts. Later, when you are satisfied with your content and organization, you can smooth out these confusing or unintentionally humorous constructions. At first you may agree with well-known essayist Annie Dillard, who notes that writing sometimes feels like alligator wrestling: "With your two bare hands, you hold and fight a sentence's head while its tail tries to knock you over." By practicing good revision skills, however, you soon should be able to wrestle your sentence problems to the ground. (◆ For additional examples of misplaced and dangling modifiers, see page 562 in the Handbook.)

Avoid Mixed Constructions and Faulty Predication

Sometimes you may begin with a sentence pattern in mind and then shift, midsentence, to another pattern—a change that often results in a generally confusing sentence. In many of these cases, you will find that the subject of your sentence simply doesn't fit with the rest of the sentence (the predicate). Look at the following examples and note their corrections:

Faulty	Financial aid is a growing problem for many college students. [Financial aid itself isn't a problem; rather, it's the lack of aid.]
Revised	College students are finding it harder to obtain financial aid.
Faulty	Pregnant cows are required to teach a portion of two courses in Animal Science, AS100 (Breeding of Livestock) and AS200 (Problems in Reproduction of Cattle). [Obviously, the cows will not be the instructors for the classes.]

Revised   The Animal Science Department needs to purchase pregnant cows for use in two courses, AS100 (Breeding of Livestock) and AS200 (Problems in Reproduction of Cattle).

Faulty   Love is when you start rehearsing dinner-date conversation before breakfast. [A thing is never a "when" or a "where"; rewrite all "is when" or "is where" constructions.]

Revised   You're in love if you start rehearsing dinner-date conversation before breakfast.

Faulty   My math grade is why I'm so depressed. [A grade is not a "why"; rewrite "is why" constructions.]

Revised   I'm so depressed because of my math grade.

Faulty   "Fans, don't fail to miss tomorrow's game." [A contorted line from Dizzy Dean, baseball star and sportscaster]

Revised   "Fans, don't miss tomorrow's game."

Many mixed constructions occur when a writer is in a hurry; read your rough drafts carefully to see if you have sentences in which you started one pattern but switched to another. (◆ For more help on faulty predications and mixed constructions, see pages 571–572 in Part Four.)

Clear, straightforward sentences keep readers from feeling as though they are lost in an Escher maze. *Convex and Concave*, 1955, by M. C. Escher.

© Art Resource, NY

awareness. For instance, using your very first thoughts, fill in the blanks in the following sentence:

> After years of service, my old car finally _____, _____, and _____ by the side of the road.

If your immediate responses were the three words printed at the bottom of page 177, don't be surprised! Most people who have taken this simple test responded that way too, either entirely or in part. So what's the problem, you might ask. The writer describing the car wanted her readers to see *her* particular old car, not some bland image identically reproduced in her readers' minds. To show readers her car—as opposed to thousands of other old cars—she needs to substitute specific, "showing" language for the Insta-Prose.* (Retest yourself: what might she have said about this car that would allow you, the reader, to see what happened that day?)

As a writer, you also want your readers to "see" your specific idea and be engaged by your prose rather than skipping over canned-bland images. When you are drafting for ideas early in the writing process, Insta-Prose pours out—and that's to be expected because you are still discovering your thoughts. But, later, when you revise your drafts, be sensitive to predictable language in all its forms. Stamp out Insta-Prose! Cook up some fresh language to delight your reader.

Don't use trendy expressions or slang in your essays. Slang generally consists of commonly used words made up by special groups to communicate among themselves. Slang has many origins, from sports to space travel; for example, surfers gave us the expression "to wipe out" (to fail), soldiers lent "snafu" (from the first letters of "situation normal—all fouled up"), and astronauts provided "A-OK" (all systems working).

Although slang often gives our speech color and vigor, it is unacceptable in most writing assignments for several reasons. First, slang is often part of a private language understood only by members of a particular professional, social, or age group. Second, slang often presents a vague picture or one that changes meanings from person to person or from context to context. More than likely, each person has a unique definition for a particular slang expression, and although these definitions may overlap, they are not precisely the same. Consequently, your reader could interpret your words in one way although you intend them in another, a dilemma that might result in total miscommunication.

Too often, beginning writers rely on vague, popular phrases ("The party was way awesome") instead of thinking of specific words to explain specific ideas. Slang expressions frequently contain nontraditional grammar and diction that are inappropriate for college work. Moreover, slang becomes dated quickly, and almost nothing sounds worse

---

*Some prose is so familiar that it is now a joke. The phrase "It was a dark and stormy night," the beginning of an 1830 novel by Edward George Bulwer-Lytton, has been parodied in the *Peanuts* comic strip (plagiarized without shame by Snoopy). It also prompted a bad-writing contest sponsored since 1982 by the English Department at San José State University, in which entrants are challenged to "compose the opening sentence to the worst of all possible novels."

than yesterday's "in" expressions. (Can you seriously imagine calling a friend "Daddy-O" or telling someone you're "feelin' groovy"?)

Try to write so that your prose will be as fresh and pleasing ten years from now as it is today. Don't allow slang to give your writing a tone that detracts from a serious discussion. Putting slang in quotation marks isn't the solution—omit the slang and use precise words instead.

Refrain from using texting language and Webspeak in your academic or professional writing. Millions of people worldwide are chatting daily online and through their cell phone screens, with the number of messages increasing with each technological advance. But the language often used there—with its shorthand spelling (GR8, C U 2morrow), abbreviations (BTW, IMO, IDK), pictograms (what's ^?, I <3 U), and incomplete or "imposter" words (txtspk, cuz)—is not appropriate for your college assignments or traditional business correspondence.

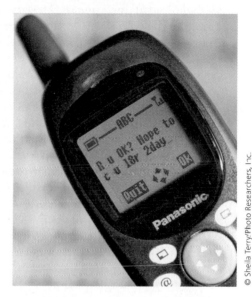

© Sheila Terry/Photo Researchers, Inc.

Texting lingo thrives because it is easy to type on a palm-sized keypad and quickly reduces content in small-screen messages that may be confined to a limited number of characters (for example, Twitter's 140-character cap for "tweets"). Despite its easy use in casual messaging, such language is too informal for many other writing situations and audiences. More importantly, some readers may not understand all the techno-language words, and even commonly used abbreviations may be misinterpreted (Does LOL here mean "laughing out loud" or "lots of love"? Is B/F a best friend or boyfriend?). In addition, some readers may see incomplete or misspelled words simply as errors or as indications of carelessness; other readers may wonder if a lack of proper capitalization or incorrect punctuation reveals ignorance rather than chat-style. Still others may regard such language as juvenile slang, since keyboard symbols and emoticons [:-)] are so frequently used by younger teens.

Good writers understand that standards and levels of English vary from situation to situation and that to be successful in their communications, all effective writers must both respect and respond to the needs of different kinds of readers. Keep your shorthand symbols in their appropriate informal places, not in your college and professional work. But anywhere, at any time, if there's a chance the meaning of your message might be lost, take the extra minute to write out those words!

Do select simple, direct words your readers can easily understand. Don't use pompous or pseudo-sophisticated language in place of plain speech. Wherever possible, avoid *jargon*—that is, words and phrases that are unnecessarily technical, pretentious, or abstract.

Technical jargon—terms specific to one area of study or specialization—should be omitted or clearly defined in essays directed to a general audience because such language is often inaccessible to anyone outside the writer's particular field. By now, most of us are familiar with bureaucratese, journalese, and psychobabble, in addition to gobbledygook from business, politics, advertising, and education. If, for example, you worry that "a self-actualized person such as yourself cannot transcend either your hostile environment or your passive-aggressive behavior to make a commitment to a viable lifestyle and meaningful interpersonal relationships," you are indulging in psychological or sociological jargon; if you "review existing mechanisms of consumer input, thruput, and output via the consumer communications channel module," you are speaking business jargon. Although most professions do have their own terms, you should limit your use of specialized language to writing aimed solely at your professional colleagues; always try to avoid technical jargon in prose directed at a general audience.

Today the term "jargon" also refers to prose containing an abundance of abstract, pretentious, multisyllabic words. The use of this kind of jargon often betrays a writer's attempt to sound sophisticated and intellectual; actually, it only confuses meaning and delays communication. Here, for instance, is a sample of incomprehensible jargon from a college president who obviously prefers twenty-five-cent words to simple, straightforward, nickel ones: "We will divert the force of this fiscal stress into leverage energy and pry important budgetary considerations and control out of our fiscal and administrative procedures." Or look at the thirty-eight-word definition of "exit" written by an Occupational Safety and Health Administration bureaucrat: "That portion of a means of egress which is separated from all spaces of the building or structure by construction or equipment as required in this subpart to provide a protected way of travel to the exit discharge." Such language is not only pretentious and confusing but almost comic in its wordiness.

Legal jargon, complicating even the smallest transaction, has become so incomprehensible that some lawmakers and consumers have begun to fight back. Today in Texas, for example, any firm lending $500 or less must use a model plain-English contract or submit its contract for approval to the Office of Consumer Credit. The new, user-friendly contract replaces "Upon any such default, and at any time thereafter, Secured party may declare the entire balance of the indebtedness secured hereby, plus any other sums owed hereunder, immediately due and payable without demand or notice, less any refund due, and Secured Party shall have all the remedies of the Uniform Commercial Code" with a clear, easy-to-understand statement: "If I break any of my promises in this document, you can demand that I immediately pay all that I owe." Hooray for the gobbledygook squashers in the Lone Star State!

To avoid such verbal litter in your own writing, follow these rules:

1. Always select the plainest, most direct words you know.

   Jargon   The editor wanted to halt the proliferation of the product because she discovered an error on the page that terminates the volume.

   Revised   The editor wanted to stop publishing the book because she found an error on the last page.

2. Replace nominalizations (nouns that are made from verbs and adjectives, usually by adding endings such as *-tion*, *-ism*, *-ness*, or *-al*) with simpler verbs and nouns.

> **Jargon**   The departmental head has come to the recognition that the utilization of verbose verbalization renders informational content inaccessible.
>
> **Revised**   The head of the department recognizes that wordiness confuses meaning.

3. Avoid adding *-ize* or *-wise* to verbs and adverbs.

> **Jargon**   *Weatherwise*, it looked like a good day to *finalize* her report on wind tunnels.
>
> **Revised**   The day's clear weather would help her finish her report on wind tunnels.

4. Drop out meaningless tack-on words such as "factor," "aspect," and "situation."

> **Jargon**   The convenience *factor* of the neighborhood grocery store is one *aspect* of its success.
>
> **Revised**   The convenience of the neighborhood grocery store contributes to its success.

Remember that good writing is clear and direct, never wordy, cloudy, or ostentatious. (◆ For more hints on developing a clear style, see pages 126–133.)

Do call things by their proper names. Don't sugarcoat your terms by substituting *euphemisms*—words that sound nice or pretty applied to subjects some people find distasteful. For example, you've probably heard someone say, "she passed away" instead of "she died" or "he was under the influence of alcohol" instead of "he was drunk." Flight attendants refer to a "water landing" rather than an ocean crash. "Senior Citizens" (or, worse, the "chronologically advantaged") may receive special discounts. Often, euphemisms are used to soften names of jobs: "sanitary engineer" for garbage collector, "field representative" for salesperson, "information processor" for typist, "vehicle appearance specialist" for car washer, and so forth.

Some euphemisms are dated and now seem plain silly: in Victorian times, for example, the word "leg" was considered unmentionable in polite company, so people spoke of "piano limbs" and asked for the "first joint" of a chicken. The phrases "white meat" and "dark meat" were euphemisms some people used to avoid asking for a piece of chicken breast or thigh.

Today, euphemisms still abound. Though our generation is perhaps more direct about sex and death, many current euphemisms gloss over unpleasant or unpopular business, military, and political practices. Some stockbrokers, for example, once referred to an October market crash as "a fourth-quarter equity retreat," and General Motors didn't really shut down one of its plants—the closing was merely a "volume-related production schedule adjustment." Similarly, Chrysler didn't lay off workers; it simply "initiated a career alternative enhancement program." Nuclear power plants no longer have dumps; they have "containment facilities" with radiation "migration" rather than leaks and "inventory discrepancies" rather than thefts of plutonium. Simple products are now complex technology: clocks are "analog temporal displacement monitors," toothbrushes are "home plaque removal instruments," sinks are part of the "hygienic hand-washing media," and pencils are "portable handheld communications inscribers." Vinyl is now "vegetarian leather."

Euphemisms abound in governments and official agencies when those in charge try to hide or disguise the truth from the public. On the national level, a former budget director gave us "revenue enhancements" instead of new taxes, and a former Secretary of Health, Education, and Welfare once tried to camouflage cuts in social services by calling them "advance downward adjustments." Wiretaps once became "technical collection sources" used by "special investigators units" instead of burglars, and plain lying became on one important occasion merely "plausible deniability." Other lies or exaggerations have been "strategic misrepresentations" and convenient "reality augmentations." Interestingly enough, even Washington staff members in charge of prettying up the truth for the public have earned their own euphemistic title: "spin doctors."

In a large Southwestern city, people might have been surprised to learn that there were no potholes in the streets—only "pavement deficiencies." Garbage no longer stinks; instead, it "exceeds the odor threshold." In some jails, a difficult prisoner who once might have been sent to solitary confinement is now placed in the "meditation room" or the "adjustment center." In some hospitals, sick people do not die—they experience "negative patient care outcome"; if they died because of a doctor's mistake, they underwent a "diagnostic misadventure of a high magnitude." Incidentally, those patients who survive no longer receive greeting cards; instead, they open "social expression products." During their recovery, patients might watch the "choreographed reality" of TV wrestling, while their dogs enjoy "play activities" at a local "pet lodge."

Perhaps the military is the all-time winner of the "substitute-a-euphemism" contest. Over the years, the military has used a variety of words, such as "neutralization," "pacification," and "liberation," to mean the invasion and destruction of towns, countries, and governments. During the first Gulf War with Iraq, for example, bombs that fell on civilians were referred to as "incontinent ordnance," with the dead becoming "collateral damage." Earlier, to avoid publicizing a retreat, the military simply called for "backloading our augmentation personnel." On the less serious side, the Navy changes ocean waves into "climatic disturbances at the air-sea interface," and the Army, not to be outdone, transforms the lowly shovel into a "combat emplacement evacuator."*

Although many euphemisms seem funny and harmless, too many of them are not, because people—often those with power to shape public opinion—have intentionally designed them to obscure the reality of a particular situation or choice of action. Because euphemisms can be used unscrupulously to manipulate people, you should always avoid them in your own prose and be suspicious of them in the writing of others. As Aldous Huxley, author of *Brave New World*, noted, "An education for freedom is, among other things, an education in the proper uses of language."

In addition to weakening the credibility of one's ideas, euphemisms can make prose unnecessarily abstract, wordy, pretentious, or even silly. For a clear and natural prose style, use terms that are straightforward and simple. In other words, call a spade a spade, not "an implement for use in horticultural environments."

Avoid sexist language. Most people will agree that language helps shape thought. Consequently, writers should avoid using language that promotes any kind of exclusion or demeaning gender stereotypes. In particular, sexist language, by consistently identifying certain groups, jobs, or actions as male, subtly suggests that only men, rather

---

* ◆ For more examples of euphemisms and doublespeak, see the "To the Student" essay in the front of this text.

than both men and women, appear in those roles. To make your writing as inclusive and unbiased as possible, here are some simple suggestions for writing nonsexist prose:

1. Try using plural nouns to eliminate the need for the singular pronouns "he" and "she":

   Original Today's *doctor* knows *he* must carry extra malpractice insurance.
   Revision Today's *doctors* know *they* must carry extra malpractice insurance.

2. Try substituting gender-neutral occupational titles for those ending in "man" or "woman":

   Original The *fireman* and the *saleslady* watched the *policeman* arrest the former *chairman* of the Physics Department.
   Revision The *firefighter* and the *sales clerk* watched the *police officer* arrest the former *chair* of the Physics Department.

3. Don't contribute to stereotyping by assigning particular roles solely to men or women:

   Original *Mothers* concerned about the possibility of Reyes syndrome should avoid giving aspirin to their sick children.
   Revision *Parents* concerned about the possibility of Reyes syndrome should avoid giving aspirin to their sick children.

4. Try substituting such words as "people," "persons," "one," "voters," "workers," "students," and so on, for "man" or "woman":

   Original Any *man* who wants to become a corporation executive before thirty should buy this book.
   Revision *Anyone* who wants to become a corporation executive before thirty should buy this book.

5. Don't use inappropriate diminutives:

   Original In the annual office picture, the photographer asked the men to stand behind the *girls*.
   Revision In the annual office picture, the photographer asked the men to stand behind the *women*.

6. Consider avoiding words that use "man" to describe the characteristics of a group or that refer to people in general.

   Original Rebuilding the space shuttle will call for extra money and *manpower*, but such an endeavor will benefit *mankind* in the generations to come.
   Revision Rebuilding the space shuttle will call for extra money and *employees*, but such an endeavor will benefit future *generations*.

   Similarly, substitute more specific words for "man" used as a verb or as an adjective.

   Original We needed someone to *man* the booth at the fair where we were selling *man-made* opals.
   Revision We needed someone to *staff* the booth at the fair where we were selling *synthetic* opals.

7. Be consistent in your treatment of men's and women's names, marital status, professional titles, and physical appearances:

Original Neither Herman Melville, the inspired novelist, nor *Miss* Emily Dickinson, the *spinster poetess* of Amherst, gained fame or fortune in their lifetimes.

Revision Neither Herman Melville, the novelist, nor Emily Dickinson, the *poet*, gained fame or fortune in their lifetimes.

8. If a situation demands multiple hypothetical examples, consider including or alternating references to both genders, when appropriate.

Original In a revision workshop, one writer may request help with *his* concluding paragraph. Another writer may want reaction to *his* essay's introduction.

Revision In a revision workshop, one writer may request help with *his* concluding paragraph. Another writer may want reaction to *her* essay's introduction.

Revising your writing to eliminate certain kinds of gender-specific references does not mean turning clear phrases into awkward or confusing jumbles of "he/she told him/her that the car was his/hers." By following the previous suggestions, you should be able to make your prose both clear and inoffensive to all members of your audience.*

Do enliven your writing with figurative language, when appropriate. Figurative language produces pictures or images in a reader's mind, often by comparing something unfamiliar to something familiar. The two most common figurative devices are the simile and the metaphor. A *simile* is a comparison between two people, places, feelings, or things, using the word "like" or "as"; a more forceful comparison, omitting the word "like" or "as," is a *metaphor.* Here are two examples:

Simile George eats his meals like a hog.
Metaphor George is a hog at mealtime.

In both sentences, George, whose eating habits are unfamiliar to the reader, is likened to a hog, whose sloppy manners are generally well known. By comparing George to a hog, the writer gives the reader a clear picture of George at the table. Figurative language not only can help you present your ideas in clear, concrete, economical ways but also can make your prose more memorable—especially if the image or picture you present is a fresh, arresting one. Here are some examples of striking images designed to catch the reader's attention and to clarify the writer's point:

- An hour away from him felt like a month in the country.
- The atmosphere of the meeting room was as tense as a World Series game tied in the ninth inning.
- The woman's earrings were as big as butter plates.
- The angry accusation flew like a spear: once thrown, it could not be retrieved and it cut deeply.

---

*Some writers now use "s/he" to promote gender inclusivity in their informal prose. Be aware, however, that this usage is nontraditional and not accepted universally. Always check with your instructors, or the publication for which you are writing, for the appropriate and preferred style.

- Out of the night came the convoy of brown trucks, modern-day buffalo thundering single file across the prairie, eyes on fire.
- Behind her broad polished desk, Matilda was a queen bee with a swarm of office drones buzzing at her door.
- The factory squatted on the bank of the river like a huge black toad.

Sometimes, in appropriate writing situations, exaggerated similes and metaphors may be used humorously to underscore a particular point: "I felt so stupid that day. I'm sure my colleagues thought my brain was so small that if they placed it on the head of a pin, it would roll around like a marble on a six-lane highway."

Figurative language can spice up your prose, but like any spice, it can be misused, thus spoiling your soup. Therefore, don't overuse figurative language; not every point needs a metaphor or simile for clarity or emphasis. Too many images are confusing. Moreover, don't use stale images. (Clichés—discussed on pages 163–164—are often tired metaphors or similes: "snake in the grass," "hot as fire," "quiet as a mouse," etc.) If you can't catch your readers' attention with a fresh picture, don't bore them with a stale one.

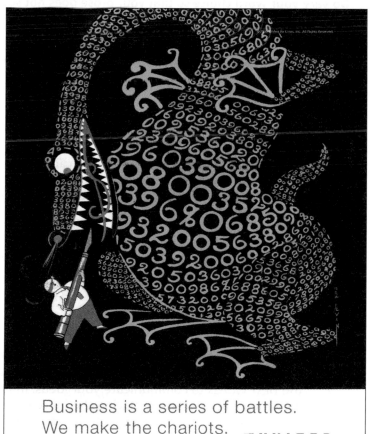

Advertising often uses figurative language to sell products. What is the metaphor in this ad?

Courtesy of United Airlines

of decisions regarding organization, development, and style, just as you do when you write. By asking questions (Why did the writer begin the essay this way? Why compare this event to that one? Why use a personal example in that paragraph?), you will begin to see how the writer put the essay together—and that knowledge will help you plan and shape your own essay. Questioning the rhetorical choices of other writers should also help you revise your prose because it promotes the habit of asking yourself questions that consider the reader's point of view (Does the point in paragraph 3 need more evidence to convince my reader? Will the reader be confused if I don't add a smoother transition from paragraph 4 to 5? Does the conclusion fall flat?).

© Michael Newman/PhotoEdit

In other words, the skills you practice as an analytical reader are those you'll use as a good writer.

How Can I Become an Analytical Reader?

Becoming an analytical reader may, at first, demand more time—and involvement—than you have previously devoted to a reading assignment. Analytical reading requires more than allowing your eyes to pass over the words on the page; it's not like channel surfing through late-night TV shows, stopping here or there as interest strikes. Analytical reading asks you not only to understand the writer's ideas, but also to consider *how* those ideas were presented, *why* the writer presented them that way, and whether that presentation was *effective*. Consequently, to improve your understanding of the reading-writing connection, you should plan on two readings of the assigned essay, some note-taking, and some marking of the text (called *annotating*). This procedure may seem challenging at first, but the benefits to you as both reader and writer will be well worth the extra minutes.

Steps to Reading Well

1. Before you begin the essay itself, note the *publication information* and *biographical data* on the author in the paragraph that precedes each selection in this text. Where and when was the essay originally published? Was it directed toward a particular or a general audience? Was it written in response to some event or controversy? Is the essay still timely or is it dated? Does the author seem qualified to write about this subject? Does the introduction offer any other information that might help you assess the essay's effectiveness?

2. Next, note the *title* of the essay. Does it draw you into the essay? Does it suggest a particular tone or image?

3. You're now ready to begin your first reading of the essay. Some readers like to read through the essay without stopping; others feel comfortable at this point underlining a few main ideas or making checks in the margins. You may also have to make a dictionary stop if words you don't know appear in key places in the essay. Many times you can figure out definitions from context—that is, from the words and ideas surrounding the unknown word—but don't miss the point of a major part of an essay because of failure to recognize an important word, especially if that word is repeated or emphasized in some way.

   When you finish this reading, write a sentence or two summarizing your general impression of the essay's content or ideas. Consider the author's *purpose*: what do you think the writer was trying to do? Overall, how well did he or she succeed? (A typical response might be "argued for tuition hike—unconvincing, boring—too many confusing statistics.")

   Now prepare to take another, closer look at the essay. Make some notes in the margins or in another convenient place as you respond to the following tasks and questions. Remember that analytical reading is not a horse race: there are no trophies for finishing quickly! Fight the bad habit of galloping at breakneck speed through an essay; slow down to admire the verbal roses the writer has tried to place in your path.

4. Look at the *title* (again) and at the essay's *introductory paragraph(s)*. Did they effectively set up your expectations? Introduce the essay's topic, main idea, tone? (Would some other title or introductory "hook" have worked better?)

5. Locate the writer's main point or *thesis*; this idea may be stated plainly or it may be clearly implied. If you didn't mark this idea on your first reading, do so now by placing a "T" in the margin so you can refer to the thesis easily. (If the thesis is implied, you may wish to mark places that you think most clearly indicate the writer's stance.)

6. As you reread the essay, look for important statements that support or illustrate the thesis. (As you know, these are often found as *topic sentences* occurring near the beginning or end of the body paragraphs.) Try numbering these supporting points or ideas and jotting a key word by each one in the margin.

7. As you identify each important supporting point, ask yourself how the writer develops, explains, or argues that idea. For example, does the writer clarify or support the point by providing examples, testimony, or statistics? By comparing or contrasting one idea to another? By showing a cause-effect relationship? Some other method? A combination of methods? A writer may use one or many methods of development, but each major point in an essay should be explained clearly and logically. Make brief marginal notes to indicate how well you think the writer has succeeded ("convincing example," "generalization without support," "questionable authority cited," "good comparison," etc.). Practice using marginal symbols, such as stars (for especially effective statements, descriptions, arguments) or question marks (for passages you think are confusing, untrue, or exaggerated). Make up your own set of symbols to help yourself remember your evaluations of the writer's ideas and techniques.

8. Look back over the essay's general *organization*. Did the writer use one of the expository, descriptive, narrative, or argumentative strategies to structure the essay? Some combination of strategies? Was this choice effective? (Always consider alternative ways: would another choice have allowed the writer to make his or her main point more emphatically? Why or why not?)

9. Does the essay flow logically and coherently? If you are having trouble with *unity* or *coherence* in your own essays, look closely at the transitional devices used in a few paragraphs; bracketing transitional words or phrases you see might show you how the writer achieved a sense of unity and flow.

10. Consider the writer's *style* and the essay's *tone*. Does the writer use figurative language in an arresting way? Specialized diction for a particular purpose? Repetition of words or phrases? Any especially effective sentence patterns? Does the writer's tone of voice come through clearly? Is the essay serious, humorous, angry, consoling, happy, sad, sarcastic, or something else? Is the tone appropriate for the purpose and audience of this essay? Writers use a variety of stylistic devices to create prose that is vivid and memorable; you might mark new uses of language you would like to try in essays of your own.

   Now is also the time to look up meanings of any words you felt you could skip during your first time through the essay, especially if you sense that these words are important to the writer's tone or use of imagery.

Once you have completed these steps and added any other comments that seem important to the analysis of the essay, review your notes. Is this an effective essay? Is the essay's thesis explained or supported adequately with enough logically developed points and evidence? Is the essay organized as effectively as it could have been? What strengths and weaknesses did you find after this analytical reading? Has your original evaluation of this essay changed in any way? If so, write a new assessment, adding any other notes you want to help you remember your evaluation of this essay.

Finally, after this close reading of the essay, did you discover any new ideas, strategies, or techniques you might incorporate into *your* current piece of writing?

Sample Annotated Essay

Here is a professional essay annotated according to the steps listed on the previous pages.

By closely reading and annotating the professional essays in this text, you can improve your own writing in numerous ways. Once you have practiced analyzing essays by other writers, you may discover that you can assess your own drafts' strengths and weaknesses with more confidence.

Our Youth Should Serve

Steven Muller

title forecasts thesis

Steven Muller is President Emeritus of The Johns Hopkins University, founded in *educator*
1876 in Baltimore, Maryland. This essay first appeared in *Newsweek* in 1978 and *general audience*
has been reprinted often.

1   Too many young men and women now leave school without a well-developed sense of purpose. If they go right to work after high school, many are not properly prepared for careers. But if they enter college instead, many do not really know what to study or what to do afterward. Our society does not seem to be doing much to encourage and use the best instincts and talents of our young.

Introductory paragraphs present the problem

2   On the other hand, I see the growing problems of each year's new generation of high-school graduates. After twelve years of schooling—and television—many of them want to participate actively in society; but they face either a job with a limited future or more years in educational institutions. Many are wonderfully idealistic: they have talent and energy to offer, and they seek the meaning in their lives that comes from giving of oneself to the common good. But they feel almost rejected by a society that has too few jobs to offer them and that asks nothing of them except to avoid trouble. They want to be part of a new solution; instead society perceives them as a problem. They seek a cause; but their elders preach only self-advancement. They need experience on which to base choice; yet society seems to put a premium on the earliest possible choice, based inescapably on the least experience.

Problem for youth: idealism, talent, and energy but too few jobs and too little experience.

3   On the other hand, I see an American society sadly in need of social services that we can afford less and less at prevailing costs of labor. Some tasks are necessary but constitute no career; they should be carried out, but not as anyone's lifetime occupation. Our democracy profoundly needs public spirit, but the economy of our labor system primarily encourages self-interest. The Federal government spends billions on opportunity grants for post-secondary education, but some of us wonder about money given on the basis only of need. We ask the young to volunteer for national defense, but not for the improvement of our society. As public spirit and public services decline, so does the quality of life. So I ask myself why cannot we put it all together and ask our young people to volunteer in peacetime to serve America.

Problem for society: social services are needed but labor costs are high

✱ *Thesis: Youth should volunteer to serve America's public service needs*

4   I recognize that at first mention, universal national youth service may sound too much like compulsory military service or the Hitler Youth or the Komsomol. I do not believe it has to be like that at all. It need not require uniforms or camps, nor a vast new Federal bureaucracy, nor vast new public expenditures. And it should certainly not be compulsory.

¶ clarifies proposal by contrast: not like military, not political, not required (Komsomol: youth section of the Soviet Communist Party)

5 A voluntary program of universal national youth service does of course require compelling <u>incentives</u>. Two could be provided. Guaranteed <u>job training</u> would be one. Substantial <u>Federal assistance toward post-secondary education</u> would be the other. This would mean that today's complex measures of Federal aid to students would be ended, and that there would also be no need for tuition tax credits for post-secondary education. Instead, prospective <u>students would *earn* their assistance</u> for post-secondary education by volunteering for national service, and only those who earned assistance would receive it. Present Federal expenditures for the assistance of students in post-secondary education would be converted into a <u>simple grant program</u>, modeled on the post–World War II GI Bill of Rights.

1. Incentives
—job training
— Federal money for
college

Comparison: education grants like those given to returning WWII soldiers

6 But what, you say, would <u>huge numbers of high-school graduates do as volunteers in national service?</u> They could be interns in public agencies, local, state, and national. They could staff day-care programs, neighborhood health centers, centers to counsel and work with children; help to maintain public facilities, including highways, railbeds, waterways and airports; engage in neighborhood-renewal projects, both physical and social. Some would elect military service, others the Peace Corps. Except for the latter two alternatives and others like them, they could <u>live anywhere</u> they pleased. They would not wear uniforms. They would be employed and supervised by people already employed locally in public-agency careers.

2. Kinds of jobs

examples

7 Volunteers would <u>be paid only a subsistence wage</u>, because they would receive the benefits of job training (not necessarily confined to one task) as well as assistance toward post-secondary education if they were so motivated and qualified. If cheap mass <u>housing</u> for some groups of volunteers were needed, supervised participants in the program could rebuild decayed dwellings in metropolitan areas. . . .

3. Support costs
—wages
—housing
problem?

8 The ⟨<u>direct benefits</u>⟩ of such a universal national-youth-service program would be significant. Every young man and woman would face a <u>meaningful role in society</u> after high school. Everyone would receive <u>job training</u>, and the right to <u>earn assistance</u> toward post-secondary education. Those going on to post-secondary education would have their education interrupted by a constructive <u>work experience</u>. There is ⟨evidence⟩ that they would thereby <u>become more highly motivated and successful students</u>, particularly if their work experience related closely to subsequent vocational interests. Many participants might <u>locate careers</u> by means of their national-service assignments.

✱ 4. Direct benefits for youth:
—meaningful role in society
—job training
—money for education
—work experience
—success in school
—career direction

such as?

9 No union jobs need be lost, because skilled workers would be needed to give job training. Many <u>public services would be performed by cheap labor</u>, but there would be no youth army. And the intangible indirect benefits would be the greatest of all. Young people could regard themselves as more <u>useful and needed</u>. They could serve this country for a <u>two-year period</u> as volunteers, and <u>earn job</u>

addresses possible criticism

training and/or assistance toward post-secondary education. <u>There is more self-esteem and motivation in earned than in unearned benefits.</u> Universal national youth service may be no panacea. But in my opinion the idea merits serious and imaginative consideration.

Conclusion summarizes advantages, emphasizes the benefit of earning self-esteem, and calls for consideration of this proposal

First impression: Muller proposes a volunteer youth corps to provide some public services. Many benefits for both country and young people.

Notes: Muller uses comparisons, contrasts, and examples to explain the proposed youth corps, and he clearly shows the benefits (training, grants, self-esteem). His arguments might be even more effective if he had added some specific examples and testimony from students and people in social services. Or maybe from participants in similar kinds of programs, such as VISTA?

Personal response: Although the low wages might be a problem for many people, I like this program. It might have helped me decide on a career path sooner and definitely would help with tuition now.

(panacea: cure for all ills)

PRACTICING WHAT YOU'VE LEARNED

Select one of the professional essays reprinted in this text, and annotate it according to the steps described in this chapter. Note at least one strength in the essay that you would like to incorporate into your own writing.

ASSIGNMENT

Select one of the professional essays in this text to read analytically and annotate. Then write a one-page explanation of the essay's major strengths (or weaknesses), showing how the writer's rhetorical choices affected you, the reader.

Writing a Summary

Frequently, writing teachers will ask students to read an essay and briefly summarize it. A *summary* is an objective, condensed version of a reading selection, containing the author's main ideas. Although summaries are always more concise than the original texts, the length of a particular summary often depends on the length and complexity of the original reading and the purpose of the summary.

Chapter 8 Summary

Here is a brief summary of what you should remember about the reading–writing connection.

1. Reading and analyzing essays can improve your writing skills.

2. Learning to recognize and evaluate the strategies and stylistic techniques of other writers will help you plan and shape your own essays.

3. Reading analytically takes time and practice but is well worth the extra effort.

4. Learning to summarize reading material accurately and objectively is an important skill, useful in school and at work.

5. Active participation in class discussions of sample essays can help you strengthen your own writing.

Part One Summary:
The Basics of the Short Essay

Here are ten suggestions to keep in mind while you are working on the rough drafts of your essay:

1. Be confident that you have something important and interesting to say.

2. Identify your particular audience and become determined to communicate effectively with them.

3. Use prewriting techniques to help you focus on one main idea that will become the thesis of your essay.

4. Organize your essay's points logically, in a persuasive and coherent order.

5. Develop each of your ideas with enough evidence and specific details.

6. Delete any irrelevant material that disrupts the smooth flow from idea to idea.

7. Compose sentences that are clear, concise, and informative; choose accurate, vivid words.

8. Improve your writing by learning to read analytically.

9. Revise your prose.

10. Revise your prose!

PART 2

Purposes, Modes, and Strategies

Communication may be divided into four types (or "modes" as they are often called): exposition, argumentation, description, and narration. Although each one will be explained in greater detail in this section of the text, the four modes may be defined briefly as follows:

Exposition

The writer intends to explain or inform.

Argumentation

The writer intends to convince or persuade.

Description

The writer intends to create in words a picture of a person, place, object, or feeling.

Narration

The writer intends to tell a story or recount an event.

Although we commonly refer to exposition, argumentation, description, and narration as the basic types of prose, in

193

reality it is difficult to find any one mode in a pure form. In fact, almost all essays are combinations of two or more modes; it would be virtually impossible, for instance, to write a story—narration—without including description or to argue without also giving some information. Nevertheless, by determining a writer's main purpose, we can usually identify an essay or prose piece as primarily exposition, argumentation, description, or narration. In other words, an article may include a brief description of a new mousetrap, but if the writer's main intention is to explain how the trap works, then we may designate the essay as exposition. In most cases, the primary mode of any essay will be readily apparent to the reader.

In Part Two of this text, you will study each of the four modes in detail and learn some of the patterns of development, called *strategies*, that will enable you to write the kind of prose most frequently demanded in college and professional work. Mastering the most common prose patterns in their simplest forms now will help you successfully assess and organize any kind of complex writing assignment you may face in the future. Chapter 13 concludes this section by discussing the more complex essay, developed through use of multiple strategies.

CHAPTER 9

Exposition

xposition refers to prose whose primary purpose is giving information. Some familiar examples of expository writing include encyclopedias, dictionaries, news magazines, and textbooks. In addition, much of your own college work may be classified as exposition: book reports, political analyses, laboratory and business reports, and most essay exams, to cite only a few of the possibilities.

Although expository writing does present information, a good expository essay is more than a collection of facts, figures, and details. First, each essay should contain a thesis statement clarifying the writer's purpose and position. Then the essay should be organized so that the body paragraphs explain and support that thesis. In an expository essay the writer says, in effect, here are the facts *as I see them*; therefore, the writer's main purpose is not only to inform readers but also to convince them that this essay explains the subject matter in the clearest, most logical way.

The Strategies of Exposition

There are a variety of ways to organize an expository essay, depending on your purpose. The most common strategies, or patterns, of organization include development by *example*, *process analysis*, *comparison and contrast*, *definition*, *classification*, and *causal analysis*. However, an essay is rarely developed completely by a single strategy (an essay developed by comparison and contrast, for instance, may also contain examples; a classification essay may contain definitions, and so forth); therefore, as in the case of the four modes, we identify the kind of expository essay by its *primary* strategy of development. To help you understand every expository strategy thoroughly before going on to the next, each is presented here separately. Each discussion section follows a similar pattern, which includes explanation of the strategy, advice on developing your essay, a list of essay topics, a topic proposal sheet, a revision checklist, sample essays (by students and by professional writers), and a progress report.

Strategy One: Development by Example

Perhaps you've heard a friend complain lately about a roommate. "Tina is an inconsiderate boor, impossible to live with," she cries. Your natural response might be to question your friend's rather broad accusation: "What makes her so terrible? What does she do that's so bad?" Your friend might then respond with specific examples of Tina's insensitivity: she never washes her dishes, she ties up the bathroom for hours, and she borrows clothes without asking. By citing several examples, your friend clarifies and supports her general criticism of Tina, thus enabling you to understand her point of view.

Examples in an essay work precisely the same way as in the preceding hypothetical story: they *support, clarify, interest,* and *persuade.*

In your writing assignments, you might want to assert that dorm food is cruel and inhuman punishment, that recycling is a profitable hobby, or that the cost of housing is rising dramatically. But without some carefully chosen examples to show the truth of your statements, these remain unsupported generalities or mere opinions. Your task, then, is to provide enough specific examples to support your general statements, to make them both clear and convincing. Here is a statement offering the reader only hazy generalities:

> Our locally supported TV channel presents a variety of excellent educational shows. The shows are informative on lots of different subjects for both children and adults. The information they offer makes channel 19 well worth the public funds that support it.

Rewritten, the same paragraph explains its point clearly through the use of specific examples:

> Our locally supported TV channel presents a variety of excellent educational shows. For example, young children can learn their alphabet and numbers from *Sesame Street*; imaginative older children can be encouraged to create by watching *Kids' Writes*, a show on which four hosts read and act out stories written and sent in by youngsters from eight to fourteen. Adults may enjoy learning about antiques and collectibles from a program called *The Collector*; each week the show features an in-depth look at buying, selling, trading, and displaying collectible items, from Depression glass to teddy bears to Shaker furniture. Those folks wishing to become handy around the home can use information on repairs from plumbing to wiring on *This Old House*, while the nonmusical can learn the difference between scat singing and arias on such programs as *Jazz!* and *Opera Today*. Money-minded viewers may profit from the tips dropped by stockbrokers who appear on *Wall Street Week*. The information offered makes these and other educational shows on channel 19 well worth the public funds that support the station.

Although the preceding example is based on real shows, you may also use personal experiences, hypothetical situations, anecdotes, research material, facts, testimony, or any combination thereof, to explain, illustrate, or support the points in your essays.

In some cases you may find that a series of short examples fits your purpose, illustrating clearly the idea you are presenting to your reader:

> In the earlier years of Hollywood, actors aspiring to become movie stars often adopted new names that they believed sounded more attractive to the public. Frances Ethel Gumm, for instance, decided to change her name to Judy Garland long before she flew over any rainbows, and Alexander Archibald Leach became Cary Grant on his way from England to America. Alexandra Cymboliak and Merle Johnson, Jr., might not have set teenage hearts throbbing in the early 1960s, but Sandra Dee and Troy Donahue certainly did. Although some names were changed to achieve a smoother flow (Frederic Austerlitz to Fred Astaire, for example), some may have also been changed to ensure a good fit on movie theater marquees as well as a place in their audience's memory: the teenage Turner girl, Julia Jean Mildred Frances, for instance, became just Lana.

Or you may decide that two or three examples explained in some detail provide the best support for your topic, rather than a series of short examples. In the paragraph that follows, the writer chose to develop two examples to illustrate her point about the unusual dog her family owned when she was a young girl in the late 1970s:

> Our family dog Sparky always let us know when he wasn't getting enough attention. For instance, if he thought we were away from home too much, he'd perform his record trick. While we were out, Sparky would push an album out of the record rack and then tap the album cover in just such a way that the record would roll out. Then he would chomp the record! We'd return to find our favorite LP (somehow, always our current favorite) chewed into tiny bits of black vinyl scattered about the room. Another popular Sparky trick was the cat-sit. If the family was peacefully settled on the porch, not playing with him, Sparky would grab the family cat by the ear and drag her over to the steps, whereupon he would sit on top of her until someone paid attention to him. He never hurt the cat; he simply sat on her as one would sit on a fine cushion, with her head poking out under his tail, and a silly grin on his face that said, "See, if you'd play with me, I wouldn't get into such mischief."

You may also find that in some cases, one long, detailed example (called an *extended example*) is more useful than several shorter ones. If you were writing a paragraph urging the traffic department to install a stop sign at a particularly dangerous corner, you probably should cite numerous examples of accidents there. On the other hand, if you were praising a certain kind of local architecture, you might select one representative house and discuss it in detail. In the following paragraph, for instance, the writer might have supported his main point by citing a number of cases in which lives had been saved by seat belts; he chose instead to offer one detailed example, in the form of a personal experience:

> Wearing seat belts can protect people from injury, even in serious accidents. I know because seat belts saved me and my dad two years ago when we were driving to see my grandparents who live in California. Because of the distance, we had to travel late on a rainy, foggy Saturday night. My dad was driving, but what he didn't know was that there was a car a short way behind us driven by a drunk who was following our car's taillights in order to keep himself on the road. About midnight, my dad decided to check the map to make sure we were headed in the right direction,

Topic sentence one: Trip teaches respect for environment

2   The most important lesson a rafting trip teaches students is respect for the environment. When students are exposed to the outdoors, they can better learn to appreciate its beauty and feel the need to preserve it. For example, I went on a rafting trip three summers ago with the biology department at my high school. Our trip lasted seven days down the Green River through the isolated Desolation Canyon in Utah. After the first day of rafting, I found myself surrounded by steep canyon walls and saw virtually no evidence of human life. The starkly beautiful, unspoiled atmosphere soon became a major influence on us during the trip. By the second day I saw classmates, whom I had previously seen fill an entire room with candy wrappers and empty soda cans, voluntarily inspecting our campsite for trash. And when twenty-four high school students sacrifice washing their hair for the sake of a suds-less and thus healthier river, some new, better attitudes about the environment have definitely been established.

Two brief examples illustrating respect:
1. Cleaning up trash
2. Foregoing suds in river

Topic sentence two: Trip teaches cooperation

3   In addition to the respect for nature a rafting trip encourages, it also teaches the importance of group cooperation. Since school-associated trips put students in command of the raft, the students find that in order to stay in control, each member must be reliable, be able to do his or her own part, and be alert to the actions of others. These skills are quickly learned when students see the consequences of noncooperation. Usually this occurs the first day, when the left side of the raft paddles in one direction, and the right the other way, and half the crew ends up seasick from going in circles. An even better illustration is another experience I had on my river trip. Because an upcoming rapid was usually not too rough, our instructor said a few of us could jump out and swim in it. Instead of deciding as a group who should go, though, five eager swimmers bailed out. This left me, our angry instructor, and another student to steer the raft. As it turned

Two examples of the need for cooperation:

1. Difficulties in paddling raft

out, the rapid was fairly rough, and we soon found ourselves heading straight for a huge hole (a hole is formed from swirling funnel-like currents and can pull a raft under). The combined effort of the three of us was not enough to get the raft completely clear of the hole, and the raft tipped up vertically on its side, spilling us into the river. Luckily, no one was hurt, and the raft did not topple over, but the near loss of our food rations for the next five days, not to mention the raft itself, was enough to make us all more willing to work as a group in the future.

2. A near accident

4   Despite the obvious benefits rafting offers, the number of river permits issued to school groups continues to decline because of financial cutbacks. It is a shame that those in charge of these cutbacks do not realize that in addition to having fun and making discoveries about themselves, students are learning valuable lessons through rafting trips—lessons that may help preserve the rivers for future rafters.

Conclusion: Importance of lessons

Professional Essay*

So What's So Bad about Being So-So?

Lisa Wilson Strick

Lisa Wilson Strick is a freelance writer who publishes in a variety of magazines, frequently on the subjects of family and education. She is co-author of *Learning Disabilities, A to Z: A Parent's Complete Guide to Learning Disabilities from Preschool to Adulthood* (1997). This essay first appeared in *Woman's Day* in 1984.

1   The other afternoon I was playing the piano when my seven-year-old walked in. He stopped and listened awhile, then said: "Gee, Mom, you don't play that thing very well, do you?"

2   No, I don't. I am a piano lesson dropout. The fine points of fingering totally escape me. I play everything at half-speed, with many errant notes. My performance

---

* ◆ To help you read this essay analytically, review pages 180–182.

would make any serious music student wince, but I don't care. I've enjoyed playing the piano badly for years.

3   I also enjoy singing badly and drawing badly. (I used to enjoy sewing badly, but I've been doing that so long that I finally got pretty good at it.) I'm not ashamed of my incompetence in these areas. I do one or two other things well and that should be enough for anybody. But it gets boring doing the same things over and over. Every now and then it's fun to try something new.

4   Unfortunately, doing things badly has gone out of style. It used to be a mark of class if a lady or a gentleman sang a little, painted a little, played the violin a little. You didn't have to be *good* at it; the point was to be fortunate enough to have the leisure time for such pursuits. But in today's competitive world we have to be "experts"—even in our hobbies. You can't tone up your body by pulling on your sneakers and slogging around the block a couple of times anymore. Why? Because you'll be laughed off the street by the "serious" runners—the ones who log twenty-plus miles a week in their headbands, sixty-dollar running suits and fancy shoes. The shoes are really a big deal. If you say you're thinking about taking up almost any sport, the first thing the aficionados will ask is what you plan to do about shoes. Leather or canvas? What type of soles? Which brand? This is not the time to mention that the gym shoes you wore in high school are still in pretty good shape. As far as sports enthusiasts are concerned, if you don't have the latest shoes you are hopelessly committed to mediocrity.

5   The runners aren't nearly so snobbish as the dance freaks, however. In case you didn't know, "going dancing" no longer means putting on a pretty dress and doing a few turns around the ballroom with your favorite man on Saturday night. "Dancing" means squeezing into tights and a leotard and leg warmers, then sweating through six hours of warm-ups and five hours of ballet and four hours of jazz classes. Every week. Never tell anyone that you "like to dance" unless this is the sort of activity you enjoy. (At least the costume isn't so costly, as dancers seem to be cultivating a riches-to-rags look lately.)

6   We used to do these things for fun or simply to relax. Now the competition you face in your hobbies is likely to be worse than anything you run into on the job. "Oh, you've taken up knitting," a friend recently said to me. "Let me show you the adorable cable-knit, popcorn-stitched cardigan with twelve tiny reindeer prancing across the yoke that I made for my daughter. I dyed the yarn myself." Now why did she have to go and do that? I was getting a kick out of watching my yellow stockinette muffler grow a couple of inches a week up till then. And all I wanted was something to keep my hands busy while I watched television anyway.

7   Have you noticed what this is doing to our children? "We don't want that dodo on our soccer team," I overheard a ten-year-old sneer the other day. "He doesn't know a goal kick from a head shot." As it happens, the boy was talking about my son, who did not—like some of his friends—start soccer instruction at age three (along with preschool diving, creative writing and Suzuki clarinet). I'm sorry, Son, I guess I blew it. In *my* day when we played softball on the corner lot, we expected to give a little instruction to the younger kids who didn't know how. It didn't matter if they were terrible; we weren't out to slaughter the other team. Sometimes we didn't even keep score. To us, sports were just a way of having a *good time*. Of course we didn't have some of the nifty things kids have today—such as matching

uniforms and professional coaches. All we had was a bunch of kids of various ages who enjoyed each other's company.

8   I don't think kids have as much fun as they used to. Competition keeps getting in the way. The daughter of a neighbor is a nervous wreck worrying about getting into the *best* gymnastics school. "I was a late starter," she told me, "and I only get to practice five or six hours a week, so my technique may not be up to their standards." The child is nine. She doesn't want to *be* a gymnast when she grows up; she wants to be a nurse. I asked what she likes to do for fun in her free time. She seemed to think it was an odd question. "Well, I don't actually *have* a lot of free time," she said. "I mean homework and gymnastics and flute lessons kind of eat it all up. I have flute lessons three times a week now, so I have a good shot at getting into the all-state orchestra."

9   Ambition, drive and the desire to excel are all admirable within limits, but I don't know where the limits are anymore. I know a woman who has always wanted to learn a foreign language. For years she has complained that she hasn't the time to study one. I've pointed out that an evening course in French or Italian would take only a couple of hours a week, but she keeps putting it off. I suspect that what she hasn't got the time for is to become completely fluent within the year—and that any lesser level of accomplishment would embarrass her. Instead she spends her evenings watching reruns on television and tidying up her closets—occupations at which no particular expertise is expected.

10   I know others who are avoiding activities they might enjoy because they lack the time or the energy to tackle them "seriously." It strikes me as so silly. We are talking about *recreation*. I have nothing against self-improvement. But when I hear a teenager muttering "practice makes perfect" as he grimly makes his four-hundred-and-twenty-seventh try at hooking the basketball into the net left-handed, I wonder if some of us aren't improving ourselves right into the loony bin.

11   I think it's time we put a stop to all this. For sanity's sake, each of us should vow to take up something new this week—and to make sure we never master it completely. Sing along with grand opera. Make peculiar-looking objects out of clay. I can tell you from experience that fallen soufflés still taste pretty good. The point is to enjoy being a beginner again; to rediscover the joy of creative fooling around. If you find it difficult, ask any two-year-old to teach you. Two-year-olds have a gift for tackling the impossible with zest; repeated failure hardly discourages them at all.

12   As for me, I'm getting a little out of shape so I'm looking into tennis. A lot of people I know enjoy it, and it doesn't look too hard. Given a couple of lessons I should be stumbling gracelessly around the court and playing badly in no time at all.

Questions on Content, Structure, and Style

1. Why does Strick begin her essay with the comment from her son and the list of activities she does badly?

2. What is Strick's thesis? Is it specifically stated or clearly implied?

3. What examples does Strick offer to illustrate her belief that we no longer take up hobbies for fun? Are there enough well-chosen examples to make her position clear?

4. What is the effect, according to Strick, of too much competition on kids? In what ways does she show this effect?

5. Does Strick use enough details in her examples to make them clear, vivid, and persuasive? Point out some of her details to support your answer.

6. What does Strick gain by using dialogue in some of her examples?

7. What solution to the problem does Strick offer? How does she clarify her suggestion?

8. Characterize the tone of Strick's essay. Is it appropriate for her purpose and for her intended audience? Why or why not?

9. Evaluate Strick's conclusion. Does it effectively wrap up the essay?

10. Do you agree or disagree with Strick? What examples could you offer to support your position?

Suggestions for Writing

Try using Lisa Strick's essay "So What's So Bad about Being So-So?" as a stepping-stone, moving from one or more of her ideas to a subject for your own essay. For instance, you might write an essay based on your personal experience that illustrates or challenges Strick's view that competition is taking all the fun out of recreation. Or perhaps Strick's advice urging her readers to undertake new activities might lead you to an essay about your best or worst "beginner" experience. Look through Strick's essay once more to find other springboard ideas for *your* writing.

Vocabulary*

errant (2)   mediocrity (4)   fluent (9)
incompetence (3)   excel (9)   zest (11)
aficionados (4)

© Ryan McVay/Photodisc/ Getty Images

A Revision Worksheet

As you write your rough drafts, consult Chapter 5 for guidance through the revision process. In addition, here are a few questions to ask yourself as you revise your example essay:

1. Is the essay's thesis clear to the reader?

2. Do the topic sentences support the thesis?

3. Does each body paragraph contain examples that effectively illustrate the claim of the topic sentence rather than offering mere generalities?

4. Are there enough well-chosen examples to make each point clear and convincing?

---

*Numbers in parentheses following vocabulary words refer to paragraphs in the essay.

5. Is each example developed in enough specific detail? Where could more details be added? More precise language?

6. If a paragraph contains multiple examples, are they arranged in the most effective order, with a smooth transition from one to another?

7. If a paragraph contains an extended example, does the discussion flow logically and with coherence?

Collaborative Activity: After you've revised your essay extensively, exchange rough drafts with a classmate and answer these questions for each other, making specific suggestions for improvement wherever appropriate. (◆ For advice on productive participation in classroom workshops, see pages 115–120.)

Reviewing Your Progress

After you have completed your essay developed by examples, take a moment to measure your progress as a writer by responding to the following questions. Such analysis will help you to recognize growth in your writing skills and may enable you to identify areas that are still problematic.

1. What is the best feature of your essay? Why?

2. After considering your essay's supporting examples, which one do you think most effectively explains or illustrates your ideas? Why?

3. What part of your essay gave you the most trouble? How did you overcome the problem?

4. If you had more time to work on this essay, what would receive additional attention? Why?

5. What did you learn about your topic from writing this essay? About yourself as a writer?

Strategy Two: Development by Process Analysis

Process analysis identifies and explains what steps must be taken to complete an operation or procedure. There are two kinds of process analysis essays: directional and informative.

A *directional process* tells the reader how to do or make something. In simple words, it gives directions. You are more familiar with directional process than you might think. For example, when you open a telephone book or cell phone user's guide, you may see pages explaining how to make a multiparty call. When you tell friends how to find your house, you're asking them to follow a directional process. If you use a computer, you can learn how to transfer files or download attachments or any one of hundreds of other options by following step-by-step directions often found on a "Help" menu. The most widely read books in American libraries fall into the how-to-do-it (or how-to-fix-it) category: how to wire a house, how to repair a car, how to play winning poker, how to become a millionaire overnight, and so forth. And almost every home contains at least one cookbook full of recipes providing directions for preparing various dishes. (Even Part One of this text is, in detailed fashion, a directional process telling how to write a short essay, beginning with the selection of a topic and concluding with advice on revision.)

An *informative process* tells the reader how something is or was made or done or how something works. Informative process differs from directional process in that it is not designed primarily to tell people how to do it; instead, it describes the steps by which someone other than the reader does or makes something (or how something was made or done in the past). For example, an informative process essay might describe how scientists discovered polio vaccine, how a bill passes through Congress, how chewing gum is made, how contact lenses were invented, or how an engine propels a jet. In other words, this type of essay gives information on processes that are not intended to be—or cannot be—duplicated by the individual reader.

Developing Your Essay

Of all the expository essays, students usually agree that the process paper is the easiest to organize, mainly because it is presented in simple, chronological steps. To prepare a well-written process essay, however, you should remember the following advice:

Select an appropriate subject. First, make sure you know your subject thoroughly; one fuzzy step could wreck your entire process. Second, choose a process that is simple and short enough to describe in detail. In a 500-to-800-word essay, for instance, it's better to describe how to build a ship in a bottle than how to construct a life-size replica of Noah's Ark. On the other hand, don't choose a process so simpleminded, mundane, or mechanical that it insults your readers' intelligence or bores them silly. (Some years ago at a large state university, students were directed to write a process essay on "How to Sharpen a Pencil"; with the assignment of such stirring, creative topics, it's a wonder that particular English department produced any majors at all that year.)

Describe any necessary equipment and define special terms. In some process essays, you will need to indicate what equipment, ingredients, or tools are required. Such information is often provided in a paragraph following the thesis, before the process itself is described; in other cases the explanation of proper equipment is presented as the need arises in each step of the process. As the writer, you must decide which method is best for your subject. The same is true for any terms that need defining. Don't lose your reader by using terms only you, the specialist, can comprehend. Always remember that you're trying to tell people about a process they don't understand.

State your steps in a logical, chronological order. Obviously, if someone wanted to know how to bake bread, you wouldn't begin with "Put the prepared dough in the oven." Start at the beginning and carefully follow through, step by step, until the process is completed. Don't omit any steps or directions, no matter how seemingly insignificant. Without complete instructions, for example, the would-be baker might end up with a gob of dough rather than a loaf of bread—simply because the directions didn't say to heat the oven to a certain temperature.

Explain each step clearly, sufficiently, and accurately. If you've ever tried to assemble a child's toy or a piece of furniture, you probably already know how frustrating—and infuriating—it is to work from vague, inadequate directions. Save your readers from tears and tantrums by describing each step in your process as clearly as possible. Use enough specific details to distinguish one step from another. As the readers finish each step, they should know how the subject matter is supposed to look, feel, smell, taste, or sound at that stage of the process. You might also explain why each step is necessary ("Cutting back the young avocado stem is necessary to prevent a spindly plant"; "Senator Snort then had to win over the chair of the Arms Committee to be sure his bill would go to the Senate floor for a vote"). In some cases, especially in directional processes, it's helpful to give warnings ("When you begin tightrope walking, the condition of your shoes is critical; make sure the soles are not uneven or slick") or descriptions of errors and how to rectify them ("If you pass a white church, you've gone a block too far, so turn right at the church and circle back on Candle Lane"; "If the sauce appears thin, add one teaspoon more of cornstarch to thicken the gravy").

Organize your steps effectively. If you have a few big steps in your process, you probably will devote a paragraph to each one. On the other hand, if you have several small steps, you should organize them into a few manageable units. For example, in the essay "How to Prepare Fresh Fish," the list of small steps on the left has been grouped into three larger units, each of which becomes a body paragraph:

1. scaling	I. Cleaning
2. beheading	A. scaling
3. gutting	B. beheading
4. washing	C. gutting
5. seasoning	II. Cooking
6. breading	A. washing
7. frying	B. seasoning
8. draining	C. breading
9. portioning	D. frying
10. garnishing	III. Serving
	A. draining
	B. portioning
	C. garnishing

In addition, don't forget to use enough transitional devices between steps to avoid the effect of a mechanical list. Some frequently used linking words in process essays include the following:

next	first, second, third, etc.
then	at this point
now	following
to begin	when
finally	at last
before	afterward

Vary your transitional words sufficiently so that your steps are not linked by a monotonous repetition of "and then" or "next."

Problems to Avoid

Don't forget to include a thesis. You already know, of course, that every essay needs a thesis, but the advice bears repeating here because for some reason some writers often omit the statement in their process essays. Your thesis might be (1) your reason for presenting this process—why you feel it's important or necessary for the readers to know it ("Because rescue squads often arrive too late, every adult should know how to administer CPR to accident victims") or (2) an assertion about the nature of the process itself ("Needlepoint is a simple, restful, fun hobby for both men and women"). Here are some other subjects and sample theses:

- Donating blood is not the painful process one might suspect.
- The raid on Pearl Harbor wasn't altogether unexpected.
- Returning to school as an older-than-average student isn't as difficult as it may look.
- Sponsoring a five-mile run can be a fun way for your club or student organization to raise money for local charities.
- Challenging an undeserved speeding ticket can be a time-consuming, energy-draining, but financially rewarding endeavor.
- The series of escalating demonstrations outside the White House influenced the 1920 passage of the Nineteenth Amendment, giving American women the right to vote.

Presenting a thesis and referring to it appropriately gives your essay unity and coherence, as well as ensuring against a monotonous list of steps.

Pay special attention to your conclusion. Don't allow your essay to grind to an abrupt halt after the final step. You might conclude the essay by telling the significance of the completed process or by explaining other uses it may have. Or, if it is appropriate, finish your essay with an amusing story or emphatic comment. However you conclude, leave the reader with a feeling of satisfaction, with a sense of having completed an interesting procedure. (◆ For more information on writing good conclusions, see pages 86–90.)

© Inspirestock/CORBIS

ESSAY TOPICS

Here are suggested topics for both directional and informative process essays. Some of the topics may be used in humorous essays, such as "How to Flunk a Test," "How to Remain a Bench Warmer," or "How to Say Nothing in Eight Hundred Words." ◆ For additional ideas, turn to the "Suggestions for Writing" sections following the professional essays (page 223 and page 226).

1. How you arrived at a major decision or solved an important problem

2. How to survive the first week of college

3. How to begin a collection or hobby or acquire a skill

4. How to buy a computer, cell phone, camera, or other product

5. How a popular product or fad originated or grew

6. How to manage stress, stage fright, homesickness, or an irrational fear

7. How something in nature works or was formed

8. How a company makes or markets a product

9. How a piece of equipment or a machine works

10. How to cure a cold, the hiccups, insomnia, or some other common ailment

11. How to improve physical fitness or a mental activity (e.g., study habits; ways to remember all those passwords)

12. How to stop smoking (or break some other bad habit)

13. How to select a car (new or used), house, apartment, roommate

14. How to earn money quickly or easily (and legally)

15. How a famous invention or discovery occurred

16. How to lodge a complaint and win

17. How to succeed or fail in a job or class (or in some other important endeavor)

18. How to build or repair a household item or create something online (e.g., blog, Web site, social network page)

19. How to plan the perfect party, wedding, holiday, birthday, or date

20. How a historical event occurred or an important law was passed (e.g., Rosa Parks's arrest; the 1773 Boston Tea Party; the passage of Title IX, ensuring equal athletic opportunities for female students)

Rosa Parks, whose refusal to give up her bus seat in Montgomery, Alabama, in 1955 helped to ignite the Civil Rights Movement.

© Bettmann/CORBIS

A Topic Proposal for Your Essay

Selecting the right subject matter is important to every writer. To help you clarify your ideas and strengthen your commitment to your topic, here is a proposal sheet that asks you to describe some of your preliminary ideas about your subject before you begin drafting. Although your ideas may change as you write (they will almost certainly become more refined), thinking through your choice of topic now may help you avoid several false starts.

1. What process will you explain in your essay? Is it a directional or an informative process? Can you address the complexity of this process in a short essay?

2. Why did you select this topic? Are you personally or professionally interested in this process? Cite at least one reason for your choice.

3. Why do you think this topic would be of interest to others? Who might find it especially informative or enjoyable?

4. Describe in one or two sentences the ideal response from your readers. What would you like them to do or know after reading about your topic?

5. List at least three of the larger steps or stages in the process.

6. What difficulties might this topic present during your drafting? Will this topic require any additional research on your part?

Sample Student Essay

The following essay is a directional process telling readers how to run a successful garage sale. To make the instructions clear and enjoyable, the writer described seven steps and offered many specific examples, details, and warnings.

CATCHING GARAGE SALE FEVER

Introduction:
A series of
questions to
hook the reader

1   Ever need some easy money fast? To repay those incredible overdue library fines you ran up writing your last research paper? Or to raise money for that much-needed vacation to Florida you put on credit cards last Spring Break? Or maybe you feel you simply have to clear out some junk before the piles block the remaining sunlight from your windows? Whether the problem is cash flow or trash flow, you can solve it easily by holding what is fast becoming an all-American sport: the weekend garage sale. As a veteran of some half-dozen successful

ventures, I can testify that garage sales are the easiest way to make quick money, with a minimum of physical labor and the maximum of fun.

Thesis

2 Most garage sale "experts" start getting ready at least two weeks before the sale by taking inventory. Look through your closets and junk drawers to see if you actually have enough items to make a sale worthwhile. If all you have is a mass of miscellaneous small items, think about waiting or joining a friend's sale, because you do need at least a couple of larger items (furniture is always a big seller) to draw customers initially. Also, consider whether the season is appropriate for your items: sun dresses and shorts, for example, sell better in the spring and summer; coats and boots in the fall. As you collect your items, don't underestimate the "saleability" of some of your junk—the hideous purple china bulldog Aunt Clara gave you for Christmas five years ago may be perfect for someone's Ugly Mutt Collection.

Step one: Taking inventory

3 As you sort through your closets, begin thinking about the time and place of your sale. First, decide if you want a one- or two-day sale. If you opt for only one day, Saturdays are generally best because most people are free that day. Plan to start early—by 8 A.M. if possible—because the experienced buyers get up and get going so they can hit more sales that way. Unless you have nothing else to do that day, plan to end your sale by mid-afternoon; most people have run out of buying energy (or money) by 3 P.M. Deciding on the location of your sale depends, of course, on your housing situation, but you still might need to make some choices. For instance, do you want to put your items out in a driveway, a front yard, or actually in the garage (weather might affect this decision)? Or perhaps a side yard gets more passers-by? Wherever you decide, be sure that there are plenty of

Step two: Deciding when and where

places for customers to park close by without blocking your neighbors' driveways.

Step three:
Advertising
the sale

4   Unless you live in a very small town or on a very busy street, you'll probably want to place an inexpensive ad in the "garage sale" column of your local newspaper, scheduled to run a day or two before, and the day of, your sale. Your ad should tell the times and place of the sale (give brief directions or mention landmarks if the location is hard to find) as well as a short list of some of your items. Few people will turn out for "household goods" alone; some popular items include bookcases, antiques, books, fans, jewelry, toys, baby equipment, and name-brand clothes. One other piece of advice about the ad copy:

A warning

it should include the phrase "no early sales" unless you want to be awakened at 6:30 A.M., as I was one Saturday, by a bunch of semipro garage sale buyers milling restlessly around in your yard, looking like zombies out of a George Romero horror movie. In addition to your newspaper ad, you may also wish to put up posters in places frequented by lots of people; laundromats and grocery stores often have bulletin boards for such announcements. You can also put up signs on nearby

Another warning

well-traveled streets, but one warning: in some towns it's illegal to post anything on utility poles or traffic signs, so be sure to check your local ordinances first.

Step four:
Pricing the
merchandise

5   Tagging your items with their prices is the least fun, and it can take a day or a week depending on how many items you have and how much time each day you can devote to the project. You can buy sheets of little white stickers or use pieces of masking tape to stick on the prices, but if you want to save time, consider grouping some items and selling them all for the same price—all shirts, for example, are 50¢. Be realistic about your prices; the handcrafted rug from Greece may have been expensive and important to you, but to others, it's a worn doormat. Some experts suggest pricing your articles at about one-fourth their original value, unless you have special reasons not to (an antique or a popular collectors' item, for instance, may be more valuable now than when you bought it). Remember that you can always come down on your prices if someone is interested in a particular item.

6   By the day before your sale you should have all your items clean and tagged. One of the beauties of a garage sale is that there's very little equipment to collect. You'll need tables, benches, or boards supported by bricks to display your goods; a rope tied from side to side of your garage can double as a clothes rack. Try to spread out your merchandise rather than dumping articles in deep boxes; customers don't want to feel like they're rummaging through a trash barrel. Most important, you'll need a chair and a table to hold some sort of money box, preferably one with a lock. The afternoon before the sale, take a trip to the bank if you need to, to make sure you have enough one-dollar bills and coins to make plenty of change. The evening before the sale, set up your items on your display benches in the garage or indoors near the site of your sale so that you can quickly set things out in the morning. Get a good night's sleep so you can get up to open on time: the early bird does get the sales in this business.

Step five: Setting up your sale

A note on equipment

7   The sale itself is, of course, the real fun. Half the enjoyment is haggling with the customers, so be prepared to joke and visit with the shoppers. Watching the different kinds of people who show up is also a kick—you can get a cross section from college students on a tight budget to harried mothers toting four kids to real eccentrics in fancy cars who will argue about the price of a 75¢ item (if you're a creative writer, don't forget to take notes for your next novel). If the action slows in the afternoon, you can resort to a half-price or two-for-one sale by posting a large sign to that effect; many shoppers can't resist a sale at a sale!

Step six: Running the sale

Vocabulary

docility (1)	*raison d'être* (3)	pliable (8)
perpetuation (1)	ingenious (5)	semblance (11)
inherent (2)	cadaver (5)	ravages (11)
mandatory (2)	somatic (7)	stippling (12)
intractable (3)	rudimentary (7)	emaciation (13)
reticence (3)	dispel (7)	

II. The Directional Process Essay

Preparing for the Job Interview: Know Thyself

Katy Piotrowski

Katy Piotrowski, M.Ed., is the owner of Career Solutions Group, through which she provides career and job-search support, and the author of five books in the *Career Cowards Guide* series. Her essay, which originally appeared in 2005 in her "On the Job" column for the Fort Collins, Colorado, *Coloradoan* newspaper, has been slightly revised for this text.

1   "I have a job interview this afternoon!" Shawn told me. "Are you ready for it?" I asked. "I'm not sure," she confessed. So, drawing on my work as a career-search consultant, I helped her through an interview-readiness procedure, a quick, six-step process that can successfully prepare almost anyone for a job interview.

2   First, I asked, can you identify the top two or three responsibilities of the job? Shawn hesitated, so I asked her to reread the position description and tell me which parts or key words stood out most. "Evaluating the effectiveness of health-care programs" and "coordinating information exchange in the hospital," she determined. With the key responsibilities in mind, we were ready for the next step. For each of the primary responsibilities, can you describe at least three examples from your past that demonstrate your expertise in those areas? Shawn had one example ready to share, but she needed more. "Tell me about a time when you evaluated the effectiveness of health-care or coordinated information among people or agencies," I prompted her. Within minutes, she'd created a longer list of examples.

3   Moving on, I asked Shawn to think of other experiences in her professional background that would show her as an attractive candidate for this job. Shawn's responses were unfocused, so I taught her a simple three-step STAR process for answering a number of interview questions: 1) describe the **s**ituation or **t**asks, 2) talk about the **a**ctions you took, 3) finish with the **r**esults of your efforts. Try to frame your answers concisely but in a compelling way, using action verbs that show leadership, such as "designed," "coordinated," "implemented," "created," and "managed," when such words are appropriate. Shawn practiced the process, and soon her answers were much more effective.

4   In addition to questions about specific qualifications, interviewers often ask general questions designed to reveal a candidate's "fit" as an employee in their business. "Tell me a little about yourself" is a common request; it may even come at the beginning of an interview when you are the most nervous, so it helps to have some prepared (though not stiffly memorized) thoughts. Shawn's response

included highlights of her work history, information about her education, and a statement about why she was excited about the job opening. Variations on this line of questioning might include "As a worker in this field, what is your greatest strength? Biggest weakness?" or "How have you handled a difficult situation?" Shawn had impressive responses to these kinds of questions; she just needed to practice them several more times.

5   As well as presenting themselves to companies, interviewees also need to know something about the companies to which they are applying. Whether you are asked directly or not, it's important to be acquainted with the goals, products, and services of your prospective employer. A quick online search may lead you to a company Web page and any recent publicity. Knowing current information about your prospective employer may better help you respond to questions such as "What knowledge or skills can you bring to our company?" with specific answers that happily fit their needs.

6   Often interviewers' final question may be "Do you have any questions for us?" so the last step in your preparation process calls for thinking of at least one good response. You might ask about the ways this position fits into the larger organization or the company's future plans or ask for more details about the advertised position. You might ask them to describe the most successful employees they've ever hired for this job. (At this time, you probably do not want to negotiate salary, especially if you are an entry-level applicant.) If it seems appropriate, you may also ask how you should proceed: would they prefer for you to contact them or to wait for their response? Is there any other information you can provide that would be helpful in furthering your application for this job? (Don't forget, I reminded Shawn, at the close of your meeting, to thank the interviewers for their time.)

7   Within an hour, following these few steps, Shawn was much more prepared for her interview. Though few people can be totally relaxed during an interview, she was calmed with the knowledge that she was ready to effectively give meaningful responses to a variety of questions. And, yes, she *did* get the job.

Questions on Content, Structure, and Style

1. What process is explained in this essay? What is Piotrowski's main purpose?

2. Although Piotrowski describes her conversation with Shawn, why may this article be considered a directional process essay for its readers?

3. What are the primary steps in this process?

4. Piotrowski uses an actual job applicant, Shawn, to show how the interview-preparation process works. What benefits for the reader does this choice of organization present?

5. Consider ways in which Piotrowski explains each step of the process. How does she clarify her advice by using examples?

6. Cite some ways Piotrowski moves her reader from one step in the preparation process to the next. What transitional words or phrases help guide the reader through the steps?

7. Effective writers of process essays often offer warnings or point out what not to do. Where does Piotrowski use this technique?

8. In paragraph 3, how does Piotrowski use an *acronym* (a word formed from the first letters or parts of other words) to explain her advice?

9. Describe Piotrowski's tone or "voice" in this essay. Is it appropriate and effective? Cite some examples of her language to support your answer.

10. Evaluate Piotrowski's conclusion. How does it wrap up the essay? In particular, what is the effect of the last sentence?

Suggestions for Writing

Try using Piotrowski's essay as a stepping-stone to your own writing. Think of a job that you would like to have soon, perhaps this summer or after you finish your education. Following Piotrowski's procedure for interview preparation, write an essay showing why you are the best candidate for the position. Keep this essay for later use when you face a real interview or for help designing a résumé. (Or, if you prefer, try writing a light-hearted, tongue-in-cheek process essay that makes a serious point by humorously advising readers what *not* to do in the workplace: how not to impress your boss, how not to cooperate with your co-workers, how not to get a raise, and so on.)

Vocabulary

expertise (2)
implemented (3)
prospective (5)

A Revision Worksheet

© Ryan McVay/Photodisc/
Getty Images

As you write your rough drafts, consult Chapter 5 for guidance through the revision process. In addition, here are a few questions to ask yourself as you revise your process essay:

1. Is the essay's purpose clear to the reader?

2. Has the need for any special equipment been noted and explained adequately? Are all terms unfamiliar to the reader defined clearly?

3. Does the essay include all the steps (and warnings, if appropriate) necessary to understanding the process?

4. Is each step described in enough detail to make it understandable to all readers? Where could more detail be effectively added?

5. Are all the steps in the process presented in an easy-to-follow chronological order, with smooth transitions between steps or stages?

6. Are there any steps that should be combined in a paragraph describing a logical stage in the process?

7. Does the essay have a pleasing conclusion?

Collaborative Activity: After you've revised your essay extensively, exchange rough drafts with a classmate and answer the preceding questions for each other, making specific suggestions for improvement wherever appropriate. (◆ For advice on productive participation in classroom workshops, see pages 115–120.)

Reviewing Your Progress

After you have completed your process essay, take a moment to measure your progress as a writer by responding to the following questions. Such analysis will help you to recognize growth in your writing skills and may enable you to identify areas that are still problematic.

1. Which part of your essay is most successful? Why?

2. Select two details that contribute significantly to the clarity of your explanation. Why are these details effective?

3. What part of your essay gave you the most trouble? How did you overcome the problem?

4. If you had more time to work on this essay, what would receive additional attention? Why?

5. What did you learn about your topic from writing this essay? About yourself as a writer?

Strategy Three: Development by Comparison and Contrast

Every day you exercise the mental process of comparison and contrast. When you get up in the morning, for instance, you may contrast two choices of clothing—a short-sleeved shirt versus a long-sleeved one—and then make your decision after hearing the weather forecast. Or you may contrast and choose between Sugar-Coated Plastic Pops and Organic Millet Kernels for breakfast, between the health advantages of walking to campus and the speed afforded by your car or bicycle. Once on campus, preparing to register, you may first compare both professors and courses; similarly, you probably compared the school you attend now to others before you made your choice. In short, you frequently use the process of comparison and contrast to come to a decision or make a judgment about two or more objects, persons, ideas, or feelings.

When you write a comparison or contrast essay, your opinion about the two elements* in question becomes your thesis statement; the body of the paper then shows why you arrived at that opinion. For example, if your thesis states that Mom's Kum-On-Back Hamburger Haven is preferable to McPhony's Mystery Burger Stand, your body paragraphs might contrast the two restaurants in terms of food, service, and atmosphere, revealing the superiority of Mom's on all three counts.

---

*It is possible to compare or contrast more than two elements. But until you feel confident about the organizational patterns for this kind of essay, you should probably stay with the simpler format.

Developing Your Essay

There are two principal patterns of organization for comparison or contrast essays. For most short papers you should choose one of the patterns and stick with it throughout the essay. Later, if you are assigned a longer essay, you may want to mix the patterns for variety as some professional writers do, but do so only if you can maintain clarity and logical organization.

Pattern One: Point by Point

This method of organization calls for body paragraphs that compare or contrast the two subjects first on point one, then on point two, then point three, and so on. Study the following example:

Thesis: Mom's Hamburger Haven is a better family restaurant than McPhony's because of its superior food, service, and atmosphere.

Point 1: Food
A. Mom's
B. McPhony's

Point 2: Service
A. Mom's
B. McPhony's

Point 3: Atmosphere
A. Mom's
B. McPhony's

Conclusion

If you select this pattern of organization, you must make a smooth transition from subject "A" to subject "B" in each discussion to avoid a choppy seesaw effect. Be consistent: present the same subject first in each discussion of a major point. In the essay just outlined, for instance, Mom's is always introduced before McPhony's.

Pattern Two: The Block

This method of organization presents body paragraphs in which the writer first discusses subject "A" on points one, two, three, and so on, and then discusses subject "B" on the same points. The following model illustrates this Block Pattern:

Thesis: Mom's Hamburger Haven is a better family restaurant than McPhony's because of its superior food, service, and atmosphere.

A. Mom's
  1. Food
  2. Service
  3. Atmosphere

B. McPhony's
  1. Food
  2. Service
  3. Atmosphere

Conclusion

If you use the Block Pattern, you should discuss the three points—food, service, atmosphere—in the same order for each subject. In addition, you must include in your discussion of subject "B" specific references to the points you made earlier about subject "A" (see outline). In other words, because your statements about Mom's superior food may be several pages away by the time your comments on McPhony's food appear, the readers may not remember precisely what you said. Gently, unobtrusively, remind them with a specific reference to the earlier discussion. For instance, you might begin your paragraph on McPhony's service like this: "Unlike the friendly, attentive help at Mom's, service at McPhony's features grouchy employees who wait on you as if they consider your presence an intrusion on their privacy." The discussion of atmosphere might begin, "McPhony's atmosphere is as cold, sterile, and plastic as its decor, in contrast to the warm, homey feeling that pervades Mom's." Without such connecting phrases, what should be one unified essay will look more like two distinct mini-essays, forcing readers to do your job of comparing or contrasting for themselves.

Which Pattern Should You Use?

As you prepare to compose your first draft, you might ask yourself, "Which pattern of organization should I choose—Point by Point or Block?" Indeed, this is not your simple "paper or plastic" supermarket choice. It's an important question—to which there is no single, easy answer.

For most writers, choosing the appropriate pattern of organization involves thinking time in the prewriting stage, before beginning a draft. Many times, your essay's subject matter itself will suggest the most effective method of development. The Block Method might be the better choice when a complete, overall picture of each subject is desirable. For example, you might decide that your "then-and now" essay (your disastrous first day at a new job contrasted with your success at that job today) would be easier for your readers to understand if your description of "then" (your first day) was presented in its entirety, followed by the contrasting discussion of "now" (current success). Later in this section, you will see that Mark Twain chose this method in his essay "Two Ways of Viewing the River" to contrast his early and later impressions of the Mississippi.

On the other hand, your essay topic might best be discussed by presenting a number of distinct points for the reader to consider one by one. Essays that evaluate, that argue the superiority or advantage of one thing over another ("A cat is a better pet for students than a dog because . . ."), often lend themselves to the Point-by-Point Method because each of the writer's claims may be clearly supported by the side-by-side details. "Bringing Back the Joy of Market Day," a student essay in this section, employs this method to emphasize three ways in which a small food cooperative is preferable to a chain grocery store.

However, none of the preceding advice always holds true. There are no hard-and-fast rules governing this rhetorical choice. Each writer must decide which method of organization works best in any particular comparison/contrast essay. Before drafting begins, therefore, writers are wise to sketch out an informal outline or rough plan using one method and then the other to see which is more effective for their topic, their purpose, and their audience. By spending time in the prewriting stage "auditioning" each method of development, you may spare yourself the frustration of writing an entire draft whose organization doesn't work well for your topic.

No benefits at Lane Grocer contrasted to two benefits at the co-op

Direct selling offers two advantages for producers: they get a better price for their wares than by selling them through wholesalers, and at the same time they establish an independent reputation for their business, which can be immensely valuable to their success later on. In Fort Collins, for example, Luna tofu (bean curd) stands out as an excellent illustration of this kind of mutual support. Several years ago my friend Carol Jones began making tofu in small batches to sell to the co-op as a way to earn a part-time income as well as to contribute to the co-op. Her enterprise has now grown so well that last year her husband quit his job to go into business with her full time. She currently sells to distributors and independent stores from here to Denver; even Lane Grocer, which earlier would not consider selling her tofu even on a trial basis, is now thinking about changing its policy.

Conclusion: Summarizing the advantages of co-ops over chain stores

6   Of course, not all co-ops are like the one here in Fort Collins, but that is one of their best features. Each one reflects the personalities of its members, unlike the supermarket chain stores that vary only slightly. Most important, though, while each has a distinctive character, co-ops share common goals of providing members with high-quality, low cost food in a friendly, cooperative spirit.

II. The Block Pattern

After thinking through both methods of development, a second student writer chose the Block Pattern to contrast two kinds of backyards. He felt it was more effective to give his readers a complete sense of his first backyard, with its spirit of wildness, instead of addressing each point of the contrast separately, as did the first student writer in this section. Do you agree with his choice? Why or why not? Note, too, the ways in which this writer tries to avoid the "split essay" problem by making clear connections between the new yard and the older one.

BACKYARDS: OLD AND NEW

1   Most of the time I like getting something new—new clothes, new CDs, new video games. I look forward to making new friends and visiting new places. But sometimes new isn't better than old. Five years ago, when my family moved to a house in a new area, I learned that a new, neat backyard can never be as wonderful as a rambling, untamed yard of an older house.

Thesis

2   My first yard, behind our older house, was huge, the size of three normal backyards, but completely irregular in shape. Our property line zagged in and out around old, tall trees in a lot shaped like a large pie piece from which some giant had taken random bites. The left side was taken up by a lopsided garden that sometimes grew tomatoes but mainly wild raspberries, an odd assortment of overgrown bushes, and wildflowers of mismatched shapes and sizes. The middle part had grass and scattered shade trees, some that were good for climbing. The grassy part drifted off into an area with large old evergreen trees surrounded by a tall tangle of vines and bushes that my parents called "the Wild Spot," which they had carefully ignored for years. The whole yard sloped downhill, which with the irregular shape and the trees, made my job of mowing the grass a creative challenge.

Block A: The older, "untamed" backyard

(Landscape variety: Irregular lot size and shape; trees, rambling mix of bushes, flowers, berries, and vines)

3   Despite the mowing problem, there was something magical about that untamed yard. We kids made a path through the Wild Spot and had a secret hideout in the brush. Hidden from adult eyes, my friends and I sat around a pretend fire ring, made up adventures (lost in the jungle!), asked each other Important Questions (better to be a rock star or a baseball player?), and shared our secret fears (being asked to dance). The yard's grassy section was big enough for throwing a football with my brother (the here-and-there trees made catching long passes even more

(Family activities)

spectacular), and my twin sisters invented gymnastic routines that rolled them downhill. Mom picked vegetables and flowers when she felt like it. It seemed like someone, family or friend, was always in our yard doing something fun.

Transition to Block B: The new backyard (contrasting bland landscape)

4   When all the kids were teenagers, my parents finally decided we needed more space, so we moved into a house in a new development. Although the house itself was better (more bathrooms), the new backyard, in comparison to our older one, was a total disappointment. New Backyard was neat, tidy, tiny, flat, square, and completely fenced. There were not only no big old trees for shade or for climbing—there were no trees at all. My parents had to plant a few, which looked like big twigs stuck in the ground. No untamed tangles of bushes and flowers there—only identical fire hydrant–sized shrubs planted evenly every few feet in narrow, even beds along the fence. The rest of this totally flat yard was grass, easy to mow in mere minutes, but no challenge either. No wild berry bushes or rambling vegetable gardens were allowed in the new development. No wild anything at all, to be exact.

5   Nothing wild and no variety: that was the problem. To put it bluntly, the yard was neat but boring. Every inch of it was open to inspection; it held no secret spaces for the imagination to fill. There was no privacy either as our yard looked directly into the almost duplicate bland yards of the neighbors on all sides. The yard was too small to do any real physical activity in it; going out for a long pass would mean automatic collision with the chain link fence in any direction. My sisters' dance routines soon dissolved under our

(Few activities)

neighbors' eyes, and our tomatoes came from the grocery store. With no hidden nooks, no interesting landscape, and no tumbling space, our family just didn't go into the backyard very often. Unlike the older, overgrown backyard that was always inviting someone to play, the new backyard wasn't fun for anyone.

6   Over the last five years, the trees have grown and the yard looks better, not so sterile and empty. I guess all new yards are on their way to becoming old yards eventually. But it takes decades and that is too slow for me. New houses have lots of modern conveniences, but I hope if I am lucky enough to own my own place someday, I will remember that when it comes to backyards, old is always better than new.

Conclusion: A future preference based on essay's thesis

Professional Essays*

Because there are two common ways to develop comparison/contrast essays, this section offers two professional essays so that each pattern is illustrated.

I. The Point-by-Point Pattern

Grant and Lee: A Study in Contrasts

Bruce Catton

Bruce Catton, an authority on the Civil War, won both the Pulitzer Prize for historical work and the National Book Award in 1955. He wrote numerous books, including *Mr. Lincoln's Army* (1951), *A Stillness at Appomattox* (1953), *Never Call Retreat* (1966), and *Gettysburg: The Final Fury* (1974). This essay is a chapter of *The American Story* (1956), a collection of essays by noted historians.

1   When Ulysses S. Grant and Robert E. Lee met in the parlor of a modest house at Appomattox Court House, Virginia, on April 9, 1865, to work out the terms for the surrender of Lee's Army of Northern Virginia, a great chapter in American life came to a close, and a great new chapter began.

2   These men were bringing the Civil War to its virtual finish. To be sure, other armies had yet to surrender, and for a few days the fugitive Confederate government would struggle desperately and vainly, trying to find some way to go on living now that its chief support was gone. But in effect it was all over when Grant and Lee signed the papers. And the little room where they wrote out the terms was the scene of one of the poignant, dramatic contrasts in American history.

3   They were two strong men, these oddly different generals, and they represented the strengths of two conflicting currents that, through them, had come into final collision.

---

* ◆ To help you read these essays analytically, review pages 180–182.

4   Back of Robert E. Lee was the notion that the old aristocratic concept might somehow survive and be dominant in American life.

5   Lee was tidewater Virginia, and in his background were family, culture, and tradition . . . the age of chivalry transplanted to a New World which was making its own legends and its own myths. He embodied a way of life that had come down through the age of knighthood and the English country squire. America was a land that was beginning all over again, dedicated to nothing much more complicated than the rather hazy belief that all men had equal rights, and should have an equal chance in the world. In such a land Lee stood for the feeling that it was somehow of advantage to human society to have a pronounced inequality in the social structure. There should be a leisure class, backed by ownership of land; in turn, society itself should be keyed to the land as the chief source of wealth and influence. It would bring forth (according to this ideal) a class of men with a strong sense of obligation to the community; men who lived not to gain advantage for themselves, but to meet the solemn obligations which had been laid on them by the very fact that they were privileged. From them the country would get its leadership; to them it could look for the higher values—of thought, of conduct, of personal deportment—to give it strength and virtue.

6   Lee embodied the noblest elements of this aristocratic ideal. Through him, the landed nobility justified itself. For four years, the Southern states had fought a desperate war to uphold the ideals for which Lee stood. In the end, it almost seemed as if the Confederacy fought for Lee; as if he himself was the Confederacy . . . the best thing that the way of life for which the Confederacy stood could ever have to offer. He had passed into legend before Appomattox. Thousands of tired, underfed, poorly clothed Confederate soldiers, long-since past the simple enthusiasm of the early days of the struggle, somehow considered Lee the symbol of everything for which they had been willing to die. But they could not quite put this feeling into words. If the Lost Cause, sanctified by so much heroism and so many deaths, had a living justification, its justification was General Lee.

7   Grant, the son of a tanner on the Western frontier, was everything Lee was not. He had come up the hard way, and embodied nothing in particular except the eternal toughness and sinewy fiber of the men who grew up beyond the mountains. He was one of a body of men who owed reverence and obeisance to no one, who were self-reliant to a fault, who cared hardly anything for the past but who had a sharp eye for the future.

8   These frontier men were the precise opposites of the tidewater aristocrats. Back of them, in the great surge that had taken people over the Alleghenies and into the opening Western country, there was a deep, implicit dissatisfaction with a past that had settled into grooves. They stood for democracy, not from any reasoned conclusion about the proper ordering of human society, but simply because they had grown up in the middle of democracy and knew how it worked. Their society might have privileges, but they would be privileges each man had won for himself. Forms and patterns meant nothing. No man was born to anything, except perhaps to a chance to show how far he could rise. Life was competition.

9   Yet along with this feeling had come a deep sense of belonging to a national community. The Westerner who developed a farm, opened a shop, or set up in

business as a trader could hope to prosper only as his own community prospered—and his community ran from the Atlantic to the Pacific and from Canada down to Mexico. If the land was settled, with towns and highways and accessible markets, he could better himself. He saw his fate in terms of the nation's own destiny. As its horizons expanded, so did his. He had, in other words, an acute dollars-and-cents stake in the continued growth and development of his country.

10   And that, perhaps, is where the contrast between Grant and Lee becomes most striking. The Virginia aristocrat, inevitably, saw himself in relation to his own region. He lived in a static society which could endure almost anything except change. Instinctively, his first loyalty would go to the locality in which that society existed. He would fight to the limit of endurance to defend it, because in defending it he was defending everything that gave his own life its deepest meaning.

11   The Westerner, on the other hand, would fight with an equal tenacity for the broader concept of society. He fought so because everything he lived by was tied to growth, expansion, and a constantly widening horizon. What he lived by would survive or fall with the nation itself. He could not possibly stand by unmoved in the face of an attempt to destroy the Union. He would combat it with everything he had, because he could only see it as an effort to cut the ground out from under his feet.

12   So Grant and Lee were in complete contrast, representing two diametrically opposed elements in American life. Grant was the modern man emerging; beyond him, ready to come on the stage, was the great age of steel and machinery, of crowded cities and a restless, burgeoning vitality. Lee might have ridden down from the old age of chivalry, lance in hand, silken banner fluttering over his head. Each man was the perfect champion of his cause, drawing both his strengths and his weaknesses from the people he led.

13   Yet it was not all contrast, after all. Different as they were—in background, in personality, in underlying aspiration—these two great soldiers had much in common. Under everything else, they were marvelous fighters. Furthermore, their fighting qualities were really very much alike.

14   Each man had, to begin with, the great virtue of utter tenacity and fidelity. Grant fought his way down the Mississippi Valley in spite of acute personal discouragement and profound military handicaps. Lee hung on in the trenches at Petersburg after hope itself had died. In each man there was an indomitable quality . . . the born fighter's refusal to give up as long as he can still remain on his feet and lift his two fists.

15   Daring and resourcefulness they had, too; the ability to think faster and move faster than the enemy. These were the qualities which gave Lee the dazzling campaigns of Second Manassas and Chancellorsville and won Vicksburg for Grant.

16   Lastly, and perhaps greatest of all, there was the ability, at the end, to turn quickly from war to peace once the fighting was over. Out of the way these two men behaved at Appomattox came the possibility of a peace of reconciliation. It was a possibility not wholly realized, in the years to come, but which did, in the end, help the two sections to become one nation again . . . after a war whose bitterness might have seemed to make such a reunion wholly impossible. No part of either man's life became him more than the part he played in their brief meeting

in the McLean house at Appomattox. Their behavior there put all succeeding generations of Americans in their debt. Two great Americans, Grant and Lee—very different, yet under everything very much alike. Their encounter at Appomattox was one of the great moments of American history.

Questions on Content, Style, and Structure

1. What is Catton's thesis?

2. According to Catton, how did Lee view society? Summarize the aristocratic ideal that Lee symbolized.

3. Who did Grant represent? How did they view the country's social structure?

4. After carefully studying paragraphs 4 through 16, describe the pattern of organization Catton uses to present his discussion.

5. What new means of development begins in paragraph 13?

6. How does Catton avoid the choppy seesaw effect as he compares and contrasts his subjects? Point out ways in which Catton makes a smooth transition from point to point.

7. Evaluate Catton's ability to write unified, coherent paragraphs with clearly stated topic sentences. Are his paragraphs adequately developed with enough specific detail? Cite evidence to support your answer.

8. What is the advantage or disadvantage of having only one sentence in paragraph 3? In paragraph 4?

9. What is Catton's opinion of these men? Select words and passages to support your answer. How does Catton's attitude affect the tone of this essay? Is his tone appropriate? Why or why not?

10. Instead of including a separate paragraph, Catton presents his concluding remarks in paragraph 16, in which he discusses his last major point about Grant and Lee. Many essays lacking concluding paragraphs end too abruptly or merely trail off; how does Catton avoid these weaknesses?

Suggestions for Writing

Try using Bruce Catton's "Grant and Lee: A Study in Contrasts" as a stepping-stone to your writing. Comparing public figures is a familiar activity. People often discuss the styles and merits of various politicians, writers, business leaders, humanitarians, sports celebrities, and media stars. Write your own essay about two public figures who interest you. Similar or different, these people may have lived in the same times (Winston Churchill and Franklin D. Roosevelt, Ernest Hemingway and F. Scott Fitzgerald, Babe Didrikson Zaharias and Babe Ruth), or you might choose two people from different eras (Clara Barton and Mother Teresa, Mozart and Madonna, Susan B. Anthony and Cesar Chavez, Harriet Tubman and Martin Luther King, Jr.). The possibilities are endless and thought-provoking; use your essay to make an interesting specific point about the fascinating (and perhaps heretofore unrecognized) differences/similarities between the people you choose.

Vocabulary

chivalry (5)	tenacity (11)	indomitable (14)
deportment (5)	diametrically (12)	reconciliation (16)
embodied (6)	burgeoning (12)	

II. The Block Pattern

Two Ways of Viewing the River

Samuel Clemens

Samuel Clemens, whose pen name was Mark Twain, is regarded as one of America's most outstanding writers. Well known for his humorous stories and books, Twain was also a pioneer of fictional realism and local color. His most famous novel, *Adventures of Huckleberry Finn* (1884), is often hailed as a masterpiece. This selection is from the autobiographical book *Life on the Mississippi* (1883), which recounts Clemens' job as a riverboat pilot.

1   Now when I had mastered the language of this water and had come to know every trifling feature that bordered the great river as familiarly as I knew the letters of the alphabet, I had made a valuable acquisition. But I had lost something, too. I had lost something which could never be restored to me while I lived. All the grace, the beauty, the poetry, had gone out of the majestic river! I still kept in mind a certain wonderful sunset which I witnessed when steamboating was new to me. A broad expanse of the river was turned to blood; in the middle distance the red hue brightened into gold, through which a solitary log came floating, black and conspicuous; in one place a long, slanting mark lay sparkling upon the water; in another the surface was broken by boiling, tumbling rings, that were as many-tinted as an opal; where the ruddy flush was faintest, was a smooth spot that was covered with graceful circles and radiating lines, ever so delicately traced; the shore on our left was densely wooded and the somber shadow that fell from this forest was broken in one place by a long, ruffled trail that shone like silver; and high above the forest wall a clean-stemmed dead tree waved a single leafy bough that glowed like a flame in the unobstructed splendor that was flowing from the sun. There were graceful curves, reflected images, woody heights, soft distances, and over the whole scene, far and near, the dissolving lights drifted steadily, enriching it every passing moment with new marvels of coloring.

2   I stood like one bewitched. I drank it in, in a speechless rapture. The world was new to me and I had never seen anything like this at home. But as I have said, a day came when I began to cease from noting the glories and the charms which the moon and the sun and the twilight wrought upon the river's face; another day came when I ceased altogether to note them. Then, if that sunset scene had been repeated, I should have looked upon it without rapture, and should have commented upon it inwardly after this fashion: "This sun means that we are going to have wind tomorrow; that floating log means that the river is rising, small thanks to it; that slanting mark on the water refers to a bluff reef which is going to kill somebody's steamboat one of these nights, if it keeps on stretching out like that;

those tumbling 'boils' show a dissolving bar and a changing channel there; the lines and circles in the slick water over yonder are a warning that that troublesome place is shoaling up dangerously; that silver streak in the shadow of the forest is the 'break' from a new snag and he has located himself in the very best place he could have found to fish for steamboats; that tall dead tree, with a single living branch, is not going to last long, and then how is a body ever going to get through this blind place at night without the friendly old landmark?"

3   No, the romance and beauty were all gone from the river. All the value any feature of it had for me now was the amount of usefulness it could furnish toward compassing the safe piloting of a steamboat. Since those days, I have pitied doctors from my heart. What does the lovely flush in a beauty's cheek mean to a doctor but a "break" that ripples above some deadly disease? Are not all her visible charms sown thick with what are to him the signs and symbols of hidden decay? Does he ever see her beauty at all, or doesn't he simply view her professionally and comment upon her unwholesome condition all to himself? And doesn't he sometimes wonder whether he has gained most or lost most by learning his trade?

Questions on Content, Structure, and Style

1. What is Clemens contrasting in this essay? Identify his thesis.
2. What organizational pattern does he choose? Why is this an appropriate choice for his purpose?
3. How does Clemens make a smooth transition to his later view of the river?
4. Why does Clemens refer to doctors in paragraph 3?
5. What is the purpose of the questions in paragraph 3? Why is the last question especially important?
6. Characterize the language Clemens uses in his description in paragraph 1. Is his diction appropriate?
7. Point out several examples of similes in paragraph 1. What do they add to the description of the sunset?
8. How does the language in the description in paragraph 2 differ from the diction in paragraph 1? What view of the river is emphasized there?
9. Identify an example of personification in paragraph 2. Why did Clemens add it to his description?
10. Describe the tone of this essay. Does it ever shift?

Suggestions for Writing

Try using Samuel Clemens' "Two Ways of Viewing the River" as a stepping-stone to your own writing. Consider, as Clemens did, writing about a subject before and after you experienced it from a more technically informed point of view. Did your appreciation of your grandmother's quilt increase after you realized how much skill went into making it? Did a starry night have a different appeal after your astronomy course? Did your admiration of a story or poem diminish or increase after you studied its craft? Clemens felt that a certain loss came with his expertise, but was this the case in your experience?

Vocabulary

trifling (1)   ruddy (1)

acquisition (1)   wrought (2)

conspicuous (1)   compassing (3)

© Ryan McVay/Photodisc/Getty Images

A Revision Worksheet

As you write your rough drafts, consult Chapter 5 for guidance through the revision process. In addition, here are a few questions to ask yourself as you revise your comparison/contrast essay:

1. Does the essay contain a thesis that makes a significant point instead of a "so-what" thesis?

2. Is the material organized into the best pattern for the subject matter?

3. If the essay is developed by the Point-by-Point Pattern, are there enough transitional words used to avoid the seesaw effect?

4. If the essay is developed by the Block Pattern, are there enough transitional devices and references connecting the two subjects to avoid the split-essay problem?

5. Are the points of comparison/contrast presented in a logical, consistent order that the reader can follow easily?

6. Are both subjects given a reasonably balanced treatment?

7. Are both subjects developed in enough specific detail so that the reader clearly understands the comparison or contrast? Where might more detail be added?

Collaborative Activity: After you've revised your essay extensively, exchange rough drafts with a classmate and answer these questions for each other, making specific suggestions for improvement wherever appropriate. (◆ For advice on productive participation in classroom workshops, see pages 115–120.)

A Special Kind of Comparison: The Analogy

In the past few pages of this text, you've learned about essays developed by comparison/contrast, which generally point out similarities and differences between two things with enough common ground to merit meaningful discussion (two apartments, two computers, a book and its movie, etc.). In comparison/contrast essays, two subjects ("X" and "Y") are explained to make a point. An *analogy* is slightly different: it is a comparison that uses one thing ("X") only to clarify or argue a second thing ("Y"). In an analogy, one element is the main focus of attention.

You've probably heard several colorful analogies this week. Perhaps a friend who holds a hectic, dead-end job has tried to explain life at that moment by comparing herself to a crazed gerbil on a cage treadmill—always running, getting nowhere, feeling trapped in a never-changing environment. Or perhaps your science teacher explained the behavior of cancer cells by comparing them in several ways to an invading army on a destructive mission. If you read the Preface to this text, you were asked to see your writing instructor as a coach who helps you practice your skills, gives constructive criticism, and encourages your successes. Analogies are plentiful in our conversations and in both our reading and writing.

Writers often find analogies useful in three ways:

1. *To clarify and explain:* Most often writers use analogies to clarify an abstract, unfamiliar, or complex element by comparing it to something that is familiar to the reader, often something that is more concrete or easier to understand. For example, raising children has often been compared to nourishing baby birds, with parents feeding and nurturing but ultimately nudging offspring out of the nest. A relationship might be explained as having grown from a seed that eventually blossomed into a flower (or a weed!). Popular novelist Stephen King has used a roller coaster analogy to explain some people's enjoyment of horror movies.

   Frequently, scientific and medical topics profit from analogies that a general audience of readers can more readily understand. A technical discussion of the human eye, for instance, might be explained using the analogy of a camera lens; photosynthesis might be compared to the process of baking bread. One biology teacher explains the semipermeability of a cell membrane with a football analogy: the offensive line wants to let out the running back with the ball but keep the defensive line in. In short, analogies can make new or difficult material easier to grasp.

2. *To argue and persuade:* Writers often use analogies to try to convince their audience that what is true about "X" would also be true about "Y" because the two elements have so many important similarities. For example, someone against new anti-drug laws might argue that they are similar to those passed under Prohibition, the banning of alcohol in the 1930s, and thus the drug laws are doomed to failure. Or perhaps a NASA official might argue for more money for space exploration by comparing trips into outer space with those expeditions to the New World by explorers such as Columbus. How convincing an analogy is depends to a large extent on how similar the two elements appear to be. Remember, however, that analogies by themselves cannot *prove* anything; they can merely suggest similarities between two cases or things.

3. *To dramatize or capture an image:* Writers (and speakers) often use analogies because they wish their audience to remember a particular point or to see something in a new way. Using a vivid analogy—sometimes referred to as an extended metaphor or simile—can effectively impress an image upon the reader's or listener's mind ("Using crack is like burning down your own house. And the insurance policy ran out a long time ago . . ."). Analogies can be enjoyable too for their sheer inventiveness and their colorful language. Perhaps one of the most well-known analogies in American literature is Thoreau's description, in *Walden*, of a battle between two ant colonies, with the tiny creatures drawn as rival warriors fighting to the death in classical epic style. Analogies may even be used for comic effect in appropriate situations (moving into your basement apartment in sweltering August heat as analogous to a trip to the Underworld, for instance). Fresh, creative analogies can delight your readers and hold their attention.

Although analogies can be helpful and memorable, they can also present problems if they are trite, unclear, or illogical. Analogies can be especially harmful to a writer's credibility in an argument if readers don't see enough logical similarities to make the comparison convincing. Some faulty analogies may seem acceptable on first glance but fall apart when the details of the comparison are considered closely. For example, perhaps you have seen a bumper sticker that reads "Giving money and power to the government is like giving whisky and car keys to teenage boys." Are the two situations really alike? Do government agencies/officials and adolescents share many similarities in maturity, experience, and goals? Does financial support have the same effect as alcohol? If too many points of comparison are weak, readers will not find the analogy persuasive. Or perhaps you have read that "America is like a lifeboat already full of people; letting in more immigrants will cause the boat to sink." If readers do not accept the major premise—that America, a country with many renewable resources, closely resembles a lifeboat, a confined space with unchanging dimensions—they are likely to reject the argument.

Also be wary of those writers who try to substitute an analogy in place of any other kind of evidence to support their points in an argument, and be especially suspicious of those using analogies as "scare tactics" ("This proposed legislation is just like laws passed in Nazi Germany"). As a writer, use only those analogies that will help your reader understand, remember, or accept your ideas; as a reader, always protect yourself by questioning the validity of the analogy offered to you. (◆ For more on *faulty analogy* as a logical fallacy, see page 299.)

To illustrate use of analogy, here are three examples from professional writers. In each case, what was the writer's purpose? How is "X" used to clarify or argue for "Y"? Which of these analogies do you find the most effective, and why?

> A good lab course is an exercise in *doing* science. As such it differs totally in mission from a good lecture course where the object is learning *about* science. In the same way that one can gain vastly greater insight into music by learning to play an instrument, one can experience the doing of science only by going into the lab and trying one's hand at measurement.
>
> —*Miles Pickering, "Are Lab Courses a Waste of Time?"*

> For a long time now, since the beginning, in fact, men and women have been sparring and dancing around with each other, each pair trying to get it together and boogie to the tune called Life. For some people, it was always a glide, filled with grace and ease. For most of us, it is a stumble and a struggle, always trying to figure out the next step, until we find a partner whose inconsistencies seem to fit with ours, and the two of us fit into some kind of rhythm. Some couples wind up struggling and pulling at cross purposes; and of course, some people never get out on the floor, just stand alone in the corners, looking hard at the dancers.
>
> —*Jay Molishever, "Changing Expectations of Marriage"*

> One afternoon while we were there at that lake a thunderstorm came up. It was like the revival of an old melodrama that I had seen long ago with childish awe. The second-act climax of the drama of the electrical disturbance over a lake in America had not changed in any important respect. This was the big scene, still the big scene. The whole thing was so familiar, the first feeling of oppression and heat and a general air around camp of not wanting to go very far away. In midafternoon (it was all the same) a curious darkening of the sky, and a lull in everything that had made life tick; and then the way the boats suddenly swung the other way at their moorings with the coming of a breeze out of the new quarter, and the premonitory rumble.

Then the kettle drum, then the snare, then the bass drum and cymbals, then crackling light against the dark. . . . Afterward the calm, the rain steadily rustling in the calm lake, the return of light and hope and spirits, and the campers running out in joy.

—*E. B. White, "Once More to the Lake"*

Analogies come in a variety of lengths, from several sentences to an entire essay, depending upon the writer's purpose. As you practice your writing in this composition class, you may find that incorporating an analogy into one of your essays is an effective way to explain, emphasize, or help support an idea.

Reviewing Your Progress

After you have completed your essay developed by comparison/contrast, take a moment to measure your progress as a writer by responding to the following questions. Such analysis will help you to recognize growth in your writing skills and may enable you to identify areas that are still problematic.

1. Which part of your essay do you like the best? Why?

2. Which point of comparison or contrast do you think is the most successful? Why is it effective?

3. What part of your essay gave you the most trouble? How did you overcome the problem?

4. If you had more time to work on this essay, what would receive additional attention? Why?

5. What did you learn about your topic from writing this essay? About yourself as a writer?

Strategy Four: Development by Definition

Frequently in conversation we must stop to ask, "What do you mean by that?" because in some cases our failure to comprehend just one particular term may lead to total misunderstanding. Suppose, for example, in a discussion with a friend, you refer to a new law as a piece of "liberal legislation"; if you and your friend do not share the same definition of "liberal," your remark may be completely misinterpreted. Here's another example: if you tell your grandparents that you are "headed for the man-cave for some plasma and tweets," will they think you are going for a blood transfusion and bird watching in a natural area or that you are headed to the basement rec room for TV and text messaging? In other words, a clear understanding of terms or ideas is often essential to meaningful communication.

Sometimes a dictionary definition or a one- or two-sentence explanation is all a term needs (Hemingway, for example, once defined courage as "grace under pressure"). And sometimes a brief, humorous definition can cut right to the heart of the matter (comedian Robin Williams, for instance, once defined "cocaine" as "God's way of saying you're making too much money").*

---

*Even graffiti employ definition. One bathroom wall favorite: "Death is Nature's way of telling you to slow down." Another, obviously written by an English major: "A double negative is a no-no."

Frequently, however, you will find it necessary to provide an *extended definition*—that is, a longer, more detailed explanation that thoroughly defines the subject. Essays of extended definitions are quite common; think, for instance, of the articles you've seen on "mercy killing," "assisted suicide," or abortion that define "life" in a variety of ways. Other recent essays have grappled with defining such complex concepts as free speech, animal rights, pornography, affirmative action, and gun control.

Discussions of many nationwide issues often contain confusing or controversial terms. Hearing about the state of American finances, you might wish for a clearer understanding of words such as "recession," "bailout," or "toxic assets." Ecological proposals often talk about "sustainability" and "green" choices. Following the events of September 11, 2001, the definitions of many divisive words continue to be debated nationally. Who is a "terrorist"? Are procedures such as waterboarding "enhanced interrogation techniques" or "torture"? What is the difference between an "enemy combatant," a "detainee," and a "political prisoner"? Is it "patriotic" to oppose military actions of one's country? Today we need to clearly understand specific meanings of language before we can make intelligent decisions or take appropriate actions.

Why Do We Define?

Essays of extended definition are usually written for one or more of the following reasons:

1. To clarify an abstract term or concept ("hero," "success," "friendship," "loyalty")
2. To provide a personal interpretation of a term that the writer feels is vague, controversial, misused, or misunderstood ("feminist," "eco-terrorist," "Feng Shui," "multiculturalism")
3. To explain a new or unusual term or phrase found in popular culture, slang, dialect, or within a particular geographic area or cultural group ("hip-hop," "helicopter parent," "McJobs," "boomerang kids," "lagniappe")
4. To make understandable the language or technical terms of a particular field of study, a profession, or an industry ("deconstruction," "identity spoofing," "retinitis pigmentosa," "subprime mortgage")
5. To offer information about a term or an idea to a particular interested audience (antique collectors learning about "Depression glass," movie buffs understanding "film noir")
6. To inform and entertain by presenting the colorful history, uses, effects, or examples of a word, expression, or concept ("comfort food," "Zydeco music," "urban legends," "Kwanzaa")

Developing Your Essay

Here are four suggestions to help you prepare your essay of extended definition:

Know your purpose. Sometimes we need to define a term as clearly and objectively as possible. As a laboratory assistant, for instance, you might need to explain a technical measuring instrument to a group of new students. At other times, however, we may wish to persuade as well as inform our readers. People's interpretations of words, especially abstract or controversial terms, can, and often do, differ greatly depending on their point of view. After all, one person's protest march can be another person's street riot. Consequently, before you begin writing, decide on your purpose. If your readers need objective information only, make your definition as unbiased as you can; if your goal is to convince them that your point of view is the right or best one, you may adopt a variety of persuasive techniques as well as subjective (or even humorous) language. For example, readers of a paper entitled "The Joys of Catching Broncomania" should quickly realize they are not getting an objective medical analysis of Colorado football fever.

Give your readers a reason to read. One way to introduce your subject is to explain the previous use, misuse, or misunderstanding of the term; then present your new or better interpretation of the term or concept. An introduction and thesis defining a new word in popular usage might state, "Although people who suffer from weak immune systems might suddenly fear breathing the same air as someone suffering from affluenza, they needn't worry. 'Affluenza' isn't germ-laden; it's simply a colorful term describing the out-of-control consumerism spreading like an epidemic through America today." Or consider this introduction and thesis aimed at a word the writer feels is unclear to many readers: "When the credits roll at the end of a movie, much of the audience may be perplexed to see the job of 'best boy' listed. No, the 'best boy' isn't the nicest kid on the set—he (or she) is, in fact, the key electrician's first assistant, who helps arrange the lights for the movie's director of photography."

Keep your audience in mind to anticipate and avoid problems of clarity. Because you are trying to present a new or improved definition, you must strive above all for clarity. Ask yourself, "Who is my intended audience? What terms or parts of my definition are strange to them?" You don't help your audience, for example, by defining one campus slang expression in terms of other bits of unfamiliar slang. If, in other words, you discuss "mouse potatoes" as "Google bombers," you may be confusing some readers more than you are informing them. If your assignment doesn't specify a particular audience, you may find it useful to imagine one. You might pretend, for instance, that you're defining current campus slang for your parents, clarifying a local expression for a foreign visitor, or explaining a computer innovation to a technophobic friend. Remember that your definition is effective only if your explanation is clear not just to you but to those unfamiliar with the term or concept under discussion.

Use as many strategies as necessary to clarify your definition. Depending on your subject, you may use any number of the following methods in your essay to define your term:

1. Describe the parts or distinguishing characteristics*
2. Offer some examples
3. Compare to or contrast with similar terms
4. Explain an operation or a process

---

*With some topics, it may also be useful to describe the genus, class, or species to which the subject belongs.

5. State some familiar synonyms

6. Define by negation (that is, tell what the term doesn't mean)

7. Present the history or trace its development or changes from the original linguistical meaning

8. Discuss causes or effects

9. Identify times/places of use or appearance

10. Associate it with recognizable people, places, or ideas

To illustrate some of the methods suggested here, let's suppose you want to write an extended definition of "crossover" country music. You might choose several of these methods:

- Describe the parts: lyrics, musical sound, instruments, typical subject matter
- Compare to or contrast with other kinds of music, such as traditional country music, Western swing, or "pop"
- Give some examples of famous "crossover" country songs and artists
- Trace its historical development from traditional country music to its present state

In the paper on "crossover" country music or in any definition essay, you should, of course, use only those methods that will best define your term. Never include methods purely for the sake of exhibiting a variety of techniques. You, the writer, must decide which method or methods work best, which should receive the most emphasis, and in which order the chosen methods of definition should appear.

Problems to Avoid

Here is a list of "don'ts" for the writer of extended-definition essays:

Don't present an incomplete definition. An inadequate definition is often the result of choosing a subject too broad or complex for your essay. You probably can't, for instance, do a good job of defining "twentieth-century modern art" in all its varieties in a short essay; you might, however, introduce your reader to some specific school of modern art, such as Cubism or Surrealism. Always narrow your subject to a manageable size and then define it as thoroughly as possible.

Don't begin every definition essay by quoting Webster. If you must include a standard definition of your term, try to find a unique way of blending it into your discussion, perhaps as a point of contrast to your explanation of the word's meaning. Dictionary definitions are generally so overused as opening sentences that they can drive composition teachers to seek more interesting jobs, such as measuring spaghetti in a pasta factory. Don't bore your audience to death; it's a terrible way to go.

Don't define vaguely or by using generalities. As always, use specific, vivid details to explain your subject. If, for example, you define a shamrock as "a green plant with three leaves," you have also described hundreds of other plants, including poison ivy.

Consequently, you must select details that will make your subject distinct from any other. Including concrete examples is frequently useful in any essay but especially so when you are defining an abstract term, such as "pride," "patriotism," or "prejudice." To make your definition both interesting and clear, always add as many precise details as possible. (◆ For a review of using specific, colorful language, see pages 127, 141, and 161–164.)

Don't offer circular definitions. To define a poet as "one who writes poetry" or the American Dream as "the dream most Americans hold dear" is about as helpful as a doctor telling a patient, "Your illness is primarily a lack of good health." Explain your subject; don't just rename it.

© Inspirestock/CORBIS

ESSAY TOPICS

Here are several suggestions for terms or concepts whose meanings might be unclear to a particular audience. Narrow any topic that seems too broad for your assignment, and decide before writing whether your definition will be objective or subjective. (Student writers, by the way, often note that abstract concepts are harder to define than the more concrete subjects, so proceed at your own risk, and remember to use plenty of specific detail in your essay.) ◆ For additional ideas, turn to the "Suggestions for Writing" section following the professional essay (page 259).

1. A current slang, campus, local, or popular culture expression

2. A term from your field of study

3. A slob (or some other undesirable kind of roommate or friend)

4. Success or failure

5. A good/bad teacher, clerk, coach, friend, parent, date, or spouse

6. Heroism or cowardice

7. A term from science or technology

8. A kind of music, painting, architecture, or dance

9. A social label ("Goth," "Prep," "Skater," etc.)

10. A current fad or style or one from the past

11. A rebel or conformist

12. A family or hometown expression

13. A good/bad restaurant, store, movie theater, nightspot, class

14. Self-respect

15. Prejudice or discrimination

16. An important historical movement or group

17. A controversial political idea or term

18. A term from a hobby or sport

19. A medical term or condition

20. Select a painting or photograph in which you think the artist offers a visual definition of the subject matter (e.g., heroism, sorrow, mortality, prosperity). Explain this definition by examining the artist's choice and arrangement of details in the picture. For example, study George Tooker's painting *The Subway*. What aspect of urban life is represented here? What parts of the picture illustrate and clarify this point of view? Or consider another picture in this text, such as *Migrant Mother* (page 339) or *The Scream* (page 121). (A list of artworks follows the Table of Contents.)

Photography copyright © 2000, Whitney Museum of American Art. Collection of the Whitney Museum of American Art, New York. Photography by Geoffrey Clements, NY.

The Subway, 1950, by George Tooker

A Topic Proposal for Your Essay

Selecting the right subject matter is important to every writer. To help you clarify your ideas and strengthen your commitment to your topic, here is a proposal sheet that asks you to describe some of your ideas about your subject before you begin drafting. Although your ideas may change as you write (they will almost certainly become more refined), thinking through your topic now may help you avoid several false starts.

1. What subject will your essay define? Will you define this subject objectively or subjectively? Why?

2. Why are you interested in this topic? Do you have a personal or professional connection to the subject? State at least one reason for your choice of topic.

3. Is this a significant topic of interest to others? Why? Who specifically might find it interesting, informative, or entertaining?

4. Is your subject a controversial, ambiguous, or new term? What will readers gain by understanding this term as defined from your point of view?

5. Writers use a variety of techniques to define terms. At this point, list at least two techniques you think you might use to help readers understand your topic.

6. What difficulties, if any, can you foresee during the drafting of this essay? For example, do you need to do any additional reading or interviewing to collect information for your definition?

Sample Student Essay

A student with an interest in running wrote the following essay defining "runner's high." Note that he uses several methods to define his subject, one that is difficult to explain to those who have not experienced it firsthand.

BLIND PACES

Introduction: An example and a general definition of the term

1   After running the Mile-Hi ten-kilometer race in my hometown, I spoke with several of the leading runners about their experiences in the race. While most of them agreed that the course, which passed through a beautifully wooded yet overly hilly country area, was difficult, they also agreed that it was one of the best races of their running careers. They could not, however, explain why it was such a wonderful race but could rather only mumble something about the tall trees, cool air, and sandy path. When pressed, most of them didn't even remember specific details about the course, except the start and finish, and ended their descriptions with a blank—but contented—stare. This self-satisfied, yet almost indescribable, feeling is often the result of an experienced runner running, a feeling often called, because of its similarities to other euphoric experiences, "runner's high."

2   Because this experience is seemingly impossible to define, perhaps a description of what runner's high is not might, by contrast, lead to

---

a better understanding of what it is. I clearly remember—about five years ago—when I first took up running. My first day, I donned my tennis shorts, ragged T-shirt, and white discount-store tennis shoes somewhat ashamedly, knowing that they were symbolic of my novice status. I plodded around my block—just over a half mile—in a little more than four minutes, feeling and regretting every painful step. My shins and thighs revolted at every jarring move, and my lungs wheezed uncontrollably, gasping for air, yet denied that basic necessity. Worst of all, I was conscious of every aspect of my existence—from the swinging of my arms to the slap of my feet on the road, and from the sweat dripping into my eyes and ears and mouth, to the frantic inhaling and exhaling of my lungs. I kept my eyes carefully peeled on the horizon or the next turn in the road, judging how far away it was, how long it would take me to get there, and how much torture was left before I reached home. These first few runs were, of course, the worst—as far from any euphoria or "high" as possible. They did, however, slowly become easier as my body became accustomed to running.

Definition by negation, contrast

3   After a few months, in fact, I felt serious enough about this new pursuit to invest in a pair of real running shoes and shorts. Admittedly, these changes added to the comfort of my endeavor, but it wasn't until two full years later that the biggest change occurred—and I experienced my first real "high." It was a fall day. The air was a cool sixty-five degrees, the sun was shining intently, the sky was a clear, crisp blue, and a few dead leaves were scattered across the browning lawn. I stepped out onto the road and headed north towards a nearby park for my routine jog. The next thing I remember, however, was not my run through the park, but rather my return, some forty-two minutes and six miles later, to my house. I woke, as if out of a dream, just as I slowed to a walk, cooling down from my run. The only memory I had of my

Personal example

Effects of
the "high"

run was a feeling of floating on air—as if my real self were somewhere above and detached from my body, looking down on my physical self as it went through its blind paces. At first, I felt scared—what if I had run out in front of a car? Would I have even known it? I felt as if I had been asleep or out of control, that my brain had, in some real sense, been turned off.

4   Now, after five years of running and hundreds of such mystical experiences, I realize that I had never lost control while in this euphoric state—and that my brain hadn't been turned off, or, at least, not completely. But what does happen is hard to prove. George Sheehan, in a column for *Runner's World*, suggests that "altered states," such as runner's high, result from the loss of conscious control, from the temporary cessation of left-brain messages and the dominance of right-brain activity (the left hemisphere being the seat of reason and rationality; the right, of emotions and inherited archetypal feelings) (14). Another explanation comes from Dr. Jerry Lynch, who argues, in his book *The Total Runner*, that the "high" results from the secretion of natural opiates, called beta endorphins, in the brain (213). My own explanation draws on both these medical explanations and is perhaps slightly more mystical. It's just possible that indeed natural opiates do go to work and consequently our brains lose track of the ins and outs of everyday activities—of jobs and classes and responsibilities. And because of this relaxed, drugged state, we are able to reach down into something more fundamental, something that ties us not only to each other but to all creation, here and gone. We rejoin nature, rediscovering the thread that links us to the universe.

Possible causes
of the feeling:
Two authorities

The writer's
explanation

5   My explanation is, of course, unscientific and therefore suspect. But I found myself, that day of the Mile-Hi Ten K run, eagerly trying to discuss my experience with the other runners: I wanted desperately to discover where I had been and what I had been doing during the race for which

I received my first trophy. I didn't discover the answer from my fellow runners that day, but it didn't matter. I'm still running and still feeling the glow—whatever it is.

Conclusion: An incomplete understanding doesn't hamper enjoyment

Works Cited*

Lynch, Jerry. *The Total Runner: A Complete Mind-Body Guide to Optimal Performance*. Englewood Cliffs: Prentice, 1987. Print.

Sheehan, George. "Altered States." *Runner's World* Aug. 1988: 14. Print.

Professional Essay**

The Munchausen Mystery

Don R. Lipsitt

As a clinical professor of psychiatry at Harvard Medical School, Don R. Lipsitt has written over one hundred articles on mental health and coedited four books, including *Hypochondriasis: Modern Perspectives on an Ancient Malady* (2001) and the *Handbook of Studies on General Hospital Psychiatry* (1991). In 2001 he was awarded a Lifetime Achievement Award from the Association of Academic Psychiatry. He published this article in *Psychology Today* in 1983.

1   In Thomas Mann's *Confessions of Felix Krull, Confidence Man*, young Felix fabricates an illness and convinces both his mother and the family doctor that he is sick. Felix describes the intense pleasure that his performance brings him. "I was delirious with the alternate tension and relaxation necessary to give reality, in my own eyes and others, to a condition that did not exist."

2   I estimate that in any given year in the United States, every general hospital with 100 or more beds admits an average of two patients who deliberately mimic symptoms of disease so convincingly that they deceive reasonably competent physicians. The patients' ages range from 11 to 60, but most are men in their 20s and 30s. Often these strange imposters wander from hospital to hospital, but even if we count only one patient per hospital, we are left with the staggering figure of approximately 4,000 people each year who devote their energies to fooling medical practitioners. If each incurs a cost of $1,000 to $10,000—bills that are not unusual, and that are rarely paid—the annual drain on health services alone is between $4 million and $40 million.

---

*Editor's note: In a formal research paper, the "Works Cited" list appears on a separate page.

** ◆ To help you read this essay analytically, review pages 180–182.

3   What do these people hope to gain? Nothing more, experience and research suggest, than the opportunity to assume the role of patient—in some cases, all the way to the operating table.

4   Unlike hypochondriacs, who really believe that they are ill, these people intentionally use varied and often sophisticated deceptions to duplicate medical problems. These deceptions include: blood "spit up" from a rubber pouch concealed in the mouth; genital bleeding deliberately caused by sharp objects; hypoglycemia (low blood sugar) induced by insulin injections; and skin infections or abscesses caused by injecting oneself with feces, sputum, or laboratory cultures of bacteria. A patient who called himself "the Duncan Hines of American hospitals" logged about 400 admissions in 25 years. Another patient, dubbed the "Indiana cyclone," was hospitalized in at least 12 states and two countries. The dramatic fabrication and extensive wandering often observed in such individuals prompted the late British physician Richard Asher in 1951 to label their "condition" the Munchausen Syndrome, after a flamboyant 18th-century teller of tall tales fictionalized in *The Adventures of Baron von Munchausen*, by Rudolph Erich Raspe. But as Asher himself came to realize, the name is somewhat misleading. While stories of the Baron's escapades are always palpably absurd, the accounts of patients whose condition bears his name are generally quite feasible. "Indeed," says Asher, "it is the credibility of their stories that makes these patients such a perpetual and tedious problem."

5   For obvious reasons, Munchausen patients have been difficult to study—they usually flee once their fictions are exposed. But research to this point provides a minimal portrait. In addition to being primarily men in their 20s and 30s, most have high IQs (as their imaginative inventions indicate), often abuse but are not necessarily addicted to drugs, come from a background in which a doctor was an important figure, are employed in health care, and are productive citizens between episodes.

6   What produces their medical madness? There are three main explanations:

7   The psychoanalytic interpretation draws attention to the unconscious. The Munchausen patient, by feigning illness, presents himself simultaneously as victim and victimizer, and compulsively re-enacts unresolved conflicts: The weak child/patient is challenging and even defying the strong father/surgeon. Paradoxically, the weak patient controls the surgeon/parent—and risks death!—by "making" the doctor perform needless surgery. The psychoanalytic view also sees in the syndrome an attempt to continue into adulthood the game of "doctor," which characterizes a phase of childhood development.

8   A second explanation locates the source of Munchausen behavior in a personality trait known as borderline character disorder. According to Otto Kernberg, a psychoanalyst at Cornell who has most fully researched this trait, the core problems are untamed (often unconscious) rage and chronic feelings of boredom, two emotions that work against each other. The Munchausen character, for example, presents himself as a "sick" patient, a condition that should appeal to a dedicated physician—yet no accepting relationship can grow between a deceptive patient and a suspecting physician who is alternately idealized and despised.

9   The third explanation looks to excessive stress as the trigger that starts Munchausen patients on their medical odyssey. Many of them began their "wandering" and symptom mimicry in response to cumulative major disappointments, losses, or damage to self-image. One patient first sought surgery for questionable persistent stomach pains after being jilted by a medical-student lover, beginning a long string of lies and hospitalizations.

10   We are beginning to identify the reasons for the behavior of Munchausen patients, but we are still far from knowing how to free them of their remarkably creative compulsion for self-destructive behavior.

Questions on Content, Structure, and Style

1. Why does Lipsitt begin his essay with reference to Thomas Mann's character in *Confessions of Felix Krull, Confidence Man*?

2. What effect does the essay's title have on readers? Why didn't Lipsitt simply call this essay "Munchausen Syndrome"?

3. Why does Lipsitt feel this syndrome is important to understand? How does this problem affect the health-care system?

4. Why explain the origin of the syndrome's name?

5. Why does Lipsitt use specific examples of "deceptions" to develop his extended definition?

6. Similarly, why does Lipsitt offer examples of actual patients? Would additional examples be helpful?

7. How does Lipsitt use contrast as a technique of definition in paragraph 4?

8. What other strategy of definition does Lipsitt employ in paragraphs 6–9? Why might readers interested in understanding this syndrome want such discussion?

9. Evaluate the essay's conclusion. Is it an effective choice for this essay?

10. After reading Lipsitt's descriptive details, examples, and analysis, do you feel you now have a general understanding of a new term? If the writer were to expand his definition, what might he add to make your understanding even more complete? More statistics? Case studies? Testimony from doctors or patients themselves?

Suggestions for Writing

Try using Don Lipsitt's "The Munchausen Mystery" as a stepping-stone to your essay. Select a puzzling or "mysterious" subject from a field of study (e.g., black holes in space) or from an interest you have explored (or would like to explore). Write an extended definition, as Lipsitt did, that explains this mystery for your readers. As appropriate, include information about its characteristics, parts, history, possible causes, effects, solutions, benefits, or dangers. Or investigate a well-known mystery, such as Stonehenge, the Bermuda Triangle, the Nazca path drawings, the Marfa lights, King Tut's "curse," Bigfoot, the Easter Island statues, or perhaps even a famous local ghost. Remember that your essay should offer in-depth explanation, not just general description.

Vocabulary

fabricates (1)   sputum (4)   psychoanalytic (7)
mimic (2)   palpably (4)   paradoxically (7)
incurs (2)   feasible (4)   odyssey (9)
hypochondriacs (4)

© Ryan McVay/Photodisc/
Getty Images

A Revision Worksheet

As you write your rough drafts, consult Chapter 5 for guidance through the revision process. In addition, here are a few questions to ask yourself as you revise your extended-definition essay:

1. Is the subject narrowed to manageable size, and is the purpose of the definition clear to the readers?

2. If the definition is objective, is the language as neutral as possible?

3. If the definition is subjective, is the point of view obvious to the readers?

4. Are all the words and parts of the definition itself clear to the essay's particular audience?

5. Are there enough explanatory methods (examples, descriptions, history, causes, effects, etc.) used to make the definition clear and informative?

6. Have the various methods been organized and ordered in an effective way?

7. Does the essay contain enough specific details to make the definition clear and distinct rather than vague or circular? Where could additional details be added?

Collaborative Activity: After you've revised your essay extensively, exchange rough drafts with a classmate and answer these questions for each other, making specific suggestions for improvement wherever appropriate. (◆ For advice on productive participation in classroom workshops, see pages 115–120.)

Reviewing Your Progress

After you have completed your essay developed by definition, take a moment to measure your progress as a writer by responding to the following questions. Such analysis will help you to recognize growth in your writing skills and may enable you to identify areas that are still problematic.

1. What do you like best about your essay? Why?

2. After considering the various methods of definition you used in your essay, which one do you think offered the clearest or most persuasive explanation of your topic? Why was that particular technique effective in this essay?

3. What part of your essay gave you the most trouble? How did you overcome the problem?

4. If you had more time to work on this essay, what would receive additional attention? Why?

5. What did you learn about your topic from writing this essay? About yourself as a writer?

Strategy Five: Development by Division and Classification

To make large or complex subjects easier to comprehend, we frequently apply the principles of *division* or *classification*.

Division

Division is the act of separating something into its component parts so that it may be better understood or used by the reader. For example, consider a complex subject such as the national budget. Perhaps you have seen a picture on television or in the newspaper of the budget represented by a circle or a pie that has been divided into parts and labeled: a certain percentage or "slice" of the budget designated for military spending, another slice for social services, another for education, and so on. By studying the budget after it has been divided into its parts, taxpayers may have a better sense of how their money is being spent.

As a student, you see division in action in many of your college courses. A literature teacher, for instance, might approach a particular drama by dividing its plot into stages such as exposition, rising action, climax, falling action, and dénouement. Or your chemistry lab instructor may ask you to break down a substance into its components to learn how the parts interact to form the chemical compound. Even this textbook is divided into chapters to make it easier for you to use. When you think of *division*, then, think of dividing, separating, or breaking down one subject (often a large or complex or unfamiliar one) into its parts to help people understand it more easily.

Classification

While the principle of division calls for separating one thing into its parts, *classification* systematically groups a number of things into categories to make the information easier to grasp. Without some sort of imposed system of order, a body of information can be a jumble of facts and figures. For example, at some point you've probably turned to the classified ads in the newspaper; if the ads were not classified into categories such as "houses to rent," "cars for sale," and "help wanted," you would have to search through countless ads to find the service or item you needed.

Classification occurs everywhere around you. As a student, you may be classified as a freshman, sophomore, junior, or senior; you may also be classified by your major. If you vote, you may be categorized as a Democrat, Republican, Independent, Socialist, or something else; if you attend religious services, you may be classified as Baptist, Methodist, Catholic, Jewish, and so on. The books you buy may be grouped and shelved by the bookstore into "mysteries," "Westerns," "biographies," "science fiction," and other categories; the movies you see have already been typed as "G," "PG," "PG-13," "R," or "NC-17." Professionals classify almost every kind of knowledge: ornithologists classify birds; etymologists classify words by origins; botanists classify plants; zoologists classify animals. Remember that *classification* differs from division in that it sorts and organizes *many* things into appropriate groups, types, kinds, or categories. *Division* begins with *one* thing and separates it into its parts.

Developing Your Essay

A classification or division paper is generally easy to develop. Each part or category is identified and described in a major part of the body of the essay. Frequently, one body paragraph will be devoted to each category. Here are three additional hints for writing your essay:

Select one principle of classification or division and stick to it. If you are classifying students by major, for instance, don't suddenly switch to classification by college: French, economics, psychology, *arts and sciences*, math, and chemistry. A similar error occurs in this classification of dogs by breeds because it includes a physical characteristic: spaniels, terriers, *long-haired*, hounds, and retrievers. Decide on what basis of division you will classify or divide your subject and then be consistent throughout your essay.

Make the purpose of your division or classification clear to your audience. Don't just announce that "There are four kinds of 'X'" or that "'Z' has three important parts." Why does your particular audience need this information? Consider these sample thesis statements:

- By recognizing the three kinds of poisonous snakes in this area, campers and backpackers may be able to take the proper medical steps if they are bitten.
- Knowing the four types of spinning reels will help those new to mullet fishing purchase the equipment best suited to their needs.
- Although karate has become a popular form of exercise as well as of self-defense, few people know what the five levels of achievement—or "belts" as they are called—actually stand for.

Organize your material for a particular purpose and then explain to your readers what that purpose is.

Account for all the parts in your division or classification. Don't, for instance, claim to classify all the evergreen trees native to your hometown and then leave out one or more species. For a short essay, narrow your ruling principle rather than omit categories. You couldn't, for instance, classify all the architectural styles in the United States in a short paper, but you might discuss the major styles on your campus. In the same manner, the enormous task of classifying all types of mental illness might be narrowed to the most common forms of childhood schizophrenia. However you narrow your topic, remember that in a formal classification, all the parts must be accounted for.

Like most rules, the preceding one has an exception. If your instructor permits, you can also write a satirical or humorous classification. In this sort of essay, you make up your own categories as well as your thesis. One writer, for example, recently wrote about the kinds of moviegoers who spoil the show for everyone else, such as "the babbling idiot," "the laughing hyena," and "the wandering dawdler." Another female student described blind dates to avoid, including "Mr. Neanderthal," "Timothy Timid," "Red, the Raging Rebel," and "Frat-Rat Freddie," among others. Still another student classified the various kinds of people who frequent the school library at 2 A.M. In this kind of informal essay, in which you're making a humorous or satirical point about your subject, your classification should be more than random silliness. Effective humor should ultimately make good sense, not nonsense.

Problems to Avoid

Avoid underdeveloped categories. A classification or division essay is not a mechanical list; each category should contain enough specific details to make it clearly recognizable and interesting. To present each category or part, you may draw on the methods of development you already know, such as example, comparison and contrast, and definition. Try to use the same techniques in each category so that no one category or part of your essay seems underdeveloped or unclear.

Avoid indistinct categories. Each category should be a separate unit; there should be no overlap among categories. For example, in a classification of shirts by fabric, the inclusion of flannel with silk, nylon, and cotton is an overlap because flannel is a kind of cotton. Similarly, in a classification of soft drinks by flavor, to include sugar-free with cola, root beer, orange, grape, and so on, is misleading because sugar-free drinks come in many different flavors. In other words, make each category unique.

Avoid too few or too many categories. A classification essay should have at least three categories, avoiding the either-or dichotomy. On the other hand, too many categories give a short essay the appearance of a list rather than a discussion. Whatever the number, don't forget to use transitional devices for easy movement from category to category.

ESSAY TOPICS

Narrow and focus your subject by selecting an appropriate principle of division or classification. Some of the following suggestions may be appropriate for humorous essays ("The Three Best Breeds of Cats for Antisocial People"). ◆ For additional ideas, see the "Suggestions for Writing" section following the professional essays (pages 270 and 272).

1. Friends or relatives

2. First-year college students

3. Heroes in a particular field

4. Summer or part-time jobs

5. Attitudes toward a current controversy

6. Kinds of popular tattoos

7. Specializations in your field of study

continued on next page

1. A pet peeve or bad habit
2. A change of mind about some important issue or belief
3. An accident, illness, or misadventure
4. A family story/tradition or an influential book
5. A trip or an experience in a different country or culture
6. The best gift you ever received or ownership of a particular possession
7. A radical change in your appearance
8. A hobby, sport, or class
9. The best (or worst) advice you ever gave, followed, or rejected
10. An important decision or choice
11. An act of heroism or sacrifice
12. An important idea, event, or discovery in your field of study
13. A superstition or irrational fear
14. A currently popular kind of entertainment (e.g., reality TV, superhero movies, Sudoku, graphic novels)
15. A disappointment or a success
16. Racism or sexism or some other kind of discrimination or prejudice
17. An influential person (teacher, coach, friend, etc.)
18. A political action (campus, local, state, national), historical event, or social movement
19. A popular cultural trend (tattooing, piercing, clothing or hair styles)

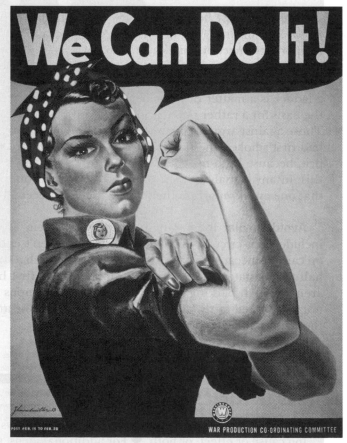

The poster *Rosie the Riveter*, by graphic artist J. Howard Miller, was created in 1943 as part of a government campaign to encourage women to enter the factory workforce during World War II.

© CORBIS

20. A piece of visual art promoting a particular cause or point of view (Consider, for example, the famous image of Rosie the Riveter, who first appeared on a poster sponsored by the War Production Committee during World War II [see previous page]. Considering the gender roles of the time, why was such a poster needed? What effects was this image designed to have on both its male and female viewers? What specific elements in this picture produce these effects? What effect does this image have on viewers today? If you prefer, select another visual image reproduced in this text, such as *Migrant Mother* [page 339] or *The Third of May, 1808* [page 488], and analyze its major effects on the viewer. A list of all artworks in this text follows the Table of Contents. ◆ For help writing about art, see Chapter 17.)

A Topic Proposal for Your Essay

Selecting the right subject matter is important to every writer. To help you clarify your ideas and strengthen your commitment to your topic, here is a proposal sheet that asks you to describe some of your preliminary ideas about your subject before you begin drafting. Although your ideas may change as you write (they will almost certainly become more refined), thinking through your choice of topic now may help you avoid several false starts.

1. What is the subject and purpose of your causal analysis essay? Is this subject appropriately narrowed and focused for a discussion of major causes or effects?

2. Will you develop your essay to emphasize primarily the effects or the causes of your topic? Or is a causal chain the most appropriate method of development?

3. Why are you interested in this topic? Do you have a personal or professional connection to the subject? State at least one reason for your choice of topic.

4. Is this a significant topic of interest to others? Why? Who specifically might find it interesting, informative, or entertaining?

5. List at least two major causes or effects that you might develop in the discussion of your topic.

6. What difficulties, if any, might arise during your drafting on this topic? For example, how might you convince a skeptical reader that your causal relationship is not merely a temporal one?

Sample Student Essay

In the following essay, a student explains why working in a local motel damaged her self-esteem, despite her attempts to do a good job. Note that the writer uses many vivid examples and specific details to show the reader how she was treated and, consequently, how such treatment made her feel.

It's Simply Not Worth It

Introduction:
Her job as a
motel maid

1   It's hard to find a job these days, and with our county's unemployment rate reaching as high as 8 percent, most people feel obligated to "take what they can get." But after working as a maid at a local motel for almost a year and a half, I decided no job is worth keeping if it causes a person to doubt his or her worth. My hard work rarely received recognition or appreciation, I was underpaid, and I was required to perform some of the most disgusting cleaning tasks imaginable. These factors caused me to devalue myself as a person and ultimately motivated me to return to school in hope of regaining my self-respect.

Thesis: No
appreciation,
low pay,
disgusting tasks
(causes) produce
damaged
self-esteem and
action (effects)

Cause one: Lack
of appreciation

2   It may be obvious to say, but I believe that when a maid's hours of meticulous cleaning are met only with harsh words and complaints, she begins to lose her sense of self-esteem. I recall the care I took in making the motel's beds, imagining them as globs of clay and molding them into impeccable pieces of art. I would teeter from one side of a bed to the other, over and over again, until I smoothed out every intruding wrinkle or tuck. And the mirrors—I would vigorously massage the glass, erasing any toothpaste splotches or oil smudges that might draw my customer's disapproval. I would scrutinize the mirror first from the left side, then I'd move to the right side, once more to the left until every possible angle ensured an unclouded reflection. And so my efforts went, room after room. But, without fail, each day more than one customer would approach me, not with praise for my tidy beds or spotless mirrors, but with nitpicking complaints that undermined my efforts: "Young lady, I just checked into room 143 and it only has one ashtray. Surely for $69.95 a night you people can afford more ashtrays in the rooms."

3   If it wasn't a guest complaining about ashtrays, it was an impatient customer demanding extra towels or a fussy stay-over

insisting his room be cleaned by the time he returned from breakfast at 8:00 A.M. "Can't you come to work early to do it?" he would urge thoughtlessly. Day after day, my spotless rooms went unnoticed, with no spoken rewards for my efforts from either guests or management. Eventually, the ruthless complaints and thankless work began wearing me down. In my mind, I became a servant undeserving of gratitude.

4 The lack of spoken rewards was compounded by the lack of financial rewards. The $7.30/hour appraisal of my worth was simply not enough to support my financial needs or my self-esteem. The measly $3.65 I earned for cleaning one room took a lot of rooms to add up, and by the end of the month I was barely able to pay my bills and buy some food. (My mainstay became ninety-two cent, generic macaroni and cheese dinners.) Because the flow of travelers kept the motel full for only a few months of the year, during some weeks I could only work half time, making a mere $584.00 a month. As a result, one month I was forced to request an extension on my rent payment. Unsympathetically, my landlord threatened to evict me if I didn't pay. Embarrassed, yet desperate, I went to a friend and borrowed money. I felt uneasy and awkward and regretted having to beg a friend for money. I felt like a mooch and a bum; I felt degraded. And the constant reminder from management that there were hundreds of people standing in unemployment lines who would be more than willing to work for minimum wage only aided in demeaning me further.

Cause two: Low pay

5 In addition to the thankless work and the inadequate salary, I was required to clean some of the most sickening messes. Frequently, conventions for high school clubs booked the motel. Once I opened the door of a conventioneer's room one morning and almost gagged at the odor. I immediately beheld a trail of vomit that began at the bedside and ended just short of the bathroom door. At that moment

Cause three: Repulsive duties

I cursed the inventor of shag carpet, for I knew it would take hours to comb this mess out of the fibers. On another day I spent thirty minutes dislodging the bed linen from the toilet where it had been stuffed. And I spent what seemed like hours removing from one of my spotless mirrors the lipstick-drawn message that read, "Yorktown Tigers are number one." But these inconsiderate acts were relaying another message, a message I took personally: "Lady, you're not worth the consideration—you're a maid and you're not worth respecting."

Conclusion: Review of the problem and a brief explanation of the solution she chose

6   I've never been afraid to work hard or do jobs that weren't particularly "fun." But the line must be drawn when a person's view of herself becomes clouded with feelings of worthlessness. The thankless efforts, the inadequate wage, and the disgusting work were just parts of a total message that degraded my character and caused me to question my worth. Therefore, I felt compelled to leave this demeaning job in search of a way to rebuild my self-confidence. Returning to school has done just that for me. As my teachers and fellow students take time to listen to my ideas and compliment my responses, I feel once again like a vital, valued, and worthwhile person. I feel human once more.

Professional Essay*

Some Lessons from the Assembly Line

Andrew Braaksma

Andrew Braaksma, from Portage, Michigan, was a junior at the University of Michigan studying history and French in the College of Literature, Science, and Arts when he won first place in a "Back to School" essay contest sponsored by *Newsweek* magazine. The award-winning essay was then published in *Newsweek*'s "My Turn" column on September 12, 2005.

1   Last June, as I stood behind the bright orange guard door of the machine, listening to the crackling hiss of the automatic welders, I thought about how different my life had been just a few weeks earlier. Then, I was writing an essay about French

* ◆ To help you read this essay analytically, review pages 180–182.

literature to complete my last exam of the spring semester at college. Now I stood in an automotive plant in southwest Michigan, making subassemblies for a car manufacturer.

2 I have worked as a temp in the factories surrounding my hometown every summer since I graduated from high school, but making the transition between school and full-time blue-collar work during the break never gets any easier. For a student like me who considers any class before noon to be uncivilized, getting to a factory by 6 o'clock each morning, where rows of hulking, spark-showering machines have replaced the lush campus and cavernous lecture halls of college life, is torture. There my time is spent stamping, cutting, welding, moving or assembling parts, the rigid work schedules and quotas of the plant making days spent studying and watching "SportsCenter" seem like a million years ago.

3 I chose to do this work, rather than bus tables or fold sweatshirts at the Gap, for the overtime pay and because living at home is infinitely cheaper than living on campus for the summer. My friends who take easier, part-time jobs never seem to understand why I'm so relieved to be back at school in the fall or that my summer vacation has been anything but a vacation.

4 There are few things as cocksure as a college student who has never been out in the real world, and people my age always seem to overestimate the value of their time and knowledge. After a particularly exhausting string of 12-hour days at a plastics factory, I remember being shocked at how small my check seemed. I couldn't believe how little I was taking home after all the hours I spent on the sweltering production floor. And all the classes in the world could not have prepared me for my battles with the machine I ran in the plant, which would jam whenever I absent-mindedly put in a part backward or upside down. As frustrating as the work can be, the most stressful thing about blue-collar life is knowing your job could disappear overnight. Issues like downsizing and overseas relocation had always seemed distant to me until my co-workers at one factory told me that the unit I was working in would be shut down within six months and moved to Mexico, where people would work for 60 cents an hour.

5 Factory life has shown me what my future might have been like had I never gone to college in the first place. For me, and probably many of my fellow students, higher education always seemed like a foregone conclusion: I never questioned if I was going to college, just where. No other options ever occurred to me. After working 12-hour shifts in a factory, the other options have become brutally clear. When I'm back at the university, skipping classes and turning in lazy rewrites seems like a cop-out after seeing what I would be doing without school. All the advice and public-service announcements about the value of an education that used to sound trite now ring true.

6 These lessons I am learning, however valuable, are always tinged with a sense of guilt. Many people pass their lives in the places I briefly work, spending 30 years where I spend only two months at a time. When fall comes around, I get to go back to a sunny and beautiful campus, while work in the factories continues. At times I feel almost voyeuristic, like a tourist dropping in where other people make their livelihoods. My lessons about education are learned at the expense of those who weren't fortunate enough to receive one. "This job pays well, but it's hell on the body," said one co-worker. "Study hard and keep reading," she added, nodding at

the copy of Jack Kerouac's *On the Road** I had wedged into the space next to my machine so I could read discreetly when the line went down.

7   My experience will stay with me long after I head back to school and spend my wages on books and beer. The things that factory work has taught me—how lucky I am to get an education, how to work hard, how easy it is to lose that work once you have it—are by no means earth-shattering. Everyone has to come to grips with them at some point. How and when I learned these lessons, however, has inspired me to make the most of my college years before I enter the real world for good. Until then, the summer months I spend in the factories will be long, tiring and every bit as educational as a French-lit class.

Questions on Content, Structure, and Style

1. What cause-effect relationship is presented in this essay? Does this essay focus primarily on causes or effects?

2. What are some of the important lessons Braaksma has learned? Learning these lessons at this point in his life inspired Braaksma in what new way?

3. What strategy does Braaksma use to begin his essay, and why? How is this strategy continued throughout the essay?

4. In paragraph 2, what descriptive details and verbs are particularly effective in characterizing the work that Braaksma did at the factories?

5. What specific examples does Braaksma include to help the reader understand his experiences and reactions?

6. Why does Braaksma often characterize himself and other college students in less than positive ways? Is such a characterization likely to appeal to or offend his readers?

7. Why does Braaksma mention that his lessons are "tinged with a sense of guilt"?

8. What does the use of dialogue in paragraph 6 add to this essay?

9. Evaluate Braaksma's conclusion. Why does he refer to his French-lit class?

10. Overall, how effective is Braaksma's essay? Did his causal analysis change or reconfirm any of your beliefs about work or school?

Suggestions for Writing

Use Andrew Braaksma's essay "Some Lessons from the Assembly Line" as a stepping-stone to your essay. If you have held full- or part-time jobs, think of how one affected you in specific ways that led to new insight or encouraged you to take new action. Perhaps your work changed your mind about your major or future profession, or perhaps your job helped you decide to begin or return to school (a topic explored in the student essay on pages 280–282). Or, if you prefer, consider any volunteer work you've done that made a difference in your life or in the lives of others. To help your readers understand the cause-effect relationship you're presenting, be sure to include enough logical explanation and vivid details to show clearly how "X" caused "Y."

---

*American novelist and poet Jack Kerouac was one of the 1950s "Beat Generation" writers.

Vocabulary

blue-collar (2)	cocksure (4)	voyeuristic (6)
lush (2)	downsizing (4)	discreetly (6)
cavernous (2)	tinged (6)	

© Ryan McVay/Photodisc/ Getty Images

A Revision Worksheet

As you write your rough drafts, consult Chapter 5 for guidance through the revision process. In addition, here are a few questions to ask yourself as you revise your causal analysis essay:

1. Is the thesis limited to a reasonable claim that can be supported in the essay?

2. Is the organization clear and consistent so that the reader can understand the purpose of the analysis?

3. Does the essay focus on the most important causes or effects, or both?

4. If the essay has a narrative form, is each step in the chain reaction clearly connected to the next?

5. Does the essay convincingly show the reader *how* or *why* relationships between the causes and effects exist, instead of merely naming and describing them?

6. Does the essay provide enough evidence to show the connections between causes and effects? Where could additional details be added to make the relationships clearer?

7. Has the essay avoided the problems of oversimplification, circular logic, and the *post hoc* fallacy?

Collaborative Activity: After you've revised your essay extensively, exchange rough drafts with a classmate and answer these questions for each other, making specific suggestions for improvement wherever appropriate. (◆ For advice on productive participation in classroom workshops, see pages 115–120.)

Reviewing Your Progress

After you have completed your essay developed by causal analysis, take a moment to measure your progress as a writer by responding to the following questions. Such analysis will help you to recognize growth in your writing skills and may enable you to identify areas that are still problematic.

1. What do you like best about your essay? Why?

2. After considering your essay's presentation of the major causes or effects, which part of your analysis do you think readers will find the most convincing? Why?

3. What part of your essay gave you the most trouble? How did you overcome the problem?

4. If you had more time to work on this essay, what would receive additional attention? Why?

5. What did you learn about your topic from writing this essay? About yourself as a writer?

CHAPTER 10

Argumentation

Almost without exception, each of us, every day, argues for or against something with somebody. The discussions may be short and friendly ("Let's go to this restaurant rather than that one") or long and complex ("Mandatory motorcycle helmets are an intrusion on civil rights"). Because we do argue our viewpoints so often, most of us realized long ago that shifting into high whine did not always get us what we wanted. On the contrary, we've learned that we usually have a much better chance at winning a dispute or having our plan adopted or changing someone's mind if we present our side of an issue in a calm, logical fashion, giving sound reasons for our position. This approach is just what a good argumentative essay does: it presents logical reasoning and solid evidence that will persuade your readers to accept your point of view.

Some argumentative essays declare the best solution to a problem ("Raising the drinking age will decrease traffic accidents"); others argue a certain way of looking at an issue ("Beauty pageants degrade women"); still others may urge adoption of a specific proposal or plan of action ("Voters should pass ordinance 10 to fund the new ice rink"). Whatever your exact purpose, your argumentative essay should be composed of a clear thesis and body paragraphs that offer enough sensible reasons and persuasive evidence to convince your readers to agree with you.

Developing Your Essay

Here are some suggestions for developing and organizing an effective argumentative essay:

Choose an appropriate topic. Selecting a good topic for any essay is important. Choosing a focused, appropriate topic for your argument essay will save you enormous time and energy even before you begin prewriting. Some subjects are simply too large and complex to be adequately treated in a three-to-five-page argumentative essay; selecting such a subject might produce a rough draft of generalities that will not be persuasive. If you have an interest in a subject that is too general or complex for the length of your assignment, try to find a more focused, specific issue within it to argue. For example, the large, controversial (and rather overdone) subject "capital punishment" might be narrowed and focused to a paper advocating time limits for the death-row appeal process or required use of DNA testing. A general opinion on "unfair college grading" might become a more interesting persuasive essay in which the writer takes a stand on the use of pluses and minuses (A–, B+, B–, etc.) on transcript grades. Your general annoyance with smokers might move from "All smoking should be outlawed forever" to an essay focused on the controversial smoking bans in open-air sports stadiums. The complex subject of gun control might be narrowed into an essay arguing support for or against new laws regarding concealed weapons on campuses or in national parks. In other words, while we certainly do debate large issues in our lives, in a short piece of writing it may be more effective, and often more interesting, to choose a focused topic that will allow for more depth in the arguments. You must ultimately decide whether your choice of subject is appropriate for your assignment, but taking a close, second look at your choice now may save you frustration later.

Explore the possibilities . . . and your opinions. Perhaps you have an interesting subject in mind for your argumentative essay, but you don't as yet have a definite opinion on the controversy. Use this opportunity to explore the subject! Do some research, talk to appropriate people, investigate the issues. By discovering your own position, you can address others who may be similarly uncertain about the subject.

Many times, however, you may want to argue for a belief or position you already hold. But before you proceed, take some time to consider the basis of your strong feelings. Not surprisingly, we humans have been known, on various occasions, to spout opinions we can't always effectively support when challenged to do so. Sometimes we hold an opinion simply because on the surface it seems to make good sense to us or because it fits comfortably with our other social, ethical, or political beliefs. Or we may have inherited some of our beliefs from our families or friends, or perhaps we borrowed ideas from well-known people we admire. In some cases, we may have held an opinion for so long that we can't remember why we adopted it in the first place. We may also have a purely sentimental or emotional attachment to some idea or position. Whatever the origins of our beliefs, we need to examine the real reasons for thinking what we do before we can effectively convince others.

If you have a strong opinion you want to write about, try jotting down a list of the reasons or points that support your position. Then study the list—are your points logical and persuasive? Which aren't, and why not? After this bit of prewriting, you may discover that although you believe something strongly, you really don't have the kinds of factual evidence or reasoned arguments you need to support your opinion. In some cases, depending on your topic, you may wish to talk to others who share your position or you may decide to research your subject (◆ for help with research or interviewing, see Chapter 14); in other cases, you may just need to think longer and harder about your topic and your reasons for maintaining your attitude toward it. Keep an open mind; your exploration may lead you to a surprising new position. (Remember the words of humorist F. G. Burgess: "If in the last few years you haven't discarded a major opinion or acquired a new one, check your pulse. You may be dead.") But with or without formal research, the better you know your subject, the more confident you will be about writing your argumentative essay.

Anticipate opposing views. An argument assumes that there is more than one side to an issue. To be convincing, you must be aware of your opposition's views on the subject and then organize your essay to answer or counter those views. If you don't have a good sense of the opposition's arguments, you can't effectively persuade your readers to dismiss their objections and see matters your way. Therefore, before you begin your first rough draft, write down all the opposing views you can think of and an answer to each of them so that you will know your subject thoroughly. If you are unfamiliar with the major objections to your position, now is the time to investigate your subject further. (For the sake of clarity throughout this chapter, your act of responding to those arguments against your position will be called *refuting the opposition*; "to refute" means "to prove false or wrong," and that's what you will try to do to some of the arguments of those who disagree with you.)

Know and remember your audience. Although it's important to think about your readers' needs and expectations whenever you write, it is essential to consider carefully the audience of your argumentative essay both before and as you write your rough drafts. Because you are trying to persuade people to adopt some new point of view or perhaps to take some action, you need to decide what kinds of supporting evidence will be most convincing to your particular readers. Try to analyze your audience by asking yourself a series of questions. What do they already know about your topic? What information or terms do they need to know to understand your point of view? What biases might they already have for or against your position? What special concerns might your readers have that influence their receptiveness? ◆ To be convincing, you should consider these questions and others by carefully reviewing the discussion of audience on pages 19–22 *before* you begin your drafts.

Decide which points of argument to include. Once you have a good sense of your audience, your own position, and your opposition's strongest arguments, try making a Pro-and-Con Sheet to help you sort out which points you will discuss in your essay.

Let's suppose you want to write an editorial on the sale-of-class-notes controversy at your school. Should professional note-takers be allowed to sit in on a course and then sell their notes to class members? After reviewing the evidence on both sides, you have decided to argue that your school should prohibit professional note-taking services from attending large lecture classes and selling notes. To help yourself begin planning your essay, you list all the pro-and-con arguments you can think of concerning the controversy:

My Side: Against the Sale of Class Notes

1. Unfair advantage for some students in some classes
2. Note-taking is a skill students need to develop
3. Rich students can afford and poor can't
4. Prevents students from learning to organize for themselves
5. Encourages class cutting
6. Missing class means no chance to ask questions, participate in discussions
7. Notes taken by others are often inaccurate
8. Some professors don't like strangers in classroom
9. Students need to think for themselves

My Opposition's Side: For the Sale of Class Notes

1. Helps students to get better test, course grades
2. Helps students to learn, organize material
3. Helps if you're sick and can't attend class
4. Shows students good models for taking notes and outlining them
5. Other study guides are on the market, so why not these?
6. Gives starving graduate students jobs
7. No laws against sale of notes, free country

After making your Pro-and-Con Sheet, look over the list and decide which of your strongest points you want to argue in your paper and also which of your opposition's claims you want to refute. At this point you may also see some arguments on your list that might be combined and some that might be deleted because they're irrelevant or unconvincing. (Be careful not to select more arguments or counter-arguments to discuss than the length of your writing assignment will allow. It's far better to present a persuasive analysis of a few points than it is to give an underdeveloped, shallow treatment of a host of reasons.)

Let's say you want to cover the following points in your essay:

- Professional note-taking services keep students from developing their own thinking and organizational skills (combination of 4 and 9)

- Professional note-taking services discourage class attendance and participation (5 and 6)

- Unfair advantages to some students (1 and 3)

Your assignment calls for an essay of 750 to 1,000 words, so you figure you'll only have space to refute your opposition's strongest claim. You decide to refute this claim:

- Helps students to learn and organize material (2)

The next step is to formulate a working thesis. At this stage, you may find it helpful to put your working thesis in an "although-because" statement so you can clearly see both your opposition's arguments and your own. An "although-because" thesis for the note-taking essay might look something like this:

> *Although* some students maintain that using professional note-taking services helps them learn more, such services should be banned from our campus *because* they prevent students from developing their own thinking and organizational skills, they discourage class attendance, and they give unfair advantages to some students.

Frequently, your "although-because" thesis will be too long and awkward to use in the later drafts of your essay. But for now, it can serve as a guide, allowing you to see your overall position before the writing of the first draft begins. (◆ To practice compiling a

Pro-Con Sheet and writing an "although-because" thesis, turn to the exercise on pages 299–300.)

Organize your essay clearly. Although there is no set model of organization for argumentative essays, here are some common patterns that you might use or that you might combine in some effective way.

Important note: For the sake of simplicity, the first two outlines present two of the writer's points and two opposing ideas. Naturally, your essay may contain any number of points and refuted points, depending on the complexity of your subject and the assigned length of your essay.

In Pattern A, you devote the first few body paragraphs to arguing points on your side and then turn to refuting or answering the opposition's claims.

Pattern A: Thesis

Body paragraph 1: you present your first point and its supporting evidence

Body paragraph 2: you present your second point and its supporting evidence

Body paragraph 3: you refute your opposition's first point

Body paragraph 4: you refute your opposition's second point
Conclusion

Sometimes you may wish to clear away the opposition's claims before you present the arguments for your side. To do so, you might select Pattern B:

Pattern B: Thesis

Body paragraph 1: you refute your opposition's first point

Body paragraph 2: you refute your opposition's second point

Body paragraph 3: you present your first point and its supporting evidence

Body paragraph 4: you present your second point and its supporting evidence
Conclusion

In some cases, you may find that the main arguments you want to present are the very same ones that will refute or answer your opposition's primary claims. If so, try Pattern C, which allows each of your argumentative points to refute one of your opposition's claims in the same paragraph:

Pattern C: Thesis

Body paragraph 1: you present your first point and its supporting evidence, which also refutes one of your opposition's claims

Body paragraph 2: you present a second point and its supporting evidence, which also refutes a second opposition claim

Body paragraph 3: you present a third point and its supporting evidence, which also refutes a third opposition claim

Conclusion

Now you might be thinking, "What if my position on a topic as yet has no opposition?" Remember that almost all issues have more than one side, so try to anticipate objections and then answer them. For example, you might first present a thesis that calls for a new traffic signal at a dangerous intersection in your town and then address hypothetical counter-arguments, such as "The City Council may say that a stoplight at Lemay and Columbia will cost too much, but the cost in lives will be much greater" or "Commuters may complain that a traffic light there will slow the continuous flow of north-south traffic, but it is precisely the uninterrupted nature of this road that encourages motorists to speed." By answering hypothetical objections, you impress your readers by showing them you've thought through your position thoroughly before you asked them to consider your point of view.

You might also be thinking, "What if my opposition actually has a valid objection, a legitimate point of criticism? Should I ignore it?" Hoping that an obviously strong opposing point will just go away is like hoping the IRS will cancel income taxes this year—a nice thought but hardly likely. Don't ignore your opposition's good point; instead, acknowledge it, but then go on quickly to show your readers why that reason, though valid, isn't compelling enough by itself to motivate people to adopt your opposition's entire position. Or you might concede that one point while simultaneously showing why your position isn't really in conflict with that criticism, but rather with other, more important, parts of your opponent's viewpoint. By admitting that you see some validity in your opposition's argument, you can again show your readers that you are both fair-minded and informed about all aspects of the controversy.

If you are feeling confident about your ability to organize an argumentative essay, you might try some combination of patterns, if your material allows such a treatment. For example, you might have a strong point to argue, another point that simultaneously answers one of your opposition's strongest claims, and another opposition point you want to refute. Your essay organization might look like this:

Combination: Thesis

Body paragraph 1: a point for your side

Body paragraph 2: one of your points, which also refutes an opposition claim

Body paragraph 3: your refutation of another opposition claim
Conclusion

In other words, you can organize your essay in a variety of ways as long as your paper is logical and clear. Study your Pro-and-Con Sheet and then decide which organization best presents the arguments and counter-arguments you want to include. Try sketching out your essay following each of the patterns; look carefully to see which pattern (or variation of one of the patterns) seems to put forward your particular material most persuasively, with the least repetition or confusion. Sometimes your essay's material will clearly fall into a particular pattern of organization, so your choice will be easy. More often, however, you will have to arrange and rearrange your ideas and counter-arguments until you see the best approach. Don't be discouraged if you decide to change patterns after you've begun a rough draft; what matters is finding the most effective way to persuade the reader to your side.

If no organizational pattern seems to fit at first, ask yourself which of your points or counter-arguments is the strongest or most important. Try putting that point in one of the two most emphatic places: either first or last. Sometimes your most important discussion will lead the way to your other points and, consequently, should be introduced first; perhaps more often, effective writers and speakers build up to their strongest point, presenting it last as the climax of their argument. Again, the choice depends on your material itself, though it's rare that you would want to bury your strongest point in the middle of your essay.

Now let's return to the essay on note-taking first discussed on page 289. After selecting the most important arguments and counter-arguments (page 290), let's say that you decide that your main point concerns the development of students' learning skills. Since your opposition claims the contrary, that their service does promote learning, you see that you can make your main point as you refute theirs. But you also wish to include a couple of other points for your side. After trying several patterns, you decide to put the "thinking skills" rebuttal last for emphasis and present your other points first. Consequently, Pattern A best fits your plan. A sketchy outline might look like this:

- *Revised working thesis and essay map:* **Professional note-taking services should be banned from our campus. Not only do they give some students unfair advantages and discourage class attendance, they prevent students from developing and practicing good learning skills**

- *Body paragraph 1 (a first point for the writer's side):* **Services penalize some students—those who haven't enough money or take other sections or enroll in classes without lectures.**

- *Body paragraph 2 (another point for the writer's side):* **Services encourage cutting class so students miss opportunities to ask questions, participate in discussion, talk to instructor, see visual aids, etc.**

- *Body paragraph 3 (rebuttal of the opposition's strongest claim):* **Services claim they help students learn more, but they don't because they're doing the work students ought to be doing themselves. Students must learn to think and organize for themselves.**

Once you have a general notion of where your essay is going, plan to spend some more time thinking about ways to make each of your points clear, logical, and persuasive to your particular audience. (If you wish to see how one student actually developed an essay based on the preceding outline, turn to the sample student paper on pages 304–306.)

Argue your ideas logically. To convince your readers, you must provide sufficient reasons for your position. You must give more than mere opinion—you must offer logical arguments to back up your assertions. Some of the possible ways of supporting your ideas should already be familiar to you from writing expository essays; listed here are several methods and illustrations:

1. Give examples (real or hypothetical): "Cutting class because you have access to professional notes can be harmful; for instance, you might miss seeing some slides or graphics essential to your understanding of the lecture."

2. Present a comparison or contrast: "In contrast to reading 'canned' notes, outlining your own notes helps you remember the material."

3. Show a cause-and-effect relationship: "Dependence on professional notes may mean that some students will never learn to organize their own responses to classroom discussions."

4. Argue by definition: "Passively reading through professional notes isn't a learning experience in which one's mind is engaged."

The well-thought-out arguments you choose to support your case may be called *logical appeals* because they appeal to, and depend on, your readers' ability to reason and to recognize good sense when they see it. But there is another kind of appeal often used today: the *emotional appeal*.

Emotional appeals are designed to persuade people by playing on their feelings rather than appealing to their intellect. Rather than using thoughtful, logical reasoning to support their claims, writers and speakers using *only* emotional appeals often try to accomplish their goals by distracting or misleading their audiences. Frequently, emotional appeals are characterized by language that plays on people's fears, material desires, prejudices, or sympathies; such language often triggers highly favorable or unfavorable responses to a subject. For instance, emotional appeals are used constantly in advertising, where feel-good images, music, and slogans ("Come to Marlboro Country"; "The Heartbeat of America Is Today's Chevy Truck") are designed to sway potential customers to a product without their thinking about it too much. Some politicians also rely heavily on emotional appeals, often using scare tactics to disguise a situation or to lead people away from questioning the logic of a particular issue.

But in some cases, emotional appeals can be used for legitimate purposes. Good writers should always be aware of their audience's needs, values, and states of mind, and they may be more persuasive on occasion if they can frame their arguments in ways that appeal to both their readers' logic and their emotions. For example, when Martin Luther King, Jr., delivered his famous "I Have a Dream" speech to the crowds gathered in Washington, D.C., in 1963 and described his vision of little children of different races walking hand in hand, being judged not "by the color of their skin but by the content of their character," he certainly spoke with passion that was aimed at the hearts of his listeners. But King was not using an emotional appeal to keep his audience from thinking about his message; on the contrary, he presented powerful emotional images that he hoped would inspire people to act on what they already thought and felt, their deepest convictions about equality and justice.

Appeals to emotions are tricky: you can use them effectively in conjunction with appeals to logic and with solid evidence, but only if you use them ethically. Too many appeals to the emotions are also overwhelming; readers tire quickly from excessive tugs on the heartstrings. To prevent your readers from suspecting deception or feeling manipulated, support your assertions with as many logical arguments as you can muster, and use emotional appeals only when they legitimately advance your cause.

Offer evidence that effectively supports your claims. In addition to presenting thoughtful, logical reasoning, you may wish to incorporate a variety of convincing evidence to persuade your readers to your side. Your essay might profit from including, where appropriate, some of the following kinds of supporting evidence:

- Personal experiences
- The experiences or testimony of others whose opinions are pertinent to the topic
- Factual information you've gathered from research
- Statistics from current, reliable sources
- Hypothetical examples
- Testimony from authorities and experts
- Charts, graphs, or diagrams

You'll need to spend quite a bit of your prewriting time thinking about the best kinds of evidence to support your case. Remember that not all personal experiences or research materials are persuasive. For instance, the experiences we've had (or that our friends have had) may not be representative of a universal experience and consequently may lead to unconvincing generalizations. Even testimony from an authority may not be convincing if the person is not speaking on a topic from his or her field of expertise; famous football players, for instance, don't necessarily know any more about panty hose or soft drinks than anyone else. Always put yourself in the skeptical reader's place and ask, "Does this point convince me? If not, why not?" (◆ For more information on incorporating research material into your essays, see Chapter 14. For more advice on the selection of evidence, see the section on critical thinking in Chapter 5.)

Find the appropriate tone. Sometimes when we argue, it's easy to get carried away. Remember that your goal is to persuade and perhaps change your readers, not alienate them. Instead of laying on insults or sarcasm, present your ideas in a moderate let-us-reason-together spirit. Such a tone will persuade your readers that you are sincere in your attempts to argue as truthfully and fairly as possible. If your readers do not respect you as a reasonable person, they certainly won't be swayed to your side of an issue. Don't preach or pontificate either; no one likes—or respects—a writer with a superior attitude. Write in your natural "voice"; don't adopt a pseudo-intellectual tone. In short, to argue effectively you should sound logical, sincere, and informed. (◆ For additional comments on tone, review pages 156–158.)

Consider using Rogerian techniques, if they are appropriate. In some cases, especially those involving tense situations or highly sensitive issues, you may wish to incorporate some techniques of the noted psychologist Carl Rogers, who developed a procedure for presenting what he called the nonthreatening argument. Rogers believed that people involved in a debate should strive for clear, honest communication so that the problem under discussion could be resolved. Instead of going on the defensive and trying to "win" the argument, each side should try to recognize common ground and then develop a solution that will address the needs of both parties.

A Rogerian argument uses these techniques:

1. A clear, objective statement of the problem or issue
2. A clear, objective summary of the opposition's position that shows you understand its point of view and goals

3. A clear, objective summary of your point of view, stated in nonthreatening language

4. A discussion that emphasizes the beliefs, values, and goals that you and your opposition have in common

5. A description of any of your points that you are willing to concede or compromise

6. An explanation of a plan or proposed solution that meets the needs of both sides

By showing your opposition that you thoroughly understand its position and that you are sincerely trying to effect a solution that is in everyone's—not just your—best interests, you may succeed in some situations that might otherwise be hopeless because of their highly emotional nature. Remember, too, that you can use some of these Rogerian techniques in any kind of argument paper you are writing, if you think they would be effective.

Problems to Avoid

Writers of argumentative essays must appear logical or their readers will reject their point of view. Here is a short list of some of the most common *logical fallacies*—that is, errors in reasoning. Check your rough drafts carefully to avoid these problems.

Students sometimes ask, "If a logical fallacy works, why not use it? Isn't all fair in love, war, and argumentative essays?" The honest answer is maybe. It's quite true that speakers and writers do use faulty logic and irrational emotional appeals to persuade people every day (one needs only to look at television or a newspaper to see example after example). But the cost of the risk is high: if you do try to slide one by your readers and they see through your trick, you will lose your credibility instantly. On the whole, it's far more effective to use logical reasoning and strong evidence to convince your readers to accept your point of view.

Common Logical Fallacies

Hasty generalization: The writer bases the argument on insufficient or unrepresentative evidence. Suppose, for example, you have owned two poodles and they have both bitten you. If you declare that all poodles are vicious dogs, you are making a hasty generalization. There are, of course, thousands of poodles who have not attacked anyone. Similarly, you're in error if you interview only campus athletes and then declare, "University students favor a new stadium." What about the opinions of the students who aren't athletes? In other words, when the generalization is drawn from a sample that is too small or select, your conclusion isn't valid.

Non sequitur **("it doesn't follow"): The writer's conclusion is not necessarily a logical result of the facts.** An example of a *non sequitur* occurs when you conclude, "Professor Smith is a famous chemist, so he will be a brilliant chemistry teacher." As you may have realized by now, the fact that someone knows a subject well does not automatically mean that he or she can communicate the information clearly in a classroom; hence, the conclusion is not necessarily valid.

Begging the question: The writer presents as truth what is not yet proven by the argument. For example, in the statement "All useless laws such as Reform Bill 13 should be repealed," the writer has already pronounced the bill useless without assuming responsibility for proving that accusation. Similarly, the statement "Professor Austin, one of the many instructors on our campus using their classrooms solely for preaching their political ideas, should be fired" begs the question (that is, tries like a beggar to get something for nothing from the reader) because the writer gives no evidence for what must first be argued, not merely asserted—that there are in fact professors on that particular campus using class time solely for spreading their political beliefs.

Red herring: The writer introduces an irrelevant point to divert the readers' attention from the main issue. This term originates from the old tactic used by escaped prisoners of dragging a smoked herring, a strong-smelling fish, across their trail to confuse tracking dogs by making them follow the wrong scent. For example, roommate A might be criticizing roommate B for his repeated failure to do the dishes when it was his turn. To escape facing the charges, roommate B brings up times in the past when the other roommate failed to repay some money he borrowed. Although roommate A may indeed have a problem with remembering his debts, that discussion isn't relevant to the original argument about sharing the responsibility for the dishes. (By the way, you might have run across a well-known newspaper photograph of a California environmentalist group demonstrating for more protection of dolphins, whales, and other marine life; look closely to see, over in the left corner, almost hidden by the host of placards and banners, a fellow slyly holding up a sign that reads "Save the Red Herring!" Now, who says rhetoricians don't have a good sense of humor?)

Post hoc, ergo propter hoc. See page 277.

Argument *ad hominem* ("to the man"): The writer attacks the opponent's character rather than the opponent's argument. The statement "Dr. Bloom can't be a competent marriage counselor because she's been divorced" may not be valid. Bloom's advice to her clients may be excellent regardless of her own marital status.

Faulty use of authority: The writer relies on "authorities" who are not convincing sources. Although someone may be well known in a particular field, he or she may not be qualified to testify in a different area. A baseball player in an ad for laser surgery may stress his need for correct vision, but he may be no more knowledgeable about eye care than anyone else on the street. In other words, name recognition is not enough. For their testimony to count with readers, authorities must have expertise, credentials, or relevant experience in the area under discussion. (◆ See also pages 295, 389–391, and "transfer of virtue" in the discussion of "bandwagon appeal" on page 298.)

Argument *ad populum* ("to the people"): The writer evades the issues by appealing to readers' emotional reactions to certain subjects. For example, instead of arguing the facts of an issue, a writer might play on the readers' negative response to such words as "socialism," "terrorist," or "radical," and their positive response to words like "God," "country," "liberty," or "patriotic." In the statement "If you are a true American, you will vote against the referendum on flag burning," the writer avoids any discussion of the merits or weaknesses of the bill and merely substitutes an emotional appeal. Other popular "virtue words" include "duty," "common sense," "courage," and "healthy." (Advertisers, of course, also play on consumers' emotions by filling their ads with pictures of babies, animals, status objects, and sexually attractive men and women.)

Circular thinking. See page 277.

Either/or: The writer tries to convince readers that there are only two sides to an issue—one right, one wrong. The statement "If you don't go to war against Iceland, you don't love your country" is irrational because it doesn't consider the other possibilities, such as patriotic people's right to oppose war as an expression of love for their country. A classic example of this sort of oversimplification was illustrated in the 1960s bumper sticker that was popular during the debate over the Vietnam War: "America: Love It or Leave It." Obviously, there are other choices ("Change It or Lose It," for instance, to quote another either/or bumper sticker of that era).

Hypostatization: The writer uses an abstract concept as if it were a concrete reality. Always be suspicious of a writer who frequently relies on statements beginning "History has always taught us . . ." or "Science has proven . . ." or "Research shows. . . ." The implication in each case is that history or science (or any other discipline) has only one voice, one opinion. On the contrary, "history" is written by a multitude of historians who hold a variety of opinions; doctors and scientists also frequently disagree. Instead of generalizing about a particular field, quote a respected authority or simply qualify your statement by referring to "many" or "some" scientists, historians, or other professionals.

Bandwagon appeal: The writer tries to validate a point by intimating that "everyone else believes in this." Such a tactic evades discussion of the issue itself. Advertising often uses this technique: "Everyone who demands real taste smokes Phooey cigarettes"; "Discriminating women use Smacky-Mouth lipstick." (The ultimate in "bandwagon" humor may have appeared on a recent Colorado bumper sticker: "Eat lamb—could 1000s of coyotes be wrong?") A variation of the "bandwagon" fallacy is sometimes referred to as "transfer of virtue," the sharing of light from someone else's sparkle. Advertisers often use this technique by paying attractive models or media stars to endorse their product. The underlying premise is this:

> Popular/beautiful/"cool"/rich people use/buy/wear "X"; if you use "X," you too will be popular/beautiful/etc.

Intelligent readers and consumers know, of course, to suspect such doubtful causal relationships.

Straw man: The writer selects the opposition's weakest or most insignificant point to argue against, to divert the readers' attention from the real issues. Instead of addressing the opposition's best arguments and defeating them, the writer "sets up a straw man"—that is, the writer picks out a trivial (or irrelevant) argument against his or her own position and easily knocks it down, just as one might easily push over a figure made of straw. Perhaps the most famous example of the "straw man" occurred in

1952 when, during his vice-presidential campaign, Richard Nixon was accused of misappropriating campaign funds for his personal use. Addressing the nation on television, Nixon described how his six-year-old daughter, Tricia, had received a little cocker spaniel named Checkers from a Texas supporter. Nixon went on about how much his children loved the dog and how, regardless of what anyone thought, by gosh, he was going to keep that cute dog for little Tricia. Of course, no one was asking Nixon to return the dog; they were asking about the $18,000 in missing campaign funds. But Nixon's canine gift was much easier for him to defend, and the "Checkers" speech is now famous as one of the most notorious "straw man" diversions.

Faulty analogy: The writer uses an extended comparison as proof of a point. Look closely at all extended comparisons and metaphors to see if the two things being compared are really similar. For example, in a recent editorial a woman protested new laws requiring parents to use car seats for small children, arguing that if the state could require the seats, they could just as easily require mothers to breast-feed instead of using formula. Are the two situations alike? Car accidents are the leading cause of death of children under four; is formula deadly? Or perhaps you've read that putting teenagers in sex education classes is like taking an alcoholic to a bar. Is it? Is stem cell research the same as Nazi medical experiments, as the leader of a family-outreach group has claimed? If readers don't see a close similarity, the analogy may not be persuasive. Moreover, remember that even though a compelling analogy may suggest similarities, it alone cannot *prove* anything. (◆ For more discussion of analogy, see pages 245–248.)

Quick fix: The writer leans too heavily on catchy phrases or empty slogans. A clever turn of phrase may grab one's attention, but it may lose its persuasiveness when scrutinized closely. For instance, a banner at a recent rally to protest a piece of antigun legislation read, "When guns are outlawed, only outlaws will have guns." Although the sentence had nice balance, it oversimplified the issue. The legislation in question was not trying to outlaw all guns, just the sale of the infamous Saturday Night Specials, most often used in crimes and domestic violence; the sale of guns for sport, such as hunting rifles, would remain legal. Other slogans sound good but are simply irrelevant: a particular soft drink, for example, may be "the real thing," but what drink isn't? Look closely at clever lines substituted for reasoned argument; always demand clear terms and logical explanations.*

PRACTICING WHAT YOU'VE LEARNED

A. Imagine that you are writing an argumentative essay addressing the controversial question "Should home-schooled students be allowed to play on public school athletic teams?" You have investigated the topic and have noted the variety of

continued on next page

© Canstock Images, Inc./ Index Stock Imagery

---

*Sometimes advertisers get more for their slogans than they bargained for. According to one news source, a popular soft-drink company had to spend millions to revise its slogan after introducing its product into parts of China. Apparently the slogan "Come alive! Join the Blah-Blah-Cola Generation!" translated into some dialects as "Blah-Blah Cola Brings Your Ancestors Back from the Dead!"

opinions listed here. Arrange the statements into two lists: a "Pro" list (those statements that argue for allowing home schoolers to play) and a "Con" list (those statements that are against allowing home schoolers to play). Cross off any inappropriate or illogical statements you find; combine any opinions that overlap.

1. Parents of home schoolers pay the same taxes as public school parents.

2. Public school kids must meet grade requirements to be eligible.

3. School rules prohibit nonenrolled youth on campus.

4. Home schoolers shouldn't get the benefits of a school they've rejected.

5. Public school kids are bad influences on home schoolers.

6. Home schoolers need the social interaction.

7. Public school teams can always use more good athletes.

8. More students will overburden athletic facilities.

9. Home schoolers miss their public school friends, and vice versa.

10. Ten states allow home schoolers to play on teams.

11. Home schoolers will displace public school students on teams.

12. Public school students have to meet attendance rules to be eligible.

13. Athletic competition is good for everybody.

14. Home schoolers often have controversial political beliefs that will cause fights.

15. Team members need to share the same community on a daily basis.

16. Home schoolers aren't as invested in school pride.

Once you have your two lists, decide your own position on this topic. Then select two points you might use to argue your position and one opposing criticism you might refute. Put your working thesis into an "although-because" format, as explained on page 290. Compare your choices to those of your classmates.

B. Errors in reasoning can cause your reader to doubt your credibility. In the following mock essay, for example, the writer includes a variety of fallacies that undermine his argument; see if you can identify all his errors.

Ban Those Books!

1   A serious problem faces America today, a problem of such grave importance that our very existence as a nation is threatened. We must either cleanse our

schools of evil-minded books, or we must reconcile ourselves to seeing our children become welfare moochers and homeless bums.

2   History has shown time and time again that placement of immoral books in our schools is part of an insidious plot designed to weaken the moral fiber of our youth from coast to coast. In Wettuckett, Ohio, for example, the year after books by Mark Twain, such as *Tom Sawyer* and *Huckleberry Finn*, were introduced into the school library by liberal free-thinkers and radicals, the number of students cutting classes rose by 6 percent. And in that same year, the number of high school seniors going on to college dropped from thirty to twenty-two.

3   The reason for this could be either a natural decline in intelligence and morals or the influence of those dirty books that teach our beloved children disrespect and irresponsibility. Since there is no evidence to suggest a natural decline, the conclusion is inescapable: once our children read about Twain's characters skipping school and running away from home, they had to do likewise. If they hadn't read about such undesirable characters as Huckleberry Finn, our innocent children would never have behaved in those ways.

4   Now, I am a simple man, a plain old farm boy—the pseudo-intellectuals call me redneck just like they call you folks. But I can assure you that, redneck or not, I've got the guts to fight moral decay everywhere I find it, and I urge you to do the same. For this reason I want all you good folks to come to the ban-the-books rally this Friday so we can talk it over. I promise you all your right-thinking neighbors will be there.

© CORBIS

ASSIGNMENT

Collaborative Activity: Out of class, search for one of the following:

1. An example of an advertisement that illustrates one or more of the fallacies or appeals discussed on pages 296–299

2. An example of illogical or fallacious reasoning in a piece of writing (you might try looking at the editorial page or "Letters to the Editor" section of your local or campus newspaper)

3. An example of a logical, persuasive point in a piece of writing

Be prepared to explain your analysis of your sample, but do not write any sort of identifying label or evaluation on the sample itself. Bring your ad or piece of writing to class and exchange it with that of a classmate. After ten minutes, compare notes. Do you and your classmate agree on the evaluation of each sample? Why or why not?

ESSAY TOPICS

Write a convincing argument attacking or defending one of the following statements, or use them to help you think of your own topic. Remember to narrow and focus the topic as necessary. (◆ Note that essays on some of the topics presented here might profit from research material; see Chapter 14 for help.) For additional ideas, see the "Suggestions for Writing" section following the professional essays (page 309).

1. Students should/should not work throughout high school.

2. Plastic shopping sacks should/should not be legally banned from grocery and other retail stores.

3. Sixteen-year-olds should/should not be issued limited-privilege or "graduated" driver's licenses.

4. American students should/should not be required to take more foreign language courses in public school.

5. All adoption records should/should not be open to adopted people over 18.

6. A school voucher system should/should not be used in this state.

7. Students who do poorly in their academic courses should/should not be allowed to participate in athletic programs.

8. All schools should/should not adopt a "repeat/delete" policy, allowing students to retake a course and substitute a higher grade on their record.

9. Televised instant replays should/should not be used to call plays in football, baseball, and other sports.

10. Drivers' use of cell phones while vehicles are in motion should/should not be prohibited.

11. Sodas and high-sugar foods should/should not be sold in public school vending machines.

12. Off-road recreational vehicles should/should not be banned from our national parks.

13. Americans should/should not be required to perform a year of public service after high school graduation.

14. Public school students should/should not be required to wear uniforms.

15. The New Jersey law requiring drivers under twenty-one to display identifying decals on their vehicles should/should not be adopted nationwide.

16. Controversial names or symbols of athletic teams ("Redskins," the Confederate flag, the tomahawk chop) should/should not be changed.

© Inspirestock/CORBIS

17. A bill increasing the minimum wage (or some other controversial bill or policy) should/should not be approved.

18. Individuals under age fourteen charged with crimes should/should not be tried as adults.

19. Men and women in the military should/should not serve in separate units.

20. Advertising for "Product X" rarely/often relies on use of emotional appeals and faulty logic. (Focus on one kind of product—cars, cosmetics, computers, soft drinks, cell phones, etc.—or on one especially popular brand, and collect a number of its ads to analyze. What does your analysis reveal about the major ways the product is advertised to its target audience? Do the ads appeal to consumers' reason or do they employ logical fallacies? Some combination? Which ads are more effective, and why? If it's helpful, consider the appeals of ads reprinted in this text. A list of the ads follows the Table of Contents.)

A Topic Proposal for Your Essay

Selecting the right subject matter is important to every writer. To help you clarify your ideas and strengthen your commitment to your topic, here is a proposal sheet that asks you to describe some of your preliminary ideas about your subject before you begin drafting. Although your ideas may change as you write (they will almost certainly become more refined), thinking through your choice of topic now may help you avoid several false starts.

1. What is the subject of your argumentative essay? Write a rough statement of your opinion on this subject.

2. Why are you interested in this topic? Is it important to your personal, civic, or professional life? State at least one reason for your choice of topic.

3. Is this a significant topic of interest to others? Why? Is there a particular audience you would like to address?

4. At this point, can you list at least two reasons that support your opinion of your topic?

5. Who opposes your opinion? Can you state clearly at least one of your opposition's major criticisms of your position?

6. What difficulties, if any, might arise during drafting? For example, might you need to collect any additional evidence through reading, research, or interviewing to support your points or to refute your opposition?

Sample Student Essay

The student who wrote this essay followed the steps for writing an argumentative paper discussed in this chapter. His intended audience was the readers of his school newspaper, primarily students but instructors as well. To argue his case, he chose Pattern A, presenting two of his own points and then concluding with a rebuttal of an important opposing view. Notice that this writer uses a variety of methods to convince his readers, including hypothetical examples, causal analysis, analogy, and testimony. Does the writer persuade you to his point of view? Which are his strongest and weakest arguments? What might you change to make his essay even more persuasive?

STUDENTS, TAKE NOTE!

Introduction: Presenting the controversy

Thesis

Essay map

1   A walk across campus this week will reveal students, professors, and administrators arguing about class notes like never before. But they're not engaged in intellectual debates over chemical formulas or literary images. They're fighting over the taking of the notes themselves, as professional note-taking services in town are applying for permission to sit in on large lecture courses and then sell their notes to the students in those classes. Although the prospect of having "canned" notes looks inviting to many students, our administration should nevertheless ban these services from campus. Not only do such businesses give certain students unfair advantages and discourage class attendance, but they also prohibit the development of students' important learning skills, despite the services' claims to the contrary.

A point for the writer's position: Note-taking services are unfair to some students

2   What is bothersome for many of us about the professional-notes option is our sense of fair play. Let's face it: like it or not, school is, among other things, a place of competition, as students vie for the best academic records to send to prospective employers, graduate and professional schools, and in some cases, paying parents. In today's classes, all students have an equal opportunity to come to class, take notes, study, and pass or fail on their own merits. But the expensive professional notes, already organized and outlined, may give those with plenty of money some advantages that poorer students—those on scholarships or with families, for example—just can't afford. In addition, the notes may be available only to those students who take certain sections of a course and not others, thus giving some students an extra advantage. The same is true

---

for students who satisfy a requirement by taking one course that has notes available rather than another that has not. Knowing that you're doing your own work may make you feel morally superior to a classmate who isn't, but frankly, on some other level, it just plain feels irritating and unfair, sort of like watching your roommate getting away with plagiarizing his paper for a class after you spent weeks researching yours.

3   In addition to being a potential source of conflict among students, the professional-note services aren't winning many friends among the faculty, either. Several instructors have complained that the availability of notes will encourage many students, especially the weaker ones, to cut classes, assuming that they have all the material necessary for understanding the lecture, discussion, or lab. But anyone who has ever had to use borrowed notes knows something vital is not there. Someone else's interpretation of the information is often hard or impossible to follow, especially if you must understand complex relationships and problems. Moreover, skipping class may mean missed opportunities for students to ask questions or to participate in experiments or in group discussions, all of which often help clarify concepts under study. Not seeing visual aids or diagrams in person can also result in problems understanding the material. And, last, missing class can mean failure to become comfortably acquainted with the teacher, which, in turn, may discourage a student from asking for individual help when it's needed. All these possibilities are real; even Jeff Allridge, owner of the Quotable Notes service, has admitted to a campus reporter, "There *is* an incentive to skip class."

Another point for the writer's position: Professional notes discourage students from attending and participating in class

4   Despite the admission that professional note-taking encourages class-cutting, the services still promote themselves by claiming that students using their notes learn more. They support this claim by arguing that their notes offer students clearly organized information and, according to one advertising brochure, "good models" for students to follow in other classes. But such arguments miss the larger point: students should be

Presentation and rebuttal of the opposition's claim that students learn more using professional notes

learning how to develop their own note-taking, organizing, and thinking skills rather than swallowing the material whole as neatly packaged and delivered. Memorizing class material as outlined can be important, but it's not really as valuable in the long run as learning how to think about the material and use it to solve problems or come up with new ideas later. Taking your own notes teaches you how to listen and how to spot the important concepts; organizing your own notes teaches you how to pull ideas together in a logical way, all skills students will need in other classes, on jobs, and in life in general. Having memorized the outlines but not really mastered the thinking skills won't help the medical student whose patient's symptoms vary from the textbook description or the engineer whose airplane wings suddenly fail the stress test for no apparent reason.

Conclusion:
Restatement
of thesis,
ending
on pun to
emphasize
the main idea

5   By appealing to students who believe professional notes will help them accomplish their educational goals easier and quicker, a variety of note-taking services now have franchises across the country. But our campus shouldn't allow them to move in. Students need to recognize that the difference between the services' definition of "learning" and the real learning experiences college can provide is of notable importance.

Professional Essays*

The following essays on the four-day public school week were first published together in *USA Today* in a "Today's Debate" column (2009). The first essay represents the views of the newspaper's editorial board; the second essay was written by Gregory A. Schmidt, superintendent of MACRAY Public Schools, a multicommunity district in west central Minnesota.

Although you may already hold an opinion on this controversy, try to remain objective as you analyze the strengths and weaknesses of both essays. Which points are most and least persuasive, and why?

USA Today: Four Is Not Enough

1   Hit by falling property values and slumping tax receipts, school districts are feeling the economic downturn. Nearly half are trimming budgets; 20% have laid off staff. About 100 districts in 17 states—mostly rural systems facing stiff fuel costs for buses—have gone so far as to shift to four-day school weeks.

---

* ◆ For help reading these essays analytically, review pages 180–182.

2   The trend could spread. Earlier this month in Arizona, some of the state's biggest districts began calculating the savings they might achieve from a four-day week. Tough times demand innovative responses, but this one is troubling. A shorter school week could threaten educational achievement, burden working parents and endanger latch-key children. While there's no direct evidence—yet—that the four-day week hurts students, plenty of good research shows that U.S. schoolchildren benefit enormously when school districts ramp up classroom time.

3   If anything, U.S. students spend too little time in school. Compared with 39 other developed countries, the United States ranks near the bottom on average weekly instruction time. Measured over 12 years, the difference adds up to a full year of instruction. The best evidence that boosting learning time pays off comes from Massachusetts. There, 10 schools recently lengthened their instructional days by 25%, a strategy that raised state scores in math, English and science in all grades. Math, especially, is a subject where more time on task pays off, a recent Brookings Institution study concluded. The rationale used by the districts that have gone to four-day weeks—that adding more hours to the four-day week leaves learning untouched—is questionable.

4   What about the learning losses from a three-day school break? What about the stiff penalty a student faces when sick or absent for one of those four days? What about the family costs of day care for a child home alone on a weekday, or the potential for an unattended child to get into trouble?

5   Adopting a four-day week, as has been done in Minnesota's sprawling MAC-CRAY public school district, means that school districts have officially abandoned any move to boost learning time. MACCRAY students, it should be noted, score significantly below the Minnesota state average in both math and reading. Given that most of the district's budget is tied up in teacher salaries, the savings from a shift to four days may be as little as 2%, a recent study by the Southern Regional Education Board found.

6   Most of the four-day conversions were initially prompted by this summer's skyrocketing fuel prices. With gas prices now tumbling toward $2 a gallon, it's time for the four-day districts to reconsider.

Gregory A. Schmidt's Opposing View: We Like the Four-Day Week

1   The MACCRAY Public Schools made the decision to transition to a four-day school week as a result of tight finances and the desire to keep its academic program intact. Although MACCRAY is currently the only Minnesota district that has opted to use a modified schedule, districts in at least 17 other states are on a four-day schedule.

2   MACCRAY's leadership team researched the pros and cons of making a change by contacting leadership from districts in states that use a four-day schedule. Their research showed that not only was the four-day week well accepted, but standardized test scores had not declined and other measures of academic progress had not suffered (and in some cases had improved) as the result of having fewer instructional days. Another unanticipated benefit realized in many districts is that student

and staff attendance improved due to better morale and the ability to schedule appointments on the days off.

3   Despite reducing the number of instructional days from 172 to 149, MACCRAY students have gained more than 17 hours of instructional time by adding 65 minutes to each instructional day. Because there are fewer days, there are fewer breaks for recess, lunch, and time between classes—making more time for academic pursuits.

4   The district expects to save between $85,000 and $100,000 in 2008–09 because of the modified schedule. The contract with its transportation provider assures the district of $65,000 in savings. That's nearly $3,000 per day. Other savings will result by reducing electrical usage and having fewer days that furnaces are required to heat the buildings to a comfortable level.

5   I trust that MACCRAY's experience will be similar to that of other districts— that students will not suffer academically as the result of the modified schedule.

6   Despite my optimism, we intend to evaluate our experience from a variety of angles. MACCRAY's leadership and board will assess academic progress, attendance of students and staff, and energy cost savings, as well as solicit input from parents, students, staff and community members to determine whether or not to continue using a modified schedule beyond 2008–09.

Questions on Content, Structure, and Style

1. Why are some school districts throughout the country changing their academic schedules? Briefly summarize the problem and proposed solution under discussion in these essays.

2. What is the *USA Today* editorial board's position on a four-day week for public schools? What is Superintendent Schmidt's opinion regarding his district's change?

3. What is the editorial board's primary objection to the shortened-week trend?

4. Why did the editors cite the Massachusetts schools and refer to the Brookings Institution and the Southern Regional Education Board?

5. What is the purpose of the series of questions in paragraph 4?

6. In what ways do the editors address their opposition's claims in paragraph 5? Is their rebuttal persuasive? Why/why not?

7. According to Superintendent Schmidt, what are the primary benefits of their change in schedule?

8. Evaluate Schmidt's discussion of the district's predecision research, which appears in paragraph 2. Where might some specific data have been used to increase the persuasiveness of these claims?

9. How does Schmidt address the objection of the *USA Today* editorial board regarding the loss of learning time?

10. Of the two essays, which do you find more persuasive, and why? How might your response to these essays differ depending on whether you are a teacher, a parent working outside the home, or a student facing longer school days in a shorter week?

Suggestions for Writing

Use the essays by the *USA Today* editorial board and by Gregory A. Schmidt as a stepping-stone to your essay. Perhaps drawing in part on your response to question 10, write an essay arguing your own position on high school schedules. Or if you prefer, argue for or against some other rule or regulation at a previous or current school that you think affects academic success (a particular course requirement? an attendance policy?). Or perhaps argue for a change in some academic support service or campus office. (◆ For topics that would profit from support from interviews or questionnaires, see the section *Conducting Primary Research* in Chapter 14, pages 379–386.)

Vocabulary

USA Today essay:

innovative (2)
latch-key children (2)
rationale (3)
conversions (6)
solicit (6)

Schmidt's essay:

standardized (2)
unanticipated (2)
morale (2)
instructional (3)

Analyzing Advertisements

Because they are designed to be persuasive, advertisements use a variety of logical and emotional appeals. Ads might be considered arguments in brief form, as they frequently try to convince the public to buy a product, take an action, vote for or against something, join a group, or change an attitude or a behavior. By analyzing the ads that follow, you can practice identifying a variety of persuasive appeals and evaluating their effectiveness. After discussing these ads, apply what you've learned about logical appeals, target audiences, and choice of language to your argumentative essay.*

Conflicting Positions: Gun Control

The three advertisements that follow address the controversial subject of gun control. The first ad is one of a series published by the National Rifle Association (NRA) to tell the public about its organization and its interpretation of the Second Amendment; other ads in this series have featured author Tom Clancy and basketball star Karl Malone. The second ad ("Well-Regulated Militia") counters the NRA position. This ad features Sarah Brady, who, following the shooting of her husband, White House Press Secretary James Brady, during an assassination attempt on President Ronald Reagan, became chair of the Center to Prevent Handgun Violence. The third ad uses an expository strategy and statistics to make its point about handgun regulation in America. Analyze the appeals used in each advertisement. Which methods of persuasion do you think are the most effective, and why? Do you find any of the logical fallacies previously described in this chapter?

---

* ◆ For additional practice analyzing the arguments and appeals of other advertisements that appear in this text, see the list that follows the Table of Contents.

REP. ALBERTO GUTMAN: Florida Legislator, Businessman, Husband, Member of the National Rifle Association.

"Being from a country that was once a democracy and turned communist, I really feel I know what the right to bear arms is all about. In Cuba, where I was born, the first thing the communist government did was take away everybody's firearms, leaving them defenseless and intimidated with fear. That's why our constitutional right to bear arms is so important to our country's survival.

"As a legislator I have to deal with reality. And the reality is that gun control does not work. It actually eliminates the rights of the law-abiding citizen, not the criminal. Criminals will always have guns, and they won't follow gun control laws anyway. I would like to see tougher laws on criminals as opposed to tougher laws on legitimate gun owners. We need to attack the problem of crime at its roots, instead of blaming crime on gun ownership and citizens who use them lawfully.

"It's a big responsibility that we face retaining the right to bear arms. That's why I joined the NRA. The NRA is instrumental in protecting these freedoms. It helps train and educate people, supporting legislation that benefits not only those who bear arms but all citizens of the United States. The NRA helps keep America free." **I'm the NRA.**

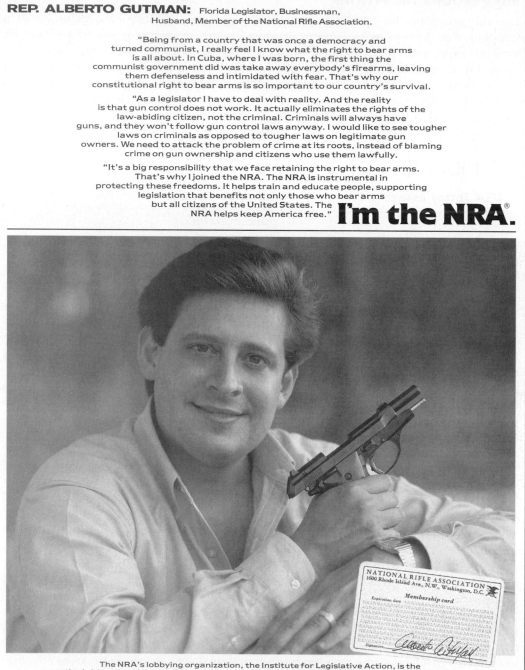

The NRA's lobbying organization, the Institute for Legislative Action, is the nation's largest and most influential protector of the constitutional right to keep and bear arms. At every level of government and through local grassroots efforts, the Institute guards against infringement upon the freedoms of law-abiding gun owners. If you would like to join the NRA or want more information about our programs and benefits, write J. Warren Cassidy, Executive Vice President, P.O. Box 37484, Dept. AG-15, Washington, D.C. 20013.

Paid for by the members of the National Rifle Association of America. Copyright 1986.

Reprinted with permission of the National Rifle Association

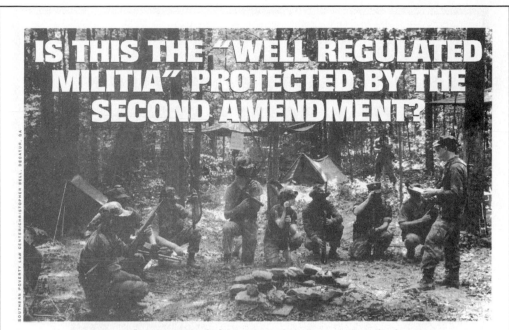

IS THIS THE "WELL REGULATED MILITIA" PROTECTED BY THE SECOND AMENDMENT?

"A well regulated Militia, being necessary to the security of a free State, the right of the people to keep and bear Arms, shall not be infringed."

—*Second Amendment to the U.S. Constitution*

For years, the National Rifle Association has spread the myth that gun control laws violate the Second Amendment. Now self styled "citizen militias" invoke the Second Amendment as they stockpile weapons and train for warfare against what they perceive as a "tyrannical" federal government. The NRA declares that the paramilitary activity of these groups is an exercise of their "right to keep and bear arms." Echoing the extremist rhetoric of the "militias," an NRA official has called the Second Amendment "a loaded gun…held to the head of government." This is a perversion of our Constitution.

When our Founding Fathers wrote the Second Amendment more than 200 years ago, the "well regulated militia" was not a privately organized army formed to resist the government of the United States. It was the military arm of state government, formed to maintain public order.

The Supreme Court has ruled that the "obvious purpose" of the Second Amendment was to protect the "militia which the States were expected to maintain and train," and that "the National Guard is the modern militia."

Because laws regulating firearms do not interfere with the modern militia, no gun control law has ever been overturned by the federal courts on Second Amendment grounds. That's why former Supreme Court Chief Justice Warren Burger has called the NRA's Second Amendment propaganda a "fraud on the American public."

The Second Amendment is not a barrier to reasonable gun control laws. Nor is it a license for those who disagree with government policies to resist them by force of arms. It's time for the NRA to stop its Second Amendment fraud.

The Second Amendment protects the National Guard, not private armies preparing to take the law into their own hands.

Sarah Brady, Chair of the Center to Prevent Handgun Violence

Dear Sarah, I want to support your national education campaign to fight the NRA's Second Amendment fraud. Enclosed is my contribution for:

☐ $15   ☐ $25   ☐ $50   ☐ Other _____

NAME _____

ADDRESS _____

CITY, STATE, ZIP _____

E-MAIL _____

Return to: Center to Prevent Handgun Violence, 1225 Eye Street, NW, Room 1100, Washington, DC 20005

Contributions to the Center to Prevent Handgun Violence are tax-deductible.

☐ **I'd like more information on the Second Amendment and the Center to Prevent Handgun Violence.**

NAME _____

ADDRESS _____

CITY, STATE, ZIP _____

Return to: Center to Prevent Handgun Violence
1225 Eye Street, NW, Room 1100
Washington, DC 20005

Brought to you by the Center to Prevent Handgun Violence, Sarah Brady, Chair

Courtesy of the Center to Prevent Handgun Violence

TEDDY BEARS
HAVE TO MEET CONSUMER HEALTH & SAFETY STANDARDS

1 At least four types of federal safety standards cover teddy bears: sharp edges and points, small parts, hazardous materials, and flammability.

2 From 1994 to 1997, eight models of teddy bears were recalled by the United States Consumer Product Safety Commission due to possible choking hazards. The total number of teddy bears manufactured during this period was more than 750,000.

3 Teddy bears killed no one in the United States in 1997. From 1994 to 1997 there were 71 toy-related deaths in the United States.

BUT GUNS DON'T!

1 There are no federal safety standards for the domestic manufacture of firearms.

2 No federal health and safety agency has the authority to recall defective firearms or force changes in design.

3 Guns killed 32,436 people in the United States in 1997. From 1994 to 1997 there were 140,938 gun-related deaths in the United States. In 1997, for every time a firearm was used by a civilian to kill in self-defense, there were 4 unintentional deaths, 43 criminal homicides, and 75 suicides involving firearms.

THE SOLUTION

The Firearms Safety and Consumer Protection Act would end the gun industry's deadly exemption from health and safety regulation. Only then will America experience a meaningful reduction in firearms violence.

981 unintentional
367 undetermined
13,322 homicides
17,566 suicides

Violence Policy Center • 1140 19th Street • NW • Suite 600 • Washington • DC • 20036 • www.vpc.org

Courtesy of the Violence Policy Center, Washington, DC

Competing Products: Sources of Energy

The advertisement by the Metropolitan Energy Council that follows argues for the use of oil to provide heating. What arguments are offered? What emotional appeals does this ad incorporate? To whom are these appeals directed? How does the next ad for Xcel Energy, a large Midwestern and Western natural gas utility company, try to respond to some of the first ad's arguments against using gas heat? Why might Xcel run a newspaper advertisement that appears to be primarily a public safety announcement?

The third advertisement (page 316) is part of a series sponsored by the U.S. Council for Energy Awareness to promote the building of more nuclear energy plants. How does it argue against both oil and gas? What emotional appeals do you see in this ad?

Considering both the language and the visual appeals of all three advertisements, which ad do you find the most persuasive, and why?

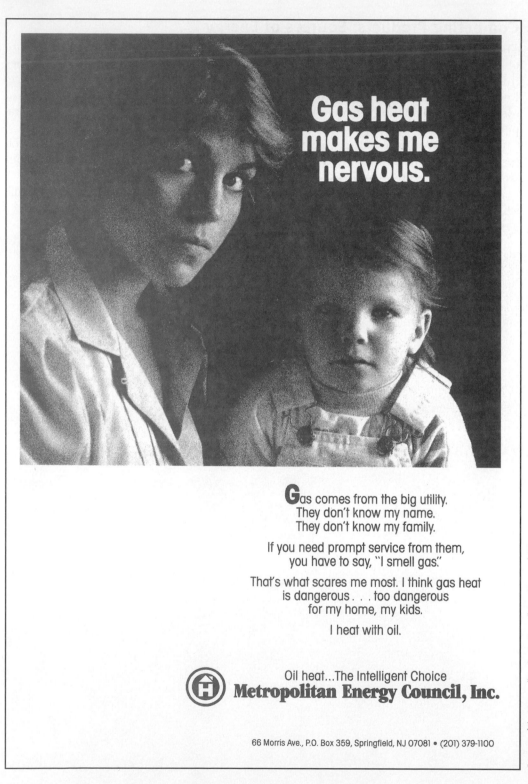

Courtesy of the Metropolitan Energy Council, Inc., Norwood, NJ www.xcelenergy.com   ©2005 Xcel Energy Inc.

"WE COULD MAKE NATURAL GAS SMELL LIKE LILACS OR BACON COOKING IN THE MORNING. BUT THAT WOULDN'T GET YOU OUT OF THE HOUSE."

"Natural gas is naturally odorless. So we mix a harmless chemical in with it that smells like sulfur or rotten eggs. If you ever smell that in your house, you could well have a dangerous gas leak. That's when you have to get everyone out of the house immediately, get to a neighbor's house, and call 1-800-895-2999 to get one of our inspectors over. In an emergency, call 911 first. Most people don't know this either, but if you suspect you have a leak, you should NEVER turn lights or appliances on or off. And NEVER use your phone or cell phone in a house that may be filling with gas. The spark from a switch or phone could cause an explosion. By the same token, don't be lighting a match or opening windows. Just get out of there. Then make that call for help. Remember: Stay away. Stay alive."

Timio, Lead Welder
For more safety tips, visit our website at www.xcelenergy.com.

Xcel Energy

Every time you flip a switch or turn a dial, you tap into the energy of over 12,000 people working to make your life better. Xcel Energy. You get all of our energy.

Courtesy of Xcel Energy

SOME ARGUMENTS FOR NUCLEAR ENERGY ARE SMALLER THAN OTHERS.

Around the nuclear electric plant on Florida's Hutchinson Island, endangered wildlife have a safe haven. The baby sea turtles hatching on nearby beaches are more evidence of the truth about nuclear energy: it peacefully coexists with the environment.

America's 110 operating nuclear plants don't pollute the air, because they don't burn anything to generate electricity. Nor do they eat up valuable natural resources such as oil and natural gas.

Still, more plants are needed—to help satisfy the nation's growing need for electricity without sacrificing the quality of our environment. For a free booklet on nuclear energy, write to the U.S. Council for Energy Awareness, P.O. Box 66080, Dept. TR01, Washington, D.C. 20035.

NUCLEAR ENERGY MEANS CLEANER AIR.

© 1992 USCEA

As seen in April 1992 issues of The Washington Post, FORTUNE, and National Journal; May 1992 issues of TIME, Newsweek, Washington Post National Weekly and Congressional Quarterly; June 1992 issues of National Geographic, Smithsonian, New Choices and Christian Science Monitor; July 1992 issue of Forbes; August 1992 issue of World Monitor; September 1992 issue of Ladies' Home Journal and Natural History; October 1992 issues of Good Housekeeping, Atlantic and American Heritage; and November 1992 issue of Reader's Digest.

This advertisement is provided courtesy of the United States Council for Energy Awareness, Washington, DC

Popular Appeals: Spending Our Money

How do all three of the following advertisements employ variations of the "bandwagon" appeal? In the American Century ad, what sort of company identity is created with the story of the boss's lunch? Why might an investment service want this image? To what kind of person does this ad appeal?

The Omega watch ad appeals to a different audience in its use of movie star Pierce Brosnan, known for his portrayal of adventurous characters such as 007 spy James Bond. What effect is "Brosnan's choice" intended to have on the reader? What does the name of the watch style ("Seamaster Aqua Terra") contribute to the appeal of this ad?

The advertisement on page 320, sponsored by People for the Ethical Treatment of Animals (PETA), is one of a series of anti-fur ads featuring media celebrities, such as Oscar-winning Charlize Theron (shown here), Simon Cowell (judge on TV's *American Idol*), and Goran Visnjic (actor on TV show *ER*). In addition to its bandwagon appeal, this ad argues its cause by setting up what comparison or analogy (X is like Y) in the reader's mind? Do you find this ad's argument logical and persuasive? Why or why not? (◆ If it's helpful, review the discussions of analogies on pages 245–248 and 299.)

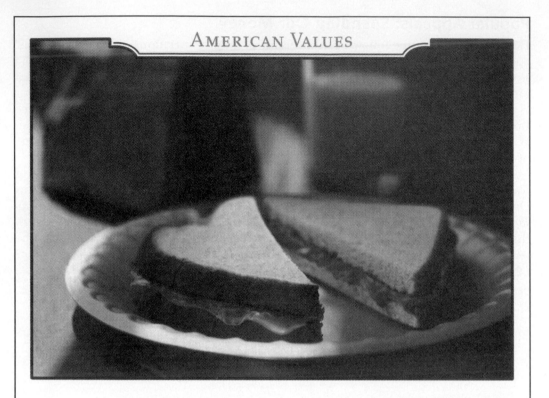

AMERICAN VALUES

Every day, our founder has the same lunch. It isn't lobster tail. ═══════

It's a true story. At noon, he sits down in the cafeteria and eats a peanut butter sandwich. When he's done, he folds up his paper sack so it can be used again tomorrow.

It's a tradition around here. One of the many we've created in our 44 years of managing investments. Over time we've grown, but two things have remained constant. His lunch. And our values. Your success is still our first priority. The proof is in the peanut butter.

AMERICAN CENTURY.

Investment Managers

American Century Investment Services, Inc. © 2002 American Century Services Corporation

Courtesy of American Values

PIERCE BROSNAN'S CHOICE

www.omegawatches.com

SEAMASTER AQUA TERRA
Co-Axial Escapement
3 year extended warranty

The name Omega has always been closely associated with quality and reliability. The Seamaster Aqua Terra upholds this pioneering spirit. Its classic design houses the latest in watchmaking technology: the unique Co-Axial Escapement movement, which offers unrivalled long-term accuracy.

Ω OMEGA

Courtesy of Omega

Courtesy of PETA, Washington, DC

PRACTICING WHAT YOU'VE LEARNED

Continue practicing your critical thinking skills by analyzing the 1920s advertisement that appears here. Who was the likely target audience in terms of gender, age, socioeconomic group, and marital status? Why might this ad have appealed to its audience at that time in our country? After analyzing this ad, compare it to an advertisement for one of today's cars, SUVs, or trucks. Has the audience changed? What kinds of arguments, appeals, and language are employed to sell the vehicle in the current ad? In what ways do you find the two ads similar and different in their persuasive techniques?

A Revision Worksheet

As you write your rough drafts, consult Chapter 5 for guidance through the revision process. In addition, here are a few questions to ask yourself as you revise your argumentative essay:

1. Does this essay present a clear thesis limited to fit the assigned length of this paper?

2. Does this essay contain a number of strong, persuasive points in support of its thesis?

3. Is the essay organized in an easy-to-follow pattern that avoids repetition or confusion?

4. Does the essay present enough supporting evidence to make each of its points convincing? Where could additional examples, factual information, testimony, or other kinds of supporting material be added to make the arguments even more effective?

5. Will all the supporting evidence be clear to the essay's particular audience? Do any terms or examples need additional explanation or special definition?

6. Has at least one major opposing argument been addressed?

7. Does the essay avoid any logical fallacies or problems in tone?

Collaborative Activity: After you've revised your essay extensively, exchange rough drafts with a classmate and answer these questions for each other, making specific suggestions for improvement wherever appropriate. (◆ For advice on productive participation in classroom workshops, see pages 115–120.)

Reviewing Your Progress

After you have completed your argument essay, take a moment to measure your progress as a writer by responding to the following questions. Such analysis will help you to recognize growth in your writing skills and may enable you to identify areas that are still problematic.

1. Which part of your essay do you like best? Why?

2. After analyzing your essay's reasoning and evidence, which particular argument or point do you consider the strongest? What makes it so convincing?

3. What part of your essay gave you the most trouble? How did you overcome the problem?

4. If you had more time to work on this essay, what would receive additional attention? Why?

5. What did you learn about your topic from writing this essay? About yourself as a writer?

CHAPTER 11

Description

The writer of description creates a word-picture of people, places, objects, and emotions, using a careful selection of details to make an impression on the reader. If you have already written expository or argumentative essays in your composition course, you almost certainly have written some descriptive prose. Nearly every essay, after all, calls for some kind of description; for example, in the student comparison/contrast essay (pages 233–236) the writer describes two kinds of stores; in the professional process essay (pages 218–222) the writer describes the embalming procedure in great detail. To help you write better description in your other essays, however, you may want to practice writing descriptive paragraphs or a short descriptive essay.

How to Write Effective Description

When descriptive prose is called for in your writing, consider these four basic suggestions:

Recognize your purpose. Description is not free-floating; it appears in your writing for a particular reason: to help you inform, clarify, persuade, or create a mood. In some essays you will want your description as *objective*—without personal impressions—as you can make it; for example, you might describe a scientific experiment or a business transaction in straight factual detail. Other times, however, you will want to convey a particular attitude toward your subject; this approach to description is called *subjective* or *impressionistic*. Note the differences between the following two descriptions of a tall, thin boy: the objective writer sticks to the facts by saying, "The eighteen-year-old boy was 6'1" and weighed 155 pounds," whereas the subjective writer gives an impressionistic description: "The young boy was as tall and scrawny as a birch tree in winter." Before you begin describing anything, you must first decide your purpose and whether it calls for objective or subjective reporting.

Describe clearly, using specific details. To make any description clear to your reader, you must include a sufficient number of details that are specific rather than fuzzy or vague. If, for example, your family dog were missing, you wouldn't call the animal shelter to ask if they'd seen a "big brown dog with a short tail"—naturally, you'd mention every distinguishing detail about your pet you could think of: size, color, breed, cut of ears, and special markings. Similarly, if your car had been stolen, you'd give the police as clear and as complete a description of your vehicle as possible. Look at the following sentence. Does it clearly identify a vaulting horse?

> A vaulting horse is a thing usually found in gyms that has four legs and a beam and is used by gymnasts making jumps.

If you didn't already know what a vaulting horse was, you might have trouble picking it out in a gymnasium crowded with equipment. A description with additional details would help you locate it:

> A vaulting horse is a piece of equipment used by gymnasts during competition to help propel them into the air when they perform any of a variety of leaps known as vaults. The gymnasts usually approach the vaulting horse from a running start and then place their hands on the horse for support or for a push off as they perform their vaults. The horse itself resembles a carpenter's sawhorse, but the main beam is made of padded leather rather than wood. The rectangular beam is approximately 5 feet, 3 inches long and 13½ inches wide. Supported by four legs usually made of steel, the padded leather beam is approximately 4 feet, ½ inch above the floor in men's competitions and 3 feet, 7 inches in women's competitions. The padded leather beam has two white lines marking off three sections on top: the croup, the saddle, and the neck. The two end sections—the croup and the neck—are each 15½ inches long. Gymnasts place their hands on the neck or croup, depending on the type of vault they are attempting.

Moreover, the reader cannot imagine your subject clearly if your description is couched in vague generalities. The following sentence, for example, presents only a hazy picture:

> Larry is a sloppy dresser.

Revised, the picture is now sharply in focus:

> Larry wears dirty, baggy pants, shirts too small to stay tucked in, socks that fail to match his pants or each other, and a stained coat the Salvation Army rejected as a donation.

Specific details can turn cloudy prose into crisp, clear images that can be reproduced in the mind like photographs.

Select only appropriate details. In any description the choice of details depends largely on the writer's purpose and audience. However, many descriptions—especially the more subjective ones—will present a *dominant impression*; that is, the writer selects primarily those details that communicate a particular mood or feeling to the reader. The dominant impression is the controlling focus of a description; for example, if you wrote a description of your grandmother to show her thoughtfulness, you would select only those details that convey an impression of a sweet, kindly old lady. Here are two brief descriptions illustrating the concept of dominant impression. The first writer tries to create a mood of mystery:

> Down a black winding road stands the abandoned old mansion, silhouetted against the cloud-shrouded moon, creaking and moaning in the wet, chill wind.

The second writer tries to present a feeling of joy and innocence.

> A dozen kites filled the spring air, and around the bright picnic tables spread with hot dogs, hamburgers, and slices of watermelon, Tom and Annie played away the warm April day.

In the description of the deserted mansion, the writer would have violated the impression of mystery had the sentence read,

> Down the black winding road stands the abandoned old mansion, surrounded by bright, multicolored tulips in early bloom.

Including the cheerful flowers as a detail in the description destroys the dominant mood of blackness and mystery. Similarly, the second example would be spoiled had the writer ended it this way:

> Tom and Annie played away the warm April day until Tom got so sunburned he became ill and had to go home.

Therefore, remember to select only those details that advance your descriptive purpose. Omit any details you consider unimportant or distracting.

See if you can determine the dominant impression of each of the following descriptions:

> The wind had curled up to sleep in the distant mountains. Leaves hung limp and motionless from the silent trees, while birds perched on the branches like little statues. As I sat on the edge of the clearing, holding my breath, I could hear a squirrel scampering through the underbrush. Somewhere far away a dog barked twice, and then the woods were hushed once more.

> This poor thing has seen better days, but one should expect the sofa in a fraternity house den to be well worn. The large, plump, brown corduroy pillows strewn lazily on the floor and propped comfortably against the threadbare arms bear the pencil-point scars of frustrated students and foam-bleeding cuts of multiple pillow wars. No fewer than four pairs of rotting Nikes stand twenty-four-hour guard at the corners of its carefully mended frame. Obviously the relaxed, inviting appearance masks the permanent odors of cheap cigars from Thursday night poker parties; at least two or three guests each weekend sift through the popcorn kernels and Doritos crumbs, sprawl face down, and pass out for a nap. However, frequent inhabitants have learned to avoid the brown stains courtesy of the house pup and the red fruit punch designs of the chapter klutz. Habitually, they strategically lunge over the back of the sofa to an unsoiled area easily identifiable in flight by the large depression left by previous regulars. The quiet *hmmph* of the cushions and harmonious squeal of the exhausted springs signal a perfect landing and utter a warm greeting from an old and faithful friend.

Make your descriptions vivid. By using clear, precise words, you can improve any kind of writing. ◆ Chapters 7 (on words) and 6 (on sentences) offer a variety of tips on clarifying your prose style. In addition to the advice given there, here are two other ways to enliven your descriptions, particularly those that call for a subjective approach:

Use sensory details. If it's appropriate, try using images that appeal to your readers' five senses. If, for example, you are describing your broken leg and the ensuing stay in a hospital, tell your readers how the place smelled, how it looked, what your cast felt like, how your pills tasted, and what noises you heard. Here are some specific examples using sensory details:

Sight	The clean white corridors of the hospital resembled the set of a sci-fi movie, with everyone scurrying around in identical starched uniforms.
Hearing	At night, the only sounds I heard were the quiet squeakings of sensible white shoes as the nurses made their rounds.
Smell	The green beans on the hospital cafeteria tray smelled stale and waxy, like crayons.
Touch	The hospital bedsheet felt as rough and heavy as a feed sack.
Taste	Every four hours they gave me an enormous gray pill whose aftertaste reminded me of the stale licorice my great-aunt kept in candy dishes around her house.

By appealing to the readers' senses, you better enable them to imagine the subject you are describing. Joseph Conrad, the famous nineteenth-century novelist, agreed, believing that all art "appeals primarily to the senses, and the artistic aim when expressing itself in written words must also make its appeal through the senses, if its highest desire is to reach the secret spring of responsive emotions." In other words, to make your readers feel, first make them "see."

Use figurative language when appropriate. As you may recall from Chapter 7, figurative language produces images or pictures in the readers' minds, helping them to understand unfamiliar or abstract subjects. Here are some devices you might use to clarify or spice up your prose:

1. Simile: a comparison between two things using the words "like" or "as" (◆ see also pages 170–172)

    Example Seeing exactly the video game he wanted, he moved as quickly as a starving teenager spotting pie in a refrigerator full of leftover vegetables.

2. Metaphor: a direct comparison between two things that does not use "like" or "as" (◆ see also pages 170–172)

    Example I was a puppet with my father controlling all the financial strings.

3. Personification: the attribution of human characteristics and emotions to inanimate objects, animals, or abstract ideas

    Example The old teddy bear sat in a corner, dozing serenely before the fireplace.

4. Hyperbole: intentional exaggeration or overstatement for emphasis or humor

    Example The cockroaches in my kitchen had now grown to the size of carry-on luggage.

5. Understatement: intentional representation of a subject as less important than the facts would warrant (◆ see also irony, pages 156–157)

   Example   "The reports of my death are greatly exaggerated."—Mark Twain

6. Synecdoche: a part of something used to represent the whole

   Example   A hundred tired feet hit the dance floor for one last jitterbug. [Here "feet" stand for the dancing couples themselves.]

7. Allusion: a brief reference to real or fictitious people, places, events, or things to produce certain associations in the reader's mind

   Example   She proofread her essay again and again, searching for errors with the tenacity of Captain Ahab. [Ahab, the ship captain in the novel *Moby-Dick*, was obsessively devoted to hunting the white whale.]

If you do choose to include figurative language in your descriptions, be sure you are creating the specific image and tone you want to convey. These similes, taken from actual student papers, may have a distracting (and/or humorous) effect:

- She grew on him like she was a colony of E. coli, and he was room-temperature Canadian beef.
- He had a deep, throaty, genuine laugh, like the sound a dog makes just before it throws up.
- He was deeply in love and when she spoke, he heard bells, as if she were a garbage truck backing up.
- Her face was a perfect oval, like a circle that had its two sides gently compressed by a ThighMaster.

And sometimes, as in the following case, a feeble comparison is worse than nothing at all!

   The little boat gently drifted across the pond exactly the way a bowling ball wouldn't.

Used sparingly and with careful crafting, however, figures of speech can make your prose enjoyable (as expensive chocolate?) and memorable (as your best weekend ever?). (◆ For more discussion of figurative language, including mixed metaphors, see pages 170–172.)

Problems to Avoid

Keep in mind these three pieces of advice to solve problems that frequently arise in description:

Remember your audience. Sometimes the object of our description is so clear in our minds that we forget that our readers haven't seen it, too. Consequently, the description we write turns out to be vague, bland, or skimpy ("The big tree was beautiful"). Ask yourself about your audience: what do they need to know to see this sight as clearly as I do? Then fill in your description with ample, precise details that reveal the best picture possible. Don't forget to define or explain any terms you use that may be puzzling to your audience. (◆ For more advice on clear, vivid language, see Chapter 7.)

Avoid an erratic organization of details. Too often, descriptions are a hodgepodge of details, jotted down randomly. When you write a lengthy description, you should select a plan that will arrange your details in an orderly fashion. Depending on your subject matter and your purpose, you might adopt a plan calling for a description of something from top to bottom, left to right, front to back, and so on. For example, a description of a woman might begin at the head and move to the feet; furniture in a room might be described as your eyes move from one side of the room to another. A second plan for arranging details presents the subject's outstanding characteristics first and then fills in the lesser information; a child's red hair, for example, might be his most striking feature and therefore would be described first. A third plan presents details in the order you see them approaching: dust, then a car, then details about the car, its occupants, and so on. Or you might describe a subject as it unfolds chronologically, as in some kind of process or operation. Regardless of which plan of organization you choose, the reader should feel a sense of order in your description.

Avoid any sudden change in perspective. If, for example, you are describing the White House from the outside, don't suddenly include details that could be seen only from the inside. Similarly, if you are describing a car from a distance, you might be able to tell the car's model, year, and color, but you could hardly describe the upholstery or reveal the mileage. It is, of course, possible for you—or your observer—to approach or move around the subject of your description, but the reader must be aware of this movement. Any shift in point of view must be presented clearly and logically, with no sudden, confusing leaps from a front to a back view, from outside to inside, and so on.

© Canstock Images, Inc./ Index Stock Imagery

PRACTICING WHAT YOU'VE LEARNED

A. The following paragraphs are from *Pilgrim at Tinker Creek* (1974), by well-known naturalist Annie Dillard. What is Dillard's attitude toward the poisonous copperhead she watched one evening? Fear, repulsion, or something else entirely? How is her point of view presented through her choice of descriptive details? Is her description objective or subjective, or both? What descriptive words or phrases stand out for you, and why?

Snake

Annie Dillard

1 There was a snake at the quarry with me tonight. It lay shaded by cliffs on a flat sandstone ledge above the quarry's dark waters. I was thirty feet away, sitting on the forest path overlook, when my eye caught the dark scrawl on the rocks, the lazy sinuosity that can only mean snake. I approached for a better look, edging my way down the steep rock cutting, and saw that the snake was only

twelve or thirteen inches long. Its body was thick for its length. I came closer still, and saw the unmistakable undulating bands of brown, the hourglasses: copperhead.

2   I never step a foot out of the house, even in winter, without a snakebite kit in my pocket. Mine is a small kit in rubber casing about the size of a shotgun shell; I slapped my pants instinctively to fix in my mind its location. Then I stomped hard on the ground a few times and sat down beside the snake.

3   The young copperhead was motionless on its rock. Although it lay in a loose sprawl, all I saw at first was a camouflage pattern of particolored splotches confused by the rushing speckles of light in the weeds between us, and by the deep twilight dark of the quarry pond beyond the rock. Then suddenly the form of its head emerged from the confusion: burnished brown, triangular, blunt as a stone ax. Its head and the first four inches of its body rested on airy nothing an inch above the rock. I admired the snake. Its scales shone with newness, bright and buffed. Its body was perfect, whole and unblemished. I found it hard to believe it had not just been created on the spot, or hatched fresh from its mother, so unscathed and clean was its body, so unmarked by any passage.

4   Did it see me? I was only four feet away, seated on the weedy cliff behind the sandstone ledge; the snake was between me and the quarry pond. I waved an arm in its direction: nothing moved. Its low-forehead glare and lipless reptile smirk revealed nothing. How could I tell where it was looking, what it was seeing? I squinted at its head, staring at those eyes like the glass eyes of a stuffed warbler, at those scales like shields canted and lapped just so, to frame an improbable, unfathomable face.

5   Yes, it knew I was there. There was something about its eyes, some alien alertness . . . what on earth must it be like to have scales on your face? All right then, copperhead. I know you're here, you know I'm here. This is a big night. I dug my elbows into rough rock and dry soil and settled back on the hillside to begin the long business of waiting out a snake.

The venomous copperhead

© Robert Zappalorti / Photo Researchers, Inc.

B. Choose sensory details (sight, taste, smell, touch, and hearing) and/or figurative language (similes, metaphors, personification, etc.) to vividly describe each of the following. Avoid clichés and Insta-Prose by creating memorable new images (serious or humorous) for your reader.

1. A dessert

2. A pair of jeans

3. A pet

4. The floor of a theater following a kids' movie

5. A sunset

6. February

7. A scene in nature or in the city

8. Your favorite pillow

9. A dentist's office

10. Yourself in either a happy or grouchy mood

C. *Collaborative Activity:* Bring a small (palm-sized), inexpensive, unbreakable object from home to class. This might be a household or personal item (such as a fork or a key) or perhaps something from nature (a rock or leaf) or even something left over from your lunch (a piece of fruit or candy). All students will deposit their objects in a large bag or cardboard box that your instructor has brought. Join two other students and direct a group representative to choose, without peeking, an object from the bag or box, one item that no one in your group contributed to the collection. Together, practice your objective descriptive skills by composing a detailed, factual picture of this object in a paragraph of at least five sentences. If time permits, write another paragraph describing the same object subjectively, using colorful language to offer a dominant impression. Which description was easier for your group? Be ready to read your paragraphs to the rest of the class.

ASSIGNMENT

Use the painting reproduced here to practice your descriptive writing skills. Often influenced by his Russian-Jewish heritage, artist Marc Chagall (1887–1985) painted this picture titled *Birthday* in 1915. Describe what you feel is the dominant mood of this picture, pointing out some of the details that communicate that tone to you. Consider the painting's people, setting, colors, and even shapes. In a short descriptive essay, re-create this painting as you see it for someone unfamiliar with the work. To get you started, ponder this: some viewers have questioned whether the male figure is "floating on air" with happiness or is instead an imaginary guest, perhaps even someone deceased. What do *you* think? (◆ For more help writing about art, see Chapter 17.)

Birthday (L'Anniversaire), 1915, by Marc Chagall

(◆ For additional advice and exercises designed to improve descriptive writing skills, see pages 140–144 and 161–165 in Part One of this text.)

ESSAY TOPICS

Here are some suggestions for a descriptive paragraph or essay; focus your topic to fit your assignment. Don't forget that every description, whether objective or subjective, has a purpose and that your details should support that purpose. ◆ For additional ideas, see "Suggestions for Writing" on page 339.

1. A favorite painting, photograph, or sculpture (Or choose one of the many artworks in this textbook. A list of the visual art follows the Table of Contents.)

continued on next page

2. One dish or foodstuff that should be forever banned

3. A piece of equipment important to your major, a hobby, or a favorite sport

4. A campus or a local building you admire

5. Your best/worst job

6. Yourself (how you looked at a certain age or on a memorable occasion or in a particular photograph)

7. Your most precious material possession

8. The ugliest/most beautiful place on your campus

9. A holiday, celebration, or ritual in your family

10. Your first or worst car or apartment

11. A piece of clothing that reveals the real "you" (or a favorite costume)

12. A common object with uncommon beauty

13. A poster for a movie, concert, or campus event or a CD album cover by your favorite band

14. Your favorite recreation area (beach, hiking trail, park, etc.)

15. An unforgettable moment

16. An event, element, or creature in nature

17. A shopping mall, student cafeteria, or other crowded public place

18. The inside of your refrigerator, your closet, or some other equally loathsome place in your home

19. A treasure from a personal collection or a family heirloom

20. Your Special Place (Perhaps your place offers you solitude, beauty, or renewed energy. The scene shown here was painted over a half-dozen different ways by nineteenth-century

The Water-Lily Pond, 1899, by Claude Monet

© National Gallery, London, England/SuperStock

artist Claude Monet, who loved this tranquil lily pond near his farmhouse in France. Re-create your special place for your readers by choosing the right descriptive words, just as Monet did with each brushstroke of color.)

A Topic Proposal for Your Essay

Selecting the right subject matter is important to every writer. To help you clarify your ideas and strengthen your commitment to your topic, here is a proposal sheet that asks you to describe some of your preliminary ideas about your subject before you begin drafting. Although your ideas may change as you write (they will almost certainly become more refined), thinking through your choice of topic now may help you avoid several false starts.

1. What subject will your essay describe? Will you describe this subject objectively or subjectively? Why?

2. Why are you interested in this topic? Do you have a personal or professional connection to the subject? State at least one reason for your choice of topic.

3. Is this a significant topic of interest to others? Why? Who specifically might find it interesting, informative, or entertaining?

4. What is the main purpose of your description? In one or two sentences describe the major effect you'd like your descriptive essay to have on your readers. What would you like for them to understand or "see" about your subject?

5. List at least three details that you think will help clarify your subject for your readers.

6. What difficulties, if any, might arise during drafting? For example, what organizational strategy might you think about now that would allow you to guide your readers through your description in a coherent way?

Sample Student Essay

In her descriptive essay, this student writer recalls her childhood days at the home of her grandparents to make a point about growing up. Notice that the writer uses both figurative language and contrasting images to help her readers understand her point of view.

TREECLIMBING

1   It was Mike's eighteenth birthday and he was having a little bit of a breakdown. "When was the last time you made cloud pictures?" he asked me absently as he stared up at the ceiling before class started. Before I could answer, he continued, "Did you know that by the time you're an

Introduction: The conversation that triggers her memory

---

adult, you've lost 85 percent of your imagination?" He paused. "I don't want to grow up." Although I doubted the authenticity of his facts, I understood that Mike—the hopeless romantic with his long ponytail, sullen black clothes, and glinting dark eyes—was caught in a Peter Pan complex. He drew those eyes from the ceiling and focused on me: "There are two types of children. Tree children and dirt children. Kids playing will either climb trees or play in the dirt. Tree children are the dreamers—the hopeful, creative dreamers. Dirt children, they just stay on the ground. Stick to the rules." He trailed off, and then picked up again: "I'm a tree child. I want to make cloud pictures and climb trees. And I don't ever want to come down." Mike's story reminded me of my own days as a tree child, and of the inevitable fall from the tree to the ground.

2   My childhood was a playground for imagination. Summers were spent surrounded by family at my grandparents' house in Milwaukee, Wisconsin. The rambling Lannonstone bungalow was located on North 46th Street at Burleigh, a short drive from center-city Milwaukee and the historic Schuster's department store. In the winter, all the houses looked alike, rigid and militant, like white-bearded old generals with icicles hanging from their moustaches. One European-styled house after the other lined the streets in strict parallel formation, block after block.

The grandparents' neighborhood remembered in military images and sensory details

3   But in the summer it was different . . . softer. No subzero winds blew lonely down the back alley. Instead, kids played stickball in it. I had elegant, grass-stained tea parties with a neighborhood girl named Shelly, while my grandfather worked in his thriving vegetable garden among the honeybees, and watched sprouts grow. An ever-present warming smell of yeast filtered down every street as the nearby breweries pumped a constant flow of fresh beer. Above, the summer sky looked like an Easter egg God had dipped in blue dye.

4   Those summer trips to Milwaukee were greatly anticipated events back then. My brother and I itched with repressed energy throughout the long plane ride from the West Coast. We couldn't wait to see Grandma and Papa.

We couldn't wait to see what presents Papa had for us. We couldn't wait to slide down the steep, blue-carpeted staircase on our bottoms, and then on our stomachs. Most of all, we couldn't wait to go down to the basement.

Use of parallel sentences to emphasize anticipation

5   The basement was better than a toy store. Yes, the old-fashioned milk cabinet in the kitchen wall was enchanting, and the laundry chute was fun because it was big enough to throw down Ernie, my stuffed dog companion, so my brother could catch him below in the laundry room, as our voices echoed up and down the chute. But the basement was better than all of these, better even than sliding down those stairs on rug-burned bottoms.

6   It was always deliciously cool down in the basement. Since the house was built in the 1930s, there was no air conditioning. Upstairs, we slept in hot, heavy rooms. My nightgown stuck to the sheets, and I would lie awake, listening to crickets, inhaling the beer-sweet smell of the summer night, hoping for a cool breeze. Nights were forgotten, however, as my brother and I spent hours every day in the basement. There were seven rooms in the basement; some darker rooms I had waited years to explore. There was always a jumbled heap of toys in the middle room, most of which were leftovers from my father's own basement days. It was a child's safe haven; it was a sacred place.

The basement in contrast to other parts of the house

7   The hours spent in the basement were times of a gloriously secure childhood. Empires were created in a day with faded colored building blocks. New territories were annexed when either my brother or I got the courage to venture into one of those Other Rooms—the dark, musty ones without windows—and then scamper back to report of any sightings of monsters or other horrific childhood creatures. In those basement days everything seemed safe and wholesome and secure, with my family surrounding me, protecting me. Like childhood itself, entering the basement was like entering another dimension.

Adventures in the basement

8   Last summer I returned to Milwaukee to help my grandparents pack to move into an apartment. I went back at 17 to find the house—my

The house
and
neighborhood
years later

kingdom—up for sale. I found another cycle coming to a close, and I found myself separated from what I had once known. I looked at the house. It was old; it was crumbling; it needed paint. I looked down the back alley and saw nothing but trash and weeds. I walked to the corner and saw smoke-choked, dirty streets and thick bars in shop windows, nothing more than another worn-out midwestern factory city. I went back to the house and down to the basement, alone.

The
basement
years later

9   It was gray and dark. Dust filtered through a single feeble sunbeam from a cracked window pane. It was empty, except for the overwhelming musty smell. The toys were gone, either packed or thrown away. As I walked in and out of rooms, the quietness filled my ears, but in the back of my head the sounds of childhood laughter and chatter played like an old recording.

10   The dark rooms were filled not with monsters but with remnants of my grandfather's business. A neon sign was propped against the wall in a corner: Ben Strauss Plumbing. Piles of heavy pipes and metal machine parts lay scattered about on shelves. A dusty purple ribbon was thumbtacked to a door. It said SHOOT THE WORKS in white letters. I gently took it down. The ribbon hangs on my door at home now, and out of context it somehow is not quite so awe-inspiring and mystifying as it once was. However, it does serve its purpose, permanently connecting me to my memories.

Conclusion: A
return to the
introduction's
images and
some advice

11   All children are tree children, I believe. The basement used to be my tree, the place I could dream in. That last summer I found myself, much to Mike's disappointment, quite mature, quite adult. Maybe Mike fell from his tree and was bruised. Climbing down from that tree doesn't have to be something to be afraid of. One needn't hide in the tree for fear of touching the ground and forgetting how to climb back up when necessary. I think there is a way to balance the two extremes. Climb down gracefully as you grow up, and if you fall, don't land in quicksand. I like to think I'm more of a shrubbery child: not so low as to get stuck in the mud and just high enough to look at the sky and make cloud pictures.

Professional Essay*

Still Learning from My Mother

Cliff Schneider

Cliff Schneider is a graduate of Cornell and a retired freshwater fisheries biologist who worked for the Department of Environmental Conservation in New York. Much of his research and writing has focused on his work studying Lake Ontario. This essay, a personal tribute to his seventy-nine-year-old mother, was first published in the "My Turn" column of *Newsweek* magazine in March 2000.

1   When I was a young boy growing up on New York's Long Island in the 1950s, it was common to see boys and their fathers gathering in the roads in front of their homes on warm summer evenings to "have a catch." That was the term we had for tossing a baseball while we talked about school, jobs and life in general. Although my dad and I had many catches together, my most memorable ones were with my mother. She would happily grab a glove, run out to the road and then fire fastballs at me that cracked my glove and left my hand stinging. She never showed any motherly concern, though, just a broad grin with the tip of her tongue exposed in the corner of her mouth. This was her game face. I can still recall how delighted I was tossing the ball with Mom and hearing the comments from my friends and neighbors: "Where did your mother learn to throw a ball like that?"

2   My mother, you see, was a jock long before Title IX unleashed the explosion of modern women's athletics. She lettered in field hockey and basketball while attending Hofstra University in the late 1930s. This was a time when it wasn't very fashionable for women to go running after a ball and work up a sweat. Luckily for me, Mom never worried about what was fashionable. She loved sports, loved being active and, most of all, loved the competition. Mom was kind to her kids until we played ball. Then we'd notice this gleam in her eye, the broad grin and the familiar tongue that told us she was ready for action and ready to have some fun. No matter what game she played, Mom had class. She played hard, she laughed a lot and, win or lose, she was always gracious.

3   The years have diminished Mom's physical abilities, as they would have for anyone who is about to become an octogenarian. Her back is a little bent, and she complains occasionally about her hip. Her biggest concession to the aging process, however, is that she has had to lighten up on her bowling ball. As a young mother in suburban bowling leagues she toted a 15-pound ball, carried a 160 average and had a high game of 212. As she's grown older, her scores have declined. In recent years she's had to start using an eight-pound ball, which she protests is too light and "doesn't give enough pin action."

4   For years I have had to listen to my mother's perennial battle cry as she begins each new bowling season—"This is the year I'm going to bowl a 200 game!" I've always smiled and nodded in agreement, which was my way of acknowledging her

---

* ◆ To help you read this essay analytically, review pages 180–182. For two other professional essays in Part Two that make extensive use of description, see "To Bid the World Farewell" (pages 218–222) and "Two Ways of Viewing the River" (pages 243–244).

determination. During our regular Thursday-evening phone conversations (she bowls on Thursdays), she gives me a frame-by-frame description of her games, and gripes that she can't bowl the way she used to. She almost always slips in the comment "I'm going to make 200 if it kills me." I try to explain that she should be satisfied that she is at least able to play the game. "Try to make some concession to your age, Mom," I say. Of course, she will have none of this talk and this year bought a 10-pound ball in pursuit of her dream. Vince Lombardi would be proud.

5   A week after she started bowling with her new ball, I called to check on her progress. She no sooner said "Hi" than I could tell something big had happened in her life. I could feel the smile all the way from Hendersonville, N.C., to upstate New York. I shouted, "You bowled a 200 game!" knowing it could be the only reason for such a happy voice. She corrected me: "Not a 200 game; I got a 220." It was her highest score ever! She gave me a strike-by-strike description of her game, and we both celebrated over the phone. As she signed off and said her goodbyes, I could still sense the smile on her face. Her grin will probably fade in another month or two.

6   After some reflection, I am amazed by my mother's accomplishment. Whether it is baseball, tennis, golf or even bowling, I have never heard of anyone's peaking at 79. Yes, there is some degree of luck in every game, but in Mom's case she had the best game of her life because she persevered. Mom's achievement has lifted her spirits and made her feel young again. For someone who is too frequently reminded that she can't do what she used to, this experience could not have come at a better time in her life. I guess I'm not surprised that I can still learn from Mom—that you are never too old to dream and never too old to realize those dreams. I am not surprised, either, that in our most recent calls she talks about bowling a 250 game.

Questions on Content, Structure, and Style

1. Is Schneider's description of his mother primarily objective or subjective? Cite an example of his language to support your answer.

2. Why was his mother's behavior unusual in the 1950s? What does "before Title IX" (paragraph 2) mean?

3. What "dominant impression" of his mother does Schneider present in this essay? What are some of the details Schneider provides to help us understand this woman's character?

4. How does Schneider physically describe his mother so that readers can easily imagine those early games of catch? Why does she have "class"?

5. Examine some of Schneider's word choices. What, for example, is the effect of writing that his mother would "fire fastballs at me that cracked my glove and left my hand stinging" (paragraph 1) instead of "Mom could throw very hard"?

6. What does his mother's "perennial battle cry" at age seventy-nine reveal about her? Why does Schneider think football coach Vince Lombardi—for whom the Super Bowl trophy is named—would be proud of her?

7. What does Schneider's occasional use of dialogue add to this essay? Why, for example, does he quote his neighbors in paragraph 1 and his mother in paragraphs 3 and 4?

8. Why does Schneider organize his essay by starting with a description of his mother's younger days and concluding with a reference to "a 250 game"? How does this organization contribute to our understanding of his mother?

9. What has Schneider learned from his mother? In what way is this lesson an important part of this essay's purpose?

10. Did Schneider successfully create a picture of his mother? Could you suggest some ways he might improve his description? What language might have been more specific or vivid?

Suggestions for Writing

Try using Cliff Schneider's "Still Learning from My Mother" as a stepping-stone to your essay. Describe an unusual-but-wonderful relative or friend you admire for a particular trait. Consider including ample physical details, dialogue, and actions illustrating personality, as Schneider did, to make your description of this person vivid for your reader. Or write a description of an ancestor whose photograph has always intrigued you. What is the dominant impression of this picture? What does this person's face (or posture or choice of clothing) say to you about his or her character or style?

Perhaps you might choose to describe another mother figure, whose face is forever identified with the Great Depression. In 1936 photographer Dorothea Lange stopped on a dirt road in California to take a half-dozen pictures of a thirty-two-year-old woman and her children as they huddled in the rain under a lean-to tent. The woman told Lange they had been living off birds the children had killed and that she had just sold the tires off their car to buy food. Why do you think *Migrant Mother*, shown here, is considered one of the most affecting photographs of all time?

Migrant Mother, 1936, by Dorothea Lange

Copyright © the Dorothea Lange Collection, Oakland Museum of California

Vocabulary

Title IX (2)   octogenarian (3)   toted (3)
diminished (3)   concession (3)   perennial (4)

© Ryan McVay/Photodisc/ Getty Images

A Revision Worksheet

As you write your rough drafts, consult Chapter 5 for guidance through the revision process. In addition, here are a few questions to ask yourself as you revise your description:

1. Is the descriptive essay's purpose clear to the reader?

2. Are there enough specific details in the description to make the subject matter distinct to readers who are unfamiliar with the scene, person, or object? Where might more detail be added?

3. Are the details arranged in an order that's easy to follow?

4. If the assignment called for an objective description, are the details as "neutral" as possible?

5. If the assignment called for a subjective description, does the writer's particular attitude come through clearly with a consistent use of well-chosen details or imagery?

6. Could any sensory details or figurative language be added to help the reader "see" the subject matter?

7. Does this essay end with an appropriate conclusion or does description merely stop?

Collaborative Activity: After you've revised your essay extensively, exchange rough drafts with a classmate and answer these questions for each other, making specific suggestions for improvement wherever appropriate. (◆ For advice on productive participation in classroom workshops, see pages 115–120.)

Reviewing Your Progress

After you have completed your descriptive essay, take a moment to measure your progress as a writer by responding to the following questions. Such analysis will help you recognize growth in your writing skills and may enable you to identify areas that are still problematic.

1. What is the best part of your essay? Why?

2. Which one descriptive detail or image do you think is the clearest or most vivid in your essay? Why does that one stand above the others?

3. What part of your essay gave you the most trouble? How did you overcome the problem?

4. If you had more time to work on this essay, what would receive additional attention? Why?

5. What did you learn about your topic from writing this essay? About yourself as a writer?

CHAPTER 12

Narration

When many people hear the word "narrative," they think of a made-up story. But not all stories are fiction. In this chapter we are not concerned with writing literary short stories—that's a skill to develop in a creative writing class— but rather with nonfiction *expository narratives,* stories that are used to explain or prove a point. We most often use two kinds of these stories:

1. the *extended narrative*—a long episode that by itself illustrates or supports an essay's thesis

2. the *brief narrative*—a shorter incident that is often used in a body paragraph to support or illustrate a particular point in an essay.

Let's suppose, for example, you want to write an essay showing how confusing the registration system is at your school. To illustrate the problems vividly, you might devote your entire essay to the retelling of a friend's seven-hour experience signing up for classes last fall, thus making use of extended narration. Or take another example: in an argumentative essay advocating mandatory use of side-door air bags in automobiles, you might include a brief narrative about a car wreck to support a paragraph's point about air bags' ability to save lives. Regardless of which type of narrative best fits your purpose, the telling of a story or an incident can be an interesting, persuasive means of informing your readers.

Writing the Effective Narrative Essay

Know your purpose. What are you trying to accomplish by writing this narrative essay? Are you, for example, offering an *objective* retelling of a historical event (the dropping of the atomic bomb) to inform your readers who may not be acquainted with the facts? Or are you presenting a *subjective* narrative, which persuasively tells a story (Susan

343

B. Anthony's 1872 arrest for voting) from a clearly defined point of view? Perhaps your narrative is a personal story, whose lesson you wish readers to share. Whatever your choice—an objective, factual retelling or a subjective interpretation—your narrative's purpose should be clear to your readers, who should never reach the end of the story wondering "What was that all about?" Knowing your purpose will help you select the information and language best suited to meet your audience's needs.

Present your main point clearly. To ensure that readers understand their purpose, many writers first state a thesis claim followed by a narrative that supports it. Sometimes writers begin with their narrative and use their concluding paragraph to state or sum up the point or "lesson" of their story. Still others choose to imply a main point or attitude through the unfolding action and choice of descriptive details. An implied thesis is always riskier than a stated one, so unless you are absolutely convinced that your readers could not possibly fail to see your point, work on finding a smooth way to incorporate a statement of your main idea into your essay.

Follow a logical time sequence. Many narrative essays—and virtually all brief stories used in other kinds of essays—follow a chronological order, presenting actions as they naturally occur in the story. Occasionally, however, a writer will use the flashback technique, which takes the readers back in time to reveal an event that occurred before the present scene of the essay. If you decide to use shifts in time, use transitional phrases or other signals to ensure that your readers don't become confused or lost.

Use sensory details to hold your readers' interest. For example, if the setting plays an important role in your story, describe it in vivid terms so that your readers can imagine the scene easily. Suppose you are pointing out the necessity of life preservers on sailboats by telling the story of how you spent a stormy night in the lake, clinging to a capsized boat. To convince your readers, let them "feel" the stinging rain and the icy current trying to drag you under; let them "see" the black waves and the dark menacing sky; let them "hear" the howling wind and the gradual splitting apart of the boat. Effective narration often depends on effective description, and effective description depends on vivid, specific detail. (◆ For more help on writing description, see Chapter 11; review Chapter 7 for advice on word choice.)

Create authentic characters. Again, the use of detail is crucial. Your readers should be able to visualize the people (or animals) in your narrative clearly; if your important characters are drawn too thinly or if they seem phony or stereotyped, your readers will not fully grasp the meaning of your story. Show your readers the major characters as you see them by commenting unobtrusively on their appearances, speech, and actions. In addition, a successful narrative may depend on the reader's understanding of people's motives—why they act the way they do in certain situations. A narrative about your hometown's grouchiest miser who suddenly donated a large sum of money to a poor family isn't very believable unless we know the motive behind the action. In other words, let your readers know what is happening to whom by explaining or showing why.

Use dialogue realistically. Writers often use dialogue, their characters' spoken words, to reveal action or personality traits of the speakers. By presenting conversations, writers show rather than tell, often creating emphasis or a more dramatic effect. Dialogue may also help readers identify with or feel closer to the characters or action by creating a sense of "you are there." If your narrative would profit from dialogue, be certain the word choice and the manner of speaking are in keeping with each character's education, background, age, location, and so forth. Don't, for example, put a sophisticated philosophical treatise into the mouth of a ten-year-old boy or the latest campus slang into the speech of a fifty-year-old auto mechanic from Two Egg, Florida. Also, make sure that your dialogue doesn't sound wooden or phony. The right dialogue can help make your story more realistic and interesting, provided that the conversations are essential to the narrative and are not merely padding the plot. (◆ For an example of dialogue in a narrative, read Langston Hughes' "Salvation" on pages 352–353. For help in punctuating dialogue, see pages 586–588 in the Handbook.)

Problems to Avoid

Weak, boring narratives are often the result of problems with subject matter or poor pacing; therefore, you should keep in mind the following advice:

Choose your subject carefully. Most of the best narrative essays come from personal experience or study, and the reason is fairly obvious: it's difficult to write convincingly about something you've never seen or done or read about. You probably couldn't, for instance, write a realistic account of a bullfight unless you'd seen one or at least had studied the subject in great detail. The simplest, easiest, most interesting nonfiction narrative you can write is likely to be about an event with which you are personally familiar. This doesn't mean that you can't improvise many details or create a hypothetical story to illustrate a point. Even so, you will probably still have more success basing your narrative—real or hypothetical—on something or someone you know well.

Limit your scope. When you wish to use an extended narrative to illustrate a thesis, don't select an event or series of actions whose retelling will be too long or complex for your assignment. In general, it's better to select one episode and flesh it out with many specific details so that your readers can clearly see your point. For instance, you may have had many rewarding experiences during the summer you worked as a lifeguard, but you can't tell them all. Instead, you might focus on one experience that captures the essence of your attitude toward your job—say, the time you saved a child from drowning—and present the story so vividly that the readers can easily understand your point of view.

Don't let your story lag or wander. At some time you've probably listened to a storyteller who became stuck on some insignificant detail ("Was it Friday or Saturday the letter came? Let's see now . . ."; "Then Joe said to me—no, it was Sally—no, wait, it was . . ."). And you've probably also heard bores who insist on making a short story long by including too many unimportant details or digressions. These mistakes ruin the *pacing* of their stories; in other words, the story's tempo or movement becomes bogged down until the readers are bored witless. To avoid creating a sleeping tonic in word form, dismiss all unessential information and focus your attention—and use of detail—on the important events, people, and places. Skip uneventful periods of time by using such phrases as "A week went by before Mr. Smith called . . ." or "Later that evening, around nine o'clock. . . ." In short, keep the story moving quickly enough to hold the readers' interest. Moreover, use a variety of transitional devices to move the readers from one action to another; don't rely continuously on the "and then . . . and then . . ." method.

PRACTICING WHAT YOU'VE LEARNED

A. To practice collecting details that will strengthen your narrative, try this activity. First, study the accompanying painting, *Tornado Over Kansas* by John Steuart Curry, and then list as many specific, descriptive details about the scene as you can see or imagine. For example, what do details about the setting and the family's appearance reveal about these people and where they live? What unusual noises, colors, and smells might be present and how might they be vividly described? What does each person's facial expression and body language tell you about his or her thoughts at this very moment? What words might be spoken by each person and in what tone of voice? What role do the animals play in this scene?

Tornado Over Kansas (oil on canvas), 1929, by John Steuart Curry

© Canstock Images, Inc./ Index Stock Imagery

Collection of the Muskegon Museum of Art, Michigan, Hackley Picture Fund Purchase, 1935.4

Now think of a time in which you experienced a narrow escape or conquered a fearful moment, some event in your life that might be retold in an exciting narrative essay. Using the impressions recorded from the painting as a guide to prompt your memory, compile a similar list of vivid, sensory details describing the people, setting, dialogue, and action at the most dramatic point of your story.

B. *Collaborative Activity:* Think of an important event in your life that you would like known to future generations of your family. Or perhaps there is a story about your ancestors that you want to record so it is not forgotten. Draft some notes about your story, and then, in class, pair with another student. Take turns telling your stories; as each person talks, the partner should ask for more details. Simple questions such as "What did he look like at that moment?" or "Why was that decision so important?" or "What exactly did you say then?" can help a writer shape and invigorate a narrative. Incorporate any useful new details, descriptions, or dialogue into the final draft of your essay.

© Inspirestock/CORBIS

ESSAY TOPICS

Use one of the following topics to suggest an essay that is developed by narration. Remember that each essay must have a clear purpose. ◆ For additional ideas, see the "Suggestions for Writing" section following the professional essay (page 354); the quotations on pages 43–45 may also spark topics.

1. An act of courage or devotion

2. An event of historical, medical, or scientific importance

3. An interaction that changed your thinking on a particular subject

4. Your best holiday or road trip; a meaningful first or last day (school, job, camp, etc.)

5. A random act of kindness

6. Your worst accident or brush with danger

7. An unforgettable childhood experience

8. A memorable event governed by nature or an entertaining pet story

9. A time you gained self-confidence or changed your self-image

10. A meaningful event experienced in another culture or country

11. The day everything went wrong (or right)

12. An event that led to an important decision

continued on next page

13. Your experience with prejudice or with an act of charity or friendship

14. A blessing in disguise

15. A gain or loss of something or someone important

16. A risk that paid off (or a triumph against the odds)

17. A nonacademic lesson learned at school, on a job, or on a team

18. An episode marking your passage from one stage of your life to another

19. A habit that got you into (or out of) trouble

20. Your participation in a civic event, social justice activity, or charity (an election campaign, voter registration work, Red Cross blood drive, Habitat for Humanity, etc.), showing how you were informed or changed

For many people, a first involvement in an exciting political campaign or in a helpful volunteer service organization can be a life-changing experience.

© Win McNames/Getty Images News

A Topic Proposal for Your Essay

Selecting the right subject matter is important to every writer. To help you clarify your ideas and strengthen your commitment to your topic, here is a proposal sheet that asks you to describe some of your preliminary ideas about your subject before you begin drafting. Although your ideas may change as you write (they will almost certainly become more refined), thinking through your choice of topic now may help you avoid several false starts.

1. In a sentence or two, briefly state the subject of your narrative. Did you or someone you know participate in this story?

2. Why did you select this narrative? Does it have importance for you personally, academically, or professionally? In some other way? Explain your reason, or purpose, for telling this story.

3. Will others be informed or entertained by this story? Who might be especially interested in hearing your narrative? Why?

4. What is the primary effect you would like your narrative to have on your readers? What would you like them to feel or think about after they read your story? Why?

5. What is the critical moment in your story? At what point, in other words, does the action reach its peak? Summarize this moment in a few descriptive words.

6. What difficulties, if any, might this narrative present as you are drafting? For example, if the story you want to tell is long or complex, how might you focus on the main action and pace it appropriately?

Sample Student Essay

In this narrative a student uses a story about a sick but fierce dog to show how she learned a valuable lesson in her job as a veterinarian's assistant. Notice the student's good use of vivid details that make this well-paced story both clear and interesting.

NEVER UNDERESTIMATE THE LITTLE THINGS

1   When I went to work as a veterinarian's assistant for Dr. Sam Holt and Dr. Jack Gunn last summer, I was under the false impression that the hardest part of veterinary surgery would be the actual performance of an operation. The small chores demanded before this feat didn't occur to me as being of any importance. As it happened, I had been in the veterinary clinic only a total of four hours before I met a little animal who convinced me that the operation itself was probably the easiest part of treatment. This animal, to whom I owe thanks for so enlightening me, was a chocolate-colored chihuahua of tiny size and immense perversity named Smokey.

Introduction: A misconception

Thesis: Small preliminary details can be as important as the major action

2   Smokey could have very easily passed for some creature from another planet. It wasn't so much his gaunt little frame and overly large head, or his bony paws with nearly saberlike claws, as it was his grossly infected eyes. Those once-shining eyes were now distorted and swollen into grotesque balls of septic, sightless flesh. The only vague similarity they had to what we'd normally think of as the organs of vision was a slightly

Description of the main character: His appearance

His personality

upraised dot, all that was left of the pupil, in the center of a pink and purply marble. As if that were not enough, Smokey had a temper to match his ugly sight. He also had surprisingly good aim, considering his largely diminished vision, toward any moving object that happened to place itself unwisely before his ever-inquisitive nose; with sudden and wholly vicious intent, he would snap and snarl at whatever blocked the little light that could filter through his swollen and ruptured blood vessels. Truly, in many respects, Smokey was a fearful dog to behold.

The difficulty of moving the dog to the surgery room

3   Such an appearance and personality did nothing to encourage my already flagging confidence in my capabilities as a vet's assistant. How was I supposed to get that little demon out of his cage? Jack had casually requested that I bring Smokey to the surgery room, but did he really expect me to put my hands into the cage of that devil dog? I suppose it must have been my anxious expression that saved me, for as I turned uncertainly toward the kennel, Jack chuckled nonchalantly and accompanied me to demonstrate how professionals in his line of work dealt with professionals in Smokey's. He took a small rope about four feet long with a no-choke noose at one end and unlatched Smokey's cage. Then cautiously he reached in and dangled the noose before the dog's snarling jaws. Since Smokey could only barely see what he was biting at, his attacks were directed haphazardly in a semicircle around his body. The tiny area of his cage led to his capture, for during one of Smokey's forward lunges, Jack dropped the noose over his head and moved the struggling creature out onto the floor. The fight had only just begun for Smokey, however, and he braced his feet against the slippery linoleum tiling and forced us to drag him, like a little pull toy on a string, to the surgery.

The difficulty of moving the dog to the table

4   Once Smokey was in the surgery, however, the question that hung before our eyes like a veritable presence was how to get the dog from the floor to the table. Simply picking him up and plopping him down was

out of the question. One glance at the quivering little figure emitting ominous and throaty warnings was enough to assure us of that. Realizing that the game was over, Jack grimly handed me the rope and reached for a muzzle. It was a doomed attempt from the start: the closer Jack dangled the tiny leather cup to the dog's nose, the more violent did Smokey's contortions and rage-filled cries become and the more frantic our efforts became to try to keep our feet and fingers clear of the angry jaws. Deciding that a firmer method had to be used, Jack instructed me to raise the rope up high enough so that Smokey would have to stand on his hind legs. This greatly reduced his maneuverability but served to increase his tenacity, for at this the little dog nearly went into paroxysms of frustration and rage. In his struggles, however, Smokey caught his forepaw on his swollen eye, and the blood that had been building up pressure behind the fragile cornea burst out and dripped to the floor. In the midst of our surprise and the twinge of panic startling the three of us, Jack saw his chance and swiftly muzzled the animal and lifted him to the operating table.

5   Even at that point it wasn't easy to put the now terrified dog to sleep. He fought the local anesthesia and caused Jack to curse as he was forced to give Smokey more of the drug than should have been necessary for such a small beast. After what seemed an eternity, Smokey lay prone on the table, breathing deeply and emitting soft snores and gentle whines. We also breathed deeply in relief, and I relaxed to watch fascinated, while Jack performed a very delicate operation quite smoothly and without mishap.

The difficulty of putting the dog to sleep before the surgery

6   Such was my harrowing induction into the life of a veterinary surgeon. But Smokey did teach me a valuable lesson that has proven its importance to me many times since: wherever animals are concerned, even the smallest detail is important and should never be taken for granted.

Conclusion: The lesson she learned

Professional Essay*

Salvation

Langston Hughes

Langston Hughes is a poet and fiction writer who was an important part of the Harlem Renaissance of the 1920s. Creating innovative poetry that often incorporated the rhythms of jazz and vibrant dialect into his work, Hughes is admired for his insightful presentations of black life in America; his most famous poem is known as "Dream Deferred." This essay was first published as part of his autobiography, *The Big Sea* (1940).

1   I was saved from sin when I was going on thirteen. But not really saved. It happened like this. There was a big revival at my Auntie Reed's church. Every night for weeks there had been much preaching, singing, praying, and shouting, and some very hardened sinners had been brought to Christ, and the membership of the church had grown by leaps and bounds. Then just before the revival ended, they held a special meeting for children, "to bring the young lambs to the fold." My aunt spoke of it for days ahead. That night I was escorted to the front row and placed on the mourners' bench** with all the other young sinners, who had not yet been brought to Jesus.

2   My aunt told me that when you were saved you saw a light, and something happened to you inside! And Jesus came into your life! And God was with you from then on! She said you could see and hear and feel Jesus in your soul. I believed her. I had heard a great many old people say the same thing and it seemed to me they ought to know. So I sat there calmly in the hot, crowded church, waiting for Jesus to come to me.

3   The preacher preached a wonderful rhythmical sermon, all moans and shouts and lonely cries and dire pictures of hell, and then he sang a song about the ninety and nine safc in the fold, but one little lamb was left out in the cold. Then he said: "Won't you come? Won't you come to Jesus? Young lambs, won't you come?" And he held out his arms to all us young sinners there on the mourners' bench. And the little girls cried. And some of them jumped up and went to Jesus right away. But most of us just sat there.

4   A great many old people came and knelt around us and prayed, old women with jet-black faces and braided hair, old men with work-gnarled hands. And the church sang a song about the lower lights are burning, some poor sinners to be saved. And the whole building rocked with prayer and song.

5   Still I kept waiting to *see* Jesus.

6   Finally all the young people had gone to the altar and were saved, but one boy and me. He was a rounder's son named Westley. Westley and I were surrounded by sisters and deacons praying. It was very hot in the church, and getting late now. Finally Westley said to me in a whisper: ". . . I'm tired o' sitting here. Let's get up and be saved." So he got up and was saved.

---

*◆ To help you read this essay analytically, review pages 180–182.

**At some revivals, a bench near the front of the church provided reserved seating for repentant sinners and others in sorrow.

7   Then I was left all alone on the mourners' bench. My aunt came and knelt at my knees and cried, while prayers and song swirled all around me in the little church. The whole congregation prayed for me alone, in a mighty wail of moans and voices. And I kept waiting serenely for Jesus, waiting, waiting—but he didn't come. I wanted to see him, but nothing happened to me. Nothing! I wanted something to happen to me, but nothing happened.

8   I heard the songs and the minister saying: "Why don't you come? My dear child, why don't you come to Jesus? Jesus is waiting for you. He wants you. Why don't you come? Sister Reed, what is this child's name?"

9   "Langston" my aunt sobbed.

10   "Langston, why don't you come? Why don't you come and be saved? Oh, Lamb of God! Why don't you come?"

11   Now it was really getting late. I began to be ashamed of myself, holding everything up so long. I began to wonder what God thought about Westley, who certainly hadn't seen Jesus either, but who was now sitting proudly on the platform, swinging his knickerbockered legs and grinning down at me, surrounded by deacons and old women on their knees praying. God had not struck Westley dead for taking his name in vain or for lying in the temple. So I decided that maybe to save further trouble, I'd better lie, too, and say that Jesus had come, and get up and be saved.

12   So I got up.

13   Suddenly the whole room broke into a sea of shouting, as they saw me rise. Waves of rejoicing swept the place. Women leaped in the air. My aunt threw her arms around me. The minister took me by the hand and led me to the platform.

14   When things quieted down, in a hushed silence, punctuated by a few ecstatic "Amens," all the new young lambs were blessed in the name of God. Then joyous singing filled the room.

15   That night, for the last time in my life but one—for I was a big boy twelve years old—I cried. I cried, in bed alone, and couldn't stop. I buried my head under the quilts, but my aunt heard me. She woke up and told my uncle I was crying because the Holy Ghost had come into my life, and because I had seen Jesus. But I was really crying because I couldn't bear to tell her that I had lied, that I had deceived everybody in the church, that I hadn't seen Jesus, and that now I didn't believe there was a Jesus any more, since he didn't come to help me.

Questions on Content, Structure, and Style

1. What is Hughes' main purpose in this narrative? Why do you think this event was important in his life?

2. How does Hughes create the scene in the revival meeting? Which sensory details of sight and sound are particularly effective in helping the reader feel present at the church?

3. Which people in his life are pressuring the twelve-year-old Hughes to be "saved"?

4. Why does Hughes resist going to the altar with the rest of the children? What sense of conflict does he feel?

5. What does Hughes' use of dialogue add to his story? Which people speak directly and how do their words help the reader understand Hughes' emotional state?

6. Why does Hughes single out Westley's actions for description?

7. What are Hughes' reasons for finally joining the other children? Does he explain his thinking clearly enough for you to understand his decision?

8. How does Hughes use figurative language to capture a particular moment? (See, for example, "a sea of shouting . . . waves of rejoicing" in paragraph 13.)

9. Why is Hughes crying in bed after the service? How does his aunt perceive his tears?

10. Overall, how effective is Hughes' story about this childhood event? At the narrative's conclusion, did you empathize with him or have a different reaction?

Suggestions for Writing

Try using Langston Hughes' essay as a stepping-stone to your writing. Remember a time you resisted or gave in to peer or family pressure. What insight did you gain from this experience? Given a second chance, would you make the same decision or a different one? Imagine that you are writing to an audience of high school or college students who might profit from hearing your story. Consider using sensory details, dialogue, or imagery, as Hughes did, to help your readers understand the people, places, and actions in your narrative.

Vocabulary

revival (1)
dire (3)
deacons (6)
serenely (7)
knickerbockered (11)

© Ryan McVay/Photodisc/
Getty Images

A Revision Worksheet

As you write your rough drafts, consult Chapter 5 for guidance through the revision process. In addition, here are a few questions to ask yourself as you revise your narrative:

1. Is the narrative essay's purpose clear to the reader?

2. Is the thesis plainly stated or at least clearly implied?

3. Does the narrative convincingly support or illustrate its intended point? If not, how might the story be changed?

4. Does the story maintain a logical point of view and an understandable order of action? Are there enough transitional devices used to give the story a smooth flow?

5. Are the characters, actions, and settings presented in enough vivid detail to make them clear and believable? Where could more detail be effectively added? Would use of dialogue be appropriate?

6. Is the story coherent and well paced, or does it wander or bog down in places because of irrelevant or repetitious details? What might be condensed or cut? Could any bland or wordy description be replaced?

7. Does the essay end in a satisfying way, or does the action stop too abruptly?

Collaborative Activity: After you've revised your essay extensively, you might exchange rough drafts with a classmate and answer these questions for each other, making specific suggestions for improvement wherever appropriate. (◆ For advice on productive participation in classroom workshops, see pages 115–120.)

Reviewing Your Progress

After you have completed your narrative essay, take a moment to measure your progress as a writer by responding to the following questions. Such analysis will help you to recognize growth in your writing skills and may enable you to identify areas that are still problematic.

1. What do you like best about your narrative essay? Why?

2. After reading through your essay, select the description, detail, or piece of dialogue that you think best characterizes a major figure or most effectively advances the action in your story. Explain the reason for your choice in one or two sentences.

3. What part of your essay gave you the most trouble? How did you overcome the problem?

4. If you had more time to work on this essay, what would receive additional attention? Why?

5. What did you learn about your topic from writing this essay? About yourself as a writer?

CHAPTER 13

Writing Essays Using Multiple Strategies

In Part Two of this text you have been studying essays developed primarily by a single mode or expository strategy. You may have, for example, written essays primarily developed by multiple examples, process analysis, or comparison/contrast. Concentrating on a single strategy in your essays has allowed you to practice, in a focused way, each of the patterns of development most often used in writing tasks. Although practicing each strategy in isolation this way is somewhat artificial, it is the easiest, simplest way to master the common organizational patterns. Consider the parallels to learning almost any skill: before you attempt a complex dive with spins and flips, you first practice each maneuver separately. Having understood and mastered the individual strategies of development, you should feel confident about facing any writing situation, including those that would most profit from incorporating multiple strategies to accomplish their goal.

Most essays *do* call upon multiple strategies of development to achieve their purpose, a reality you have probably discovered for yourself as you studied various essays in this text. In fact, you may have found it difficult—or impossible—to avoid combining modes and strategies in your own essays. As noted in the introduction to Part Two, writers virtually always blend strategies, using examples in their comparisons, description in their definitions, causal analysis in their arguments, and so on. Therein is the heart of the matter: the single patterns of development you have been practicing are *thinking* strategies—ways of considering a subject and generating ideas—as well as organizing tools. Successful writers study their tasks and choose the strategies that will most effectively accomplish their purpose.

In addition, some writing tasks, often the longer ones, will clearly profit from combining multiple strategies in distinct ways to thoroughly address the essay's subject,

357

purpose, and audience. Suppose, for example, you are given a problem-solving assignment in a business class: selling the City Council on a plan to build a student housing project in a particular neighborhood. You might call on your writing resources and use multiple strategies to

- Describe the project
- Explain the causes (the need for such a project)
- Argue its strengths; deflect opposing arguments
- Contrast it to other housing options
- Cite similar successful examples in other towns
- Explain its long-term beneficial effects on tenants, neighbors, businesses, etc.

Or perhaps you are investigating recent disciplinary action taken against Colorado high school seniors for decorating their graduation caps and gowns. Your essay might combine strategies by first presenting examples of the controversy, explaining its causes and effects, and then contrasting the opinions of administrators, students, and parents. You might even conclude with a suggested process for avoiding future problems. In other words, many essay assignments—including the widely assigned summary-response paper*—might call for a multistrategy response.

As a writer who now knows how to use a variety of thinking and organizational methods, you can assess any writing situation and select the strategy—or strategies—that will work best for your topic, purpose, and audience.

Choosing the Best Strategies

To help you choose the best means of development for your essay, here is a brief review of the modes and strategies accompanied by some pertinent questions:

1. Example: Would real or hypothetical illustrations make my subject more easily understood?
2. Process: Would a step-by-step procedural analysis clarify my subject?
3. Comparison/Contrast: Would aligning or juxtaposing my subject to something else be helpful?
4. Definition: Would my subject profit from an extended explanation of its meaning?
5. Division/Classification: Would separating my subject into its component parts or grouping its parts into categories be useful?
6. Causal Analysis: Would explaining causes or effects add important information?
7. Argument: Would my position be advanced by offering logical reasons and/or addressing objections?
8. Description: Would vivid details, sensory images, or figurative language help readers visualize my subject?
9. Narrative: Would a story best illustrate some idea or aspect of my subject?

---

* ◆ For an in-depth look at this popular assignment, see pages 448–451.

Use these nine questions as prompts to help you generate ideas and select those strategies that best accomplish your purpose.

Problems to Avoid

Avoid overkill. Being prepared to use any of the writing strategies is akin to carrying many tools in your carpenter's bag. But just because you own many tools doesn't mean you must use all of them in one project; rather, you select only the ones you need for the specific job at hand. If you do decide to use multiple strategies in a particular essay, avoid a hodgepodge of information that runs in too many directions. Sometimes your essay's prescribed length means you cannot present all you know; again, let your main purpose guide you to including the best or most important ideas.

Organize logically. If you decide that multiple strategies will work best, you must find an appropriate order and coherent flow for your essay. In the hypothetical problem-solving essay on the housing project mentioned earlier, for instance, the writer must decide whether the long-term effects of the project should be discussed earlier or later in the paper. In the student essay that follows, the writer struggled with the question of discussing kinds of vegetarians before or after reasons for adopting vegetarianism. There are no easy answers to such questions—each writer must experiment with outlines and rough drafts to find the most successful arrangement, one that will offer the most effective response to the particular material, the essay's purpose, and the audience's needs. Be patient as you try various ways of combining strategies into a coherent rather than choppy paper.

PRACTICING WHAT YOU'VE LEARNED

To help you recognize how writers often use multiple strategies in their writing, select one of the professional essays in Chapter 9 of this text. Identify at least two strategies at work, explaining their effectiveness and why you think the writer chose to make his or her point in this way.

© Canstock Images, Inc./ Index Stock Imagery

Sample Student Essay

In the essay that follows, the student writer responds to an assignment that asked her to write about an important belief or distinguishing aspect of her life. The purpose, audience, and development of her essay were left to her; the length was designated as 750 to 1,000 words. As a confirmed vegetarian for well over a decade, she often found herself questioned about her beliefs. After deciding to clarify (and encourage) vegetarianism for an audience of interested but often puzzled fellow students, she developed her essay by drawing on many strategies, including causal analysis, example, classification, contrast, argument, and process analysis. Because she found her early draft too long, the writer edited out an extended narrative telling the story of her own "conversion" to vegetarianism, viewing that section as less central to her essay's main purpose than the other parts.

PASS THE BROCCOLI—PLEASE!

Introduction: Famous examples

1   What do Benjamin Franklin, Charles Darwin, Leonardo da Vinci, Percy Bysshe Shelley, Mohandas Gandhi, Albert Einstein, and I have in common? In addition to being great thinkers, of course, we are all vegetarians, people who have rejected the practice of eating animals. Vegetarianism is growing rapidly in America today, but some people continue to see it as a strange choice. If you are thinking of making this decision yourself or are merely curious, taking time to learn about vegetarianism is worthwhile.

Thesis, purpose, audience

Contrast to other parts of the world

2   In a land where hamburgers, pepperoni pizza, and fried chicken are among our favorite foods, just why do Americans become vegetarians anyway? Worldwide, vegetarianism is often part of religious faith, especially to Buddhists, Hindus, and others whose spiritual beliefs emphasize nonviolence, karma, and reincarnation. But in this country the reasons for becoming vegetarian are more diverse. Some people cite ecological reasons, arguing that vegetarianism is best for our planet because it takes less land and food to raise vegetables and grain than livestock. Others choose vegetarianism because of health reasons. Repeated studies by groups such as the American Heart Association and the American Medical Association show that diets lower in animal fats and higher in fiber decrease the risk of heart disease, cancer, diabetes, hypertension, and osteoporosis.

Causal analysis: 3 reasons

3   Still other people's ethical beliefs bring them to vegetarianism. These people object to the ways that some animals, such as cows and chickens, are confined and are often fed various chemicals, such as growth hormones, antibiotics, and tranquilizers. They object to the procedures of slaughterhouses. They object to killing animals for consumption or for their decorative body parts (hides, fur, skins, tusks, feathers, etc.) and to their use in science or cosmetic experiments. These vegetarians believe that animals feel fear and pain and that it is morally wrong for one

species to inflict unnecessary suffering on another. I count myself among this group; consequently, my vegetarian choices extend to wearing no leather or fur, and I do not use household or cosmetic products tested on animals.

Personal example

4   Regardless of reasons for our choice, all vegetarians reject eating meat. However, there are actually several kinds of vegetarians, with the majority falling into three categories:

1. Ovo-lacto vegetarians eat milk, cheese, eggs, and honey;
2. Lacto vegetarians do not eat eggs but may keep other dairy products in their diet;
3. Vegans do not eat dairy products or any animal by-products whatsoever.

Classification: Three types

Many people, including myself, begin as ovo-lacto vegetarians but eventually become vegans, considered the most complete or pure type.

5   Perhaps the most common objection to any type of vegetarianism comes from a misconception about deficiencies in the diet, particularly protein. But it is a mistake to think only meat offers us protein. Vegetarians who eat dairy products, grains, vegetables, beans, and nuts receive more than enough nutrients, including protein. In fact, according to the cookbook *The Higher Taste*, cheese, peanuts, and lentils contain more protein per ounce than hamburger, pork, or a porterhouse steak. Many medical experts think that Americans actually eat too much protein, as seen in the revised food pyramid that now calls for an increase in vegetables, fruits, and grains over meat and dairy products. A vegetarian diet will not make someone a limp weakling. Kevin Eubanks, long-time *Tonight Show* band leader, is, for example, not only a busy musician but also a weightlifter. Some members of the Denver Broncos football team, according to their manager, no longer eat red meat at their training table.

Argument: Refutation, evidence, examples

6   For those who would like to give vegetarianism a try, here are a few suggestions for getting started:

Process:
4 steps to begin

1. Explore your motives. If you are only becoming a vegetarian to please a friend, for example, you won't stick with it. Be honest with yourself: the reasons behind your choice have a lot to do with your commitment.

2. Read more. The library can provide you with answers to your questions and concerns. There are hundreds of books full of ecological, medical, and ethical arguments for vegetarianism.

(More argument
and examples)

3. Eat! Another popular misconception is that vegetarianism means a life of eating tasteless grass; nothing could be less true. Visit a vegetarian restaurant several times to see how many delicious dishes are available. Even grocery stores now carry a variety of vegetarian entrees. Or try one of the many vegetarian cookbooks on the market today. You may be surprised to discover that tofu enchiladas, soy burgers, and stuffed eggplant taste better than you could ever imagine.

4. Start slowly. You don't have to become a vegan overnight if it doesn't feel right. Some people begin by excluding just red meat from their diets. Feeling good as time goes by can direct your choices. Books, such as *The Beginning Vegetarian*, and magazines, such as *Vegetarian Times*, can offer encouragement.

7   It's never too late to change your lifestyle. Nobel Prize–winning author Isaac Bashevis Singer became a vegetarian at age fifty-eight. Making this choice now may allow you to live longer and feel better. In fifty years you may be like playwright George Bernard Shaw, who at twenty-five was warned against a vegetarian diet. As a vigorous old man, Shaw wanted to tell all those people they were wrong, but noted he couldn't: "They all passed away years ago"!

Conclusion:
Additional famous
examples, witty
quotation

Professional Essay*

Don't Let Stereotypes Warp Your Judgments

Robert L. Heilbroner

Robert L. Heilbroner was a Professor of Economics at the New School for Social Research in New York City for over fifty years. He was well known for his *New Yorker* essays and for over twenty books, including *The Worldly Philosophers* (1953), whose revised editions are still widely used in economics classes. This essay, published in *Reader's Digest*, uses multiple strategies to expose a social problem, explain its causes and effects, and offer some practical suggestions for change.

1   Is a girl called Gloria apt to be better-looking than one called Bertha? Are criminals more likely to be dark than blond? Can you tell a good deal about someone's personality from hearing his voice briefly over the phone? Can a person's nationality be pretty accurately guessed from his photograph? Does the fact that someone wears glasses imply that he is intelligent?

2   The answer to all these questions is obviously, "No."

3   Yet, from all the evidence at hand, most of us believe these things. Ask any college boy if he'd rather take his chances with a Gloria or a Bertha, or ask a college girl if she'd rather blind-date a Richard or a Cuthbert. In fact, you don't have to ask: college students in questionnaires have revealed that names conjure up the same images in their minds as they do in yours—and for as little reason.

4   Look into the favorite suspects of persons who report "suspicious characters" and you will find a large percentage of them to be "swarthy" or "dark and foreign-looking"—despite the testimony of criminologists that criminals do *not* tend to be dark, foreign or "wild-eyed." Delve into the main asset of a telephone stock swindler and you will find it to be a marvelously confidence-inspiring telephone "personality." And whereas we all think we know what an Italian or a Swede looks like, it is the sad fact that when a group of Nebraska students sought to match faces and nationalities of 15 European countries, they were scored wrong in 93 percent of their identifications. Finally, for all the fact that horn-rimmed glasses have now become the standard television sign of an "intellectual," optometrists know that the main thing that distinguishes people with glasses is just bad eyes.

5   Stereotypes are a kind of gossip about the world, a gossip that makes us prejudge people before we ever lay eyes on them. Hence it is not surprising that stereotypes have something to do with the dark world of prejudice. Explore most prejudices (note that the word means prejudgment) and you will find a cruel stereotype at the core of each one.

6   For it is the extraordinary fact that once we have typecast the world, we tend to see people in terms of our standardized pictures. In another demonstration of the power of stereotypes to affect our vision, a number of Columbia and Barnard students were shown 30 photographs of pretty but unidentified girls, and asked to rate

---

*   ◆ For help reading this essay analytically, review pages 180–182.

Can you find Cuthbert?

each in terms of "general liking," "intelligence," "beauty" and so on. Two months later, the same group were shown the same photographs, this time with fictitious Irish, Italian, Jewish and "American" names attached to the pictures. Right away the ratings changed. Faces which were now seen as representing a national group went down in looks and still farther down in likability, while the "American" girls suddenly looked decidedly prettier and nicer.

7   Why is it that we stereotype the world in such irrational and harmful fashion? In part, we begin to type-cast people in our childhood years. Early in life, as every parent whose child has watched a TV Western knows, we learn to spot the Good Guys from the Bad Guys. Some years ago, a social psychologist showed very clearly how powerful these stereotypes of childhood vision are. He secretly asked the most popular youngsters in an elementary school to make errors in their morning gym exercises. Afterwards, he asked the class if anyone had noticed any mistakes during gym period. Oh, yes, said the children. But it was the *unpopular* members of the class—the "bad guys"—they remembered as being out of step.

8   We not only grow up with standardized pictures forming inside of us, but as grown-ups we are constantly having them thrust upon us. Some of them, like the half-joking, half-serious stereotypes of mothers-in-law, or country yokels, or psychiatrists, are dinned into us by the stock jokes we hear and repeat. In fact, without such stereotypes, there would be a lot fewer jokes. Still other stereotypes are perpetuated by the advertisements we read, the movies we see, the books we read.

9   And finally, we tend to stereotype because it helps us make sense out of a highly confusing world, a world which William James* once described as "one great, blooming, buzzing confusion." It is a curious fact that if we don't *know* what we're looking at, we are often quite literally unable to *see* what we're looking at. People who recover their sight after a lifetime of blindness actually cannot at first tell a triangle from a square. A visitor to a factory sees only noisy chaos where the

---

*William James (1842–1910) was an American philosopher and psychologist.

superintendent sees a perfectly synchronized flow of work. As Walter Lippmann* has said, "For the most part we do not first see, and then define; we define first, and then we see."

10   Stereotypes are one way in which we "define" the world in order to see it. They classify the infinite variety of human beings into a convenient handful of "types" towards whom we learn to act in stereotyped fashion. Life would be a wearing process if we had to start from scratch with each and every human contact. Stereotypes economize on our mental effort by covering up the blooming, buzzing confusion with big recognizable cutouts. They save us the "trouble" of finding out what the world is like—they give it its accustomed look.

11   Thus the trouble is that stereotypes make us mentally lazy. As S. I. Hayakawa, the authority on semantics, has written: "The danger of stereotypes lies not in their existence, but in the fact that they become for all people some of the time, and for some people all the time, *substitutes for observation*." Worse yet, stereotypes get in the way of our judgment, even when we do observe the world. Someone who has formed rigid preconceptions of all Latins as "excitable," or all teenagers as "wild," doesn't alter his point of view when he meets a calm and deliberate Genoese,** or a serious-minded high school student. He brushes them aside as "exceptions that prove the rule." And, of course, if he meets someone true to type, he stands triumphantly vindicated. "They're all like that," he proclaims, having encountered an excited Latin, an ill-behaved adolescent.

12   Hence, quite aside from the injustice which stereotypes do to others, they impoverish ourselves. A person who lumps the world into simple categories, who type-casts all labor leaders as "racketeers," all businessmen as "reactionaries," all Harvard men as "snobs," and all Frenchmen as "sexy," is in danger of becoming a stereotype himself. He loses his capacity to be himself—which is to say, to see the world in his own absolutely unique, inimitable and independent fashion.

13   Instead, he votes for the man who fits his standardized picture of what a candidate "should" look like or sound like, buys the goods that someone in his "situation" in life "should" own, lives the life that others define for him. The mark of the stereotype person is that he never surprises us, that we do indeed have him "typed." And no one fits this strait-jacket so perfectly as someone whose opinions about *other people* are fixed and inflexible.

14   Impoverishing as they are, stereotypes are not easy to get rid of. The world we type-cast may be no better than a Grade B movie, but at least we know what to expect of our stock characters. When we let them act for themselves in the strangely unpredictable way that people do act, who knows but that many of our fondest convictions will be proved wrong?

15   Nor do we suddenly drop our standardized pictures for a blinding vision of the Truth. Sharp swings of ideas about people often just substitute one stereotype for another. The true process of change is a slow one that adds bits and pieces of reality to the pictures in our heads, until gradually they take on some of the blurriness of life itself. Little by little, we learn not that Jews and Negroes and Catholics and Puerto Ricans are "just like everybody else"—for that, too, is a stereotype—but

*Walter Lippmann (1889–1974) was an American journalist.
**"Genoese" refers to a citizen of Genoa, Italy.

that each and every one of them is unique, special, different and individual. Often we do not even know that we have let a stereotype lapse until we hear someone saying, "all so-and-so's are like such-and-such," and we hear ourselves saying, "Well—maybe."

16   Can we speed the process along? Of course we can.

17   First, we can become *aware* of the standardized pictures in our heads, in other peoples' heads, in the world around us.

18   Second, we can become suspicious of all judgments that we allow exceptions to "prove." There is no more chastening thought than that in the vast intellectual adventure of science, it takes but one tiny exception to topple a whole edifice of ideas.

19   Third, we can learn to be chary of generalizations about people. As F. Scott Fitzgerald* once wrote: "Begin with an individual, and before you know it you have created a type; begin with a type, and you find you have created—nothing."

20   Most of the time, when we type-cast the world, we are not in fact generalizing about people at all. We are only revealing the embarrassing facts about the pictures that hang in the gallery of stereotypes in our own heads.

Questions on Content, Structure, and Style

1. Why does Heilbroner begin his essay with a series of questions, references to criminal reports, and the Nebraska study? How does this introduction set up Heilbroner's thesis?

2. How does Heilbroner define stereotypes in paragraph 5? What do the studies at Barnard and Columbia University and at the elementary school (paragraphs 6 and 7) illustrate about prejudice?

3. Why does Heilbroner use "we" and "us" so often in this essay instead of referring to "people who stereotype"? Is his choice a good one?

4. What explanation of causes does Heilbroner offer? How do stereotypes contribute to the ways we try to "define" the world?

5. In addition to the injustice inflicted on others, what negative effects does stereotyping have on those who employ it?

6. Throughout his essay, Heilbroner uses vivid, specific examples, both real and hypothetical. Cite and explain some of his most effective uses of this strategy.

7. Why does Heilbroner include a three-step process near the end of his essay?

8. Why does Heilbroner quote such well-known figures as William James, S. I. Hayakawa, Walter Lippmann, and F. Scott Fitzgerald in various places in his essay? What purposes do their words serve?

9. Evaluate this essay's conclusion. How does Heilbroner use figurative language to make a memorable last impression on his readers?

---

*F. Scott Fitzgerald (1896–1940) was an American writer, best known for his novel *The Great Gatsby*.

10. List the main strategies Heilbroner uses to develop his essay. Which do you find the most effective? If Heilbroner were to extend his essay, what other strategies might he incorporate in his exploration of stereotyping?

Suggestions for Writing

Try using Robert Heilbroner's "Don't Let Stereotypes Warp Your Judgments" as a stepping-stone to an essay of your own. Have you ever been the victim of someone's irrational or harmful stereotyping? Has anyone ever devalued your job or belittled your choice of activities? Or have you yourself been guilty of misjudging someone else? Remember that not all stereotypes are racial or ethnic; typecasting surrounds economic status (the "welfare moocher"), gender (the "dumb blonde"), locations (the redneck Texan), professions (the mousey accountant), and extracurricular activities (the "jock"), to name only a few areas. Write an essay that explores the topic of stereotyping or prejudice; use any of the modes or strategies you find helpful. You might, for example, describe an incident, discuss causes or effects, argue for ways to solve the problem, or explain steps you once took to escape "the gallery of stereotypes" in your own head.

Vocabulary

swarthy (4)	semantics (11)	chastening (18)
dinned (8)	vindicated (11)	edifice (18)
perpetuated (8)	impoverish (12)	chary (19)
synchronized (9)		

© Ryan McVay/Photodisc/ Getty Images

A Revision Worksheet

As you write your rough drafts, consult Chapter 5 for guidance through the revision process. In addition, here are a few questions to ask yourself before and during the early stages of your writing:

1. What is my main purpose in writing this particular essay? Who is my audience?

2. Does my assignment or the subject itself suggest a primary method of development or would combining several strategies be more effective?

3. Have I considered my subject from multiple directions, as suggested by the questions on page 358?

4. Have I selected the best strategies to meet the needs of my particular audience?

5. Would blending strategies help my readers understand my topic and my essay's purpose? Or am I trying to include too many approaches, move in too many directions, resulting in an essay that seems too scattered?

6. Have I considered an effective order for the strategies I've chosen? Do the parts of my essay flow together smoothly?

7. Have I avoided common weaknesses such as vague examples, fuzzy directions, circular definitions, overlapping categories, or logical fallacies, as discussed in the "Problems to Avoid" sections of Chapters 9–12?

Collaborative Activity: After you've revised your essay extensively, exchange rough drafts with a classmate and answer these questions for each other, making specific suggestions for improvement wherever appropriate. (◆ For advice on productive participation in classroom workshops, see pages 115–120.)

Reviewing Your Progress

After you have completed your essay, take a moment to measure your progress as a writer by responding to the following questions. Such analysis will help you recognize growth in your writing skills and may enable you to identify areas that are still problematic.

1. What do you like best about your essay? Why?

2. After considering the multiple strategies of development used in your essay, which one do you find most effective and why?

3. What part of your essay gave you the most trouble? How did you overcome the problem?

4. If you had more time to work on this essay, what would receive additional attention? Why?

5. What did you learn about your topic from writing this essay? About yourself as a writer?

PART 3

Special Assignments

The third section of this text addresses several kinds of assignments frequently included in composition classes and in many other college courses. Chapter 14 will first explain ways to conduct formal research on a topic and then show you how to best incorporate your research into your essay. Chapter 15, "Writing in Class: Exams and 'Response' Essays," confronts the anxiety that writing under pressure may bring by helping you respond quickly but effectively to a variety of timed essays and exams. This chapter also addresses one of the most widely used in-class assignments, the summary-response (or reaction) essay. Chapter 16, "Writing about Literature," illustrates several uses of poetry and short stories in the composition classroom and provides some guidelines for both close reading and analytical thinking. Chapter 17, "Writing about Visual Arts," offers suggestions for essays analyzing paintings, photographs, and sculptures. Chapter 18, "Writing about Film," is focused on thoughtful analysis of movies. The last chapter in Part

Three, "Writing in the World of Work," presents advice for effective business letters, memos, electronic-mail messages, and résumés.

If you have worked through Parts One and Two of this book, you have already practiced many of the skills demanded by these special assignments. Information in the next six chapters will build on what you already know about good writing.

CHAPTER 14

Writing a Paper Using Research

Although the words "research paper" have been known to produce anxiety worse than that caused by the sound of a dentist's drill, you should try to relax. A research paper is similar to the kinds of expository and argumentative essays described in the earlier parts of this book, the difference being the use of documented source material to support, illustrate, or explain your ideas. Research papers still call for thesis statements, logical sequences of paragraphs, well-developed evidence, smooth conclusions—or in other words, all the skills you've been practicing throughout this book. By citing sources in your essays or reports, you merely show your readers that you have investigated your ideas and found support for them. In addition, using sources affords your readers the opportunity to look into your subject further if they so desire, consulting your references for additional information.

The process described in the next few pages should help you write a paper using research that is carefully and effectively documented. This chapter also contains sample citation forms for a variety of research sources, illustrated by sample student writing using both MLA and APA styles.

Focusing Your Topic

In some cases, you will be assigned your topic, and you will be able to begin your research right away. In other cases, however, you may be encouraged to select your own subject, or you may be given a general subject ("health-care reform," "recycling," "U.S. immigration policies") that you must narrow and then focus into a specific, manageable topic. If the topic is your choice, you need to do some preliminary thinking about what interests you;

as in any assignment, you should make the essay a learning experience from which both you and your readers will profit. Therefore, you may want to brainstorm for a while on your general subject before you go to the library, asking yourself questions about what you already know and don't know. Some of the most interesting papers are argumentative essays in which writers set out to find an answer to a controversy or to find support for a solution they suspected might work. Other papers, sometimes called "research reports," expose, explain, or summarize a situation or a problem for their audience.

Throughout this chapter, we will track the research and writing process of Kira Anzai, a composition student whose writing assignment called for an examination of major influences on the works of a noteworthy artist, musician, or writer. As an art major, Kira developed an interest in Frida Kahlo after discovering the painting *The Two Fridas*, found on page 493 in this textbook. From popular culture and her prior reading in an art history class, Kira was somewhat familiar with the arresting images of Frida Kahlo, but she knew very little about the artist's life. As she began her investigation of Kahlo's biography, Kira was able to think about her topic in terms of some specific *research questions*: What would research tell her about Frida Kahlo's personal life and career? How did the experiences and relationships in Kahlo's life influence her art? (◆ Kira's completed essay with MLA documentation appears on pages 423–430 and with APA documentation on pages 431–440.)

Beginning Your Library Research

Once you have a general topic (and perhaps have some research questions in mind), your next step is familiarizing yourself with the school or public library where you may do all or part of your research. Most college libraries today have both print and electronic resources to offer researchers, as well as access to the Internet. Your library most likely has an online central information system, which may include a catalog of its holdings, a number of selected databases, gateways to other libraries, and other kinds of resources. With appropriate computer connections, this system may be accessed from other places on or off campus, which is handy for those times when you cannot be in the library.

Most libraries also have information (printed or online) that will indicate the location of important areas, and almost all have reference librarians who can explain the various kinds of programs and resources available to you. The smartest step you may take is asking a librarian for help before you begin searching. Library staff members may be able to save you enormous amounts of research time by pointing you in just the right direction. Do not be shy about asking the library staff for help at any point during your research!

Once you are familiar with your library, you may find it useful to consult one or more of the following research tools.

General Reference Works

If you need a general overview of your subject, or perhaps some background or historical information, you might begin your library research by consulting an encyclopedia, a collection of biographical entries, or even a statistical or demographic yearbook. You might use a comprehensive or specialized dictionary if your search turns up terms that are unfamiliar to you. These and many other library reference guides (in print and online) may also help you find a specific focus for your essay if you feel your topic is still too large or undefined at this point.

Online Catalogs

Today the online catalog has replaced the print catalog system as the primary guide to a library's holdings. You can access a library's catalog through on-site computer terminals or, in many cases, connect from off-site locations through the Internet to the library's Web page.

Most computer catalogs allow you to look for information by subject, author, and title as well as by keyword(s), by the ISBN (publisher's book number), by the call number, or by a series title (Time-Life books, for example). On-screen prompts will guide you through the process of searching. Because no two library catalog systems are exactly alike, never hesitate to ask a librarian for help if you need it.

Unless you are already familiar with authorities or their works on your topic, you might begin your search by typing in keywords or your general subject. For example, Kira Anzai began her search by typing in the subject words "Frida Kahlo," which produced a listing of sixty-five entries related to the artist. One book entitled *Frida Kahlo: The Brush of Anguish* looked particularly promising, so she pulled up the following screen to see more information.

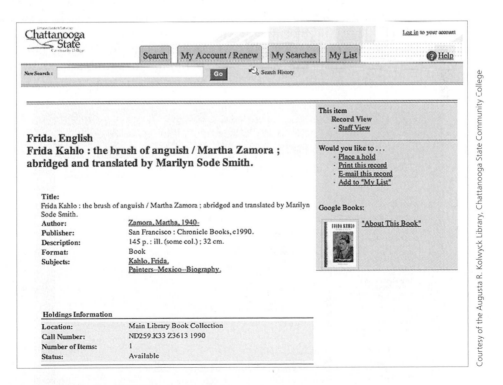

Courtesy of the Augusta R. Kolwyck Library, Chattanooga State Community College

If you find a relevant book, as Kira did, look at the catalog record's *Subject* line to see additional headings ("Frida Kahlo" and "Painters–Mexico–Biography") that may lead you to other useful resources. Often these subject headings are linked to the online catalog, and, by clicking on one, you will be taken to resources related to the topic. For example, when Kira clicked on the "Frida Kahlo" subject heading, the library's online catalog provided a listing of more than a dozen alphabetically arranged categories, including "Kahlo, Frida Correspondence," "Kahlo, Frida Criticism and Interpretation," "Kahlo, Frida Diaries," and "Kahlo, Frida Exhibitions." Once you have a call number for a particular book, a library map will help you find its location on the shelves.

Databases

Most libraries across the country subscribe to a wide variety of information services that lead researchers to appropriate databases for their subjects. After you access your library's Web site, you might find an alphabetically arranged listing of the available databases. A list of this nature is often quite lengthy and not very easily navigated, so many libraries also provide headings (such as those shown in the following list) to organize the options into categories that are more easily searched.

Databases by Subject   Databases by Type
Full-Text Resources   Multidisciplinary Resources

If, indeed, you encounter these options and pursue the "Databases by Subject" link, you might find several headings (e.g., Business, Health, Literature, Music, Science, Social Sciences). Many of these categories might include other subheadings; for example, under "Science" you might find Biology, Chemistry, Environmental Science, and Physics. As you might expect, the organization of Web sites varies from library to library, so when you first visit your library's Web site, devote some time to getting acquainted with the layout. And, of course, be willing to ask a librarian for assistance.

Courtesy of the Augusta R. Kolwyck Library, Chattanooga State Community College

At your library's Web site, you're likely to find one or more of the popular general databases, including *Academic Search Premier, Academic OneFile, General OneFile,* and *Info-Trac.* Each of these will serve as an excellent starting point for your research. Many college and university libraries subscribe to these databases because they provide access to millions of articles related to an exhaustive range of topics and derived from thousands of publications.

If your library's Web site also provides a listing of specialized categories, look for those that seem most appropriate to your topic. Because many college students write research papers about authors and their literary works, you might find that your library includes "Literature" among its specialized categories. Under this heading, many libraries place *Literature Resource Center,* which provides extensive information in this area. Consider these *Literature Resource Center* features, which make this a useful tool for many students: full-text scholarly articles, book reviews, and biographical essays.

Online databases are updated frequently—most on a daily basis—and almost certainly provide you with the most current sources for your research. Do note, however, that because libraries contract and pay a fee for database services, they must restrict most database access to on-site use or use by particular patrons (for example, enrolled students, faculty, and staff). Know, too, that each database may have its own search method. Always ask a librarian to help if you are struggling with a database search.

As you search your electronic sources, remember that you may have to try a variety of keywords (and their synonyms) to find what you need. Sometimes your keyword search may turn up too few leads—and sometimes you may be overwhelmed with too many matches! To save time and effort, you may be able to broaden or narrow your search by typing in words called *Boolean operators,** as illustrated here:

AND (Frida Kahlo AND Diego Rivera)—narrows your search to those references containing both Frida Kahlo and her husband, well-known artist Diego Rivera
OR (Frida Kahlo OR Diego Rivera)—broadens search to find items containing either term
NOT (Frida Kahlo NOT movie)—excludes items irrelevant to your search
NEAR (Frida Kahlo NEAR Surrealism)—finds references in which the terms occur within a set number of words (This option is not always available.)

Not all databases respond to Boolean operators, however, so it's always best to consult the searching advice offered by your particular information system.

While her school's library offered several database options, Kira selected *General One-File.* After accessing the *General OneFile* database, Kira clicked on the "Subject Guide Search" tab, typed "Frida Kahlo AND biography" in the "FIND" field, and limited the results "to documents with full text." This search yielded more than 400 potential sources—a bit overwhelming—but fortunately they were arranged in slightly over a dozen "subdivisions." Although Kira had begun her search with "biography" in mind, by clicking on the "subdivisions" link, she found several topics that she had not considered. The most promising, "Criticism and Interpretations," listed more than twenty potential sources spread among five categories (Academic Journals, Magazines, Books, News, and Multimedia).

---

*Named for the nineteenth-century British mathematician and logician George Boole.

Kira also wanted to learn more about Kahlo's paintings, so she used *General OneFile*'s "Basic Search" option (rather than the "Subject Guide Search" that she used for "biography") and entered the keywords "Frida Kahlo AND paintings." Here is the *General OneFile* "keyword" search screen Kira used to look for more information on the important "Frida Kahlo AND paintings":

Copyright © 2009 Cole/Cengage Learning. Reprinted with permission.

This search produced more than ninety potential sources, spread among the same five categories (Academic Journals, Magazines, Books, News, and Multimedia) that Kira had encountered in the "biography" search. With this list of ninety sources, Kira realized that she had some weeding out to do. Hoping to make the list more manageable, Kira sought advice from one of her school's librarians, who recommended that Kira sort the results by "relevance" as opposed to "publication date" (through a drop-down window located to the right and immediately below the category tabs). Selecting the "relevance" classification proved especially important in helping Kira quickly locate the most valuable articles for this particular topic. From the results, Kira came across the journal article shown at the top of the next page.

When Kira accessed the full-text version of this article (consisting of more than four thousand words), she found that it appeared on a single "page," making it difficult to include useful specific citations. She suspected that the article might also be available on the Smithsonian Institution's Web site, and a quick visit confirmed her suspicion. At the Web site, she found a version of the article spread over six numbered pages, so she was able to develop far more specific citations when she incorporated the article in her essay.

Once you have found useful information, remember that libraries have printers available to print out the on-screen data you wish to keep; you may have to pay a small fee for this printing, so it's a good idea to take some cash along, preferably in correct change. (Sometimes library users with personal computers at home can avoid this expense by e-mailing data to themselves.)

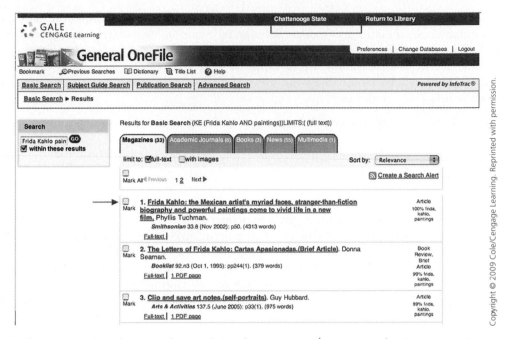

Copyright © 2009 Cole/Cengage Learning. Reprinted with permission.

And once again, the very best advice bears repeating: never hesitate to ask your library staff for help.

The Internet

You may have access to the Internet through your library, through your school network, or through a personal account with a service provider of your choice. The Internet can offer great research opportunities, but in many cases, it may only supplement—not replace—the information you will need to collect through library sources.

The most effective approach to discovering useful material on the Internet may be through the use of search engines that produce a list of potential electronic documents or Web sites in response to your search. After you type in your keyword(s), the search engine explores its database for word or phrase matches; it then presents you with a list of potential sources, which include the Internet addresses (called URLs—"uniform resource locators"). You may access the sources that seem most promising (often those that appear first on the list), and you may also connect to other material by clicking on any highlighted words (hypertext links) appearing within the text of a particular document.

At this time, the most popular search engine is Google, but there are many, many more worldwide, including Yahoo!, AlltheWeb, Bing, and Ask; you might prefer meta-search engines (such as MetaCrawler, KartOO, Clusty), which simultaneously search the Internet's top search engines. Because each search engine pulls its results from a different (but often overlapping) pool of Web pages, and because each one offers distinct "extra features," it pays to try more than one. (If you aren't satisfied with your results, try another set of keywords before moving on.)

Most search engines have their own searching tips; to improve your chances for success, it's well worth the time to read the advice on conducting advanced searches. For example, Google and Yahoo! focus search results by allowing you to fill in such fields as "exact phrase," "all of the words," "at least one of the words," or "none of the words."

Other options narrow the search by designating certain languages, specific dates, or particular kinds of materials. (Google Scholar, for example, will search among academic books, journals, theses, and abstracts.)

Some search engines allow use of Boolean operators (see page 375) to narrow or broaden your search. Some allow the use of plus and minus signs to show connected terms or unwanted matches:

> Frida Kahlo + Diego Rivera (find sources containing both Frida Kahlo and her artist husband)
>
> Frida Kahlo – movie (find sources about Frida Kahlo but exclude those that include the word "movie")

Some programs request quotation marks around a key term of multiple words ("Anne Frank"); some are case sensitive (capitalize proper nouns or not?); some use truncation to find various forms of a word ("myth*" will return "mythology" and "mythical"). Other search engines, such as Ask, allow users to ask questions in natural language ("Who was Frida Kahlo?"). As technology continues to improve, searching will no doubt become easier, so always take a moment to look at each search engine's current directions.

Here is one more hint for searching the Web: sometimes you can guess the URL you need. Simply fill in the name of a specific company, college, agency, or organization. Do not put spaces between words (usnews.com).

- **Businesses:** www.nameofcompany.com
- **Colleges:** www.nameofcollege.edu
- **Government agencies:** www.nameofagency.gov
- **Organizations:** www.nameoforganization.org

You may also consult specialized directories to discover the addresses you need.

Once you find a useful document, you may print it, add the reference to your "bookmarks" or "favorites" list, or copy it to a USB drive or to a home file if you are using your own computer. Whether at the library or at home, always keep a list of your important sites, their addresses, and the date you accessed them. You may need this information for an easy return to a particular document and also for your working bibliography.

To explore other ways to use the Internet for research, check your library's home page, which most likely will offer links to helpful search advice.

Words of Caution for Internet Users: Be Afraid, Be Very Afraid. . . . The Internet offers researchers a wealth of information incredibly fast. However, the Internet poses problems, too. It may offer a great deal of information on your essay topic—but it may not offer the *best* information, which might be found in a classic text on your library shelf. Background information or historical perspective may not be available; Web site information may be out of date. Moreover, simply finding the specific information you need can be frustrating and time-consuming, especially if your keywords and links don't lead in useful directions. The information superhighway is congested with scores of irrelevant distractions, so beware the wild Web chase.

There is, however, another much more serious problem: not all material found on the Internet is accurate or reliable. When an article is printed in a respected journal, for example, readers have assurances that editors have reviewed the information, writers have checked their facts, and authorities have been quoted correctly. However, Web sites may be created by anyone on any subject, from gene splicing to Elvis sightings, without any sort of editorial review. Opinions—wise or crackpot—may be presented as facts; rumors may be presented as reality.

Because there is no "quality control" of Web sites, writers of research papers must evaluate their sources extremely carefully to avoid gathering unreliable information. For example, as Kira Anzai searched for information about Frida Kahlo, she consulted the *Wikipedia* Web site after hearing so much about it from her classmates. But she soon found information that she knew was inaccurate because it contradicted information that she was able to verify and confirm in several other published sources. While *Wikipedia* often provides useful and accurate information, Kira realized that virtually anyone in the world can contribute to articles and edit their content, making it easy for erroneous information and personal bias to slip in. With this insight, Kira decided not to depend on *Wikipedia* as a source for her essay.

Always ask these questions of each source:

- What is the purpose of this Web site? (To inform, persuade, market a product or service, share an interest, entertain?) To whom is this site primarily directed, and why?

- Who is the sponsor, author, or creator of the site? (A business, an educational institution, a nonprofit organization, a government agency, a news bureau, an individual?) Is the sponsor or author known and respected in the particular content area?

- Does the sponsor or author reveal a clear bias or strong opinion? Does such a slant undercut the usefulness of the information?

- When was this site produced? When was it last updated or revised? If links exist, are they still viable? Up to date?

- Is the information accurate? How might the material be cross-checked and verified?

If you have doubts about the accuracy of any material you discover on the Internet, find another authoritative source to validate the information or omit it from your essay. ◆ Following the guidelines on pages 389–391 will help you evaluate *all* your potential research sources.

Special Collections

Your library may contain special collections that will help you research your subject. Some libraries, for example, have extensive collections of government documents or educational materials or newspapers from foreign cities. Other libraries may have invested in manuscripts from famous authors or in a series of works on a particular subject, such as your state's history. Remember, too, that some libraries contain collections of early films, rare recordings, or unique photographs. Consult your librarian or the information sources describing your library's special holdings.

Conducting Primary Research

To illustrate and support their points, most writers of research papers draw heavily on material found in articles, books, and other library sources. However, researchers sometimes find it useful to gather their own information. Collecting data firsthand is called *primary research* or *original research*, and it is valuable because it provides information not available from other sources.

Students often conduct primary research in a variety of college classes. For example, a chemistry major may gain new knowledge from a lab experiment; an English major may discover original insights reading a work of literature; a political science major may produce thoughtful analysis after studying local election results. In each case, the investigator collects information that was not already in existence.

Although there are many ways to conduct primary research, this section will present suggestions for conducting two strategies composition students may find most helpful: the *interview* and the *questionnaire*.

The Personal Interview

Depending on your choice of topic, you may find all the information you need for your essay by exploring sources through library and online research. However, sometimes you may discover that an authority on your subject lives in your town or works on your campus. In this case, you may wish to conduct a *personal interview* to gather valuable information for your essay.

Preparation is the key word governing a good interview. Here are some suggestions to help you collect useful data in the most effective way possible.

Before You Interview:

1. *Know your purpose.* If you have only a vague notion of why you are talking to the interviewee, you will waste everyone's time as the conversation roams like a lost hiker wandering from one clearing to the next. A close look at your essay's outline or your early drafts should tell you why and how this person might contribute to your research. Be certain that the person you have selected for an interview is, in fact, the best source for the kind of information you are seeking. For example, if you are writing a paper on the campus program that assists students with learning disabilities, you might interview the program's director to obtain expert opinion; on the other hand, if you wish to know some specific ways in which the program has helped its participants, you might interview a student actively involved in the program for his or her personal response.

2. *Make an appointment.* Calling for an interview may make you a bit nervous, but remember that most people like to be asked for their opinions and are usually willing to help students with their research, if their schedules permit. Be sure the interviewee understands who you are, why you are asking for an interview, and approximately how much time you are requesting. Whenever possible, allow the interviewee to select the hour and place most convenient for him or her. Do adjust your schedule to give yourself time after the meeting in case the interview runs long and to allow yourself a few minutes to review and fill in your notes.

3. *Educate yourself.* Before the interview, read about your topic and your interviewee. You want to appear knowledgeable about your subject; you can also save time by skipping questions that have already been answered in print. Busy experts appre-

ciate not having to explain basic information that you could have—and should have—already looked up.

4. *Plan some questions.* Unless you have an excellent memory, it is best to jot down some specific questions to which you can refer during the interview. Some interviewers write each question at the top of an index card, and then use the rest of the card for their notes on the answer. Others use a notebook in which they write a question (or key words) at the top of each page. Try to create questions that are specific, clear, and logically ordered. Avoid "yes/no" questions that don't lead to discussion. If you have a complicated or convoluted issue you want to discuss, try breaking it into a series of simpler questions that can be tackled by the interviewee one at a time.

During the Interview:

5. *Make a good first impression.* Always arrive on time, prepared with pens, paper, or other documents you need. Some interviewers like to use a recorder, but you first must secure your interviewee's permission to use this equipment. (A recorder makes some people uncomfortably self-conscious and hesitant to speak freely, so consider whether the accuracy it may provide is more important than the spontaneity it may kill.) Always begin by thanking your interviewee for his or her time and briefly say again why you think he or she can provide helpful information to you.

6. *Ask, listen, ask.* Begin asking your prepared questions, but don't rush through them. Listen attentively to your interviewee's answers, and although it takes practice, try to maintain eye contact as you jot down abbreviated notes on the answers. Allow the interviewee to do almost all the talking; after all, you are there to collect information, not participate in a debate. Do politely ask for clarification (unfamiliar terms, spelling of names, unclear references, and so on) when you need it.

7. *Be flexible.* Sometimes your interviewee will talk about something fascinating that never occurred to you when you prepared your original list of questions. Be ready to adapt your plan and ask new questions that follow up on unexpected commentary.

8. *"Silence is golden," but* . . . If an interviewee is quiet or hesitates to give the kind of detailed responses you are seeking, you may need to use phrases of this kind to draw out longer answers:

   Can you elaborate on that?

   Tell me more about X.

   Why did you think that?

   How did you react to that?

   When did you realize . . . ?

   Why do you believe that?

   What's your reading of that situation?

   Would you explain that for me?

As you ask for more details, try to use a friendly, conversational tone that will put your interviewee at ease.

On the other hand, sometimes interviewees talk too much! They become stuck on one aspect of a topic, going into unnecessary depth, or perhaps they begin to drift off the subject completely. Be courteous but firm in your resolve to redirect the flow of conversation. To get back to your topic, you may need to re-ask the original question, using slightly different words.

9. *Conclude thoughtfully.* At the end of the interview, ask for any additional comments the interviewee would like to offer and for any information (or other sources) he or she thinks you might find useful. Ask the interviewee if you may contact him or her again if you should have another brief question; if such permission is granted, ask for the best means of contact (a telephone number or e-mail address). Give the interviewee your most sincere thanks for his or her time and assistance.

After the Interview:

10. *Review your notes immediately.* Fill in gaps in your notes while your memory is fresh, and write out acronyms or abbreviations whose meanings you might forget in a few days. Make some notes to yourself about using the information in your essay.

Later, if the interview figures prominently in your essay, consider sending your interviewee a copy of your work. Within days of the interview, however, it is ALWAYS polite to send your interviewee a short thank-you note, acknowledging his or her help with your research project.

The Questionnaire

A questionnaire is a series of questions or statements designed to obtain people's opinions about certain ideas, products, issues, activities, or even other people. You have, no doubt, responded to a number of questionnaires yourself: in your school, you may have filled out course evaluation forms; in a store, you may have answered questions about a new product or service; at home, you may have replied to political pollsters or participated in a marketing survey.

Designing effective questionnaires is a complex business. There are, in fact, entire college courses devoted to the analysis and development of polls and surveys, courses often required for marketing majors and political science students. As daunting as composing a questionnaire may sound, student writers often find it useful to conduct small-scale surveys to gain wider opinions on a topic under research. For example, let's assume you've been assigned a paper calling for a specific recommendation to improve a campus service or agency. You have chosen the composition computer lab and, although you have a few ideas of your own, you think it would be valuable to know what other users of the lab would most like to see changed. You design a questionnaire asking lab users to identify their chief areas of concern, and, using that information, you write a persuasive essay calling for a specific change.

Here are some suggestions for designing, administering, and analyzing questionnaires, whose results might prove useful in your research.

Developing the Questionnaire

1. *Know your purpose and identify your target audience.* Writers of effective question-naires have a specific goal in mind; articulating that goal clearly in writing will help you create the best survey questions. Ask yourself: what do I most want to know from this particular group of people? Which group of people will give me the information I want? Hint: Asking a particular population (computer lab users) to focus on a single issue (computer lab hours) will often produce the most precise responses.

2. *Encourage participation.* At the top of your questionnaire, briefly state your pur-pose and your request for response, giving pertinent (but not personal) informa-tion. People are more likely to participate if they know who is conducting the survey ("student in English 121"), what you want ("collecting composition stu-dents' opinions on . . ."), and how the results will be used ("data for essay whose purpose is . . ."). Some respondents will be naturally sympathetic to a hardwork-ing student; others may need an answer to "what's in this for me?" If it's appropri-ate, you can appeal to your respondents' sense of the Common Good. In the case of the computer lab survey, for example, respondents might be encouraged to answer the questions if they thought the essay's recommendations would actually go to the lab supervisor, thus creating the possibility of improved service for all.

3. *Choose the most effective type of questionnaire for your purpose.* There are several kinds of questions or statements you may use to generate information; in a short survey, choose only one or two types to avoid confusing your participants.

   Common methods include the following:

   - **Yes/No Answers**
     Example: Do you use the computer lab at least once a week?
                ( ) Yes
                ( ) No

   - **Multiple Choice**
     Example: Check one answer. How often do you use the computer lab?
                ( ) Once a week?
                ( ) Twice a week?
                ( ) More than twice a week?

   - **Checklist**
     Example: Check all the statements with which you agree.
                ___ The current lab hours of operation are convenient for me.
                ___ The lab should be open on the weekends.
                ___ The lab needs extended evening hours.
                Etc.

   - **Rank Order**
     Example: In the following list, identify the issues most important to you by marking the most important as "1" and the least important as "5."
                ___ Hours of operation
                ___ Updated equipment
                ___ Technical assistance available
                Etc.

- **Rating System**
  Example: Rate the following statements as SA (Strongly Agree), A (Agree),
  D (Disagree), SD (Strongly Disagree), or N (No Opinion).
  ___ The lab should be open on the weekends.
  ___ The lab should be open later at night.
  ___ The lab should have extended hours during final exams.
  Etc.

- **Open Questions**
  Example: If you could change the lab's hours of operation, what would an ideal
  schedule look like for you? Why would these hours be better than the
  current schedule?

Designers of questionnaires should note that although open questions may produce the most interesting answers to read, they are also the most difficult to tally objectively. Multiple-choice questionnaires may be the easiest to score, and their numbers may quickly be converted to percentages.

Once you have decided which method will best retrieve the kind of information you are seeking, clearly state the directions for following that method at the top of your questionnaire, after your statement of purpose. Consider using bold type to emphasize any important words in the instructions.

4. *Watch your language.* It's unfortunately easy to confuse your respondents or "contaminate" your survey with careless use of words or phrases. Avoid problems by remembering the following advice:

   - Clarify vague references and avoid abbreviations your participants may not know.
     Unclear   Are you in favor of or opposed to the proposed SB128?
     Better   Are you in favor of or opposed to Colorado Senate Bill 128,
                          which would raise the technology fees at this college by 2
                          percent?

   - Rewrite any "loaded" questions or leading statements that attempt to shape the respondent's answer.
     Biased   Should the university continue to waste your money on new,
                          overpriced computer equipment?
     Objective   Should the university purchase new computer equipment?

   - Ask for one piece of information at a time.
     Double question   Are the technical assistants at the lab helpful and friendly?
                            Yes/No
                            [Respondents might find the assistants friendly but not
                            particularly helpful, or vice versa, so a single "yes" or a
                            "no" answer would be misleading.]
     Better questions   Do you find the technical assistants at the lab helpful?
                            Yes/No
                            Do you find the technical assistants in the lab friendly?
                            Yes/No

5. *Keep it short, simple, and smooth.* People often cooperate with pollsters, but they don't want to be imposed on for too long. After you've drafted a number of potential questions for your survey, cut your list down to the most important

ones. Unless you have an overwhelming reason to ignore this advice, limit your questionnaire to a single page. (Some pollsters also advise placing your most important questions first, in case respondents tire of answering and turn in incomplete forms.) Ask your questions in the clearest, most direct way possible to get the most straightforward answers.* Just as you know how to write coherent, smoothly linked paragraphs in your essays, group questions logically to move your respondents' thoughts easily from issue to issue.

Administering the Questionnaire

6. *Secure a valid sampling.* To get meaningful responses, you must survey the right people, ones with the knowledge or opinions that matter to your research. But at this point you must also ask yourself two other vitally important questions: are the people taking my survey truly representative of my target group as a whole? Does my sample—the number of people contacted—comprise a large enough part of the target group to merit the conclusions I might draw from their comments?

    For valid results, first make sure that you are taking a *random sample*; that is, you must ensure that each member of the population has a fair and equal chance of being selected. In a survey on the computer center hours, for example, you would not get an accurate cross-section of opinions if you sampled only the work-study students staffing the lab or your best friends who feel as you do. Similarly, if you sample only a tiny fraction of the students who use the lab, your results will not provide strong support for any broad claims about student opinion. As you prepare to distribute your questionnaire, be sure you will address a significant number of randomly selected people who compose a cross section of your target group.

7. *Perform a test run.* If time permits, ask several people in your target group to take the survey before you distribute it widely. If the questionnaire has problems or confusing spots, they will surface in time for you to fix them.

8. *Be prepared.* Plan ahead to discover how best to distribute your questionnaires. If you are handing them out on school or private property, be sure you have permission to do so. If you are placing the questionnaires in a public place for respondents to pick up at their leisure, think about a secure drop-box for completed surveys that you can empty frequently. (If your respondents are answering by hand, don't forget to provide an extra-large number of pencils or pens as they do "walk off" with great regularity.)

Totaling and Reporting Results

9. *Analyze your responses.* Depending on your method of surveying, you may simply add up the totals for each answer (in multiple-choice or checklist questionnaires, for example), or you may need to spend some time pondering the nuances of written comments. All returned, completed questionnaires must be included in your

---

*Some national pollsters believe that to obtain the most truthful responses, questionnaires should be answered anonymously; others suggest making signatures optional.

analysis. If you wish to convert questionnaire numbers into percentages, divide the number of responses to a particular answer by the total number of questionnaires returned and then multiply that figure by 100 (Example: five responses to one multiple-choice answer out of 25 questionnaires would be 0.20; multiplying $0.20 \times 100 = 20\%$). As you study your results, look for emerging patterns and repeated ideas. What conclusions can you draw based on these responses?

10. *Accurately report your findings.* If you base your essay's assertions, arguments, conclusions, or recommendations on your questionnaire's results, your readers will certainly need a clear understanding of how those results were obtained. To be persuaded that your research is valid, they may wish to know how the questionnaire was designed and why, how many were distributed and completed, how the respondents were chosen, and other such information. Such explanations may appear within the body of your essay or in appropriately marked sections (such as "Purpose and Design," "Results," "Recommendations") or in an appendix; whichever method you choose, always attach a blank sample copy of the questionnaire to your essay.

Conducting research through the distribution of a questionnaire is a challenging but fascinating way to collect information about current unexplored topics. If you have collected data that would be valuable to people on your campus, at your workplace, or in your community, by all means communicate it to them. Your primary research, and your conclusions, could help someone make an important decision.

Preparing a Working Bibliography

As you search for information about your essay topic, keep a list of sources that you may want to use in your essay. This list, called a *working bibliography*, will grow as you discover potential sources, and it may shrink if you delete references that aren't useful. Ultimately, this working bibliography will become the list of references presented at the end of your essay.

There are several ways to record your sources. Some students prefer to make an index card for each title; others compile a list in a research notebook; still others prefer to create a computer file or a folder of printouts. As you add sources to your working bibliography, note the following information as appropriate.

Book
1. Author's or editor's full name (and name of translator if given)
2. Complete title, including subtitle if one exists
3. Edition number
4. Volume number if the book is part of a series
5. City of publication and name of publisher
6. Date of publication
7. For reading or article in an anthology, title and author
8. Page numbers of the information you need
9. Library call number or location of source

Article in a Journal, Magazine, or Newspaper

1. Author's full name (if given)
2. Title of the article
3. Title of the journal, magazine, or newspaper
4. Volume and issue number of the journal or magazine
5. Date of publication
6. Page numbers of the article (section and page numbers for newspaper)

Electronic Sources

1. Author's full name or name of sponsoring organization
2. Title of document
3. Information about print publication (book: place, publisher, date; periodical: title, volume and issue if given, date, pages)
4. Information about electronic publication (source, such as database or Web site; name of service; date of publication or most recent update)
5. Access information (URL and date of access)

Interview

1. Interviewee's name and title
2. Interviewee's organization or company, job description, or other information regarding his or her expertise, including pertinent publications, studies, presentations, and so forth.
3. Subject of interview
4. Date, place, and method of interview (e.g., in person, by telephone, by e-mail)

Here are four sample index cards that might appear in Kira Anzai's working bibliography:

Book

Zamora, Martha
Abridged and translated by Marilyn Sode Smith
Frida Kahlo: The Brush of Anguish
Chronicle Books, 1990
San Francisco, California
Call number: ND259.K33 Z3613 1990
TCU Library, Main Stacks

Article in a Scholarly Journal

Baddeley, Oriana
"'Her Dress Hangs Here': De-Frocking the Kahlo Cult"
Oxford Art Journal   Volume 14   Number 1   1991
pages 10-17
TCU Library, Periodicals

Electronic Source

Johnston, Jill
"Self-Portrait"
Rev. of The Diary of Frida Kahlo: An Intimate Self-Portrait
by Sarah M. Lowe
Art in America Volume 84   Number 3   March 1996
pages 31 and 33 (page 32 is skipped)
General OneFile   Gale
Accessed 24 March 2009

Interview

Bryant, Jennifer (Dr.)
Professor of Art History
TCU Department of Art and Art History
Teaches ART 20093, Art of Mexico from 1500 to the Present
Interview subject: Frida Kahlo
In-person interview: March 9, 2009

Credentials:
—specialist in Latin American art of the 20th c
—attended symposium on Mexican Modernism held in
   Mexico City
—saw exhibition of paintings by Frida Kahlo, Diego Rivera

Choosing and Evaluating Your Sources

After you have found a number of promising sources, take a closer look at them. The strength and credibility of your research paper will depend directly on the strength and credibility of your sources. In short, a research paper built on shaky, unreliable sources will not convince a thoughtful reader. Even one suspect piece of evidence may lead your reader to wonder about the validity of other parts of your essay.

To help you choose your print and online sources, ask yourself the following questions as you try to decide which facts, figures, and testimonies will best support or illustrate your ideas.

What do I know about the author? Does this person have any expertise or particular knowledge about the subject matter? If the author of an article about nuclear fusion is a physics professor at a respected university, her views may be more informed than those of a writer of popular science. Although books and scholarly journals generally cite their author's qualifications, the credentials of journalists and magazine writers may be harder to evaluate. Internet sources, as mentioned earlier, may be highly suspect. In cases in which the background of a writer is unknown, you might examine the writer's use of his or her own sources. Can sources for specific data or opinions be checked or verified? In addition, the objectivity of the author must be considered: some authors are clearly biased and may even stand to gain economically or politically from taking a particular point of view. The president of a tobacco company, for instance, might insist that secondary smoke from the cigarettes of others will not harm nonsmokers, but does he or she have an objective opinion? Try to present evidence only from those authors whose views will sway your intelligent readers.

What do I know about the publisher? Who published your sources? Major, well-known publishing houses can be one indication of a book's credibility. (If you are unfamiliar with a particular publisher, consult a librarian or professor in that field.) Be aware that there are many publishers who publish books supporting only a specific viewpoint; similarly, many organizations support Web sites to further their causes. The bias in such sources may limit their usefulness to your research.

For periodicals, consider the nature of the journal, magazine, or newspaper. Who is its intended audience? A highly technical paper on sickle-cell anemia, for example, might be weakened by citing a very general discussion of the disease from *Health Digest*; an article from the *Journal of the American Medical Association*, however, might be valuable. Is it a publication known to be fairly objective (the *New York Times*) or does it have a particular cause to support (the *National Sierra Club Bulletin*)? Looking at the masthead of a journal or other publication will often tell you whether articles are subjected to stringent review before acceptance for publication. In general, articles published in "open" or nonselective publications should be examined closely for credibility. For example, the newsletter for Mensa—a well-known international society for individuals who have documented IQs in the top 2 percent of the population—once created a furor when an article appeared recommending the euthanasia of the mentally and physically disabled, the homeless, and other so-called "nonproductive" members of society. The newsletter editor's explanation was that all articles submitted for publication were generally accepted.

Is my research reasonably balanced? Your treatment of your subject—especially if it is a controversial one—should show your readers that you investigated all sides of the issue before reaching a conclusion. If your sources are drawn only from authorities well known for voicing one position, your readers may be skeptical about the quality of your research. For instance, if in a paper arguing against a new gun-control measure, you cite only the opinions voiced by the officers of the National Rifle Association, you may antagonize the reader who wants a thorough analysis of all sides of the question. Do use sources that support your position, but don't overload your argument with obviously biased sources.

Are my sources reporting valid research? Is your source the original researcher, or is he or she reporting someone else's study?* If the information is being reported secondhand, has your source been accurate and clear? Is the original source named or referenced in some way so that the information could be checked?

A thorough researcher might note the names of authorities frequently cited by other writers or researchers and try to obtain the original works by those authorities. This tip was useful for Kira Anzai as she found researcher Hayden Herrera, whose exhaustive book, *Frida: A Biography of Frida Kahlo*, was mentioned in a number of magazine articles. Once she obtained a copy of this often-quoted book, she had additional information to consider for her paper.

Look too at the way information in your source was obtained in the first place. Did the original researchers themselves draw logical conclusions from their evidence? Did they run their study or project in a fair, impartial way? For example, a survey of people

---

*Interviews, surveys, studies, and experiments conducted firsthand are referred to as *primary sources*; reports and studies written by someone other than the original researcher are called *secondary sources*.

whose names were obtained from the rolls of the Democratic Party will hardly constitute a representative sampling of voters' opinions on an upcoming election.

Moreover, be especially careful with statistics because they can be manipulated quite easily to give a distorted picture. A recent survey, for instance, asked a large sample of people to rate a number of American cities based on questions dealing with quality of life. Pittsburgh—a lovely city to be sure—came out the winner, but only if one agrees that all the questions should be weighted equally; that is, the figures gave Pittsburgh the highest score only if one rates "weather" as equally important as "educational opportunities," "number of crimes," "cultural opportunities," and other factors. In short, always evaluate the quality of your sources' research and the validity of their conclusions before you decide to incorporate their findings into your own paper. (And don't forget Mark Twain's reference to "lies, damned lies, and statistics.")

Are my sources still current? Although some famous experiments or studies have withstood the years, many topics demand research as current as possible. What was written two years or even two weeks ago may have been disproved or surpassed since, especially in our rapidly changing political world and ever-expanding fields of technology. A paper on the status of the U.S. space program, for example, demands recent sources, and research on personal computer use in the United States might be severely weakened by the use of a text published as recently as last year for "current" statistics.

If they're appropriate, journals and other periodicals may contain more up-to-date reports than books printed several years ago; library database searches can often provide the most current information. On the other hand, you certainly shouldn't ignore a "classic" study on your subject, especially if it is the one against which all the other studies are measured. A student researching the life of Abraham Lincoln, for instance, might find Carl Sandburg's multivolume biography of over seventy years ago as valuable as more recent works. Be aware, too, that even though Web sites can be continually revised, they are sometimes neglected; always check to see if a "last updated" date has been posted or if the material contains current dates or references. In some cases, an elusive "last update" may be determined by typing the following in the address field: javascript:alert(document:lastModified).

> ◆ REMEMBER: For more advice to help you think critically about your sources, see pages 104–106 in Chapter 5.

Preparing an Annotated Bibliography

While you are gathering and assessing your sources, you may be asked to compile an annotated bibliography—a description of each important source that includes the basic bibliographic facts as well as a brief summary of each entry's content. After reading multiple articles or books on your subject over a period of days or even weeks, you may discover that the information you've found has begun to blur in your head. Annotating each of your sources will help you remember the specific data in each one so that you can locate the material later in the planning and drafting stages of your writing process.

Here is a sample taken from Kira Anzai's annotated bibliography:

Herrera, Hayden. *Frida: A Biography of Frida Kahlo.* 1983. New York: Perennial-
    Harper, 2002. Print.
        Art historian Hayden Herrera's detailed biography of Frida Kahlo explores her
    personal life, career, and vibrant personality within the context of Mexico's cultural
    and political atmosphere. The book frequently draws on Kahlo's own writing—her
    diary entries, letters, and poetry—as well as the views of her friends, relatives, and
    other contemporaries.

Compiling an annotated bibliography will also give you a clear sense of how complete
and balanced your sources are in support of your ideas, perhaps revealing gaps in your
evidence that need to be filled with additional research data. Later, when your essay is
finished, your annotated bibliography might provide a useful reference for any of your
readers who are interested in exploring your subject in more depth.

Taking Notes

As you evaluate and select those sources that are both reliable and useful, you will begin
taking notes on their information. Most researchers use one or more of the following
three methods of note-taking.

1. Some students prefer to make their notes on index cards rather than on notebook
    paper because a stack of cards may be added to, subtracted from, or shuffled
    around more easily when it's time to plan the essay. You may find it useful to label
    each card with a short topic heading that corresponds to a major idea in your
    essay. Then, as you read, put pertinent information on its appropriate card. Be
    sure to identify the source of all your notes. (Hint 1: If you have used bibliography
    cards, take your notes on cards of different sizes or colors to avoid any confusion;
    write on only one side of each card so that all your information will be in sight
    when you draft your essay.)

2. Other students rely on photocopies or printouts of sources, highlighting or
    underlining important details. (Hint 2: Copy a source's title page and other front
    matter so that you can clip complete bibliographic information to your pages.)

3. Students with personal computers may prefer to store their notes as computer
    files because of the easy transfer of quoted material from file to essay draft. (Hint
    3: This is a great use for a USB drive. Always make a hard copy of your notes and
    back up your files frequently in case of a crash!) You will probably find yourself
    taking notes by hand on those occasions when you are without your computer
    (classroom, interview, public speech, etc.), so carry index cards with you and tran-
    scribe your notes into your files later.

Whichever note-taking method you choose, always remember to record bibliographic
information and the specific page numbers (in printed sources) or paragraph numbers
(in some electronic sources) from which your material is taken. Your notes may be one
of the following kinds:

1. *Direct quotations.* When you use material word for word, you must always enclose it in quotation marks and note the precise page number of the quotation, if given.* If the quoted material runs from one printed page onto another, use some sort of signal to yourself, such as a slash bar (child/abuse) or arrow ($\rightarrow$ p. 162) at the break so if you use only part of the quoted material in your paper, you will know on which page it appeared. If the quoted material contains odd, archaic, or incorrect spelling, punctuation marks, or grammar, insert the word *sic* in brackets next to the item in question; [*sic*] means "this is the way I found it in the original text," and such a symbol will remind you later that you did not miscopy the quotation. In any case, always double-check to make sure you did copy the material accurately and completely to avoid having to come back to the source as you prepare your essay. If the material you want to quote is lengthy or complex, you will find it easier—though not cheaper—to photocopy (or print out) the text rather than transcribe it.

2. *Paraphrase.* You paraphrase when you put into your own words what someone else has written or said. Please note: *paraphrased ideas are borrowed ideas, not your original thoughts, and, consequently, they must be attributed to their owner just as direct quotations are.*

   To remind yourself that certain information in your notes is paraphrased, always introduce it with some sort of notation, such as a handwritten ℗ or a typed P//. Quotation marks will always tell you what you borrowed directly, but sometimes when writers take notes one week and write their first draft a week or two later, they cannot remember if a note was paraphrased or if it was an original thought. Writers occasionally plagiarize unintentionally because they erroneously believe that only direct quotations and statistics must be attributed to their proper sources, so make your notes as clear as possible. (◆ For more information on avoiding plagiarism, see pages 397–399.)

3. *Summary.* You may wish to condense a piece of writing so you can offer it as support for your own ideas. Using your own words, you should present in shorter form the writer's thesis and supporting ideas. You may find it helpful to include a few direct quotations in your summary to retain the flavor of the original work. Of course, you will tell your readers what you are summarizing and by whom it was written. Remember to make a note (sum:) to yourself to indicate summarized, rather than original, material. (◆ For more information on writing a summary, see also pages 185–186.)

4. *Your own ideas.* Your notes may also contain your personal comments (judgments, flashes of brilliance, questions, notions of how to use something you've just read, notes to yourself about connections between sources, and so forth) that will aid you in the writing of your paper. In handwritten notes, you might jot these down in a different-colored pen or put them in brackets that you've initialed, so that you will recognize them later as your own responses.

---

*All tables, graphs, and charts that you copy must also be directly attributed to their sources, though you do not enclose graphics in quotation marks.

Distinguishing Paraphrase from Summary

Because novice writers sometimes have a hard time understanding the difference between paraphrase and summary, here is an explanation and a sample of each. The original paragraph that appears here was taken from a magazine article describing an important 1984 study still frequently cited:

> Another successful approach to the prevention of criminality has been to target very young children in a school setting before problems arise. The Perry Preschool Program, started 22 years ago in a low socioeconomic area of Ypsilanti, Michigan, has offered some of the most solid evidence to date that early intervention through a high-quality preschool program can significantly alter a child's life. A study released this fall tells what happened to 123 disadvantaged children from preschool age to present. The detention and arrest rate for the 58 children who had attended the preschool program was 31 percent, compared to 51 percent for the 65 who did not. Similarly, those in the preschool program were more likely to have graduated from high school, have enrolled in postsecondary education programs and be employed, and less likely to have become pregnant as teenagers.
>
> —from "Arresting Delinquency,"
> *Dan Hurley,* Psychology Today
> *March 1985, page 66*

Paraphrase

A *paraphrase* puts the information in the researcher's own words, but it does follow the order of the original text, and it does include the important details:

> Quality preschooling for high-risk children may help stop crime before it starts. A 1984 study from the Perry Preschool Program located in a poor area of Ypsilanti, Michigan, showed that of 123 socially and economically disadvantaged children, the 58 who attended preschool had an arrest rate of 31 percent compared to 51 percent for those 65 who did not attend. The adults with preschool experience had also graduated from high school in larger numbers; in addition, more of them had attended postsecondary education programs, were employed, and had avoided teenage pregnancy (Hurley 66).

Summary

A *summary* is generally much shorter than the original; the researcher picks out the key ideas but often omits many of the supporting details:

> A 1984 study from the Perry Preschool Program in Michigan suggests that disadvantaged children who attend preschool are less likely to be arrested as adults. They choose more education, have better employment records, and avoid teenage pregnancy more often than those without preschool (Hurley 66).

> REMEMBER: Both paraphrased and summarized ideas must be attributed to their sources, even if you do not reproduce exact words or figures.

Incorporating Your Source Material

Be aware that a research paper is not a massive collection of quotations and paraphrased or summarized ideas glued together with a few transitional phrases. It is, instead, an essay in which you offer your thesis and ideas based on and supported by your research. Consequently, you will need to incorporate and blend in your reference material in a variety of smooth, persuasive ways. Here are some suggestions:

Use your sources in a clear, logical way. Make certain that you understand your source material well enough to use it in support of your own thoughts. Once you have selected the best references to use, be as convincing as possible. Ask yourself if you're using enough evidence and if the information you're offering really does clearly support your point. As in any essay, you need to avoid oversimplification, hasty generalizations, *non sequiturs*, and other problems in logic (◆ For a review of common logical fallacies, see pages 296–299). Resist the temptation to add quotations, facts, or statistics that are interesting but not really relevant to your paper.

Don't overuse direct quotations. It's best to use a direct quotation *only* when it expresses a point in a far more impressive, emphatic, or concise way than you could say it yourself. Suppose, for instance, you were analyzing the films of a particular director and wanted to include a sample of critical reviews:

> As one movie critic wrote, "This film is really terrible, and people should ignore it" (Dennison 14).

The direct quotation above isn't remarkable and could be easily paraphrased. However, you might be tempted to quote the following line to show your readers an emphatically negative review of this movie:

> As one movie critic wrote, "This film's plot is so idiotic it's clearly intended for people who move their lips not only when they read but also when they watch TV" (Dennison 14).

When you do decide to use direct quotations, don't merely drop them into your prose as if they had fallen from a tall building onto your page. Instead, lead into them smoothly so that they obviously support or clarify what you are saying.

| Dropped in | Scientists have been studying the ill effects of nitrites on test animals since 1961. "Nitrites produced malignant tumors in 62 percent of the test animals within six months" (Smith 109). |
| Better | Scientists have been studying the ill effects of nitrites on test animals since 1961. According to Dr. William Smith, head of the Farrell Institute of Research, who conducted the largest experiment thus far, "Nitrites produced malignant tumors in 62 percent of the test animals within six months" (109). |

Vary your sentence pattern when you present your quotations. Here are some sample phrases for quotations:

> In her introduction to *The Great Gatsby*, Professor Wilma Smith points out that Fitzgerald "wrote about himself and produced a narcissistic masterpiece" (5).

Wilma Smith, author of *Impact*, summarized the situation this way: "Eighty-eight percent of the sales force threaten a walkout" (21).

"Only the President controls the black box," according to White House Press Secretary Wilma Smith.

As drama critic Wilma Smith observed last year in the *Saturday Review*, the play was "a rousing failure" (212).

Perhaps the well-known poet Wilma Smith expressed the idea best when she wrote, "Love is a spider waiting to entangle its victims" (14).

"Employment figures are down 3 percent from last year," claimed Senator Wilma Smith, who leads opposition to the tax cut (32).

In other words, don't simply repeat "Wilma Smith said," "John Jones said," "Mary Brown said."

Punctuate your quotations correctly. The proper punctuation will help your reader understand who said what. ◆ For information on the appropriate uses of quotation marks surrounding direct quotations, see pages 586–588 in Part Four. If you are incorporating a long quoted passage into your essay, one that appears as more than four typed lines in your manuscript, you should present it in block form without quotation marks, as described on pages 402–403. To omit words in a quoted passage, use ellipsis points, explained on pages 595–596.

Make certain your support is in the paper, not still in your head or back in the original source. Sometimes when you've read a number of persuasive facts in an article or a book, it's easy to forget that your reader doesn't know them as you do now. For instance, the writer of the following paragraph isn't as persuasive as she might be because she hides the support for her controversial point in the reference to the article, forgetting that the reader needs to know what the article actually said:

An organ transplant from one human to another is becoming a common occurrence, an operation that is generally applauded by everyone as a lifesaving effort. But people are overlooking many of the serious problems that come with the increase in transplant surgery. A study shows that in Asia there may be a risk of traffic in organs on the black market. Figures recorded recently are very disturbing (Wood 35).

For the reader to be persuaded, he or she needs to know what the writer learned from the article: what study? What figures and what exactly do they show? Who has recorded these? Is the source reliable? Instead of offering the necessary support in the essay, the writer merely points to the article as proof. Few readers will take the time to look up the article to find the information they need to understand or believe your point. Therefore, when you use source material, always be sure that you have remembered to put your support on the page, *in the essay itself*, for the reader to see. Don't let the essence of your point remain hidden, especially when the claim is controversial.

Don't let reference material dominate your essay. Remember that your reader is interested in *your* thesis and *your* conclusions, not just in a string of references. Use your researched material wisely whenever your statements need clarification, support, or amplification. But don't use quotations, paraphrases, or summarized material at every turn, just to show that you've done your homework.

Avoiding Plagiarism

Unfortunately, most discussions of research must include a brief word about plagiarism. Novice writers often unintentionally plagiarize, as noted before, because they fail to recognize the necessity of attributing paraphrased, summarized, and borrowed ideas to their original owners. And indeed it is sometimes difficult after days of research to know exactly what one has read repeatedly and what one originally thought. Also, there's frequently a thin line between general or common knowledge ("Henry Ford was the father of the automobile industry in America") that does not have to be documented and those ideas and statements that do ("USX reported an operating loss of four million dollars in its last quarter"). As a rule of thumb, ask yourself whether the majority of your readers would recognize the fact or opinion you're expressing or if it's repeatedly found in commonly used sources; if so, you may not need to document it. For example, most people would acknowledge that the Wall Street crash of 1929 ushered in the Great Depression of the 1930s, but the exact number of bank foreclosures in 1933 is not common knowledge and, therefore, needs documenting. Similarly, a well-known quotation from the Bible or Mother Goose or even the Declaration of Independence might pass without documentation, but a line from the Vice President's latest speech needs a reference to its source. Remember, too, that much of the material on the Internet is copyrighted. When in doubt, the best choice is to document anything that you feel may be in question.

To help you understand the difference between plagiarism and proper documentation, here is a passage taken from the book *Criminal Investigation*, followed by both incorrect and correct ways of using its information in a paper of your own:

Original As bicycles have increased in popularity, so has bicycle theft. According to the Web site of the National Bike Registry (www.nationalbikeregistry .com), more than 1.5 million bicycles, worth an estimated $200 million, are stolen each year in the United States. Experienced thieves can steal a locked bike in less than 20 seconds. And while nearly 50 per cent of all stolen bicycles are recovered every year by law enforcement, only 5 per cent are returned to their owners, because most bikes are unregistered.

—*from* Criminal Investigation *(8th edition)*
Wayne W. Bennett and Karen M. Hess
Wadsworth, 2007, page 400

Plagiarized As more people ride bicycles today, bike theft is on the rise. Over 1.5 million bikes are stolen every year in the United States, at a loss of approximately $200 million. A locked bike can be stolen by a good thief in as little as 20 seconds, and even though police recover almost half of them, only 5 percent of owners ever see their rides again because the bikes are unregistered.

The writer of the preceding paragraph paraphrased the original—changed some words and sentences. But because the writer borrowed the ideas and the statistics without crediting the original source, the passage is plagiarized.

Also plagiarized   Got a nice bicycle? Watch out, as it may become one of the 1.5 million bikes stolen this year alone, with bike theft on the rise (Bennett and Hess 400). Campus is a prime place for such theft, as I know from personal experience, despite use of a heavy lock and chain. But even if police or campus cops find your bike—and they do recover nearly half of them—you still may not get your transportation back if you are one of the 95 percent who have not registered your bike. You'll join the other U.S. bikers who all together will lose some $200 million this year.

The writer of the preceding paragraph did show the source of the number of stolen bikes, but the rest of the paragraph contains borrowed material that also must be clearly attributed.

Properly documented   This week campus police are holding their annual bicycle registration drive. Unfortunately, too many students ignore this simple procedure—and pay the price. I know I did last year when my new bike was stolen from the rack in front of the Chemistry Building, despite its heavy lock and chain. I'm not the only one to lose my transportation, of course. According to figures from the National Bike Registry, over 1.2 million bikes are stolen each year, but, more importantly, despite recovery of almost half of them, only 5 percent of owners could claim their recovered bikes through proper registration (Bennett and Hess 400). Learn from my mistake: it's worth the five-minute hassle of filling out a form. Walk—or ride the bike you want to keep—over to the Student Center any afternoon this week from 2 to 4.

The writer of the preceding paragraph used the properly documented information to support her own point about the value of campus bike registration. She has not tried to pass off any of the facts about national bike loss and recovery as her own, and her readers will know where to find the data should they wish more information.

Although plagiarism is often unintentional, it's your job to be as honest and careful as possible. If you're in doubt about your use of a particular idea, study, statistics or any other kind of borrowed material, consult your instructor for a second opinion.

Here's a suggestion that might help you avoid plagiarizing by accident. When you are drafting your essay and come to a spot in which you want to incorporate the ideas of someone else, think of the borrowed material as if it were in a window.* Always frame the window at the top with some sort of introduction that identifies the author (or source) and frame the window on the bottom with a reference to the location of the material, as illustrated on the following page.

---

*I am indebted to John Clark Pratt, Professor Emeritus of English, Colorado State University, for this useful suggestion. Professor Pratt is the author of *Writing from Scratch: The Essay* (1987), published by Hamilton Press, and the editor of the *Writing from Scratch* series.

Introductory phrase
identifies author or source
(According to art critic Jane Doe,) ——————— Top
Frame

Quotation
or
Paraphrase
or
Summary ——————— Window

Location of material
(*Media* 42) ——————— Bottom
Frame

A sample might look like this:

Introductory phrase identifies author

As humorist Mike McGrady once said about housekeeping, "Any job that requires six hours to do and can be undone in six minutes by one small child carrying a plate of crackers and a Monopoly set—this is not a job that will long capture my interest" (13).

Window

Location

In a later draft, you'll probably want to vary your style so that all your borrowed material doesn't appear in exactly the same "window" format (◆ see pages 395–396 for suggestions). But until you acquire the habit of always documenting your sources, you might try using the "window" technique in your early drafts.

PRACTICING WHAT YOU'VE LEARNED

© Canstock Images, Inc./
Index Stock Imagery

A. As Kira Anzai researched the life of Frida Kahlo, she found the following opinion including commentary on one of the artist's paintings. To practice some of the skills you've learned, read the passage and perform the tasks that follow it.

Another Mexican artist, Frida Kahlo, moved in a different direction than the Mexican muralists. Although her work has been associated with the Surrealists, she was an independent like Klee and Miro. Using the visual vocabulary of Mexican folk art, she drew directly on the events of her life, particularly the accident that left her partly crippled and in pain. In *Self-Portrait with Thorn Necklace and Hummingbird* . . . the prickly thorns represent the ache of body and soul. The monkey and the cat refer to the jungle and the fact that she was part

continued on next page

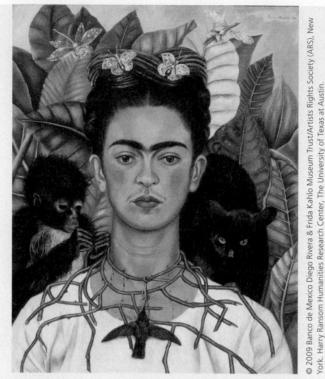

© 2009 Banco de Mexico Diego Rivera & Frida Kahlo Museum Trust/Artists Rights Society (ARS), New York. Harry Ransom Humanities Research Center, The University of Texas at Austin.

Self-Portrait with Thorn Necklace and Hummingbird, 1940, by Frida Kahlo

Indian. The hummingbird that hangs around her neck is a symbol of those who have lost love. In particular, it refers to her recent divorce from muralist Diego Rivera, whom she soon remarried.

1. The book from which the passage was taken contains the following information. Select the appropriate data and prepare a working bibliography card.

Fleming's Arts & Ideas
Tenth Edition
Wadsworth/Cengage Learning, publishers
Boston, MA
Printed in the USA by Graphic World Inc.
23 chapters plus glossary, 704 pages
Library of Congress Control Number 2004107621
Chapter 21
Copyright 2005
Authors: Mary Warner Marien, Professor, Syracuse University, and
    William Fleming, Professor Emeritus, Syracuse University
Pages 585–586
ISBN 0-534-61381-0

2. Paraphrase the first three sentences, showing how you would credit the source of your words in an essay of your own.

3. Practice summarizing the paragraph; do not quote directly from it.

4. Select an idea from the passage to quote directly. Using the "window" technique described on pages 398–399, lead into the quotation with a smooth acknowledgment of its source or authors in the top frame and conclude with the correct location of the material in the bottom frame.

5. Select an idea or take a direct quotation from the passage and use it as support for a point of your own, being careful not to plagiarize the borrowed material.

B. In your library, look up a newspaper* from any city or state and find the issue published on the day of your birth or on some other significant date. Prepare a bibliography card and then summarize an important article from the front page. (Don't forget to acknowledge the source of your summary.)

© CORBIS

ASSIGNMENT

A. To practice searching for and choosing source material, find three recent works on your essay topic available in your library. If you don't have an essay topic yet, pick a subject that interests you, one that is likely to appear in both print and electronic sources (Baseball Hall of Fame, stamp collecting, the *Titanic* disaster, king cobras, etc.). If possible, try to find three different kinds of sources, such as a book, a journal or magazine article, and a Web site. After you have recorded bibliographic information for each source, locate and evaluate the works. Do all of these sources provide relevant, reliable information? In a few sentences explain why you believe each one would or would not be an appropriate source for your research essay.

B. *Collaborative Activity:* To help you focus your essay topic, engage in a "talk-write" session with another student. Before class, review your research thus far, selecting the most interesting, surprising, or puzzling piece of information you have found. In class, explain your findings to a classmate, and together brainstorm about ways this information might be most effectively incorporated into your essay. Take notes on any useful suggestions or unexpected reactions that might help you see a new possibility for the direction of your essay. Also, if time permits, help each other problem-solve any difficulties with a particular research method or source.

*If the newspaper is not accessible, you might substitute a weekly news magazine, such as *Time* or *Newsweek*.

Choosing the Documentation Style for Your Essay

Once you begin to write your paper incorporating your source material, you need to know how to show your readers where your material came from. You may have already learned a documentation system in a previous writing class, but because today's researchers and scholars use a number of different documentation styles, it's important that you know which style is appropriate for your current essay. In some cases, your instructors (or the audience for whom you are writing) will designate a particular style; at other times, the choice will be yours.

In this chapter, we will look at two widely used systems—MLA style and APA style—and also briefly review the use of the traditional footnote/bibliography format.

MLA Style

Most instructors in the humanities assign the documentation form prescribed by the Modern Language Association of America (MLA). Since 1984, the MLA has recommended a form of documentation that no longer uses traditional footnotes or endnotes to show references.* The current form calls for *parenthetical documentation*, most often consisting of the author's last name and the appropriate page number(s) in parentheses immediately following the source material in your paper. At the end of your discussion, readers may find complete bibliographic information for each source on a Works Cited page, a list of all the sources in your essay.

MLA Citations in Your Essay

Here are some guidelines for using the MLA parenthetical reference form within your paper.

1. If you use a source by one author, place the author's name and page number after the quoted, paraphrased, or summarized material. Note that the parentheses go *before* the end punctuation, and there is no punctuation between the author's name and the page number. (Use the author's name and omit the page reference when citing a complete work or a one-page work.)

   Example   Although pop art often resembles the comic strip, it owes a debt to such painters as Magritte, Matisse, and de Kooning (Rose 184).

2. If you use a source by one author and give credit to that author by name in your paper, you need only give the page number in the parentheses.

   Example   According to art critic Barbara Rose, pop art owes a large debt to such painters as Magritte, Matisse, and de Kooning (184).

3. If you are directly quoting material of more than four typed lines, indent the material one inch from the left margin, double-space, and do not use quotation marks. Do not change the right margin. Note that in this case, the parentheses appear *after* the punctuation that ends the quoted material.

---

*If you wish a more detailed description of the current MLA form, ask your local bookstore or library for the *MLA Handbook for Writers of Research Papers*, 7th ed. (New York: MLA, 2009) and also the *MLA Style Manual and Guide to Scholarly Publishing*, 3rd ed. (New York: MLA, 2008). The most up-to-date documentation information may be found on the MLA Web site <http://www.mla.org>.

Example   In addition to causing tragedy for others, Crane's characters who are motivated by a desire to appear heroic to their peers may also cause themselves serious trouble. For example, Collins, another Civil War private, almost causes his own death because of his vain desire to act bravely in front of his fellow Union soldiers. (Hall 16)

4. If you are citing more than one work by the same author, include a short title in the parentheses.

   Example   Within fifty years, the Inca and Aztec civilizations were defeated and overthrown by outside invaders (Thomas, *Lost Cultures* 198).

5. If you are citing a work by two or three authors, use all last names and the page number.

   Examples   Prisons today are overcrowded to the point of emergency; conditions could not be worse, and the state budget for prison reforms is at an all-time low (Smith and Jones 72).

   Human infants grow quickly, with most babies doubling their birth weight in the first six months of life and tripling their weight by their first birthday (Pantell, Frics, and Vickery 52).

6. For more than three authors, use all the last names or use the last name of the first author plus "et al." (Latin for "and others") and the page number. There is no comma after the author's name.

   Example   Casualties of World War II during 1940-45 amounted to more than twenty-five million soldiers and civilians (Blum et al. 779).

7. If you cite a work that has no named author, use the work's title and the page number.

   Example   Each year 350,000 Americans will die of a heart attack before reaching a hospital ("First Aid for Heart Attacks" 88).

8. If the work you are citing appears in a series, include the volume and page number with the author's name.

   Example   On August 28, 1963, King delivered his "I Have a Dream" address to more than 200,000 civil rights supporters in Washington, DC, a speech that added momentum to the passage of the 1964 Civil Rights Act (Lopez 1: 270).

9. If your source is an electronic document, treat it as you would a print source. If you are citing an entire work from an electronic source that has no page, paragraph, or screen numbers, it is preferable to use the name of the author or editor in the text, rather than in a parenthetical reference. If the author's or editor's name is unavailable, use the work's title (shortened or in full).

   Example   Cannon College Economics Professor John Thompson argues a different view of the Chinese role in Indonesia's economy.

   Some electronic documents include paragraph or screen numbers. When citing these documents, include the appropriate number, preceded by "par." or "pars." for paragraph(s), or "screen." If the paragraphs are not numbered in the original source, however, do not impose your own numbering system.

Example   The Chinese in Indonesia account for only 4% of the population but control 70% of the economy (Thompson, par. 6).

10. If the material you are citing contains a passage quoted from another source, indicate your source for the quotation in the parentheses.

Example   According to George Orwell, "Good writing is like a window-pane" (qtd. in Murray 142).

11. If the work you are citing is a nonprint source with no reference markers, such as an interview, lecture, television show, film, or performance, include in the text the name of the person or the title (e.g., *60 Minutes*) that begins the corresponding entry in the Works Cited list.

Example   In a March 12, 2009, telephone interview, Stefan Jacoby, President and CEO of Volkswagen Group of America, expressed his satisfaction with the progress being made in the site preparation for VW's Chattanooga production facility.

Compiling a Works Cited List: MLA Style

If you are using the MLA format, at the end of your essay you should include a Works Cited page—a formal listing of the sources you used in your essay. (If you wish to show all the sources you consulted, but did not cite, add a Works Consulted page.) Arrange the entries alphabetically by the authors' last names; if no name is given, alphabetize the source by the first important word of its title. Double-space each entry, and double-space between entries. If an entry takes more than one line, indent the subsequent lines one-half inch. Current MLA guidelines indicate one space following end punctuation marks. (Some instructors still prefer two spaces, however, so you might check with your teacher on this issue.) See the sample entries that follow.

Sample Entries: MLA Style

Here are some sample entries to help you prepare a Works Cited page according to the MLA guidelines. Please note that MLA style recommends using shortened forms of publishers' names and omitting business descriptions, such as Inc., Co., Press, or House.

- For publishers' names that include the name of one person:

    Alfred A. Knopf becomes Knopf   John Wiley becomes Wiley

- For publishers' names that include the name of more than one person:

    Harper and Row becomes Harper   Houghton Mifflin becomes Houghton

- To cite a university press, use "U" and "P" appropriately:

    Oxford UP for Oxford University Press
    U of Illinois P for University of Illinois Press
    UP of Florida for University Press of Florida

- For publishers' names that include articles, business abbreviations, and descriptive words:

    The Denali Press becomes Denali   Stemmer House Publishers, Inc. becomes Stemmer

Remember, too, when you type your paper on a computer, the titles of books and journals should be italicized. The titles of articles, essays, and chapters should be enclosed in quotation marks. Capitalize the first word, last word, and all important words in a title or subtitle. Do not capitalize the following parts of speech (unless they appear as the first or last word):

articles ("a," "an," "the," as in "Crossing the Bar")

prepositions (e.g., "across," "behind," "at," "of," "up," "down," as in "The Jilting of Granny Weatherall")

coordinating conjunctions ("and," "but," "for," "nor," "or," "so," "yet," as in *Romeo and Juliet*)

the "to" in infinitives ("A Good Man Is Hard to Find")

Books

- **A book with one author**

  Davis, Bertram H. *A Proof of Eminence: The Life of Sir John Hawkins.* Bloomington: Indiana UP, 1973. Print.

- **Two books by the same author**

  Davis, Bertram H. *A Proof of Eminence: The Life of Sir John Hawkins.* Bloomington: Indiana UP, 1973. Print.

  ---. *Thomas Percy: A Scholar-Cleric in the Age of Johnson.* Philadelphia: U of Pennsylvania P, 1989. Print.

  Include the author's name in only the first entry. In each subsequent entry, type three hyphens followed by a period. The three hyphens stand for exactly the same name as in the preceding entry. The hyphens do not represent any role other than author (for example, a comma and "ed." are added after the hyphens to indicate the role as editor). Such a label (e.g., "comp.," "ed.," or "trans.") does not affect the order in which the entries appear. For works listed under the same name, alphabetize them by title.

- **A book with two or three authors**

  McDonough, James Lee, and Thomas L. Connelly. *Five Tragic Hours: The Battle of Franklin.* Knoxville: U of Tennessee P, 1983. Print.

  Note that only the name of the first author is inverted.

- **A book with more than three authors**

  Guerin, Wilfred L., et al. *A Handbook of Critical Approaches to Literature.* 5th ed. New York: Oxford UP, 2004. Print.

  Guerin, Wilfred L., Earle Labor, Lee Morgan, Jeanne C. Reesman, and John R. Willingham. *A Handbook of Critical Approaches to Literature.* 5th ed. New York: Oxford UP, 2004. Print.

  You may use "et al." (meaning "and others") for the other names, or you may give all names in full in the order they appear on the book's title page.

- **A book with author and editor**

  Chaucer, Geoffrey. *The Tales of Canterbury.* Ed. Robert Pratt. Boston: Houghton, 1974. Print.

- **A book with corporate authorship**

  National Fire Safety Council. *Stopping Arson before It Starts.* Washington: Edmondson, 1992. Print.

  Omit any initial article ("A," "An," "The") in the name of the corporate author, and do not abbreviate its name.

- **A book with an editor**

  Knappman, Edward W., ed. *Great American Trials: From Salem Witchcraft to Rodney King.* Detroit: Visible Ink, 1994. Print.

- **A selection or chapter from an anthology or a collection with an editor**

  O'Connor, Flannery. "A Good Man Is Hard to Find." *Literature: Reading, Reacting, Writing.* Ed. Laurie G. Kirszner and Stephen R. Mandell. 7th ed. Boston: Wadsworth-Cengage, 2010. 447-57. Print.

  Following the date of publication and period, include the page numbers on which the work appears.

- **One volume of a multivolume work**

  Delaney, John J., ed. *Encyclopedia of Saints.* Vol. 4. New York: Doubleday, 1998. Print.

- **A work in more than one volume**

  Piepkorn, Arthur C. *Profiles in Belief: The Religious Bodies of the United States and Canada.* 2 vols. New York: Harper, 1976-78. Print.

  If the volumes were published over a period of years, give the inclusive dates after the publisher's name.

- **A work in a series**

  Vance, John A. *Joseph and Thomas Warton.* Ed. Sarah Smith. Boston: Twayne-Hall, 1983. Print. Twayne English Authors Ser. 380.

  After the medium of publication, include the series name and the series number (if any) followed by a period.

- **A translation**

  Zamora, Martha. *Frida Kahlo: The Brush of Anguish.* Trans. Marilyn Sode Smith. San Francisco: Chronicle, 1990. Print.

- **A reprint**

  Thaxter, Celia. *Among the Isles of Shoals.* 1873. Ed. Leslie Dunn. Hampton: Heritage, 1978. Print.

  Note that this citation presents two dates: the date of original publication (1873) and the date of the reprinted work (1978).

- **An introduction, preface, foreword, or afterword**

  Soloman, Barbara H. Introduction. *Herland.* By Charlotte Perkins Gilman. New
  York: Penguin, 1992. xi-xxxi. Print.

  Begin the citation with the name of the writer of the section you are citing;
  then identify the section but do not italicize or use quotation marks around
  the word. Next, give the name of the book and the name of its author, preceded by the word "By" and followed by a period.

Periodicals (Magazines, Journals, Newspapers)

MLA guidelines stipulate that you should omit any introductory article in the title of
an English-language magazine (*New Republic* rather than *The New Republic*) or scholarly
journal (*Kenyon Review* rather than *The Kenyon Review*). In citing an English-language
newspaper, give the name as it appears on the masthead, but omit any introductory
article (*New York Times* rather than *The New York Times*; *Washington Post* rather than *The
Washington Post*).

Scholarly journals require volume and issue numbers; magazines and newspapers do
not.

If an article is not printed on consecutive pages (for example, if the article begins on
page 51, runs through page 55, resumes on page 112, and concludes on page 113), use
the first page number and a plus sign with no space between them.

Except for May, June, and July, the months of the year are abbreviated. Use the first
three letters for each month (e.g., Jan., Feb., Mar.), but use Sept. for September.

- **A signed article in a magazine published every week or every two weeks**

  Walsh, Bryan. "The Gusty Superpower." *Time* 16 Mar. 2009: 42-44. Print.

  Note that the magazine title is not followed by a period.

- **An unsigned article in a magazine published every week or every two weeks**

  "Exit Ramp Poses Difficulty for Local Residents." *East Hamilton Weekly* 16 Mar.
  2009: 42-44. Print.

- **An article in a magazine published every month or every two months**

  Kunhardt, Philip B. "Lincoln's Contested Legacy." *Smithsonian* Feb. 2009: 32-38.
  Print.

  To cite this article from an electronic source, refer to "An article in an
  online monthly magazine" and "An article in a periodical publication in an
  online database" later in this section.

- **A review in a magazine published every month or every two months**

  Andrews, Donald. "Religious Traditions in the Tennessee Valley." Rev. of
  Lasting Influences, by Joel Henderson. *Chattanooga's History* Jan.
  2009: 15-17. Print.

- **A signed article in a scholarly journal**

  Webb, Allen. "Digital Texts and the New Literacies." *English Journal* 97.1
  (2007): 83-88. Print.

Note that the journal title is not followed by a period. One space after the title of a scholarly journal, include the volume and issue numbers separated by a period. The year but not the month of publication is placed inside parentheses.

- **A signed article in a newspaper**

  Sohn, Pam. "City, County Burning Ban Begins Friday." *Chattanooga Times Free Press* 27 Apr. 2009: B1+. Print.

  Brooks, Jennifer. "Belmont to Stop Selling Bottled Water at School." *Tennessean* [Nashville] 22 Apr. 2009: 1B+. Print.

Note that the newspaper title is not followed by a period. When it is not a part of the newspaper's title, add the city name in brackets after the title. Omit any introductory article (*Chattanooga Times Free Press* instead of *The Chattanooga Times Free Press*; *Miami Herald* instead of *The Miami Herald*). Note that section designation and page number are often combined (B1 or 1B); record the page numbers exactly as they appear.

- **An unsigned article in a newspaper**

  "De La Hoya Calls End to Golden Ring Career." *Atlanta Journal-Constitution* 15 Apr. 2009: C4. Print.

- **A signed editorial in a newspaper**

  Ball, George. "We Can't Spring Forward Fast Enough to Catch Nature." Editorial. *Atlanta Journal-Constitution* 15 Apr. 2009: A11. Print.

- **An unsigned editorial in a newspaper**

  "Environmental Rules at Risk." Editorial. *Chattanooga Times Free Press* 30 Apr. 2009: B6. Print.

- **A letter to the newspaper**

  Byrd, Charles. Letter. *Denver Post* 10 May 2009: A10. Print.

Encyclopedias, Pamphlets, Dissertations

- **A signed article in an encyclopedia (full reference)**

  Collins, Dean R. "Light Amplifier." *McGraw-Hill Encyclopedia of Science and Technology.* Ed. Justin Thyme. 3 vols. Boston: McGraw, 1997. Print.

Use full publication information for reference works, such as encyclopedias and dictionaries, unless they are familiar and often revised. Volume and page numbers are not needed if the information is in alphabetical order.

- **An unsigned article in a well-known encyclopedia**

  "Sailfish." *Encyclopedia Americana.* 18th ed. 1998. Print.

- **A pamphlet**

  Young, Leslie. *Baby Care Essentials for the New Mother.* Austin: Hall, 2006. Print.

  Atlanta Builders Association. *Have Confidence in Your Builder.* Atlanta: Brown, 2009. Print.

- **A government document**

  United States. National Institute on Drug Abuse. *Drug Abuse Prevention.*
  Washington: GPO, 2008. Print.

  Many documents issued by the U.S. government are published by the Government Printing Office (GPO) in Washington, DC.

- **An unpublished dissertation or thesis**

  Harmon, Gail A. "Poor Writing Skills at the College Level: A Program for
  Correction." Diss. U of Colorado, 2006. Print.

Films, Television, Radio, Performances, Recordings

- **A film**

  Frida. Dir. Julie Taymor. Perf. Salma Hayek and Alfred Molina. Miramax, 2002.
  Film.

  Begin with the title (italicized) followed by the director, the distributor, the year of release, and the medium (Film). You may also include other data, such as the star performers, writer, or producer.

  Taymor, Julie, dir. *Frida.* Perf. Salma Hayek and Alfred Molina. 2002. Miramax,
  2003. DVD.

  If you are referring to the contribution of a particular individual, such as the director, writer, actor, or composer, begin with that person's name. Cite a videocassette, DVD, or laser disc as a film but also include its distributor, its distribution date, and its medium.

- **A television or radio show**

  Antiques Roadshow. PBS. WGBH, Boston, 19 Apr. 2009. Television.

  Conan, Neal, narr. "The 'Lost Magic' of the Irish Pub." *Talk of the Nation.* Natl.
  Public Radio. WSMC, Collegedale, 16 Mar. 2009. Radio.

  Dugan, David, dir. "Lord of the Ants." Narr. Harrison Ford. *NOVA.* PBS. WTCI,
  Chattanooga, 9 June 2009. Television.

  "The One with the Late Thanksgiving." By Shana Goldberg-Meehan. Dir.
  Gary Halvorson. Perf. Jennifer Aniston, Courteney Cox, Lisa Kudrow,
  Matt LeBlanc, Matthew Perry, David Schwimmer. *Friends.* Fox. WDSI,
  Chattanooga, 6 Apr. 2009. Television.

  If you are referring to a particular episode or person associated with the show, cite that name first, before the show's name.

- **Performances (plays, concerts, ballets, operas)**

  Messiah. By George Frideric Handel. Cond. Laurie Redmer Minner. Perf. Julie
  Penner, Martha Boutwell, Michael Kull, and Brett Hyberger. Collegedale
  Church of Seventh-day Adventists, Collegedale. 1 Apr. 2009. Performance.

  Cardillo, Ken, cond. "Rhapsody in Blue." By George Gershwin. Perf. Beth
  Douglass. Chattanooga Symphony Orch. Tivoli Theatre, Chattanooga.
  18 May 2009. Performance.

  If you are referring to the contribution of a particular person associated with the performance, put that person's name first.

- **A sound recording**

Celtic Woman. *The Greatest Journey: Essential Collection.* Perf. Chloë Agnew,
Órla Fallon, Lynn Hilary, Lisa Kelly, Méav Ni Mhaolchatha, Máiréad
Nesbitt, and Alex Sharpe. Manhattan Records, 2008. CD.

Zapen, Rebecca. "Shower #2." Rec. 2 Feb. 2004. *Japanese Bathhouse.* Bashert
Records, 2005. CD.

You may cite an entire sound recording (with its title italicized) or a specific
song (with its title in quotation marks). Depending on what information you
wish to emphasize, you may begin with the composer, conductor, or performers, followed by the title of the recording, artists other than the group
or person listed first, the manufacturer, and the year of issue. Conclude
with the medium (Audiocassette, CD [compact disc], or LP [long-playing
record]), neither italicized nor in quotation marks.

Letters, Lectures, and Speeches

- **An unpublished letter, archived**

Steinbeck, John. Letter to Elizabeth R. Otis. 11 Nov. 1944. TS. Steinbeck
Collection. Stanford U Lib., Stanford.

- **A letter received by the author**

Hall, Katherine. Letter to the author. 10 May 2009. MS.

For a letter, indicate the form by including "TS" for typescript (prepared by
machine) or "MS" for manuscript (written by hand).

- **A lecture or speech**

Dippity, Sarah N. "The Importance of Prewriting." CLAS Convention. President
Hotel, Colorado Springs. 15 Feb. 2009. Keynote speech.

Give the speaker's name and, if known, the title of the presentation (in quotation marks) followed by the meeting and the sponsoring organization (if
appropriate), the location, the date, and the delivery format (e.g., Address,
Lecture, Reading), neither italicized nor in quotation marks.

Interviews

- **A broadcast or published interview**

Catanzaro, James L. Interview by Ray Bertani. *Around the Scenic City.* PBS.
WTCI, Chattanooga. 28 Mar. 2009. Television.

Hewlett, F. D. "Expansion along the River." Interview by Tim Dills. *Chattanooga
Times Free Press* 15 Feb. 2009: C12. Print.

Cite the person interviewed first and the title of the interview, if any. Use the
word "Interview" (neither italicized nor in quotation marks) if the interview
has no title. The interviewer's name may be added if relevant. Conclude with
the publication or broadcast information and medium of publication.

- **A personal interview**

   Adkins, Camille. Personal interview. 11 Jan. 2009.

   Payne, Linda. Telephone interview. 13 Apr. 2009.

   Give the name of the person interviewed, the kind of interview, and the date.

Electronic Sources: MLA Style

The purpose of a citation for an electronic source is the same as that for printed matter: identification of the source and the best way to locate it. All citations basically name the author and the work and identify publication information. Citations for various types of electronic sources, however, must also include different kinds of additional information to help researchers locate the sources in the easiest way.

It's important to remember, too, that forms of electronic sources continue to change rapidly. As technology expands, new ways of documenting electronic sources must also be created. The problem is further complicated by the fact that some sources will not supply all the information you might like to include in your citation. In these cases, you simply have to do the best you can by citing what is available.

The guidelines and sample entries that follow are designed merely as an introduction to citing electronic sources according to MLA style. If you need additional help citing other kinds of electronic sources, consult the most up-to-the-minute documentation guide available, such as the current *MLA Handbook for Writers of Research Papers* or the MLA Web site.

Before looking at the sample citations given here, you should be familiar with the following information regarding dates, addresses, and reference markers in online sources.

Use of multiple dates. Because online sources may change or be revised, a citation may contain more than one date. For a document that appeared previously in print form, use the original date. For a Web-only document, use the date of its electronic publication. If no date is given, use "n.d." Your entry should also include a "date of access," indicating the day you found the particular source.

Use of network addresses. The *MLA Handbook* no longer requires the inclusion of a URL (uniform resource locator) in a Works Cited entry. But MLA guidelines continue to encourage that URLs be included when the reader probably cannot locate the sources without it. If you choose to include the URL, place it immediately following the date of access, a period, and a space. Enclose the URL in angle brackets and conclude with a period. If you must divide a URL at the end of a line, break it only after a slash mark. Do not use a hyphen at the break as this will distort the address. URLs are often long and easy to misread, so take extra time to ensure that you are copying them correctly.

Important note: Many online databases and some online library catalogs now include a persistent link or URL to their records; do use this link in your citations for online works.

Use of reference markers. Unfortunately, many online sources do not use markers such as page or paragraph numbers. If such information is available to you, include it in your citations by all means; if it does not exist, readers must fend for themselves when accessing your sources. (Some readers might locate particular information in a document by using the "Find" tool in their computer program, but this option is not always available or useful.)

Nonperiodical Publications

Most works on the Web are classified as "nonperiodical publications" because they are not released on a regular schedule (i.e., weekly or monthly). An entry for a nonperiodical publication includes the following information, *if available*: name of the author, editor, or compiler; title of the work; title of the Web site (italicized) if distinct from the title of the work; version or edition number; publisher or sponsor of the Web site; date of publication; medium of publication, and date of access.

> Cohen, Elizabeth. "Five Ways to Avoid Germs While Traveling." *CNN.com.* Cable
> News Network, 27 Nov. 2008. Web. 14 Mar. 2009.

> Harmon, William, ed. *The Columbia Granger's World of Poetry.* Columbia UP, n.d.
> Web. 7 May 2009.

> Neary, Lynn. "Did Shakespeare Want to Suppress His Sonnets?" *Morning Edition.*
> Nat'l. Public Radio, 20 May 2009. Web. 22 May 2009.

> Parker, Deborah, gen. ed. *The World of Dante.* Inst. for Advanced Technology in the
> Humanities, U of Virginia, n.d. Web. 7 May 2009.

If a Web site indicates no date of publication, include "n.d." (neither italicized nor in quotation marks) where the date of publication would ordinarily appear.

Also within this group are Web sites sponsored by newspapers and magazines (discussed in the following section), which can post updated revisions after the original print version as well as reporters' blogs written only for the Web site.

Articles in Online Periodicals (Magazines and Newspapers)

Guidelines for citing online magazines and newspapers are based on the guidelines for citing their print counterparts. Begin with the author's name; if no author is given, begin with the title of the article (in quotation marks) and continue with the name of the periodical (italicized). At this point, the guidelines vary from those for the print version. After the name of the periodical, provide the sponsor of the publication, date of publication, medium of publication (Web), and date of access. Note that page numbers are not included in citations for online magazines and newspapers.

- **An article in an online monthly magazine**

  > Kunhardt, Philip B. "Lincoln's Contested Legacy." *Smithsonian.* Smithsonian
  > Inst., Feb. 2009. Web. 30 Apr. 2009.

  After the publication (*Smithsonian*) is the publisher or sponsor of the site (Smithsonian Inst.) followed by a comma and the date of publication. Next is the medium of publication (Web) followed by the date of access. Note that periods follow each item—except after the publisher or sponsor of the site. Page numbers are not included.

- **A signed article in an online weekly magazine**

  > Underwood, Anne. "Cellular Healing." *Newsweek.* Newsweek, 6 May 2009.
  > Web. 7 May 2009.

After the publication (*Newsweek*) is the publisher or sponsor of the site (Newsweek) followed by a comma and the date of publication. Next is the medium of publication (Web) followed by the date of access. Note that periods follow each item—except after the publisher or sponsor of the site. Page numbers are not included.

- **An unsigned article in an online weekly magazine**

  "10 Things You Didn't Know about Abraham Lincoln." *U.S.News.com.* U.S. News & World Report, 10 Feb. 2009. Web. 7 May 2009.

  Because this title begins with a numeral, the article should be alphabetized as if the numeral were spelled out ("Ten Things You Didn't Know about Abraham Lincoln").

- **An article in an online newspaper**

  Lubell, Sam. "Of the Sea and Air and Sky." *New York Times.* New York Times, 26 Nov. 2008. Web. 14 Mar. 2009.

  Spirrison, Brad. "Biotech 'Moon Shot' Starts in Classroom." *Chicago Sun-Times.* Sun-Times News Group, 27 Apr. 2009. Web. 27 Apr. 2009.

  After the publication (*New York Times* or *Chicago Sun-Times*) is the publisher or sponsor of the site (New York Times or Sun-Times News Group) followed by a comma and the date of publication. Next is the medium of publication (Web) followed by the date of access. Note that periods follow each item—except after the publisher or sponsor of the site. Page numbers are not included.

- **An editorial in an online newspaper**

  "Cash for Old Cars Is a Clunker of an Idea." Editorial. *DenverPost.com.* Denver Post, 19 Apr. 2009. Web. 23 Apr. 2009.

- **A review in an online newspaper**

  Wisniewski, Mary. "Sundance's Girlfriend." Rev. of *Etta*, by Gerald Kolpan. *Chicago Sun-Times.* Sun-Times News Group, 5 Apr. 2009. Web. 23 Apr. 2009.

Articles in Online Scholarly Journals

As with online magazines and newspapers, the guidelines for citing online scholarly journals are based on the guidelines for citing their print counterparts. Begin with the author's name; if no author is given, begin with the title of the article (in quotation marks) and continue with the name of the periodical (italicized), the volume and issue numbers (if available), the year of publication (in parentheses) followed by a colon, and the page numbers followed by a period. At this point, the guidelines vary from those for the print version. Conclude the entry with the medium of publication (Web) and date of access.

- **An article in an online scholarly journal**

  Fetters, Allison. "Intrigue in Shakespeare's Sonnets." *Midlothian Review* 28.3 (2009): 17-27. Web. 6 Apr. 2009.

  Shapiro, Stephen. "Intellectual Labor Power, Cultural Capital, and the Value of Prestige." *South Atlantic Quarterly* 108.2 (2009): 249-64. Web. 9 May 2009.

Wright, Patrick. "Coleridge's Translucence: A Failed Transcendence." *RaVoN: Romanticism and Victorianism on the Net* 50 (2008): n. pag. Web. 7 May 2009.

If the page numbers are not indicated, you should include "n. pag." (neither italicized nor in quotation marks)] to indicate "no pagination." Place "n. pag." where the page numbers would ordinarily appear.

Articles Accessed through an Online Database

To cite a source that you have found through one of your library's databases, begin by following the guidelines for citing their print counterparts. To this information, add the title of the database (italicized), medium of publication (Web), and date of access. For all periodical publications—magazines, newspapers, and scholarly journals—accessed through a database, provide the page numbers. If this information is not available, use "n. pag." (no pagination).

- **An article in a periodical publication in an online database**

Kunhardt, Philip B. "Lincoln's Contested Legacy." *Smithsonian* Feb. 2009: n. pag. *General OneFile.* Web. 30 Apr. 2009.

Compare this Kunhardt entry with other Kunhardt entries found at "An article in a magazine published every month or every two months" and at "An article in an online monthly magazine" earlier in this section. All three entries refer to the same *Smithsonian* article about Abraham Lincoln—one in print, one from the publication's Web site, and one accessed through an online database.

- **A review in a periodical publication in an online database**

Johnston, Jill. "Self-Portrait." Rev. of *The Diary of Frida Kahlo: An Intimate Self-Portrait*, by Sarah M. Lowe. *Art in America* Mar. 1996: 31, 33. *General OneFile.* Web. 24 Mar. 2009.

Personal or Professional Web Sites

In citing Web sites, begin with the name of the person who created the site, if appropriate. If no name is given, begin with the title of the work (italicized if the work is independent; in quotation marks if the work is part of a larger work). For an untitled work, use a descriptive label such as "Advertisement," "Home page," "Online posting," or "Preface" (but do not italicize or enclose a description in quotation marks). Next, provide the title of the overall Web site (italicized), if it is different from the title of the work. Then, if appropriate, identify the version or edition. Continue with the Web site's publisher or sponsor; if this information is not available, use "N.p." (not italicized or enclosed in quotation marks). Then include the date of publication; if this information is not available, use "n.d." (not italicized nor enclosed in quotation marks). Conclude with the medium of publication (Web) and the date of access.

"Humanities and Fine Arts." *Chattanooga State Technical Community College.* Chattanooga State Technical Community College, 25 Feb. 2009. Web. 9 May 2009.

Williford, Sandra. Home page. *Teach Yourself to Paint Portraits.* N.p. 29 Sept. 2008. Web. 22 Apr. 2009.

Online Books

With the texts of countless books now available online, many students prefer to access copies in this economic format. To cite an online version of a book, begin the entry with the author's name, the book's name, and any publication information given in the source (city of publication, publisher, date). Then list the title of the Web site (italicized), the medium of publication, and the date of access.

> Dickens, Charles. *Oliver Twist.* London, 1897. *Electronic Text Center, U of Virginia.* Web. 22 May 2009.

> Goldsmith, Oliver. *The Vicar of Wakefield.* 1766. *Google Book Search.* Web. 22 May 2009.

Nonperiodical Publications on CD-ROM, Diskette, or Magnetic Tape

Nonperiodical electronic citations are similar to those for a print book, but also include the medium of publication (CD-ROM, Diskette, Magnetic tape). If you are citing a specific entry, article, essay, poem, or short story, enclose the title in quotation marks.

> "Acupuncture." *Oxford English Dictionary.* 2nd ed. Oxford: Oxford UP, 1992. CD-ROM.

> Ontag, Jennifer. "Aphra Behn's Spark." *Eighteenth-Century Drama.* Ed. Erica Lux. Knoxville: U of Tennessee P, 2009. CD-ROM.

E-Mail Communications

Begin with the writer's name, followed by the title from the subject line, "Message to" with recipient's name (or "Message to the author"), date of the message, and medium.

> Bray, Joseph P. "Lincoln Celebration." Message to Scott Douglass. 12 Feb. 2009. E-mail.

APA Style

The American Psychological Association (APA) recommends a documentation style for research papers in the social sciences.* Your instructors in psychology and sociology classes, for example, may prefer that you use the APA form when you write essays for them.

If you are using APA style in an academic paper, put your work's title, your name, the school's name, the instructor's name, the course name and section number, and the date on a title page, numbered as page 1. Writers following APA guidelines often include an *abstract* on page 2. An abstract is a short summary of your research; it may contain the following parts: a statement of the problem or your reason for undertaking this topic; your research methods; the results, findings, or product of this work; your conclusions; and, if appropriate, a statement of any larger implications. The essay itself begins on page 3. The APA style manual recommends inclusion of a shortened version (maximum 50 characters) of the essay's title as a running head in uppercase letters in the top left corner of all pages. Insert "Running head:" before the running head on the title page.

---

*If you wish a more detailed description of the APA style, consult the *Publication Manual of the American Psychological Association*, 6th ed. (Washington, DC: American Psychological Association, 2010); your school's library probably has a copy. The most up-to-date documentation forms may be found on the APA Web site <http://www.apastyle.org>.

Some papers using APA style also include headings to identify major sections ("Methods," "Results") or key points in the discussion.

The APA style is similar to the MLA style in that it calls for parenthetical documentation within the essay itself, although the information cited in the parentheses differs slightly from that presented according to the MLA format. For example, you will note that in the APA style the date of publication follows the author's last name and precedes the page number in the parentheses. Instead of a Works Cited page, the APA style uses a References page at the end of the essay to list those sources cited in the text. In some instances, your instructor might prefer that you include a Bibliography page, which differs from the References page by listing all works that were consulted. Another important difference concerns capitalization of book and article titles in the reference list: in the MLA style, the first letter of each important word is capitalized, but in the APA style, only proper names, the first word of titles, and the first word appearing after a colon are capitalized.

APA Citations in Your Essay

Here are some guidelines for using the APA parenthetical form within your paper:

1. APA style typically calls for an "author–publication year" method of citation, with the name and date inserted in the text at an appropriate place in the reference.

   Examples A recent study (Jones, 2009) found no discernible differences in the absentee rate of men and women students on the main campus.

   Jones (2009) contrasted the absentee rates of men and women students on the main campus but found no discernible differences.

2. When you are quoting directly, place the author's name, the publication year, and the page number in parentheses following the quoted material. Note that in APA style, you place commas between the items in the parentheses, and you do include the "p." and "pp." abbreviations for "page" and "pages" (these are omitted in MLA style).

   Example One crucial step in developing an anti-social personality may, in fact, be "the experience of being caught in some act and consequently being publicly labeled as a deviant" (Becker, 2008, p. 31).

3. If you use a print source by one author and give credit to that author by name within your paper, you need give only the date and the page number in parentheses. Note that the publication date follows directly after the name of the author.

   Example According to Green (2006), gang members from upper-class families are rarely convicted for their crimes and are "almost never labeled as delinquent" (p. 101).

4. If you are citing a work with more than two authors, but fewer than six, list all names in the first reference; in subsequent references, use only the first author's last name and "et al." (which means "and others"). For six or more authors, use only the last name of the first author followed by "et al." for all citations, including the first. Note the use of "&" instead of "and" within parentheses.

   Example *First reference:* After divorce, men's standard of living generally rises some 75%, whereas women's falls to approximately 35% of what it once was (Bird, Gordon, & Smith, 1992, p. 203).

Subsequent references: Almost half of all the poor households in America today are headed by single women, most of whom are supporting a number of children (Bird et al., 1992, p. 285).

5. If you cite a work that has a corporate author, cite the group responsible for producing the work.

Example   In contrast, the State Highway Research Commission (2004) argues, "The return to the sixty-five-mile-an-hour speed limit on some of our state's highways has resulted in an increase in traffic fatalities" (p. 3).

6. Private interviews, e-mail messages, and other personal communications should be referred to in your text but *not* in your reference list. Provide the initials and last name of the communicator, the words "personal communication," and the date in your paper.

Example   Sierra Club leader C. L. Byrd confirmed that the fall trip to Cinque Terre would be June 12, 2009 (personal communication, May 20, 2009).

Compiling a Reference List: APA Style

If you are using the APA style, at the end of your essay you should include a page labeled References—a formal listing of the sources you cited in your essay. Arrange the entries alphabetically by the authors' last names; use initials for the authors' first and middle names. All authors' names are inverted (Forst, M. L, & Hall, S. L.). Note that with two to seven authors, an ampersand (&) appears before the last author. If a work has more than seven authors, APA lists the first six followed by an ellipsis and the last author's name, omitting the customary ampersand (&). If there are two or more works by one author, list them chronologically, beginning with the earliest publication date. If an author published two or more works in the same year, the first reference alphabetically is designated "a," the second "b," and so on (Feinstein 1999a; Feinstein 1999b). APA style uses the half-inch hanging indent method (as does the MLA style).

Remember that in APA style, you italicize book and journal titles, volume numbers, and their associated punctuation, but you do not put the names of articles in quotation marks. Although you do capitalize the major words in the titles of magazines, newspapers, and journals, you do not capitalize any words in the titles of books or articles except the first word in each title, the first word following a colon or dash, and all proper names.

In a reference entry that includes the publisher, APA requires the publisher's location—city and state for those in the United States (using the official two-letter U.S. Postal Service abbreviation), and city and country for those outside the United States. If the publisher is a university press whose name includes the state, don't repeat the state in the publisher location. Use the full names of publishers, including the words "Books" and "Press," but omit terms such as "Publishers," "Co.," or "Inc."

Sample Entries: APA Style
Books

- **Book with one author**

  Isaacson, W. (2007). *Einstein: His life and universe.* New York, NY: Simon & Schuster.

- **Book with two authors**

  Forst, M. L., & Blomquist, M. (1991). *Missing children: Rhetoric and reality*. New York, NY: Lexington Books.

- **Books by one author published in the same year**

  Hall, S. L. (2005a). *Attention deficit disorder*. Denver, CO: Bald Mountain Press.

  Hall, S. L. (2005b). *Taming your adolescent*. Detroit, MI: Morrison Books.

- **Book with an editor**

  Banks, A. S. (Ed.). (1988). *Political handbook of the world*. Binghamton, NY: CSA.

- **Chapter from book with an editor**

  Newcomb, T. M. (1958). Attitude development as a function of reference groups: The Bennington study. In E. Maccoby, T. M. Newcomb, & E. L. Hartley (Eds.), *Readings in social psychology* (pp. 10–12). New York, NY: Holt, Rinehart and Winston.

- **A book with a corporate author**

  Mentoring Group. (1997). *The new mentors and protégés: How to succeed with the new mentoring partnerships*. Grass Valley, CA: Author.

  This method indicates that the corporate author is also the publisher.

- **A reference book**

  Rothman, B. K. (Ed.) (1993). *Encyclopedia of childbearing: Critical perspectives*. Phoenix, AZ: Oryx Press.

  Remember that reference books are not cited in the body of the essay.

Articles in Print

APA reference entries for articles in periodicals follow a pattern similar to that used for books. The author is followed by the date of publication (in parentheses). Note that journals include only the year; magazines and newspapers include the complete date. Do not abbreviate names of months. Next is the article's title, capitalizing the first word and any proper nouns. Then provide the periodical's name and volume number, italicized. If each issue of the journal begins on page one, place the issue number in parentheses immediately following the volume number. Use "p." or "pp." with page numbers in newspapers but not in magazines or journals. Unlike MLA style, numbers are not clipped in APA style (e.g., APA prefers 360–378, while MLA favors 360–78).

APA guidelines for citing print versions of periodicals differ from MLA style in a significant way. The APA recommends the inclusion of the DOI (digital object identifier) if it is available. Publishers who participate in the DOI system assign each publication a unique alphanumeric sequence. To help you recognize a DOI, understand that it begins with a "10" and often appears on the article's first page.

If the DOI is available, include it in the citation at the location indicated in the following examples. Because the DOI is extremely long, be sure to copy and paste the DOI for accuracy. If the DOI is not available, conclude the entry with the page numbers.

- **An article in a journal with DOI**

  Haugh, K. H., & Salyer, J. (2007). Needs of patients and families during the wait for a donor heart. *Heart & Lung: The Journal of Acute and Critical Care, 36*, 319–329. doi:10.1016/j.hrtlng.2006.11.003

  Because this journal does not begin each issue on page one, the issue number is not included after the volume number. Note that a space does not follow the colon after "doi."

- **An article in a journal without DOI**

  Morrison, G. B., & Byers, B. D. (2007). Criminal justice career fairs: Addressing recruiting challenges through practitioner and academic collaboration. *Law Enforcement Executive Forum, 7*(5), 107–124.

  Because this journal begins each issue on page one, the issue number in parentheses follows immediately after the volume number.

- **An article in a newspaper**

  Gascay, G. (2009, June 19). Strong winds, hail damage crops in three counties. *The Athens Eagle*, p. C1.

  Note the inclusion of the newspaper's entire title as it appears on the masthead. For newspaper articles, page numbers should be preceded by "p," or "pp."

- **An unsigned article in a newspaper**

  City unveils plans for tourist information center. (2009, May 21). *The Central Courier*, pp. D2, D10–D11.

  If an article is not printed on consecutive pages (for example, if the article begins on page D2, continues on page D10, and concludes on page D11), provide all page numbers separated by a comma and a space.

- **An article in a magazine**

  Halverson, N. (2009, May). Home gardening: Therapy for the heart and mind. *Today's Gardener, 25*(5), 22–31.

Electronic Sources: APA Style

As with print versions of periodicals, APA guidelines for citing electronic versions of periodicals differ considerably from MLA methods. For all electronic sources, the APA prefers to include the DOI (digital object identifier) if it is available. Publishers who participate in the DOI system assign each publication a unique alphanumeric sequence intended to provide a persistent link to its location on the Internet. To help you recognize a DOI, understand that it begins with a "10" and is often placed on the first page of the electronic journal article, near the copyright notice.

If the DOI is available, include it in the citation at the location indicated in the following examples. Because the DOI is extremely long, be sure to copy and paste the DOI for accuracy. If you use the DOI, no further retrieval information (such as the URL) is necessary to identify or locate the content.

If the DOI is not available, the APA prefers that you include the home page URL of the journal or of the book publisher. Before the URL, include "Retrieved from" and do not include angle brackets or conclude with a period (to avoid confusion that it is part of the URL). Break a URL only before a period or slash mark (but retain "http://" as a unit). Note that the location of this separation point differs from MLA guidelines.

For more about APA guidelines related to electronic citations, visit the APA Web site at <http://www.apastyle.org/learn/faqs/index.aspx>.

- **An electronic version of a print book**

  Isaacson, W. (2007). *Einstein: His life and universe*. Retrieved from http://ebookstore.sony.com

- **An electronic-only book**

  Stevens, K. (n.d.). *The dreamer and the beast*. Retrieved from http://www.onlineoriginals.com/

  Because no publication date is provided for this online book, "n.d." appears in parentheses where the year of publication would appear if it were available.

- **A signed entry in an online reference work**

  Brownlee, K. (2007). Civil disobedience. In E. N. Zalta (Ed.), *The Stanford encyclopedia of philosophy* (Fall 2008 ed.). Retrieved from http://plato.stanford.edu/entries/civil-disobedience/

- **An article in an online journal with DOI**

  Kubzansky, L. D., Martin, L. T., & Buka, S. L. (2009). Early manifestations of personality and adult health: A life course perspective. *Health Psychology, 28*, 364–372. doi:10.1037/a0014428

  Note that a space does not follow the colon after "doi."

- **An article in an online journal without DOI**

  Lane, A. M., Thelwell, R., & Devonport, T. J. (2009). Emotional intelligence and mood states associated with optimal performance. *E-Journal of Applied Psychology, 5*(1), 67–73. Retrieved from http://ojs.lib.swin.edu.au/index.php/ejap/index

  Because no DOI has been assigned, the URL for the journal's home page is included. Each issue of the journal begins on page one, so the issue number is included in parentheses. No retrieval date is necessary.

- **An article in an online magazine**

  Martin, S. (2009, July). A new day for practice: At a historic summit, psychology practitioners took a first step in defining how to adapt to a fast-changing world. *Monitor on Psychology, 40*(7). Retrieved from http://www.apa.org/monitor/

- **An article in an online newspaper**

  Murray, S. (2009, July 17). Health bill advances in the House. *The Washington Post*. Retrieved from http://www.washingtonpost.com/

To avoid complex URLs that might move or be modified over time, APA recommends providing the URL of the home page when the online version of the article is available by search.

Footnote and Bibliography Form

Most research papers today use a parenthetical documentation style, as illustrated in the MLA and APA sections of this chapter. However, in the event you face a writing situation that calls for use of traditional footnotes and bibliography page, here is a brief description of one version of that format. This section will also help you understand the citation system of older documents you may be reading, especially those using Latin abbreviations.

If you are writing a paper using this format, each idea you borrow and each quotation you include must be attributed to its author(s) in a footnote that appears at the bottom of the appropriate page.* Number your footnotes consecutively throughout the essay (do not start over with "1" on each new page), and place the number in the text to the right of and slightly above the end of the passage, whether it is a direct quotation, a paraphrase, or a summary. Place the corresponding superscript number, indented one-half inch, before the note at the bottom of the page. Single-space each entry, and double-space after each footnote if more than one appears on the same page. Once you have provided a first full reference, subsequent footnotes for that source may include only the author's last name and page number. (See the examples that follow. Please note that today many word-processing programs include a function for formatting footnotes.)

You may notice the use of Latin abbreviations in the notes of some documents, such as "ibid." ("in the same place") and "op. cit." ("in the work cited"). In such documents, "ibid." indicates the same author's name, title, and publication information as in the preceding footnote; there will be a new page number only if the reference differs from the one in the previous footnote. Writers use "op. cit." with the author's name to substitute for the title in second and subsequent references.

In the Bibliography at the end of the document, sources are listed by author in alphabetical order (or by title if no author is given). The first lines are flush left; subsequent lines are indented a half-inch.

First footnote reference

    [5]Garrison Keillor, *Leaving Home* (New York: Viking, 1987) 23.

Next footnote

    [6]Keillor 79.

Later reference

    [12]Keillor 135.

Bibliographic entry

Keillor, Garrison. *Leaving Home.* New York: Viking, 1987.

---

*Some documents use endnotes that appear in a list on a page immediately following the end of the essay, before the bibliography page.

© Canstock Images, Inc./
Index Stock Imagery

PRACTICING WHAT YOU'VE LEARNED

Collaborative Activity: Increase your understanding of documentation styles and practice your editing skills by exchanging your MLA Works Cited page (or APA Reference list or Bibliography page) with a classmate. Using the sample entries on the appropriate pages of this chapter, check the accuracy of the forms on the page. Circle any errors you see, but do not correct the problems. Use both the feedback you give and receive as encouragement to proofread your own documentation carefully several more times.

Using Supplementary Notes

Sometimes when writers of research papers wish to give their readers additional information about their topic or about a particular piece of source material, they include *supplementary notes.* If you are using the MLA or APA format, these notes should be indicated by using a superscript number in your text (The study seemed incomplete at the time of its publication.[2]); the explanations appear on a page called "Notes" that precedes the Works Cited page (MLA) or "Footnotes" that follows the References page (APA). If you are using traditional footnote form, simply include the supplementary notes in your list of footnotes at the bottom of the page or in the list of endnotes following your essay's conclusion.

Supplementary notes can offer a wide variety of additional information.

Examples (MLA Style)

1. For a different interpretation of this imagery, see Spiller 63-67.

2. Simon and Brown have also contributed to this area of investigation. For a description of their results, see *Report on the Star Wars Project* 98-102.

3. It is important to note here that Brown's study followed Smith's by at least six months.

4. Later in his report Carducci himself contradicts his earlier evaluation by saying, "Our experiment was contaminated from the beginning" (319).

Use supplementary notes only when you think the additional information would be truly valuable to your readers. Obviously, information critical to your essay's points should go in the appropriate body paragraphs. (◆ See pages 429 and 440 for additional examples.)

Sample Student Essay Using MLA Style

Here is the result of Kira Anzai's research on the biographical events influencing the art of painter Frida Kahlo. To see the portrait that inspired Kira's essay, *The Two Fridas*, turn to page 493 in Chapter 17; another portrait mentioned in this essay, *Self-Portrait with Thorn Necklace and Hummingbird*, appears on page 400.

As you read this essay, evaluate its effectiveness: does Kira successfully support her thesis? Point out major strengths and any weaknesses you see. If you wanted more information on Kahlo's life and work, how might Kira's sources help you begin your search? Remember that the paragraphs in Kira's essay have been numbered for easy reference during class discussion. Do *not* number the paragraphs in your own essay.

1"   ½"

Anzai 1

1"   Kira Anzai

Professor Andrews

English 1010-07

6 April 2009

Double-space

1"

Indent
½"

Frida Kahlo: A Life on Canvas

1   Speaking of the vibrant images fraught with pain and fantasy that filled her canvas, Frida Kahlo commented that "I paint my own reality" (qtd. in Herrera xi). Many viewers must wonder what sort of "reality" prompted the artist to paint pictures such as *The Two Fridas*, a double self-portrait in which her two selves—one in a snow-white dress, the other draped in colorful Mexican costume—sit connected by clasped hands, a blood-dripping artery, and mirrored expressions accentuated by distinctive dark eyebrows. An exploration of Frida Kahlo reveals that her art did indeed reflect her life, which was largely characterized by physical and emotional anguish. A tragic accident in her youth and a tumultuous marriage, mingled with deep personal and political ties to her native country, shaped the woman and work that continue to captivate viewers today.

2   Born on July 6, 1907, Kahlo passed her childhood and adolescence on the outskirts of Mexico City. She would always identify herself as a daughter of the Mexican Revolution, which broke out in 1910 and exposed her to scenes of violent fighting in the streets near her home (Herrera 4). At age six, however, a severe bout with polio confined her indoors for nine months, leaving her socially isolated (14). The girlish Kahlo who appears in paintings created years later usually stands by herself, evidence that the artist's "painted memories contain much truth about the past" (16). Loneliness would be a recurring theme throughout her life and art. Nevertheless, by the time Kahlo entered the National Preparatory School in 1922, she was a mischievous extrovert aspiring to a

Thesis: Kahlo's often-tragic life influenced her art

Essay Map: Accident, marriage, heritage

Early life in Mexico

1"

future in medicine. Her study of anatomy lent accuracy to later paintings, including the detailed human heart in *The Two Fridas* (Tuchman 2). Beyond her intellectual pursuits, Kahlo delighted in practical joking and frequently targeted Diego Rivera, the famous muralist commissioned to paint the school auditorium. She teasingly nicknamed him Panzón ("fat belly") and entertained romantic notions in spite of their twenty-one-year age difference (Herrera 31-32).

Traumatic
accident,
lifelong pain

3   The desired liaison did not materialize, for Kahlo's life was altered by a tragic accident at age eighteen. On September 17, 1925, she and her boyfriend, Alejandro, hopped onto a wooden bus just before it was rammed by a trolley car. Alejandro recalled that the bus "burst into a thousand pieces," sending an iron handrail through Kahlo's abdomen; her "screaming was louder than the siren" of the arriving ambulance (qtd. in Herrera 48). The trauma broke her spine in three places, crushed her pelvis, and severely damaged her right leg and foot. Against all odds, Kahlo began a slow recovery, but the images of intense agony that characterized her art in ensuing years largely reflected her unending battle with physical pain. For the next three decades, she wore various plaster corsets to support her improperly healed spine and underwent taxing operations that provided temporary relief at best (Tuchman 2). Ironically, the accident that haunted Kahlo with thoughts of death was critical to rousing the artist inside her. During the months of her recuperation, she began painting portraits to pass the time, taking her first steps as an artist while still physically bedridden (Zamora 26-27).

Marriage to
famous painter

4   After she regained mobility, financial difficulties prevented Kahlo's return to school, but an interest in leftist politics renewed her acquaintance with the highly political Diego Rivera in 1928 (Zamora 31). Kahlo sought the muralist's assessment of her paintings, and he

Anzai 3

instantly recognized her inborn talent. Rivera was equally drawn to the petite young woman—no longer a schoolgirl—whose "delicate face" was adorned by graceful black eyebrows he admirably compared to "the wings of a blackbird" (qtd. in Tuchman 3). In contrast, the heavyset Rivera was commonly described as having the features of a frog (Hardin 37). Despite these sharp contrasts, the mismatched couple struck up a courtship that led to their marriage on August 21, 1929. Rivera had a significant impact on his wife's artistic development. By observing his creation of historical murals, she "learned how to tell a story in paint," an ability that contributed to the frequently autobiographical nature of her later art (Tuchman 4).

5   After their wedding, Kahlo followed Rivera to the United States, where he accepted a series of commissions while she honed her portraiture and garnered public attention for her native Mexican attire. Bright blouses and skirts, stone bead necklaces, and upswept braids appeased Rivera's preference that she dress in the Tehuana Indian style and, more importantly, allowed Kahlo to openly celebrate her culture and nationalist sentiments (Baddeley 12-13). Most of the self-portraits she painted in subsequent decades, including her colorfully costumed self in *The Two Fridas*, capture this personal identification with Mexico. Despite the gratifying attention of the American press, the Riveras' time in the States was marred by tragedy when Kahlo suffered a miscarriage in 1932.[1] Her bloody and fantastical portrayal of the experience in the painting *Henry Ford Hospital* diverged from the portraits that typify her body of work up to that point. The loss of her child, accompanied by her mother's death the same year, marked a shift in Kahlo's subject matter. Elements of fantasy increasingly appeared in the paintings, which were "beginning to emphasize terror, suffering, wounds, and pain," both physical and psychological (Zamora 46).

Identification with heritage

Loss of child and mother

6   The return to Mexico in 1933 brought Kahlo some relief but did not
restore her happiness, as her marriage felt the mounting pressure of her
husband's infidelity. Although she had long tolerated Rivera's string of
casual affairs, Kahlo's increasing anguish prompted her to move into her
own apartment for several months (Zamora 46-47). Author Terri Hardin
argues that Rivera's betrayal and the couple's ensuing separation freed
her from convention and "removed the final impediments to her progress
as an artist" whose vision was inimitable (49). Kahlo returned to Rivera
in 1935, but their reconciliation left Kahlo far from comfortable. To cope
with the duress of this situation, Kahlo channeled her feelings into her art
(Zamora 50). The productive years that followed led to the inclusion of
two paintings in a 1938 exhibit in Paris, where their shocking fantastical
elements earned her praise as a Surrealist (56).[2] Fresh devastation
replaced her confidence, however, when, shortly after her return from
France, Rivera requested a divorce (62).

Tumultuous marriage, divorce, remarriage reflected in her art

7   The dissolution of their disintegrating marriage in 1939 coincided
with the creation of emotionally charged paintings like *The Two Fridas*.
Some critical interpretations of the double self-portrait conclude that it
directly responded to the divorce, hence the depiction of the left-hand
Kahlo wearing Rivera's favored Tehuana costume. She shares a severed
artery with the opposing white-clad Kahlo, who displays a "broken"
heart in her bisected chest; this second self stops the artery's blood flow
with a clamp, suggesting that "the Frida independent of Rivera holds the
means of self-rescue" (Hardin 68). *The Two Fridas*, in essence, conveys
two sides of the artist's personality, a hallmark of additional self-portraits
(captured on canvas and in her diary) that explore her distinct feminine
and masculine identities. In *Self-Portrait with Cropped Hair*, completed
the year after her divorce, Kahlo poses in a man's suit, as opposed to her
typical Mexican dress and flower-bedecked braids. She is surrounded by

Anzai 5

long strands of sheared-off hair, a sign of despair and retaliation against Rivera (Johnston 33). *Self-Portrait with Thorn Necklace and Hummingbird*, painted in 1940, likewise expresses her woe through the symbolism of the dead bird hanging from her neck (Hardin 70-71). Without her husband, Kahlo felt an isolation reminiscent of her childhood and explained her profusion of self-portraits by stating simply, "I am all alone" (qtd. in Zamora 102). Regardless of their former troubles, Rivera was likewise plagued by separation from Kahlo, and they chose to remarry in 1940 (70). Kahlo expressed her renewed devotion to Rivera in the 1943 painting *Roots*, symbolically binding herself to the landscape where they built a home together (Herrera 312-14).

8   The last several years of Kahlo's life were disrupted by numerous operations as her health declined, but she continued to paint her signature self-portraits and fantastical scenes. In *The Dream* (1940), the skeleton over her canopied bed speaks to the psychological effects of her physical condition, while *The Wounded Deer* (1946) suggests her identification with a bleeding animal, as her head is fixed to a deer's arrow-pierced body (Hardin 70, 103). The pain that began in her youth now became unbearable, and Kahlo's reliance on stimulants and strong medication for relief revealed itself in her slightly frenetic brushwork (Tuchman 5). In 1953, her ailing lower right leg was amputated, but the restraints of an artificial limb and wheelchair did not prevent Kahlo from resolutely accompanying Rivera to leftist political demonstrations. Similarly, she had insisted upon attending her long-awaited one-person exhibition in Mexico City earlier that year despite serious illness. Kahlo was delivered to the gallery by ambulance and enjoyed the festive event from the comfort of a canopied bed (Hardin 108). She told attentive reporters for *Time* magazine, "I am not sick. I am broken. But I am happy to be alive as long as I can paint" (qtd. in Zamora 126).

Broken health and pain influence portraits

Conclusion: Shaped by pain and a beloved heritage, Kahlo's art continues to fascinate

9   Kahlo's artistic career was cut short by her death on July 13, 1954, when she was forty-seven years old, but over the course of three decades, she completed approximately two hundred paintings (Tuchman 1).[3] They have since fascinated a worldwide audience with their striking originality, which must be attributed to a life and artistic vision shaped by painful personal experiences and deep ties to Mexico. Kahlo consistently exhibited a concern with keeping her memory alive in people's minds, frequently beseeching her acquaintances, "Don't forget me!" (qtd. in Zamora 102). Her evocative images ensure that Frida Kahlo—the woman and the artist—will continue to be remembered by the legacy she left on canvas.

1"

½"

Anzai 7

Double-space

Notes

Indent
½"

1. Kahlo's inability to bear children to term is generally blamed on the injuries she sustained in the bus accident. The horrific nature of the 1932 miscarriage caused her significant emotional duress. Many biographers have noted her lifelong struggle with frustrated maternity, and, in particular, the couple's concern about the physical toll of pregnancy on Kahlo's weakened body (Zamora 91).

2. Surrealism was a movement that valued the dreamlike imagery recurrent in Kahlo's paintings. *The Two Fridas* was displayed at the "International Exhibition of Surrealism" in Mexico City in 1940. Although Kahlo acknowledged her artistic similarities to the Surrealists, she always maintained her insistence that she painted reality, not dreams (Herrera 255).

1"

1"

3. In the absence of a postmortem, the cause of Kahlo's death remains disputed; although her death certificate mentions a pulmonary embolism, an accidental or intentional overdose of stimulants and medication has also been suspected (Zamora 130).

1"

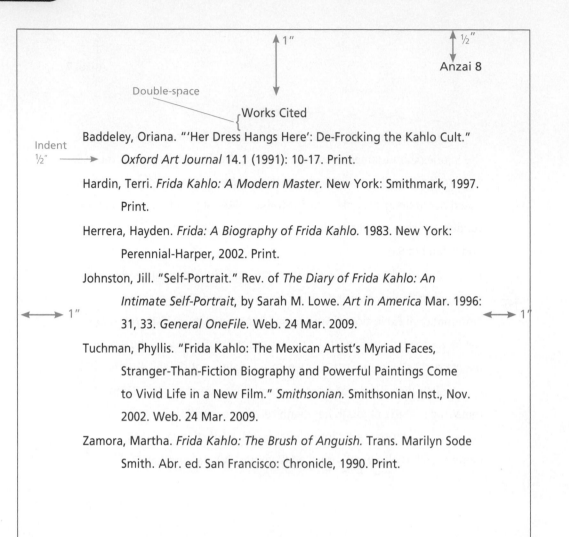

1"

½"

Double-space

Works Cited

Indent
½"

Baddeley, Oriana. "'Her Dress Hangs Here': De-Frocking the Kahlo Cult."

Oxford Art Journal 14.1 (1991): 10-17. Print.

Hardin, Terri. *Frida Kahlo: A Modern Master.* New York: Smithmark, 1997.

Print.

Herrera, Hayden. *Frida: A Biography of Frida Kahlo.* 1983. New York:

Perennial-Harper, 2002. Print.

Johnston, Jill. "Self-Portrait." Rev. of *The Diary of Frida Kahlo: An*

Intimate Self-Portrait, by Sarah M. Lowe. *Art in America* Mar. 1996:

31, 33. *General OneFile.* Web. 24 Mar. 2009.

Tuchman, Phyllis. "Frida Kahlo: The Mexican Artist's Myriad Faces,

Stranger-Than-Fiction Biography and Powerful Paintings Come

to Vivid Life in a New Film." *Smithsonian.* Smithsonian Inst., Nov.

2002. Web. 24 Mar. 2009.

Zamora, Martha. *Frida Kahlo: The Brush of Anguish.* Trans. Marilyn Sode

Smith. Abr. ed. San Francisco: Chronicle, 1990. Print.

1"

1"

1"

Sample Student Essay Using APA Style

To illustrate the differences between MLA and APA documentation styles, here is the student essay from the previous pages rewritten to show the most current APA guidelines for in-text citations and a References page. To see the portrait that inspired Kira's essay, *The Two Fridas*, turn to page 493 in Chapter 17; another portrait mentioned in this essay, *Self-Portrait with Thorn Necklace and Hummingbird*, appears on page 400.

As you read this essay, evaluate its effectiveness: does Kira successfully support her thesis? Point out major strengths and any weaknesses you see. If you wanted more information on Kahlo's life and work, how might Kira's sources help you begin your search? Remember that the paragraphs in Kira's essay have been numbered for easy reference during class discussion. Do *not* number the paragraphs in your own essay.

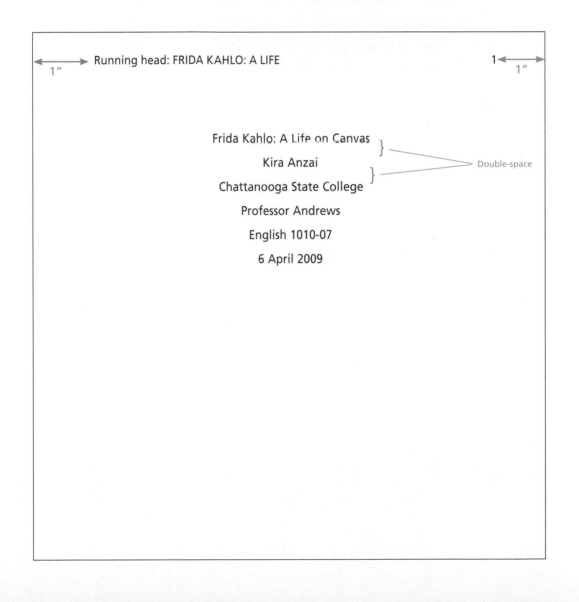

Running head: FRIDA KAHLO: A LIFE 1

1" 1"

Frida Kahlo: A Life on Canvas

Kira Anzai

Chattanooga State College

Professor Andrews

English 1010-07

6 April 2009

Double-space

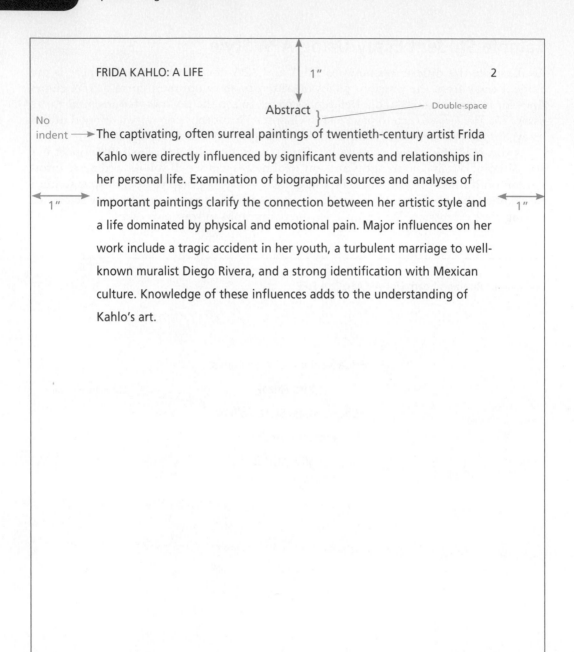

FRIDA KAHLO: A LIFE 1" 2

Abstract } Double-space

No indent → The captivating, often surreal paintings of twentieth-century artist Frida Kahlo were directly influenced by significant events and relationships in her personal life. Examination of biographical sources and analyses of important paintings clarify the connection between her artistic style and a life dominated by physical and emotional pain. Major influences on her work include a tragic accident in her youth, a turbulent marriage to well-known muralist Diego Rivera, and a strong identification with Mexican culture. Knowledge of these influences adds to the understanding of Kahlo's art.

1" 1"

1"

FRIDA KAHLO: A LIFE   1″   3

Indent
½″

Frida Kahlo: A Life on Canvas }   Double-space

1   Speaking of the vibrant images fraught with pain and fantasy that

filled her canvas, Frida Kahlo commented that "I paint my own reality"

(Herrera, 2002, p. xi). Many viewers must wonder what sort of "reality"

1″   prompted the artist to paint pictures such as *The Two Fridas*, a double   1″

self-portrait in which her two selves—one in a snow-white dress, the

other draped in colorful Mexican costume—sit connected by clasped

hands, a blood-dripping artery, and mirrored expressions accentuated by   Thesis: Kahlo's

distinctive dark eyebrows. An exploration of Frida Kahlo reveals that her   often-tragic

life influenced

art did indeed reflect her life, which was largely characterized by physical   her art

and emotional anguish. A tragic accident in her youth and a tumultuous

marriage, mingled with deep personal and political ties to her native   Essay Map:
Accident,

country, shaped the woman and work that continue to captivate viewers   marriage,
heritage

today.

2   Born on July 6, 1907, Kahlo passed her childhood and adolescence   Early life in
Mexico

on the outskirts of Mexico City. She would always identify herself as

a daughter of the Mexican Revolution, which broke out in 1910 and

exposed her to scenes of violent fighting in the streets near her home

(Herrera, 2002, p. 4). At age six, however, a severe bout with polio

confined her indoors for nine months, leaving her socially isolated

(Herrera, 2002, p. 14). The girlish Kahlo who appears in paintings

created years later usually stands by herself, evidence that the artist's

"painted memories contain much truth about the past" (Herrera, 2002,

p. 16). Loneliness would be a recurring theme throughout her life and

art. Nevertheless, by the time Kahlo entered the National Preparatory

School in 1922, she was a mischievous extrovert aspiring to a future in

medicine. Her study of anatomy lent accuracy to later paintings, including

1″

the detailed human heart in *The Two Fridas* (Tuchman, 2002, p. 2). Beyond her intellectual pursuits, Kahlo delighted in practical joking and frequently targeted Diego Rivera, the famous muralist commissioned to paint the school auditorium. She teasingly nicknamed him Panzón ("fat belly") and entertained romantic notions in spite of their twenty-one-year age difference (Herrera, 2002, pp. 31–32).

Traumatic accident, lifelong pain

3   The desired liaison did not materialize, for Kahlo's life was altered by a tragic accident at age eighteen. On September 17, 1925, she and her boyfriend, Alejandro, hopped onto a wooden bus just before it was rammed by a trolley car. Alejandro recalled that the bus "burst into a thousand pieces," sending an iron handrail through Kahlo's abdomen; her "screaming was louder than the siren" of the arriving ambulance (Herrera, 2002, p. 48). The trauma broke her spine in three places, crushed her pelvis, and severely damaged her right leg and foot. Against all odds, Kahlo began a slow recovery, but the images of intense agony that characterized her art in ensuing years largely reflected her unending battle with physical pain. For the next three decades, she wore various plaster corsets to support her improperly healed spine and underwent taxing operations that provided temporary relief at best (Tuchman, 2002, p. 2). Ironically, the accident that haunted Kahlo with thoughts of death was critical to rousing the artist inside her. During the months of her recuperation, she began painting portraits to pass the time, taking her first steps as an artist while still physically bedridden (Zamora, 1990, pp. 26-27).

Marriage to famous painter

4   After she regained mobility, financial difficulties prevented Kahlo's return to school, but an interest in leftist politics renewed her acquaintance with the highly political Diego Rivera in 1928 (Zamora,

FRIDA KAHLO: A LIFE   5

1990, p. 31). Kahlo sought the muralist's assessment of her paintings, and he instantly recognized her inborn talent. Rivera was equally drawn to the petite young woman—no longer a schoolgirl—whose "delicate face" was adorned by graceful black eyebrows he admirably compared to "the wings of a blackbird" (Tuchman, 2002, p. 3). In contrast, the heavyset Rivera was commonly described as having the features of a frog (Hardin, 1997, p. 37). Despite these sharp contrasts, the mismatched couple struck up a courtship that led to their marriage on August 21, 1929. Rivera had a significant impact on his wife's artistic development. By observing his creation of historical murals, she "learned how to tell a story in paint," an ability that contributed to the frequently autobiographical nature of her later art (Tuchman, 2002, p. 4).

5   After their wedding, Kahlo followed Rivera to the United States, where he accepted a series of commissions while she honed her portraiture and garnered public attention for her native Mexican attire. Bright blouses and skirts, stone bead necklaces, and upswept braids appeased Rivera's preference that she dress in the Tehuana Indian style and, more importantly, allowed Kahlo to openly celebrate her culture and nationalist sentiments (Baddeley, 1991, pp. 12–13). Most of the self-portraits she painted in subsequent decades, including her colorfully costumed self in *The Two Fridas*, capture this personal identification with Mexico. Despite the gratifying attention of the American press, the Riveras' time in the States was marred by tragedy when Kahlo suffered a miscarriage in 1932.[1] Her bloody and fantastical portrayal of the experience in the painting *Henry Ford Hospital* diverged from the portraits that typify her body of work up to that point. The loss of her child, accompanied by her mother's death the same year, marked a shift

Identification with heritage

Loss of child and mother

FRIDA KAHLO: A LIFE   8

brushwork (Tuchman, 2002, p. 5). In 1953, her ailing lower right leg was amputated, but the restraints of an artificial limb and wheelchair did not prevent Kahlo from resolutely accompanying Rivera to leftist political demonstrations. Similarly, she had insisted upon attending her long-awaited one-person exhibition in Mexico City earlier that year despite serious illness. Kahlo was delivered to the gallery by ambulance and enjoyed the festive event from the comfort of a canopied bed (Hardin, 1997, p. 108). She told attentive reporters for *Time* magazine, "I am not sick. I am broken. But I am happy to be alive as long as I can paint" (Zamora, 1990, p. 126).

Conclusion: Shaped by pain and a beloved heritage, Kahlo's art continues to fascinate

9   Kahlo's artistic career was cut short by her death on July 13, 1954, when she was forty-seven years old, but over the course of three decades, she completed approximately two hundred paintings (Tuchman, 2002, p. 1).[3] They have since fascinated a worldwide audience with their striking originality, which must be attributed to a life and artistic vision shaped by painful personal experiences and deep ties to Mexico. Kahlo consistently exhibited a concern with keeping her memory alive in people's minds, frequently beseeching her acquaintances, "Don't forget me!" (Zamora, 1990, p. 102). Her evocative images ensure that Frida Kahlo—the woman and the artist—will continue to be remembered by the legacy she left on canvas.

Tumultuou marriage, divorce, remarriage reflected ir her art

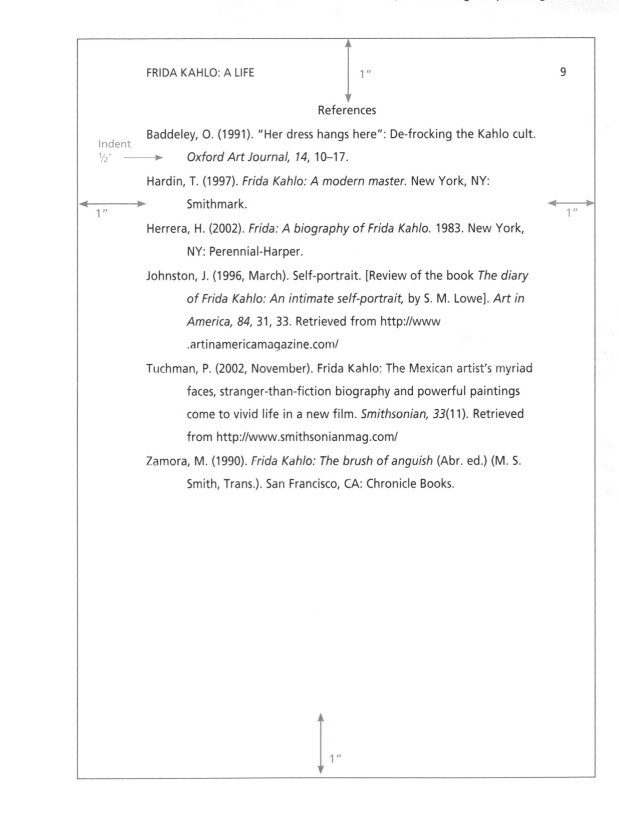

FRIDA KAHLO: A LIFE   1″   9

References

Baddeley, O. (1991). "Her dress hangs here": De-frocking the Kahlo cult.

Indent ½″ →   *Oxford Art Journal, 14*, 10–17.

Hardin, T. (1997). *Frida Kahlo: A modern master.* New York, NY:

1″   Smithmark.

Herrera, H. (2002). *Frida: A biography of Frida Kahlo.* 1983. New York,

NY: Perennial-Harper.

Johnston, J. (1996, March). Self-portrait. [Review of the book *The diary*

of Frida Kahlo: An intimate self-portrait, by S. M. Lowe]. *Art in*

America, 84, 31, 33. Retrieved from http://www

.artinamericamagazine.com/

Tuchman, P. (2002, November). Frida Kahlo: The Mexican artist's myriad

faces, stranger-than-fiction biography and powerful paintings

come to vivid life in a new film. *Smithsonian, 33*(11). Retrieved

from http://www.smithsonianmag.com/

Zamora, M. (1990). *Frida Kahlo: The brush of anguish* (Abr. ed.) (M. S.

Smith, Trans.). San Francisco, CA: Chronicle Books.

Dir

Illu
Pro
Sho
Sup

Ex
Ex
Ou
Tra
Re
Giv

Dis
Sho
Giv
Ex
Dis
Sh

Co
Co
Sh
Di
Sh
Re

De
Re
Di
Ex

Ag
Do
O
Pr
C
E
St
Ju
W

D
Sl
A
C

D
E
Ic
C

*

5. As you **begin writing**, remember what you have learned about paragraphing, topic sentences, and supporting evidence. If you have been given multiple tasks, be sure that you are responding to all parts of the assignment. If the assignment asks you to present your own opinion, focus your answer accordingly. In timed-writing situations, you can't take on the world, but you can offer intelligent commentary on selected ideas. If you have only an hour or less to complete your essay, consider aiming for three well-developed points of discussion. You may be writing a rather conventional five-paragraph essay, but such a clear pattern of organization frequently works best when nervous writers are under pressure and time is short.

Two more suggestions:

- If you are writing by hand, it may be a good idea to compose on one side of your paper only, leaving wide margins on both sides; consider, too, leaving extra lines between paragraphs. If you discover that you have time after finishing your essay, you might wish to add additional information to your exam answer or perhaps another persuasive example to a body paragraph. Leaving plenty of blank spaces will allow you to insert information neatly instead of jamming in handwriting too small for your instructor to decipher.

- If you are writing an essay (rather than a short answer), do try to conclude in a satisfactory way. Your conclusion may be brief, but even a few sentences are better than an abrupt midsentence halt when time runs out.

6. In the time remaining after writing the complete draft of your essay, **read what you have written**. Aim for sufficient, appropriate content and clear organization. Insert, delete, or make changes neatly. Once you are reasonably satisfied with the essay's content and flow, take a few minutes to proofread and edit. Although most instructors do not expect an in-class essay to be as polished as one written out of class, you are responsible for the best spelling, grammar, and punctuation you can muster under the circumstances. Take care to apply what you know to sentence problems, especially the run-ons, comma splices, and twisted predicates that tend to surface when writers are composing in a hurry. After all, information too deeply hidden in a contorted sentence is information that may not be counted in your favor.

7. **Tips.** Before you turn in your work, be sure your name is on every page of your essay or exam so your instructor will know whom to praise for a job well done. If appropriate, include other pertinent information, such as your class section number or your student number. Always number and clip or staple the loose pages of your essay or exam (do *not* rely on folded corners to hold your pages together!).

© Stockbyte/SuperStock

Problems to Avoid

Misreading the assignment. Always read the directions and the assignment completely and carefully before you start prewriting. Mark key and directional words. Do you have multiple tasks? Consider numbering the tasks to avoid overlooking any parts. Important choices to make? Neatly put a line through the options you don't want. Grossly misreading your assignment may give you as much chance at success as a pig at a barbecue.

Incomplete essay. Don't begin writing an in-class essay without a plan, even if you are excited about the topic and want to dive right in. Having a plan and budgeting your time accordingly will avoid the common problem of not finishing, which, in the end, may cost you dearly. Don't allow yourself to ramble off on a tangent in one part of the assignment. Stay focused on your plan and complete the entire essay or exam. If you have left blank space as described previously, you can return to a part of the essay to add more information if time permits. Wear a watch and consult it regularly! Don't depend on a classmate or your instructor to advise you of the time remaining.

Composition amnesia. Writing essays under time pressure causes some students suddenly to forget everything they ever knew about essay organization. This memory loss often wreaks havoc on paragraphing skills, resulting in a half-dozen one- and two-sentence string-bean paragraphs without adequate development; at other times, it results in one long super-paragraph that stretches for pages before the eye like the Mojave Desert, no relief or rest stop in sight. Emphasize your good ideas by presenting them in a recognizable organizational structure, just as you would do in an out-of-class assignment.

Gorilla generalizations. Perhaps the biggest problem instructors find is the lack of adequate, specific evidence to explain or support shaggy, gorilla-sized generalities roaming aimlessly through students' essays. If, for example, you argue, "Team sports are good for kids because they build character," *why* do you believe this? What particular character traits do you mean? Can you offer a personal example or a hypothetical case to clarify and support your claim? ◆ Remember what you learned in Chapter 3 about using evidence—examples, personal experience, testimony—to illustrate or back up any general claims you are making. Your goal is to be as clear and persuasive as you can be—*show* what you know!

© Mark Newman/Photo Researchers, Inc.

Develop and support your large claims!

PRACTICING WHAT YOU'VE LEARNED

Underline the key words and circle the directional words or phrases in the following assignments. What pattern(s) of development are suggested in each assignment?

1. Discuss three examples of flower imagery as they clarify the major themes of Toni Morrison's novel *The Bluest Eye*.

2. Trace the events that led to the Bay of Pigs invasion of Cuba.

3. Discuss Louis B. Mayer's major influences on the American film industry during the "Golden Age of Moviemaking."

4. Agree or disagree with the following statement: "The 1957 launching of the Russian satellite *Sputnik* caused important changes in the American educational system."

5. Consider the similarities and differences between the expressionistic techniques of American painters Jaune Quick-to-See Smith and Audrey Flack. Illustrate your answer with references to important works of both artists.

ASSIGNMENT

Practice planning an in-class essay by selecting one of the quotations on pages 43–45 in Chapter 2 as a brief "prompt" for a personal opinion essay developed by any method(s) you find appropriate. Allow yourself only ten minutes to write a working thesis and a sketch outline for your essay. Would you then be ready to turn your plan into a clearly organized and well-developed in-class essay? Continue to practice responding to the prompts in Chapter 2 until you gain confidence in your ability to think, plan, and write under time pressure.

Writing the Summary-and-Response Essay

The "summary-and-response essay" is such a common assignment today that it merits additional discussion and illustration. As noted earlier in this chapter, this kind of assignment frequently asks students to read a professional article,* summarize its thesis and main points, and write a response expressing agreement or disagreement with the article's ideas.

You may have had experience with some form of this assignment before now. Many college entrance examinations have adopted this kind of essay to evaluate both reading

---

*To avoid confusion in this discussion between the professional essay used as a prompt and the student's response essay, the word "article" will be used to refer to the professional reading.

comprehension and writing skills. Many colleges also use this format as their composition placement exam, to direct students into the appropriate writing class. Still other schools employ this kind of essay as a final exam or exit test for their composition requirement. And although this format is often assigned as in-class writing, it certainly is not limited to this use. Many composition classes and other academic courses include this type of essay as an out-of-class paper.

Though the format of this assignment may vary slightly depending on its purpose and occasion, throughout your college and professional life you will almost certainly be asked on more than one occasion to read information, summarize it for others, and then present your reaction to its ideas. To help you prepare for this kind of thinking and writing activity, here are a few suggestions, divided into three sections for clarity:

Reading the Assignment and the Article

1. Read your assignment's directions carefully to discover exactly what you are being asked to do. For example, are you being asked to present a one-paragraph summary of a professional article first and then write a personal response? Or are you being asked to respond to the professional article's major points one at a time? Perhaps you are being asked to critique the author's style as well as ideas. Because formats vary, be sure you understand your complete assignment—all its required parts—before you begin writing.

2. Before you can intelligently respond to any reading you need to thoroughly understand its ideas. ◆ To review suggestions for close reading, take the time now to review Chapter 8, "The Reading-Writing Connection," in this text. This chapter will help you identify and evaluate an article's thesis, main points, supporting evidence, and other rhetorical techniques.

3. If you are given an article to read out of class, study it carefully, annotating it as outlined in Chapter 8. If reading the article is part of the in-class activity, you may have only enough time to read it carefully once, underlining and annotating as you move through each paragraph. Minimally, you should mark the thesis and the main ideas of the body paragraphs. Underline or star important claims or supporting evidence. Are the claims logical and well supported, or does the author rely on generalizations or other faulty reasoning? Overall, do you agree or disagree with the article? Would you call it a weak or strong piece of writing? Why? (◆ For help evaluating claims and supporting evidence, review the discussion of logical fallacies in Chapter 10, pages 296–299.)

Writing the Summary Section

If you are to begin with a brief summary of the article, follow the guidelines listed under "Writing a Summary" on pages 185–186 of Chapter 8. Remember that a good summary presents the author's name and full title of the article in the first sentence, which also frequently presents the article's thesis (In his article "Free Speech on Campus," author Clarence Page argues that . . .). The next sentences of your summary should present the article's main ideas, found in the article's body paragraphs. Unless you need to quote a word or phrase for clarity or emphasis, use your own words to present a concise version of the article. Normally, your summary will be an objective treatment of the article's ideas, so save your opinions for the "response" section.

Writing the Response Section

1. Before you begin writing the "response" part of your essay, look at the underlining and any marginal notes you made on the article. What was your general assessment of the article? Do you agree or disagree with the author? Perhaps you only agree with some points and disagree with others? Or perhaps you agree with the main ideas but think that this particular essay is a weak defense of those ideas? After looking over the article and your notes, decide on your overall reaction to this article. This assessment will become your thesis in the "response" portion of your essay.

2. Once you have a working thesis in mind, plan the rest of your essay. For example, if you disagree with the article, you might want to note two or three reasons you reject the author's opinion; these reasons may become the basis for your own body paragraphs. Important: be sure you have evidence of your own to support your positions. Responding with personal examples is perhaps the most common kind of support for essays written in class, but if you know facts, statistics, testimony, or other information that would support your position, you may certainly include them.

3. If you have begun your essay with a summary, start the next paragraph with a sentence that clearly indicates the "response" section is now beginning. Present a smooth transition to your thesis and consider using an "essay map" to indicate to your readers the points you will discuss.

   Example   Although in his article "Test!" Paul Perez correctly identifies a growing drug problem in our public schools, his plan to drug-test all students involved in campus activities should be rejected. Such a test could not be implemented fairly and is an unreasonable invasion of students' privacy.

4. In each of your own body paragraphs make clear which of the author's claims or ideas you are refuting or supporting by using "tag lines" to remind the reader.

   Example   Although Foxcroft argues that the proposed tuition increase will not discourage prospective students, she fails to understand the economic situation of most IBC applicants, who are sacrificing income to return to school. In a recent survey. . . .

5. Once you have signaled the point in question and stated your position, develop each body paragraph with enough specific supporting evidence to make your claim convincing. If you disagree with a point, you must show why and present your position logically (◆ you may wish to review Chapter 10 on argument). If you agree with the article, beware a tendency to simply restate the positions with which you are in agreement ("I think Brower is right when she says housing is too expensive on campus. She is also right about the lack of housing choices . . ."). Find examples, reasons, or information that lend support to the points that you and the author think are valid.

6. Many assignments call for a straightforward personal opinion or "agree-disagree" response. In other assignments, you may be given the option of criticizing or praising an author's logic, style, or even tone. You might, for example, show that a particular argument is ineffective because it is based on a mass of overstated generalities, or you might show why the author's sarcastic tone alienates the reader. On the other hand, an author might deserve credit for a particularly effective supporting example or a brilliantly clever turn of phrase that captures the essence of an idea. Always check your assignment to see if this sort of critique is welcome or even required in your response.

7. Don't forget to write a brief concluding paragraph. If appropriate, you might emphasize the value of the article in question, or call for action for or against its ideas, or project its effects into the future (◆ other suggestions for conclusions appear in Chapter 4). However you end your essay, your conclusion should always be consistent with your overall assessment of the article and its ideas.

Sample Student Essay

The essay that follows was written by a student who was assigned the article "Our Youth Should Serve" by Steven Muller (pages 183–185 in Chapter 8) and then asked to write a one-paragraph summary and a response essay, expressing her opinion of the article's proposal. Although the student thought the article itself could have been stronger, she liked Muller's suggestion for a volunteer youth service. Her approval of his proposal became her essay's thesis, which she then developed through use of her own experience.

After you read Muller's article and the student's summary-and-response essay, what suggestions for revision might you offer her?

YOUTH SERVICE: AN IDEA WHOSE TIME HAS COME

1   In "Our Youth Should Serve," former university president Steven Muller proposes a national volunteer youth service. This program would perform some of our country's public service tasks and also help high school graduates who have to choose between low-paying jobs or starting college with no clear direction. Although the pay would be low, volunteers would benefit through job training and by earning federal grants for college. Muller also argues that youth service would motivate volunteers to become better students and perhaps help them find a career. The greatest benefit, according to Muller, would

Summary

be the self-esteem volunteers would gain from earning these benefits themselves.

Response begins

2   Although Muller's article might have been more persuasive with some specific examples supporting its claims, Muller's national volunteer youth service is still a good idea, especially for students who have no money for college and no work experience. I was one of those students, and because of the year I spent after high school graduation working in a boring, dead-end job, I believe the Youth Service should be started as soon as possible.

Thesis

3   After I graduated from high school, I didn't go to college because I didn't have any money saved and I was tired of school. I decided to work for a while to save up, but I didn't have any training for anything so I took a minimum-wage sales job in a mall clothing store. I had to look good for work, but since my wardrobe consisted of jeans and T-shirts, I had to buy new clothes. With clothes and transportation to work and other bills, I was barely breaking even. If I had been in Muller's program, my pay would also have been low but at least I would have been earning grant money for college at the same time.

Response to the benefit of earning grant money

4   Muller also makes a good point about people needing to feel that what they are doing is important or meaningful. My job at the store wasn't meaningful or challenging; it was, in fact, repetitive and boring. For example, a typical day during the summer months consisted of cleaning out dressing rooms and hanging up two-piece swim suits thrown all over the floor. It took forever to match up the right size tops and bottoms and then hang them back up on these crazy little double hangers so that everything was facing the right way with all the straps untwisted. In the winter it was pants and sweaters. Unlike Muller's volunteers who would be helping society while getting some valuable training themselves, I wasn't contributing to anything meaningful, and I sure wasn't learning any skills for a better future.

Response to the benefits of meaningful work, skills

5   It didn't take me long to figure out that I wanted more out of life than a low-paying, boring, going-nowhere job. So I talked to a counselor here at Logan [Community College] who helped me explore some of my interests, and now I am enrolled in the pre-nursing program. In Muller's program I might have discovered this career earlier by volunteering at a hospital or nursing home, plus getting some on-the-job experience. I would have tuition grant money instead of going into major debt from student loans like I am now. I might also have worked for someone who might even hire me later. And I'm absolutely positive I would have felt more useful and had better self-esteem than I did hanging up clothes for eight months!

Response to career benefits

and increased self-esteem

6   Although this program wasn't there to help me, my sister is getting ready to graduate and she is in the same situation I was two years ago—no money, no skills, no solid future goals. If Muller's program existed today, I'd tell her to look into it. The benefits of college money, job training, and better self-esteem are just too good to pass up.

Conclusion emphasizes benefits to a future volunteer

PRACTICING WHAT YOU'VE LEARNED

A. After reading Steven Muller's article "Our Youth Should Serve" (pages 183–185), write your own summary-and-response essay, drawing on your own knowledge and experience to support or reject his proposed program. In your opinion, would this be a worthwhile, feasible program? Why or why not?

B. *Collaborative Activity:* Review Muller's "Our Youth Should Serve" and practice your analytical skills by composing a short list of the essay's major strengths and weaknesses. What are the essay's most effective points? How might Muller have improved his arguments and supporting evidence? Pair with a classmate and compare lists. Pretend Muller is a partner in a peer revision workshop who has asked you two for help; give him feedback that includes at least one compliment on something well done and one specific suggestion for an effective change. How does your advice to Muller compare to the recommendations of the other students in the class?

© Canstock Images, Inc./ Index Stock Imagery

© CORBIS

ASSIGNMENT

Read and annotate the selection "So What's So Bad about Being So-So?" on pages 205–207 of this textbook and then write your own summary-and-response essay, agreeing or disagreeing (wholly or in part) with the writer's view of competition today. Remember to support your position with logical reasons, persuasive examples, or relevant facts. (If you prefer, you may select some other professional essay from this textbook or from another source, such as a newspaper or magazine, but be sure to obtain your instructor's approval of your selection in advance.)

CHAPTER 16

Writing about Literature

People read literature for many, many reasons, including amusement, comfort, escape, new ideas, exploration of values, intellectual challenge, and on and on. Similarly, people write about literature to accomplish a variety of purposes. Literary essays may inform readers about the ideas in a work, analyze its craft, or focus on the work's relationship to the time or culture in which it was written. Other essays might explore biographical, psychological, archetypal, or personal readings of a work.

Although approaches to literature are diverse and may be studied in depth in other English courses, writing essays about literature is worthwhile in the composition classroom as well. Writing about literature offers an opportunity to practice the important skills of close reading, critical thinking, and effective expression of ideas.

Using Literature in the Composition Classroom

Teachers of writing most often use literature in their courses in two ways: as "prompts" to inspire personal essay topics and as subjects of interpretative essays.

1. *Prompts:* You might be asked to read a poem or short story and then use some aspect of it—its ideas or characters, for example—as a springboard to discover an essay topic of your own. For instance, after reading John Updike's "A & P," a story about a rather naive young man who receives a real-world lesson, you might write about a coming-of-age experience you had. Or your teacher might assign Shirley Jackson's "The Lottery" and ask you to agree or disagree with the author's views on unexamined conformity to tradition.

2. *Literary Analysis:* Rather than responding to a piece of literature in a personal essay, you might be assigned a literary analysis, asking you to study a piece of literature and then offer your interpretation—that is, your insight into the work (or some important part of it). Your insight becomes your thesis; the body of your

essay explains this reading, supported by textual evidence (material from the work) to help your reader understand your view and perhaps gain greater pleasure from, and appreciation of, the work itself.

Literary analysis assignments may be focused in different ways, as well. Some common examples include essays whose main purpose is to show:

- how the various parts or elements of a piece of literature work together to present the main ideas (for example, how the choices of narrator, stanza form, and figurative language in a poem effectively complement each other);

- how one element fits into the complex whole (for example, how setting contributes to a story);

- how two works or two elements may be profitably read together (two poems with similar ideas but different forms; two characters from one story);

- how one interpretation is more insightful than another reading;

- how a work's value has been overlooked or misunderstood.

There are as many possibilities for essay topics as there are readers!

Regardless of the exact assignment, you should feel confident about writing an essay of literary analysis. Working through Part Two of this text, you have already practiced many of the strategies required. For example, to present a particular reading of a poem, you may organize your discussion by *dividing* it into its major literary elements: point of view, setting, structure, language, and so on. Your essay may offer specific lines or images from the work as *examples* illustrating your reading. Working with more than one piece of literature or literary element calls for *comparison and contrast* techniques. And every paper—whether it is a personal response or literary analysis—uses the skills you learned in Part One of this text: a clear thesis, adequate development of ideas, coherent organization, and effective use of language.

Suggestions for Close Reading of Literature

Writing about literature begins with careful reading—and, yes, rereading. The steps suggested here are certainly not exhaustive; one can ask literally hundreds of questions about a complex piece of literature. Rather, these questions are intended to give you a start. Practicing close reading and annotation should help you generate ideas and lead you to additional questions of your own.

Our discussion in this chapter is limited to poems and short stories because composition courses frequently do not have the time to include novels and plays (or long narrative poems, for that matter). However, many of the suggestions for reading short stories and poems may be applied to the reading of longer fiction and drama.

Before you begin reading the suggestions that follow, let's dispel the myth about "hidden meanings." A work of literature is not a trick or puzzle box wherein the author has hidden a message for readers to discover if they can just uncover the right clues. Literary works are open to discussion and interpretation; that's part of their appeal. They contain ideas and images that the author thought important, and some ideas or elements the writer may not have consciously been aware of. You, as the reader, will have insights into a poem or story that your classmates don't. It's your job as the writer of your literary analysis to explain not only *WHAT* you see but also *WHY* and *HOW*, supporting your interpretation in ways that seem reasonable, persuasive, and satisfying to your readers.

Steps to Reading a Story

If possible, make your own copy of the story and read with pen in hand. Prepare to make notes, underline important lines, circle revealing words or images, and put stars, question marks, or your own symbols in the margins.

1. Before you begin the piece, read any *biographical information* that may accompany the story. Knowing information about the author and when the story was written or published may offer some insight. Also, note the *title*. Does it offer intriguing hints about the story's content?

2. Read through the story at least once to clearly acquaint yourself with its *plot*, the series of actions and events that make up the narrative. In other words, what happened and to whom? Is there a conflict of some sort? Is it resolved or is the story left open-ended?

3. Many times in a story you'll see words you don't know. Sometimes you can figure them out from their context, but if you find unknown words that might indeed have a critical bearing on your understanding of a character, for example, look these up now.

4. Jot a few notes describing your initial reactions to the story's main idea(s) or major *theme(s)*. (If it's helpful, think of the story in terms of its "about-ness." What do you as reader think this story is about? Loss of innocence? The bitterness of revenge? The power of sympathy? Tragic lack of communication? The wonder of first love?) In other words, what comments or observations does this story make about the human condition?

5. As you review the story, begin to think about its parts, always asking yourself "why?": why did the author choose to do it this way? What is gained (or lost) by writing it this way? What does "X" contribute to my understanding of the story? You might begin noting *point of view*—that is, who is narrating this story? Is a character telling this story or is it told by an all-knowing (omniscient) narrator? A narrator who is partially omniscient, seeing into the thoughts of only some characters? If the story is told by a character, is this narrator informed and trustworthy or "unreliable" to some degree because of ignorance, bias, psychological state, age (a young child, for example), or some other factor? What is gained through the story's choice of narration?

6. Is the story's *structure* in chronological order, or does the writer shift time sequences through flashbacks or multiple points of view? Does the story contain foreshadowing, early indications in the plot that signal later developments? Again, think about the author's choices in terms of communicating the story's ideas.

7. Think about the *characters*, their personalities, beliefs, motivations. How do they interact? Do any of them change—refuse or fail to change? Look closely at their descriptions, thoughts, and dialogue. Sometimes names are revealing, too.

8. What is the relationship between the *setting* of the story and its action or characters? Remember that setting can include place, time of year, hour of day or night, weather or climate, terrain, culture, and so on. Settings can create mood and even function symbolically to reveal character or foreshadow a coming event.

9. Look closely at the *language* of the story, paying attention to revealing images, metaphors, and similes (◆ for help identifying these, see pages 326–327). Note any use of *symbols*—persons, places, or things that bear a significant meaning beyond their usual meaning. (For example, in a particular story, a dreary rain might be associated with a loss of hope; a soaring bird might emphasize new possibilities.) Overall, would you characterize the story's *style* as realistic or something else? What is the *tone* of the story? Serious? Humorous? Does irony, the discrepancy between appearance and reality, play a part?

10. After you've looked at these and any other important elements of the reading, review your initial reactions. How would you now describe the main ideas or major themes of this story? How do the parts of the story work together to clarify those themes?

Remember to add your own questions to this list, ones that address your specific story in a meaningful way. ◆ To continue improving your reading skills, turn to the "Practicing What You've Learned" exercise on pages 473–480, which offers two stories for your analysis. Before you write an essay of literary analysis, see the guidelines on pages 471–473.

Annotated Story

Using the preceding guidelines, a composition student annotated the story that follows. Some of the notes she made on imagery became the basis for her short essay, which appears on pages 462–464. Before you read the story, however, cover the marginal notes with a sheet of paper. Then read the story, making your own notes. Next, uncover the student's notes and reread the story. Compare your reactions to those of the student writer. What new or different insights did you have?

The Story of an Hour

Kate Chopin

Kate Chopin was a nineteenth-century American writer whose stories appeared in such magazines as the *Atlantic Monthly, Century,* and the *Saturday Evening Post*. She published two collections of short stories and two novels; one of her novels, *The Awakening* (1899), was considered so shocking in its story of a married woman   *similar theme* who desired a life of her own that it was removed from some library shelves. "The Story of an Hour" was first published in 1894.

1   Knowing that Mrs. Mallard was afflicted with a heart trouble, great care was taken to break to her as gently as possible the news of her husband's death.

foreshadowing

2   It was her sister Josephine who told her, in broken sentences, veiled hints that revealed in half concealing. Her husband's friend Richards was there, too, near her. It was he who had been in the newspaper office when intelligence of the railroad disaster was received, with Brently Mallard's name leading the list of "killed." He had only taken the time to assure himself of its truth by a second telegram, and had hastened to forestall any less careful, less tender friend in bearing the sad message.

3   She did not hear the story as many women have heard the same, with a paralyzed inability to accept its significance. She wept at once, with sudden, wild abandonment, in her sister's arms. When the storm of grief had spent itself she went away to her room alone. She would have no one follow her.

storm imagery

4   There stood, facing the open window, a comfortable, roomy armchair. Into this she sank, pressed down by a physical exhaustion that haunted her body and seemed to reach into her soul.

Setting: closed room but open window
—spring trees, air
—songs
—blue sky

5   She could see in the open square before her house the tops of trees that were all aquiver with the new spring life. The delicious breath of rain was in the air. In the street below a peddler was crying his wares. The notes of a distant song which some one was singing reached her faintly, and countless sparrows were twittering in the eaves.

6   There were patches of blue sky showing here and there through the clouds that had met and piled each above the other in the west facing her window.

7   She sat with her head thrown back upon the cushion of the chair quite motionless, except when a sob came up into her throat and shook her, as a child who has cried itself to sleep continues to sob in its dreams.

8   She was young, with a fair, calm face, whose lines bespoke repression and even a certain strength. But now there was a dull stare in her eyes, whose gaze was fixed away off yonder on one of those patches of blue sky. It was not a glance of reflection, but rather indicated a suspension of intelligent thought.

Mrs M.: repression and strength

3rd person narrator—readers know her feelings

9   There was something coming to her and she was waiting for it, fearfully. What was it? She did not know; it was too subtle and elusive to name. But she felt it, creeping out of the sky, reaching toward her through the sounds, the scents, the color that filled the air.

new insight from spring sky

10   Now her bosom rose and fell tumultuously. She was beginning to recognize this thing that was approaching to possess her, and she was striving to beat it back with her will—as powerless as her two white slender hands would have been.

conflict within herself

11   When she abandoned herself a little whispered word escaped her slightly parted lips. She said it over and over under her breath: "Free, free, free!" The vacant stare and the look of terror that had followed it went from her eyes. They stayed keen and bright. Her pulses beat fast, and the coursing blood warmed and relaxed every inch of her body.

Revelation: freedom

images of vitality

12   She did not stop to ask if it were not a monstrous joy that held her. A clear and exalted perception enabled her to dismiss the suggestion as trivial.

13   She knew that she would weep again when she saw the kind, tender hands folded in death; the face that had never looked save with love upon her, fixed and gray and dead. But she saw beyond that bitter moment a long procession of years to come that would belong to her absolutely. And she opened and spread her arms out to them in welcome.

more "open" imagery

14   There would be no one to live for during those coming years; she would live for herself. There would be no powerful will bending her in that blind persistence with which men and women believe they have a right to impose a private will upon a fellow creature. A kind intention or a cruel intention made the act seem no less a crime as she looked upon it in that brief moment of illumination.

***self-assertion, wants to control her own life*

15   And yet she had loved him—sometimes. Often she had not. What did it matter! What could love, the unsolved mystery, count for in face of this possession of self-assertion which she suddenly recognized as the strongest impulse of her being.

16   "Free! Body and soul free!" she kept whispering.

17   Josephine was kneeling before the closed door with her lips to the keyhole, imploring for admission. "Louise, open the door! I beg; open the door—you will make yourself ill. What are you doing, Louise? For heaven's sake open the door."

closed door, illness imagery vs "elixir of life" (potion that cures all), open window

18   "Go away. I am not making myself ill." No; she was drinking in a very elixir of life through that open window.

19   Her fancy was running riot along those days ahead of her. Spring days, and summer days, and all sorts of days that would be her own. She breathed a quick prayer that life might be long. It was only yesterday she had thought with a shudder that life might be long.

future: seasons of life, growth

20   She arose at length and opened the door to her sister's importunities. There was a feverish triumph in her eyes, and she carried herself unwittingly like a goddess of Victory. She clasped her sister's waist, and together they descended the stairs. Richards stood waiting for them at the bottom.

victory imagery

21   Some one was opening the front door with a latchkey. It was Brently Mallard who entered, a little travel-stained, composedly carrying his gripsack and umbrella. He had been far from the scene of accident, and did not even know there had been one.

Is he associated with rain?

He stood amazed at Josephine's piercing cry; at Richards' quick motion to screen him from the view of his wife.

22   But Richards was too late.

23   When the doctors came they said she had died of heart dis-ease—of joy that kills.

Irony: She may die from a "broken" heart all right, but readers know it's not from joy.

Initial reactions: Mrs. Mallard is sad about her husband's death, though I'm not sure she really loved him all that much. He wasn't a bad guy—she just wants to be a "free" woman, back when women had few rights, little control over their lives. She dies—of shock? disappointment?—when he turns up alive.

After rereading: I think Chopin wanted readers to see how confined some nineteenth-century women felt in their traditional roles. I felt sorry for Mrs. Mallard, whose realization that life will not be hers after all is so traumatic that it kills her.

Open window—lets in spring scenes, color, sounds of new life—symbol of future possibilities. Also, lots of sick-versus-well and life-versus-death imagery.

Question: Why is she named "Mallard"—a duck?

Repose, 1911, by John Singer Sargent

Nonchaloir (Repose) by John Singer Sargent, 1911. Oil on canvas. 63.8 x 76.2 cm (25 12/8" x 30"). National Gallery, Washington, DC. Gift of Curt H. Reisinger. 1948.16.1

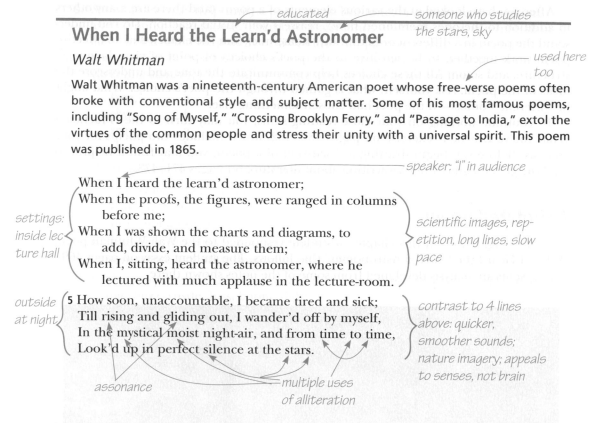

When I Heard the Learn'd Astronomer

educated — *someone who studies the stars, sky*

Walt Whitman

Walt Whitman was a nineteenth-century American poet whose free-verse poems often broke with conventional style and subject matter. Some of his most famous poems, including "Song of Myself," "Crossing Brooklyn Ferry," and "Passage to India," extol the virtues of the common people and stress their unity with a universal spirit. This poem was published in 1865.

used here too

speaker: "I" in audience

When I heard the learn'd astronomer;
When the proofs, the figures, were ranged in columns
    before me;
When I was shown the charts and diagrams, to
    add, divide, and measure them;
When I, sitting, heard the astronomer, where he
    lectured with much applause in the lecture-room.

5 How soon, unaccountable, I became tired and sick;
Till rising and gliding out, I wander'd off by myself,
In the mystical moist night-air, and from time to time,
Look'd up in perfect silence at the stars.

settings: inside lecture hall

scientific images, repetition, long lines, slow pace

outside at night

contrast to 4 lines above: quicker, smoother sounds; nature imagery; appeals to senses, not brain

assonance — *multiple uses of alliteration*

Initial reaction: The speaker of the poem (a student?) is listening to an astronomer's lecture—lots of facts and figures. He gets tired (bored?) and goes outside and looks at the nice night himself.

After rereading: I see two ways of looking at the sky here, two ways of understanding. You can learn academically and you can use your own senses. I think Whitman prefers the personal experience in this case because the language and images are much morre positive in the last lines of the poem when the speaker is looking at nature for himself.

The poem shows the contrast between the two ways by using two stanzas with different styles and tones. Cold vs. warm. Passive vs. active. Facts vs. personal experience.

Sample Student Essay

After studying the Whitman poem, the student writer wrote this essay to show how many poetic elements work together to present the main idea. Do you agree with his analysis? Which of his claims seems the most or least persuasive, and why? What different interpretation(s) might you suggest?

TWO WAYS OF KNOWING

1   In the poem "When I Heard the Learn'd Astronomer," nineteenth-century American poet Walt Whitman contrasts two ways people may study the world around them. They can approach the world through lectures and facts, and they can experience nature firsthand through their own senses. Through the use of contrasting structures, imagery, diction, and sound devices in this poem, Whitman expresses a strong preference for personal experience.

Introduction: Title, author, brief overview of content

Thesis and essay map

2   The poem's structure clearly presents the contrast between the two ways of experiencing the world, or in this specific case, two ways of studying the heavens. The eight-line, free-verse poem breaks into two stanzas, with the first four lines describing an indoor academic setting, followed by a one-line transition to three concluding lines describing an outdoor night scene. The two parts are unified by a first-person narrator who describes and reacts to both scenes.

Two-part structure

3   In the first four lines the narrator is described as sitting in "the lecture-room" (l. 4) as part of an audience listening to an astronomer's talk. The dominant imagery of lines 2–3 is scientific and mathematical: "proofs," "figures," "charts," and "diagrams" are presented so that the audience "may add, divide, and measure them" (l. 3). The words, mostly nouns, appear without any colorful modifiers; the facts and figures are carefully arranged "in columns" (l. 2) for objective analysis. This approach to learning is clearly logical and systematic.

Stanza 1: Inside lecture hall

4   The structure and word choice of the first four lines of the poem also subtly reveal the narrator's attitude toward the lecture, which he finds dry and boring. To emphasize the narrator's emotional uninvolvement with the material, Whitman presents him passively "sitting" (l. 4), subject of the passive verb "was shown" (l. 3). Lines 2,

first-person "I." So that your readers may easily follow your discussion, include a copy of the work or at least indicate publication information describing the location of the work (the name of volume, publisher, date, pages, and so forth).

Within your essay, it's also helpful to include a poem's line number following a direct quotation: "the silent schoolyard" (1. 10). Some instructors also request paragraph or page numbers in essays on fiction.

4. **Organize effectively.** Your method of organization may depend heavily on your subject matter. A poem, for example, might be best discussed by devoting a paragraph to each stanza; on the other hand, another work might profit from a paragraph on imagery, another on point of view, another on setting, and so on. You must decide what arrangement makes the best sense for your readers. Experiment by moving your ideas around in your prewriting outlines and drafts.

5. **Use ample evidence.** Remember that you are, in essence, arguing your interpretation—you are saying to your reader, "Understand this work the way I do." Therefore, it is absolutely essential that you offer your reader convincing evidence, based on reasonable readings of words in the work itself. The acceptance of your views depends on your making yourself clear and convincing. To do so, include plenty of references to the work through direct quotation and paraphrase. Don't assume that your reader sees what you see—or sees it in the way you do. You must *fight* for your interpretation by offering clearly explained readings substantiated with references to the work.

> *Unsupported claim:* Robert feels sorry for himself throughout the story.

> *Claim supported with text:* Robert's self-pity is evident throughout the story as he repeatedly thinks to himself, "No one on this earth cares about me" (4) and "There isn't a soul I can turn to" (5).

Ask yourself as you work through your drafts: am I offering enough clear, specific, convincing evidence here to persuade my reader to accept my reading?

6. **Find a pleasing conclusion.** At the end of your literary analysis, readers should feel they have gained new knowledge or understanding of a work or some important part of it. You might choose to wrap up your discussion with a creative restatement of your reading, its relation to the writer's craft, or even your assessment of the work's significance within the author's larger body of writing. However you conclude, the readers should feel intellectually and emotionally satisfied with your discussion.

Problems to Avoid

Don't assign meanings. By far the most common problem in essays of literary analysis involves interpretation without clear explanation of supporting evidence. Remember that your readers may not see what you see in a particular line or paragraph; in fact, they may see something quite different. The burden is on you to show cause—how you derived your reading and why it is a valid one. Don't represent claims as truth without support even if they ever-so-conveniently fit your thesis: "It is clear that the moon is used here as a symbol of her family's loss." Clear to whom besides you? If it helps, each time you make an interpretative claim, imagine a classmate who immediately says, "Uh, sorry, but I don't get it. Show me how you see that?" Or imagine a hostile reader with a completely different reading who sneers, "Oh yeah, says who? Convince me."

Use quoted material effectively. Many times your supporting evidence will come from quotations from the text you're analyzing. But don't just drop a quoted line onto your page, as if it had suddenly tumbled off a high cliff somewhere. You run the risk of your readers reading the quoted material and still not seeing in it what you do. Blend the quoted material smoothly into your prose, in a way that illustrates or supports your clearly stated point:

Dropped in: Miranda is twenty-four years old. "After working for three years on a morning newspaper she had an illusion of maturity and experience" (280). [What exact point do you want your reader to understand?]

Point clarified: Although Miranda is twenty-four and has worked on a newspaper for three years, she is not as worldly wise as she thinks she is, having acquired only the "illusion of maturity and experience" (280).

◆ Review pages 395–396 for some ways to blend your quotations into your prose. Always double-check to ensure you are quoting accurately; refer to pages 402–403 and 586–588 for help with proper punctuation and block indention of longer quoted material.

Analysis is not plot summary. Sometimes you may want to offer your readers a brief overview of the work before you begin your in-depth analysis. And certainly there will be times in the body of your essay, especially if you are writing about fiction, that you will need to paraphrase actions or descriptions rather than quote long passages directly. Paraphrasing can indeed provide effective support, but do beware a tendency to fall into unproductive plot-telling. Remember that the purpose of your paper is to provide insight into the work's ideas and craft—not merely to present a rehash of the story line. Keep your eye on each of your claims and quote or paraphrase only those particular lines or important passages that illustrate and support your points. Use your editing pen as a sharp stick to beat back plot summary if it begins taking over your paragraphs.

PRACTICING WHAT YOU'VE LEARNED

© Canstock Images, Inc./ Index Stock Imagery

Practice your skills of literary analysis on one or both of the following stories. A few questions about each story are offered here to start your thinking.

"Geraldo No Last Name" is an excerpt from Sandra Cisneros' award-winning novel *The House on Mango Street* (1984), which presents a series of vignettes often told by Esperanza, a young girl growing up in Chicago. In this story, Esperanza's older teenage friend Marin has a chance meeting with Geraldo. How does this story comment on stereotyping and human misunderstanding? Overall, what new insights do you think Cisneros wanted her readers

continued on next page

CHAPTER 17

Writing about Visual Arts

Today, more than at any time in the history of the world, we live in a visual culture. On a daily basis we receive information and messages from images on television, on the Internet, in magazines and newspapers, in movies, in galleries, and in advertisements, just to name a few sources. Artistic visual images may enrich our lives by bringing beauty, retrieving memories, posing questions, stirring action, or offering new ideas that awaken our minds to different possibilities.

Learning to analyze visual art is an important skill; understanding how and why images affect us in specific ways helps us evaluate the messages we are being given and our reactions to them. Writing about art is an excellent way to practice careful observation, analytical thinking, and the ability to organize and clearly communicate ideas.

Close scrutiny of visual images is generally a pleasant activity; for example, most of us enjoy looking at the photographs we've taken, the art we hang on our walls, and even the computer desktop wallpaper we've selected. Although there are many kinds of visual arts, this chapter will focus primarily on the analysis of paintings, with additional brief advice about responding to sculpture and photography. Chapter 18 is entirely devoted to writing about film.

To practice applying the advice outlined here, you may find it helpful to look at some of the many artworks reprinted in this and other chapters in this text; a list of paintings and photographs may be found following the table of contents.

Using Visual Arts in the Composition Classroom

Because writing about art is such a good way to practice valuable thinking and writing skills, composition teachers often assign one of the following kinds of essays:

1. *A personal response:* You might be assigned a discussion of a particular picture or be asked to select one of your choice. Your thesis would be your interpretation of the

Artists may paint scenes of ordinary human life (such as *Nighthawks* or Jacob Lawrence's *The Library*, page 51), or they may choose more turbulent action scenes (such as John S. Curry's *Tornado Over Kansas*, page 346). In addition, artists have frequently painted historical events as they saw or imagined them. For example, in the age before photography, Napoleon paid artist Jacques-Louis David to paint his and Empress Josephine's coronation (when Napoleon's mother couldn't attend the event, David obliged Napoleon by painting her into the scene anyway). In *The Raft of the Medusa*, Theodore Gericault transformed the news story of an 1816 shipwreck into a visual image, showing the wretchedness of survivors adrift at sea. Throughout the ages, many artworks have made clear social or political statements. J. M. W. Turner's *The Slave Ship*, painted in 1840, criticized the English slave trade; Francisco Goya's painting *The Third of May, 1808* (below) focused attention on executions in Spain. Still other paintings present scenes from well-known myths (the birth of Venus), literature (death of Ophelia from *Hamlet*), or cultural or religious events (the crucifixion of Jesus). A little research may help you better understand paintings with historical, political, or literary subject matter.

- *A portrait:* Rather than a broader scene, your painting might be a closer, more focused representation of a particular person.* Is the person well

© Scala/Art Resource, NY

The Third of May, 1808, painted by Francisco Goya in 1814, recorded the mass executions of Spanish civilians who had rebelled against the occupation of Napoleon's French troops; the painting has been called the first modern image of war.

---

*A portrait may also contain more than one figure; artists often paint couples, children, entire families, small groups of workers or officials, etc. If there are multiple people in the portrait you are analyzing, take into consideration the connection of the people to each other. Is there, for example, an obvious power relationship captured in the picture?

known (e.g., a portrait of George Washington) or specifically identified by name or relationship to the artist (the painter's mother)? Perhaps the artist chose to paint a portrait of someone representing a universal human type (an innocent child, for example). Remember, too, that artists also frequently paint self-portraits, often at different times in their lives. Portraits capture not only faces but also personalities and attitudes; such paintings may also present commentary on the status and values of their subjects, as well as the time and culture in which they live.

As you study a portrait, note your reaction to the person and consider the following questions: when, where, and for what purpose was this picture painted? Is the subject identified or unidentified? What do the person's facial expression and posture say to you—that is, do the facial features and angle of the body imply power, superiority, gentleness, aloofness, boredom, innocence, or something else? What sort of clothing or accessories (jewelry or hat, for example) characterize this person and his or her social class? Note too both the immediate setting and the background of the portrait. Painters often include objects that offer insight into their subject: books, dogs, and food surrounding a figure in a richly furnished room might reveal a wealthy eighteenth-century landowner with leisure time. Consider too the size of the person within the frame and the direction of the figure's gaze (straight at you or away?), both of which may affect your feelings toward the subject.

At this point if you wish to practice this advice, turn to *Repose*, a 1911 portrait of his niece by John Singer Sargent, reprinted on page 461 of this text. What is your impression of this woman and her status in life, and how do her expression, posture, clothes, and other details in the portrait communicate that impression? What is the effect of the artist's decision to make her dress occupy so much of the picture?

- *A landscape:* Paintings of nature and other outdoor scenes are generally called "landscapes," even though their specific subject matter varies widely from woods to meadows, mountains, rivers, roads, fields of crops, villages, clouds and sky, and so on. Landscapes may also contain people, animals, and buildings, though these are sometimes included to give the viewer a sense of proportion, emphasizing the majesty or vastness of Nature (a small figure by a tall waterfall, for example).

If the painting you are analyzing may be considered a landscape, explore the artist's interpretation of this view. Is the scene tranquil and inviting or dark and foreboding? Does it emphasize the calming powers of nature or capture its raw power? Its mystery, its grandeur, or something else? Does the artist seem to invite the viewer to simply enjoy a beautiful natural experience or is there a feeling of paradise lost? Is anything in the picture used symbolically, such as crossroads or a storm? If there are people in the picture, what is their purpose? To show proportion or to illustrate a reaction to the scene? Do the people or buildings emphasize a contrast—perhaps between town and country, civilization and the natural world?

For examples of outdoor scenes, in both painting and photography, look at Caspar David Friedrich's *Early Snow* (page 45), Claude Monet's *The Water-Lily Pond* (page 332), Vincent van Gogh's *Starry Night* (page 467), and Ansel

As was previously noted, this list is by no means comprehensive. Look at your painting again and again, allowing it to suggest other questions and ideas as you study its design. Consider grouping your responses by topics (e.g., the painting's use of colors) so that later, when you are ready to write your essay's first draft, your thoughts may be somewhat organized in support of a larger point. (For a sample of responses to some of the preceding questions, see the notes on *Nighthawks* on page 501.)

7. **If possible, identify the painting's period style or "school."** Some paintings may be recognized by common characteristics as belonging to a particular group or era of painters. Recognizing your painting as part of, or influenced by, a particular artistic movement may help you better understand important elements of its composition and design. For example, Monet's *The Water-Lily Pond* (page 332) shows variations of color as reflected in natural light that often characterize paintings of the late nineteenth-century movement called Impressionism. Other artistic movements of the last 150 years include Cubism, Surrealism, Art Nouveau, Art Deco, Expressionism, Abstract Expressionism, and Pop Art, to name only a few; art from earlier periods may be identified with Classical, Romantic, or Renaissance styles, or any one of many others. If you are analyzing a well-known work, art history books or Web sites may help you identify the major style of your painting.

Once you have studied the subject matter, composition, and style of your painting, reassess your first reactions. Is your interpretation of the painting the same? Has your analysis broadened or changed your understanding or appreciation of the artwork and the ways its parts work together to communicate a dominant impression or main idea?

Additional Advice about Sculpture and Photography

Much of the advice for close analysis of paintings can be applied to sculpture and to professional photography. Use as many of the questions in the preceding pages as possible to shed light on the work you have selected. Here are a few more suggestions.

Sculptures may represent a wide variety of forms, including humans, animals, mythical creatures, everyday objects, and abstract or whimsical shapes. Sculptures of the human form or face have been found since the Stone Age, and people continue to be the dominant subject matter of sculpture today.

Some human subjects are specific, well-known people (e.g., Abraham Lincoln); others may honor a group of people (e.g., WWII soldiers); still others may represent universal types (e.g., a young girl on a swing). Some human sculptures, especially ones from earlier Greek, Roman, and Egyptian cultures, may be idealized (or culturally stylized) to varying degrees, often to express harmony of body and mind, leadership qualities, or even a link to divinity. In addition to a statue's facial features, consider such factors as the pose (standing, sitting, in action?), clothing or drapery, and the size of the figure. In some cases, the advice on analyzing portraits (pages 488–489) may be especially helpful.

Sculptures may be composed of a wide variety of materials, such as marble, bronze, stone, clay, pewter, plaster, wire, or wood, and both the choice of material (its texture, color, and weight) and the sculptor's technique often contribute significantly to the work's dominant impression. Polished white marble, for instance, might be the best choice for a statue of a mythical goddess because of its soft, smooth classical beauty; sturdy, roughed bronze might be better used to communicate the strength and ruggedness of a golden grizzly bear; light-weight plastics or fiberglass might be used appropriately in an abstract sculpture of a kite dancing in the wind. Whether the sculpture is a representational ("realistic"), symbolic, or abstract piece, the selection and treatment of its material are important parts of its effect.

Remember, too, that unlike paintings, sculptures may be seen from multiple angles, so do walk around the artwork, if possible. Does the change in perspectives affect your understanding or appreciation of the work? If the base, pedestal, or wall/ceiling connection is part of the artwork, include its contribution in your analysis. Sometimes, especially in sculpture that has been commissioned for a particular purpose, the site of a sculpture is noteworthy; consider, for example, the kinds of sculpture one might find in a public park as opposed to an older cemetery or college library. How does your piece of sculpture blend with or complement its location?

Photography, like painting, may show people, places, things, or pleasing combinations of colors, shadows, and shapes. Like paintings, photos may tell a story, illustrate or document a news or historical event, capture a mood or feeling, make a political statement, encourage social action, or accomplish some other purpose. Whether you are analyzing an example of photojournalism or a fine art photograph, always collect the identifying information: the name of the photographer, the name of the photograph (if given), the subject matter, the place and date of the photo, the place of first publication or exhibition, and any other pertinent background details.

© SCHOMBURG CENTER/Art Resource, NY

Meta Warrick Fuller's sculpture *Ethiopia Awakening* (1914) shows a woman in a queen's headdress emerging from the wrappings of an ancient mummy, with Fuller's design celebrating a renaissance of pride in African American women's heritage.

In addition to analyzing the composition of the photograph using some of the suggestions outlined in previous pages, be aware that the circumstance and method by which the photo was made may also affect a viewer's response. Some prize-winning news photographs have been taken on the run in risky circumstances (battle scenes, for example) or as the result of chance meetings (◆ see the story of Dorothea Lange's *Migrant Mother*, page 339); other fine art photographs are the product of long patience waiting for the perfect shot. Still other photos are staged (still lifes such as Edward Weston's peppers) or posed (portraits of William Wegman's costumed dogs). Others are produced with complex camera manipulation or crafted through computer technology to achieve desired effects.

Analysis of photographs also invites special attention to their use of lighting and color or absence of color. A photo taken with black-and-white film produces a different effect from one in high-speed color often used for action shots (compare, for example,

© Ansel Adams Publishing Rights Trust/CORBIS

In *Moonrise, Hernandez, New Mexico* (1941), Ansel Adams captures a small village graveyard dwarfed by the vast sky above, perhaps offering a comment on the brevity of life contrasted to a seemingly infinite universe.

© Thomas Dworzak, Magnum Photos

Photojournalist Thomas Dworzak's dramatic picture of both flood and fire in New Orleans following Hurricane Katrina was selected as one of *Time* magazine's "Best Photos of 2005."

Migrant Mother, page 339, or *Moonrise, Hernandez, New Mexico*, page 496, to the color photo of Hurricane Katrina's destruction in New Orleans, also on page 496). Exposure time, depth of field (use of focus), angle and range of vision may also affect an image's appearance and meaning. Although no one expects you to be an expert on cameras or photo technology, do plan to explore the effects on you, the viewer, of the photograph's arrangement of subject matter, sharp/soft or blurry focus, wide or close angle, or any one of many other factors that make the particular picture effective.

As in the discussion of paintings, these suggestions for analyzing photography and sculptures are only a start, prompting your own closer investigation of the work you are analyzing.

© Canstock Images, Inc./Index Stock Imagery

PRACTICING WHAT YOU'VE LEARNED

A. Using the steps outlined on pages 487–494 in this chapter, practice your analytical skills by responding to a piece of art whose picture is reproduced in this textbook (a list of the artworks follows the table of contents). First, record your selection's title, artist, medium, and other pertinent information; then briefly describe the work. In a few sentences, explain the dominant effect or theme of the artwork as you see it and identify the important elements in the work that support your interpretation.

B. *Collaborative Activity:* Study the painting *The Subway* on page 253 of this text, and record your personal reaction to it. Then write a few sentences explaining why you might have responded in this way to the painting. In a group with two other students, compare your reactions, noting both similarities and differences. In addition to the painter's choice of detail, arrangement, and medium, how much does personal experience shape one's view of an artwork? How might each of you support your own interpretation? (If the group prefers, study the painting *Nighthawks*, on page 500, and then compare your group's responses to the notes of the student writer on page 501.)

Guidelines for Writing about Artworks

Whether you are analyzing a painting, drawing, photograph, or piece of sculpture, you may find the following advice helpful as you write your essay.

1. **In the beginning . . .** Consider starting your essay with a brief interest-catching lead-in, perhaps an arresting descriptive detail, a hint of controversy, or a reference to the artwork's appeal or popularity. However you begin, your introduction should always clearly identify the work by title, full name of the artist, date (if available), and any other information you deem important, such as a painting's period style or a sculpture's location. Remember that names of artworks should be italicized in print media or underlined in handwritten prose.

2. **Offer a compelling thesis.** In an essay of analysis, your thesis will be the statement of your thoughtful interpretation of the work—what you see as its dominant effect, theme, main ideas, appeal, or commentary—and your discussion will show how the various elements of the piece work together to suggest that interpretation. In an essay focused on two works, you might show how the selections may be compared or contrasted to better inform the reader about the works' subject matter and/or style (for example, what interesting similarities and differences in subject and style exist in Edvard Munch's *The Scream* [page 121] and George Tooker's *The Subway* [page 253]?).

In some cases, you may find it helpful to include an essay map that will indicate the main topics of discussion. For example, your map might assert that your painting's theme, a commentary on the brutality of war, is best understood through explanation of its violent subject matter, its asymmetrical arrangement of jagged shapes and lines, and its unusual harsh colors.

3. **Present an overview of the work and, if appropriate, include pertinent background information.** Remember that your readers may be unfamiliar with the piece of art. Even though you will be analyzing important elements of it in your body paragraphs, readers may profit from a clear sense of the work in its entirety. In some cases, this overview may effectively appear in a paragraph following your introduction, just as a book or movie review might give a brief plot summary before discussing individual parts of those works. At this point in your essay you might also decide to include other relevant information about the painting's background. For example, if it is a historical painting, you might need to explain the circumstances; if a photograph captures a news event, an explanation of the situation might be in order; a statue of a particular person, real or mythological, may need identification.

4. **Organize your main points effectively.** Because artworks are unique, no one formula exists for organizing the body paragraphs of your essay. Perhaps the most helpful advice suggests that you look closely at the notes you took on the artist's choices of subject matter, composition, and design and then decide which aspects of the artwork play the most important roles in communicating the "meaning" or mood of the piece, as you see it. Try grouping your thoughts about the artwork into logical clusters; for instance, in a particular painting, one cluster might focus on the selection and arrangement of the subject matter while another addresses issues of light, shadow, and intensity of colors. With an appropriate topic sentence to introduce each one, these clusters may be shaped into effective body paragraphs in support of your thesis. In other cases artworks will suggest their own organization and order; for instance, a discussion of a portrait (if it helps, think *Mona Lisa* here) might focus first on the facial expression; then move to a paragraph on the body, clothes, and accessories; then address the location or the background. Although there are no set blueprints for organizing body paragraphs in essays analyzing visual arts, readers must always feel a sense of coherence and logical order as the essay discussion progresses.

5. **Provide clear supporting evidence.** To help your reader understand—and accept—your interpretative claims, you must provide clear explanations and descriptive details from the artwork. Make your references to particular elements

as vivid and specific as possible; describing a storm cloud looming over a ship as "huge" is not as helpful as describing it proportionally as three times the size of the ship, taking over half of the entire canvas. If you sense motion from circular images in the same storm-at-sea picture, show repetition of the shape in rounded waves, billowing sails, and whirling tufts of clouds. Remember that acceptance of your thesis—your interpretation—depends on your readers' ability to see what you see in the work.

6. **Conclude gracefully.** By the end of your essay your readers should feel that they have acquired insight into a specific work of art, and perhaps even learned new information about an artist or particular artistic style. Your conclusion might reemphasize what you see as the work's purpose or primary appeal, or you might point out its influence on other artists or later works. If you know such information, you can "situate" this selection in the artist's larger body of work. However you choose to end your essay, readers should feel they have enjoyed a reasonable, well-written analysis that has provided new understanding and appreciation of the work.

Problems to Avoid

Pay close attention to your assignment. Be sure you clearly understand the *purpose* of your essay. If you have been asked to provide a formal analysis of a painting, one that presents an interpretation by showing how the elements work together in support of that view, do not simply describe the picture. In addition, some assignments encourage research, but others request only personal response. Read your assignment carefully so that you will know exactly how to approach your essay topic. (Note too that in personal response essays, some teachers allow the use of "I," but others don't, preferring more objective references to "viewers" or "observers." Ask your instructor for guidance on this matter.)

Inform and delight readers with your own vivid description. As in any evaluation, whether it discusses a book, movie, restaurant, or artwork, it isn't enough to simply say, "I liked it. It was interesting." As someone sharing your opinion with others, you must work hard to help readers understand your point of view and the reasons for it. Explain your reasoning logically and with ample references to the artwork; be sure that those references are themselves vividly described (yes, the sky in van Gogh's *Starry Night* [page 467] is blue and green—but what shades of blue and green, and why?). Revise your own bland or fuzzy language by using action verbs and colorful adjectives and adverbs that appeal to your reader's senses. Make your prose as inviting as the artwork you are describing. (◆ For more help strengthening your prose, review pages 126–129 and 161–164.)

Annotated Painting: *Nighthawks*

Using this chapter's suggestions for analyzing paintings, a composition student took the following notes on the well-known picture *Nighthawks* (page 500), painted in 1942 by American artist Edward Hopper. Many of these notes were incorporated into the student's essay, on pages 502–503.

Nighthawks, 1942, by Edward Hopper

Photography © The Art Institute of Chicago

Notes

First Impressions: I've seen a poster of this painting somewhere. I get feelings of loneliness and depression from this picture but I like it anyway. What are these people's stories?

Basic information: Nighthawks, Edward Hopper (American artist), 1942, oil paint.

Subject matter: An all-night café in a city. Four people in the café: a couple, a man by himself, and a counter guy. In the 1940s because the guys at the counter are wearing '40s hats. Late night—empty streets, dark buildings.

The café is lit up so we can see inside. My eye is drawn to the single guy, maybe because he's in the middle of the picture, but also because he's turned away. He's separate from everyone else. The couple doesn't look too happy but at least they're together.

Colors: Shadows, dark areas, eerie green street and sidewalk. Café's walls—bleached out yellow, plain. All mostly depressing, though café does have light.

Shapes: Lots of long straight lines, rectangle shapes; even the counter and the ceiling are sort of triangle shaped. Sharp edges == harsh city life? Paint is flat, feels cold.

Note: The viewer is way back from the people (more isolation feeling?). No sky, just buildings.

What kind of birds are "nighthawks"?

Reassessment: Picture captures the loneliness of city life—maybe loneliness anywhere? The setting, figures, colors, and shapes all add to feeling of isolation. Maybe the light and café represent a small bit of hope in a hard world?

Sample Student Essay

After studying the painting *Nighthawks*, the student writer incorporated his notes into this analytical essay, offering his interpretation of the work and showing important ways in which the painting's elements effectively communicate a dominant effect. As you read this essay, what specific details help you understand the writer's main points?

NIGHT IN THE CITY AND PSYCHE

Introduction
sets the
mood

1   It's four o'clock in the morning and after studying all night, you stumble out for coffee at an ever-open café. The night outside is cold and dark, the café light is harsh, and slumped on a worn counter stool, you've never felt so alone. Could anyone else possibly understand how this moment feels? American artist Edward Hopper captured just this emotion in his 1942 oil painting *Nighthawks*. Through skillful arrangement of space, sharp angles, and muted colors, Hopper brilliantly conveys on canvas the sense of isolation and loneliness often experienced in modern life.

Thesis and
essay map
|
Overview of
painting

2   *Nighthawks* presents a late-night scene in a city café, surrounded by dark buildings and a deserted street. The viewer, at some distance from the café, can see inside through a large glass window. Only four people are in the café: three customers—a single man and a couple—sitting on bar stools at the counter and a young waiter behind the counter. There is a sense of silence in the picture, a moment frozen in time, as no one is pictured as speaking or moving, except for a slight arm motion of the waiter as he does his job.

Point One:
Use of space

3   To capture the mood of loneliness and separation, Hopper effectively arranges the figures through use of isolating space and distance. Near the center of the painting, Hopper places the single man apart from the others. Alone, faceless, with his back turned to the viewer, he represents every person who has ever felt distanced from other humans, whether

(figures)

it be in a quiet café or a noisy dorm. He isn't interacting with the waiter or the couple, who are not communicating with or even looking at each other. Though they obviously know each other, they look tired, maybe depressed, and have retreated into separate worlds. As important as the isolation of the figures within the café is the distance between the viewer and the scene. Just as the characters do not close the gap between

(viewer)

each other, the viewer too is removed, outside the café observing these nighthawks, these solitary nocturnal creatures, like birds in a glass cage.

4   Hopper's use of long straight lines and sharp geometrical shapes throughout the picture also communicates the sense of an unfriendly, stark world. Rectangle shapes appear throughout the picture: the plate glass windows; the inside door; the doorway, window, and windowsills across the street; and the street, to name a few examples. Long thin lines dominate the scene, visible in window dividers, columns, edges of doors, building trim, and the curb. Even the counter inside the café is a triangle, with a darker triangle inside of it. The angle of the roof makes the wall above the far glass window come to a point, like a thin knife blade. There are few rounded lines in this picture, and there are no trees on the street or decorations on the café walls to soften the scene. Hard buildings and concrete fill the entire canvas out to its edges, stressing again the idea of the city as a cold, confining box.

Point Two: Use of lines, shapes, angles

5   The choice of colors also adds to the depressed mood of the painting. The dark patches, in the shadows on the building across the street and in its windows, emphasize the emptiness of the street. The pale, shadowy green of the sidewalk and street gives the scene an eerie feeling in the late-night hours. The café outside is brown-black, and the counter is also brown; although the walls are lighter, the color is a faded-out yellow. The use of these dark, sickly colors adds to the gloomy atmosphere. However, Hopper does place the couple and the counter guy in more light than the single man, and the woman's red dress adds a small bit of brighter color. Perhaps Hopper means to suggest that there is still a slight hope if people try to find companionship.

Point Three: Use of colors

6   French playwright Jean Anouilh once said, "Life is very nice, but it lacks form. It's the aim of art to give it some." In *Nighthawks* Edward Hopper gives visible form to the feeling of loneliness, an emotion almost everyone has experienced at one time or another. Hopper's painting appeals to viewers because it taps into our own sense of isolation, perhaps subtly encouraging us to reach out to others before it's too late.

Conclusion: A quotation emphasizing the painting's appeal

Suggestions for Writing

1. Write an essay of analysis that presents and supports your interpretation of an artwork you find especially appealing. You might select a favorite painting, a piece of sculpture that is on your campus, or one of the many artworks reproduced in this textbook. (A list of artworks in this text follows the table of contents.) What elements of the piece make it "work" for you? (If you completed Practice A on page 497, you might expand those notes into this essay.)

2. Write an essay that compares/contrasts two artworks in such a way that both of them are clarified for your reader. For example, you might select two landscapes or two portraits and show how the style of each is similar or different, and why each is effective for its purpose. Or perhaps you might argue your preference for one over the other, explaining the reasons for your selection.

3. Write an essay that highlights the differences between two different kinds of art, such as a painting and a sculpture or a painting and a photograph. What advantages does each medium offer its subject?

4. Use this opportunity to investigate a "classic" artwork. Research an admired painting, a famous sculpture, or a Pulitzer Prize–winning photograph and discover why others have found the work so arresting. After reading about your subject (and possibly about its artist), decide if you agree with the comments you found. Do you have a better interpretation to offer?

5. Practice your descriptive writing skills by reproducing in words one of the artworks whose picture appears in this text. Your writing should be so vivid and precise that any reader could identify the artwork you chose. Or, if you prefer, allow one of the artworks in this text to suggest to you a similar scene to describe (for example, you might take a close look at Lawrence's *The Library* [page 51] and then "paint" your own library scene in colorful language).

CHAPTER 18

Writing about Film

Millions of people see films of one kind or another every day. Because the movie screen has become such an important medium of communication, it is not surprising that so many college courses have added a variety of films—from educational documentaries to commercially produced "Hollywood" movies—to their syllabi.

As you know from visiting your local movie theater, a powerful film can affect its audience in many emotional and intellectual ways, leading its viewers to thoughtful consideration of its ideas, craft, and construction. Writing about film is simply the next step from something you have probably done for years. Progressing from informally talking about movies with your friends, you can now use your analytical thinking and writing skills to put your ideas into organized essays so that a variety of readers may respond to them.

Using Film in the Composition Classroom

Writing about film in academic classes may take many forms, depending on its purpose and audience and the kind of course in which it is assigned. Here are some of the more common kinds of essay assignments using film found in composition and writing-across-the-disciplines courses:

1. *Prompted Response:* You might be shown a scene, a longer "clip" (that is, multiple shots or scenes), or a short film to help you find an interesting topic for your own writing. For example, a documentary on an inspirational figure might encourage you to write about a personal moment of courage, or you might write an essay about a memorable relative you recall after watching a fictionalized screen character or an interview with a famous author. Or perhaps you might write about one

of the important themes you saw expressed in a movie (for example, the importance of honesty or lessons learned from teamwork). Film, like literature, can be the springboard to all sorts of good essay topics.

2. *Review Essay:* Many composition courses offer students the chance to *evaluate* a commercial movie of their choice or one from an approved list. These review essays focus on why the writer does/does not think the movie is effective and whether it should be recommended to a particular audience. In these essays, writers usually select two or three important criteria by which a film may be judged (such as acting, plot, direction, special effects, etc.) and then offer evidence from the film to illustrate the reasons for their opinions. More than a simple yea/nay pronouncement, this kind of assignment is popular in writing classes because it allows writers to practice basic essay skills: a clear thesis, logical organization of persuasive claims, adequate development in support of those claims, and effective language.

3. *Strategy Practice:* You may also be offered the option of using film as subject matter in your essays as you practice mastering one or more of the organizational strategies discussed in Part Two of this text. For instance, movie reviews will certainly include examples and descriptive details from the film; a controversial film may call for an essay with a sharp argumentative edge. To practice comparison/ contrast, you might choose to write about a movie version of a literary work, an older movie and its current remake, a movie and its sequel, two movies with similar themes, or a Hollywood treatment of a historical event. Or you might practice causal analysis by explaining why a particular movie is your favorite or by showing how it influenced you at a crucial point in your life. Recalling a film you like (or hate!) can provide you with a wealth of examples and details while you practice developing essays in a number of ways.

4. *Formal Analysis:* Similar to essays of literary analysis, discussed in Chapter 16, some assignments call for interpretation of one or more of the elements that make up a film, explaining how those elements help communicate a particular idea or mood. For example, you might analyze the setting in a particular scene to show how it helps create the appropriate atmosphere (the house in *The Others*), or you might show how a minor character contributes to the viewer's understanding of a major theme (the child in the red coat in *Schindler's List*) or how a symbolic object reveals a character's transformation (the vintage car in *Gran Torino*). Other kinds of analysis essay assignments might ask specific questions about a movie's political, cultural, or social ideas ("What criticisms of 1950s American values does *Dr. Strangelove* offer its viewers?"; "Explain the concept of personal sacrifice as suggested in *It's a Wonderful Life*.").

There are, of course, many other kinds of essays written about film. In Film Studies classes, for example, you will often find students writing essays on film history (the influence of *Star Wars* on subsequent science fiction movies) or on the films of a particular actor or director (Spielberg's body of work), as well as many treatments of technical elements, such as editing, lighting, sound production, and special effects (stop-motion 3-D in *Coraline*; innovative camera angles in *Citizen Kane*). These kinds of essay topics are fascinating, but they are often dependent upon expertise gained from research and in-depth study of film theory and production; consequently, they are not usually assigned in composition classes.

Guidelines for Writing about Film

Because the purposes of writing about film vary greatly, it is difficult to list suggestions that will apply to all assignments. However, if you are writing a movie review or an essay of film analysis, you may find some of these hints helpful.

1. **Pay close attention to your assignment.** Be sure you have a clear understanding of your purpose and audience. Are you, for example, writing a complete movie review or a more formal analysis of only certain elements? Does your assignment ask you to address any specific questions? Is your intended audience a group of general viewers, perhaps other students in your class, or are you writing for a particular audience, such as parents who might wish to know if this film is appropriate for their young children? Having a good understanding of the goals for this essay will help you focus your attention on the parts of the film relevant to your assignment.

2. **Prepare in advance of your first screening.** If you are writing a movie review or formal analysis, you may need to include certain kinds of production information about the film. To save time and stress (credits roll by quickly), obtain the information you need before you watch the film. It might be helpful, for example, to know the names of the director, the major actors, the screenwriter, the studio or film company, and the date of release. Does the movie fall into a particular genre, or category, such as horror, science fiction, mystery, adventure, musical, romantic comedy, or domestic drama? Some combination of genres (comedy-adventure) or a recognizable subcategory of a genre (buddy cops 'n' robbers, teen-slasher horror flick, *film noir* mystery)? Some reviewers like to have a brief plot summary before they see the movie; other viewers want to experience the film free of preconceived ideas or expectations. (Hint: If the film is a classic, popular, or current movie, production information is often available online from the many studio, movie review, or film studies Web sites. Books on film in your library may also provide such information, although they will not contain facts about the most current movies.)

3. **Try to arrange multiple viewing opportunities.** It's difficult to write any kind of detailed treatment of a film you have seen only once, as most viewers need at least one screening just to take in plot and character development. If the choice of film is yours, you may find it much easier to write about one that is on DVD so that you can see it more than once as well as replay specific scenes for closer study. Multiple screenings may be necessary if you plan to quote dialogue, which must be presented accurately. (Remember that all kinds of films may be available, without charge, from your community's public library.)

4. **Take notes as you watch.** It's easier, of course, to take notes while watching a film at home than it is in a darkened movie theater or even in a classroom. But you can do it, even if you have to struggle to decipher some of your scrawl later. As you watch, take notes on the plot or story line, the sequence of events (told

chronologically, in flashback, or in some other nontraditional way?), the time and places in which the narrative occurs, the character development and interactions, and any cinematic elements (camera shots, lighting, sound, etc.) that seem especially striking. Jot down your reactions to key scenes, characters, or lines of dialogue in the film, and make notes on parts you may already know will be important to your particular assignment. As the film unfolds, do you see any commentary on particular values or cultural assumptions?

5. **Make more notes immediately after the screening.** While your memory is fresh, ask and try to answer questions for yourself. Did you like or dislike the film? Mixed reaction? Why? What were the best or worst parts? Try to record some specific reasons for your opinions. Begin to use your critical thinking skills here: what is the film "about"? That is, what larger themes, values, or point of view does this film communicate to its viewers? For example, does this film comment on the triumph of good over evil, the loss of innocence, the search for love in the modern world, materialism in our society? Even movies that one might view as "purely entertainment" have a point of view toward the actions and characters presented in their stories. What is your film saying about certain social, political, or personal values? Is the film positive, satiric, or cynical about these values? Do you agree or disagree with the stances taken in the film?

6. **Review your notes in light of your assignment's purpose.** At this point, do you have enough ideas to draft a tentative thesis (and perhaps an essay map) for your particular assignment? For example, if you are writing a review of a movie, do you have a clear idea of what the movie is about, your evaluation of it, and some reasons to offer for that opinion? You may need to reorganize your notes in order to focus your efforts at this stage. Remember, you can't talk about every aspect of a movie. Often movie review essays in composition classes will focus on two or three main points about the film. To help you select important discussion points, try rearranging your notes into useful groups (for example: notes on acting, notes on the screenplay, notes on the settings). Which ideas look most promising in order to illustrate and support your thesis? (One professional reviewer uses index cards to "bunch together" those notes that might make up a good discussion point; you could also type your notes on a computer and then move the similar notes together to see what you have.)

    At this stage, many writers will have a working thesis in mind but now see the wisdom of screening the movie one more time to clarify their supporting claims and to collect evidence to support those points.

7. **Watch the film again with a more analytical eye.** During this screening (and perhaps during repeated viewings of particular scenes), you can focus your attention on those aspects of the film you want to write about in your essay. If you already have a sense of the claims you want to make about the film, collect specific details you might use to illustrate and support your ideas.

    If at this stage you are still searching for your thesis or main supporting points, try posing questions for yourself before you watch the film again. What parts of the film were confusing to you (e.g., a character's decision, an ambiguous ending) and why? Concentrate on the most powerful images that stuck with you from the first viewing. Or try to analyze the three most memorable scenes. What do these images or scenes contribute to your understanding of and response to the film? Why is the film titled as it is? Asking "why" as you watch a second time may uncover interesting questions about the film that your essay will answer, responses that will inform other viewers. (◆ Writing analytically about film has much in common with literary analysis, so you may find it helpful to review pages 457–458 in Chapter 16 for some general tips regarding common elements such as characterization, setting, point of view, and narrative structure.)

8. **As you begin to draft, be aware of certain conventions particular to writing about film.** For example, most movie review essays will include a brief summary of the movie's story. It may be clearer for folks who have not seen the movie to read the summary in a paragraph near the essay's beginning, though in some essays the plot may be effectively interwoven throughout the discussion. (*Special note:* If presenting a complete plot summary would give away a surprise ending, the name of the villain, or other information that would diminish the enjoyment of the potential moviegoer, you can acknowledge that you are holding back certain information. Or you can adopt the handy phrase "Spoiler Alert," which professional reviewers use to warn readers to skip the next sentence or two if they wish to remain in the dark about a particular detail.) In addition to a brief summary, reviews usually offer some production information, such as names of the leading actors and director and the year of the film; your essay may also present pertinent background or historical information about the film if it is relevant to the assignment.

   Another consideration for the writer is whether to use "I" in a movie review essay. Although some famous movie reviewers consistently use "I" and "my" in their reviews ("I am putting this movie on my 'All-Time Worst List'"), others do not, so ask your instructor which choice is preferable for your assignment.

9. **Use clear, precise language.** As you draft and revise, assume that your readers have not watched the film and consequently cannot visualize what you have seen unless you help them. Make your discussions as clear as possible, using details and vivid language to re-create the images you are recalling. For ease of discussion, writers on film sometimes make use of a few cinematic terms to help communicate what they saw ("Hollywood Ending") or to describe how something was done on the screen ("voice-over"). A glossary at the end of this chapter provides vocabulary that might prove useful as you watch and write about film, though essays for a general audience should not become overly technical.

10. **In your final draft, it's wise to recheck the film to ensure your accuracy.** Be sure that you have the characters' names right and that any lines you quoted are correctly transcribed. (◆ For help punctuating dialogue, see the guidelines for quoted material on pages 586–588 in Part Four.) Remember that the names of films are italicized in print or underlined in handwriting, not placed within quotation marks.

Watching and thinking about films are enjoyable experiences for most people, and writing analytically about film can extend that pleasure as you offer your thoughtful opinions to others in an organized, persuasive way. Practice your good writing skills as you create an essay worthy of Four Stars!

Problems to Avoid

Don't be tempted to just "pun and run." Movie reviews are rather well known for offering critics the opportunity to throw out witty phrases or memorable one-liners to praise or slash actors, directors, or scripts. You may have read lines similar to "her acting ran the range of emotions from A to B" or "his performance was so wooden you could have boarded up the windows with it." Or perhaps you've just seen a "must flee" rather than a "must see" movie. Puns and vivid figurative language often do add humor and spice that increase our enjoyment of reading a review. However, witty one-liners, as on-target as they may be, are never a substitute for good analysis. Even if you think a movie is so frightfully bad that its screening could be used to extract confessions out of hardened serial killers, you must offer some reasons for your evaluation. It isn't enough to say of a movie, "I just liked it" or "It was a tragic waste of two hours of my life"— explain your judgment and illustrate your claims with ample details from the film.

Keep your primary purpose in mind. Although you may need to include a plot summary in your essay, don't allow it to dominate your discussion. Remember that your larger purpose in a review or analytical essay is to offer an opinion—to give readers your recommendation and/or to interpret some important parts of the film. If your reaction to a film is mixed, you may certainly say so in a review essay as long as you avoid seeming wishy-washy. It's true that most bad films have at least one redeeming feature and many good films have flaws. But even if some aspect of the film bothered you to the point of wanting to pitch your popcorn (an annoying soundtrack, for example), ask yourself if that element alone merits a main point in your discussion. If, in fairness, you feel you must mention a strength in an overall negative review or point out a weakness in a generally positive review, then do so—but keep your main purpose and thesis in mind. Focus your discussion chiefly on those parts of your film that best support your overall evaluation or interpretation.

Sample Student Essay

In this essay a student recommends one of his favorite movies to his classmates. According to this writer, his hardest task was describing the mystery's twisting plot without spoiling the movie's surprises for the potential viewers. As you read this review, do you find that his comments encourage you to see this movie?

Introduction:
Questions
lead to thesis
and map
(plot, cast,
dialogue)

CATCH THE BLACK BIRD

1　　Tired of watching movies with predictable plots, repetitive car chases,

and excessive shoot-outs? Bored with lame performances and awful dialogue?

As you stroll the aisles at your favorite movie rental store, leave those unoriginal stories and special effects behind. Reach for something new by reaching for something older. If you are looking for a crime caper with surprising plot twists, an unbeatable cast, and some of the best dialogue ever written, reach for *The Maltese Falcon* (1941).

2   Adapted from the detective novel by Dashiell Hammett, with direction and screenplay by John Huston, *The Maltese Falcon* is regarded as one of the first and best movies in the *film noir* genre, films popular from the early 1940s to the late 1950s (revisited by Hollywood more recently with *L.A. Confidential*, *Body Heat*, and *Chinatown*). These films typically tell dark stories of urban crime and are filled with seedy characters, often including a hard-boiled detective and a beautiful, treacherous woman. Frequently filmed in shadows and night scenes, these movies have a gritty visual style that emphasizes the bleak and corrupt atmosphere of their stories.

Production and genre information

3   The plot of *The Maltese Falcon* is complex and unpredictable, mainly because throughout the film almost no character tells the truth the first time around . . . or even the second. The story begins in the office of tough-guy detective Sam Spade and his partner Miles Archer, hired by a beautiful Miss Wonderly to rescue her sister from a hoodlum named Thursby. Archer trails Thursby but is shot (at close range and with his coat buttoned over his gun). Spade is suspected of killing his partner because he has had an affair with Archer's wife, but then Thursby is killed too. The plot twists when Miss Wonderly admits (after trying out a few more phony stories) that she is really a thief named Brigid O'Shaughnessy, who claims she was double-crossed by Thursby, one of a handful of shady characters searching for a statue of a jewel-encrusted bird, now covered with a black veneer. Brigid convinces Spade to help her get the stolen bird, and an uneasy romantic relationship begins to grow. In pursuit of the mysterious falcon, Spade must outwit Brigid's dangerous enemies— the "Fatman," his murderous young henchman Wilmer, and Joel Cairo—not to mention a cop who hates Spade, Archer's angry widow, and Brigid herself. Characters make alliances one minute and then betray each other the next. By the movie's famous ending, Spade faces his toughest moral dilemma: whose side is he on?

Supporting Point One: Surprising plot twists

(Brief summary)

Supporting
Point Two:
Excellent cast

A. Bogart as
antihero

4   But it's not the plot twists that ultimately make this film so watchable—it's the fascinating cast of characters and the actors who play them perfectly. The best is Humphrey Bogart as the archetypal tough guy, whose un-pretty, no-nonsense face is an ideal match for the cold, cynical Spade. Bogart is totally believable as the unsentimental antihero: his reaction to his partner's brutal murder, for example, is a flat "yeah, tough break." Street smart and confident, he won't take guff from the cops, sees through Brigid's various poses, and knows how to manipulate the criminals in his own behalf. In one scene when the Fatman won't deal with him to his liking, he convincingly throws a violent fit of anger, smashes a glass, and stalks out—then grins all the way to the elevator, laughing over his successful act.

B. Memorable
villains:
Greenstreet,
Lorre, Astor

5   The villains in the film are quirky and unforgettable too. Sidney Greenstreet is Kaspar Gutman, the huge "Fatman," whose chuckles and nice manners only partially hide his creepy obsession with the Black Bird. Peter Lorre plays bad guy Joel Cairo like a prissy little penguin with lethal craziness. And certainly Mary Astor as Brigid is much more than a Pretty Face. Like a quick-change artist, she's the Good/Bad Girl, who lies, tearfully admits her faults, and then lies again. When "helpless" Brigid begs Sam for protection, he replies, "You won't need much help . . . you're good. It's chiefly in your eyes, I think—and that throb you get in your voice. . . ." It takes a talented actress to play such a convincing liar, especially one who fools the audience every time she opens her mouth.

Supporting
Point Three:
Witty
dialogue
(examples)

6   The best part of the movie, however, may be the fast-paced, witty dialogue, full of wisecracks and sharp retorts. Sam gets most of the good lines, of course. Nobody's fool and slightly corrupt himself, he lets Brigid know he spotted her as a fake in his office from the beginning: "Oh, we didn't exactly believe your story . . . we believed your two hundred dollars." And he coolly answers an accusation of murder with the ironic question, "How'd I kill him, I forget." A lot of the humor is directed at Wilmer, the nasty young thug who is forever being needled by Spade. Relieving Wilmer of all his guns with a simple maneuver, Spade sneers, "Come on, this'll put you in solid with your boss" and then tells the Fatman how

Wilmer lost his weapons: "a crippled newsy [newsboy] took 'em away from him but I made him give them back." To quote the famous lines of the last scene here would give away too much of the film's ending, but Sam's speech to the deceitful Brigid is so full of deliciously cold-blooded (but well-deserved) sarcasm that many film buffs know it by heart.

7   The movie's surprising conclusion wraps up a near-perfect film. Though it's not a warm, happy ending, it's a just one. Sam Spade may not always play fair or by the cops' rules, and he may be tempted by desire and money. Ultimately, however, he must follow a code of his own to maintain self-respect. He remains a hard-core detective to the end. Despite all the copycat detectives in films since 1941, there is truly only one Sam Spade. And as the Fatman explains as he agrees to sell out Wilmer to the cops, "There is only one Maltese falcon." So true, and its story is one of the best movies ever made.

Conclusion: An original hero and a compelling story make a great film

Humphrey Bogart, Peter Lorre, Mary Astor, and Sydney Greenstreet star in *The Maltese Falcon* (1941).

© Bettmann/CORBIS

PRACTICING WHAT YOU'VE LEARNED

A. Evaluate the effectiveness of the movie review that follows. Does the critic present a clear recommendation and overview of *Slumdog Millionaire*? Does he offer persuasive reasons for his opinions, supported with enough convincing examples and details from the movie, or are you unconvinced? If you have seen this film, do you agree or disagree with the review, and why? If you have not seen the movie, would this review encourage you to do so?

B. *Collaborative Activity:* Working in a group with two other students, compare your assessments of Ty Burr's use of specific details to describe various parts of this movie. In addition, look closely at his tone and his use of colorful language. What are the effects, for example, of such phrases as "deep-dish audience-rouser," "blow-dried slickster," and "popcorn durability"? Be ready to report your group's analysis to the class as a whole.

Professional Essay

Cinematic Riches in *Millionaire*

Ty Burr

Ty Burr is a movie critic for the *Boston Globe* newspaper, where this review appeared in November 2008. Prior to assuming this job in 2002, he was the chief video critic at *Entertainment Weekly* for ten years. He is the author of three books on the film industry, the most recent being *The Best Old Movies for Families* (2007).

1   I'll keep this simple: Cancel whatever you're doing tonight and go see *Slumdog Millionaire* instead. Yes, you, the girl obsessed with *Twilight* and the guy still hung up on *The Dark Knight*. Take the grandparents, too, and the teenagers. Everyone can play.

2   You've never heard of the actors. A third of the film is in Hindi. Much of it takes place in the most fetid, poverty-ridden corners of the Indian subcontinent, and most of it isn't nice. Yet this sprawling, madly romantic fairy-tale epic is the kind of deep-dish audience-rouser we've long given up hoping for from Hollywood. *Slumdog* is a soaring return to form for director Danny Boyle (*Trainspotting*), but mostly it's just a miracle of mainstream pop moviemaking—the sort of thing modern filmmakers aren't supposed to make anymore. Except they just did.

3   Unfolding with the scope and brisk energy of a Dickens novel transplanted to Asia, *Slumdog Millionaire* is the tale of Jamal Malik (Dev Patel), a lanky, sad-faced Mumbai slum kid who, when we first meet him, is poised to win 20 million rupees on India's version of *Who Wants to Be a Millionaire*. He has already aced the first

rounds; tonight, the entire country will be tuning in to hear his final answer. The show's host, a blow-dried slickster played by Bollywood superstar Anil Kapoor, is not happy. So much so, in fact, that he has arranged for the local cops to give the kid a working-over.

4   Is Jamal a genius? Is he a cheat? How would a young man with no education and a life on the streets know whose picture is on a US $100 bill? That's what a police lieutenant (Irrfan Khan, the father in *The Namesake*) hopes to beat out of him. When torture doesn't work, he sits the boy down in front of a videotape of his appearances on the show and demands to know, question by question, how Jamal did it. And thus an entire life unfurls before us, as does the history of modern India itself.

5   Boyle, working from Simon Beaufoy's adaptation of a novel by Vikas Swarup, gives us Jamal's unsentimental education in head-spinning, vertiginous flashbacks that become the main story line. Each answer on the TV show becomes a key that unlocks another chapter of the boy's past, a pat narrative device kept from cliché by the deft, vital filmmaking.

6   The first sequence, prompted by a question involving a famous Indian movie star—the sort of factoid any Mumbai kid would know—shows the hero's early years as both horrifying and exuberant. Jamal (played as a child by Ayush Mahesh Khedekar) and his brother Salim (Azharuddin Mohammed Ismail) take their desperate existence as merely the soup in which they swim; Boyle and cinematographer Anthony Dod Mantle visualize that soup with an astonishing pullback that reveals the vastness of Mumbai's tin-roof chaos.

7   The siblings' innocence, such as it is, ends when their mother (Sanchita Choudary) is killed in the anti-Muslim riots of 1992–93 and they take to the streets, picking up an urchin girl named Latika (Rubina Ali) in the process. The three small musketeers are taken in by a smiling villain (Ankur Vikal) who runs a school for child beggars; what this Fagin does to create an extra-special line of underage street singers marks the grueling nadir of *Slumdog Millionaire*, yet the movie, knowing such things happen, doesn't let us look away.

8   The trio grow into adolescence and young adulthood, by which point the brothers have chosen their respective paths. The adult Salim (Madhur Mittal) has gone for quick cash and gangster glory; Latika (Freida Pinto) is the kept plaything of a mobster boss (Mahesh Manjrekar). Jamal has found work as a gofer at one of the new Mumbai's energetic, youthful call centers. He serves tea, absorbs everything around him, and, when needed, dons the headset to deal with cranky old ladies in Scotland.

9   Good brother, bad brother, childhood sweetheart torn between the underworld and true love: We've all been here before. Warner Brothers and MGM used to dine out on this stuff in the 1930s, with actors like Jimmy Cagney and Pat O'Brien and Ann Sheridan in the roles. Boyle cherishes the tale's popcorn durability, though—it's an old story because it works—and his team retrofits it, polishes it up, and sets it careening.

10   Mantle's images and Chris Dickens' editing are infused with the go-go colors and rhythms of the subcontinent; the co-direction by Loveleen Tandan adds to the sense of teeming sensory overload; the music keens with beauty and corn. (Even the

subtitles feel fresh, popping up like speech balloons all over the screen.) The characters are archetypes draped with specifics of time and place and, in Jamal's case, of character. As Patel plays him, he seems too studious—too inward-directed—to be the hero of such a big movie, yet that's why we come to love him. In the rushing slipstream of *Slumdog Millionaire,* he's our anchor.

11   This sort of headlong melodrama has long since dropped out of fashion in our irony-drenched age, and some audiences, I'm sure, will turn up their noses. There have been grumblings that the film's just too pretty, and that a movie about India directed by an Englishman can't be taken seriously. Allow me to float the idea that it's possible to talk yourself out of intense moviegoing pleasure.

12   And *Slumdog Millionaire* is a pleasure, as Jamal negotiates every obstacle before him (including, in one nerve-wracking turn of events, a psychological showdown with Kapoor's preening host), and teeters between intelligence, luck, and a destiny that he has in large part made for himself. In his story, the movie implies, is that of an entire modern nation. After the dust has settled, the Bollywood dance scene that explodes under the closing credits feels both incongruous and earned: Young India kicking up its heels.

13   You may even feel like dancing in the aisles yourself. Sure, the real world doesn't always work this way. Have you forgotten that this is one of the reasons why we go to movies in the first place?

© Fox Searchlight/Courtesy Everett Collection

Despite controversy over issues of class and gender stereotyping, *Slumdog Millionare* won the 2008 Academy Award for Best Picture.

Suggestions for Writing

1. Select a film that's available on DVD, and write a movie review that might appear in your local newspaper, addressed to a general audience. Explain your evaluation of the movie by providing at least two or three important reasons, each supported with details from the film. (Suggestion: As you decide on a movie to review, you might look at the American Film Institute Web site, containing their list of the top 100 American movies. Although you may not agree with the Institute, this ranking will suggest some films admired over the years by both critics and viewers. Now may be your chance to discover for yourself why a particular movie is considered a classic.)

2. Analyze one of your favorite movies. Write an essay explaining why you find it so satisfying. Or, if you prefer, tackle a movie that seems to be loved (or loathed) by everyone—but you. Write an essay that shows the world why your assessment is the better one.

3. Find a movie review (newspaper, magazine, online) with which you strongly disagree. Write an essay in which your analysis shows why the reviewer is off track in his or her evaluation of this movie.

4. Write an essay comparing/contrasting a literary work (novel, short story, or drama) you know well to its movie version (for example, one of the *Harry Potter* or *Lord of the Rings* movies, *The Grapes of Wrath*, or *The Curious Case of Benjamin Button*), explaining how effectively you think the original story was captured on the Big Screen.

5. Movies are often controversial for a variety of reasons, including their point of view, content, or style. Although *Slumdog Millionaire*, the movie reviewed on pages 514–516, won the Academy Award for Best Picture in 2008, some viewers criticized the film for romanticizing poverty and perpetuating stereotypes. Watch this movie or another one that has stirred debate, and then research the controversy around it; write an essay that argues your opinion but also clearly informs your readers about different reactions. (◆ For help documenting your research sources, turn to Chapter 14.)

6. Think of a film story (fictional or factual) that deeply impressed you, one that you feel presents a thoughtful message, question, or challenge to its viewers. Explore this idea in a personal essay as it applies to values or choices in your own life. Or perhaps you have seen a film that changed your mind about an important topic. Explain how the film has affected your point of view.

Glossary of Film Terms

Camera angle The position of the camera in relation to the subject being filmed. Some common camera angles include the close-up (often of a face), the long shot, and the high angle.

Deus ex machina Refers to use of an improbable plot device to save the hero from a difficult situation (the cavalry or police arrive at just the right moment, for example). The phrase, meaning "god from the machine," came from ancient Greek drama when a crisis was solved by the appearance of a god, lowered onto the stage with ropes or other equipment. Today the term is most often used to criticize an unbelievable rescue in a weak script.

Dialogue The words spoken by the characters in a film.

Editing Technically, editing is the splicing together of different pieces of film. The order in which a filmmaker links shots in a single scene, and then links scenes together, to construct the entire film plays a crucial role in communicating the film's meaning.

Fade A transitional device in which the picture on the screen gradually darkens to black before another scene begins.

Flashback A scene or sequence of scenes that take the story into the past.

Genre Movies may be categorized into recognizable types that share similarities in themes, narrative structures, characters, style, mood, and other characteristics. Some common movie genres include horror, romantic comedy, Westerns, adventure, science fiction, crime, and mystery. Many movies are a blend of more than one genre.

"Guilty Pleasure" Refers to a movie that a reviewer enjoyed in spite of recognizing that the film has serious flaws (a comedy that is fun even though it is over-the-top silly or an action movie that is thrilling even though its special effects are ridiculously unbelievable).

Hero/Antihero The hero of a film is usually a major character who displays worthy values and admirable characteristics, often including courage and self-sacrifice for the good of others. An antihero rejects traditional values or societal norms, but may nevertheless appeal to audiences because of his or her individualism or adherence to a personal code of behavior.

"Hollywood Ending" Refers to a movie's happy ending that often seems contrived or tacked on merely to make audiences feel good as they leave the theater.

Location A film that is shot "on location" is filmed in the geographical area that is present in the story rather than in a studio.

Narrative structure Refers to the way a story's plotline is constructed, through arrangement of scenes and point of view.

Scene A period of screen activity in which the action is usually confined to one time and space.

Sets Constructed physical environments in scenes.

Setting Place and time (year, hour of day, month, season, etc.) of a particular scene or entire film. Lighting and sound effects may influence the mood of a particular setting.

Shot A single image on the screen; a variety of shots may be edited to form a sequence that makes up a scene.

Slow motion Film speed is slowed to produce a desired effect on the audience; frequently used in modern movies to underscore an emotional interaction between characters or to emphasize the horror of tragedy or violence. (In contrast, *fast motion* is often used for comedic effect or to show frenzied activity in a passage of time.)

Soft focus Refers to scenes in which the images on the screen appear slightly fuzzy or out of focus to the viewer; often used to create a romantic effect.

Special effects Refers to a variety of methods, from makeup to complex computer technology, used to create characters or scenes that cannot be produced normally (e.g., space travel, superhuman powers, battle scenes, dinosaurs).

"Spoiler Alert" Phrase used by movie reviewers to warn those who have not seen the film that an important plot element (the identity of the murderer, for example) is about to be revealed.

Voice-over Refers to the commentary heard over the screen images, spoken by a narrator or character whose remarks directly address the audience.

CHAPTER 19

Writing in the World of Work

Imagine you are a manager of a business who receives the following memo from one of the sales representatives:

> Our biggest customer in Atlanta asked me to forward the shipment to the company warehouse and I said I could not realizing how serious a decision this was I changed my mind. This OK with you?

Did the salesperson mean to say that at first he thought he could send the shipment, but then changed his mind?

> Our biggest customer in Atlanta asked me to forward the shipment to the company warehouse and I said I could. Not realizing how serious a decision this was, I changed my mind.

Or did he mean he first thought he couldn't but then reconsidered?

> Our biggest customer in Atlanta asked me to forward the shipment to the company warehouse and I said I could not. Realizing how serious a decision this was, I changed my mind.

What would you do as the manager? Very probably you would stop your current work and contact the salesperson to clarify the situation before you gave final approval. Because of the unclear communication, the extra effort required will cost your business valuable time, energy, and possibly customer satisfaction.

The preceding scenario is not far-fetched; unclear writing hurts businesses and organizations in every country in the world. Consequently, here is a bold claim: *Almost all workplaces today demand employees with good communication skills.*

Although specific writing tasks vary from job to job, profession to profession, successful businesses rely on the effective sharing of information among managers, coworkers, and customers. No employer ever wants to see confusing reports or puzzling memos that result in lost production time, squandered resources, or aggravated clients. To maximize their organization's efficiency, employers look for and reward employees who can demonstrate the very writing skills you have been practicing in this composition course. Without question, your ability to communicate clearly in precise, organized prose will give you a competitive edge in the world of work.

© PhotoLibrary/Image Source

To help you address some of the most common on-the-job writing situations, this chapter offers general guidelines for business letters, office memos, and professional e-mail messages. A special section on the preparation of résumés at the end of the chapter will suggest ways to display your skills to any prospective employer.

Composing Business Letters

Letters in the workplace serve many purposes and audiences, so it isn't possible to illustrate each particular kind. However, it is important to note that all good business letters have some effective qualities in common. And although a business letter is clearly not a personal essay, they share many features: consideration of audience, development of a main idea, organized paragraphs, appropriate tone and diction, and clear, concise expression of thoughts.

Before you begin any letter, prewrite by considering these important questions:

1. What is the main purpose of this letter? What do you want this letter to accomplish? Are you applying for a job, requesting material, offering thanks, lodging a complaint? Perhaps it is you who are answering a request for information about a product, procedure, service, or policy. The occasions for written correspondence are too many to list, but each letter should clearly state its purpose for the reader, just as a thesis in an essay presents your main idea.

2. Who is your "audience," the person to whom you are writing? As discussed in detail on pages 19–22 in Chapter 1, effective writers select the kinds of information, the level of complexity, and even the appropriate "voice" in response to their readers' needs, knowledge, and attitudes. Remember that no matter who the recipient of your letter happens to be, all readers want clarity, not confusion; order, not chaos; and useful information, not irrelevant chitchat. Put yourself in the reader's place: what should she or he know, understand, or decide to do after reading this letter?

3. What overall impression of yourself do you want your letter to present? All business correspondence should be courteous, with a tone that shows your

appreciation for the reader's time and attention. Achieving this tone may be more difficult if you are writing a letter of complaint, but remember that to accomplish your purpose (a refund or an exchange of a purchase, for example), you must persuade, not antagonize, your reader. If you're too angry or frustrated to maintain a reasonable tone, give yourself some time to cool off before writing. A respectful tone should not, on the other hand, sound phony or pretentious ("It is indeed regrettable but I must hereby inform you . . ."). Choose the same level of language you would use in one of your polished academic essays. In short, good business writing is clear, courteous, and direct.

Business Letter Format

Most traditional business letters are neatly typed on one side of 8½-by-11-inch white bond paper. Margins are usually set for a minimum of 1¼ inches at the top and at least one inch on the left and right sides and at the bottom. Almost all professional letters now use the "block form"—that is, lines of type are flush with the left margin and paragraphs are not indented. Envelopes should match the letter paper.

Business letters typically have six primary parts:

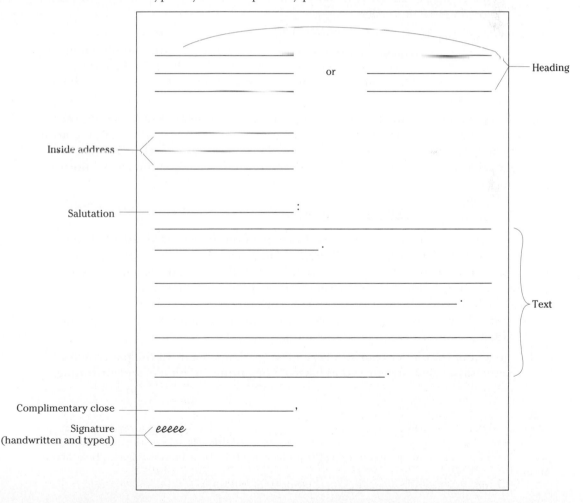

1. The **heading** of a letter is your address and the date, typed either above the inside address of the letter or in the upper right corner. If the heading is in the upper right position, the longest line should end at the one-inch margin on the right side of the page. All lines in your heading should begin evenly on the left. If you are using letterhead stationery (paper already imprinted with your business name, address, or logo), you need to add only the date.

2. The **inside address** contains the name of the person to whom you are writing, the person's title or position, the name of the company or organization, the full address (street or post office box, city, state, ZIP Code). The first line of the inside address should appear at least two lines below the last line of the heading. (The inside address information should be repeated exactly on your letter's envelope.)

   Correct use of titles and positions can be tricky. Sometimes a person has a title and an additional position; other times, the title is lengthy. In general, if a person's title has more than two words, put it on a separate line:

   > Professor Linda Payne
   > Dean, College of Liberal Arts
   > Colorado State University

   Whenever possible, direct your letter to a specific person. If you do not know the name of the person and cannot discover it before your letter must be sent, you may address the correspondence to the position held by the appropriate person(s): General Manager, Graduate Advisor, Personnel Director, City Council, and so forth.

3. The **salutation** is your letter's greeting to your reader. Begin the salutation two lines down from the inside address, and greet the person formally using the word "Dear" plus title and name (Dear Mr. Smith, Dear Ms. Jones,* Dear Dr. Black). The salutation is traditionally followed by a colon rather than the more informal comma:

   > Dear Dr. Montoya:
   > Dear Personnel Director:

   A caution: be careful to avoid sexist assumptions in your salutations. If you do not know the gender of the person to whom you are writing (initials and many first names—Chris, Pat, Jordan—are used by both men and women), do some research, if possible. When in doubt, use the title or position and last name (Dear Professor Chieu). Use of the full name (Dear Xin Chieu) or organization name (Dear Safety Council) may be preferable to the impersonal "Dear Sir or Madam," a phrase that seems stilted today.

4. The **text** of your letter consists of the message that appears in the paragraphs. As in essays, think of your text as having a beginning, a middle, and an ending.

---

*If you know that the woman you are writing prefers to be addressed as Mrs. X, address her in this way. However, if you do not know her marital status or preferred title, Ms. may be the best choice. If possible, avoid the matter altogether by using her professional title: Dear Professor Smith, Dear Mayor Alvarez.

Although there is no rule about the number of paragraphs in any business letter, most letters contain the following:

- a first paragraph that clearly states the reason for writing (think about a thesis in an essay);
- one or more paragraphs that present the necessary details or explanation of the reason for writing (think body paragraphs in an essay);
- a last paragraph that sums up the message in a positive way, offers thanks if appropriate, and, on occasion, provides information to help reader and writer make contact (think conclusion in an essay).

Because professional people receive so much mail, business letters should be brief and to the point. *Above all, readers want clarity!* Scrutinize your prose for any words or phrases that might mislead or confuse your reader. Select precise words and create trim sentences that present your message in the clearest, most straightforward way possible. (◆ For help writing clear, concise prose, review Chapters 6 and 7.)

If possible, without sacrificing clarity or necessary information, keep your letter to one page. Single-spaced paragraphs of eight lines or fewer are easiest to read. Skip a line between paragraphs. If you must go to a second page, type your name, the date, and the page number in an upper corner. If you discover that you have only one or two lines to carry over to the second page, try to condense your text or, if you must, squeeze or expand the margins just a bit. Try not to divide paragraphs between pages, and do not split a word between pages. Second and subsequent pages should be plain paper, without letterhead material.

5. The **complimentary closing** of a business letter is a conventional farewell to the reader, typed two lines below the last line of the text. The two most common phrases for closing formal business correspondence are "Sincerely" and "Yours truly." Stick with these unless you have a more informal relationship with the person you are writing. In those cases, you might use such closings as "Cordially" or "Warm regards." The first letter of the first closing word is capitalized, and the closing is followed by a comma.

6. The **signature** part of a business letter contains both your handwritten name and, beneath that, your typed name (plus your title, if appropriate). Leave approximately four lines for your handwritten name, which should be written in black ink:

> Sincerely,
>
> *Jane Doe*
>
> Jane Doe
> Professor of Philosophy

Do not forget to sign your letter! Such an oversight not only looks careless but may also suggest to the reader that this is merely a mass-produced form letter.

7. Some letters contain additional information below the signature. Typical notes include the word "enclosure" (or "encl.") to indicate inclusion of additional material (which may be named) or a distribution list to indicate other persons who

are receiving a copy of this letter. Distribution is indicated by the word "copy" or by the letters "c" or "cc" (for "courtesy copy"), followed by a colon and the name(s); if more than one person is listed, the names should appear in alphabetical order.

Copy: Mayor Sue Jones	Enclosure: résumé
or	*or*
cc: Mayor Sue Jones,	Encl.: résumé
Dr. Inga York	

If someone else types your letter, put your initials in capital letters, a slash mark, and the typist's initials in lowercase:

JCW/ma

In formal business correspondence, avoid any sort of postscript (P.S.).

Some last advice: Most business letters today are written on a word processor, whose spelling and grammar programs can help writers find and fix typos. But, as in any piece of writing, always proofread for errors carefully—and repeatedly! Never trust your spell-checker to catch all possible errors. Don't undercut the message you are sending by failing to revise misspelled words, inaccurate names, ungrammatical sentences, or sloppy punctuation. Also, be sure to select a clear, traditional type font (such as Times New Roman; no fancy script or gothic styles, please), set in a readable size (often 12 point), and use only a printer that can produce dark, high-grade type.

PRACTICING WHAT YOU'VE LEARNED

© Canstock Images, Inc. / Index Stock Imagery

Find a recent business letter you or someone you know has received. This letter might be a request for a charitable donation, an announcement of some school policy, a letter of recommendation, or even a parking-violation summons. Assess the effectiveness of the letter: is it clear? Informative? To the point? Write a one-paragraph critique of the letter that identifies both its strengths and any weaknesses you see.

ASSIGNMENT

© CORBIS

Writing business letters becomes easier with practice. Think of an upcoming occasion that will require you to write a professional letter. Perhaps you are asking for a job or accepting one? Applying for a scholarship, grant, or school loan? Requesting an interview or letter of recommendation? Complaining to your landlord? Ordering or returning a product? The choices are many, but try to select a letter that you might indeed send sometime soon. Limit your letter to one page, and revise as many times as necessary to illustrate your thorough understanding of purpose, audience, format, and style. Don't forget to proofread carefully!

Sample Business Letter

Art Tech Studio
802 West Street
Fort Collins, CO 80525
May 10, 2009

Mr. Thomas Valdez
General Manager
Harmony Products, Inc.
645 Monroe Avenue
Little Rock, AR 90056

Dear Mr. Valdez:

Thank you for your May 5 order for twenty of my hand-designed laptop sleeves and for your advance payment check of $250. I am delighted that your company wishes to stock my painted cloth sleeves in both your Little Rock and Fayetteville stores.

The sleeves are being packed in individual boxes this week and should arrive by Air Flight Mail at your main office no later than May 25. If you wish for me to use express mail for quicker arrival, please let me know.

Many thanks again for your interest in my work and for your recent order. I am planning to attend a marketing seminar in Little Rock, June 5–8; I will call you next week to see if we might arrange a brief meeting at your convenience on one of those days. Until then, should you need to contact me, please call my studio (970/555-6009).

Sincerely,

Rachel Zimmerman

Rachel Zimmerman

Enclosure: receipt

Creating Memos

A memo, short for "memorandum," is a common form of communication *within* a business or an organization. Memos, especially those sent by e-mail, are often more informal than business letters, and they may be addressed to more than one person (a committee, a sales staff, an advisory board, etc.). Memos may be sent up or down the chain of command at a particular workplace, or they may be distributed laterally, across a department or between offices. Despite the prevalence of e-mail, some companies still use paper memos for certain tasks; though the format may vary slightly from organization to organization, it often appears in this manner:

TO:	name of recipient(s) and/or title(s)
FROM:	name of sender and title; handwritten initials
DATE:	day, month, year
SUBJECT:	brief identification of the memo's subject matter

The message follows in one or more paragraphs.

Note that in paper memos the name of the sender is usually accompanied by the sender's handwritten initials, rather than a full signature as in a business letter. Also, in some memos, the term "Re" ("in reference to") may be substituted for the word "Subject."

Many memos are brief, containing important bulletins, announcements, or reminders, as illustrated in this sample:

TO:	Editorial Staff
FROM:	Louise Presaria, Editor-in-Chief *LP*
DATE:	April 22, 2009
RE:	Silver Eagle Award Banquet

Because the current snowstorm is presenting problems with public transportation and also with heating outages in our building, the annual Silver Eagle Banquet originally scheduled for tomorrow night has been postponed for one week. It is now rescheduled for Thursday, April 30, beginning at 7:30 P.M., in the Whitaker conference room.

I look forward to seeing you all there. Each of you has done a marvelous job this year and greatly deserves to share the benefits that come with our industry's most prestigious award.

Other in-house memos—those explaining policies or procedures, for example—may be long and complex. Lengthy memos may begin with a summary or statement of general purpose and may use headings (such as "Background Information," "Previous Action," or "Recommendations") to identify various parts of the discussion.

All business memos, paper or electronic, regardless of length, share a common goal: the clear, concise communication of useful information from writer to reader.

Sending Professional E-Mail

Although the world of work will never be totally paperless, more businesses today are relying on computer-based communications to send or request information, both inside and outside their organizations.

Electronic mail, or e-mail, offers a number of advantages to employees and customers. It's faster and easier than postal service (now known to many as "snail mail"), as you can compose or forward a message to one person or many people, across the building or across the country, and receive a reply almost instantly. Messages may be sent and read from a variety of sites, from desktop to portable devices. Unlike landline telephones, most e-mail programs have an "attachments" feature that allows users to send documents, forms, graphics, or pictures.

Because e-mail is useful in so many ways to different kinds of businesses and organizations, there is no one-size-fits-all format. Consequently, it's always a good idea to acquaint yourself with customary use of e-mail at your place of work. In addition, here are some suggestions for improving the quality of all electronic communications:

1. **Use a helpful subject line.** Successful business leaders today may receive scores of e-mail messages every day, so many that they are tempted to delete any unrecognizable mail that might be "spam" (an unsolicited message or sales offer) or contain a "virus" that might destroy their files. To ensure that your message will be opened and read, always use specific words in the subject line to clearly delineate the central focus or key words of your correspondence ("Project Thunderbolt contracts"). Using a specific subject line will also be helpful if your reader wants to reread your message later and needs to find it quickly in a long list of e-mails.

2. **Begin appropriately.** Unlike a business letter, e-mail needs no heading or inside address, but a new communication should begin with an appropriate greeting, depending on the formality of the occasion. For example, if you are writing an officer of another company to ask for information, you might begin with a traditional salutation (Dear Mr. Hall:). An informal memo to a coworker might have a more casual greeting, depending on your relationship to that person (Hello, Bill; Good morning, Ms. Merrill). Some companies prefer the standard To-From-Date-Subject memo form discussed earlier in this chapter.

3. **Keep your message brief.** Long messages are difficult to read on screens; all that scrolling and flipping back and forth to check information can be tiresome. If possible, confine your message to one screen. Working people are busy, so try to follow the advice given previously in this chapter regarding business letters and memos: clearly state your purpose, explain in a concise manner, and conclude gracefully.

4. **Make it easy to read.** To avoid contributing to your reader's eyestrain, write messages that are visually pleasant. Keep your paragraphs short, and skip a line between each paragraph. If your message is long, break it up with headings, numbered lists, or "bullets." Use a readable, plain font.

5. **Check your tone.** Your e-mail messages should sound professional and cordial. Unlike personal e-mail, which may contain slang, fragments, asides, or funny graphics, business e-mails should be written in good standard English and be straight to the point. If you're angry, resist the temptation to fly to the computer and "flame"; cool off and compose a thoughtful, persuasive response instead. Be especially careful about the use of irony or humor: without nonverbal clues, readers may misinterpret your words and react in a manner opposite the one you intended. In general, strive for a polite, friendly tone, using the clearest, most precise words you can muster.

6. **Sign off.** If your e-mail is performing a task similar to that of a business letter, you may wish to close in a traditional way:

> Yours truly,
> Scott Muranjan

You may also want to create a standard sign-off that not only includes your name but also your title, telephone and fax numbers, and postal and e-mail addresses. Such information is helpful for readers who wish to contact you later.

However, if your e-mail is more akin to an informal memo between coworkers, you may find it appropriate to end with a friendly thought or word of thanks and your first name:

> I'm looking forward to working with you on the Blue file. See you at Tuesday's meeting.
> Scott

Allow your sense of occasion and audience to dictate the kind of closing each e-mail requires.

7. **Revise, proofread, copy, send.** The very ease of e-mail makes it tempting to send messages that may not be truly ready to go. All your professional correspondence should look just that: professional. Take some time to revise for clarity and tone; always proofread. Double-check figures and dates, and run the spell-checker if you have one. If time permits, print out a "hard copy" of important messages to look over before you hit the Send button. If you need to keep track of your correspondence, make a computer file or a print copy for your office.

Problems to Avoid

Electronic mail has revolutionized the workplace, but it is not without its disadvantages. Computers crash, files vaporize, printers freeze, and so on. Work on developing patience and give yourself time to use other methods of communication if necessary. Meanwhile, here are two other tips:

Business e-mail is not private. Perhaps because of individual passwords or because of experience with sealed postal mail, employees often believe that their e-mail is private correspondence. It is not! Employers have the legal right to read any e-mail sent from their organizations. Moreover, you never know when someone may be peering at a screen over the shoulder of the intended recipient. And there's always the danger of hitting the wrong button, sending your thoughts to an entire list of people when you meant to contact only one. To avoid embarrassing yourself—or even endangering your job—never send inappropriate comments, angry responses, petty remarks, or personal information through your business e-mail. Never send confidential or "top secret" business information through e-mail without proper authorization. Learn to use e-mail in a productive way that protects both you and your organization.

Mind your netiquette! Although no one requires that you don your white kid gloves to hit those computer keys, rules of etiquette for e-mail writers are important. Here are a few suggestions for well-behaved writers:

- Don't "shout" your messages in all capital letters. IT'S TOO HARD TO READ A SCREEN FULL OF SAME-SIZED LETTERS. Occasionally, you may type a word in capital letters or bold for emphasis, but use this technique sparingly.

- Be cautious about using Internet and texting shorthand or in-house abbreviations ("the TR6 project"), especially in messages to other organizations. If certain shorthand signs or phrases, such as BTW (by the way), FWIW (for what it's worth), or G2G (got to go), are routinely used in casual e-mail at your place of work, feel free to adopt them. However, most business correspondence is more formal and not all abbreviations may be universally recognized. When in doubt, spell it out. Business messages depend on clarity and a mutual understanding of all terms. (◆ For more advice regarding texting and Web speak, see page 165.)

- Don't ever, ever use "emoticons" in business writing. Emoticons are typed "smiley" faces read sideways that many people find more annoying than ground glass in a sandwich. Instead of relying on these symbols to communicate emotions of happiness, sadness, surprise, or irony, find the right words instead. Show off your writing skills, not just your ability to arrange type!

- Never forward anyone else's e-mail message without permission, especially if that message contains controversial and/or hurtful statements or confidential material. (Because other people often break this rule, think twice before *you* write.)

Designing Cover Letters and Résumés

Job seekers often send *cover letters* and *résumés* to particular employers. To prepare each cover letter, follow the basic steps for writing the traditional business letter, as outlined earlier in this chapter. In the first paragraph, clearly tell your reader why you are writing: the specific job you are applying for and why. Devote one or more paragraphs in the "body" of your letter to noting your education or professional experience or both, explaining why you are a good match for the advertised position or how you might benefit the organization. Your concluding paragraph should express thanks for the employer's consideration and briefly reemphasize your interest in the job; in this paragraph you may also mention contact information or explain access to your credentials file. In some situations, you may indicate your availability for an interview. If the employer is interested, he or she will read your résumé for more details and possibly distribute copies to others involved in the hiring process.

A *résumé* is a document that presents a brief summary of your educational background, work experiences, professional skills, special qualifications, and honors; some résumés also contain a brief list of references. You may be asked to submit a résumé on a variety of occasions, most often to supplement your applications for jobs, interviews, promotions, scholarships, grants, fellowships, or other kinds of opportunities. Because prospective employers are the largest target audience for résumés, the following pages offer advice to help job seekers design the most effective document possible.

Employers today may receive hundreds of applications for a single job, so it is important to present yourself as positively as possible in your letter and résumé. If your campus has a career center, seek it out as your first step. Career centers often have extraordinary resources: sample cover letters and résumés, hints for interviews, information on electronic job searching, and much more. Because there are multiple ways to arrange a résumé, you will find it useful to familiarize yourself with some representative samples before you begin working on your own.

Although there is no single blueprint for all résumés, there is one guiding principle: *select and arrange your information in the way that most effectively highlights your strengths to your prospective employer.* Think of your résumé as a one-page advertisement for yourself.

To find the best way to "sell" yourself to an employer, you might choose to adopt one of the two most popular arrangement styles:

- *Functional format:* This arrangement places the reader's focus more directly on the job seeker's education and skills than on limited work experience. It is better suited for job seekers who are new graduates or those just entering the workforce. Most résumés of this type are one page.

- *Experiential format:* This style emphasizes professional experience by placing work history in the most prominent position, listing the current or most important employment first. This format might be best for nontraditional students who have a work history before school or for those students who have worked throughout their college careers. If the list of relevant professional experience is lengthy, this kind of résumé may extend to a second page if necessary.

Before you begin drafting your résumé, make a list of the information you want to include. Then think about the best ways to group your material, and select an appropriate title for each section. Some of the common content areas include the following:

1. **Heading.** Located at the top of your résumé, this section identifies you and presents your contact information: your full name, address, phone number, and e-mail address if you have one. You may wish to put your name in slightly bigger type or in bold letters.

2. **Employment objective.** Some job seekers choose to include a statement describing the kind of employment or specific position they are seeking. Others omit this section, making this information clear in their cover letters. If you do

include this section, always substitute a brief, specific objective for trite, over-blown language any job seeker in the world might write:

> *Trite:* Seeking employment with a company offering intellectual challenges and opportunities for professional growth
>
> *Specific:* A microbiology research position in a laboratory or center working on disease prevention and control

If you have the time and resources to customize a résumé for each job announcement you respond to, you can use this section to show that the position you most want matches the one advertised. However, if you plan to use one résumé for a variety of job applications, beware presenting an employment objective so narrowly focused that it excludes you from a particular application pool.

3. **Education.** If you have no relevant or recent work experience, this section might appear next on your résumé. Begin with the highest degree you have earned or are working on; if you are about to graduate, you may present the anticipated graduation date. Include the name of the school and its location and, if relevant, your major, minor, or special concentration. Some students with a "B" or better grade point average also include that information. This section might also contain any professional certificates or licenses (teaching, real estate, counseling, etc.) you have earned or other educational information you deem relevant to a particular job search (internships, research projects, study-abroad programs, honors classes, or other special training).

4. **Professional experience.** If you wish to emphasize your work history, place this section after your heading or employment objective, rather than your educational background. In this section, list the position title, name of employer, city and state, and employment dates, with the most current job or relevant work experience first. Some résumés include brief statements describing the responsibilities or accomplishments of each position; you may list these statements (with bullets, not numbers) if space is an issue (see page 537 for an example). If you include job descriptions, be specific ("prepared monthly payroll for 35 employees") rather than general ("performed important financial tasks monthly"); use action verbs (supervised, developed, organized, trained, created, etc.) that present your efforts in a strong way. Use past-tense verbs for work completed and present tense for current responsibilities.

   Note that résumés traditionally do not use the word "I"; beginning brief descriptive phrases with a strong verb, rather than repeating "I had responsibility for . . . " saves precious space on a résumé.

5. **Skills.** Because you want to stress your value to a prospective employer, you may wish to note relevant professional skills or special abilities you have to offer. This section may be especially important if you do not have a work history; many recent graduates place this section immediately following the education section to underscore the skills they could bring to the workplace. For example, you might list technical skills you possess or mention expertise in a foreign language if that might look useful to a company with overseas connections.

6. **Honors, awards, activities.** In this section, list awards, scholarships, honors, and prizes to show that others have recognized you as an outstanding worker, student,

writer, teacher, and so on. Here (or perhaps in a section for related skills or experiences) you might also add leadership roles in organizations, and even certain kinds of volunteer work, if mentioning these would further your case. Although you don't want to trivialize your résumé by listing irrelevant activities, think hard about your life from a "skills" angle. Coordinating a campus charity project, for example, may indicate just the kinds of managerial skills an employer is looking for. Don't pad your résumé—but don't undersell yourself either.

7. **References.** Some employers ask immediately for references, persons they may contact for more information about you and your work or academic experiences; other employers ask for references later in the hiring process. If references are requested with the initial application letter, the information may be listed at the end of the résumé or on an attached page. Reference information includes the person's full name and title or position, the name and postal address of the person's business or organization, a telephone number, and an e-mail address, if available. Do not list friends or neighbors as references; résumé references should be academics or professionals who are familiar with your work.

Critique Your Page Appeal

Once you have decided on your résumé's content, you also need to consider its visual appeal. Because employers often look over résumés quickly, your page should be not only informative but also professional looking and easy to read. Unless you have a compelling reason for another choice, always laser print your résumé on high-quality white or off-white paper. You may highlight your section titles (education, work experiences, skills, etc.) by using boldface or large print, but don't overuse such print. Balance your text and white space in a pleasing arrangement.

If you have problems arranging your material (too much information jammed on the page or so little that your text looks lonely, for example), go back to the career center to look at ways others handled similar problems (some large copy shops also have sample books). A good page design, like a good haircut, can frame your best features in the most engaging way.

Most important: Always proofread your résumé for errors in grammar, punctuation, spelling, spacing, or typing! Because you want your résumé to look as professional as possible, make a point of having several careful (human) readers proofread your final draft.

Problems to Avoid

Remain ethical. Never lie on a résumé! Never, ever! Although you want to present yourself in the best possible ways, never fib about your experience, forge credentials you don't have, take credit for someone else's work, or overstate your participation in a project. No matter what you have heard about "puffery" in résumés ("Everyone exaggerates, so why shouldn't I?"), avoid embarrassment (or even legal action) by always telling the truth. Instead of misrepresenting yourself, find ways to identify and arrange your knowledge and skills to best highlight your strengths.

Contact your references in advance. You *must* obtain permission from each person before you list him or her as a reference. Even if you know the person well, use your good manners here: in person or in a politely written note or letter, ask in advance of your job application if you may name him or her as a reference. Once permission is granted, it's smart to give your references your résumé and any other information that might help them help you if they are contacted by a prospective employer. (Although former bosses or teachers may remember you well, they may be hazy about your exact dates of employment or the semester of your course work. Give them a helpful list of places, dates, skills, and—though you may have to overcome your sense of modesty—tactfully remind them of any outstanding work you did.)

It's also good manners (and smart) to send your references a thank-you note, expressing your appreciation for their part in your job search (such notes are absolutely *required* if people write letters of recommendation for you). Thank-you notes should be written on stationery and sent through the mail; e-mail notes are not appropriate.

Add personal information thoughtfully. Federal law protects you: employers may not discriminate on the basis of ethnicity, race, religion, age, or gender. You should not include on your résumé any personal information (marital status, number of children, birth date, country of origin, etc.) that is not relevant to the job search. Although you may, if you wish, include information on your résumé about relevant personal interests (travel, theatrical experience, volunteer rescue work, etc.), you should be aware that employers may not consider such details useful. Don't squander your résumé space on unessential information! A better plan: if you've spent a great deal of your time in some after-work or extracurricular activity, identify the *skills* you have developed that will transfer to the workplace (customer relations, public speaking, editing, etc.). Instead of just describing yourself, show prospective employers what you can *do* for them.

Special note: An increasing number of Web sites are helping employers and job seekers find each other through the posting of jobs and résumés. If you do post your résumé on such a site, choose your words carefully. Many prospective employers now use applicant-tracking software to look for keywords in résumés to match their needs. For example, a business seeking an accountant to assist its offices in Paris and Rome might flag only those résumés containing the words "CPA," "French," and "Italian." So if you are interested in a particular job advertised on the web, study the language of the job description and consider repeating, where appropriate, its keywords in your résumé.

Sample Résumés

The first résumé that follows was designed by a recent college graduate. Because he did not have an extensive work record, he chose a functional format to emphasize his education, business skills, and scholastic honors. The second résumé briefly notes specific skills from previous academic and work experiences that might interest a prospective employer.

Sample Résumé #1

Brent Monroe

417 Remington Street   (970) 555-4567
Fort Collins, CO 80525   BCMonroe@aol.com

Education

B.S. in Business Administration, Colorado State University, May 2009. GPA 3.6
A.S., Front Range Community College, May 2007. GPA 3.9

Professional Skills

Accounting
Spreadsheet programs
Amortization schedules
Payroll design and verification
Contracts and invoices

Computer
Microsoft Word, Works, Access, Outlook Express
Spreadsheets: Excel, Select
Presentations: PowerPoint, Macromedia Flash
Web site design

Awards and Activities

Outstanding Student Achievement Award, College of Business, Colorado
State University, 2009
President's Scholarship, Colorado State University, 2008 and 2009
Treasurer, Business Students Association, Colorado State University, 2008

Employment

Assistant Manager, Poppa's Pizza; Ault, Colorado, 6/08–12/09

References

Professor Gwen Lesser	Professor Ralph Berber	Mr. Randy Attree
Department of Accounting	Department of Finance	Manager, Poppa's Pizza
Colorado State University	Colorado State University	630 E. Third Street
Fort Collins, CO 80523	Fort Collins, CO 80523	Ault, CO 80303
(970) 555-7890	(970) 555-2344	(970) 333-4839
Glesser@colostate.edu	Rberber@colostate.edu	

Sample Résumé #2

ROSEMARY SILVA

3000 Colorado Avenue   (720) 555-6428
Boulder, Colorado 80303   Rosesilva@netscape.net

Objective

A full-time position as a counselor at a mental health or addiction-recovery facility

Education

B.A., University of Colorado, Boulder, May 2009. Major: Psychology. Minor: Spanish.

Internship and Research Experience

Intern Detoxification Counselor, Twin Lakes Recovery Center, Boulder, Colorado; January–May 2009.

- Provided one-on-one counseling for inpatients
- Conducted admission interviews and prepared mental/physical evaluation reports
- Responded to crisis phone line
- Monitored physical vitals of patients; performed basic paramedical techniques
- Referred patients and family members to other community agencies

Psychology Research Lab Assistant, University of Colorado at Boulder, under the direction of Professor Lois Diamond; September–December 2007.

- Helped conduct experiments on CU student-volunteers to measure the relationship of memory and academic success
- Recorded student information and validated research credit slips

Employment

Night Security Dispatcher, University of Colorado, Boulder, Campus Police Department; May 2004–April 2008.

- Accurately received and responded to emergency and non-emergency calls and radio transmissions
- Communicated emergency information to appropriate agencies, such as Boulder Police and the Rape Crisis Center
- Dispatched security units and counselors to disturbances
- Wrote detailed records describing incoming calls and security patrol responses

References Available upon Request

PRACTICING WHAT YOU'VE LEARNED

Prepare a one-page résumé for your professional use at this time or in the near future. While you are in school, you might use this résumé to apply for a scholarship, an internship, a summer job, or a part-time position. Arrange your information to emphasize your strengths, and don't forget to thoroughly proofread several times before you print your final draft. (If you keep a copy of this résumé handy and revise it regularly, you will be ready to respond quickly should a job or other opportunity unexpectedly present itself.)

ASSIGNMENT

Collaborative Activity: Exchange a current résumé (perhaps the one you wrote for the preceding Practice) with that of a classmate. Role-play prospective employers, and give each other helpful feedback. Does each résumé effectively "sell" the job seeker? What specific details or action verbs might increase the chances of success? Be sure to proofread carefully, marking any typos, mechanical errors, or stylistic inconsistencies.

Preparing Interview Notes and Post-Interview Letters

If a prospective employer wishes to interview you, sketch out a few notes for yourself before the meeting. Try to anticipate questions you may be asked, such as "What are your strengths as a worker?" and "How would you fit into our organization?" You will feel much more confident if you are prepared to discuss specific experiences that show both your skills and your previous work or school successes. Think about important information you wish your interviewer to know; consider making a brief list of the reasons you are the best candidate for the job. Once you have completed your notes, jot down a few key words on a note card to review just before your appointment so you can easily recall the details you want to provide. (◆ For more good suggestions, turn to "Preparing for the Job Interview: Know Thyself" [pages 224–225] by Katy Piotrowski, a career-search consultant.)

After you interview for a job you want, consider writing a follow-up note to the prospective employer. This letter should be more than a polite thank-you for the interview, however. Use the opportunity to again emphasize your skills. Begin by thanking the person for his or her time, but move on to show that you think, now more than ever, that you are the right person for the position and for the organization. Illustrate this claim by showing that during the interview you really listened and observed: "After hearing about your goals for new product X, I know I could contribute because. . . ." Or remind your interviewer of reasons to hire you: "You stressed your company's need for someone with XYZ skills. My internship training in that area. . . ." In other words, use this follow-up letter not only to offer your thanks but also to advertise yourself (and your good writing skills) one more time.

PART 4

A Concise Handbook

Part 4 of this text begins with an overview of the parts of speech, followed by a brief discussion of sentence components and types. These pages present explanations, definitions, and illustrations to help you better understand the grammatical conventions and terms used in the handbook chapters that follow. Chapters 20, 21, and 22 will address major errors in grammar, punctuation, and mechanics, showing you how to recognize and correct these problems. Each error will be explained as simply as possible, with a minimum of technical language. Beside each rule you will find the editing mark or abbreviation that is most often used to identify that error; each rule is also numbered for easy reference. Exercises placed throughout each chapter offer opportunities to practice the advice; collaborative assignments may also promote improved editing and proofreading skills.

Parts of Speech

The following section offers an overview of the eight groups of words called *parts of speech*. Knowing how a word or phrase is properly used may help you produce sentences that are clear, correct, and pleasing to your readers. In addition, recognizing commonly used grammatical terms may make it easier for you to understand your instructor's advice as well as the explanations of major errors in usage and punctuation that appear in the following handbook chapters.

The eight parts of speech are *nouns, pronouns, verbs, adjectives, adverbs, prepositions, conjunctions,* and *interjections.** The group to which a word belongs is determined by its function in a particular sentence; consequently, a word may be one part of speech in one sentence and a different part of speech in another. (For example, note that "rock" is a noun—a thing—in "Put down that rock!" but a verb—a word expressing action—in "Don't rock the boat!")

Here is a brief introduction to the parts of speech. You will also see some of these definitions repeated in the various sections on grammatical errors in Chapter 20. Moving back and forth between this overview and the advice in that chapter should help you improve your grammatical skills as you draft and revise your sentences.

1. **Nouns** name persons, places, things, and concepts. *Proper nouns* are the names of particular people, places, and things and should be capitalized; *common nouns,* referring to any person, place, or thing, are not capitalized. *Gerunds* are nouns formed from verbs ending in "-ing."

   Examples of common nouns The *girl* sold her *car* in *town*.
   Examples of proper nouns *Rachel* sold her *Honda* in *Denver*.
   Example of a gerund *Dancing* is fun.

   (◆ For additional information on the uses of nouns, see pages 555–556.)

2. **Pronouns** take the place of nouns. By using pronouns, you can avoid repeating nouns in the same sentence or group of sentences.

   Example We saw Hortense across the parking lot and waved to *her*. [Use of "her" avoids the awkward repetition of "We saw Hortense across the parking lot and waved to Hortense."]

   There are several classes of pronouns, including these six important kinds:

   • *Personal pronouns* refer to specific people; they include such words as "I," "you," "he," "her," "it," and "them." (*Compound personal pronouns*—sometimes called reflexive pronouns—add "-self" or "-selves" to some of the simple personal ones: "himself," "herself," "themselves.")

   Example *You* and *I* will meet *him* at the movies.

*Some authorities claim nine parts of speech, adding the group of words called *articles*: "a," "an," and "the." In English "a" generally precedes nouns beginning with consonants (*a* cat); "an" generally precedes nouns beginning with vowels (*an* island).

- *Indefinite pronouns* refer to nonspecific people or things and include such words as "everyone," "everything," "someone," "anyone," and "anybody."

  Example   *Everyone* should use caution crossing that busy street.

- *Possessive pronouns* (such as "his," "hers," "its," "ours," "theirs") show ownership.

  Example   *His* passport was about to expire; *its* renewal deadline was March 15.

- *Demonstrative pronouns* refer the reader to previous references.

  Example   *That* is my house, *those* are my prize roses, and *this* is my cat.

- *Interrogative pronouns* introduce questions.

  Example   *Which* house? *What* roses? *Who* is asking all these questions?

- *Relative pronouns* join a dependent clause to the main clause of a sentence and describe a previous noun or pronoun. Commonly used relative pronouns are "who," "which," "that," and "whose."

  Examples   The singer *who* won the competition is holding a free concert.
  I found the purse *that* I thought I had lost at the restaurant.

(◆ For more information on the uses of pronouns, see pages 556–559.)

3. **Verbs** express action ("walk," "yell," "swim") and states of being ("am," "is," "are"). A verb phrase may be composed of several words: "should have written," "might have called."

   Three important kinds of verbs include the following:

   - *Action verbs* express physical or mental activity.

     Examples   Birds *fly* through the yard.
     I *dream* of beaches in Hawaii.

   - *Linking verbs* (such as "is, "are," "was," "were,") show states of being; they may also show connections between ideas or relationships of one thing to another.

     Examples   Shameka *is* twenty-eight years old.
     Austin *was* the youngest child.

   - *Auxiliary verbs* are sometimes referred to as "helper verbs" because they assist the main verbs in communicating meaning or time of action. Common auxiliary verbs include forms of "do," "have," "may," "can," and "will."

     Examples (auxiliary + main verbs)   Good students *do proofread* their essays.
     Revising *will help* your writing.

   Also note that verbs may be described as being in the *active voice* or the *passive voice*.

   - Active voice denotes that the subject of the verb is performing the action: The house-sitter *watered* the lawn.

   - Passive voice denotes that the subject of the verb is acted upon: The lawn *was watered* by the house-sitter.

Verbs come in many forms, but three to remember as you revise your prose include the *infinitive*, the *participle*, and the *gerund*.

- An infinitive is a verb introduced by the word "to": I like *to read*.
- A participle may share the properties of both a verb and a modifier; present participles end in "-ing": *Watching* the rain fall, anticipated summer flowers.
- A gerund is a verb plus "-ing" used as a noun: *Swimming* is wonderful exercise.

(◆ For advice addressing some of the common errors with verbs, see pages 549–551.)

4. **Adjectives** modify or describe nouns and pronouns. *Proper adjectives* derived from proper nouns are usually capitalized. *Predicate adjectives* may follow the word they modify.

   Examples   I bought a *red* sweater, just the *perfect* weight for *Colorado* evenings.
   Her answer was *wrong*.

5. **Adverbs** most often modify or describe verbs, adjectives, and other adverbs. They frequently answer "how" or "how much" and end in "-ly."

   Examples   My father drove *slowly*. ["Slowly" modifies the verb, describing how he drove.]
   Her answer was *partially* wrong. ["Partially" modifies the adjective "wrong," describing how incorrect the answer was.]
   She appeared *mildly* amused. ["Mildly" modifies the adverb "amused," describing the extent of her delight.]

   (◆ For additional information on the use of adjectives and adverbs, see pages 560–561.)

6. **Prepositions** are words that most often show locations and relationships in time, place, and direction. The following are some common prepositions:

to	under	in	during
on	with	at	upon
about	by	for	since
between	through	from	after
of	before	over	

   A preposition and its object make up a *prepositional phrase*, which may be used as an adjective or adverb.

   Example   *During Spring Break*, we took a vacation *to the city*. [The first prepositional phrase is used as an adverb to tell when and the other is used as an adjective to describe the place of the vacation.]

   Writers should avoid ending sentences with prepositions when possible. Recast the sentence, or simply drop an unnecessary (and ungrammatical) preposition: "Where are you sitting at?" becomes "Where are you sitting?"

7. **Conjunctions** connect words ("dogs *and* cats") or groups of words ("please return the acceptance card *or* send a note of regret").

There are two kinds of conjunctions for you to recognize:

- *Coordinating conjunctions* connect two words, phrases, or clauses of equal kind or rank. The most commonly used coordinating conjunctions are "for," "and," "nor," "but," "or," "yet," and "so."

  Examples   He promises an evening of singing *and* dancing. [connecting two words]
  We can either hail a cab *or* catch the subway. [connecting two phrases]
  I have to be home early, *but* you can stay out late. [connecting two clauses]

- *Subordinating conjunctions* connect two clauses of unequal rank; as their name indicates, they connect one clause that is subordinate to—that is, dependent for meaning upon—its main clause. Common subordinating conjunctions include "because," "when," "if," "as," "since," "after," and "although."

  Example   *Because* his songs promote violence, I won't buy albums by that recording artist.

  In most cases when a subordinate clause begins the sentence, it is followed by a comma, as shown previously.

(◆ Understanding how to use coordinating and subordinating conjunctions is important as you learn to create sentence variety and also how to avoid fragment, run-on, or spliced sentences. For more information, see pages 564, 566, and 567.)

8. **Interjections** are exclamatory words that frequently express strong, sudden, or contrary emotions. They may stand alone or they may be part of a sentence.

  Examples   *Ouch! Help!* Call an ambulance!
  Oh, never mind. The movie was, *alas*, already sold out.

Sentence Components and Classifications

In addition to recognizing the parts of speech, you may find it helpful to understand some of the grammatical terms used to describe sentence components and types. Here are a few common terms, their definitions, and examples.

1. A *sentence* is most often a group of words that expresses a complete thought.
   - The squirrel ate the bird seed.

2. A sentence contains a *subject* and a *predicate*, either expressed or understood. The subject is the performer or receiver of the action or state of being expressed in the predicate, which gives information about the subject.
   - The squirrel [subject] ate the bird seed [predicate].

   A subject may be implied rather than stated.
   - Stop talking! Run for your life! ["You" is implied.]

3. A *direct object* receives the action of the verb. It often answers the question "what?"
   - We caught a skunk [direct object] in a trap from the Humane Society.

4. An *indirect object* names the person or thing to whom or for whom the action is done.
   - We gave the *dog* [indirect object] some special treats [direct object].

5. A *modifier* is a word or group of words used to describe, characterize, or change the meaning of other words in the sentence. Adjectives and adverbs are common modifiers.
   - The *starving* teenager *happily* gobbled the *cold* pizza.

6. A *phrase* is a group of related words in a sentence that do not contain a subject or predicate. Phrases do not stand alone. Common forms include prepositional, infinitive, and verbal phrases.
   - He accidentally set up the tent *on an ant hill.* [prepositional phrase]
   - *Waving frantically,* he ran toward the river. [verbal phrase, using participle "ing" form of the verb "wave"]

7. A *clause* is a group of related words in a sentence that do have a subject and a predicate. Independent clauses stand alone and are complete thoughts; they are, in essence, what we call sentences. Dependent clauses, on the other hand, need to be attached for their meaning to a main clause; they are considered fragments if they stand alone.
   - Abraham Lincoln was the first president to sport a beard. [independent clause]
   - Although my history book fails to mention this fact [dependent clause], Abraham Lincoln was the first president to sport a beard [independent clause].

8. The word "compound" is often used to indicate parts of sentences that appear in multiple forms, such as compound subjects, predicates, clauses, and objects.

   • *Sarah* and *Kate* received their Master's Degrees on the same day. [compound subject]

   • The girls *found interesting jobs* and *moved to different states*. [compound predicate]

9. Sentences themselves may be classified according to their structures as four types: simple, compound, complex, and compound-complex.

   A *simple sentence* has one independent clause.

   • She practices yoga.

   A *compound sentence* has two or more independent clauses. (Expressed another way, a compound sentence is two simple sentences joined by a conjunction.)

   • Sarah moved to Berkeley, and Kate stayed in Washington.

   A *complex sentence* may consist of one independent clause and one or more dependent clauses.

   • If we are thoughtful enough [dependent clause], we usually can find an important lesson in every disappointment [independent clause].

   A *compound-complex* sentence includes two or more independent clauses and at least one dependent clause.

   • Thomas Jefferson is a much-admired president [independent clause], but he is especially honored in Virginia [independent clause], where he founded the state university [dependent clause].

10. Sentences may also be classified by purpose:

    Declarative: makes a statement (The day is sunny.)
    Imperative: gives a command (Do not pass that car.)
    Interrogative: asks a question (Why are you here?)
    Exclamatory: expresses strong emotion (How lovely you look tonight!)

CHAPTER 20

Major Errors in Grammar

Errors with Verbs

Verbs express action ("run," "walk," "kick") or state of being ("is," "are," "was").

20a Faulty Agreement S-V Agr

Make your verb agree in number with its subject; a singular subject takes a singular verb, and a plural subject takes a plural verb.

Incorrect	*Lester Peabody*, principal of the Kung Fu School of Grammar, *don't* agree that gum chewing should be banned in the classroom.
Correct	*Lester Peabody*, principal of the Kung Fu School of Grammar, *doesn't* agree that gum chewing should be banned in the classroom.
Incorrect	The *actions* of the new senator *hasn't* been consistent with her campaign promises.
Correct	The *actions* of the new senator *haven't* been consistent with her campaign promises.

Compound subjects joined by "and" take a plural verb, unless the subject refers to a single person or a single unit.

Examples	*Bean sprouts* and *tofu are* dishes Jim Bob won't consider eating. ["Bean sprouts" and "tofu" are a compound subject joined by "and"; therefore, use a plural verb.]
	The *winner* and *new champion refuses* to give up the microphone at the news conference. ["Winner" and "champion" refer to a single person; therefore, use a singular verb.]

Listed here are some of the most confusing subject-verb agreement problems:

1. With a collective noun: a singular noun referring to a collection of elements as a unit generally takes a singular verb.

   Incorrect   During boring parts of the Transcendental Vegetation lecture, the *class* often *chant* to the music of Norman Bates and the Shower Heads.

   Correct   During boring parts of the Transcendental Vegetation lecture, the *class* often *chants* to the music of Norman Bates and the Shower Heads.

   Incorrect   The *army* of the new nation *want* shoes, bullets, and weekend passes.

   Correct   The *army* of the new nation *wants* shoes, bullets, and weekend passes.

2. With a relative pronoun ("that," "which," and "who") used as a subject: the verb agrees with its antecedent, the word being described.

   Incorrect   The boss rejected a shipment of *shirts, which was* torn.

   Correct   The boss rejected a shipment of *shirts, which were* torn.

3. With "each," "everybody," "everyone," and "neither" as the subject: use a singular verb even when followed by a plural construction.

   Incorrect   *Each* of the children *think* Mom and Dad are automatic teller machines.

   Correct   *Each* of the children *thinks* Mom and Dad are automatic teller machines.

   Incorrect   Although only a few of the students saw the teacher pull out his hair, *everybody know* why he did it.

   Correct   Although only a few of the students saw the teacher pull out his hair, *everybody knows* why he did it.

   Incorrect   *Neither have* a dime left by the second of the month.

   Correct   *Neither has* a dime left by the second of the month.

4. With "either . . . or" and "neither . . . nor": the verb agrees with the nearer item.

   Incorrect   Neither rain nor dogs nor *gloom of night keep* the mail carrier from delivering bills.

   Correct   Neither rain nor dogs nor *gloom of night keeps* the mail carrier from delivering bills.

   Incorrect   Either Betty or her *neighbors is* hosting a come-as-you-are breakfast.

   Correct   Either Betty or her *neighbors are* hosting a come-as-you-are breakfast.

5. With "here is (are)" and "there is (are)": the verb agrees with the number indicated by the subject following the verb.

   Incorrect   *There is* only two good *reasons* for missing this law class: death and jury duty.

   Correct   *There are* only two good *reasons* for missing this law class: death and jury duty.

   Incorrect   To help you do your shopping quickly, Mr. Scrooge, *here are* a *list* of gifts under a dollar.

   Correct   To help you do your shopping quickly, Mr. Scrooge, *here is* a *list* of gifts under a dollar.

6. With plural nouns intervening between subject and verb: the verb still agrees with the subject.

Incorrect	The *jungle*, with its poisonous plants, wild animals, and biting insects, *make* Herman long for the sidewalks of Topeka.
Correct	The *jungle*, with its poisonous plants, wild animals, and biting insects, *makes* Herman long for the sidewalks of Topeka.

7. With nouns plural in form but singular in meaning: a singular verb is usually correct.

Examples	*News travels* slowly if it comes through the post office.
	Charades is the exhibitionist's game of choice.
	Politics is often the rich person's hobby.

8. As you revise your prose, use a dictionary if you need help determining whether a word is singular or plural. For example, two common subject-verb agreement errors occur with the words "media" and "data," which, despite colloquial usage, should be treated as plurals in formal writing.

Correct	The *data were* faulty.
	The media often *influence* public opinion polls.

PRACTICING WHAT YOU'VE LEARNED

Errors with Verbs: Subject-Verb Agreement

The following sentences contain subject-verb agreement errors. Correct the problems by changing the verbs. Some sentences contain more than one error.

1. A recent report on Cuban land crabs show that they can run faster than horses.

2. The team from Snooker Hollow High School are considering switching from basketball to basket weaving because passing athletics are now required for graduation.

3. Neither of the students know that both mystery writer Agatha Christie and inventor Thomas Edison was dyslexic.

4. Each of the twins have read about Joseph Priestley's contribution to the understanding of oxygen, but neither were aware that he also invented the pencil eraser.

5. Clarity in speech and writing are absolutely essential in the business world today.

6. Historical data suggests that the world's first money, in the form of coins, were made in Lydia, a country that is now part of Turkey.

7. Bananas, rich in vitamins and low in fat, is rated the most popular fruit in America.

8. There is many children in this country who appreciate a big plate of hot grits, but none of the Hall kids like this Southern dish.

continued on next page

© Canstock Images, Inc./ Index Stock Imagery

9. Either the Labrador Retriever or the Yorkshire Terrier hold the honor of being the most popular breed of dogs in the United States, say the American Kennel Club.

10. Many people considers Johnny Appleseed a mythical figure, but now two local historians, authors of a well-known book on the subject, argues that he was a real person named John Chapman.

20b   Subjunctive   V Sub

When you make a wish or a statement that is contrary to fact, use the subjunctive verb form "were."

Incorrect   I wish I *was* queen so I could levy a tax on men who spit.

Correct   I wish I *were* queen so I could levy a tax on men who spit. [This expresses a wish.]

Incorrect   If "Fightin' Henry" *was* a foot taller and thirty pounds heavier, we would all be in trouble.

Correct   If "Fightin' Henry" *were* a foot taller and thirty pounds heavier, we would all be in trouble. [This proposes a statement contrary to fact.]

20c   Tense Shift   T

In most cases, the first verb in a sentence establishes the tense of any later verb. Keep your verbs within the same time frame to avoid confusing your readers.

Incorrect   Big Joe *saw* the police car coming up behind, so he *turns* into the next alley.

Correct   Big Joe *saw* the police car coming up behind, so he *turned* into the next alley.

Incorrect   Horace *uses* an artificial sweetener in his coffee all day, so he *felt* a pizza and a hot-fudge sundae *were* fine for dinner.

Correct   Horace *uses* an artificial sweetener in his coffee all day, so he *feels* a pizza and a hot-fudge sundae *are* fine for dinner.

Incorrect   Rex the Wonder Horse *was* obviously very smart because he *taps* out the telephone numbers of the stars with his hoof.

Correct   Rex the Wonder Horse *was* obviously very smart because he *tapped* out the telephone numbers of the stars with his hoof.

20d   Split Infinitive   Sp I

Many authorities insist that "to" never be separated from its verb; today, however, some grammarians allow the split infinitive except in the most formal kinds of writing.

Nevertheless, because the split offends some readers, it is probably best to avoid the construction unless clarity or emphasis is clearly served by its use.

Traditional   A swift kick is needed *to start* the machine properly.
Untraditional A swift kick is needed *to* properly *start* the machine.

Traditional   The teacher wanted Lori *to communicate* her ideas clearly.
Untraditional The teacher wanted Lori *to* clearly *communicate* her ideas.

20e Double Negatives   D Neg

1. Rewrite sentences that use two negatives to communicate a single negative idea.

Incorrect   He *don't* need *no* fancy car to impress her.
Correct   He *doesn't* need a fancy car to impress her.

Incorrect   They *couldn't* find *no* record of my purchase.
Correct   They *could* find *no* record of my purchase.
Also Correct They *couldn't* find *any* record of my purchase.

2. Don't use a negative verb and a negative qualifier ("hardly," "barely," "scarcely") together.

Incorrect   I *can't hardly* wait until Jim Bob gets his jaw out of traction, so I can challenge him to a bubblegum-blowing contest.
Correct   I *can hardly* wait until Jim Bob gets his jaw out of traction, so I can challenge him to a bubblegum-blowing contest.

Incorrect   Even when he flew his helicopter upside-down over her house, she *wouldn't barely* look at him.
Correct   Even when he flew his helicopter upside-down over her house, she *would barely* look at him.

20f Passive Voice   Pass

"Active voice" refers to sentences in which the subject performs the action. "Passive voice" refers to sentences in which the subject is acted upon.

Active   The police *pulled over* the van full of stolen ski sweaters.
Passive   The van full of stolen ski sweaters *was pulled over* by the police.

The passive voice is a logical construction when the person or thing performing the action is unknown or of lesser importance than the event or action.

Examples   My car was stolen last night.

The soldier was buried with full military honors.

Some disciplines, particularly those in science and engineering, may prefer the passive voice: "All results were triple verified." Nevertheless, your prose style will improve if you choose strong, active-voice verbs over wordy, awkward, or unclear passive constructions.

Awkward passive construction   The call for volunteers was responded to by many students.

Active verb   Many students responded to the call for volunteers.

| Unclear passive construction | Much protest is being voiced over the new electric fireworks. [Who is protesting?] |
| Active verb | Members of the Fuse Lighters Association are protesting the new electric fireworks. |

(◆ For more examples of active- and passive-voice verbs, see page 138.)

20g Irregular Verbs Irreg V

Most verbs form their past tense by adding "-ed" ("ask/asked," "walk/walked"). However, some verbs form their past tenses by changing a vowel ("begin/began," "write/wrote"); others indicate past tense with an entirely new spelling or word ("go/went," "strike/struck").

Consult your dictionary when you are uncertain of the correct verb form you need. Remember that some verbs simply do not behave themselves!

Incorrect	Irregular verbs have *creeped* into our language.
Correct	Irregular verbs have *crept* into our language.
Incorrect	She *shaked* the piggy bank as hard as she could.
Correct	She *shook* the piggy bank as hard as she could.
Incorrect	I don't know the current price of ant farms because I haven't *boughten* one since grade school.
Correct	I don't know the current price of ant farms because I haven't *bought* one since grade school.

© Cansock Images, Inc./
Index Stock Imagery

PRACTICING WHAT YOU'VE LEARNED

Errors with Verbs: Form, Tense Shift, and Double Negatives

A. The following sentences contain incorrect verb forms, tense shifts, and double negatives. Correct any problems you see, and rewrite any sentences whose clarity or conciseness would be improved by using active rather than passive verbs.

1. He couldn't hardly wait to hear country star Sue Flay sing her version of "I've Been Flushed from the Bathroom of Your Heart."

2. "If you was in Wyoming and couldn't hear no wind blowing, what would people call you?" asked Jethro. "Dead," replies his buddy Herman.

3. It was believed by Aztec ruler Montezuma that chocolate had magical powers and can act as an aphrodisiac.

4. Tammy's favorite band is Opie Gone Bad, so she always was buying their concert tickets, even though she can't hardly afford to.

> 5. Suspicions of arson are being raised by the Fire Department following the burning of the new Chip and Dale Furniture Factory.
>
> **B.** Revise any incorrect verbs in the following sentences.
>
> 1. I seen what she was hiding behind her back.
>
> 2. He come around here yesterday asking questions, but we're use to that.
>
> 3. Having forget the combination to the safe, the burglar quietly snuck out the back door.
>
> 4. Austin don't like to be awokened until noon.
>
> 5. The kids done good work all day.

Errors with Nouns   N

Nouns name people, places, and things ("boy," "kitchen," "car"). Proper nouns name specific people, places, and things ("Zora Neale Hurston," "Texas," "Chevrolet") and are capitalized.

20h   Possessive with "-ing" Nouns

When the emphasis is on the action, use the possessive pronoun plus the "-ing" noun.

Example   He hated *my* singing around the house, so I made him live in the garage. [The emphasis is on *singing*.]

When the emphasis is not on the action, you may use a noun or pronoun plus the "-ing" noun.

Example   He hated *me* singing around the house, so I made him live in the garage. [The emphasis is on the person singing—me—not the action; he might have liked someone else singing.]

20i   Misuse of Nouns as Adjectives

Some nouns may be used as adjectives modifying other nouns ("horse show," "movie star," "theater seats"). But some nouns used as adjectives sound awkward or like jargon. To avoid such awkwardness, you may need to change the noun to an appropriate adjective or reword the sentence.

Awkward   The group decided to work on local *environment* problems.
Better   The group decided to work on local *environmental* problems.

Jargon   The executive began a *cost estimation comparison study* of the two products.
Better   The executive began a *comparison study* of the two products' costs.

(◆ For more information on ridding your prose of multiple nouns, see page 143.)

20j Plurals of Proper Nouns

Add an "s" to indicate plural proper nouns.

Examples Both *Keishas* volunteered for the charity drive.

The *Halls* were home for the holidays, enjoying their new *Frisbees* every afternoon.

(◆ For practice correcting errors with nouns, turn to pages 559–560.)

Errors with Pronouns

A pronoun ("he," "she," "it") takes the place of a noun. Possessive pronouns ("his," "hers," "its," "theirs") show ownership.

20k Faulty Agreement Pro Agr

A pronoun should agree in number and gender with its antecedent (that is, the word the pronoun stands for).

Incorrect To get a temperamental *actress* to sign a contract, the director would lock *them* in the dressing room.

Correct To get a temperamental *actress* to sign a contract, the director would lock *her* in the dressing room.

Use the singular pronoun with "everyone," "anyone," and "each."

Incorrect When the belly dancer asked for a volunteer partner, *everyone* in the men's gym class raised *their* hand.

Correct When the belly dancer asked for a volunteer partner, *everyone* in the men's gym class raised *his* hand.

Incorrect *Each* of the new wives decided to keep *their* own name.

Correct *Each* of the new wives decided to keep *her* own name.

In the past, writers have traditionally used the masculine pronoun "he" when the gender of the antecedent is unknown, as in the following: "If a *spy* refuses to answer questions, *he* should be forced to watch James Bond movies until *he* cracks." Today, however, some authorities prefer the nonsexist "she or he," even though the construction can be awkward when maintained over a stretch of prose. Perhaps the best solution is to use the impersonal "one" when possible or simply rewrite the sentence in the plural: "If *spies* refuse to answer questions, *they* should be forced to watch James Bond movies until *they* crack." (◆ For more advice and examples, see pages 168–170.)

20l Vague Reference Ref

Your pronoun references should be clear.

Vague If the trained seal won't eat its dinner, throw *it* into the lion's cage. [What goes into the lion's cage?]

Clear If the trained seal won't eat its dinner, throw *the food* into the lion's cage.

Vague	After the dog bit Harry, *he* raised such a fuss at the police station that the sergeant finally had *him* impounded. [Who raised the fuss? Who was impounded?]
Clear	After being bitten, *Harry* raised such a fuss at the police station that the sergeant finally had the *dog* impounded.

Sometimes you must add a word or rewrite the sentence to make the pronoun reference clear:

Vague	I'm a lab instructor in the biology department and am also taking a statistics course. *This* has always been difficult for me. [What is difficult?]
Clear	I'm a lab instructor in the biology department and am also taking statistics, a *course* that has always been difficult for me.
Clear	I'm a lab instructor in the biology department and am also taking a statistics course. Being a teacher and a student at the same time has always been difficult for me.

In many cases, simply inserting a noun after a vague use of "this" or "that" will clarify meaning.

Vague	I visited with my grandmother while we watched the lunar eclipse. That was so special. [What was special? The visit? The eclipse?]
Clear	I visited with my grandmother while we watched the lunar eclipse. That *evening* was so special.

As you revise your prose, train yourself to catch any sentences that begin with "this" or "that" and see whether adding a noun or phrase will help communicate your meaning more effectively.

20m   Shift in Pronouns   P Sh

Be consistent in your use of pronouns; don't shift from one person to another.

Incorrect	*One* shouldn't eat pudding with *your* fingers.
Correct	*One* shouldn't eat pudding with *one's* fingers.
Correct	*You* shouldn't eat pudding with *your* fingers.
Incorrect	*We* left-handed people are at a disadvantage because most of the time *you* can't rent left-handed golf clubs or bowling balls.
Correct	*We* left-handed people are at a disadvantage because most of the time *we* can't rent left-handed golf clubs or bowling balls.

(◆ For additional examples, see pages 143–144.)

20n   Incorrect Case   Ca

1. The case of a pronoun is determined by its function in the particular sentence. If the pronoun is a subject, use the nominative case: "I," "he," "she," "we," and "they"; if the pronoun is an object, use the objective case: "me," "him," "her," "us," and "them." To check your usage, all you need to do in many instances is isolate the pronoun in the manner shown here and determine whether it sounds correct alone.

Incorrect	Give the treasure map to Frankie and *I*.
Isolated	Give the treasure map to *I*. [awkward]
Correct	Give the treasure map to Frankie and *me*.

Incorrect	Bertram and *her* suspect that the moon is hollow.
Isolated	*Her* suspects that the moon is hollow. [awkward]
Correct	Bertram and *she* suspect that the moon is hollow.

Incorrect	The gift is from Annette and *I*.
Isolated	The gift is from *I*. [awkward]
Correct	The gift is from Annette and *me*.

Sometimes the "isolation test" doesn't work, so you just have to remember the rules. A common pronoun problem involves use of the preposition "between" and the choice of "me" or "I." Perhaps you can remember this rule by recalling there is no "I" in "between," only "e's" as in "me."

| Incorrect | Just *between you and I*, the Russian housekeeper is a good cook, but she won't iron curtains. |
| Correct | Just *between you and me*, the Russian housekeeper is a good cook, but she won't iron curtains. |

In other cases, to determine the correct pronoun, you will need to add implied but unstated sentence elements:

Examples	Mother always liked Dickie more than *me*. [Mother liked Dickie more than *she liked* me.]
	She is younger than *I* by three days. [She is younger than I *am* by three days.]
	Telephone exchange: May I speak to Kate? This is *she*. [This is she *speaking*.]

2. To solve the confusing *who/whom* pronoun problem, first determine the case of the pronoun in its own clause in each sentence.

A. If the pronoun is the subject of a clause, use "who" or "whoever."

Examples	I don't know *who* spread the peanut butter on my English paper. ["Who" is the subject of the verb "spread" in the clause "who spread the peanut butter on my English paper."]
	Rachel is a librarian *who* only likes books with pictures. ["Who" is the subject of the verb "likes" in the clause "who only likes books with pictures."]
	He will sell secrets to *whoever* offers the largest sum of money. ["Whoever" is the subject of the verb "offers" in the clause "whoever offers the largest sum of money."]

B. If the pronoun occurs as the object of a preposition, use "whom," especially when the preposition immediately precedes the pronoun.

Examples	*With whom* am I speaking?
	To whom is the letter addressed?
	Do not ask *for whom* the bell tolls.

C. If the pronoun is the object of a verb, use "whom" or "whomever."

Examples   Sid is a man *whom* I distrust. ["Whom" is the direct object of the verb "distrust."]

Who's calling *whom* a sore loser now? ["Whom" is the direct object of the verb "calling."]

20o   Incorrect Compound Forms

Compound personal pronouns are formed by adding "-self" or "-selves" to some of the simple personal pronouns ("my," "you," "her," "him"). Use a dictionary if you are unsure of a correct form.

Correct   myself, yourself, himself, themselves
Incorrect   hisself, theirselves

PRACTICING WHAT YOU'VE LEARNED

Errors with Nouns and Pronouns

A. In the following sentences, select the proper nouns and pronouns.

1. Please buy a copy of the book *The Celery Stalks at Midnight* for my sister and (I, me).

2. Between you and (I, me), some people define a Freudian slip as saying one thing but meaning your mother.

3. (Who, Whom) is the singer of the country song "You Can't Make a Heel Toe the Mark"?

4. Aunt Beulah makes better cookies than (I, me).

5. (Her and me, She and I) are going to the movies to see *Attack of the Killer Crabgrass.*

6. I'm giving my accordion to (whoever, whomever) is carrying a grudge against our new neighbors, the (Smith's, Smiths).

7. The Botox surprise party was given by Paige Turner, Justin Case, and (I, me).

8. She is the kind of person for (who, whom) housework meant sweeping the room with a glance.

9. (Her and him, She and he) are twins (who, whom) are always finding (theirselves, themselves) in financial trouble.

10. The judge of the ugly feet contest announced (his self, him self, himself) the winner.

continued on next page

B. The following sentences contain a variety of errors with nouns and pronouns. Some sentences contain more than one error; skip any correct sentences you may find.

1. Clarence and me have an uncle who is so mean he writes the name of the murderer on the first page of mystery novels that are passed around the family.

2. Of whom did Oscar Wilde once say, "He hasn't a single redeeming vice"?

3. It was a surprise to both Mary and I to learn that Switzerland didn't give women the right to vote until 1971.

4. Each of the young women in the Family Life class decided not to marry after they read that couples today have 2.3 children.

5. Jim Bob explained to Frankie that the best way for him to avoid his recurring nosebleeds was to stay out of his cousin's marital arguments.

6. Those of us who'd had the flu agreed that one can always get a doctor to return your call quicker if you get in the shower, but let's keep this tip confidential between you and I.

7. The stranger gave the free movie tickets to Louise and I after he saw people standing in line to leave the theater.

8. The personnel director told each of the employees, most of who opposed him, to signify their "no" vote by saying, "I resign."

9. A person knows he's in trouble when their salary undergoes a modification reduction adjustment of 50 percent.

10. One of the first movies to gross over one million dollars was *Tarzan of the Apes* (1932), starring Johnny Weissmuller, a former Olympic star who became an actor. This didn't happen often in the movie industry at that time.

Errors with Adverbs and Adjectives

20p   Incorrect Usage   Adv   Adj

Incorrect use of adverbs and adjectives often occurs when you confuse the two modifiers. Adverbs qualify the meanings of verbs, adjectives, and other adverbs; they often answer the questions "how?" "when?" or "where?" and they frequently end in "-ly."

Incorrect   After Kay argued with the mechanic, she drove *slow* all the way home.
Correct   After Kay argued with the mechanic, she drove *slowly* all the way home.

Adjectives, on the other hand, commonly describe or qualify the meanings of nouns only.

Example   The *angry* mechanic neglected to put oil into Kay's *old* car.

One of the most confusing pairs of modifiers is "well" and "good." We often use "good" as an adjective modifying a noun and "well" as an adverb modifying a verb.

Examples   A *Sap's Fables* is a *good* book for children, although it is not *well* organized.

Bubba was such a *good* liar his wife had to call in the children at suppertime.

After eating Rocky Mountain oysters, Susie yodels exceptionally *well*.

Did you do *well* on your math test?

If you cannot determine whether a word is an adverb or an adjective, consult your dictionary.

20q   Faulty Comparison   Comp

When you compare two elements to a higher or lower degree, you often add "-er" or "-r" to the adjective.

Incorrect   Of the two sisters, Selene is the *oldest*.
Correct   Of the two sisters, Selene is the *older*.

When you compare more than two elements, you often add "-est" to the adjective.

Example   Selene is the *oldest* of the four children in the family.

Other adjectives use the words "more," "most," "less," and "least" to indicate comparison.

Examples   Béla Lugosi is *more* handsome than Lon Chaney but *less* handsome than Vincent Price.

Of all the horror film stars, Boris Karloff is the *most* handsome, and Christopher Lee is the *least* handsome.

Beware using a double comparison when it is unnecessary:

Incorrect   It was the *most saddest* song I've ever heard.
Correct   It was the *saddest* song I've ever heard.

Note, too, that for most authorities, the word "unique" is a special adjective, one without a degree of comparison. Despite common usage to the contrary, an experience or thing may be unique—that is, one of a kind—but it may not be "very unique."

© Canstock Images, Inc./
Index Stock Imagery

PRACTICING WHAT YOU'VE LEARNED

Errors with Adverbs and Adjectives

Choose the correct adverbs and adjectives in the following sentences.

1. After the optometrist pulled her eye tooth, Hortense didn't behave very (good, well) in the waiting room.

2. Which is the (worser, worse, worst) food, liver or buttermilk?

continued on next page

3. I didn't do (good, well) on my nature project because my bonsai sequoia tree grew (bad, badly) in its tiny container.

4. Don't forget to dress (warm, warmly) for the Arctic freestyle race.

5. Of the twins, Teensie is (more tall, taller) than Egore.

6. Watching Joe Bob eat candied fruit flies made Jolene feel (real, really) ill, and his table manners did not make her feel (more better, better).

7. The Roman toothpick holder was (very unique, the uniquest, unique).

8. That was the (funniest, most funniest) flea circus I have ever seen.

9. Does the instructional guide *Bobbing for Doughnuts* still sell (good, well)?

10. The Fighting Mosquitoes were trained (well, good), but they just didn't take practices (serious, seriously).

Errors in Modifying Phrases

20r Dangling Modifiers DM

A modifying—or descriptive—phrase must have a logical relationship to some specific words in the sentence. When those words are omitted, the phrase "dangles" without anything to modify. Dangling modifiers frequently occur at the beginnings of sentences and often can be corrected by adding the proper subjects to the main clauses.

Dangling	Not knowing how to swim, buying scuba gear was foolish.
Correct	Not knowing how to swim, *we* decided that buying scuba gear was foolish.
Dangling	Feeling too sick to ski, her vacation to the mountains was postponed.
Correct	Feeling too sick to ski, *she* postponed her vacation to the mountains.

(◆ For additional examples, see pages 130–132.)

20s Misplaced Modifiers MM

When modifying words, phrases, or clauses are not placed near the word they describe, confusion or unintentional humor often results.

Misplaced	Teddy swatted the fly still dressed in his pajamas.
Correct	Still dressed in his pajamas, Teddy swatted the fly.
Misplaced	There are many things people won't eat, especially children.
Correct	There are many things people, especially children, won't eat.

(◆ For additional examples, see pages 130–132.)

PRACTICING WHAT YOU'VE LEARNED

Errors in Modifying Phrases

Correct the errors in dangling and misplaced modifiers by rearranging or rewriting the following sentences.

1. After boarding Hard Luck Airlines, the meals convinced us to return by ship.

2. Here is the new telephone number for notifying the fire department of any fires that may be attached to your telephone.

3. The prize-winning ice sculptor celebrated her new open-air studio in Aspen, where she lives with her infant daughter, purchased for $10,000.

4. The movie star showed off letters from admirers that were lying all over his desk.

5. Running too fast during a game of "Kick the Can," my face collided with the flagpole.

6. Eloise bought a computer from her neighbor with faulty memory.

7. Baggy, wrinkled, and hopelessly out of style, Jean tossed the skirt from her closet.

8. Forgetting to pack underwear, the suitcase had to be reopened.

9. Blanche plans to teach a course next spring incorporating her research into the mating habits of Big Foot on the campus of Slippery Rock College.

10. After spending all night in the library, Kate's friends knew she'd need a trip to Special Coffee.

11. Squeezing the can, the tomatoes didn't seem ripe to DeeDee.

12. From birth to twelve months, parents don't have to worry about solid food.

13. He didn't think the bicycles would make it over the mountains, being so old.

14. I've read that a number of modern sailors, like Thor Heyerdahl, have sailed primitive vessels across the ocean in books from the public library.

15. Proofreading carefully, dangling modifiers may be spotted and corrected easily.

© Canstock Images, Inc./ Index Stock Imagery

Errors in Sentences

20t   Fragments   Frag

A complete sentence must contain a subject and a verb. A fragment is an incomplete sentence; it is often a participial ("-ing") phrase or dependent clause that belongs to the preceding sentence. To check for fragments, try reading your prose one sentence at a time, starting at the *end* of your essay. If you find a "sentence" that makes no sense alone, it's probably a fragment that should be either rewritten or connected to another sentence.

Incorrect	Bubba's parents refuse to send him to a psychiatrist. Although they both know he eats shoelaces and lightbulbs.
Correct	Bubba's parents refuse to send him to a psychiatrist, although they both know he eats shoelaces and lightbulbs.
Incorrect	This recording of the symphony's latest concert is so clear you can hear every sound. Including the coughs and whispers of the audience.
Correct	This recording of the symphony's latest concert is so clear you can hear every sound, including the coughs and whispers of the audience.
Incorrect	Francis named her new mutt Super Dog. Because he could leap fences in a single bound.
Correct	Francis named her new mutt Super Dog because he could leap fences in a single bound.

You can also try this test to see whether a group of words is a fragment: say the phrase "It is true that" in front of the words in question. In most cases, a complete sentence will still make sense, but a fragment won't.

Examples	Francis named her new mutt Super Dog. Because he could leap fences in a single bound. [Which is a fragment?]
	It is true that *Francis named her new mutt Super Dog.* [This sentence makes sense so it is not a fragment.]
	It is true that *because he could leap fences in a single bound.* [Yes, this is the fragment.]

Sentence fragments are often used in conversations ("yes," "maybe," "just a minute") and in informal or personal writing (notes, letters, e-mail, etc.). In some professional and academic writing, *intentional fragments* or abbreviated sentences may be used occasionally for emphasis or to convey a particular tone, such as playfulness, anger, or scorn. However, intentional fragments should be just that: created on purpose to achieve a specific rhetorical goal.

Intentional fragments	After cleaning out the attic, Eloise felt terrible. *Hot. Tired. Cranky with the world.*
	She agreed to hand over the jewels. *Just exactly what he had had in mind all along.*

As a general rule, fragments should be avoided in formal writing. Ask your instructor whether intentional fragments are permitted in your essays.

(◆ For more discussion of fragments, see pages 129–130.)

PRACTICING WHAT YOU'VE LEARNED

Fragment Sentence Errors

A. Using the "It is true that" test, identify the fragments and the complete sentences in the following samples.

1. The first drive-in theaters opened in New Jersey in 1933. Which was in the middle of the Great Depression when money was scarce.

2. By 1958 there were over 4,000 drive-ins in the United States. As recorded by the United Drive-in Theatre Owners Association.

3. The number of drive-ins has fallen drastically. Perhaps because escalating land prices make property too valuable for use in this way. Or the fact that they are open only during the summer months in some areas.

4. There are only 430 drive-ins left in the country. Including the American territories.

5. Other outdoor summer activities are also endangered. For instance, the miniature golf industry, down from 50,000 courses in the 1930s to fewer than 15,000 today.

B. Rewrite the following sentences so that there are no fragments.

1. The idea of a credit card first appeared in 1887. According to Lawrence M. Ausbel, author of "Credit Cards," in the *McGraw-Hill Encyclopedia of Economics*.

2. Originally an imaginary concept in a futurist novel by Edward Bellamy. The card allowed characters to charge against future earnings.

3. Around the turn of the twentieth century some American stores issued paper or metal "shoppers' plates." Although they were only used by retailers to identify their credit customers.

4. The first real credit card was issued in 1947 by a New York bank and was a success. Despite the fact that customers could charge purchases only in a two-block area in Brooklyn.

5. Travel and entertainment cards soon appeared that allowed customers to charge items and services across the country. For example, the American Express card in 1958 and Carte Blanche in 1959.

© Canstock Images, Inc./ Index Stock Imagery

20u   Run-on (or Fused) Sentence   R-O

Don't run two sentences together without any punctuation. Use a period, a semicolon, or a comma plus a coordinating conjunction (if appropriate), or subordinate one clause.

Incorrect	The indicted police chief submitted his resignation the mayor accepted it gratefully.
Correct	The indicted police chief submitted his resignation. The mayor accepted it gratefully.
Correct	The indicted police chief submitted his resignation; the mayor accepted it gratefully.
Correct	The indicted police chief submitted his resignation, and the mayor accepted it gratefully.
Correct	When the indicted police chief submitted his resignation, the mayor accepted it gratefully.

Do not try to correct a run-on by inserting a comma between the two sentences; doing so without a coordinating conjunction will produce an error called a *comma splice*, discussed on pages 567 and 575. Punctuate correctly or rewrite the run-on to best communicate your meaning.

Incorrect (run-on)	Victoria Woodhull was the first American woman to run for the presidency she was defeated in 1872 by Ulysses S. Grant.
Incorrect (comma splice)	Victoria Woodhull was the first American woman to run for the presidency, she was defeated in 1872 by Ulysses S. Grant.
Correct	Victoria Woodhull was the first American woman to run for the presidency. She was defeated in 1872 by Ulysses S. Grant.
Correct	Victoria Woodhull was the first American woman to run for the presidency; she was defeated in 1872 by Ulysses S. Grant.
Correct	Victoria Woodhull was the first American woman to run for the presidency, but she was defeated in 1872 by Ulysses S. Grant.
Correct	Victoria Woodhull, the first American woman to run for the presidency, was defeated in 1872 by Ulysses S. Grant.

PRACTICING WHAT YOU'VE LEARNED

Run-On Errors

Correct the following run-on sentences. Try to use several different methods of correcting the errors.

1. Workers in the United States take an average of thirteen days of vacation a year in Italy they take forty-two.

2. In 1901 a schoolteacher named Annie Edson Taylor became the first person to go over Niagara Falls in a wooden barrel she is the only woman known to have survived this risky adventure.

© Canstock Images, Inc./ Index Stock Imagery

3. The minister preached his farewell sermon the choir sang "Break Forth into Joy."

4. The first microwave oven marketed in 1959 was a built-in unit it cost a whopping $2,595.

5. Coffee was considered a food in the Middle Ages travelers who found it growing in Ethiopia mixed it with animal fat.

(◆ For additional practice, turn to exercise "B" on pages 579–580.)

20v   Comma Splice   CS

A comma splice occurs when two sentences are linked with a comma. To correct this error, you can (1) separate the two sentences with a period, (2) separate the two sentences with a semicolon, (3) insert a coordinating conjunction ("for," "but," "and," "or," "nor," "so," "yet") after the comma, or (4) subordinate one clause.

Incorrect	Grover won a stuffed gila monster at the church raffle, his mother threw it away the next day while he was in school.
Correct	Grover won a stuffed gila monster at the church raffle. His mother threw it away the next day while he was in school.
Correct	Grover won a stuffed gila monster at the church raffle; his mother threw it away the next day while he was in school.
Correct	Grover won a stuffed gila monster at the church raffle, but his mother threw it away the next day while he was in school.
Correct	Although Grover won a stuffed gila monster at the church raffle, his mother threw it away the next day while he was in school.

(◆ For more help on correcting comma splices, see page 575 in the following chapter on punctuation; coordination and subordination are discussed in detail on pages 146–148.)

© Canstock Images, Inc./ Index Stock Imagery

PRACTICING WHAT YOU'VE LEARNED

Comma Splice Errors

A. Correct the comma splices that appear in the following sentences. Use more than one method of correcting the errors.

1. Most people know that the likeness of Susan B. Anthony appeared on an American dollar coin in the 1990s, fewer people know exactly who she was or why she is so important.

2. For most of her life Anthony fought for women to obtain the right to vote, she was an organizer of the world's first women's rights convention in 1848.

continued on next page

568 Part 4 A Concise Handbook

3. Anthony often risked her safety and her freedom for her beliefs, she was arrested in 1872 for the crime of voting in an election.

4. She also worked to secure laws to protect working women, at that time all of a woman's wages automatically belonged to her husband.

5. Unfortunately, Anthony did not live to see the 1920 passage of the Nineteenth Amendment giving women the right to vote, she died in 1906.

B. Correct any run-on sentences or comma splice errors you see. Skip any correct sentences you find.

1. My mother is very politically conservative, she's written in King George III for president in the last two elections.

2. Mary Lou decided not to eat the alphabet soup the letters spelled out "botulism."

3. A dried gourd containing seeds probably functioned as the first baby rattle, ancient Egyptian wall paintings show babies with such gourds clutched in their fingers.

4. Opportunists who came to the South after the Civil War were often called "carpetbaggers," they carried their belongings in cheaply produced travel bags made of Belgian carpet.

5. A friend of mine offers a good definition of nasty theater critics on opening night, according to him, they're the people who can't wait to stone the first cast.

6. When English scientist James Smithson died in 1829, he willed his entire fortune to the United States to establish a foundation for knowledge, that's how the Smithsonian Institution was started.

7. The word "jack-o'-lantern" may have come from the legend of Irish Jack, a mean old man in life, he was condemned after death to wander the earth carrying a hollow turnip with a lump of burning coal inside.

8. People forget how large the blue whale is it has a heart as large as a Volkswagen Beetle and can hold an elephant on its tongue.

9. According to a study by the Fish and Wildlife Service, Americans' favorite animals are dogs, horses, swans, robins, and butterflies; their least favorite are cockroaches, mosquitos, rats, wasps, and rattlesnakes.

10. The famous Eiffel Tower, built for the 1889 Paris Exposition, has inspired many crazy stunts, for example, in 1891 Silvain Dornon climbed the 363 steps on stilts.

© CORBIS

ASSIGNMENT

Collaborative Activity: To continue practicing revision of major sentence errors, join two classmates, each with a current essay draft in hand. Each person should select and then study independently one of these sections in this chapter: sentence fragments (page 564), run-on sentences (page 566), or comma splices (page 567). After a study period of ten minutes, regroup and take turns explaining each error—and a way to eliminate it. Next, pass around and read all three essay drafts, marking the particular sentence error you studied if you find it in a classmate's paper. How might you help your classmate correct this error?

20w   Faulty Parallelism   //

Parallel thoughts may be expressed in similar grammatical constructions. Repeated sentence elements, such as verbs, nouns, pronouns, and phrases, often appear in parallel form to emphasize meaning and to promote sentence fluency.

Examples
Parallel verbs: In his vaudeville act he *sang, danced, and juggled.*
Parallel prepositional phrases: She ran *through the door, across the yard,* and *into the limo.*

You might find it helpful to isolate the repeated elements in a sentence to see whether they are parallel.

She ran

(1) through the door
(2) across the yard   } parallel
(3) into the limo

Faulty Parallelism	Boa constrictors like *to lie* in the sun, *to hang* from limbs, and *swallowing* small animals.
Isolated	(1) to lie (2) to hang (3) swallowing [not parallel to #1 and #2]
Revised	Boa constrictors like *to lie* in the sun, *to hang* from limbs, and *to swallow* small animals.
Faulty Parallelism	Whether *working* on his greasy car, *fistfighting* at the hamburger stand, or *in bed*, my brother always kept his hair combed.
Revised	Whether *working* on his greasy car, *fistfighting* at the hamburger stand, or *lounging* in bed, my brother always kept his hair combed.

PRACTICING WHAT YOU'VE LEARNED

Errors in Parallelism

Revise the following sentences so that the parallel ideas are expressed in similar grammatical constructions.

1. Is it true that Superman could leap tall buildings, run faster than a locomotive, and that bullets would bounce off his skin?

2. To celebrate the canned pork product called Spam, we attended the Texas Spamarama Festival to participate in the Spambalaya cook-off, the Spam slab toss, the Spam relay race, and were dancing to such favorites as "Twist and Snout."*

3. My Aunt Clara swears she has seen Elvis snacking at the deli, browsing at the supermarket, munching at the pizza parlor, and in the cookbook section of a local bookstore.

4. According to my husband, summer air in Louisiana is 2 percent oxygen, 8 percent water, and the rest is mosquitoes, about 90 percent.

5. Many teachers believe that the most important keys to success for students in college include attending class, keep up with reading assignments, and being brave enough to ask questions.

6. Yoga encourages its participants to work on their flexibility, strength, and how they can reduce their stress levels.

7. Drivers should hang up their cell phones, refrain from eating, and drinking too, leaving the radio buttons alone.

8. Smart people learn from their own mistakes; learning from the mistakes of others is what even smarter people do.

9. Theater class helped me overcome my shyness, make new friends, and my confidence to do other activities was improved.

10. The writer Oscar Wilde, the dancer Isadora Duncan, the painter Max Ernst, and Jim Morrison, who was a rock star, are all buried in the same Paris cemetery.

*Yes, readers, there really is a Spamarama Festival, a silly outdoor event in Austin, Texas, with music and games (the Spamolympics) for all ages. Held annually around April Fool's Day for over twenty-five years, the Festival raises money for charity.

20x   False Predication   Pred

This error occurs when the predicate (that part of the sentence that says something about the subject) doesn't fit properly with the subject. Illogical constructions result.

If it's helpful in some cases, remember that the verbs "is" and "was" often mean "equates to."

Incorrect	Energy is one of the world's biggest problems. ["Energy" itself is not a problem.]
Correct	The lack of fuel for energy is one of the world's biggest problems.
Incorrect	My roommate is why I'm moving to a new apartment. [A roommate is not a reason.]
Correct	My roommate's habit of talking nonstop is driving me to find a new apartment.
Also Correct	Because of my annoying roommate, I'm moving to a new apartment.
Incorrect	Her first comment after winning the lottery was exciting. [Her comment wasn't exciting; she was excited.]
Correct	Her first comment after winning the lottery expressed her excitement.
Incorrect	True failure is when you make an error and don't learn anything from it. [Avoid all "is when" and "is where" constructions. The subject does not denote a time, so the predicate is faulty.]
Correct	You have truly failed only when you make an error and don't learn anything from it.

(◆ For other examples of faulty predication, see pages 132–133.)

20y   Mixed Structure   Mix S

"Mixed structure" is a catchall term that applies to a variety of sentence construction errors. Usually, the term refers to a sentence in which the writer begins with one kind of structure and then shifts to another in midsentence. Such a shift often occurs when writers are in a hurry and their minds have already jumped ahead to the next thought.

Confused	By the time one litter of cats is given away seems to bring a new one.
Clear	Giving away one litter of cats seems to tell the mother cat that it's time to produce a new batch.
Confused	The bank robber realized that in his crime spree how very little fun he was having.
Clear	The bank robber realized that he was having very little fun in his crime spree.
Confused	The novel is too difficult for what the author meant.
Clear	The novel is too difficult for me to understand what the author meant.
Confused	Children with messages from their parents will be stapled to the bulletin board.
Clear	To find messages from their parents, children should look at the bulletin board.

(◆ For other examples of mixed structure, see pages 132–133.)

PRACTICING WHAT YOU'VE LEARNED

Errors of False Predication and Mixed Structure

Rewrite the following sentences so that each one is clear and coherent.

1. The team's quarterback A. M. Hall's broken finger, which sidelined him last week for the Raiders' game, is expected to play in tonight's game.

2. The groom is a graduate of Centerville High School where he lived all his life.

3. On my way to the doctor's office, my universal joint went out, causing even more body damage after hitting the tree.

4. An example of his intelligence is when he brought home a twenty-pound block of ice after ice fishing all day.

5. For those new residents who have children and don't know about it, the town offers low-cost daycare services.

6. According to the nineteenth-century cynic Ambrose Bierce, marriage is when there is "a master, a mistress, and two slaves, making in all, two."

7. Another situation when I get so mad is the plumber showing up three hours late.

8. My drama teacher is a big reason why I am a star today.

9. Some folks argue that sound travels slower than light such as when advice parents give their teenagers doesn't reach them until they're forty.

10. Hearing his cries for help is how he came to be found in a ditch by some stray cows.

CHAPTER 21

A Concise Guide to Punctuation

Punctuation marks do not exist, as one student recently complained, to make your life complicated. They are used to clarify your written thoughts so that the reader understands your meaning. Just as traffic signs and signals tell a driver to slow down, stop, or go, so punctuation is intended to guide the reader through your prose. Look, for example, at the confusion in the following sentences when the necessary punctuation marks are omitted:

Confusing	Has the tiger been fed Bill? [Bill was the tiger's dinner?]
Clear	Has the tiger been fed, Bill?
Confusing	After we had finished raking the dog jumped into the pile of leaves. [Raking the dog?]
Clear	After we had finished raking, the dog jumped into the pile of leaves.
Confusing	The coach called the swimmers names. [Was the coach fired for verbally abusing the swimmers?]
Clear	The coach called the swimmers' names.

Because punctuation helps you communicate clearly with your reader, you should familiarize yourself with the following rules.

21a The Period (.)   P

1. Use a period to end a sentence that makes a statement.

Examples   Employees at that company are not allowed to go on coffee breaks.

It takes too long to retrain them.

2. Use a period at the end of a sentence that makes a direct command or request.

Examples   Don't walk on the grass.

Please give me your new address.

3. Use a period after initials and many abbreviations.

Examples   W. B. Yeats, 12 a.m., Dr., etc., Ms.

4. Only one period is necessary if the sentence ends with an abbreviation.

Examples   The elephant was delivered C.O.D.

To find a good job, you should obtain a B.S. or B.A.

21b   The Question Mark (?)   P

1. Use a question mark after every direct question.

Examples   May I borrow your boots?

Is the sandstorm over now?

2. No question mark is necessary after an indirect question.

Examples   Jean asked why no one makes a paper milk carton that opens without tearing.

Dave wondered how the television detective always found a parking place next to the scene of the crime.

21c   The Exclamation Point (!)   P

The exclamation point follows words, phrases, or sentences to show strong feelings.

Examples   Fire! Call the rescue squad!

The Broncos finally won the Super Bowl!

PRACTICING WHAT YOU'VE LEARNED

Errors Using Periods, Question Marks, and Exclamation Points

Correct the following sentences by adding, deleting, or changing periods, question marks, or exclamation points, where appropriate.

1. The space program sent some cows into orbit last year I think they are now known as the herd shot around the world

2. Ms Anita Bath wants to know why erasers never outlast their pencils?

3. Her French class at St Claire's School on First Ave was taught by Madame Beau V Rhee, Ph.D. .

4. Where do all the birds go when it's raining

5. I have wonderful news I won the lottery

© Canstock Images, Inc./
Index Stock Imagery

21d   The Comma (,)   P

1. Use a comma to separate two independent clauses* joined by a coordinating conjunction. To remember the coordinating conjunctions, think of the acronym FANBOYS: "for," "and," "nor," "but," "or," "yet," and "so." Always use one of the FANBOYS and a comma when you join two independent clauses.

Examples   You can bury your savings in the backyard, *but* don't expect Mother Nature to pay interest.

I'm going home tomorrow, *and* I'm never coming back.

After six weeks Louie's diet was making him feel lonely and depressed, *so* he had a bumper sticker printed that said, "Honk if you love groceries."

Do *not* join two sentences with a comma only; such an error is called a *comma splice.* Use a comma plus one of the coordinating conjunctions listed previously, a period, a semicolon, or subordination.

Comma splice	Beatrice washes and grooms the chickens, Samantha feeds the spiders.
Correct	Beatrice washes and grooms the chickens, and Samantha feeds the spiders.
Correct	Beatrice washes and grooms the chickens. Samantha feeds the spiders.
Correct	Beatrice washes and grooms the chickens; Samantha feeds the spiders.
Correct	When Beatrice washes and grooms the chickens, Samantha feeds the spiders.
Comma splice	Juan doesn't like singing groups, he won't go with us to hear Fed Up with People.
Correct	Juan doesn't like singing groups, so he won't go with us to hear Fed Up with People.
Correct	Juan doesn't like singing groups. He won't go with us to hear Fed Up with People.
Correct	Juan doesn't like singing groups; he won't go with us to hear Fed Up with People.
Correct	Because Juan doesn't like singing groups, he won't go with us to hear Fed Up with People.

(◆ For additional help, see page 567; for practice exercises, see pages 567–568 and 579–580.)

Beware the tricky word "however." "However" is *not* one of the FANBOYS (coordinating conjunctions) and consequently can never be used to join two independent clauses. Incorrect use of "however" most often results in a comma splice.

---

*An independent clause looks like a complete sentence; it contains a subject and a verb, and it makes sense by itself.

Comma splice	The police arrested the thief, *however*, they had to release him because the plant wouldn't talk.
Correct	The police arrested the thief; *however*, they had to release him because the plant wouldn't talk.
Also correct	The police arrested the thief. *However*, they had to release him because the plant wouldn't talk.

2. Set off with a comma an introductory phrase or clause.

Examples	After we had finished our laundry, we discovered that one sock was missing.
	According to the owner of the Hall Laundry House, customers have conflicting theories about missing laundry.
	For example, one man claims his socks make a break for freedom when no one is watching the dryers.

3. Set off nonessential phrases and clauses. If the information can be omitted without changing the meaning of the main clause, then the phrase or clause is nonessential. Do not set off clauses or phrases that are essential to the meaning of the main clause.

Essential	He looked worse than my friend *who gets his clothes from the "lost and found" at the bus station*. [The "who" clause is essential to explain which friend.]
	The storm *that destroyed Mr. Peartree's outhouse* left him speechless with anger. [The "that" clause is essential to explain which storm angered Mr. Peartree.]
	The movie *now showing at the Ritz* is very obscene and very popular. [The participial phrase is essential to identify the particular movie.]
Nonessential	Joe Medusa, *who won the jalapeno-eating contest last year*, is this year's champion cow-chip tosser. [The "who" clause is nonessential because it only supplies additional information to the main clause.]
	Black widow spiders, *which eat their spouses after mating*, are easily identifiable by the orange hourglass design on their abdomens. [The "which" clause is nonessential because it only supplies additional information.]
	The jukebox, *now reappearing in local honky-tonks*, first gained popularity during the 1920s. [The participial phrase is nonessential because it only supplies additional information.]

4. Conjunctive adverbs, such as "however," "moreover," "thus," "consequently," and "therefore," are used to show continuity and are frequently set off by commas when they appear in midsentence.

Examples	She soon discovered, *however*, that he had stolen her monogrammed towels in addition to her pet avocado plant.
	She felt, *consequently*, that he was not trustworthy.

When a conjunctive adverb occurs at the beginning of a sentence, it may be followed by a comma, especially if a pause is intended. If no pause is intended, you may omit the comma, but inserting the comma is never wrong.

Examples   *Thus*, she resolved never to speak to him again.
Thus she resolved never to speak to him again.
Therefore, he resolved never to speak to her again.
Therefore he resolved never to speak to her again.

(◆ For practice of comma rules 1–4, turn to page 579.)

5. Use commas to separate items in a series of words, phrases, or clauses.

Examples   Julio collects coins, stamps, bottle caps, erasers, and pocket lint.

Mrs. Jones chased the burglar out the window, around the ledge, down the fire escape, and into the busy street.

Do note that there is no comma separating "such as" and the first word in the list of items that follow.

Incorrect   Sarah eats a variety of vegetarian foods, such as, tofu, nuts, and fruit.

Correct   Sarah eats a variety of vegetarian foods, such as tofu, nuts, and fruit.

Although journalists and some grammarians permit the omission of the last comma before the "and," many authorities believe the comma is necessary for clarity. For example, how many pints of ice cream are listed in the sentence below?

Please buy the following pints of ice cream: strawberry, peach, coffee, vanilla and chocolate swirl.

Four or five pints? Without a comma before the "and," the reader doesn't know whether vanilla and chocolate swirl are (is?) one item or two. By inserting the last comma, you clarify the sentence:

Please buy the following pints of ice cream: strawberry, peach, coffee, vanilla, and chocolate swirl.

6. Use commas to separate adjectives of equal emphasis that modify the same noun. To determine whether a comma should be used, see if you can insert the word "and" between the adjectives; if the phrase still makes proper sense with the substituted "and," use a comma.

Examples   She finally moved out of her cold, dark apartment.

She finally moved out of her cold and dark apartment.

I have a sweet, handsome husband.

I have a sweet and handsome husband.

He called from a convenient telephone booth.
But not: He called from a convenient and telephone booth. ["Convenient" modifies the unit "telephone booth," so there is no comma.]

Hand me some of that homemade pecan pie.
But not: Hand me some of that homemade and pecan pie. ["Homemade" modifies the unit "pecan pie," so there is no comma.]

7. Set off a direct address with commas.

Examples Gentlemen, keep your seats.

Car fifty-four, where are you?

Not now, Eleanor, I'm busy.

8. Use commas to set off items in addresses and dates.

Examples The sheriff followed me from Austin, Texas, to question me about my uncle.

He found me on February 2, 1978, when I stopped in Fairbanks, Alaska, to buy sunscreen.

9. Use commas to set off a degree or title following a name.

Examples John Dough, M.D., was audited when he reported only $5.68 in taxable income last year.

The Neanderthal Award went to Samuel Lyle, Ph.D.

10. Use commas to set off dialogue from the speaker.

Examples Alexander announced, "I don't think I want a second helping of possum."

"Eat hearty," said Marie, "because this is the last of the food."

Note that you do not use a comma before an indirect quotation or before titles in quotation marks following the verbs "read," "sang," or "wrote."

Incorrect Bruce said, that cockroaches have portions of their brains scattered throughout their bodies.

Correct Bruce said that cockroaches have portions of their brains scattered throughout their bodies.

Incorrect One panel member read, "Aunt Jennifer's Tigers," and the other sang, "Song for My Father."

Correct One panel member read "Aunt Jennifer's Tigers," and the other sang "Song for My Father."

11. Use commas to set off "yes," "no," "well," and other weak exclamations.

Examples Yes, I am in the cat condo business.

No, all the units with decks are sold.

Well, perhaps one with a pool will do.

12. Set off interrupters or parenthetical elements appearing in the middle of a sentence. A parenthetical element is additional information placed as explanation or comment within an already complete sentence. This element may be a word (such as "certainly" or "fortunately"), a phrase ("for example" or "in fact"), or a clause ("I believe" or "you know"). The word, phrase, or clause is parenthetical if the sentence parts before and after it fit together and make sense.

Examples Jack is, *I think*, still a compulsive gambler.

Harvey, *my brother*, sometimes has breakfast with him.

Jack cannot, *for example*, resist shuffling the toast or dealing the pancakes.

13. Resist the temptation to pepper your prose with commas when you have no good reason to use them. Not all sentences containing "and" take a comma. In the following sentence, for example, "and" separates a compound predicate; it is not used as one of the FANBOYS (a coordinating conjunction) separating two independent clauses.

Incorrect	She ate a biscuit, and drank a cup of tea. [The comma here incorrectly separates the verb "drank" from its subject "she."]
Correct	She ate a biscuit and drank a cup of tea.

On the other hand, writers may use commas when necessary to improve sentence clarity.

Confusing	Unlike Mary Jo never learned to cook.
Clear	Unlike Mary, Jo never learned to cook.
Confusing	Whatever will be will be.
Clear	Whatever will be, will be.

© Canstock Images, Inc./
Index ·tock Imagery

PRACTICING WHAT YOU'VE LEARNED

Comma Errors

A. Study the comma rules numbered 1–4 on pages 575–577. Correct any comma errors you see in the following sentences.

1. In 1886 temperance leader Harvey Wilcox left Kansas, he purchased 120 acres near Los Angeles to develop a new town.

2. Although there were no holly trees growing in that part of California Mrs. Wilcox named the area Hollywood.

3. Mrs. Wilcox may have named the place after a home, owned by a friend living in Illinois.

4. During the early years settlers who shared the Wilcoxes' values moved to the area and banned the recreational drinking of alcoholic beverages, however, some alcohol consumption was allowed for medicinal purposes.

5. Nevertheless by 1910 the first film studio opened its doors inside a tavern on Sunset Boulevard, within seven short years the quiet community started by the Wilcoxes had vanished.

B. Study the comma rules 5–13 on pages 577–579. Correct any comma errors you see in the following sentences.

1. Yes Hortense in the 1920s young women did indeed cut their hair raise their hemlines dab perfume behind their knees and dance the Charleston.

continued on next page

2. In 1873 Cornell University cancelled the school's first intercollegiate football game with Michigan when the president announced "I will not permit thirty men to travel four hundred miles merely to agitate a bag of wind."

3. Jane Marian Donna Ann and Cissy graduated from high school on June 5 1964 in Texarkana Texas in the old Walnut Street Auditorium.

4. "I may be a man of few opinions" said Henry "but I insist that I am neither for nor against apathy."

5. Did you know for instance that early American settlers once thought the tomato was so poisonous they used the plant only for decoration?

C. The following sentences contain many kinds of comma errors, including the comma splice. Correct any errors you see by adding, deleting, or changing the commas as needed.

1. The father decided to recapture his youth, he took his son's car keys away.

2. Although ice cream didn't appear in America until the 1700s our country now leads the world in ice cream consumption, Australia is second I think.

3. Last summer the large friendly family that lives next door flew Discount Airlines and visited three cities on their vacation, however, their suitcases visited five.

4. Researchers in Balboa, Panama have discovered that the poisonous, yellow-belly, sea snake which descended from the cobra, is the most deadly serpent in the world.

5. Lulu Belle, my cousin, spent the week of Sept. 1–7, 1986 in the woods near Dimebox, Texas looking for additions to her extinct, butterfly collection, however she wasn't at all successful in her search.

(◆ For additional practice correcting comma splice errors, see pages 567–568 in Chapter 20.)

21e   The Semicolon (;)   P

1. Use a semicolon to link two closely related independent clauses.

Examples   Anthropologists believe popcorn originated in Mexico; they have found popcorn poppers that are over 1,500 years old.

Kate's mother does not have to begin a jogging program; she gets all the exercise she needs by worrying in place.

Avoid a "semicolon fragment" error by making sure there is an independent clause—a complete sentence, not a fragment—on either side of the semicolon.*

---

*Some folks have noted that the semicolon might be better named the "semi-period" in that it functions like a weak period, joining two complete sentences together but with a weaker stop between thoughts than a period demands.

Semicolon fragment	Cutting your lawn with a push mower burns 420 calories; according to *Vitality* magazine. ["According to *Vitality* magazine" is a fragment. In this case, a comma, not a semicolon, is needed.]
Correct	Cutting your lawn with a push mower burns 420 calories, according to *Vitality* magazine.

◆ If you are unsure about recognizing a fragment, try using the "It is true that" test as described on page 564.

2. Use a semicolon to avoid a comma splice when connecting two independent clauses with words like "however," "moreover," "thus," "therefore," and "consequently."

Examples	Vincent van Gogh sold only one painting in his entire life; however, in 1987 his *Sunflowers* sold for almost $40 million.
	All Esmeralda's plants die shortly after she gets them home from the store; consequently, she has the best compost heap in town.
	This town is not big enough for both of us; therefore, I suggest we expand the city limits.

3. Use a semicolon in a series between items that already contain internal punctuation.

Examples	Last year the Wildcats suffered enough injuries to keep them from winning the pennant, as Jake Pritchett, third baseman, broke his arm in a fight; Hugh Rosenbloom, starting pitcher, sprained his back on a trampoline; and Boris Baker, star outfielder, ate rotten clams and nearly died.
	Her children were born a year apart: Moe, 1936; Curley, 1937; and Larry, 1938.

© Canstock Images, Inc /
Index Stock Imagery

PRACTICING WHAT YOU'VE LEARNED

Semicolon Errors

Correct the sentences that follow by adding, deleting, or changing the semicolons.

1. The soloist sang the well-known hymn "I Will Not Pass This Way Again" at her concert last night the audience was delighted.

2. Apples have long been associated with romance for example, one legend says if you throw an apple peel over your shoulder, it will fall into the shape of your true love's initial.

3. According to an 1863 book of etiquette, the perfect hostess will see to it that the works of male and female authors are properly separated on her bookshelves, however, if the authors happen to be married, their proximity may be tolerated.

continued on next page

4. Today, there are some 60,000 Americans older than 100 in 1960, there were only 3,222; according to Health magazine.

5. The sixth-grade drama club will present their interpretation of Hamlet tonight in the school cafeteria all parents are invited to see this tragedy.

6. Some inventors who named weapons after themselves include Samuel Colt, the Colt revolver, Henry Deringer, Jr., the derringer pistol, Dr. Richard J. Gatling, the crank machine gun, Col. John T. Thompson, the submachine or "tommy" gun, and Oliver F. Winchester, the repeating rifle.

7. My doctor failed in his career as a kidnapper, no one could read his ransom notes.

8. The highest point in the United States is Mt. McKinley at 20,320 feet, in contrast, the lowest point is Death Valley at 282 feet below sea level.

9. As we drove down the highway, we saw a sign that said "See the World's Largest Prairie Dog Turn Right at This Exit," therefore we immediately stopped to look.

10. The next billboard read "See Live Jackalopes"; making us want to stop again.

21f   The Colon (:)   P

1. Use a colon to introduce a long or formal list, but do not use one after "to be" verbs.

Correct	Please pick up these items at the store: garlic, wolfbane, mirrors, a prayer book, a hammer, and a wooden stake.
Incorrect	Jean is such a bad cook that she thinks the four basic food groups are: canned, frozen, ready-to-mix, and take-out.
Correct	Jean is such a bad cook that she thinks the four basic food groups are canned, frozen, ready-to-mix, and take-out.

Avoid needless colons.

Incorrect	At the store I couldn't find: wolfbane or a wooden stake.
Correct	At the store I couldn't find wolfbane or a wooden stake.

2. A colon may be used to introduce a quotation or definition.

Examples	Nineteenth-century writer Ambrose Bierce offers this definition of a bore: "A person who talks when you wish him to listen."
	Critic Dorothy Parker was unambiguous in her review of the book: "This is not a novel to be tossed aside lightly; it should be thrown with great force."
	In singer Jimmy Buffett's Margaritaville store in Key West, a sign warns: "Shoplifters will be forced to listen to Barry Manilow."

3. Use a colon to introduce a word, phrase, or sentence that emphatically or humorously explains, summarizes, or amplifies the preceding sentence.

Examples   To her delight, we fed our pet lamb her favorite dish: shepherd's pie.

According to Kira, Colorado has four seasons: last winter, this winter, next winter, and July.

After marrying nine times, glamour queen Zsa Zsa Gabor had simple advice for becoming a marvelous housekeeper: every time you leave a relationship, keep the house.

4. Use a colon in the salutations of business or professional correspondence. Colons may also follow headings in memos.

Examples   Dear Professor Stallones:
To: Subject: Date:

PRACTICING WHAT YOU'VE LEARNED

Errors with Colons

Correct the following errors by adding, deleting, or substituting colons for faulty punctuation. Skip any correct sentences.

1. Experts have discovered over thirty different kinds of clouds but have separated them into three main types cirrus, cumulus, and stratus.

2. To those folks who may talk too much, Abraham Lincoln gives the following advice: "It is better to remain silent and be thought a fool than to speak out and remove all doubt."

3. A recent Gallup poll found that Americans consider only one activity more stressful than visiting the dentist hosting a dinner party.

4. Mr. and Mrs. Garden Slug loved their wedding gift a set of salt and pepper shakers.

5. Please remember to buy the following at the pet store, one pound of cat food, two flea collars, kitty fang floss, a bag of catnip, and thirty-six lint rollers.

6. A Director of Academic Services at Pennsylvania State University once nominated this sentence for Punctuation Error of the Year; "I had to leave my good friend's behind and find new ones."

7. Some of the cars manufactured between 1907 and 1912 that didn't achieve the popularity of the Model T were: the Black Crow, the Swallow, the Bugmobile, and the Carnation.

8. There's only one thing that can make our lawn look as good as our neighbor's; snow.

continued on next page

© Canstock Images, Inc./
Index Stock Imagery

9. In a Thurmont, Maryland, cemetery can be found this epitaph "Here lies an Atheist, all dressed up, and no place to go."

10. George Bernard Shaw, the famous playwright, claimed he wanted the following epitaph on his tombstone: "I knew if I stayed around long enough, something like this would happen."

21g   The Apostrophe (') AP

1. Use an apostrophe to indicate omitted letters in a contraction ("cannot" = "can't").

   Examples   *It's* too bad your car burned.

   Wouldn't the insurance company believe your story?

   Many people today confuse "it's" (the contraction for "it is") and "its" (the possessive pronoun, which never takes an apostrophe).

   Its = shows possession, functioning like "his" or "her"
   It's = contraction for "it is"

   Examples   The car is old, but *its* paint is new. ["Its" shows the car's possession of paint.]

   The car is old, but *it's* reliable. ["It's" is a contraction for "it is."]

   If you are ever in doubt about your choice, read the sentence aloud, saying the words "it is" in place of the *its/it's* in question. If the sentence becomes nonsensical (The car is old but it is coat of paint is new), then the possessive form "its" is probably what you need.

   Special note: There is no "its'." No such word exists in the English language! Forget you even thought about it!

2. Add an apostrophe plus "s" to a noun to show possession.

   Examples   *Jack's* dog ate the *cat's* dinner.

   The *veterinarian's* assistant later doctored the *puppy's* wounds.

3. Add only an apostrophe to a plural noun ending in "s" to show possession.

   Examples   Goldilocks invaded the *bears'* house.

   She ignored her *parents'* warning about breaking and entering.

4. To show joint possession between two people or things, you need to add an apostrophe and "-s" only to the second noun. To show separate ownership, add an apostrophe plus "-s" to both nouns.

   Examples   Isabel and *Sharona's* design project will be presented today. [one project]

   Isabel's and *Sharona's* design projects will be presented today. [separate projects]

5. Be careful to avoid adding an apostrophe when the occasion simply calls for the plural use of a word.

Incorrect	*Apple's* are on sale now.
Correct	*Apples* are on sale now.
Incorrect	We ordered *chip's* and dip.
Correct	We ordered *chips* and dip.

6. In some cases you may add an apostrophe plus "s" to a singular word ending in "s," especially when the word is a proper name or for ease of pronunciation.

Examples	*Doris's* name was popular in the 1950s.
	The silent screen *actress's* favorite flowers were mums.

7. To avoid confusion, you may use an apostrophe plus "s" to form the plurals of letters and words discussed as words. An apostrophe is not used on plural numbers (1960s, 80s, nines) or abbreviations (MAs, DVDs, CDs).

Examples	He made four "*C's*" last fall. [or "*Cs*"]
	You use too many "*and's*" in your sentence. [or "*ands*"]

© Carstock Images, Inc./Index Stock Imagery

PRACTICING WHAT YOU'VE LEARNED

Errors with Apostrophes

A. Correct the apostrophe errors you see in the following phrases.

1. A horses' pajamas
2. The queens throne
3. A families' vacation
4. Ten students grades
5. The Depression of the 1930s' was over.
6. That dress of hers'
7. The childrens' toys
8. Worm's for sale
9. Bill Jones car
10. All essay's are due today.
11. Sign both the painters and the roofer's contracts.
12. Womens hats with feather's for decoration

continued on next page

PRACTICING WHAT YOU'VE LEARNED
Errors with Parentheses, Brackets, and Dashes

Show that you understand the different uses of parentheses, brackets, and dashes by selecting the best choice in the sentences that follow. Skip any correct sentences you see. (◆ For additional practice, see also the exercise that appears on pages 596–597.)

1. George Eliot (the pen name of Mary Ann Evans) wrote the novel *Middlemarch.*

2. The Apostrophe Protection Society, founded in London in 2001, fights against the gross misuse of this mark of punctuation. Editor's note: For help with apostrophes, see pages 584–585 in this text.

3. A Russian woman holds the record for the highest number of children born to one mother: sixty-nine babies in a total of twenty-seven pregnancies sixteen pairs of twins, seven sets of triplets, and four sets of quadruplets.

4. More men holding first-class tickets on the *Titanic* were saved than childrens (sic) in the third-class section of the ship.

5. Billy Clyde could stay married to Maybelle as long as he played his cards right [his Visa card, his Mastercard, his American Express card.]

21 The Hyphen (-)* P

1. Use a hyphen to join words into a single adjective before a noun.

   Examples   a wind-blown wig

   the mud-caked sneakers

   a made-for-television movie

   a well-written essay

   a five-year-old boy

   Do not use a hyphen when the modifier ends in "-ly."

   Examples   a highly regarded worker

   a beautifully landscaped yard

2. Writers who create original compound adjectives often join the words with hyphens.

   Examples   Compulsive shoppers suffer from stuff-lust syndrome.

   She prefers novels with they-lived-wretchedly-ever-after endings.

---

*Do not confuse the hyphen with the dash. In typed work, a hyphen is indicated by *one* bar mark ("-"); a dash is indicated by *two* bar marks ("--").

3. Some compound words are always spelled with a hyphen; check your dictionary when you're in doubt. Note that compound numbers from twenty-one to ninety-nine use a hyphen.

   Examples   mother-in-law

   president-elect

   runner-up

   good-for-nothing

   twenty-nine

   Compound words made from combining verb forms are frequently hyphenated: The psychiatrist insisted his birthday presents be *shrink-wrapped.*

4. Some words with prefixes use a hyphen; again, check your dictionary if necessary. (Hint: If the second word begins with a capital letter, a hyphen is almost always used.)

   Examples   ex-wife

   self-esteem

   all-American

   non-English

5. In a series of compound adjectives, place a space (or a comma and a space, when appropriate) following the hyphen in every item except the last one.

   Examples   They surveyed students at both two- and four-year colleges.

   She found herself on both the best- and the worst-dressed lists.

   He suffered first-, second-, and third-degree burns on his arms.

6. Use a hyphen to mark the separation of syllables when you divide a word at the end of a line. Do not divide one-syllable words; do not leave one or two letters at the end of a line. (In most dictionaries, dots are used to indicate the division of syllables: va • ca • tion.)

   Examples   In your essays you should avoid using fragment sentences.

   Did your father try to help you with your homework?

© Canstock Images, Inc./
Index Stock Imagery

PRACTICING WHAT YOU'VE LEARNED

Errors with Hyphens

Correct the errors in the phrases that follow by adding, deleting, or changing hyphens. Skip any correct uses you see.

1. A first class event

2. The well done steak

3. A self employed person

continued on next page

2. Three points with spaces may be used to show an incomplete or interrupted thought.

Example My wife is an intelligent, beautiful woman who wants me to live a long time. On the other hand, Harry's wife . . . oh, never mind.

3. If you omit any words at the end of a quotation and you are also ending your sentence, use three points plus a fourth to indicate the period. There should be no space before the first point.

Example Lincoln wrote, "Four score and seven years ago our fathers brought forth, upon this continent, a new nation. . . ."

Note: If a parenthetical reference follows ellipses at the end of your sentence, use three points with a space before each and put a period after the parenthesis:

Lincoln wrote, "Four score and seven years ago our fathers brought forth, upon this continent, a new nation . . ." (139-140).

4. If the omission of one or more sentences occurs at the end of a quoted sentence, use four points with no space before the first point.

Example "The Lord is my shepherd; I shall not want. . . . he leadeth me in the paths of righteousness for his name's sake."

5. Use a row of ellipsis points to indicate one or more missing lines of poetry.

Example Failing to fetch me at first keep encouraged.

. . . .

I stop somewhere waiting for you.
    —Walt Whitman, "Song of Myself"

6. Ellipsis points can occasionally be used to show hesitation or a pause in thought.

Example "Yes, I'm leaving . . . I need to find myself," said Waldo.

21o The Slash (/) P

1. Use a slash between terms to indicate that either is acceptable. Do not put a space on either side of the slash.

Examples Bring a salad *and/or* a dessert to share at the picnic.

     Be careful to avoid the *either/or* fallacy in your argument paper.

2. Use a slash to mark line divisions in quoted poetry. Do use a space both before and after the slash.

Example In this poem Shakespeare describes love as "an ever-fixed mark / That looks on tempests and is never shaken."

© Canstock mages, Inc./
Index Stock Imagery

PRACTICING WHAT YOU'VE LEARNED

**Errors with Parentheses, Brackets, Dashes,
Hyphens, Italics, Ellipses, and Slashes**

Correct the following errors by adding, changing, or deleting
parentheses, brackets, dashes, hyphens, italics, ellipsis points, and slashes.

1. Many moviegoers know that the ape in King Kong the original 1933 version, not the re-make was only an eighteen inch tall animated figure, but not everyone realizes that the Red Sea Moses parted in the 1923 movie of The Ten Commandments was a quivering slab of Jell O sliced down-the-middle.

2. We recall the last words of General John B. Sedgwick at the Battle of Spotsylvania in 1864: "They couldn't hit an elephant at this dist ."

3. In a person to person telephone call the twenty five year old starlet promised the hard working gossip columnist that she would "tell the truth . . . and nothing but the truth" about her highly-publicized feud with her exhusband, editor in chief of Meat Eaters Digest.

4. While sailing across the Atlantic on board the celebrity filled yacht Titanic II, Dottie Mae Haskell she's the author of the popular new self help book Finding Wolves to Raise Your Children confided that until recently she thought chutzpah was an Italian side dish.

5. During their twenty four hour sit in at the melt down site, the anti-nuclear protestors began to sing, "Oh, say can you see . . ."

6. Few people know that James Arness later Matt Dillon in the long running television series Gunsmoke got his start by playing the vegetable creature in the postwar monster movie The Thing 1951.

7. If you do not pay your rent on time, your landlord has the right to charge a late fee and-or begin an eviction procedure.

8. A French chemist named Georges Claude invented the first neon sign in 1910. For additional information on his unsuccessful attempts to use seawater to generate electricity, see pages 200–205.

9. When Lucille Ball, star of I Love Lucy, became pregnant with her first child, the network executives decided that the word expecting could be used on the air to refer to her condition, but not the word pregnant.

10. In mystery stories the detective often advises the police to cherchez la femme. Editor's note: Cherchez la femme means "look for the woman."

CHAPTER 22

A Concise Guide
to Mechanics

22a   Capitalization   Cap

1. Capitalize the first word of every sentence.

> **Example**   The lazy horse leans against a tree all day.

2. Capitalize proper nouns—the specific names of people, places, and products—and also the adjectives formed from proper nouns.

> **Examples**   John Doe
> Austin, Texas
> First National Bank
> the Eiffel Tower
> Chevrolets
> Japanese cameras
> Spanish class
> an English major

3. Always capitalize the days of the week, the names of the months, and holidays.

> **Examples**   Saturday, December 14
> Tuesday's meeting
> Halloween parties

Special events are often capitalized: Super Bowl, World Series, Festival of Lights.

4. Capitalize titles when they are accompanied by proper names.

> **Examples**   President Jones, Major Smith, Governor Brown, Judge Wheeler,
> Professor Plum, Queen Elizabeth

5. Capitalize all the principal words in titles of books, articles, stories, plays, movies, and poems. Prepositions, articles, and conjunctions are not capitalized unless they begin or end the title.

   Examples   "The Face on the Barroom Floor"

   A Short History of the Civil War

   For Whom the Bell Tolls

6. Capitalize the first word of a direct quotation.

   Examples   Shocked at actor John Barrymore's use of profanity, the woman said, "Sir, I'll have you know I'm a lady!"

   Barrymore replied, "Your secret is safe with me."

7. Capitalize "east," "west," "north," and "south" when they refer to particular sections of the country but not when they merely indicate direction.

   Examples   The South has produced many excellent writers, including William Faulkner and Flannery O'Connor. ["South" here refers to a section of the country.]

   If you travel south for ten miles, you'll see the papier-mâché replica of the world's largest hamburger. [In this case, "south" is a direction.]

8. Capitalize a title when referring to a particular person;* do not capitalize a title if a pronoun precedes it.

   Examples   The President announced a new national holiday honoring Frank H. Fleer, inventor of bubble gum.

   The new car Dad bought is guaranteed for 10,000 miles or until something goes wrong.

   My mother told us about a Hollywood party during which Zelda and F. Scott Fitzgerald collected and boiled all the women's purses.

9. Capitalize important historic movements, documents, and events.

   Examples   the Civil Rights Movement

   World War I

   Impressionism

   Declaration of Independence

   D-Day

10. Capitalize the names of religions, their followers, revered books, and holidays.

   Examples   Islam

   Methodists

   Torah

   Bible

   Easter

---

*Some authorities disagree; others consider such capitalization optional.

11. Capitalize the letters that make up abbreviations for organizations, companies, agencies, and well-known people, places, and events.

Examples	NFL
	CBS
	FEMA
	JFK
	USA
	WW II

© Canstock Images, Inc./
Index Stock Imagery

PRACTICING WHAT YOU'VE LEARNED

Errors with Capitalization

A. Correct the errors in capitalization in the following phrases.

1. delicious chinese food

2. memorial day memories

3. fiery southwestern salsa

4. his latest novel, entitled *a prince at work*

5. bible study at the baptist church

6. count Dracula's castle in transylvania

7. african american heritage

8. a dodge van driven across the golden gate bridge

9. sunday morning programs on abc

10. the british daughter-in-law of senator Snort

B. Write a sentence in which the following pairs of words are capitalized correctly. Example: He joined the U.S. Navy wearing his best white shirt and navy pants.

1. street, Street

2. lake, Lake

3. mustang, Mustang

4. south, South

5. president, President

Abbreviations   Ab

1. Abbreviate the titles "Mr.," "Mrs.," "Ms.," "St.," and "Dr." when they precede names.

Examples   Dr. Scott, Ms. Steinham, Mrs. White, St. Jude

2. Abbreviate titles and degrees when they follow names.

Examples   Charles Byrd, Jr.; David Hall, Ph.D.; Dudley Carpenter, D.D.S.

3. You may abbreviate the following in even the most formal writing: "A.M." (*ante meridiem*, before noon), "P.M." (*post meridiem*, after noon), "A.D." (*anno Domini*, in the year of our Lord), "B.C." (before Christ), "C.E." (common era), "B.C.E." (before the common era), "etc." (*et cetera*, and others), "i.e." (*id est*, that is), and "e.g." (*exempli gratia*, for example).

4. In formal writing, do *not* abbreviate the names of days, months, centuries, states, countries, or units of measure. Do *not* use an ampersand (&) unless it is an official part of a title.

Incorrect in formal writing	Tues., Sept., 18th century, Ark., Mex., lbs.
Correct	Tuesday, September, eighteenth century, Arkansas, Mexico, pounds
Incorrect	Tony & Gus went to the store to buy ginseng root.
Correct	Tony *and* Gus went to the A & P to buy ginseng root. [The "&" in "A & P" is correct because it is part of the store's official name.]

5. In formal writing, do *not* abbreviate the words "page," "chapter," "volume," and so forth, except in footnotes and bibliographies, which have prescribed rules of abbreviation.

6. Except in formal writing, it is often permissible to use abbreviations or acronyms for well-known organizations or people. However, you should spell out the abbreviation the first time, to avoid any confusion.

Examples   Franklin Delano Roosevelt (FDR)

National Public Radio (NPR)

North Atlantic Treaty Organization (NATO)

(For additional information on proper abbreviation, consult your dictionary.)

22c   Numbers   Num

1. Use figures for dates; street, room, and apartment numbers; page numbers; telephone numbers; percentages, and decimals.

Examples   April 22, 1946

710 West 14th Street

page 242

room 17

476-1423

40 percent

3.78 GPA

2. Use figures for hours with "A.M." and "P.M." but write out the time when you use "o'clock."

Examples   8.00 A.M. or 8 A.M.

eight o'clock in the morning

3. Some authorities say to spell out numbers that can be expressed in one or two words; others say to spell out numbers under one hundred.

Examples   ten thousand dollars or $10,000

twenty-four hours

thirty-nine years

five partridges

$12.99 per pair

1,294 essays

4. When several numbers are used in a short passage, use figures.

Examples   In the anchovy-eating contest, Jennifer ate 22, Juan ate 21, Pete ate 16, and I ate 6.

According to the U.S. Census Bureau, on an average day 11,000 babies are born, 6,000 people die, 7,000 couples marry, and 3,000 couples divorce.

5. Never begin a sentence with a figure.

Incorrect   50 spectators turned out to watch the surfing exhibition at Niagara Falls.

Correct   Fifty spectators turned out to watch the surfing exhibition at Niagara Falls.

6. When a date containing a day and a year appears within a sentence, always set off the year by placing commas on each side.

Examples   She married her first husband on February 2, 1978, in Texas.

The first birth on a commercial airliner occurred on October 28, 1929, as the plane cruised over Miami.

© Canstock Images, Inc. / Index Stock Imagery

PRACTICING WHAT YOU'VE LEARNED

Errors in Capitalization, Abbreviations, and Numbers

Correct the following errors by adding, deleting, or changing capitals, abbreviations, and numbers. Skip any correct words, letters, or numbers you may find.

1. Speaking to students at Gallaudet university, Marian Wright Edelman, Founder and president of the Children's Defense Fund, noted that an american child is born into poverty every thirty seconds, is born to a

continued on next page

teen mother every 60 seconds, is abused or neglected every 26 seconds, is arrested for a violent crime every five minutes, and is killed by a gun every two hours.

2. My sister, who lives in the east, was amazed to read studies by Thomas Radecki, MD, showing that 12-year-olds commit 300 percent more murders than did the same age group 30 years ago.

3. In C.E. sixty-seven the roman emperor Nero entered the chariot race at the olympic games, and although he failed to finish the race, the judges unanimously declared him the Winner.

4. According to John Alcock, a Behavioral Ecologist at Arizona State University, in the U.S.A. the chance of being poisoned by a snake is 20 times less than that of being hit by lightning and 300 times less than the risk of being murdered by a fellow American.

5. The official chinese news agency, located in the city of xinhua, estimates that there are ten million guitar players in their country today, an amazing number considering that the instrument was banned during the cultural revolution, which lasted 10 years, from nineteen sixty-six to nineteen seventy-six.

6. 231 electoral votes were cast for James Monroe but only 1 for John Quincy Adams in the 1820 Presidential race.

7. The british soldier T. E. Lawrence, better known as "lawrence of arabia," stood less than 5 ft. 6 in. tall.

8. Before my 10 a.m. english class, held in wrigley field every other friday except on New Year's day, I eat 3 pieces of french pastry.

9. When a political opponent once called him "two-faced," president Lincoln retorted, "if I had another face, do you think I would wear this one?"

10. Alexander Graham Bell, inventor of the telephone, died on aug. 2, 1922 in nova scotia; 2 days later, on the day of his burial, for 1 minute no telephone in north america was allowed to ring.

ASSIGNMENT

© CORBIS

Collaborative Activity: After studying the rules in this chapter, write a paragraph of at least five sentences containing the following data. Create the information for a mythical person (Captain Glass Half-Full born in Optimism, Indiana? Your Evil Twin raised in Elbonia?). Exchange paragraphs with a classmate, and circle any errors you see in capitalization, abbreviations, or numbers. Work together to correct any errors you find.

Include this data:

City, state/province, and country of birth
Day, month, year, and century of birth
Exact time of birth
Current professional title and salary
Favorite holiday, book, and movie
Membership in a sports league or organization, name abbreviated
Number and kinds of pets

22d Spelling Sp

For some folks, learning to spell correctly is harder than trying to herd cats. Entire books have been written to teach people to become better spellers, and some of these are available at your local bookstore (and, no, not listed under witchcraft). Here, however, are a few suggestions that seem to work for many students:

1. Keep a list of the little beasties you misspell. After a few weeks, you may notice that you tend to misspell the same words again and again or that the words you misspell tend to fit a pattern—that is, you can't remember when the *i* goes before the *e* or when to change the *y* to *i* before *-ed*. Try to memorize the words you repeatedly misspell, or at least keep the list somewhere handy so you can refer to it when you're editing your last draft (listing the words in a computer file or on the inside cover of your desk dictionary also makes sense).

2. Become aware of a few rules that govern some of our spelling in English. For example, many people know the rule in the jingle "*I* before *E* except after *C* or when sounded like *A* as in *neighbor* and *weigh*." Not everyone, however, knows the follow-up line, which contains most of the exceptions to that jingle: "Neither the weird financier nor the foreigner seizes leisure at its height."

3. Here are some other rules, without jingles, for adding suffixes (new endings to words), a common plague for poor spellers:

   * Change final *y* to *i* if the *y* follows a consonant.*

     bury → buried
     marry → marries

   * But if the suffix is -*ing*, keep the *y*.

     marry + ing = marrying
     worry + ing = worrying

   * If the word ends in a single consonant after a single vowel and the accent is on the last syllable, double the consonant before adding the suffix.

     occur → occurred
     cut → cutting
     swim → swimmer

---

*Reminder: Consonants are all the letters that are not vowels (*a, e, i, o, u,* and sometimes *y*).

- If a word ends in a silent *e*, drop the *e* before adding *-able* or *-ing*.

  love + able = lovable
  believe + able = believable

4. And here's an easy rule governing the doubling of letters with the addition of prefixes (new beginning syllables): Most of the time, you simply add all the letters you've got when you mix the word and the prefix.

   mis + spell = misspell
   un + natural = unnatural
   re + entry = reentry

5. Teach yourself to spell the words that you miss often by making up your own silly rules or jingles. For instance:

   - dessert (one *s* or two?): I always want two helpings so I double the *s*.
   - apparently (apparantly?): Ap*parent*ly, my *parent* knows the whole story.
   - separate (seperate?): I'd be *a rat* to sep*a rat*e from you.
   - a lot (or alot?): A cot (not *acot*) provides *a lot* of comfort in a tent.
   - all right (or alright?): Think of the rhyme "all right, good night" and remember that both these phrases have two words. (No matter what Roger Daltrey and The Who said, the line should be "The kids are all right"!)
   - questionnaire (one *n* or two?): Questio*nn*aires have *n*umerous *n*umbered questions (two *n*'s).

   And so on.

6. Proofread your papers carefully. Anything that looks misspelled probably is and deserves to be looked up in your dictionary. Reading your paper one sentence at a time from the end helps, too, because you tend to start thinking about your ideas when you read from the beginning of your paper. If you are writing on a word processor that has a spell-checking program, don't forget to run it; however, do remember that such programs will skip over confused words (*to* for *too*, *there* for *their*) that are spelled correctly.

Although these few suggestions won't completely cure your spelling problems, they can make a dramatic improvement in the quality of your papers and give you the confidence to continue learning and practicing other rules that govern the spelling of our language. Good luck!

PART 5

Additional Readings

Part Five offers thirty-four additional readings to help you improve your writing skills. In nine chapters, three selections illustrate each of the modes and strategies previously explained in Part Two. In addition, Chapter 32 includes a speech and two essays illustrating multiple strategies and styles for further analysis; Chapter 33 offers three poems and a story to supplement literary assignments. Overall, the readings in Part Five were selected not only to model methods of development but also to illustrate a variety of styles and tones, including humor and irony.

A close reading of these selections can help you become a better writer in several ways. Identifying the various methods by which these writers focused, organized, and developed their material may spark new ideas as you plan and shape your own essay. Familiarizing yourself with different styles and tones may encourage new uses of language. Analyzing the rhetorical choices of other writers will also help you revise your prose because it promotes the habit of asking questions from the reader's point of view. Moreover, reading the opinions or sharing the experiences of these authors may suggest interesting topics for your own essays. In other words, to help yourself become a more effective writer, read as much and as often as you can.

CHAPTER 23

Exposition: Development by Example

Darkness at Noon

Harold Krents

Harold Krents was a Washington, D.C., attorney and activist for the rights of the disabled. Before his death in 1987, Krents served on the President's Committee on Employment of the Handicapped and was a member of the Vera Institute of Justice and Mainstream, Incorporated. His autobiography *To Race the Wind* was published in 1972; his life was the inspiration for the Broadway play and popular movie *Butterflies Are Free*. This essay originally appeared in the *New York Times* in 1976.

1 Blind from birth, I have never had the opportunity to see myself and have been completely dependent on the image I create in the eye of the observer. To date it has not been narcissistic.

2 There are those who assume that since I can't see, I obviously also cannot hear. Very often people will converse with me at the top of their lungs, enunciating each word very carefully. Conversely, people will also often whisper, assuming that since my eyes don't work, my ears don't either.

3 For example, when I go to the airport and ask the ticket agent for assistance to the plane, he or she will invariably pick up the phone, call a ground hostess and whisper: "Hi, Jane, we've got a 76 here." I have concluded that the word "blind" is not used for one of two reasons: Either they fear that if the dread word is spoken, the ticket agent's retina will immediately detach, or they are reluctant to inform me of my condition of which I may not have been previously aware.

4   On the other hand, others know that of course I can hear, but believe that I can't talk. Often, therefore, when my wife and I go out to dinner, a waiter or waitress will ask Kit if "*he* would like a drink" to which I respond that "indeed *he* would."

5   This point was graphically driven home to me while we were in England. I had been given a year's leave of absence from my Washington law firm to study for a diploma in law at Oxford University. During the year I became ill and was hospitalized. Immediately after admission, I was wheeled down to the X-ray room. Just at the door sat an elderly woman—elderly I would judge from the sound of her voice. "What is his name?" the woman asked the orderly who had been wheeling me.

6   "What's your name?" the orderly repeated to me.

7   "Harold Krents," I replied.

8   "Harold Krents," he repeated.

9   "When was he born?"

10   "When were you born?"

11   "November 5, 1944," I responded.

12   "November 5, 1944," the orderly intoned.

13   This procedure continued for approximately five minutes at which point even my saint-like disposition deserted me. "Look," I finally blurted out, "this is absolutely ridiculous. Okay, granted I can't see, but it's got to have become pretty clear to both of you that I don't need an interpreter."

14   "He says he doesn't need an interpreter," the orderly reported to the woman.

15   The toughest misconception of all is the view that because I can't see, I can't work. I was turned down by over forty law firms because of my blindness, even though my qualifications included a cum laude degree from Harvard College and a good ranking in my Harvard Law School class.

16   The attempt to find employment, the continuous frustration of being told that it was impossible for a blind person to practice law, the rejection letters, not based on my lack of ability but rather on my disability, will always remain one of the most disillusioning experiences of my life.

17   Fortunately, this view of limitation and exclusion is beginning to change. On April 16 [1976], the Department of Labor issued regulations that mandate equal-employment opportunities for the handicapped. By and large, the business community's response to offering employment to the disabled has been enthusiastic.

18   I therefore look forward to the day, with the expectation that it is certain to come, when employers will view their handicapped workers as a little child did me years ago when my family still lived in Scarsdale.

19   I was playing basketball with my father in our backyard according to procedures we had developed. My father would stand beneath the hoop, shout, and I would shoot over his head at the basket attached to our garage. Our next-door neighbor, aged five, wandered over into our yard with a playmate. "He's blind," our neighbor whispered to her friend in a voice that could be heard distinctly by Dad and me. Dad shot and missed; I did the same. Dad hit the rim: I missed entirely: Dad shot and missed the garage entirely. "Which one is blind?" whispered back the little friend.

20   I would hope that in the near future when a plant manager is touring the factory with the foreman and comes upon a handicapped and non-handicapped person working together, his comment after watching them work will be, "Which one is disabled?"

Black Men and Public Space

Brent Staples

Brent Staples is an editorial writer for the *New York Times* and has published essays and reviews in a number of other newspapers and magazines, including the *Chicago-Sun Times*, the *New York Review of Books*, and *Slate* magazine. He holds a Ph.D. in psychology from the University of Chicago, and his memoir *Parallel Time: Growing Up in Black and White* (1994) won the Anisfield Wolff Book Award. This essay first appeared in *Ms.* magazine in 1986.

1 My first victim was a woman—white, well dressed, probably in her late twenties. I came upon her late one evening on a deserted street in Hyde Park, a relatively affluent neighborhood in an otherwise mean, impoverished section of Chicago. As I swung onto the avenue behind her, there seemed to be a discreet, uninflammatory distance between us. Not so. She cast back a worried glance. To her, the youngish black man—a broad six feet two inches with a beard and billowing hair, both hands shoved into the pockets of a bulky military jacket—seemed menacingly close. After a few more quick glimpses, she picked up her pace and was soon running in earnest. Within seconds she disappeared into a cross street.

2 That was more than a decade ago. I was twenty-two years old, a graduate student newly arrived at the University of Chicago. It was in the echo of that terrified woman's footfalls that I first began to know the unwieldy inheritance I'd come into—the ability to alter public space in ugly ways. It was clear that she thought herself the quarry of a mugger, a rapist, or worse. Suffering a bout of insomnia, however, I was stalking sleep, not defenseless wayfarers. As a softy who is scarcely able to take a knife to a raw chicken—let alone hold one to a person's throat—I was surprised, embarrassed, and dismayed all at once. Her flight made me feel like an accomplice in tyranny. It also made it clear that I was indistinguishable from the muggers who occasionally seeped into the area from the surrounding ghetto. That first encounter, and those that followed, signified that a vast, unnerving gulf lay between nighttime pedestrians—particularly women—and me. And I soon gathered that being perceived as dangerous is a hazard in itself. I only needed to turn a corner into a dicey situation, or crowd some frightened, armed person in a foyer somewhere, or make an errant move after being pulled over by a policeman. Where fear and weapons meet—and they often do in urban America—there is always the possibility of death.

3 In that first year, my first away from my hometown, I was to become thoroughly familiar with the language of fear. At dark, shadowy intersections, I could cross in front of a car stopped at a traffic light and elicit the *thunk, thunk, thunk, thunk* of the driver—black, white, male, or female—hammering down the door locks. On less traveled streets after dark, I grew accustomed to but never comfortable with people crossing to the other side of the street rather than pass me. Then there were the standard unpleasantries with policemen, doormen, bouncers, cabdrivers, and others whose business it is to screen out troublesome individuals *before* there is any nastiness.

4 I moved to New York nearly two years ago and I have remained an avid night walker. In central Manhattan, the near-constant crowd cover minimizes tense

one-on-one street encounters. Elsewhere—in SoHo, for example, where sidewalks are narrow and tightly spaced buildings shut out the sky—things can get very taut indeed.

5   After dark, on the warrenlike streets of Brooklyn where I live, I often see women who fear the worst from me. They seem to have set their faces on neutral, and with their purse straps strung across their chests bandolier-style, they forge ahead as though bracing themselves against being tackled. I understand, of course, that the danger they perceive is not a hallucination. Women are particularly vulnerable to street violence, and young black males are drastically overrepresented among the perpetrators of that violence. Yet these truths are no solace against the kind of alienation that comes of being ever the suspect, a fearsome entity with whom pedestrians avoid making eye contact.

6   It is not altogether clear to me how I reached the ripe old age of twenty-two without being conscious of the lethality nighttime pedestrians attributed to me. Perhaps it was because in Chester, Pennsylvania, the small, angry industrial town where I came of age in the 1960s, I was scarcely noticeable against a backdrop of gang warfare, street knifings, and murders. I grew up one of the good boys, had perhaps a half-dozen fistfights. In retrospect, my shyness of combat has clear sources.

7   As a boy, I saw countless tough guys locked away; I have since buried several, too. They were babies, really—a teenage cousin, a brother of twenty-two, a childhood friend in his mid-twenties—all gone down in episodes of bravado played out in the streets. I came to doubt the virtues of intimidation early on. I chose, perhaps unconsciously, to remain a shadow—timid, but a survivor.

8   The fearsomeness mistakenly attributed to me in public places often has a perilous flavor. The most frightening of these confusions occurred in the late 1970s and early 1980s, when I worked as a journalist in Chicago. One day, rushing into the office of a magazine I was writing for with a deadline story in hand, I was mistaken for a burglar. The office manager called security and, with an ad hoc posse, pursued me through the labyrinthine halls, nearly to my editor's door. I had no way of proving who I was. I could only move briskly toward the company of someone who knew me.

9   Another time I was on assignment for a local paper and killing time before an interview. I entered a jewelry store on the city's affluent Near North Side. The proprietor excused herself and returned with an enormous red Doberman pinscher straining at the end of a leash. She stood, the dog extended toward me, silent to my questions, her eyes bulging nearly out of her head. I took a cursory look around, nodded, and bade her good night.

10   Relatively speaking, however, I never fared as badly as another black male journalist. He went to nearby Waukegan, Illinois, a couple of summers ago to work on a story about a murderer who was born there. Mistaking the reporter for the killer, police officers hauled him from his car at gunpoint and but for his press credentials would probably have tried to book him. Such episodes are not uncommon. Black men trade tales like this all the time.

11   Over the years, I learned to smother the rage I felt at so often being taken for a criminal. Not to do so would surely have led to madness. I now take precautions to make myself less threatening. I move about with care, particularly late in the

evening. I give a wide berth to nervous people on subway platforms during the wee hours, particularly when I have exchanged business clothes for jeans. If I happen to be entering a building behind some people who appear skittish, I may walk by, letting them clear the lobby before I return, so as not to seem to be following them. I have been calm and extremely congenial on those rare occasions when I've been pulled over by the police.

12   And on late-evening constitutionals I employ what has proved to be an excellent tension-reducing measure: I whistle melodies from Beethoven and Vivaldi and the more popular classical composers. Even steely New Yorkers hunching toward nighttime destinations seem to relax, and occasionally they even join in the tune. Virtually everybody seems to sense that a mugger wouldn't be warbling bright, sunny selections from Vivaldi's *Four Seasons*. It is my equivalent of the cowbell that hikers wear when they know they are in bear country.

Thank You

Alex Haley

American author Alex Haley is best known for his Pulitzer Prize–winning novel *Roots* (1976). Based on family stories of his African ancestors, *Roots* has been translated into thirty-seven languages and was made into the first week-long television mini-series. Other works include *The Autobiography of Malcolm X* (1965) and *A Different Kind of Christmas* (1990). This essay first appeared in *Parade* magazine in 1982.

1   It was 1943, during World War II, and I was a young U.S. coastguardsman, serial number 212-548, a number we never seem to forget. My ship, the USS *Murzim,* had been under way for several days. Most of her holds contained thousands of cartons of canned or dried foods. The other holds were loaded with five-hundred-pound bombs packed delicately in padded racks. Our destination was a big base on the Island of Tulagi in the South Pacific.

2   I was one of the *Murzim*'s several cooks and, quite the same as for folk ashore, this Thanksgiving morning had seen us busily preparing a traditional dinner featuring roast turkey.

3   Well, as any cook knows, it's a lot of hard work to cook and serve a big meal, and clean up and put everything away. But finally around sundown, with our whole galley crew just bushed, we finished at last and were free to go flop into our bunks in the fo'c'sle.

4   But I decided first to go out on the *Murzim*'s afterdeck for a breath of open air. I made my way out there, breathing in great, deep draughts while walking slowly about, still wearing my white cook's hat and the long apron, my feet sensing the big ship's vibrations from the deep-set, turbine diesels and my ears hearing that slightly hissing sound the sea makes in resisting the skin of a ship.

5   I got to thinking about Thanksgiving. In reflex, my thought registered the historic imagery of the Pilgrims, Indians, wild turkeys, pumpkins, corn on the cob and the rest.

6   Yet my mind seemed to be questing for something else—some way that I could personally apply to the waning Thanksgiving. It must have taken me a half hour

to sense that maybe some key to an answer could result from reversing the word "Thanksgiving"—at least that suggested a verbal direction, "Giving thanks."

7   Giving thanks—as in praying, thanking God, I thought. Yes, of course. Certainly.

8   Yet my mind continued nagging me. Fine. But something else.

9   After a while, like a dawn's brightening, a further answer did come—that there were *people* to thank, people who had done so much for me that I could never possibly repay them. The embarrassing truth was I'd always just accepted what they'd done, taken all of it for granted. Not one time had I ever bothered to express to any of them so much as a simple, sincere "Thank you."

10   At least seven people had been particularly and indelibly helpful to me. I realized, with a gulp, that about half of them had since died—so they were forever beyond any possible expression of gratitude from me. The more I thought about it, the more ashamed I became. Then I pictured the three who were still alive and, within minutes, I was down in the fo'c'sle.

11   Sitting at a mess table with writing paper and memories of things each had done, I tried composing genuine statements of heartfelt appreciation and gratitude to my dad, Simon A. Haley, a professor at the old AMNC (Agricultural Mechanical Normal College) in Pine Bluff, Ark., now a branch of the University of Arkansas; to my grandma, Cynthia Palmer, back in our little hometown of Henning, Tenn.; and to the Rev. Lonual Nelson, my grammar school principal, retired and living in Ripley, six miles north of Henning.

12   I couldn't even be certain if they would recall some of their acts of years past, acts that I vividly remembered and saw now as having given me vital training, or inspiration, or directions, if not all of these desirables rolled into one.

13   The texts of my letters began something like "Here, this Thanksgiving at sea, I find my thoughts upon how much you have done for me, but I have never stopped and said to you how much I feel the need to thank you—" and briefly I recalled for each of them specific acts performed in my behalf.

14   For instance, something uppermost about my father was how he had impressed upon me from boyhood to love books and reading. In fact, this graduated into a family habit of after-dinner quizzes at the table about books read most recently and new words learned. My love of books never diminished and later led me toward writing books myself. So many times I have felt a sadness when exposed to modern children so immersed in the electronic media that they have little to no awareness of the wondrous world to be discovered in books.

15   I reminded the Reverend Nelson how each morning he would open our little country town's grammar school with a prayer over his assembled students. I told him that whatever positive things I had done since had been influenced at least in part by his morning school prayers.

16   In the letter to my grandmother, I reminded her of a dozen ways she used to teach me how to tell the truth, to be thrifty, to share and to be forgiving and considerate of others. (My reminders included how she'd make me pull switches from a peach tree for my needed lesson.) I thanked her for the years of eating her good cooking, the equal of which I had not found since. (By now, though, I've reflected that these peerless dishes are most gloriously flavored with a pinch of nostalgia.) Finally, I thanked her simply for having sprinkled my life with stardust.

17   Before I slept, my three letters went into our ship's office mail sack. They got mailed when we reached Tulagi Island.

18   We unloaded cargo, reloaded with something else, then again we put to sea in the routine familiar to us, and as the days became weeks, my little personal experience receded. Sometimes, when we were at sea, a mail ship would rendezvous and bring us mail from home, which, of course, we accorded topmost priority.

19   Every time the ship's loudspeaker rasped, "Attention! Mail call!" two-hundred-odd shipmates came pounding up on deck and clustered about the raised hatch atop which two yeomen, standing by those previous bulging gray sacks, were alternately pulling out fistfuls of letters and barking successive names of sailors who were, in turn, hollering "Here! Here!" amid the jostling.

20   One "mail call" brought me responses from Grandma, Dad and the Reverend Nelson—and my reading of their letters left me not only astounded, but more humbled than before.

21   Rather than saying they would forgive that I hadn't previously thanked them, instead, for Pete's sake, they were thanking *me*—for having remembered, for having considered they had done anything so exceptional.

22   Always the college professor, my dad had carefully avoided anything he considered too sentimental, so I knew how moved he was to write me that, after having helped educate many young people, he now felt that his best results included his own son.

23   The Reverend Nelson wrote that his decades as a "simple, old-fashioned principal" had ended with grammar schools undergoing such swift changes that he had retired in self-doubt. "I heard more of what I had done wrong than what I did right," he said, adding that my letter had brought him welcome reassurance that his career had been appreciated.

24   A glance at Grandma's familiar handwriting brought back in a flash memories of standing alongside her white wicker rocking chair, watching her "settin' down" some letter to relatives. Frequently touching her pencil's tip to pursed lips, character by character, each between a short, soft grunt, Grandma would slowly accomplish one word, then the next, so that a finished page would consume hours. I wept over the page representing my Grandma's recent hours invested in expressing her loving gratefulness to *me*—whom she used to diaper!

25   Much later, retired from the Coast Guard and trying to make a living as a writer, I never forgot how those three "thank you" letters gave me an insight into something nigh mystical in human beings, most of whom go about yearning in secret for more of their fellows to express appreciation for their efforts.

26   I discovered in time that, even in the business world, probably no two words are more valued than "thank you," especially among people at stores, airlines, utilities and others that directly serve the public.

27   Late one night, I was one of a half-dozen passengers who straggled weary and grumbling off a plane that had been forced to land at the huge Dallas/Fort Worth Airport. Suddenly, a buoyant, cheerful, red-jacketed airline man waved us away from the regular waiting room seats, saying, "You sure look bushed. I know a big empty office where you can stretch out while you wait." And we surely did. When the weather improved enough for us to leave, "Gene Erickson" was in my notebook

and, back home, I wrote the president of that airline describing his sensitivity and his courtesy. And I received a thank you!

28   I travel a good deal on lecture tours and I urge students especially to tell their parents, grandparents, and other living elders simply "thank you" for all they have done to make possible the lives they now enjoy. Many students have told me they found themselves moved by the response. It is not really surprising, if one only reflects how it must feel to be thanked after you have given for years.

29   Now, approaching Thanksgiving . . . I have asked myself what will I wish for all who are reading this, for our nation, indeed for our whole world—since, quoting a good and wise friend of mine, "In the end we are mightily and merely people, each with similar needs." First, I wish for us, of course, the simple common sense to achieve world peace, that being paramount for the very survival of our kind.

30   And there is something else I wish—so strongly that I have had this line printed across the bottom of all my stationary: *"Find the good—and praise it."**

---

*To honor Haley for his literary achievements and service to country, the U.S. Coast Guard named a cutter after him, including his personal motto, "Find the Good and Praise It," on the ship's emblem.

CHAPTER 24

Exposition: Process Analysis

The Jeaning of America

Carin C. Quinn

Carin C. Quinn is an essayist who received her Master of Arts degree in American Studies from California State University at Los Angeles in 1976. "The Jeaning of America—and the World," was first published in *American Heritage* magazine in 1978.

1   This is the story of a sturdy American symbol which has now spread throughout most of the world. The symbol is not the dollar. It is not even Coca-Cola. It is a simple pair of pants called blue jeans, and what the pants symbolize is what Alexis de Tocqueville called "a manly and legitimate passion for equality. . . ." Blue jeans are favored equally by bureaucrats and cowboys; bankers and deadbeats; fashion designers and beer drinkers. They draw no distinctions and recognize no classes; they are merely American. Yet they are sought after almost everywhere in the world—including Russia, where authorities recently broke up a teenaged gang that was selling them on the black market for two hundred dollars a pair. They have been around for a long time, and it seems likely that they will outlive even the necktie.

2   This ubiquitous American symbol was the invention of a Bavarian-born Jew. His name was Levi Strauss.

3   He was born in Bad Ocheim, Germany, in 1829, and during the European political turmoil of 1848 decided to take his chances in New York, to which his two brothers already had emigrated. Upon arrival, Levi soon found that his two brothers had exaggerated their tales of an easy life in the land of the main chance. They were landowners, they had told him; instead, he found them pushing needles,

thread, pots, pans, ribbons, yarn, scissors, and buttons to housewives. For two years he was a lowly peddler, hauling some 180 pounds of sundries door-to-door to eke out a marginal living. When a married sister in San Francisco offered to pay his way West in 1850, he jumped at the opportunity, taking with him bolts of canvas he hoped to sell for tenting.

4   It was the wrong kind of canvas for that purpose, but while talking with a miner down from the mother lode, he learned that pants—sturdy pants that would stand up to the rigors of the digging—were almost impossible to find. Opportunity beckoned. On the spot, Strauss measured the man's girth and inseam with a piece of string and, for six dollars in gold dust, had [the canvas] tailored into a pair of stiff but rugged pants. The miner was delighted with the result, word got around about "those pants of Levi's," and Strauss was in business. The company has been in business ever since.

5   When Strauss ran out of canvas, he wrote his two brothers to send more. He received instead a tough, brown cotton cloth made in Nîmes, France—called *serge de Nîmes* and swiftly shortened to "denim" (the word "jeans" derives from Gènes, the French word for Genoa, where a similar cloth was produced). Almost from the first, Strauss had his cloth dyed the distinctive indigo that gave blue jeans their name, but it was not until the 1870s that he added the copper rivets which have long since become a company trademark. The rivets were the idea of a Virginia City, Nevada, tailor, Jacob W. Davis, who added them to pacify a mean-tempered miner called Alkali Ike. Alkali, the story goes, complained that the pockets of his jeans always tore when he stuffed them with ore samples and demanded that Davis do something about it. As a kind of joke, Davis took the pants to a blacksmith and had the pockets riveted; once again, the idea worked so well that word got around; in 1873 Strauss appropriated and patented the gimmick—and hired Davis as a regional manager.

6   By this time, Strauss had taken both his brothers and two brothers-in-law into the company and was ready for his third San Francisco store. Over the ensuing years the company prospered locally, and by the time of his death in 1902, Strauss had become a man of prominence in California. For three decades thereafter the business remained profitable though small, with sales largely confined to the working people of the West—cowboys, lumberjacks, railroad workers, and the like. Levi's jeans were first introduced to the East, apparently, during the dude-ranch craze of the 1930s when vacationing Easterners returned and spread the word about the wonderful pants with rivets. Another boost came in World War II, when blue jeans were declared an essential commodity and were sold only to people engaged in defense work. From a company with fifteen salespeople, two plants, and almost no business east of the Mississippi in 1946, the organization grew in thirty years to include a sales force of more than twenty-two thousand, with fifty plants and offices in thirty-five countries. Each year, more than 250,000,000 items of Levi's clothing are sold—including more than 83,000,000 pairs of riveted blue jeans. They have become, through marketing, word of mouth, and demonstrable reliability, the common pants of America. They can be purchased prewashed, prefaded, and pre-shrunk for the suitably proletarian look. They adapt themselves to any sort of idiosyncratic use; women slit them at the inseams and convert them into

long skirts, men chop them off above the knees and turn them into something to be worn while challenging the surf. Decorations and ornamentations abound.

7   The pants have become a tradition, and along the way have acquired a history of their own—so much so that the company has opened a museum in San Francisco. There was, for example, the turn-of-the-century trainman who replaced a faulty coupling with a pair of jeans; the Wyoming man who used his jeans as a towrope to haul his car out of a ditch; the Californian who found several pairs in an abandoned mine, wore them, then discovered they were sixty-three years old and still as good as new and turned them over to the Smithsonian as a tribute to their toughness. And then there is the particularly terrifying story of the careless construction worker who dangled fifty-two stories above the street until rescued, his sole support the Levi's belt loop through which his rope was hooked.

I Slalomly Swear

Dave Barry

Dave Barry is a contemporary humorist whose nationally syndicated newspaper column ran for twenty-five years. He has published numerous collections of his columns, including *Dave Barry's Complete Guide to Guys* (1996), *Dave Barry Is from Mars and Venus* (1998), and *Dave Barry on Dads* (2007), and two novels, *Big Trouble* (1999) and *Tricky Business* (2002). This selection first appeared in newspapers throughout the country in 1989.

1   If you're looking for a vacation concept that combines the element of outdoor fun with the element of potentially knocking down a tree with your face, you can't do better than skiing. My family just got back from a ski trip to Vermont ("The Wind Chill Factor State"), and it was an adventure I'm sure we will remember fondly for many years while our various body parts heal.

2   The key to a successful ski trip, of course, is planning, by which I mean: money. For openers, you have to buy a special outfit that meets the strict requirements of the Ski Fashion Institute, namely: (1) it must cost as much as a medium wedding reception, (2) it must make you look like the Giant Radioactive Easter Bunny From Space and (3) it must be made of a mutant fiber with a name that sounds like the villain on a Saturday-morning cartoon show, such as "Gore-Tex," so as to provide the necessary resistance to moisture, which, trust me, will be gushing violently from all of your major armpits once you start lunging down the mountain. You also have to buy ski goggles costing upward of $50 per eyeball that are specially designed to *not* fog up under any circumstances except when you put them on, at which time they become approximately as transparent as the Los Angeles telephone directory, which is why veteran skiers recommend that you do not pull them down over your eyes until just before you make contact with the tree. And you'll need ski boots, which are made from melted bowling balls and which protect your feet by preventing your blood, which could contain dangerous germs, from traveling below your shins.

3   As for the actual skis, you should rent them because of the feeling of confidence you get from reading the fine print on the lengthy legal document that the rental personnel make you sign, which states:

> The undersigned agrees that skiing is an INSANELY DANGEROUS ACTIVITY, and that the rental personnel were just sitting around minding their OWN BUSINESS when the undersigned, who agrees that he or she is a RAVING LOON, came BARGING IN UNINVITED, waving a LOADED REVOLVER and demanding that he or she be given some rental skis for the express purpose of suffering SERIOUS INJURY OR DEATH, leaving the rental personnel with NO CHOICE but to . . . , etc.

4   OK! Now you're ready to "hit the slopes." Ski experts recommend you start by taking a group lesson because otherwise they would have to get real jobs. To start the lesson, your instructor, who is always a smiling 19-year-old named "Chip," will take you to the top of the mountain and explain basic ski safety procedures until he feels that the cold has killed enough of your brain cells that you will cheerfully follow whatever lunatic command he gives you. Then he'll ski a short distance down the mountain, just to the point where it gets very steep and swoosh to a graceful stop, making it look absurdly easy. It *is* absurdly easy for Chip, because underneath his outfit he's wearing an anti-gravity device. All the expert skiers wear them. You don't actually believe that "ski jumpers" can leap off those ridiculously high ramps and just float to the ground unassisted without breaking into walnut-sized pieces, do you? Like Tinkerbell or something? Don't be a cretin.

5   After Chip stops, he turns to the group, his skis hovering as much as three inches above the snow and orders the first student to copy what he did. This is the fun part. Woodland creatures often wake up from hibernation just to watch this part because even they understand that the laws of physics, which are strictly enforced on ski slopes, do not permit a person to simply stop on the side of a snow-covered mountain if his feet are encased in bowling balls attached to what are essentially large pieces of teflon. So they greatly enjoy watching as the first student cautiously pushes himself forward and almost instantly achieves Warp Speed, becoming an almost-invisible blur as he passes Chip and proceeds on into the woods, flailing his arms like a volunteer in a nerve-gas experiment. "That was good!" shouts Chip . . . then he turns to the rest of the group and says, "Next!" The group's only rational response, of course, would be to lie down in the snow and demand a rescue helicopter. But these are not rational beings; these are ski students. And so, one by one, they, too, ski into the woods, then stagger out sometimes with branches sticking out, antlerlike, from their foreheads, and do it again. "Bend your knees this time!" advises Chip, knowing that this will actually make them go faster. He loves his work.

6   Eventually, of course, you get better at it. If you stick with your lessons, you'll become an "intermediate" skier, meaning you'll learn to fall before you reach the woods. That's the level I'm on now, in stark contrast to my 8-year-old son, who has not yet studied gravity in school and therefore became an expert in a matter of hours. Watching him flash effortlessly down the slope, I found myself experiencing pride and hope; pride in his accomplishment, and hope that someday, somehow, he'll ski near enough to where I'm lying that I'll be able to trip him with my poles.

Successful Presentations: Some Practical Advice

Margaret McDonald

Margaret McDonald is a professional speaker and author of the "Miss Communications" newspaper column and blog. She is president of Smart People Communications, a consulting and training firm that focuses on writing, speaking, and meeting skills. This article, offering guidance for clear presentations, first appeared in her *Coloradoan* newspaper column in March 2009.

1 Speaking to a group can be difficult, but listening to a bad presentation is truly a toilsome task—especially when the speaker is confusing. And what makes a speaker confusing? Failing to heed any of the following advice:

2 • Speak slowly and pause. When it comes to absorbing new information, the human brain needs a little time. First we need to hear and register the words; then we need to compare the incoming information to the stuff we already know. If the new bits seem quite different we need to pause and think—and a good speaker lets us do just that. But a breathless speaker who bolts from one idea to the next and never stops to let us draw them all in gets in the way of learning (big breath here)—and risks confusing us all. Slow it down. And breathe.

3 • Don't contradict yourself. We all occasionally start a sentence one way and then switch directions partway through—but it's devilishly difficult to follow. And it's a confusing way to teach. When you confound your listeners with opposing details such as "Louis Leakey performed his ethnographic studies—well, actually they weren't ethnographic studies and of course he didn't work alone," you leave the audience wondering when the information will be final and what part they should remember. Instead of relying on post-statement adjustments, work to get the facts clear and straight.

4 • Get organized. Delivering information randomly—jumping around from point to point as each one springs to mind—puts the onus on your listeners to make up for your lack of structure. And it's confusing for them to listen, reorganize, tidy up your mess and figure out what you're saying all at once. But building smoothly from one point to the next gives the audience an automatic memory device and helps them absorb information more easily. You can arrange things from beginning to end, small to large, top to bottom or by some other scheme—just be sure to organize.

5 • Drop the ums and ahs. Any verbal tic—whether it's "um," "ah," "like," "you know" or some other useless noise—can drive an audience crazy through repetitive use. It makes the speaker sound uncertain and unprepared, and it can leave listeners (or those who are attempting to listen) so distracted they can't pay attention. Recently I saw a presentation that was marked by so many droning ums that audience members were rolling their eyes. Was anybody grasping the intended message? Um, probably not.

6 • Bring it to a distinct close. Many speakers finish up their presentations with question-and-answer sessions, but some let the Q&A dribble on without a distinct end. The audience is often left confused about whether the meeting is over and when they can get up and leave. Do your listeners a favor by setting a time

limit on questions, and wrap up your presentation with a specific finale—even if it's something simple like, "If you have any more questions, you know where to reach me."

7 Or even more to the point, conclude your presentation with "Thanks for your time."

CHAPTER 25

Exposition: Comparison/Contrast

My Real Car

Bailey White

Georgia-born Bailey White has published stories and essays in many magazines, but she is perhaps best known as a commentator on National Public Radio's award-winning news program *All Things Considered*. Her essays and stories have been collected in *Mama Makes Up Her Mind and Other Dangers of Southern Living* (1993), *Sleeping at the Starlight Motel* (1995), and *Nothing with Strings* (2008); her first novel is *Quite a Year for Plums* (1998). This selection was originally published in *Smithsonian* magazine in 1991.

1   It really makes you feel your age when you get a letter from your insurance agent telling you that the car you bought, only slightly used, the year you got out of college is now an antique. "Beginning with your next payment, your premiums will reflect this change in classification," the letter said.

2   I went out and looked at the car. I thought back over the years. I could almost hear my uncle's disapproving voice. "You should never buy a used car," he had told me the day I brought it home. Ten years later I drove that used car to his funeral. I drove my sister to the hospital in that car to have her first baby, and I drove to Atlanta in that car when the baby graduated from Georgia Tech with a degree in physics.

3   "When are you going to get a new car?" my friends asked me.

4   "I don't need a new car," I said. "This car runs fine."

5   I changed the oil often, and I kept good tires on it. It always got me where I wanted to go. But the stuffing came out of the backseat and the springs poked through, and the dashboard disintegrated. At 300,000 miles the odometer quit

turning, but I didn't really care to know how far I had driven. A hole wore in the floor where my heel rested in front of the accelerator, and the insulation all peeled off the fire wall. "Old piece of junk," my friends whispered. The seat-belt catch finally wore out, and I tied on a huge bronze hook with a fireman's knot.

6   Then one day on my way to work, the car coughed, sputtered and stopped. "This is it," I thought, and I gave it a pat. "It's been a good car."

7   The mechanic laughed at me. "You know what's wrong with that car?" he asked. "That car is out of gas." So I slopped some gas in the tank and drove ten more years.

8   The fuel gauge never worked again after that, but I got to where I could tell when the gas was low by the smell. I think it was the smell of the bottom of the tank. There was also a little smell of brake fluid, a little smell of exhaust, a little smell of oil and, after all the years, a little smell of me. Car smells.

9   And sounds. The wonderful sound when the engine finally catches on a cold day, and an ominous *tick tick* in July when the radiator is working too hard. The windshield wipers said, "Gracie Allen Gracie Allen Gracie Allen." I didn't like a lot of conversation in the car, because I had to keep listening for a little skip that meant I needed to jump out and adjust the carburetor. I kept a screwdriver close at hand, and a pint of brake fluid and a new rotor, just in case. "She's strange," my friends whispered. "And she drives so slow."

10   I don't know how fast I drove. The speedometer had quit working years ago. But when I would look down through the hole in the floor and see the pavement, a gray blur, whizzing by just inches away from my feet, and feel the tremendous heat from the internal-combustion engine pouring back through the fire wall into my lap, and hear each barely contained explosion, just as a heart attack victim is able to hear her own heartbeat, it didn't feel like slow to me. A whiff of brake fluid would remind me just what a tiny thing I was relying on to stop myself from hurtling along the surface of the Earth at an unnatural speed. When I arrived at my destination, I would slump back, unfasten the seat-belt hook with trembling hands and stagger out. I would gather up my things and give the car a last look. "Thank you, sir," I would say. "We got here one more time."

11   But after I received that letter I began thinking about buying a new car. I read the newspaper every night. Finally I found one that sounded good. It was the same make as my car, but almost new. "Call Steve," the ad said. I went to see the car. It was parked in Steve's driveway. It was a fashionable wheat color. There was carpet on the floor and the seats were covered with soft, velvety-feeling stuff. It smelled like acrylic, and vinyl, and Steve. I turned a knob. Mozart's Concerto for Flute and Harp poured out of four speakers. "But how can you listen to the engine with music playing?" I asked Steve.

12   I turned the key. The car started instantly. I fastened my seat belt. Nothing but a click. Steve got in the passenger seat, and we went for a test drive. We floated down the road. I couldn't hear a sound, but I decided it must be time to shift gears. I stomped around on the floor and grabbed Steve's knee before I remembered the car had automatic transmission.

13   "You mean you just put it in 'Drive' and drive?" I asked. Steve scrunched himself against his door and clamped his knees together. He tested his seat belt. "Have you ever driven before?" he asked.

14   I bought it. I rolled all the windows up by mashing a button beside my elbow, set the air-conditioning on "Recirc" and listened to Vivaldi all the way home.

15   So now I have two cars. I call them my new car and my real car. Most of the time I drive my new car. But on some days I go out to the barn and get in my real car. I shoo the rats out of the backseat and crank up the engine. Even without daily practice my hands and feet know just what to do. My ears perk up, and I sniff the air. I add a little brake fluid, a little water. I sniff again. It'll need gas next week, and an oil change. I back it out and we roll down the road. People stop and look. They smile. "Neat car!" they say.

The Myth of the Latin Woman: I Just Met a Girl Named Maria

Judith Ortiz Cofer

Judith Ortiz Cofer is an award-winning poet, essayist, fiction writer, and professor of English and creative writing at the University of Georgia. Cofer often draws upon her Puerto Rican heritage as she explores cultural diversity issues in America. Her works include *A Love Story Beginning in Spanish* (2005), *The Meaning of Consuelo* (2003), and *The Latin Deli* (1993), from which this essay is taken.

1   On a bus trip to London from Oxford University, where I was earning some graduate credits one summer, a young man, obviously fresh from a pub, spotted me and as if struck by inspiration went down on his knees in the aisle. With both hands over his heart he broke into an Irish tenor's rendition of "Maria" from *West Side Story.** My politely amused fellow passengers gave his lovely voice the round of gentle applause it deserved. Though I was not quite as amused, I managed my version of an English smile: no show of teeth, no extreme contortions of the facial muscles—I was at this time of my life practicing reserve and cool. Oh, that British control, how I coveted it. But Maria had followed me to London, reminding me of a prime fact of my life: you can leave the Island, master the English language, and travel as far as you can, but if you are Latina, especially one like me who so obviously belongs to Rita Moreno's gene pool, the Island travels with you.

2   This is sometimes a very good thing—it may win you that extra minute of someone's attention. But with some people, the same things can *make you* an island— not so much a tropical paradise as an Alcatraz, a place nobody wants to visit. As a Puerto Rican girl growing up in the United States and wanting like most children to "belong," I resented the stereotype that my Hispanic appearance called forth from many people I met.

3   Our family lived in a large urban center in New Jersey during the sixties, where life was designed as a microcosm of my parents' *casas* [households] on the island. We spoke in Spanish, we ate Puerto Rican food bought at the *bodega* [grocery], and

---

West Side Story is a well-known musical (and movie) that sets the Romeo and Juliet story on the streets of New York amid gang rivalry. Rita Moreno won an Oscar for her supporting role in the film version.

we practiced strict Catholicism complete with Saturday confession and Sunday mass at a church where our parents were accommodated into a one-hour Spanish mass slot, performed by a Chinese priest trained as a missionary for Latin America.

4   As a girl I was kept under strict surveillance, since virtue and modesty were, by cultural equation, the same as family honor. As a teenager I was instructed on how to behave as a proper señorita. But it was a conflicting message girls got, since the Puerto Rican mothers also encouraged their daughters to look and act like women and to dress in clothes our Anglo friends and their mothers found too "mature" for our age. It was, and is, cultural, yet I often felt humiliated when I appeared at an American friend's party wearing a dress more suitable to a semiformal than a playroom birthday celebration. At Puerto Rican festivities, neither the music nor the colors we wore could be too loud. I still experience a vague sense of letdown when I'm invited to a "party" and it turns out to be a marathon conversation in hushed tones rather than a fiesta with salsa, laughter, and dancing—the kind of celebration I remember from my childhood.

5   I remember Career Day in our high school, when teachers told us to come dressed as if for a job interview. It quickly became obvious that to the barrio girls, "dressing up" some times meant wearing ornate jewelry and clothing that would be more appropriate (by mainstream standards) for the company Christmas party than as daily office attire. That morning I had agonized in front of my closet, try-ing to figure out what a "career girl" would wear because, essentially, except for Marlo Thomas* on TV, I had no models on which to base my decision. I knew how to dress for school: at the Catholic school I attended we all wore uniforms; I knew how to dress for Sunday mass, and I knew what dresses to wear for parties at my relatives' homes. Though I do not recall the precise details of my Career Day out-fit, it must have been a composite of the above choices. But I remember a comment my friend (an Italian American) made in later years that coalesced my impressions of that day. She said that at the business school she was attending the Puerto Rican girls always stood out for wearing "everything at once." She meant, of course, too much jewelry, too many accessories. On that day at school, we were simply made the negative models by the nuns who were themselves not credible fashion experts to any of us. But it was painfully obvious to me that to the others, in their tailored skirts and silk blouses, we must have seemed "hopeless" and "vulgar." Though I now know that most adolescents feel out of step much of the time, I also know that for the Puerto Rican girls of my generation that sense was intensified. The way our teachers and classmates looked at us that day in school was just a taste of the cul-ture clash that awaited us in the real world, where prospective employers and men on the street would often misinterpret our tight skirts and jingling bracelets as a come-on.

6   Mixed cultural signals have perpetuated certain stereotypes—for example, that of the Hispanic woman as the "Hot Tamale" or sexual firebrand. It is a one-dimensional view that the media have found easy to promote. In their special vocabulary, advertisers have designated "sizzling" and "smoldering" as the adjec-tives of choice for describing not only the foods but also the women of Latin Amer-ica. From conversations in my house I recall hearing about the harassment that

*Marlo Thomas starred in the 1965–1971 series *That Girl* as a young single woman seeking an acting career in New York City.

Puerto Rican women endured in factories where the "boss men" talked to them as if sexual innuendo was all they understood and, worse, often gave them the choice of submitting to advances or being fired.

7   It is custom, however, not chromosomes, that leads us to choose scarlet over pale pink. As young girls, we were influenced in our decisions about clothes and colors by the women—older sisters and mothers who had grown up on a tropical island where the natural environment was a riot of primary colors, where showing your skin was one way to keep cool as well as to look sexy. Most important of all, on the island, women perhaps felt freer to dress and move more provocatively, since, in most cases, they were protected by the traditions, mores, and laws of a Spanish/Catholic system of morality and machismo whose main rule was: *You may look at my sister, but if you touch her I will kill you.* The extended family and church structure could provide a young woman with a circle of safety in her small pueblo on the island; if a man "wronged" a girl, everyone would close in to save her family honor.

8   This is what I have gleaned from my discussions as an adult with older Puerto Rican women. They have told me about dressing in their best party clothes on Saturday nights and going to the town's plaza to promenade with their girlfriends in front of the boys they liked. The males were thus given an opportunity to admire the women and to express their admiration in the form of *piropos*: erotically charged street poems they composed on the spot. I have been subjected to a few *piropos* while visiting the Island and they can be outrageous, although custom dictates that they must never cross into obscenity. This ritual, as I understand it, also entails a show of studied indifference on the woman's part; if she is "decent," she must not acknowledge the man's impassioned words. So I do understand how things can be lost in translation. When a Puerto Rican girl dressed in her idea of what is attractive meets a man from the mainstream culture who has been trained to react to certain types of clothing as a sexual signal, a clash is likely to take place. The line I first heard based on this aspect of the myth happened when the boy who took me to my first formal dance leaned over to plant a sloppy overeager kiss painfully on my mouth, and when I didn't respond with sufficient passion said in a resentful tone: "I thought you Latin girls were supposed to mature early"—my first instance of being thought of as a fruit or vegetable—I was supposed to *ripen*, not just grow into womanhood like other girls.

9   It is surprising to some of my professional friends that some people, including those who should know better, still put others "in their place." Though rarer, these incidents are still commonplace in my life. It happened to me most recently during a stay at a very classy metropolitan hotel favored by young professional couples for their weddings. Late one evening after the theater, as I walked toward my room with my new colleague (a woman with whom I was coordinating an arts program), a middle-aged man in a tuxedo, a young girl in satin and lace on his arm, stepped directly into our path. With his champagne glass extended toward me, he exclaimed, "Evita!"*

10   Our way blocked, my companion and I listened as the man half-recited, half-bellowed "Don't Cry for Me, Argentina." When he finished, the young girl said:

---

*"Evita" refers to a hit musical (and movie) based on the rags-to-riches life of Eva Perón, wife of Argentinian president Juan Perón.

"How about a round of applause for my daddy?" We complied, hoping this would bring the silly spectacle to a close. I was becoming aware that our little group was attracting the attention of the other guests. "Daddy" must have perceived this too, and he once more barred the way as we tried to walk past him. He began to shout-sing a ditty to the tune of "La Bamba"—except the lyrics were about a girl named Maria whose exploits all rhymed with her name and gonorrhea. The girl kept say-ing "Oh, Daddy" and looking at me with pleading eyes. She wanted me to laugh along with the others. My companion and I stood silently waiting for the man to end his offensive song. When he finished, I looked not at him but at his daughter. I advised her calmly never to ask her father what he had done in the army. Then I walked between them and to my room. My friend complimented me on my cool handling of the situation. I confessed to her that I really had wanted to push the jerk into the swimming pool. I knew that this same man—probably a corporate executive, well educated, even worldly by most standards—would not have been likely to regale a white woman with a dirty song in public. He would perhaps have checked his impulse by assuming that she could be somebody's wife or mother, or at least *somebody* who might take offense. But to him, I was just an Evita or a Maria; merely a character in his cartoon-populated universe.

11　Because of my education and my proficiency with the English language, I have acquired many mechanisms for dealing with the anger I experience. This was not true for my parents, nor is it true for the many Latin women working at menial jobs who must put up with stereotypes about our ethnic group, such as "They make good domestics." This is another facet of the myth of the Latin woman in the United States. Its origin is simple to deduce. Work as domestics, waitressing, and factory jobs are all that's available to women with little English and few skills. The myth of the Hispanic menial has been sustained by the same media phenomenon that made Mammy from *Gone with the Wind* America's idea of the black woman for generations: Maria, the housemaid or counter girl, is now indelibly etched into the national psyche. The big and the little screens have presented us with the picture of the funny Hispanic maid, mispronouncing words and cooking up a spicy storm in a shiny California kitchen.

12　This media-engendered image of the Latina in the United States has been docu-mented by feminist Hispanic scholars, who claim that such portrayals are partially responsible for the denial of opportunities for upward mobility among Latinas in the professions. I have a Chicana friend working on a Ph.D. in philosophy at a major university. She says her doctor still shakes his head in puzzled amazement at all the "big words" she uses. Since I do not wear my diplomas around my neck for all to see, I too have on occasion been sent to that "kitchen," where some think I obviously belong.

13　One such incident that has stayed with me, though I recognize it as a minor offense, happened on the day of my first public poetry reading. It took place in Miami in a boat-restaurant where we were having lunch before an event. I was nervous and excited as I walked in with my notebook in my hand. An older woman motioned me to her table. Thinking (foolish me) that she wanted me to autograph a copy of my brand-new slender volume of verse, I went over. She ordered a cup of coffee from me, assuming that I was the waitress. Easy enough to mistake my poems for menus, I suppose. I know that it wasn't an intentional act of cruelty, yet of all the good things that happened that day, I remember that scene most clearly, because it reminded me of what I had to overcome before anyone would take me seriously. In retrospect I understand that my anger gave my reading fire, that I have almost always taken doubts in my abilities as a challenge—and that the result is, most times, a feeling of satisfaction at having won a convert when I see the cold, appraising eyes warm to my words, the body language change, the smile that indicates that I have opened some avenue for communication. That day I read to that woman and her lowered eyes told me that she was embarrassed at her little faux pas, and when I willed her to look up at me, it was my victory, and she graciously allowed me to punish her with my full attention. We shook hands at the end of the reading, and I never saw her again. She has probably forgotten the whole thing, but maybe not.

14   Yet I am one of the lucky ones. My parents made it possible for me to acquire a stronger footing in the mainstream culture by giving me the chance at an education. And books and art have saved me from the harsher forms of ethnic and racial prejudice that many of my Hispanic *compañeras* [friends] have had to endure. I travel a lot around the United States, reading from my books of poetry and my novel, and the reception I most often receive is one of positive interest by people who want to know more about my culture. There are, however, thousands of Latinas without the privilege of an education or the entrée into society that I have. For them life is a struggle against the misconceptions perpetuated by the myth of the Latina as whore, domestic, or criminal. We cannot change this by legislating the way people look at us. The transformation, as I see it, has to occur at a much more individual level. My personal goal in my public life is to try to replace the old pervasive stereotypes and myths about Latinas with a much more interesting set of realities. Every time I give a reading, I hope the stories I tell, the dreams and fears I examine in my work, can achieve some universal truth which will get my audience past the particulars of my skin color, my accent, or my clothes.

15   I once wrote a poem in which I called us Latinas "God's brown daughters." This poem is really a prayer of sorts, offered upward but also, through the human-to-human channel of art, outward. It is a prayer for communication, and for respect. In it, Latin women pray "in Spanish to an Anglo God / with a Jewish heritage," and they are "fervently hoping / that if not omnipotent, / at least He be bilingual."

Once More to the Lake (August 1941)

E. B. White

Elwyn Brooks White was an editor and writer for *The New Yorker* and a columnist for *Harper's* magazine. He is well known for his essays, collected in volumes including *One Man's Meat* (1943), *The Second Tree from the Corner* (1954), and *The Points of My Compass* (1962), and for his children's books, *Stuart Little* (1945) and *Charlotte's Web* (1952). This essay, written in 1941, originally appeared in *Harper's*.

1   One summer, along about 1904, my father rented a camp on a lake in Maine and took us all there for the month of August. We all got ringworm from some kittens and had to rub Pond's Extract on our arms and legs night and morning, and my

father rolled over in a canoe with all his clothes on; but outside of that the vacation was a success and from then on none of us ever thought there was any place in the world like that lake in Maine. We returned summer after summer—always on August 1st for one month. I have since become a salt-water man, but sometimes in summer there are days when the restlessness of the tides and the fearful cold of the sea water and the incessant wind which blows across the afternoon and into the evening make me wish for the placidity of a lake in the woods. A few weeks ago this feeling got so strong I bought myself a couple of bass hooks and a spinner and returned to the lake where we used to go, for a week's fishing and to revisit old haunts.

2   I took along my son, who had never had any fresh water up his nose and who had seen lily pads only from train windows. On the journey over to the lake I began to wonder what it would be like. I wondered how time would have marred this unique, this holy spot—the coves and streams, the hills that the sun set behind, the camps and the paths behind the camps. I was sure the tarred road would have found it out and I wondered in what other ways it would be desolated. It is strange how much you can remember about places like that once you allow your mind to return into the grooves which lead back. You remember one thing, and that suddenly reminds you of another thing. I guess I remembered clearest of all the early mornings, when the lake was cool and motionless, remembered how the bedroom smelled of the lumber it was made of and of the wet woods whose scent entered through the screen. The partitions in the camp were thin and did not extend clear to the top of the rooms, and as I was always the first up I would dress softly so as not to wake the others, and sneak out into the sweet outdoors and start out in the canoe, keeping close along the shore in the long shadows of the pines. I remembered being very careful never to rub my paddle against the gunwale for fear of disturbing the stillness of the cathedral.

3   The lake had never been what you would call a wild lake. There were cottages sprinkled around the shores, and it was in farming country although the shores of the lake were quite heavily wooded. Some of the cottages were owned by nearby farmers, and you would live at the shore and eat your meals at the farmhouse. That's what our family did. But although it wasn't wild, it was a fairly large and undisturbed lake and there were places in it which, to a child at least, seemed infinitely remote and primeval.

4   I was right about the tar; it led to within half a mile of the shore. But when I got back there, with my boy, and we settled into a camp near a farmhouse and into the kind of summertime I had known, I could tell that it was going to be pretty much the same as it had been before—I knew it, lying in bed the first morning, smelling the bedroom, and hearing the boy sneak quietly out and go off along the shore in a boat. I began to sustain the illusion that he was I, and therefore by simple transposition, that I was my father. This sensation persisted, kept cropping up all the time we were there. It was not an entirely new feeling, but in this setting it grew much stronger. I seemed to be living a dual existence. I would be in the middle of some simple act, I would be picking up a bait box or laying down a table fork, or I would be saying something, and suddenly it would be not I but my father who was saying the words or making the gesture. It gave me a creepy sensation.

5   We went fishing the first morning. I felt the same damp moss covering the worms in the bait can, and saw the dragonfly alight on the tip of my rod as it hovered a few inches from the surface of the water. It was the arrival of this fly that convinced me beyond any doubt that everything was as it always had been, that the years were a mirage and there had been no years. The small waves were the same, chucking the rowboat under the chin as we fished at anchor, and the boat was the same boat, the same color green and the ribs broken in the same places, and under the floor-boards the same fresh-water leavings and debris—the dead helgramite,* the wisps of moss, the rusty discarded fishhook, the dried blood from yesterday's catch. We stared silently at the tips of our rods, at the dragonflies that came and went. I lowered the tip of mine into the water, tentatively, pensively dislodging the fly, which darted two feet away, poised, darted two feet back, and came to rest again a little farther up the rod. There had been no years between the ducking of this dragonfly and the other one—the one that was part of memory. I looked at the boy, who was silently watching his fly, and it was my hands that held his rod, my eyes watching. I felt dizzy and didn't know which rod I was at the end of.

6   We caught two bass, hauling them in briskly as though they were mackerel, pulling them over the side of the boat in a businesslike manner without any landing net, and stunning them with a blow on the back of the head. When we got back for a swim before lunch, the lake was exactly where we had left it, the same number of inches from the dock, and there was only the merest suggestion of a breeze. This seemed an utterly enchanted sea, this lake you could leave to its own devices for a few hours and come back to, and find that it had not stirred, this constant and trustworthy body of water. In the shallows, the dark, water-soaked sticks and twigs, smooth and old, were undulating in clusters on the bottom against the clean ribbed sand, and the track of the mussel was plain. A school of minnows swam by, each minnow with its small individual shadow, doubling the attendance, so clear and sharp in the sunlight. Some of the other campers were in swimming, along the shore, one of them with a cake of soap, and the water felt thin and clear and unsubstantial. Over the years there had been this person with the cake of soap, this cultist, and here he was. There had been no years.

7   Up to the farmhouse to dinner through the teeming, dusty field, the road under our sneakers was only a two-track road. The middle track was missing, the one with the marks of the hooves and the splotches of dried, flaky manure. There had always been three tracks to choose from in choosing which track to walk in; now the choice was narrowed down to two. For a moment I missed terribly the middle alternative. But the way led past the tennis court, and something about the way it lay there in the sun reassured me; the tape had loosened along the backline, the alleys were green with plantains and other weeds, and the net (installed in June and removed in September) sagged in the dry noon, and the whole place steamed with mid-day heat and hunger and emptiness. There was a choice of pie for dessert, and one was blueberry and one was apple, and the waitresses were the same country girls, there having been no passage of time, only the illusion of it as in a dropped curtain—the waitresses were still fifteen; their hair had been washed,

*A helgramite is an insect sometimes used for bait.

that was the only difference—they had been to the movies and seen the pretty girls with the clean hair.

8   Summertime, oh summertime, pattern of life indelible, the fade-proof lake, the woods unshatterable, the pasture with the sweet-fern and the juniper forever and ever, summer without end; this was the background, and the life along the shore was the design, the cottages with their innocent and tranquil design, their tiny docks with the flagpole and the American flag floating against the white clouds in the blue sky, the little paths over the roots of the trees leading from camp to camp and the paths leading back to the outhouses and the can of lime for sprinkling, and at the souvenir counters at the store the miniature birch-bark canoes and the post cards that showed things looking a little better than they looked. This was the American family at play, escaping the city heat, wondering whether the newcomers in the camp at the head of the cove were "common" or "nice," wondering whether it was true that the people who drove up for Sunday dinner at the farmhouse were turned away because there wasn't enough chicken.

9   It seemed to me, as I kept remembering all this, that those times and those summers had been infinitely precious and worth saving. There had been jollity and peace and goodness. The arriving (at the beginning of August) had been so big a business in itself, at the railway station the farm wagon drawn up, the first smell of the pine-laden air, the first glimpse of the smiling farmer, and the great importance of the trunks and your father's enormous authority in such matters, and the feel of the wagon under you for a long ten-mile haul, and at the top of the last long hill catching the first view of the lake after eleven months of not seeing this cherished body of water. The shouts and cries of the other campers when they saw you, and the trunks to be unpacked, to give up their rich burden. (Arriving was less exciting nowadays, when you sneaked up in your car and parked it under a tree near the camp and took out the bags and in five minutes it was all over, no fuss, no loud wonderful fuss about trunks.)

10   Peace and goodness and jollity. The only thing that was wrong now, really, was the sound of the place, an unfamiliar nervous sound of the outboard motors. This was the note that jarred, the one thing that would sometimes break the illusion and set the years moving. In those other summertimes all motors were inboard; and when they were at a little distance, the noise they made was a sedative, an ingredient of summer sleep. They were one-cylinder and two-cylinder engines, and some were make-and-break and some were jump-spark, but they all made a sleepy sound across the lake. The one-lungers throbbed and fluttered, and the twin-cylinder ones purred and purred, and that was a quiet sound too. But now the campers all had outboards. In the daytime, in the hot mornings, these motors made a petulant, irritable sound; at night, in the still evening when the afterglow lit the water, they whined about one's ears like mosquitoes. My boy loved our rented outboard, and his great desire was to achieve singlehanded mastery over it, and authority, and he soon learned the trick of choking it a little (but not too much), and the adjustment of the needle valve. Watching him I would remember the things you could do with the old one-cylinder engine with the heavy flywheel, how you could have it eating out of your hand if you got really close to it spiritually. Motor boats in those days didn't have clutches, and you would make a landing by shutting off the motor at the proper time and coasting in with a dead rudder. But there was a

way of reversing them, if you learned the trick, by cutting the switch and putting it on again exactly on the final dying revolution of the flywheel, so that it would kick back against compression and begin reversing. Approaching a dock in a strong following breeze, it was difficult to slow up sufficiently by the ordinary coasting method, and if a boy felt he had complete mastery over his motor, he was tempted to keep it running beyond its time and then reverse it a few feet from the dock. It took a cool nerve, because if you threw the switch a twentieth of a second too soon you would catch the flywheel when it still had speed enough to go up past center, and the boat would leap ahead, charging bull-fashion at the dock.

11   We had a good week at the camp. The bass were biting well and the sun shone endlessly, day after day. We would be tired at night and lie down in the accumulated heat of the little bedrooms after the long hot day and the breeze would stir almost imperceptibly outside and the smell of the swamp drift in through the rusty screens. Sleep would come easily and in the morning the red squirrel would be on the roof, tapping out his gay routine. I kept remembering everything, lying in bed in the mornings—the small steamboat that had a long rounded stern like the lip of a Ubangi, and how quietly she ran on the moonlight sails, when the older boys played their mandolins and the girls sang and we ate doughnuts dipped in sugar, and how sweet the music was on the water in the shining night, and what it had felt like to think about girls then. After breakfast we would go up to the store and the things were in the same place—the minnows in a bottle, the plugs and spinners disarranged and pawed over by the youngsters from the boys' camp, the fig newtons and the Beeman's gum. Outside, the road was tarred and cars stood in front of the store. Inside, all was just as it had always been, except there was more Coca-Cola and not so much Moxie and root beer and birch beer and sarsaparilla. We would walk out with a bottle of pop apiece and sometimes the pop would backfire up our noses and hurt. We explored the streams, quietly, where the turtles slid off the sunny logs and dug their way into the soft bottom; and we lay on the town wharf and fed worms to the tame bass. Everywhere we went I had trouble making out which was I, the one walking at my side, the one walking in my pants.

12   One afternoon while we were there at that lake a thunderstorm came up. It was like the revival of an old melodrama that I had seen long ago with childish awe. The second-act climax of the drama of the electrical disturbance over a lake in America had not changed in any important respect. This was the big scene, still the big scene. The whole thing was so familiar, the first feeling of oppression and heat and a general air around camp of not wanting to go very far away. In midafternoon (it was all the same) a curious darkening of the sky, and a lull in everything that had made life tick; and then the way the boats suddenly swung the other way at their moorings with the coming of a breeze out of the new quarter, and the premonitory rumble. Then the kettle drum, then the snare, then the bass drum and cymbals, then crackling light against the dark, and the gods grinning and licking their chops in the hills. Afterward the calm, the rain steadily rustling in the calm lake, the return of light and hope and spirits, and the campers running out in the joy and relief to go swimming in the rain, their bright cries perpetuating the deathless joke about how they were getting simply drenched, and the children screaming with delight at the new sensation of bathing in the rain, and the joke

about getting drenched linking the generations in a strong indestructible chain. And the comedian who waded in carrying an umbrella.

13   When the others went swimming my son said he was going in too. He pulled his dripping trunks from the line where they had hung all through the shower, and wrung them out. Languidly, and with no thought of going in, I watched him, his hard little body, skinny and bare, saw him wince slightly as he pulled up around his vitals the small, soggy, icy garment. As he buckled the swollen belt suddenly my groin felt the chill of death.

CHAPTER 26

Exposition: Definition

Celebrating Nerdiness

Tom Rogers

A former chemical engineer, Tom Rogers now teaches advanced courses in physics, computer science, and statistics at a South Carolina high school and maintains a popular Web site, *Insultingly Stupid Movie Physics*, that has been featured on National Public Radio and in the *New York Times*. A companion book to the site was published in 2007. This essay appeared in *Newsweek* in 2000.

1   I'm a nerd. While the Internet boom has lent some respectability to the term, narrow-minded and thoughtless stereotypes still linger. Nerds are supposedly friendless, book-smart sissies who suck up to authority figures. Some of our image problems stem from our obsession with mastering every inane detail of our interests. But to call us suck-ups is nonsense. We often horrify those in authority with our inability to understand, let alone follow, societal norms.

2   Like most nerds, I didn't know I was one until I started school. There I quickly found out that my enthusiasm for answering the teacher's questions made others feel I was deliberately trying to make them look bad. My classmates were not shy about expressing their feelings on the playground. Fortunately, I was tall and stood my ground, a bluff that helped repel bullies. But mostly I survived by learning to keep quiet in the classroom.

3   I became a high-school teacher because I realized there were lots of young nerds growing up who needed to know that being a nerd was not just OK but something wonderful. Unfortunately, they weren't likely to hear this even from teachers, although virtually every modern blessing from democracy to electric motors

originated with a nerd. Some, like Thomas Paine, were idealistic; others, like Tesla, eccentric. Newton was arrogant and Einstein absent-minded. All of them are now considered geniuses. But make no mistake: 17-year-old versions of these men, placed in modern American high schools, would instantly be labeled as nerds.

4   I raised two nerd sons and a daughter, who describes herself as a nerd sympathizer, partly because I didn't have the cleverness to raise "cool" kids, but also because, selfishly, I wanted nerds to talk to. Every year I invite my Advanced Placement physics students to my house for study sessions before the AP test. Last year one student nerd's mother told me that her son had returned home and talked for hours about how awesome it was to have found a nerd family. Unfortunately, the world's response to our family has not always been so enthusiastic.

5   When my sons were still in school, they were often picked on by classmates. My older boy, a pale and unathletic kid, was an easy target. When his middle-school science teacher asked if anyone could name some elements, my son recited the periodic table from memory. Thanks to events like that, he endured nerd hell at the hands of bullies when waiting for the school bus every afternoon. We tried karate classes and pep talks to bolster his defenses, but he was never able to win his tormentors' respect. He was just too small.

6   My boys were often misunderstood by their teachers, too. My younger son's middle-school social-studies teacher rigidly insisted that he take notes. When he refused, she publicly told him he would never graduate from high school. My son was perfectly capable of taking notes, but in typical nerd fashion, he couldn't bring himself to comply because it was illogical. He could easily remember what the teacher had said. Writing it down cut into his thinking time.

7   Clearly, my son would have to give his teacher what she wanted, but it had to be done with style. We discussed options. These included taking notes in one of the foreign languages he studied as a hobby. I discouraged it because he had learned some colorful foreign terms and was capable of describing his teacher in ways that could make a sailor blush. Finally, we agreed he would write his notes backward.

8   For six months he transcribed his teacher's lectures backward. When I held my son's notes up to a mirror, they were perfectly readable. I shouldn't have been surprised. As a small child he'd entertained us by turning books upside down and reading them backward. I waited for a complaint from his teacher, but she never noticed.

9   Despite childhood trials, both of my sons remain devoted nerds. My older son became conversational in four foreign languages and has hitchhiked around Europe three times. And these days no one would mistake him for a sissy. On one occasion a group of Russian policemen threw him a party after he accepted their invitation to take a mid-December dip in a spring filled with near-freezing water.

10   My younger son proved his teacher wrong and graduated from high school. He scored 1600 on the SAT and was asked to give a speech before 500 educators and politicians who had gathered to honor education. It was his one moment of visibility. As I waited for him to talk, my stomach flip-flopped. I had no idea what he was going to say. He rose from his seat and delivered 10 minutes of stand-up comedy on being a nerd. The audience laughed until they cried. I cried. Afterward a young nerd paid him his highest compliment: "Thank you for what you've done for our people." No, our kind doesn't fit the stereotypes, but yes, there is something wonderful about being a nerd.

The Picture of Health

Kim Lute

Kim Lute lives in Georgia and, for the past twenty years, has undergone a series of serious medical procedures and surgeries, including two liver transplant operations. In this essay, published in the "My Turn" section of *Newsweek* magazine in December 2008, she questions common perceptions of the medically ill and suggests that it may be time for a new definition of what it means to be "healthy."

1   On a recent Monday morning, I underwent a routine liver biopsy. I changed into one of those awful hospital gowns, signed away a slew of legal rights should anything go amiss, withstood an IV-line placement and arranged myself into the proscribed position: lying on my back, my right arm high above my head.

2   Over the years, I've become inured to hospitals, needles, ambulance rides and promises of doom and gloom. Twenty years ago, when I was 15, I was diagnosed with autoimmune hepatitis. At 22, I underwent a liver transplant. By 24 I had developed ulcerative colitis and two years later I had my large intestine removed. These two early diseases then begat a third: primary sclerosing cholangitis. PSC, a liver disease, prompted a second liver transplant when I was 28.

3   But I don't feel put upon or see myself as some sort of "other," representing all that can go wrong. In fact, I've come to think of myself as the picture of health. Is this delusional? Perhaps. But I don't believe I'm the sum total of every unfortunate medical crisis I've ever come up against. Yes, there have been diagnoses that have complicated my young life, but where there's been disease there has also been triumph.

4   When I explained this to the nurse assisting with the biopsy, after he referred to me as very unhealthy, he balked at the idea. I guess I could understand his hesitation. Maybe I'd had brief, healthy intervals, but did I really consider myself healthy? What healthy person knows to ask for a less painful butterfly needle, and instinctively knows that in order "to get a good vein" for a blood draw, it's best to dangle your arms over the side of the chair? Besides, if I were the picture of health, I wouldn't be on a first-name basis with many of the emergency-room valets. Yet, it's precisely because of my experiences and routines that I think I'm healthy.

5   It's too elemental to define being healthy as merely the absence of illness, frailties and failings, the chance to count yourself among those who have never been on the receiving end of a frightening diagnosis. Maybe a healthy person is someone who's in constant pursuit of it, someone who's lost it and fought hard to regain it, someone who appreciates that being healthy isn't merely an abstract state of being to which some are blessed and others are deprived. Under this premise I'm fit, hard fought and hard won.

6   I cannot help that doctors will always see me in terms relative to a set of finite radiology or pathology reports, or that neighbors will always refer to me as L.J. and Deborah's daughter, the wan one, or even that most others will see me in terms of where one surgical scar ends and another begins. This is not all that I am. I see a body that heals quickly after trauma, one that mercifully forgets the pain of biopsies, surgeries and colonoscopies, one that remembers its strengths. When I'm in the throes of a spinal tap, or when friends and family are present for the

insertion of a second or third urine catheter, this confidence admittedly wanes. But it doesn't stay gone for long.

7   Perhaps it's time to redefine what it means to be healthy. In an era of great medical advances when doctors have the ability to diagnose once unidentifiable ailments and when genetic testing is becoming more acceptable, maybe the definition of what is and isn't healthy needs to be amended. Are you healthy if you can jog a mile? Are you considered well if your body has been put to some dire test from which you have emerged victorious? And how do you classify those of us who face numerous tests, but still jog two miles a day, work full time and lead otherwise "normal" lives?

8   I visit the doctor's office monthly, sometimes weekly. For me, annual doctor's exams are a quaint notion akin to 5 o'clock Sunday dinners. My health is monitored by a team of specialists always striving to improve upon the last set of results. Bone-density tests are scheduled between social events. Professional obligations yield to doctor's appointments, CT scans and X-rays. On any given day I can recite my most recent cholesterol, creatinine and potassium levels.

9   I understand many will not see me as healthy, that they'll continue to punctuate every inquiry with condolences. I'm not even sure how best to redefine the concept of what is and isn't healthy, but I hope any such definition will underscore that the presence of illness isn't nearly as important as one's ability to overcome it.

What Is Poverty?

Jo Goodwin Parker

When George Henderson, a professor at the University of Oklahoma, was writing his 1971 book, *America's Other Children: Public Schools outside Suburbia*, he received the following essay in the mail. It was signed "Jo Goodwin Parker" and had been mailed from West Virginia. No further information was ever discovered about the essay or its source. Whether the author of this essay was in reality a woman describing her own painful experiences or a sympathetic writer who had adopted her persona, Jo Goodwin Parker remains a mystery.

1   You ask me what is poverty? Listen to me. Here I am, dirty, smelly, and with no "proper" underwear on and with the stench of my rotting teeth near you. I will tell you. Listen to me. Listen without pity. I cannot use your pity. Listen with understanding. Put yourself in my dirty, worn out, ill-fitting shoes, and hear me.

2   Poverty is getting up every morning from a dirt- and illness-stained mattress. The sheets have long since been used for diapers. Poverty is living with a smell that never leaves. This is the smell of urine, sour milk, and spoiling food sometimes joined with the strong smell of long-cooked onions. Onions are cheap. If you have smelled this smell, you did not know how it came. It is the smell of the outdoor privy. It is the smell of young children who cannot walk the long dark way in the night. It is the smell of the mattresses where years of "accidents" have happened. It is the smell of the milk which has gone sour because the refrigerator long has not worked, and it costs money to get it fixed. It is the smell of rotting garbage. I could bury it, but where is the shovel? Shovels cost money.

3   Poverty is being tired. I have always been tired. They told me at the hospital when the last baby came that I had chronic anemia caused from poor diet, a bad case of worms, and that I needed a corrective operation. I listened politely—the poor are always polite. The poor always listen. They don't say that there is no money for iron pills, or better food, or worm medicine. The idea of an operation is frightening and costs so much that, if I had dared, I would have laughed. Who takes care of my children? Recovery from an operation takes a long time. I have three children. When I left them with "Granny" the last time I had a job, I came home to find the baby covered with fly specks, and a diaper that had not been changed since I left. When the dried diaper came off, bits of my baby's flesh came with it. My other child was playing with a sharp bit of broken glass, and my oldest was playing alone at the edge of a lake. I made twenty-two dollars a week, and a good nursery school costs twenty dollars a week for three children. I quit my job.

4   Poverty is dirt. You say in your clean clothes coming from your clean house, "Anybody can be clean." Let me explain about housekeeping with no money. For breakfast I give my children grits with no oleo or cornbread without eggs and oleo. This does not use up many dishes. What dishes there are, I wash in cold water and with no soap. Even the cheapest soap has to be saved for the baby's diapers. Look at my hands, so cracked and red. Once I saved for two months to buy a jar of Vaseline for my hands and the baby's diaper rash. When I had saved enough, I went to buy it and the price had gone up two cents. The baby and I suffered on. I have to decide every day if I can bear to put my cracked, sore hands into the cold water and strong soap. But you ask, why not hot water? Fuel costs money. Hot water is a luxury. I do not have luxuries. I know you will be surprised when I tell you how young I am. I look so much older. My back has been bent over the wash tubs for so long, I cannot remember when I ever did anything else. Every night I wash every stitch my school age child has on and just hope her clothes will be dry by morning.

5   Poverty is staying up all night on cold nights to watch the fire, knowing one spark on the newspaper covering the walls means your sleeping children die in flames. In summer poverty is watching gnats and flies devour your baby's tears when he cries. The screens are torn and you pay so little rent you know they will never be fixed. Poverty means insects in your food, in your nose, in your eyes, and crawling over you when you sleep. Poverty is hoping it never rains because diapers won't dry when it rains and soon you are using newspapers. Poverty is seeing your children forever with runny noses. Paper handkerchiefs cost money and all your rags you need for other things. Even more costly are antihistamines. Poverty is cooking without food and cleaning without soap.

6   Poverty is asking for help. Have you ever had to ask for help, knowing your children will suffer unless you get it? Think about asking for a loan from a relative, if this is the only way you can imagine asking for help. I will tell you how it feels. You find out where the office is that you are supposed to visit. You circle that block four or five times. Thinking of your children, you go in. Everyone is very busy. Finally, someone comes out and you tell her that you need help. That never is the person you need to see. You go see another person, and after spilling the whole shame of your poverty all over the desk between you, you find that this isn't the right office after all—you must repeat the whole process, and it never is any easier at the next place.

7   You have asked for help, and after all it has a cost. You are again told to wait. You are told why, but you don't really hear because of the red cloud of shame and the rising black cloud of despair.

8   Poverty is remembering. It is remembering quitting school in junior high because "nice" children had been so cruel about my clothes and my smell. The attendance officer came. My mother told him I was pregnant. I wasn't but she thought that I could get a job and help out. I had jobs off and on, but never long enough to learn anything. Mostly I remember being married. I was so young then. I am still young. For a time, we had all the things you have. There was a little house in another town, with hot water and everything. Then my husband lost his job. There was unemployment insurance for a while and what few jobs I could get. Soon, all our nice things were repossessed and we moved back here. I was pregnant then. This house didn't look so bad when we first moved in. Every week it gets worse. Nothing is ever fixed. We now had no money. There were a few odd jobs for my husband, but everything went for food then, as it does now. I don't know how we lived through three years and three babies, but we did. I'll tell you something, after the last baby I destroyed my marriage. It had been a good one, but could you keep on bringing children in this dirt? Did you ever think how much it costs for any kind of birth control? I knew my husband was leaving the day he left, but there were no good-byes between us. I hope he has been able to climb out of this mess somewhere. He never could hope with us to drag him down.

9   That's when I asked for help. When I got it, you know how much it was? It was, and is, seventy-eight dollars a month for the four of us; that is all I ever can get. Now you know why there is no soap, no needles and thread, no hot water, no aspirin, no worm medicine, no hand cream, no shampoo. None of these things forever and ever and ever. So that you can see clearly, I pay twenty dollars a month rent, and most of the rest goes for food. For grits and cornmeal, and rice and milk and beans. I try my best to use only the minimum electricity. If I use more, there is that much less for food.

10   Poverty is looking into a black future. Your children won't play with my boys. They will turn to other boys who steal to get what they want. I can already see them behind the bars of their prison instead of behind the bars of my poverty. Or they will turn to the freedom of alcohol or drugs, and find themselves enslaved. And my daughter? At best, there is for her a life like mine.

11   But you say to me, there are schools. Yes, there are schools. My children have no extra books, no magazines, no extra pencils, or crayons, or paper and the most important of all, they do not have health. They have worms, they have infections, they have pinkeye all summer. They do not sleep well on the floor, or with me in my one bed. They do not suffer from hunger, my seventy-eight dollars keeps us alive, but they do suffer from malnutrition. Oh yes, I do remember what I was taught about health in school. It doesn't do much good. In some places there is a surplus commodities program. Not here. The county said it cost too much. There is a school lunch program. But I have two children who will already be damaged by the time they get to school.

12   But, you say to me, there are health clinics. Yes, there are health clinics and they are in the towns. I live out here eight miles from town. I can walk that far (even if it is sixteen miles both ways), but can my little children? My neighbor will take

me when he goes; but he expects to get paid, *one way or another*. I bet you know my neighbor. He is that large man who spends his time at the gas station, the barbershop, and the corner store complaining about the government spending money on the immoral mothers of illegitimate children.

13   Poverty is an acid that drips on pride until all pride is worn away. Poverty is a chisel that chips on honor until honor is worn away. Some of you say that you would do *something* in my situation, and maybe you would, for the first week or the first month, but for year after year after year?

14   Even the poor can dream. A dream of a time when there is money. Money for the right kinds of food, for worm medicine, for iron pills, for toothbrushes, for hand cream, for a hammer and nails and a bit of screening, for a shovel, for a bit of paint, for some sheeting, for needles and thread. Money to pay *in money* for a trip to town. And, oh, money for hot water and money for soap. A dream of when asking for help does not eat away the last bit of pride. When the office you visit is as nice as the offices of other governmental agencies, when there are enough workers to help you quickly, when workers do not quit in defeat and despair. When you have to tell your story to only one person, and that person can send you for other help and you don't have to prove your poverty over and over and over again.

15   I have come out of my despair to tell you this. Remember I did not come from another place or another time. Others like me are all around you. Look at us with an angry heart, anger that will help you help me. Anger that will let you tell of me. The poor are always silent. Can you be silent too?

CHAPTER 27

Exposition: Division/ Classification

Party Manners

Richard L. Grossman

Richard L. Grossman is a psychotherapist, medical educator, and author. He has written a number of books, many on health-related issues, including *Choosing & Changing: A Guide to Self-Reliance* (1978) and *The Other Medicines* (1986). His most recent work is *A Year with Emerson* (2003), a daybook that introduces readers to the writings of philosopher-poet Ralph Waldo Emerson. This 1983 article first appeared in *Health* magazine as part of Grossman's column called "Richard's Almanac."

1   The Romans had their Colosseum, the Elizabethans their village promenades and their Globe Theater. For centuries the French and Germans had their spectacular court balls. Queens and Presidents have their state dinners, complete with chamber music. And we ordinary moderns? We have *parties*.

2   From college "mixers" to suburban cocktail "standarounds," from children's ice-cream splattered birthday celebrations to retirement dinners, from political fund-raisers to bridal showers, the party has become as ubiquitous an institution as the Internal Revenue Service. And familiar though it is, the party has a psychologically transforming effect on many of us. Somehow our attendance at a gathering called a "party" causes us to behave in ways we never do elsewhere, as though we were players in a drama meant to reveal some of the hidden parts of our personalities. The party setting seems to provide a license to unveil attitudes that we would never display at the office or the family dinner table. And though party behavior may not

be a reliable guide to all our psychological tics, it is nevertheless a place to see how we "go public" with some of our unresolved problems. Consider this cast of characters, for example:

The Cartoonist

3   Here's the person who has no other arena in his life in which to be a vocal social critic, who sees every party as an opportunity to be the local Andy Rooney.* No dancing or merrymaking for this one, but rather a steady stream of mini-lectures on the foibles and deficiencies of all the other guests. The Cartoonist is someone who does not want to be part of the crowd, but needs to keep his distance and act the reporting observer, drawing verbal caricatures of "them" as though he were sending communiqués back to Mars on the tribal rituals of the "Earthlings." What's really going on, of course, is that the fear of spontaneity and the relaxation of conventions is just too threatening, so the only safe stance is to play the part of the uninvolved expert.

The Spotter

4   This character is the familiar shopper for greener pastures. She is talking to you, but is looking over your shoulder the whole time, ever alert to someone just a little more interesting or a little more important who may be on the other side of the room. This person is usually the inside-dopester, the one who craves the latest information, who drops the trendiest names, who goes to the hottest events. The Spotter has the attention span of an alcoholic mayfly and cannot wait to move on, fearful that she is missing out on something better. The usual result, of course, is that she has a terrible time at parties and can't understand why all those other folks are laughing.

The Performer

5   He's often known as "the life of the party" and is the one for whom every party is the high school play in which he didn't get a part. Parties for this type are only an opportunity to grab the spotlight that he wants desperately but is being denied elsewhere. There are variations, of course: The Practical Joker, The Bathroom Comedian, The Barroom Baritone, The Poor Man's Rich Little**—but all are revealing only one sad fact: They are yearning for notoriety and attention.

The Wallflower

6   Here you have the reverse image of The Performer: The person who gains attention by a silent, martyred withdrawal from the center of the party. Sooner or later, someone will spot her standing in a corner with a rueful smile on her face, just waiting to be asked if something is wrong. If you should inquire, you'll hear that she "just isn't good in crowds," or "hates all that noise," or "never could learn to disco." Do not be deceived into thinking that you've discovered an authentically

---

*Andy Rooney, a television commentator on *60 Minutes* for over thirty years, is known for his cranky observations on the annoyances of everyday life.
**Rich Little is a comedian known for his impersonations of famous celebrities.

shy or lonely person. This routine is simply a device to get attention with a passive strategy. (The *really* shy one didn't come to the party.)

The Swashbuckler

7 Also known as "The Last of the Big Benders," this is a person who may be in real trouble. Something has gone drastically wrong somewhere in his life, and he is frightened or even desperate about the outcome. If he is not working on the problem in another corner of life or getting the help he really needs, then the only place for that terrified energy to go is into uncharacteristically heavy drinking and raucous, high-pitched haranguing. There are usually very real and troubling issues underlying this kind of behavior, and the party can, unfortunately, provide a convenient setting for acting out.

The Scarlet Pimpernel*

8 She's the person who sees every party invitation as an opportunity to project her romantic fantasy. Feeling frustrated by a humdrum, uneventful existence, such a person mentally writes out a script for Meryl Streep or Julie Christie** and goes off to the party prepared to try out the new role, altering the voice to sound sultry or provocative, speaking in cryptic or poetic language, gliding around the room like a visitor from the Court of St. James. Sometimes this is just playfulness or harmless flirtatiousness, but usually the pseudo-romantic is simply saying through her behavior that the rest of her life is dull and gray, and needs spicing up.

9   Now, a certain amount of nervousness and unease about going to a party is clearly normal, and it would be simple-minded to claim that even the types described above are necessarily displaying secret pathology. But if parties regularly call up odd or extraordinary behavior in you, or become a theater for exposing subterranean needs, it might be a good idea to look at the usual, non-partying areas of your life and see what's troubling you. Some parties are boring, to be sure, and a dose of silly, unplanned frolicking may liven them up. But we should remember that parties are usually designed as a means to gather in a friendly, open, genuine way; as a chance to enjoy the warmth and closeness of other human beings. If those are not reasons enough for going, if we need parties to ventilate other feelings, perhaps we should consider group therapy instead.

---

*This name is drawn from a 1905 novel by Baroness Emmuska Orczy, in which a British nobleman leads a double life as "the Scarlet Pimpernel," a sword-fighting rescuer of innocent people condemned to the guillotine during the French Revolution's Reign of Terror. Often credited as the first popular novel to establish the "dual identity" hero, the story paved the way for Superman, Batman, Zorro, and other modern superheroes in disguise.

**Meryl Streep is one of America's most highly regarded actresses, having won two Academy Awards; Julie Christie is a British actress, also an Academy Award winner, but possibly best known in this country for her role as Lara in the classic 1965 film *Dr. Zhivago*.

The Extendable Fork

Calvin Trillin

Calvin Trillin is an American essayist, humorist, and novelist, best known for his witty columns in *The New Yorker* and in newspapers across the country. He has published over twenty books, including memoirs, novels, political commentary, essay collections, and, most recently, satiric poetry (*Deciding the Next Decider*, 2008). Trillin often writes about food and eating out; this essay on "long-reach eaters" first appeared in his syndicated column in 1995.

1   In our house, news that the extendable fork had been invented was greeted with varying degrees of enthusiasm. I think it's fair to say that I was the most enthusiastic of all. I eat off other people's plates. My wife was mildly enthusiastic. She figures that if I use an extendable fork I'm less likely to come away from the table with gravy on my cuff.

2   People who eat off of other people's plates can categorized in four types—The Finisher, The Waif, The Researcher and The Simple Thief. I might as well admit right here at the beginning that I am all four.

3   The Finisher demonstrates concern that food may be left uneaten even though the starving children your mother told you about are still hungry. Once the pace of eating begins to slacken off a bit, he reaches across to spear a potato off of someone's plate a nanosecond after saying, "If you're not planning to finish these . . ."

4   The long-reach eater I think of as The Waif often doesn't order much himself at a restaurant, claiming that he's not terribly hungry or that he's trying to lose weight. Then, he gazes at his dinner companions' plates, like a hungry urchin who has his nose pressed up against the window of a restaurant where enormously fat rich people are slurping oysters and shoveling down mounds of boeuf bourguignon. Occasionally, he murmurs something like, "That looks delicious." Answering "Actually, it's not all that good" does not affect him—although it may slow down the Researcher, who, as he extends his fork usually says something like, "I'm curious how they do these fried onions."

5   The Simple Thief simply waits for his dining companions to glance away, then confidently grabs what he wants. If he's desperate, he may actually take measures to distract them, saying something like, "Is it my imagination, or could that be . . . Lisa Marie Presley at the table over by the door?"

6   That sort of subterfuge is not necessary, by the way, if the plate I have singled out as a target is my wife's. She does not object to my sampling—a reflection, I've always thought, of her generous heart. In fact, I have said in the past that if a young groom on his honeymoon reaches over for the first time to sample his bride's fettuccine only to be told, "Don't you like what you're having?" or "There really isn't that much of this," he knows he's in for a long haul.

7   Actually, my wife might be called a Finisher herself. If we're having fried chicken, she will stare at what's on my plate after I have indeed finished. "Look at all the chicken you left," she'll say. Or "There's a ton of meat still on that chicken." Oddly enough, this is precisely the sort of thing that I heard from my mother, who was also fond of saying that I didn't "do a good job" on the chicken. The way my wife eats chicken is to eat every speck of meat off the bones, so that the chicken looks as

if it had been staked out on an anthill by a tribe of crazed chicken torturers. She treats a lobster the same way. I eat more the way a shark eats—tearing off whatever seems exposed and easy to get at. I have suggested, in fact, that in fried-chicken or lobster restaurants we could economize by getting only one order, which I could start and my wife could finish.

8   My wife's approach to finishing does not, of course, require an extendable fork, but I intend to be an early customer myself. According to an item in the *New York Times*, the fork is nearly two feet long when fully opened. It's been marketed under the name of Alan's X-Tenda Fork. I might have chosen another name, but this one is, I'll admit, evocative. For me, it conjures up visions of a Limbaugh-sized man named Alan sitting in a restaurant with friends and family. He seems to be engaging in normal conversation, but his tiny eyes dart from plate to plate; occasionally, with a fork as quick as the strike of an adder, he helps with the finishing.

9   In fact, I can imagine Alan inventing other needed implements—a sort of vacuum tube, for instance, that can suck up french fries from three feet away. I can see him improving on Alan's X-Tenda Fork. He might install a tiny tape recorder in it, so when you pulled it out to its full length and moved it quickly across the table a voice said, "If you're not planning to finish these . . ."

Mother Tongue

Amy Tan

Amy Tan is a native of California, born to parents who had emigrated from China only a few years before. After receiving an M.A. in linguistics, Tan worked as a business writer but ultimately turned to fiction; her first novel, *The Joy Luck Club* (1987), became both a best-seller and the winner of the National Book Award. Other popular works include *The Kitchen God's Wife* (1991), *The Hundred Secret Senses* (1995), *The Bonesetter's Daughter* (2000), *The Opposite of Fate* (2003), and *Saving Fish from Drowning* (2005). "Mother Tongue" was a speech that was first printed in the *Threepenny Review* in 1990.

1 I am not a scholar of English or literature. I cannot give you much more than personal opinions of the English language and its variations in this country or others.

2   I am a writer. And by that definition, I am someone who has always loved language. I am fascinated by language in daily life. I spend a great deal of my time thinking about the power of language—the way it can evoke an emotion, a visual image, a complex idea, or a simple truth. Language is the tool of my trade. And I use them all—all the Englishes I grew up with.

3   Recently, I was made keenly aware of the different Englishes I do use. I was giving a talk to a large group of people, the same talk I had already given to half a dozen other groups. The nature of the talk was about my writing, my life, and my book, *The Joy Luck Club*. The talk was going along well enough, until I remembered one major difference that made the whole talk sound wrong. My mother was in the room. And it was perhaps the first time she had heard me give a lengthy speech, using the kind of English I have never used with her. I was saying things like, "The

intersection of memory upon imagination" and "There is an aspect of my fiction that relates to thus-and-thus"—a speech filled with carefully wrought grammatical phrases, burdened, it suddenly seemed to me, with nominalized forms, past perfect tenses, conditional phrases, all the forms of standard English that I had learned in school and through books, the forms of English I did not use at home with my mother.

4   Just last week, I was walking down the street with my mother, and I again found myself conscious of the English I was using, and the English I do use with her. We were talking about the price of new and used furniture and I heard myself saying this: "Not waste money that way." My husband was with us as well, and he didn't notice any switch in my English. And then I realized why. It's because over the twenty years we've been together I've often used the same kind of English with him, and sometimes he even uses it with me. It has become our language of intimacy, a different sort of English that relates to family talk, the language I grew up with.

5   So you'll have some idea of what this family talk I heard sounds like, I'll quote what my mother said during a recent conversation which I videotaped and then transcribed. During this conversation, my mother was talking about a political gangster in Shanghai who had the same last name as her family's, Du, and how the gangster in his early years wanted to be adopted by her family, which was rich by comparison. Later, the gangster became more powerful, far richer than my mother's family, and one day showed up at my mother's wedding to pay his respects. Here's what she said in part:

6   "Du Yusong having business like fruit stand. Like off the street kind. He is Du like Du Zong—but not Tsung-ming Island people. The local people call putong, the river east side, he belong to that side local people. The man want to ask Du Zong father take him in like become own family. Du Zong father wasn't look down on him, but didn't take seriously, until the man big like become a mafia. Now important person, very hard to inviting him. Chinese way, came only to show respect, don't stay for dinner. Respect for making big celebration, he shows up. Mean gives lots of respect. Chinese custom. Chinese social life that way. If too important won't have to stay too long. He come to my wedding. I didn't see, I heard it. I gone to boy's side, they have YMCA dinner. Chinese age I was nineteen."

7   You should know that my mother's expressive command of English belies how much she actually understands. She reads the Forbes report, listens to *Wall Street Week*, converses daily with her stockbroker, reads all of Shirley MacLaine's books with ease—all kinds of things I can't begin to understand. Yet some of my friends tell me they understand 50 percent of what my mother says. Some say they understand 80 to 90 percent. Some say they understand none of it, as if she were speaking pure Chinese. But to me, my mother's English is perfectly clear, perfectly natural. It's my mother tongue. Her language, as I hear it, vivid, direct, full of observation and imagery. That was the language that helped shape the way I saw things, expressed things, made sense of the world.

8   Lately, I've been giving more thought to the kind of English my mother speaks. Like others, I have described it to people as "broken" or "fractured" English. But I wince when I say that. It has always bothered me that I can think of no way to

describe it other than "broken," as if it were damaged and needed to be fixed, as if it lacked a certain wholeness and soundness. I've heard other terms used, "limited English," for example. But they seem just as bad, as if everything is limited, including people's perceptions of the limited English speaker.

9   I know this for a fact, because when I was growing up, my mother's "limited" English limited *my* perception of her. I was ashamed of her English. I believed that her English reflected the quality of what she had to say. That is, because she expressed them imperfectly her thoughts were imperfect. And I had plenty of empirical evidence to support me: the fact that people in department stores, at banks, and at restaurants did not take her seriously, did not give her good service, pretended not to understand her, or even acted as if they did not hear her.

10   My mother has long realized the limitations of her English as well. When I was fifteen, she used to have me call people on the phone to pretend I was she. In this guise, I was forced to ask for information or even to complain and yell at people who had been rude to her. One time it was a call to her stockbroker in New York. She had cashed out her small portfolio and it just so happened we were going to go to New York the next week, our very first trip outside California. I had to get on the phone and say in an adolescent voice that was not very convincing, "This is Mrs. Tan."

11   And my mother was standing in back whispering loudly, "Why he don't send me check, already two weeks late. So mad he lie to me, losing me money."

12   And then I said in perfect English, "Yes, I'm getting rather concerned. You had agreed to send the check two weeks ago, but it hasn't arrived."

13   Then she began to talk more loudly. "What he want, I come to New York tell him front of his boss, you cheating me?" And I was trying to calm her down, make her be quiet, while telling the stockbroker, "I can't tolerate any more excuses. If I don't receive the check immediately, I am going to have to speak to your manager when I'm in New York next week." And sure enough, the following week there we were in front of this astonished stockbroker, and I was sitting there red-faced and quiet, and my mother, the real Mrs. Tan, was shouting at his boss in her impeccable broken English.

14   We used a similar routine just five days ago, for a situation that was far less humorous. My mother had gone to the hospital for an appointment, to find out about a benign brain tumor a CAT scan had revealed a month ago. She said she had spoken very good English, her best English, no mistakes. Still, she said, the hospital did not apologize when they said they had lost the CAT scan and she had come for nothing. She said they did not seem to have any sympathy when she told them she was anxious to know the exact diagnosis, since her husband and son had both died of brain tumors. She said they would not give her any more information until the next time and she would have to make another appointment for that. So she said she would not leave until the doctor called her daughter. She wouldn't budge. And when the doctor finally called her daughter, me, who spoke in perfect English—lo and behold—we had assurances the CAT scan would be found, promises that a conference call on Monday would be held, and apologies for any suffering my mother had gone through for a most regrettable mistake.

15   I think my mother's English almost had an effect on limiting my possibilities in life as well. Sociologists and linguists probably will tell you that a person's

developing language skills are more influenced by peers. But I do think that the language spoken in the family, especially in immigrant families which are more insular, plays a large role in shaping the language of the child. And I believe that it affected my results on achievement tests, IQ tests, and the SAT. While my English skills were never judged as poor, compared to math, English could not be considered my strong suit. In grade school I did moderately well, getting perhaps B's, sometimes B-pluses, in English and scoring perhaps in the sixtieth or seventieth percentile on achievement tests. But those scores were not good enough to override the opinion that my true abilities lay in math and science, because in those areas I achieved A's and scored in the ninetieth percentile or higher.

16   This was understandable. Math is precise; there is only one correct answer. Whereas, for me at least, the answers on English tests were always a judgment call, a matter of opinion and personal experience. Those tests were constructed around items like fill-in-the-blank sentence completion, such as, "Even though Tom was ___, Mary thought he was ___." And the correct answer always seemed to be the most bland combinations of thoughts, for example, "Even though Tom was shy, Mary thought he was charming," with the grammatical structure "even though" limiting the correct answer to some sort of semantic opposites, so you wouldn't get answers like, "Even though Tom was foolish, Mary thought he was ridiculous." Well, according to my mother, there were very few limitations as to what Tom could have been and what Mary might have thought of him. So I never did well on tests like that.

17   The same was true with word analogies, pairs of words in which you were supposed to find some sort of logical, semantic relationship—for example, "*Sunset* is to *nightfall* as ___ is to ___." And here you would be presented with a list of four possible pairs, one of which showed the same kind of relationship: *red* is to *stoplight*, *bus* is to *arrival*, *chills* is to *fever*, *yawn* is to *boring*. Well, I could never think that way. I knew what the tests were asking, but I could not block out of my mind the images already created by the first pair, "*sunset* is to *nightfall*"—and I would see a burst of colors against a darkening sky, the moon rising, the lowering of a curtain of stars. And all the other pairs of words—red, bus, stoplight, boring—just threw up a mess of confusing images, making it impossible for me to sort out something as logical as saying: "A sunset precedes nightfall" is the same as "a chill precedes a fever." The only way I would have gotten that answer right would have been to imagine an associative situation, for example, my being disobedient and staying out past sunset, catching a chill at night, which turns into feverish pneumonia as punishment, which indeed did happen to me.

18   I have been thinking about all this lately, about my mother's English, about achievement tests. Because lately I've been asked, as a writer, why there are not more Asian Americans represented in American literature. Why are there few Asian Americans enrolled in creative writing programs? Why do so many Chinese students go into engineering? Well, these are broad sociological questions I can't begin to answer. But I have noticed in surveys—in fact, just last week—that Asian students, as a whole, always do significantly better on math achievement tests than in English. And this makes me think that there are other Asian-American students whose English spoken in the home might also be described as "broken" or

"limited." And perhaps they also have teachers who are steering them away from writing and into math and science, which is what happened to me.

19   Fortunately, I happen to be rebellious in nature and enjoy the challenge of disproving assumptions made about me. I became an English major my first year in college, after being enrolled as pre-med. I started writing nonfiction as a freelancer the week after I was told by my former boss that writing was my worst skill and I should hone my talents toward account management.

20   But it wasn't until 1985 that I finally began to write fiction. And at first I wrote using what I thought would be wittily crafted sentences, sentences that would finally prove I had mastery over the English language. Here's an example from the first draft of a story that later made its way into *The Joy Luck Club*, but without this line: "That was my mental quandary in the nascent state." A terrible line, which I can barely pronounce.

21   Fortunately, for reasons I won't get into today, I later decided I should envision a reader for the stories I would write. And the reader I decided upon was my mother, because these were stories about mothers. So with this reader in mind—and in fact she did read my early drafts—I began to write stories using all the Englishes I grew up with: the English I spoke to my mother, which for lack of a better term might be described as "simple"; the English she used with me, which for lack of a better term might be described as "broken"; my translation of her Chinese, which could certainly be described as "watered down"; and what I imagined to be her translation of her Chinese if she could speak in perfect English, her internal language, and for that I sought to preserve the essence, but neither an English nor a Chinese structure. I wanted to capture what language ability tests can never reveal: her intent, her passion, her imagery, the rhythms of her speech and the nature of her thoughts.

22   Apart from what any critic had to say about my writing, I knew I had succeeded where it counted when my mother finished reading my book and gave me her verdict: "So easy to read."

CHAPTER 28

Exposition: Causal Analysis

The Teacher Who Changed My Life

Nicholas Gage

Former investigative reporter, film producer, and author of seven books, Nicholas Gage is best known for *Eleni* (1983), the story of his mother's life and execution in 1948 during the Greek civil war. The story of this murder and Gage's subsequent search for her killers was made into a well-received movie in 1985. The story of Gage's family, *A Place for Us: Eleni's Children in America* (1989), contains a version of the following essay. Other books include *Greece: Land of Light* (1998) and *Greek Fire* (2000).

1   The person who set the course of my life in the new land I entered as a young war refugee—who, in fact, nearly dragged me onto the path that would bring all the blessings I've received in America—was a salty-tongued, no-nonsense school-teacher named Marjorie Hurd. When I entered her classroom in 1953, I had been to six schools in five years, starting in the Greek village where I was born in 1939.

2   When I stepped off a ship in New York Harbor on a gray March day in 1949, I was an undersized nine-year-old in short pants who had lost his mother and was coming to live with the father he didn't know. My mother, Eleni Gatzoyiannis, had been imprisoned, tortured, and shot by Communist guerrillas for sending me and three of my four sisters to freedom. She died so that her children could go to their father in the United States.

3   The portly, bald, well-dressed man who met me and my sisters seemed a foreign, authoritarian figure. I secretly resented him for not getting the whole family out of Greece early enough to save my mother. Ultimately, I would grow to love him and

appreciate how he dealt with becoming a single parent at the age of fifty-six, but at first our relationship was prickly, full of hostility.

4   As Father drove us to our new home—a tenement in Worcester, Mass.—and pointed out the huge brick building that would be our first school in America, I clutched my Greek notebooks from the refugee camp, hoping that my few years of schooling would impress my teachers in this cold, crowded country. They didn't. When my father led me and my eleven-year-old sister to Greendale Elementary School, the grim-faced Yankee principal put the two of us in a class for the mentally retarded. There was no facility in those days for non-English-speaking children.

5   By the time I met Marjorie Hurd four years later, I had learned English, been placed in a normal, graded class and had even been chosen for the college preparatory track in the Worcester public school system. I was thirteen years old when our father moved us yet again, and I entered Chandler Junior High shortly after the beginning of seventh grade. I found myself surrounded by richer, smarter, and better-dressed classmates who looked askance at my strange clothes and heavy accent. Shortly after I arrived, we were told to select a hobby to pursue during "club hour" on Fridays. The idea of hobbies and clubs made no sense to my immigrant ears, but I decided to follow the prettiest girl in my class—the blue-eyed daughter of the local Lutheran minister. She led me through the door marked "Newspaper Club" and into the presence of Miss Hurd, the newspaper adviser and English teacher who would become my mentor and my muse.

6   A formidable, solidly built woman with salt-and-pepper hair, a steely eye, and a flat Boston accent, Miss Hurd had no patience with layabouts. "What are all you goof-offs doing here?" she bellowed at the would-be journalists. "This is the Newspaper Club! We're going to put out a *newspaper*. So if there's anybody in this room who doesn't like work, I suggest you go across to the Glee Club now, because you're going to work your tails off here!"

7   I was soon under Miss Hurd's spell. She did indeed teach us to put out a newspaper, skills I honed during my next twenty-five years as a journalist. Soon I asked the principal to transfer me to her English Class as well. There, she drilled us on grammar until I finally began to understand the logic and structure of the English language. She assigned stories for us to read and discuss; not tales of heroes, like the Greek myths I knew, but stories of underdogs—poor people, even immigrants, who seemed ordinary until a crisis drove them to do something extraordinary. She also introduced us to the literary wealth of Greece—giving me a new perspective on my war-ravaged, impoverished homeland. I began to be proud of my origins.

8   One day, after discussing how writers should write about what they know, she assigned us to compose an essay from our own experience. Fixing me with a stern look, she added, "Nick, I want you to write about what happened to your family in Greece." I had been trying to put those painful memories behind me and left the assignment until the last moment. Then, on a warm spring afternoon, I sat in my room with a yellow pad and pencil and stared out the window at the buds on the trees. I wrote that the coming of spring always reminded me of the last time I said goodbye to my mother on a green and gold day in 1948.

9   I kept writing, one line after another, telling how the Communist guerrillas occupied our village, took our home and food, how my mother started planning

our escape when she learned that children were to be sent to re-education camps behind the Iron Curtain, and how, at the last moment, she couldn't escape with us because the guerrillas sent her with a group of women to thresh wheat in a distant village. She promised she would try to get away on her own, she told me to be brave and hung a silver cross around my neck, and then she kissed me. I watched the line of women being led down into the ravine and up the other side, until they disappeared around the bend—my mother a tiny brown figure at the end who stopped for an instant to raise her hand in one last farewell.

10   I wrote about our nighttime escape down the mountain, across the minefields, and into the lines of the Nationalist soldiers, who sent us to a refugee camp. It was there that we learned of our mother's execution. I felt very lucky to have come to America, I concluded, but every year, the coming of spring made me feel sad because it reminded me of the last time I saw my mother.

11   I handed in the essay, hoping never to see it again, but Miss Hurd had it published in the school paper. This mortified me at first, until I saw that my classmates reacted with sympathy and tact to my family's story. Without telling me, Miss Hurd also submitted the essay to a contest sponsored by the Freedoms Foundation at Valley Forge, and it won a medal. The Worcester paper wrote about the award and quoted my essay at length. My father, by then a "five-and-dime-store chef," as the paper described him, was ecstatic with pride, and the Worcester Greek community celebrated the honor to one of its own.

12   For the first time, I began to understand the power of the written word. A secret ambition took root in me. One day, I vowed, I would go back to Greece, find out the details of my mother's death, and write about her life, so her grandchildren would know of her courage. Perhaps I would even track down the men who killed her and write of their crimes. Fulfilling that ambition would take me thirty years.

13   Meanwhile, I followed the literary path that Miss Hurd had so forcefully set me on. After junior high, I became the editor of my school paper at Classical High School and got a part-time job at the Worcester *Telegram and Gazette*. Although my father could only give me $50 and encouragement toward a college education, I managed to finance four years at Boston University with scholarships and part-time jobs in journalism. During my last year of college, an article I wrote about a friend who had died in the Philippines—the first person to lose his life working for the Peace Corps—led to my winning the Hearst Award for College Journalism. And the plaque was given to me in the White House by President John F. Kennedy.

14   For a refugee who had never seen a motorized vehicle or indoor plumbing until he was nine, this was an unimaginable honor. When the Worcester paper ran a picture of me standing next to President Kennedy, my father rushed out to buy a new suit in order to be properly dressed to receive the congratulations of the Worcester Greeks. He clipped out the photograph, had it laminated in plastic, and carried it in his breast pocket for the rest of his life to show everyone he met. I found the much-worn photo in his pocket on the day he died twenty years later.

15   In our isolated Greek village, my mother had bribed a cousin to teach her to read, for girls were not supposed to attend school beyond a certain age. She had always dreamed of her children receiving an education. She couldn't be there when

I graduated from Boston University, but the person who came with my father and shared our joy was my former teacher, Marjorie Hurd. We celebrated not only my bachelor's degree but also the scholarships that paid my way to Columbia's Graduate School of Journalism. There, I met the woman who would eventually become my wife. At our wedding and at the baptisms of our three children, Marjorie Hurd was always there, dancing alongside the Greeks.

16   By then, she was Mrs. Rabidou, for she had married a widower when she was in her early forties. That didn't distract her from her vocation of introducing young minds to English literature, however. She taught for a total of forty-one years and continually would make a "project" of some balky student in whom she spied a spark of potential. Often these were students from the most troubled homes, yet she would alternately bully and charm each one with her own special brand of tough love until the spark caught fire. She retired in 1981 at the age of sixty-two but still avidly follows the lives and careers of former students while overseeing her adult stepchildren and driving her husband on camping trips to New Hampshire.

17   Miss Hurd was one of the first to call me on December 10, 1987, when President Reagan, in his television address after the summit meeting with Gorbachev, told the nation that Elena Gatzoyiannis's dying cry, "My children!" had helped inspire him to seek an arms agreement "for all the children of the world."

18   "I can't imagine a better monument for your mother," Miss Hurd said with an uncharacteristic catch in her voice.

19   Although a bad hip makes it impossible for her to join in the Greek dancing, Marjorie Hurd Rabidou is still an honored and enthusiastic guest at all our family celebrations, including my fiftieth birthday picnic last summer, where the shish kebab was cooked on spits, clarinets and *bouzoukis* wailed, and costumed dancers led the guests in a serpentine line around our Colonial farmhouse, only twenty minutes from my first home in Worcester.

20   My sisters and I felt an aching void because my father was not there to lead the line, balancing a glass of wine on his head while he danced, the way he did at every celebration during his ninety-two years. But Miss Hurd was there, surveying the scene with quiet satisfaction. Although my parents are gone, her presence was a consolation, because I owe her so much.

21   This is truly the land of opportunity, and I would have enjoyed its bounty even if I hadn't walked into Miss Hurd's classroom in 1953. But she was the one who directed my grief and pain into writing, and if it weren't for her I wouldn't have become an investigative reporter and foreign correspondent, recorded the story of my mother's life and death in *Eleni* and now my father's story in *A Place for Us*, which is also a testament to the country that took us in. She was the catalyst that sent me into journalism and indirectly caused all the good things that came after. But Miss Hurd would probably deny this emphatically.

22   A few years ago, I answered the telephone and heard my former teacher's voice telling me, in that won't-take-no-for-an-answer tone of hers, that she had decided I was to write and deliver the eulogy at her funeral. I agreed (she didn't leave me any choice), but that's one assignment I never want to do. I hope, Miss Hurd, that you'll accept this remembrance instead.

Mystery!

Nicholas Meyer

Nicholas Meyer is a novelist, screenwriter, and film director-producer. Two of his three mystery novels, *The Seven-Per-Cent Solution* (1974) and *The West End Horror* (1976), have been made into successful movies. Meyer is also known for his contributions as a director and co-writer of the popular sci-fi movies *Star Trek II, IV*, and *VI*. This essay, originally published in the *TV Guide* magazine in 1980, appeared in an earlier edition of this textbook and has returned in response to popular request.

1 Reading mysteries is a bedtime recreation for all segments of society—high, low and middle brow. It is the *divertissement** of prime ministers and plumbers. Mysteries, whether they are on television, paper or movie screens, delight almost all of us. Everyone likes to "curl up" with a good mystery, and that makes this particular kind of literature unique in its ubiquitous appeal. No other genre so transcends what might otherwise appear to be significant differences in the social, educational and economic backgrounds of its audience.

2 Why, for heaven's sake? What is there about mystery and detective stories that fascinate so many of us, regardless of age, sex, color and national origin?

3 On the surface, it seems highly improbable that detective novels should provide such broad-based satisfaction. Their jacket blurbs and ad copy contain plenty of violent, even gory, references: "The body lay inert, the limbs dangling at unnatural angles, the head bashed in, clearly the result of a blunt instrument . . ." Who wants to read this stuff? Even assuming that there is a certain segment of society that delights in sadistic imagery and rejoices in thrills and chills and things that go bump in the night, it is hard to imagine that these sensibilities are in the majority.

4 As the Great Detective** himself might have observed, "It is a singular business, Watson, and on the surface, most unlikely." Yet as Holmes was wont to remark, evidence that appears to point in one unerring direction may, if viewed from a slightly altered perspective, admit of precisely the opposite interpretation. People do, in fact, like to "curl up" with a good mystery. They take the corpses and the murderers to bed with them as favorite nighttime reading. One could hardly imagine a more intimate conjunction!

5 But the phrase "curling up" does not connote danger; say rather the reverse. It conjures up snug, warm, secure feelings. Curling up with a good mystery is not exciting or thrilling; it is in fact oddly restful. It is reassuring.

6 Now why should this be? How is it possible that detective stories, with all the murder and blackmail and mayhem and mystery that pervades them, should provide us with feelings of security, coziness and comfort?

7 Well, detective stories have other things in them besides violence and blood. They have solutions, for one thing. Almost invariably, the murderer is caught, or at the very least identified. *As sure as God made little green apples, it all adds up to*

---

*A French word for diversion or entertainment
**Sherlock Holmes

something. If it doesn't, we aren't happy with the piece. A good detective story ties up all the loose ends; we resent motives and clues left unconnected.

8   Yes, detective stories have solutions. But life does not. On the contrary, life is an anarchic proposition in which meaningless events conspire daily to alter our destiny without rhyme or reason. Your plane crashes, or the one you were booked on crashes but you missed it; a flat tire, a missed phone call, an open manhole, a misunderstanding—these are the chaotic commonplaces of everyday existence. But they have no place in the mystery novel. In detective novels, nothing happens without a reason. Detective literature, though it may superficially resemble life, in fact has effected at least one profound alteration: mystery stories *organize* life and provide it with meaning and answers. The kind of confusion in which real people are forced to exist doesn't occur in detective stories. Whatever the various people's problems, the only serious difficulty confronting them in detective stories is the fact that they are suspected of committing the crime involved. Once cleared of that lowering cloud, they are free to pursue their lives with, presumably, successful results.

9   So we see that the coziness of detective and mystery stories is not entirely incomprehensible or inappropriate, after all. If we like to take such literature to bed with us and cuddle up with it, what we are really cuddling up to is a highly stylized literary formula, which is remarkably consistent in delivering to us that reassuring picture we all crave of an ordered world.

10   Sherlock Holmes, Philip Marlow, Miss Marple or Columbo*—the stories in which these characters appear all manage to delight us by reassuring us. The victim is usually only slightly known or not very well liked. The world seems better off without him, or else he is so sorely missed that tracking his (or her) murderer will be, in Oscar Wilde's** words, more than a duty, it will be a pleasure.

11   And pleasurable indeed is the process of watching the tracking. There are some highfalutin apologists of the detective genre who would have us believe it is the intellectual exercise of following the clues along with the detective—the reader's or viewer's participation in a kind of mental puzzle—that provides the satisfaction associated with detective stories. I believe such participation is largely illusory. We don't really ever have all the pieces at our disposal and most of us are not inclined to work with them very thoroughly, even in those rare cases when the author has been scrupulously "fair" in giving them to us. We enjoy the *illusion* of participation without really doing any of the mental legwork beyond the normal wondering "Whodunit?"

12   In any event, such a theory to justify the fascination exerted by detective and mystery stories is elitist and falsely elitist into the bargain. It distracts our attention with a pretentious and tenuous explanation in place of a much more interesting and persuasive one; namely, that detective stories are appealing because they depict life not as it is but in some sense as it ought to be.

---

*These four characters are famous fictional detectives: Sherlock Holmes created by Arthur Conan Doyle; Philip Marlowe, by Raymond Chandler; Miss Marple, by Agatha Christie. Columbo solved crimes in a popular television series of the same name.

**Oscar Wilde was a nineteenth-century English author and wit.

Cell Phones and Social Graces

Charles Fisher

Charles Fisher has been a professor of English at Aims Community College in northeastern Colorado for twenty years and is the author of the composition textbook *Researching and Writing about Controversies*. He has taught a variety of college writing, research, and literature courses. Fisher uses this personal essay to spark discussion among his own composition students; it has been slightly adapted for this text.

1   I want to say first that I'm not a Luddite* like those who destroyed machinery in English factories during the Industrial Revolution. I have a computer, I manage my email, I can de-fragment my hard drive. But I draw the line at cell phones.

2   Cell phones are amazing creations. These brushed-silver and fluorescent-blue-lit devices do what home computers—not to mention *telephones*—could not do five years ago. They add and subtract. They enable Internet stock transactions. They download and play music. They allow real-time conversations through text messaging. They record videos. They identify who is calling by playing a particular tune. Last night my sister in Idaho knew I called because her phone tootled "Stars and Stripes Forever."

3   There are good reasons to own a cell phone. They provide a means to contact someone in an emergency: to call the insurance company after an accident on the interstate, to call the owner of a wandering dog with a phone number on its collar, to monitor children entrusted with the house for a day, and to coordinate pickups and deliveries in multi-car soccer families. Still, until cell phones came along, business was conducted without catastrophe, folks wanting to contact me urgently enough left a voice-mail message on my home phone. Even if they could never make contact, *life went on anyway*. Domestic problems were addressed *at home*, not in public (I didn't appreciate the woman in Borders yesterday who argued over domestic relationships, complete with profanity, in full hearing of customers desiring quiet while they browsed). Grocery lists were compiled *before* one left for the store, and if one forgot something, then one could always go back (does it save *that* much time and gas?)—all without cell phones.

4   Cell phones enable a person simply to stay in constant contact. But what demon has convinced the cell-phone generation that it is a *good* thing to be constantly available? Whatever happened to *not* being available to everyone at all times?

5   I am not in the market for a cell phone for the simplest and most logical reason: I don't need one; our conventional phone serves us well enough. There are economic and technological reasons as well. For example, it costs more per month than my land-line, there are additional "roaming charges" and other fees for "exceeding one's minutes," and awful penalties are exacted for breaking a mandatory two-year contract. A final indignity is that if I own a cell phone, *I* am charged if someone calls *me*. Thus my younger sons remind me to call only on "free days."

---

*Luddites were English workers who, having previously earned their living through handcrafts, participated in 1811–1812 raids that destroyed mechanized knitting and weaving machines. Today the term often refers to anyone who resists technology.

6 From a technological standpoint, I have yet to communicate with anyone on a cell phone when the connection wasn't muffled, garbled, wavery, barrel-like, or disconnected without warning because a cell phone battery lost energy. And of course, we're all aware of the controversial safety record of drivers using cell phones. I myself have been nearly a victim twice of drivers on cell phones who nearly ran over me while I was biking to work.

7 But I refuse to buy a cell phone primarily because I'm afraid that if I yield to the siren-call of gadgetry and instant-constant access, I, too will evolve into one of the many social troglodytes whom cell phones have created. I mourn the demise of courtesy and civility and refuse to become a life-long slave to the cell phone.

8 This slavish dependency is seen in countless ways. See me walking briskly around the local park lake on a delightful spring morning, enjoying the new duck family and the song of meadowlarks. See the woman approaching me, speed-walking with a cell-phone glued to her ear. Apparently, she cannot wait until she gets home to conduct this conversation. I don't even bother to say "Good morning"; she's not listening, anyway. So much for social interaction and pleasantries that enhance human contact.

9 Observe the Safeway shopper with a cell phone impaled in her ear, halted in the middle of the deli aisle, a far-off glaze in her eyes: "Well, as long as it has a ground-level bathroom." And why is it that people talking on cell phones in grocery stores feel the need to talk louder than normal? I'm sure *I* want to hear all about her husband's house-hunting. I simply don't want to hear about the problems a shopper is having with her husband while in the "foot remedies" aisle of Walgreens or while I'm trying to enjoy Rattlesnake Bites at the Texas Roadhouse. I would like to shop in peace and eat in peace.

10 I can no longer attend a movie without cell phones intruding like unwanted aliens into my enjoyment. If a cell phone doesn't go off, it's the sudden green glow of one in the lap in front of me because the movie patron *is forced* to respond to urgent bee-vibration at his hip. He *must* answer the call of the text message or call-back number *right now*. "Oh, sorry, I've *got* to get this," we hear often. Well, no, one *doesn't have* to get that.

11 More slavishness: When my wife and I celebrated our anniversary at Disney World two years ago, I had the urge to say to the lady bobbing on a carousel stallion with her hand glued to her ear: "Do you *really* have to talk to someone? Couldn't you have waited the two minutes before the ride's end? Couldn't you just simply *enjoy* the ride and enter into the enjoyment of your daughter next to you for *two doggone minutes?*"

12 Such slavish dependency on cell phones is accompanied by the demise of common social courtesies. Perfectly decent people will flip open their cell phone at a call, identify the caller, and simply press a button to ignore the call. A friend or family member who will open their front door to cute little girls selling cookies will ignore me—their beloved father or valued friend—on their cell phone. What heady power to make someone disappear! I can understand not answering the doorbell to a man selling SuperScrub Concrete Cleaner. But I'm not that guy. I'm a family member. I'm a friend.

13 I know it's not the cell phone—it's how people use all those candy-store options. But the choices *encourage* rudeness in far too many cases. Scene: Commencement

and graduation ceremonies at a northern California college. Two deans in full regalia are honored by being selected to pass out diplomas to students, many of whom they had in their classes. A name is called. Across the stage strides a cocky graduate, *talking to someone on his cell phone,* his hand pasted to his ear, a stupid grin on his face. He takes his diploma without making eye contact with the dean or saying so much as a "thank you" or indication of respect—he's too busy yakking as he bounds down the steps, oblivious to decorum.

14   Sadly, people I would least expect to be slavish and rude with cell phones—my church family—have committed some of the most odious offenses. A cell phone suddenly begins bleeping the brassy notes of "Für Elise" during the eulogy at a funeral several weeks ago. A few days later, while we shared prayer requests in our home Bible study, we all jumped as a rousing "Dixie" began emanating from one lady's purse—followed by the frantic fumbling to find the offending device, the embarrassed glance, and a quick apology and disabling of the phone—wait, *no!*— there was no embarrassed glance, no apology—instead, she said, "I've *got* to get this" and rushed, phone still ringing, into the hallway.

15   Yes, all of the above scenarios are the result of *choices* users make regarding their cell phones. They are sociological and cultural actions, and I don't have to do what they do if I ever do buy a cell phone. I could turn it off when I'm driving or shopping or eating, or attending a funeral or Bible study. No, I don't have to talk while at the carnival or while taking walks around the park. I don't have to know who's trying to call me, and I don't have to use instant messaging. In this cornucopia of choices, I don't have to choose *any* of those options. And I most likely wouldn't. And *that* is probably the main reason I don't have a cell phone.

CHAPTER 29

Argumentation

A Scientist: "I Am the Enemy"

Ron Kline

Ron Kline is a pediatric hematologist-oncologist in Nevada and a former director of the bone marrow transplant program at the University of Louisville. Kline published the following essay in *Newsweek* magazine's "My Turn" column in 1989 when he was a biotechnology fellow in the Experimental Immunology Branch of the National Cancer Institute in Washington, D.C.

1 I am the enemy! One of those vilified, inhumane physician-scientists involved in animal research. How strange, for I have never thought of myself as an evil person. I became a pediatrician because of my love for children and my desire to keep them healthy. During medical school and residency, however, I saw many children die of leukemia, prematurity, and traumatic injury—circumstances against which medicine has made tremendous progress, but still has far to go. More important, I also saw children, alive and healthy, thanks to advances in medical science such as infant respirators, potent antibiotics, new surgical techniques and the entire field of organ transplantation. My desire to tip the scales in favor of the healthy, happy children drew me to medical research.

2 My accusers claim that I inflict torture on animals for the sole purpose of career advancement. My experiments supposedly have no relevance to medicine and are easily replaced by computer simulation. Meanwhile, an apathetic public barely watches, convinced that the issue has no significance, and publicity-conscious politicians increasingly give way to the demands of the activists.

3   We in medical research have also been unconscionably apathetic. We have allowed the most extreme animal-rights protesters to seize the initiative and frame the issue as one of "animal fraud." We have been complacent in our belief that a knowledgeable public would sense the importance of animal research to the public health. Perhaps we have been mistaken in not responding to the emotional tone of the argument created by those sad posters of animals by waving equally sad posters of children dying of leukemia or cystic fibrosis.

4   Much is made of the pain inflicted on these animals in the name of medical science. The animal-rights activists contend that this is evidence of our malevolent and sadistic nature. A more reasonable argument, however, can be advanced in our defense. Life is often cruel, both to animals and human beings. Teenagers get thrown from the back of a pickup truck and suffer severe head injuries. Toddlers, barely able to walk, find themselves at the bottom of a swimming pool while a parent checks the mail. Physicians hoping to alleviate the pain and suffering these tragedies cause have but three choices: create an animal model of the injury or disease and use that model to understand the process and test new therapies; experiment on human beings—some experiments will succeed, most will fail—or finally, leave medical knowledge static, hoping that accidental discoveries will lead us to the advances.

5   Some animal-rights activists would suggest a fourth choice, claiming that computer models can simulate animal experiments, thus making the actual experiments unnecessary. Computers can simulate, reasonably well, the effects of well-understood principles on complex systems, as in the application of the laws of physics to airplane and automobile design. However, when the principles themselves are in question, as is the case with the complex biological systems under study, computer modeling alone is of little value.

6   One of the terrifying effects of the effort to restrict the use of animals in medical research is that the impact will not be felt for years and decades: drugs that might have been discovered will not be; surgical techniques that might have been developed will not be; and fundamental biological processes that might have been understood will remain mysteries. There is the danger that politically expedient solutions will be found to placate a vocal minority, while the consequences of those decisions will not be apparent until long after the decisions are made and the decision makers forgotten.

7   Fortunately, most of us enjoy good health, and the trauma of watching one's child die has become a rare experience. Yet our good fortune should not make us unappreciative of the health we enjoy or the advances that make it possible. Vaccines, antibiotics, insulin, and drugs to treat heart disease, hypertension, and stroke are all based on animal research. Most complex surgical procedures, such as coronary-artery by-pass and organ transplantation, are initially developed in animals. Presently undergoing animal studies are techniques to insert genes in humans in order to replace the defective ones found to be the cause of so much disease. These studies will effectively end if animal research is severely restricted.

8   In America today, death has become an event isolated from our daily existence—out of the sight and thoughts of most of us. As a doctor who has watched many children die, and their parents grieve, I am particularly angered by people capable of so much compassion for a dog or a cat, but with seemingly so little for

a dying human being. These people seem so insulated from the reality of human life and death and what it means.

9   Make no mistake, however: I am not advocating the needlessly cruel treatment of animals. To the extent that the animal-rights movement has made us more aware of the needs of these animals, and made us search harder for suitable alternatives, they have made a significant contribution. But if the more radical members of this movement are successful in limiting further research, their efforts will bring about a tragedy that will cost many lives. The real question is whether an apathetic majority can be aroused to protect its future against a vocal, but misdirected, minority.

Defining the SAT Downward

The Editorial Board of USA Today

Founded in 1982 by Allen Neuharth, *USA Today* is a national American newspaper claiming a readership of over three million, with special appeal to travelers. One of the paper's popular features is "Today's Debate," which expresses the opinion of the editors on a current topic and then offers an opposing view. This essay by the editorial board appeared in the "Debate" on March 13, 2009.

1   When thousands of high school students take the SAT on Saturday, they will have a big advantage over students in years past: If they do badly, no one has to know. No matter how many times they take the SAT, they can have only their best total score sent to their target colleges.

2   The College Board's Score Choice policy, new this month, is designed to "reduce student stress and improve the test-day experience," and that it surely will. It also brings the SAT in line with its fast-gaining competitor, the ACT. But while the College Board's decision makes business sense, it increases the bias that both the SAT and the ACT already show in favor of students from well-off families. That's because Score Choice benefits students with the means to take the test numerous times. Score Choice also harms the integrity of the SAT by reducing the amount of information colleges are getting about applicants' abilities.

3   The new policy is great for students who can repeat the test, thereby raising their score by an average of 40 points the second time around. These gains, though, have less to do with academic skill than with repetition, and with expensive tutoring and test-prep classes.

4   The College Board points out that it waives the $45 SAT fee twice for students in need, yet that doesn't necessarily solve the problem. Although the board gave high school seniors 221,962 fee waivers last year, that total doesn't account for an additional 170,000 test takers from households that earn less than $60,000 a year.

5   Score Choice isn't the only way the College Board keeps moving toward policies that give well-off students more ways to game the system, rather than toward its stated mission of measuring students' potential for academic success in college. It also offers a loophole through which some students can—and do—buy questionable diagnoses of learning disabilities, use the diagnoses to petition the College Board for extra time to complete the SAT and never reveal to their target colleges that they were given the extra time. Experts warned the board when the loophole

opened in 2003 that it would be abused, and lo and behold, the proportion of SAT takers claiming disabilities has grown 18% in the past decade.

6   Rather than define the SAT downward in a scramble for customers and repeat business, the College Board ought to redouble its efforts to measure academic potential, using proven gauges of academic success such as the standardized essay-writing portion and tests on advanced-level subjects.

7   It can do that, and move closer to reflecting a more accurate academic picture of all its test takers, particularly the underserved low-income ones. Or it can continue the downward slide, perhaps by supplementing Score Choice with Score Salad Bar, a program that could let repeat test takers pick a math score here, a verbal score there and thus, at a price, garnish their college applications with an even more attractive sprinkling of extra SAT points.

Judging by the Cover

Bonny Gainley

Bonny Gainley is a marketing and management consultant, speaker, and author who writes on topics relating to the family and the workplace. In addition to articles based on her experiences in the high-tech industry, she has published *Look Before You Step: Advice for Potential Stepparents and Their Partners* (2002). This essay originally appeared in 2003 as an opinion column in the Fort Collins, Colorado, newspaper, the *Coloradoan*.

1   Spring is in the air, and those about to graduate are looking for jobs just like many of the rest of us. Competition is tough, so jobs seekers must carefully consider their personal choices.

2   Every person has a need to be accepted, ideally just as he or she is. Our family and friends may do that, but the workplace does not. An editorial a while back in one of our high school newspapers claimed it is unfair for professions such as business, public relations, teaching and others to discourage visible tattoos. While not specifically mentioned, piercings and perhaps even certain hairstyles or garments would fall into the same category.

3   They say you can't judge a book by its cover, yet some people "cover" themselves in ways intended to convey certain messages. The message may be, "my uniform says I am a police officer" or "I like the latest fashions" or "I am a gang member."

4   We make assumptions about people based on their appearance every day, and often we assume exactly what they want us to assume. Just as people project messages about themselves with their appearance, so do businesses. Dress codes and standards exist in the professional world for a number of reasons. Sometimes the issue is safety; sometimes it is a matter of what clients will accept. As long as parents don't want pre-school teachers waving visible skull or profanity tattoos in front of their small children, those tattoos will be deemed inappropriate for that profession.

5   Some say this is an issue of human rights and freedom, but it is really about free enterprise. The bottom line is that businesses exist to make money. Whether it

seems fair or not, most employers do care about the personal appearances of the people they hire because those people represent the business to its customers.

6   Discrimination on the basis of factors an applicant can't control is wrong and illegal. Choosing the candidate who displays the attributes and skills that best match a job description is not. Just as runners would put themselves at a disadvantage by choosing to run the 100 meters in combat boots, people who choose to wear rings through their noses are putting themselves at a disadvantage in the professional job market. Each of us can choose whether to conform to the rules of any organization, but that organization is also free to choose whether they want us associated with it.

7   I don't personally have issues with visible tattoos or piercings, but as a hiring manager I was paid to choose the people who would make the best impression on our customers. It comes down to this—there are plenty of well-qualified applicants and most present themselves in a way my industry considers professional, so there was no compelling reason to choose someone who might offend my customers or poorly represent my company. Even though I may be open minded, I can't count on my customers to be.

8   If people continue to tattoo and pierce, attitudes about the appropriateness of those adornments in the professional workplace will change over time, in the same way that pants have become appropriate for women, for example. When tattoos and piercings are generally accepted in the business world, there will be new things that aren't—maybe nudity or some other trend we can't even imagine. Whether our personal choices will be accepted or not, we each have the right to make them, but must also be willing to accept the related consequences.

9   How we dress, tattoo or pierce is an expression of who we are and a message to the people we encounter. Freedom of choice is a dual-edged sword—individuals are free to present their desired image, and others are free to react to it.

10   There is nobody to blame but yourself if your set of choices does not match those desired by your preferred employers. No organization should have to change to accommodate a candidate simply because that person is unwilling to respect its standards, as long as its standards are legal.

Description

A Day at the Theme Park

W. Bruce Cameron

W. Bruce Cameron began writing humorous features for the Denver newspaper the *Rocky Mountain News* in 1999; his column is now in national syndication. His book *8 Simple Rules for Dating My Teenage Daughter* (2001) was adapted into a television show of the same name; other books include *How to Remodel a Man* (2004) and *8 Simple Rules for Marrying My Daughter* (2008). As a father of three, Cameron often writes about the challenges facing parents, as illustrated in this 1999 column.

1 One of the most endearing traits of children is their utter trust that their parents will provide them with all of life's necessities, meaning food, shelter, and a weekend at a theme park.

2   A theme park is a sort of artificial vacation, a place where you can enjoy all your favorite pastimes at once, such as motion sickness and heat exhaustion. Adult tolerance for theme parks peaks at about an hour, which is how long it takes to walk from the parking lot to the front gate. You fork over an obscene amount of money to gain entrance to a theme park, though it costs nothing to leave (which is odd, because you'd pay anything to escape). The two main activities in a theme park are (a) standing in line, and (b) sweating. The sun reflects off the concrete with a fiendish lack of mercy. You're about to learn the boiling point of tennis shoes. Your hair is sunburned, and when a small child in front of you gestures with her hand she smacks you in the face with her cotton candy; now it feels like your cheeks are covered with carnivorous sand.

3   The ride your children have selected for you is a corkscrewing, stomach-compressing roller coaster built by the same folks who manufactured the baggage

delivery system at DIA.* Apparently the theme of this particular park is "Nausea." You sit down and are strapped in so tightly you can feel your shoulders grinding against your pelvis. Once the ride begins you are thrown about with such violence it reminds you of your teenager's driving. When the ride is over your children want to get something to eat, but first the ride attendants have to pry your fingers off the safety bar. "Open your eyes, please, sir," they keep shouting. They finally persuade you to let go, though it seems a bit discourteous of them to have used pepper spray. Staggering, you follow your children to the Hot Dog Palace for some breakfast.

4   Food at a theme park is so expensive it would be cheaper to just eat your own money. Your son's meal costs a day's pay and consists of items manufactured of corn syrup, which is sugar; sucrose, which is sugar; fructose, which is sugar; and sugar, which is sugar. He also consumes large quantities of what in dog food would be called "meat byproducts." When, after a couple of rides, he announces that he feels like he is going to throw up, you're very alarmed. Having seen his meal once, you're in no mood to see it again.

5   With the exception of that first pummeling, you manage to stay off the rides all day, explaining to your children that it isn't good for you when your internal organs are forcibly rearranged. Now, though, they coax you back in line, promising a ride that doesn't twist, doesn't hang you upside down like a bat, doesn't cause your brain to flop around inside your skull; it just goes up and then comes back down. That's it, Dad, no big deal. What they don't tell you is HOW it comes back down. You're strapped into a seat and pulled gently up into acrophobia, the city falling away from you. Okay, not so bad, and in the conversation you're having with God you explain that you're thankful for the wonderful view but you really would like to get down now.

6   And that's just how you descend: NOW. Without warning, you plummet to the ground in an uncontrolled free fall. You must be moving faster than the speed of sound because when you open your mouth, nothing comes out. Your life passes before your eyes, and your one regret is that you will not have an opportunity to punish your children for bringing you to this hellish place. Brakes cut in and you slam to a stop. You gingerly touch your face to confirm it has fallen off. "Wasn't that fun, Dad?" your kids ask. "Why are you kissing the ground?"

7   At the end of the day, you let your teenager drive home. (After the theme park, you are impervious to fear.)

The Way to Rainy Mountain

N. Scott Momaday

N. Scott Momaday is a writer, teacher, poet, and artist whose Kiowa heritage frequently influences his work. After growing up on reservations in the Southwest, Momaday received his Ph.D. from Stanford University; since 1982 he has taught at the University of Arizona in Tucson. Author of eleven books and many stories, essays, and poems, Momaday won the 1969 Pulitzer Prize for his novel *House Made of Dawn*. This selection is the introduction to his 1969 book, *The Way to Rainy Mountain*.

---

*Denver International Airport

1 A single knoll rises out of the plain in Oklahoma, north and west of the Wichita Range. For my people, the Kiowas, it is an old landmark and they gave it the name Rainy Mountain. The hardest weather in the world is there. Winter brings blizzards, hot tornadic winds arise in the spring, and in the summer the prairie is an anvil's edge. The grass turns brittle and brown, and it cracks beneath your feet. There are green belts along the rivers and creeks, linear groves of hickory and pecan, willow and witch hazel. At a distance in July and August the steaming foliage seems almost to writhe in fire. Great green and yellow grasshoppers are everywhere in the tall grass, popping up like corn to sting the flesh, and tortoises crawl about on the earth going nowhere in plenty of time. Loneliness is an aspect of the land. All things in the plain are isolate; there is no confusion of objects in the eye, but *one* hill or *one* tree or *one* man. To look upon that landscape in the early morning, with the sun at your back, is to lose the sense of proportion. Your imagination comes to life, and this, you think, is where Creation was begun.

2   I returned to Rainy Mountain in July. My grandmother had died in the spring, and I wanted to be at her grave. She had lived to be very old and at last infirm. Her only living daughter was with her when she died, and I was told that in death her face was that of a child.

3   I like to think of her as a child. When she was born, the Kiowas were living the last great moment of their history. For more than a hundred years they had controlled the open range from the Smoky Hill River to the Red, from the headwaters of the Canadian to the fork of the Arkansas and Cimarron. In alliance with the Comanches, they had ruled the whole of the southern Plains. War was their sacred business, and they were among the finest horsemen the world has ever known. But warfare for the Kiowas was preeminently a matter of disposition rather than of survival, and they never understood the grim, unrelenting advance of the U.S. Cavalry. When at last, divided and ill-provisioned, they were driven onto the Staked Plains in the cold rains of autumn, they fell into panic. In Palo Duro Canyon they abandoned their crucial stores to pillage and had nothing then but their lives. In order to save themselves, they surrendered to the soldiers at Fort Sill and were imprisoned in the old stone corral that now stands as a military museum. My grandmother was spared the humiliation of those high gray walls by eight or ten years, but she must have known from birth the affliction of defeat, the dark brooding of old warriors.

4   Her name was Aho, and she belonged to the last culture to evolve in North America. Her forebears came down from the high country in western Montana nearly three centuries ago. They were a mountain people, a mysterious tribe of hunters whose language has never been positively classified in any major group. In the late seventeenth century they began a long migration to the south and east. It was a journey toward the dawn, and it led to a golden age. Along the way the Kiowas were befriended by the Crows, who gave them the culture and religion of the Plains. They acquired horses, and their ancient nomadic spirit was suddenly free of the ground. They acquired Tai-me, the sacred Sun Dance doll, from that moment the object and symbol of their worship, and so shared in the divinity of the sun. Not least, they acquired the sense of destiny, therefore courage and pride. When they entered upon the southern Plains they had been transformed. No longer were they slaves to the simple necessity of survival; they were a lordly and dangerous

society of fighters and thieves, hunters and priests of the sun. According to their origin myth, they entered the world through a hollow log. From one point of view, their migration was the fruit of old prophecy, for indeed they emerged from a sunless world.

5 Although my grandmother lived her long life in the shadow of Rainy Mountain, the immense landscape of the continental interior lay like memory in her blood. She could tell of the Crows, whom she had never seen, and of the Black Hills, where she had never been. I wanted to see in reality what she had seen more perfectly in the mind's eye, and traveled fifteen hundred miles to begin my pilgrimage.

6 Yellowstone, it seemed to me, was the top of the world, a region of deep lakes and dark timber, canyons and waterfalls. But, beautiful as it is, one might have the sense of confinement there. The skyline in all directions is close at hand, the high wall of the woods and deep cleavages of shade. There is a perfect freedom in the mountains, but it belongs to the eagle and the elk, the badger and the bear. The Kiowas reckoned their stature by the distance they could see, and they were bent and blind in the wilderness.

7 Descending eastward, the highland meadows are a stairway to the plain. In July the inland slope of the Rockies is luxuriant with flax and the buckwheat, stonecrop and larkspur. The earth unfolds and the limit of the land recedes. Clusters of trees, and animals grazing far in the distance, cause the vision to reach away and wonder to build upon the mind. The sun follows a longer course in the day, and the sky is immense beyond all comparison. The great billowing clouds that sail upon it are shadows that move upon the grain like water, dividing light. Farther down, in the land of the Crows and Blackfeet, the plain is yellow. Sweet clover takes hold of the hills and bends upon itself to cover and seal the soil. There the Kiowas paused on their way; they had come to the place where they must change their lives. The sun is at home on the plains. Precisely there does it have the certain character of a god. When the Kiowas came to the land of the Crows, they could see the dark lees of the hills at dawn across the Bighorn River, the profusion of light on the grain shelves, the oldest deity ranging after the solstices. Not yet would they veer southward to the caldron of the land that lay below; they must wean their blood from the northern winter and hold the mountains a while longer in their view. They bore Tai-me in procession to the east.

8 A dark mist lay over the Black Hills, and the land was like iron. At the top of a ridge I caught sight of Devil's Tower upthrust against the gray sky as if in the birth of time the core of the earth had broken through its crust and the motion of the world was begun. There are things in nature that engender an awful quiet in the heart of man; Devil's Tower is one of them. Two centuries ago, because they could not do otherwise, the Kiowas made a legend at the base of the rock. My grandmother said:

> Eight children were there at play, seven sisters and their brother. Suddenly the boy was struck dumb; he trembled and began to run upon his hands and feet. His fingers became claws, and his body was covered with fur. Directly there was a bear where the boy had been. The sisters were terrified; they ran, and the bear after them. They came to the stump of a great tree, and the tree spoke to them. It bade them climb upon it, and as they did so it began to rise into the air. The

bear came to kill them, but they were just beyond its reach. It reared against the tree and scored the bark all around with its claws. The seven sisters were borne into the sky, and they became the stars of the Big Dipper.

From that moment, and so long as the legend lives, the Kiowas have kinsmen in the night sky. Whatever they were in the mountains, they could be no more. However tenuous their well-being, however much they had suffered and would suffer again, they had found a way out of the wilderness.

9   My grandmother had a reverence for the sun, a holy regard that now is all but gone out of mankind. There was a wariness in her, and an ancient awe. She was a Christian in her later years, but she had come a long way about, and she never forgot her birthright. As a child she had been to the Sun Dances; she had taken part in those annual rites, and by them she had learned the restoration of her people in the presence of Tai-me. She was about seven when the last Kiowa Sun Dance was held in 1887 on the Washita River above Rainy Mountain Creek. The buffalo were gone. In order to consummate the ancient sacrifice—to impale the head of a buffalo bull upon the medicine tree—a delegation of old men journeyed into Texas, there to beg and barter for an animal from the Goodnight herd. She was ten when the Kiowas came together for the last time as a living Sun Dance culture. They could find no buffalo; they had to hang an old hide from the sacred tree. Before the dance could begin, a company of soldiers rode out from Fort Sill under orders to disperse the tribe. Forbidden without cause the essential act of their faith, having seen the wild herds slaughtered and left to rot upon the ground, the Kiowas backed away forever from the medicine tree. That was July 20, 1890, at the great bend of the Washita. My grandmother was there. Without bitterness, and for as long as she lived, she bore a vision of deicide.

10   Now that I can have her only in memory, I see my grandmother in the several postures that were peculiar to her: standing at the wood stove on a winter morning and turning meat in a great iron skillet; sitting at the south window, bent above her beadwork, and afterwards, when her vision failed, looking down for a long time into the fold of her hands; going out upon a cane, very slowly as she did when the weight of age came upon her; praying. I remember her most often at prayer. She made long, rambling prayers out of suffering and hope, having seen many things. I was never sure that I had the right to hear, so exclusive were they of all mere custom and company. The last time I saw her she prayed standing by the side of her bed at night, naked to the waist, the light of a kerosene lamp moving upon her dark skin. Her long, black hair, always drawn and braided in the day, lay upon her shoulders and against her breasts like a shawl. I do not speak Kiowa, and I never understood her prayers, but there was something inherently sad in the sound, some merest hesitation upon the syllables of sorrow. She began in a high and descending pitch, exhausting her breath to silence; then again and again—and always the same intensity of effort, of something that is, and is not, like urgency in the human voice. Transported so in the dancing light among the shadows of her room, she seemed beyond the reach of time. But that was illusion; I think I knew then that I should not see her again.

11   Houses are like sentinels in the plain, old keepers of the weather watch. There, in a very little while, wood takes on the appearance of great age. All colors wear

soon away in the wind and rain, and then the wood is burned gray and the grain appears and the nails turn red with rust. The windowpanes are black and opaque; you imagine there is nothing within, and indeed there are many ghosts, bones given up to the land. They stand here and there against the sky, and you approach them for a longer time than you expect. They belong in the distance; it is their domain.

12   Once there was a lot of sound in my grandmother's house, a lot of coming and going, feasting and talk. The summers there were full of excitement and reunion. The Kiowas are a summer people; they abide the cold and keep to themselves, but when the season turns and the land becomes warm and vital they cannot hold still; an old love of going returns upon them. The aged visitors who came to my grandmother's house when I was a child were made of lean and leather, and they bore themselves upright. They wore great black hats and bright ample shirts that shook in the wind. They rubbed fat upon their hair and wound their braids with strips of colored cloth. Some of them painted their faces and carried the scars of old and cherished enmities. They were an old council of warlords, come to remind and be reminded of who they were. Their wives and daughters served them well. The women might indulge themselves; gossip was at once the mark and compensation of their servitude. They made loud and elaborate talk among themselves, full of jest and gesture, fright and false alarm. They went abroad in fringed and flowered shawls, bright beadwork and German silver. They were at home in the kitchen, and they prepared meals that were banquets.

13   There were frequent prayer meetings, and great nocturnal feasts. When I was a child I played with my cousins outside, where the lamplight fell upon the ground and the singing of the old people rose up around us and carried away into the darkness. There were a lot of good things to eat, a lot of laughter and surprise. And afterwards, when the quiet returned, I lay down with my grandmother and could hear the frogs away by the river and feel the motion of the air.

14   Now there is a funeral silence in the rooms, the endless wake of some final word. The walls have closed in upon my grandmother's house. When I returned to it in mourning, I saw for the first time in my life how small it was. It was late at night, and there was a white moon, nearly full. I sat for a long time on the stone steps by the kitchen door. From there I could see out across the land; I could see the long row of trees by the creek, the low light upon the rolling plains, and the stars of the Big Dipper. Once I looked at the moon and caught sight of a strange thing. A cricket had perched upon the handrail, only a few inches away from me. My line of vision was such that the creature filled the moon like a fossil. It had gone there, I thought, to live and die, for there, of all places, was its small definition made whole and eternal. A warm wind rose up and purled like the longing within me.

15   The next morning I awoke at dawn and went out on the dirt road to Rainy Mountain. It was already hot, and the grasshoppers began to fill the air. Still, it was early in the morning, and the birds sang out of the shadows. The long yellow grass on the mountain shone in the bright light, and a scissortail hied above the land. There, where it ought to be, at the end of a long and legendary way, was my grandmother's grave. Here and there on the dark stones were ancestral names. Looking back once, I saw the mountain and came away.

Walking on the Moon
David R. Scott

Following two prior flights into space, USAF Colonel David R. Scott commanded the 1971 Apollo 15 mission, the first extended scientific expedition to the moon. This description of his lunar experience is excerpted from a longer article written two years later for *National Geographic* magazine. After serving in various NASA administrative positions, the former astronaut is now president of Scott Science and Technology, Inc.

1   Sixty feet above the moon, the blast of our single rocket churns up a gray tumult of lunar dust that seems to engulf us. Blinded, I feel the rest of the way down "on the gauges." With an abrupt jar, our lunar module, or LM, strikes the surface and shudders to rest. We have hit our target squarely—a large amphitheater girded by mountains and deep canyon, at the eastern edge of a vast plain.

2   As Jim Irvin and I wait for the dust to settle, I recall the twelve revolutions we have just spent in lunar orbit aboard our Apollo 15 spaceship *Endeavour.* Each two hours found us completing a full circuit of earth's ancient satellite—one hour knifing through lunar night, then sunrise and an hour of daylight. As we orbited, I found a particular fascination in that sector of the darkened moon bathed in earthshine. The light reflected by our planet illuminates the sleeping moon much more brightly than moonlight silvers our own night. The mountains and crater rims are clearly seen.

3   I will always remember *Endeavor* hurtling through that strange night of space. Before us and above us stars spangled the sky with their distant icy fire; below lay the moon's far side, an arc of impenetrable blackness that blotted the firmament. Then, as our moment of sunrise approached, barely discernible streamers of light—actually the glowing gases of the solar corona millions of miles away—played above the moon's horizon. Finally the sun exploded into our view like a visual thunderclap. Abruptly, completely, in less than a second, its harsh light flooded into the spaceship and dazzled our eyes.

4   As we looked into the early lunar morning from *Endeavor,* the moonscape stretched into the distance, everything the color of milk chocolate. Long angular shadows accentuated every hill, every crater. As the sun arched higher, the plains and canyons and mountains brightened to a gunmetal gray, while the shadows shrank. At full lunar noontide, the sun glared down upon a bleached and almost featureless world.

5   Now we have come to rest on the moon, and the last of the dust settles outside the LM. We throw the switches that convert this hybrid vehicle from spacecraft to dwelling. Thus begin our 67 hours of lunar residence. We are on a still and arid world where each blazing day and each subfreezing night stretch through 355 earth hours. We have landed in the bright morning of a moon day. When we depart, the sun will not have reached zenith. . . .

6   Opening the top hatch for a preliminary reconnaissance, I peer out at a world seemingly embalmed in the epoch of its creation. Each line, each form blends into the harmonious whole of a single fluid sculpture. Craters left by "recent" meteorites—merely millions of years ago—stand out, startlingly white, like fresh scar tissue against the soft beige of the undulating terrain.

7   I steal a moment and glance straight up into the black sky where the crystalline sphere of earth—all blue and white, sea and clouds—gleams in the abyss of space. In that cold and boundless emptiness, our planet provides the only glow of color. For 30 minutes my helmeted head pivots above the open hatch as I survey and photograph the wonderland of the lunar surface. The incredible variety of landforms in this restricted area (on the moon, the horizon lies a scant mile and a half from a viewer) fills me with pleasant surprise. To the south an 11,000-foot ridge rises above the bleak plain. To the east stretch the hulking heights of an even higher summit. On the west a winding gorge plunges to depths of more than 1,000 feet. Dominating the northeastern horizon, a great mountain stands in noble splendor almost three miles above us. Ours is the first expedition to land amid lunar mountains. Never quickened by life, never assailed by wind and rain, they loom still and serene, a tableau of forever. Their majesty overwhelms me.

8   Eight years' training in lunar geology makes me instantly aware of intriguing details. A dark line like a bathtub ring smudges the bases of the mountains. Was it left by the subsiding lake of lava that filled the immense cavity of Palus Putredinis, on the fringes of Mare Imbrium, billions of years ago? Mare Imbrium, on whose edge we have landed, stretches across the face of the moon for some 650 miles. The celestial projectile that excavated it must have been huge—perhaps as much as 50 miles across—and it slammed into the moon with a velocity many times greater than that of a rifle bullet.

9   When we descend the ladder of the LM and step onto the moon's surface, Jim and I feel a gratifying sense of freedom. For five days we have been crammed into the tight confines of the spacecraft that brought us here. Now, all at once, we regain the luxury of movement. But, we quickly discover, locomotion on the moon has its own peculiar restrictions. At one-sixth of earth's gravity, we weigh only a sixth our normal poundage. Our gait quickly evolves into a rhythmic, bounding motion that possesses all the lightness and ease of strolling on a trampoline.

10   At the same time, since the mass of our bodies and personal gear—and hence, our inertia—remains unchanged, starting and stopping require unusual exertion. I learn to get under way by thrusting my body forward, as though I were stepping into a wind. To stop, I dig in my heels and lean backward.

11   To fall on the moon—and I did several times—is to rediscover childhood. You go down in slow motion, the impact is slight, the risk of injury virtually nil. Forsaking the adult attitude that regards a fall not only as a loss of dignity but also a source of broken bones, the moon walker—like a child—accepts it as yet another diversion. Only the clinging moon dust, the untoward demand on the oxygen supply occasioned by the exertion of getting up, pall the pleasure of a tumble. Personally I find the one-sixth gravity of the moon more enjoyable than the soothing weightlessness of space. I have the same sense of buoyancy, but the moon provides a reassuringly fixed sense of up and down. . . .

12   The flowing moonscape, unmarred by a single jagged peak, reminds me of earth's uplands covered by a heavy blanket of fresh snow. Indeed, the dark-gray moon dust—its consistency seems to be somewhat between coal dust and talcum powder—mantles virtually every physical feature of the lunar surface. Our boots sink gently into it as we walk; we leave sharply chiseled footprints.

13   Color undergoes an odd transformation here. Everything underfoot or nearby is gray, yet this hue blends gradually into the uniform golden tan that characterizes distant objects. And this small spectrum moves with the walker. Most of the scattered rocks share the same gray tint as the dust, but we find two that are jet black, two of pastel green, several with sparkling crystals, some coated with glass, and one that is white. As we advance, we are surrounded by stillness. No wind blows. No sound echoes. Only shadows move. Within the space suit, I hear the reassuring purr of the miniaturized machines that supply vital oxygen and shield me from the blistering 150°F surface heat of the lunar morning. . . .

14   At first we experience a troubling deception with perspective. Without the familiar measuring sticks of our native planet—trees, telephone poles, clouds, and haze—we cannot determine whether an object stands close at hand or at a considerable distance, or whether it is large or small. Gradually our eyes learn to cope with the craters—mammoth, medium, and minuscule—that dot virtually every inch of the surface. And gradually the moon becomes a friendlier place. . . .

15   After each of our expeditions, we climb—sapped of energy—back into the LM. With its oxygen and food and water, it is a tiny artificial earth that comforts us in the void. Removing our space suits and attending to our housekeeping chores consumes two hours. For the first twenty minutes we are conscious of a pervasive odor, similar to that of gunpowder, from the moon dust we have tracked in. Our air-purifying system soon dispels the acrid scent, but the fine, adhesive dust clings to everything. Back on earth, no amount of cleaning will convert our space suits from the gray hue acquired on the moon to their once pristine and sparkling white. . . .

16   The thought haunts us that the end of the Apollo flights may mark man's last visit to the moon for a long time. American manned exploration of deep space is scheduled for an indefinite hiatus. Most scientists have already suggested that, when it resumes, all effort should concentrate upon reaching Mars and beyond. So our lunar artifacts—bypassed in the race to the planets—could remain undisturbed for eternity.

17   Clutching the ladder, I raise my eyes from the now-familiar moonscape to earth, glowing in the black heavens—that incredibly vivid sphere, so blue, so beautiful, so beloved. And so bedeviled: by ecological balances gone awry, by scattered starvation, by a shortage of energy that may motivate us to seek sources beyond our earth. Our Apollo crew believes that a technology capable of exploring space can and will help resolve such problems. We feel a sense of pride in the accomplishments of our program, yet we cannot escape a sense of deep concern for the fate of our planet and our species. This concern has led us to add certain items to the equipment we are leaving on the moon. The sum of these articles, we hope, will form a résumé of our era in the continuing story of the human race.

18   In eons to come, should astronauts from the deeps of space—from other solar systems in other galaxies—pass this way, they may find our spoor, our abandoned gear. A plaque of aluminum affixed to the deserted LM descent stage portrays the two hemispheres of our planet; upon it are engraved the name of our spacecraft, the date of our mission and a roster of the crew. From these data, the equipment, and even the dimensions of our footprints, intelligent beings will readily deduce

what kind of creatures we were and whence we came. We leave a piece of fauna—a falcon feather—and of flora—a four-leaf clover.

19   In a little hollow in the moon dust we placed a stylized figurine of a man in a space suit and beside it another metal plaque bearing the names of the 14 spacemen—Russians and Americans—who have given their lives so that man may range the cosmos. Finally we deposit a single book: the Bible.

20   Our mission ends in fatigue and elation. Amazing success has rewarded the first extended scientific expedition to the moon. After debriefing and helping in the analyses of our findings, our crew disbands. . . .

21   Occasionally, while strolling on a crisp autumn night or driving a straight Texas road, I look up at the moon riding bright and proud over the clouds. My eye picks out the largest circular splotch on the silvery surface: Mare Imbrium. There, at the eastern edge of that splotch, I once descended in a spaceship. Again I feel that I will probably never return, and the thought stirs a pang of nostalgia. For when I look at the moon I do not see a hostile, empty world. I see the radiant body where man has taken his first steps into a frontier that will never end.

CHAPTER 31

Narration

---

38 Who Saw Murder Didn't Call the Police

Martin Gansberg

Martin Gansberg was a reporter and editor for the *New York Times* for over 40 years, until his retirement in 1985. He also wrote for such magazines as *Diplomat*, *Catholic Digest*, and *Facts*. This often-reprinted article was first published in the *New York Times* in 1964, shortly after the murder of Kitty Genovese, a crime that has become synonymous with moral apathy.

1 For more than half an hour 38 respectable, law-abiding citizens in Queens watched a killer stalk and stab a woman in three separate attacks in Kew Gardens.

2 Twice the sound of their voices and the sudden glow of their bedroom lights interrupted him and frightened him off. Each time he returned, sought her out and stabbed her again. Not one person telephoned the police during the assault; one witness called after the woman was dead.

3 That was two weeks ago today. But Assistant Chief Inspector Frederick M. Lussen, in charge of the borough's detectives and a veteran of 25 years of homicide investigations, is still shocked.

4 He can give a matter-of-fact recitation of many murders. But the Kew Gardens slaying baffles him—not because it is a murder, but because the "good people" failed to call the police.

5 "As we have reconstructed the crime," he said, "the assailant had three chances to kill this woman during a 35-minute period. He returned twice to complete the job. If we had been called when he first attacked, the woman might not be dead now."

6 This is what the police say happened beginning at 3:20 A.M. in the staid, middle-class, tree-lined Austin Street area:

7 Twenty-eight-year-old Catherine Genovese, who was called Kitty by almost everyone in the neighborhood, was returning home from her job as manager of a bar in

Hollis. She parked her red Fiat in a lot adjacent to the Kew Gardens Long Island Rail Road Station, facing Mowbray Place. Like many residents of the neighborhood, she had parked there day after day since her arrival from Connecticut a year ago, although the railroad frowns on the practice.

8   She turned off the lights of her car, locked the door and started to walk the 100 feet to the entrance of her apartment at 82–70 Austin Street, which is in a Tudor building, with stores on the first floor and apartments on the second.

9   The entrance to the apartment is in the rear of the building because the front is rented to retail stores. At night the quiet neighborhood is shrouded in the slumbering darkness that marks most residential areas.

10   Miss Genovese noticed a man at the far end of the lot, near a seven-story apartment house at 82–40 Austin Street. She halted. Then, nervously, she headed up Austin Street toward Lefferts Boulevard, where there is a call box to the 102nd Police Precinct in nearby Richmond Hill.

"He Stabbed Me"

11   She got as far as a street light in front of a bookstore before the man grabbed her. She screamed. Lights went on in the 10-story apartment house at 82–67 Austin Street, which faces the bookstore. Windows slid open and voices punctuated the early-morning stillness.

12   Miss Genovese screamed: "Oh, my God, he stabbed me! Please help me! Please help me!"

13   From one of the upper windows in the apartment house, a man called down: "Let that girl alone!"

14   The assailant looked up at him, shrugged and walked down Austin Street toward a white sedan parked a short distance away. Miss Genovese struggled to her feet.

15   Lights went out. The killer returned to Miss Genovese, now trying to make her way around the side of the building by the parking lot to get to her apartment. The assailant stabbed her again.

16   "I'm dying!" she shrieked. "I'm dying!"

A City Bus Passed

17   Windows were opened again, and lights went on in many apartments. The assailant got into his car and drove away. Miss Genovese staggered to her feet. A city bus, Q-10, the Lefferts Boulevard line to Kennedy International Airport, passed. It was 3:35 A.M.

18   The assailant returned. By then, Miss Genovese had crawled to the back of the building, where the freshly painted brown doors to the apartment house held out hope of safety. The killer tried the first door; she wasn't there. At the second door, 82–62 Austin Street, he saw her slumped on the floor at the foot of the stairs. He stabbed her a third time—fatally.

19   It was 3:50 by the time the police received their first call, from a man who was a neighbor of Miss Genovese. In two minutes they were at the scene. The neighbor, a 70-year-old woman and another woman were the only persons on the street. Nobody else came forward.

20   The man explained that he had called the police after much deliberation. He had phoned a friend in Nassau County for advice and then he had crossed the

roof of the building to the apartment of the elderly woman to get her to make the call.

21   "I didn't want to get involved," he sheepishly told the police.

Suspect Is Arrested

22   Six days later, the police arrested Winston Moseley, a 29-year-old business-machine operator, and charged him with homicide. Moseley had no previous record. He is married, has two children and owns a home at 133–19 Sutter Avenue, South Ozone Park, Queens. On Wednesday, a court committed him to Kings County Hospital for psychiatric observation.

23   When questioned by the police, Moseley also said that he had slain Mrs. Annie May Johnson, 24, of 146–12 133d Avenue, Jamaica, on Feb. 29 and Barbara Kralik, 15, of 174–17 140th Avenue, Springfield Gardens, last July. In the Kralik case, the police are holding Alvin L. Mitchell, who is said to have confessed [to] that slaying.

24   The police stressed how simple it would have been to have gotten in touch with them. "A phone call," said one of the detectives, "would have done it." The police may be reached by dialing "O" for operator or SPring 7-3100. . . .

25   Today witnesses from the neighborhood, which is made up of one-family homes in the $35,000 to $60,000 range with the exception of the two apartment houses near the railroad station, find it difficult to explain why they didn't call the police. . . .

26   A housewife, knowingly if quite casually, said, "We thought it was a lover's quarrel." A husband and wife both said, "Frankly, we were afraid." They seemed aware of the fact that events might have been different. A distraught woman, wiping her hands in her apron, said, "I didn't want my husband to get involved."

27   One couple, now willing to talk about that night, said they heard the first screams. The husband looked thoughtfully at the bookstore where the killer first grabbed Miss Genovese.

28   "We went to the window to see what was happening," he said, "but the light from our bedroom made it difficult to see the street." The wife, still apprehensive, added: "I put out the light and we were able to see better."

29   Asked why they hadn't called the police, she shrugged and replied: "I don't know."

30   A man peeked out from a slight opening in the doorway to his apartment and rattled off an account of the killer's second attack. Why hadn't he called the police at the time? "I was tired," he said without emotion. "I went back to bed."

31   It was 4:25 A.M. when the ambulance arrived to take the body of Miss Genovese. It drove off. "Then," a solemn police detective said, "the people came out."

Crossing the Great Divide

Peter Fish

Peter Fish is an editor-at-large and award-winning writer for *Sunset*, a magazine of Western living that began publication in 1898. During the last decade Fish has written over two hundred articles for the magazine on a wide range of subjects including travel, history, science, food, and nature, in addition to a number of interviews and book reviews. This essay appeared in Fish's column, called "Western Wanderings," in 1998.

1   I went to South Pass, Wyoming, to mark my son's 4-month birthday and my 43rd. People might think the middle of Wyoming a strange place to commemorate passing time, but I had my reasons. At 43, you look forward and backward, like a driver shifting his gaze from windshield to rearview mirror. At 4 months, you look straight ahead. From both my son's vantage point and mine, I thought South Pass would be enlightening.

2   We followed the Oregon Trail in from the east, past Independence Rock, where the wagon trains stopped to let emigrants carve their names in splintered granite. We crossed and recrossed the Sweetwater River. We rose with Wyoming toward the sky. At the end of a dirt road was a stone slab inscribed "Old Oregon Trail 1843–57." This was South Pass. Six generations ago my son's ancestors came here on their way to new lives in the West.

3   "South Pass is almost a religious experience," Terry Del Bene had told me a few days earlier. Before I dragged my wife and son into the sagebrush, I wanted to know where I was going. So I tagged along with Del Bene. He is an archaeologist for the Bureau of Land Management, the agency that manages South Pass National Historic Landmark, and he knows the place cold.

4   If South Pass did not exist, the history of the United States would be so different as to be unimaginable. The pass rests at 7,400 feet elevation and forms a broad gap in the otherwise unbroken mountain ranges we label the Rockies. It straddles the Continental Divide—"Splash your canteen and half the water would go to the Atlantic and half to the Pacific," says Del Bene—but does so gently enough to allow wagon travel. Without South Pass, there would have been no Oregon or Mormon or California Trail. The first emigrant wagon train came through in 1843. By the time the last recorded wagons rolled west (amazingly late, in 1912), 400,000 settlers had crossed South Pass.

5   Del Bene told me all this while steering his government truck down State Highway 28. He was dressed as a 19th-century sharpie in wool pants and a vest that resembled mattress ticking. Del Bene is not above spiking his history with theater, and perhaps South Pass needs that—though a national historic landmark, it is noticeably lacking in the visitor centers, interpretive trails, and gift shops with which Americans embalm their history.

6   But when Del Bene announced we had arrived at South Pass, I thought he was joking. This is not an uncommon response. "It ill comports with the ideas we have formed of a pass through the Rocky Mountains," wrote emigrant Cecelia Adams in 1852, "being merely a vast, level and sandy plain sloping a little on each side of the summit."

7   Del Bene must have noticed my expression. Enthusiasm is one of his skills, and he went to work. "Look there," he said. "That's the trail. At the peak of the westward movement, wagons rolled through four or five abreast. The wagons tend to push dirt to the side, so you get those marks. The reason you still see them is that we have such a short growing season up here. We have the best wagon ruts in the country."

8   I squinted at where Del Bene was pointing, but, as usual when somebody tries to show me something important, I couldn't see what he was talking about. Still, South Pass began to make itself felt. The very absence of modern man's tampering helped. At South Pass it's just you and the weight of hopes so numerous they dent the earth a century and a half later.

9   For every traveler who disparaged South Pass, there was one who knew the most important landmarks are those you don't recognize at first, who understood that he or she had reached the point of no return in a great journey. Some travelers fired rifles in the air and shouted, "Huzzah!" Others turned introspective. "We have forever taken leave of the waters running toward the home of our childhood and youth," one woman recorded in her diary. Another wrote, "Now we are on the other side of the world."

10   We got back in Del Bene's truck so he could show me a sadder sight. When Charlotte Dansie traveled the trail in 1862, she was 32 and pregnant with her eighth child. She went into labor about a mile east of the pass. The child lived only long enough to be christened. Charlotte died minutes later. Wyoming was hard on the immigrants, Del Bene said. "One out of 10 died. On average there should be a grave every tenth of a mile, but most of them are unmarked. Charlotte's is marked."

11   We were looking at the gravestone when we heard the crunch of tires on gravel. Three people got out of the car: a man in his 20s, his mother, her mother. Descendants of Charlotte Dansie, they had driven up from Salt Lake City to put flowers on the grave. They knew her story, of course, but Del Bene told them things they hadn't heard. One account had her pleading with her husband: "She could stand her suffering no longer and asked him to pray to God that she might be released and return to her maker." The grandmother said it was merciful that Charlotte had died so quickly.

12   That night I went back to a motel in Rock Springs. I knew I had a long drive the next morning to pick up my wife and son, and I wanted to fall asleep. Instead I lay on the ugly brocade bedspread pondering why Charlotte Dansie's descendants had driven 300 miles to honor sorrow so old, and why I felt it imperative that my son see South Pass before, say, Toys "R" Us. Venturing into the past is never about the past but about the present—we look for the courage and purity of intent that we cannot locate in the modern world.

13   It is bright and windy when I drive back to South Pass with my wife and son. Busty cumulus clouds tumble across a blue sky, and their shadows roll across the plain. Joseph is a good traveler: cheerful, unflappable. He squirms while his mother tells him ancestral stories—her ancestors, not mine, as she takes pains to point out. They were from Illinois, advised to go west by a family friend named Abraham Lincoln. It is good story, and possibly true.

14   We follow the dirt road and stop at the pass. I unbuckle Joseph from his car seat and lift him into the windy day. The world smells of sage and clean baby. His arrival was its own continental divide, and all the rivers of my life now run in a new direction. If there was water here, I would baptize us both, sprinkling droplets from the Atlantic slope and then from the Pacific. But all we have are sky and ground. I watch him take those in. "This is South Pass," I tell him. I want him to remember this place. I want it to be something he can carry with him on the rest of his trail.

Arrival at Manzanar

Jeanne Wakatsuki Houston and James D. Houston

Born in California, Jeanne Wakatsuki Houston was seven years old when, during World War II, her family was moved to a Japanese-American internment camp, where they were held for four years. In collaboration with her husband, novelist James D. Houston, she recounts these experiences in *Farewell to Manzanar* (1973), from which this excerpt is taken. Individually and together, the couple has written a variety of books, films, and magazine articles. Wakatsuki Houston's most recent work is *Legends of Fire Horse Woman* (2004).

1   In December of 1941 Papa's disappearance didn't bother me nearly so much as the world I soon found myself in.

2   He had been a jack-of-all-trades. When I was born he was farming near Ingelwood. Later, when he started fishing, we moved to Ocean Park, near Santa Monica, and until they [the FBI] picked him up, that's where we lived, in a big frame house with a brick fireplace, a block back from the beach. We were the only Japanese family in the neighborhood. Papa liked it that way. He didn't want to be labeled or grouped by anyone. But with him gone and no way of knowing what to expect, my mother moved all of us down to Terminal Island. Woody* already lived there, and one of my older sisters had married a Terminal Island boy. Mama's first concern now was to keep the family together; and once the war began, she felt safer there than isolated racially in Ocean Park. But for me, at age seven, the island was a country as foreign as India or Arabia would have been. It was the first time I had lived among other Japanese, or gone to school with them, and I was terrified all the time. . . .

3   At the time it seemed we had been living under this reign of fear for years. In fact, we lived there about two months. Late in February the navy decided to clear Terminal Island completely. Even though most of us were American-born, it was dangerous having that many Orientals so close to the Long Beach Naval Station, on the opposite end of the island. We had known something like this was coming. But, like Papa's arrest, not much could be done ahead of time. There were four of us kids still young enough to be living with Mama, plus Granny, her mother, sixty-five then, speaking no English, and nearly blind. Mama didn't know where else she could get work, and we had nowhere else to move *to*. On February 25 the choice was made for us. We were given forty-eight hours to clear out.

4   The secondhand dealers had been prowling around for weeks, like wolves, offering humiliating prices for goods and furniture they knew many of us would have to sell sooner or later. Mama had left all but her most valuable possessions in Ocean Park, simply because she had nowhere to put them. She had brought along her pottery, her silver, heirlooms like the kimonos Granny had brought from Japan, tea sets, lacquered tables, and one fine old set of china, blue and white porcelain, almost translucent. On the day we were leaving, Woody's car was so crammed with boxes and luggage and kids we had just run out of room. Mama had to sell this china.

---

*An older brother

5   One of the dealers offered her fifteen dollars for it. She said it was a full setting for twelve and worth at least two hundred. He said fifteen was his top price. Mama started to quiver. Her eyes blazed up at him. She had been packing all night and trying to calm down Granny, who didn't understand why we were moving again and what all the rush was about. Mama's nerves were shot, and now Navy jeeps were patrolling the streets. She didn't say another word. She just glared at this man, all the rage and frustration channeled at him through her eyes.

6   He watched her for a moment and said he was sure he couldn't pay more than seventeen fifty for that china. She reached into the the red velvet case, took out a dinner plate and hurled it at the floor right in front of his feet.

7   The man leaped back shouting, "Hey! Hey, don't do that! Those are valuable dishes!"

8   Mama took out another dinner plate and hurled it at the floor; then another and another, never moving, never opening her mouth, just quivering and glaring at the retreating dealer, with tears streaming down her cheeks. He finally turned and scuttled out the door, heading for the next house. When he was gone she stood there smashing cups and bowls and platters until the whole set lay in scattered blue and white fragments across the wooden floor.

9   The American Friends Service helped us find a small house in Boyle Heights, another minority ghetto, in downtown Los Angeles, now inhabited briefly by a few hundred Terminal Island refugees. Executive Order 9066 had been signed by President Roosevelt, giving the War Department authority to define military areas in the western states and to exclude from them anyone who might threaten the war effort. There was a lot of talk about internment, or moving inland, or something like that in store for all Japanese Americans. I remember my brothers sitting around the table talking very intently about what we were going to do, how we would keep the family together. They had seen how quickly Papa was removed, and they knew now that he would not be back for quite a while. Just before leaving Terminal Island Mama had received her first letter, from Bismarck, North Dakota. He had been imprisoned at Fort Lincoln, in an all-male camp for enemy aliens.

10 Papa had been the patriarch. He had always decided everything in the family. With him gone, my brothers, like councilors in the absence of a chief, worried about what should be done. The ironic thing is, there wasn't much left to decide. These were mainly days of quiet, desperate waiting for what seemed at the time to be inevitable. There is a phrase the Japanese use in such situations, when something difficult must be endured. You would hear the older heads, the Issei, telling others very quietly, "*Shikato ga nai*" (It cannot be helped). "*Shikata ga nai*" (It must be done).

11 Mama and Woody went to work packing celery for a Japanese produce dealer. Kiyo and my sister May and I enrolled in the local school, and what sticks in my memory from those few weeks is the teacher—not her looks, her remoteness. In Ocean Park my teacher had been a kind, grandmotherly woman who used to sail with us in Papa's boat from time to time and who wept the day we had to leave. In Boyle Heights the teacher felt cold and distant. I was confused by all the moving and was having trouble with the classwork, but she would never help me out. She would have nothing to do with me.

12   This was the first time I had felt outright hostility from a Caucasian. Looking back, it is easy enough to explain. Public attitudes toward the Japanese in California were shifting rapidly. In the first few months of the Pacific war, America was on the run. Tolerance had turned to distrust and irrational fear. The hundred-year-old tradition of anti-Orientalism on the west coast soon resurfaced, more vicious than ever. Its result became clear about a month later, when we were told to make our third and final move.

13   The name Manzanar meant nothing to us when we left Boyle Heights. We didn't know where it was or what it was. We went because the government ordered us to. And, in the case of my older brothers and sisters, we went with a certain amount of relief. They had all heard stories of Japanese homes being attacked, of beatings in the streets of California towns. They were as frightened of the Caucasians as Caucasians were of us. Moving, under what appeared to be government protection, to an area less directly threatened by the war seemed not such a bad idea at all. For some it actually sounded like a fine adventure.

14   Our pickup point was a Buddhist church in Los Angeles. It was very early, and misty, when we got there with our luggage. Mama had bought heavy coats for all of us. She grew up in eastern Washington and knew that anywhere inland in early April would be cold. I was proud of my new coat, and I remember sitting on a duffel bag trying to be friendly with the Greyhound driver. I smiled at him. He didn't smile back. He was befriending no one. Someone tied a numbered tag to my collar and to the duffel bag (each family was given a number, and that became our official designation until the camps were closed), someone else passed out box lunches for the trip, and we climbed aboard.

15   I had never been outside Los Angeles County, never traveled more than ten miles from the coast, had never even ridden on a bus. I was full of excitement, the way any kid would be, and wanted to look out the window. But for the first few hours the shades were drawn. Around me other people played cards, read magazines, dozed, waiting. I settled back, waiting too, and finally fell asleep. The bus felt very secure to me. Almost half its passengers were immediate relatives. Mama and my older brothers had succeeded in keeping most of us together, on the same bus, headed for the same camp. I didn't realize until much later what a job that was. The strategy had been, first, to have everyone living in the same district when the evacuation began, and then to get all of us included under the same family number, even though names had been changed by marriage. Many families weren't as lucky as ours and suffered months of anguish while trying to arrange transfers from one camp to another.

16   We rode all day. By the time we reached our destination, the shades were up. It was late afternoon. The first thing I saw was a yellow swirl across a blurred, reddish setting sun. The bus was being pelted by what sounded like splattering rain. It wasn't rain. This was my first look at something I would soon know very well, a billowing flurry of dust and sand churned up by the wind through Owens Valley.

17   We drove past a barbed-wire fence, through a gate, and into an open space where trunks and sacks and packages had been dumped from the baggage trucks that drove out ahead of us. I could see a few tents set up, the first rows of black barracks, and beyond them, blurred by sand, rows of barracks that seemed to spread for miles across this plain. People were sitting on cartons or milling around,

with their backs to the wind waiting to see which friends or relatives might be on this bus. As we approached, they turned or stood up, and some moved toward us expectantly. But inside the bus no one stirred. No one waved or spoke. They just stared out the windows, ominously silent. I didn't understand this. Hadn't we finally arrived, our whole family intact? I opened a window, leaned out, and yelled happily. "Hey! This whole bus is full of Wakatsukis!"

18   Outside, the greeters smiled. Inside there was an explosion of laughter, hysterical, tension-breaking laughter that left my brothers choking and whacking each other across the shoulders.

19   We had pulled up just in time for dinner. The mess halls weren't completed yet. An outdoor chow line snaked around a half-finished building that broke a good part of the wind. They issued us army mess kits, the round metal kind that fold over, and plopped in scoops of canned Vienna sausage, canned string beans, steamed rice that had been cooked too long, and on top of the rice a serving of canned apricots. The Caucasian servers were thinking that the fruit poured over rice would make a good dessert. Among the Japanese, of course, rice is never eaten with sweet foods, only with salty or savory foods. Few of us could eat such a mixture. But at this point no one dared protest. It would have been impolite. I was horrified when I saw the apricot syrup seeping through my little mound of rice. I opened my mouth to complain. My mother jabbed me in the back to keep quiet. We moved on through the line and joined the others squatting in the lee of half-raised walls, dabbing courteously at what was, for almost everyone there, an inedible concoction.

20   After dinner we were taken to Block 16, a cluster of fifteen barracks that had just been finished a day or so earlier—although finished was hardly the word for it. The shacks were built of one thickness of pine planking covered with tarpaper. They sat on concrete footings, with about two feet of open space between the floorboards and the ground. Gaps showed between the planks, and as the weeks passed and the green wood dried out, the gaps widened. Knotholes gaped in the uncovered floor.

21   Each barracks was divided into six units, sixteen by twenty feet, about the size of a living room, with one bare bulb hanging from the ceiling and an oil stove for heat. We were assigned two of these for the twelve people in our family group; and our official family "number" was enlarged by three digits—6 plus the number of this barracks. We were issued steel army cots, two brown army blankets each, and some mattress covers, which my brothers stuffed with straw.

22   The first task was to divide up what space we had for sleeping. Bill and Woody contributed a blanket each and partitioned off the first room: one side for Bill and Tomi, one side for Woody and Chizu and their baby girl. Woody also got the stove, for heating formulas.

23   The people who had it hardest during the first few months were young couples like these, many of whom had married just before the evacuation began, in order not to be separated and sent to different camps. Our two rooms were crowded, but at least it was all in the family. My oldest sister and her husband were shoved into one of those sixteen-by-twenty-foot compartments with six people they had never seen before—two other couples, one recently married like themselves, the other with two teenage boys. Partitioning off a room like that wasn't easy. It was

bitter cold when we arrived, and the wind did not abate. All they had to use for room dividers were those army blankets, two of which were barely enough to keep one person warm. They argued over whose blanket should be sacrificed and later argued about noise at night—the parents wanted their boys asleep by 9:00 P.M.— and they continued arguing over matters like that for six months, until my sister and her husband left to harvest sugar beets in Idaho. It was grueling work up there, and wages were pitiful, but when the call came through camp for workers to alleviate the wartime labor shortage, it sounded better than their life at Manzanar. They knew they'd have, if nothing else, a room, perhaps a cabin of their own.

24   That first night in Block 16, the rest of us squeezed into the second room— Granny, Lillian, age fourteen, Ray, thirteen, May, eleven, Kiyo, ten, Mama, and me. I didn't mind this at all at the time. Being youngest meant I got to sleep with Mama. And before we went to bed I had a great time jumping up and down on the mattress. The boys had stuffed so much straw into hers, we had to flatten it some so we wouldn't slide off. I slept with her every night after that until Papa came back.

CHAPTER 32

Essays for Further Analysis: Multiple Strategies and Styles

I Have a Dream

Martin Luther King, Jr.

The Rev. Martin Luther King, Jr., president of the Southern Christian Leadership Conference, was the best-known leader of the civil rights movement of the 1960s and the recipient of the 1964 Nobel Peace Prize. He was assassinated in 1968. King delivered this speech in 1963 at a celebration of the Emancipation Proclamation, before a crowd of 250,000 who had marched to the Lincoln Memorial in Washington, D.C.

1   Five score years ago, a great American, in whose symbolic shadow we stand, signed the Emancipation Proclamation. This momentous decree came as a great beacon light of hope to millions of Negro slaves who had been seared in the flames of withering injustice. It came as a joyous daybreak to end the long night of captivity.

2   But one hundred years later, we must face the tragic fact that the Negro is still not free. One hundred years later, the life of the Negro is still sadly crippled by the manacles of segregation and the chains of discrimination. One hundred years later, the Negro lives on a lonely island of poverty in the midst of a vast ocean of material prosperity. One hundred years later, the Negro is still languishing in the corners of American society and finds himself an exile in his own land. So we have come here today to dramatize an appalling condition.

3   In a sense we have come to our nation's capital to cash a check. When the architects of our republic wrote the magnificent words of the Constitution and the Declaration of Independence, they were signing a promissory note to which every American was to fall heir. This note was a promise that all men would be guaranteed the unalienable rights of life, liberty, and the pursuit of happiness.

4   It is obvious today that America has defaulted on this promissory note insofar as her citizens of color are concerned. Instead of honoring this sacred obligation, America has given the Negro people a bad check; a check which has come back marked "insufficient funds." But we refuse to believe that the bank of justice is bankrupt. We refuse to believe that there are insufficient funds in the great vaults of opportunity of this nation. So we have come to cash this check—a check that will give us upon demand the riches of freedom and the security of justice. We have also come to this hallowed spot to remind America of the fierce urgency of *now*. This is no time to engage in the luxury of cooling off or to take the tranquilizing drugs of gradualism. *Now* is the time to make real the promises of Democracy. *Now* is the time to rise from the dark and desolate valley of segregation to the sunlit path of racial justice. *Now* is the time to open the doors of opportunity to all of God's children. *Now* is the time to lift our nation from the quicksands of racial injustice to the solid rock of brotherhood.

5   It would be fatal for the nation to overlook the urgency of the moment and to underestimate the determination of the Negro. This sweltering summer of the Negro's legitimate discontent will not pass until there is an invigorating autumn of freedom and equality. Nineteen sixty-three is not an end, but a beginning. Those who hope that the Negro needed to blow off steam and will now be content will have a rude awakening if the nation returns to business as usual. There will be neither rest nor tranquillity in America until the Negro is granted his citizenship rights. The whirl-winds of revolt will continue to shake the foundations of our nation until the bright day of justice emerges.

6   But there is something that I must say to my people who stand on the warm threshold which leads into the palace of justice. In the process of gaining our rightful place we must not be guilty of wrongful deeds. Let us not seek to satisfy our thirst for freedom by drinking from the cup of bitterness and hatred. We must forever conduct our struggle on the high plane of dignity and discipline. We must not allow our creative protest to degenerate into physical violence. Again and again we must rise to the majestic heights of meeting physical force with soul force. The marvelous new militancy which has engulfed the Negro community must not lead us to distrust of all white people, for many of our white brothers, as evidenced by their presence here today, have come to realize that their destiny is tied up with our destiny and their freedom is inextricably bound to our freedom. We cannot walk alone.

7   And as we walk, we must make the pledge that we shall march ahead. We cannot turn back. There are those who are asking the devotees of civil rights, "When will you be satisfied?" We can never be satisfied as long as the Negro is the victim of the unspeakable horrors of police brutality. We can never be satisfied as long as our bodies, heavy with the fatigue of travel, cannot gain lodging in the motels of the highways and the hotels of the cities. We cannot be satisfied as long as the Negro's basic mobility is from a smaller ghetto to a larger one. We can never be satisfied as

long as a Negro in Mississippi cannot vote and a Negro in New York believes he has nothing for which to vote. No, no, we are not satisfied, and we will not be satisfied until justice rolls down like waters and righteousness like a mighty stream.

8   I am not unmindful that some of you have come here out of great trials and tribulations. Some of you have come fresh from narrow jail cells. Some of you have come from areas where your quest for freedom left you battered by the storms of persecution and staggered by the winds of police brutality. You have been the veterans of creative suffering. Continue to work with the faith that unearned suffering is redemptive.

9   Go back to Mississippi, go back to Alabama, go back to South Carolina, go back to Georgia, go back to Louisiana, go back to the slums and ghettos of our northern cities, knowing that somehow this situation can and will be changed. Let us not wallow in the valley of despair.

10   I say to you today, my friends, that in spite of the difficulties and frustrations of the moment I still have a dream. It is a dream deeply rooted in the American dream.

11   I have a dream that one day this nation will rise up and live out the true meaning of its creed: "We hold these truths to be self-evident, that all men are created equal."

12   I have a dream that one day on the red hills of Georgia the sons of former slaves and the sons of former slaveowners will be able to sit down together at the table of brotherhood.

13   I have a dream that one day even the state of Mississippi, a desert state sweltering with the heat of injustice and oppression, will be transformed into an oasis of freedom and justice.

14   I have a dream that my four little children will one day live in a nation where they will not be judged by the color of their skin but by the content of their character.

15   I have a dream today.

16   I have a dream that one day the state of Alabama, whose governor's lips are presently dripping with the words of interposition and nullification, will be transformed into a situation where little black boys and black girls will be able to join hands with little white boys and white girls and walk together as sisters and brothers.

17   I have a dream today.

18   I have a dream that one day every valley shall be exalted, every hill and mountain shall be made low, the rough places will be made plain, and the crooked places will be made straight, and the glory of the Lord shall be revealed, and all flesh shall see it together.

19   This is our hope. This is the faith with which I return to the South. With this faith we will be able to hew out of the mountain of despair a stone of hope. With this faith we will be able to transform the jangling discords of our nation into a beautiful symphony of brotherhood. With this faith we will be able to work together, to pray together, to struggle together, to go to jail together, to stand up for freedom together, knowing that we will be free one day.

20   This will be the day when all of God's children will be able to sing with new meaning

> My country, 'tis of thee,
> Sweet land of liberty,
>   Of thee I sing:
> Land where my fathers died,
> Land of the pilgrims' pride,
> From every mountain-side
>   Let freedom ring.

21   And if America is to be a great nation this must become true. So let freedom ring from the prodigious hilltops of New Hampshire. Let freedom ring from the mighty mountains of New York. Let freedom ring from the heightening Alleghenies of Pennsylvania!

22   Let freedom ring from the snowcapped Rockies of Colorado!

23   Let freedom ring from the curvaceous peaks of California!

24   But not only that; let freedom ring from Stone Mountain of Georgia!

25   Let freedom ring from Lookout Mountain of Tennessee!

26   Let freedom ring from every hill and molehill of Mississippi. From every mountainside, let freedom ring.

27   When we let freedom ring, when we let it ring from every village and every hamlet, from every state and every city, we will be able to speed up that day when all of God's children, black men and white men, Jews and Gentiles, Protestants and Catholics, will be able to join hands and sing in the words of the old Negro spiritual, "Free at last! Free at last! thank God almighty, we are free at last!"

Beauty: When the Other Dancer Is the Self

Alice Walker

A poet, essayist, novelist, and teacher, Alice Walker is best known for her novel *The Color Purple*, which won both the Pulitzer Prize and the American Book Award in 1982. Some of her other works include *Possessing the Secret of Joy* (1992), *Anything We Love Can Be Saved* (1997), *Absolute Trust in the Goodness of the Earth: New Poems* (2003), *Now Is the Time to Open Your Heart* (2004), and *We Are the Ones We Have Been Waiting For* (2006). The following selection comes from her 1983 collection of essays, *In Search of Our Mothers' Gardens*.

1   It is a bright summer day in 1947. My father, a fat, funny man with beautiful eyes and a subversive wit, is trying to decide which of his eight children he will take with him to the county fair. My mother, of course, will not go. She is knocked out from getting most of us ready: I hold my neck stiff against the pressure of her knuckles as she hastily completes the braiding and then beribboning of my hair.

2   My father is the driver for the rich old white lady up the road. Her name is Miss Mey. She owns all the land for miles around, as well as the house in which we live. All I remember about her is that she once offered to pay my mother thirty-five cents for cleaning her house, raking up piles of her magnolia leaves, and washing her family's clothes, and that my mother—she of no money, eight children, and a chronic earache—refused it. But I do not think of this in 1947. I am two and a half

years old. I want to go everywhere my daddy goes. I am excited at the prospect of riding in a car. Someone has told me fairs are fun. That there is room in the car for only three of us doesn't faze me at all. Whirling happily in my starchy frock, showing off my biscuit-polished patent-leather shoes and lavender socks, tossing my head in a way that makes my ribbons bounce, I stand, hands on hips, before my father. "Take me, Daddy," I say with assurance: "I'm the prettiest!"

3   Later, it does not surprise me to find myself in Miss Mey's shiny black car, sharing the back seat with the other lucky ones. Does not surprise me that I thoroughly enjoy the fair. At home that night I tell the unlucky ones all I can remember about the merry-go-round, the man who eats live chickens, and the teddy bears, until they say: that's enough, baby Alice. Shut up now, and go to sleep.

4   It is Easter Sunday, 1950. I am dressed in a green, flocked, scalloped-hem dress (handmade by my adoring sister, Ruth) that has its own smooth satin petticoat and tiny hot-pink roses tucked into each scallop. My shoes, new T-strap patent leather, again highly biscuit-polished. I am six years old and have learned one of the longest Easter speeches to be heard that day, totally unlike the speech I said when I was two: "Easter lilies / pure and white / blossom in / the morning light." When I rise to give my speech I do so on a great wave of love and pride and expectation. People in the church stop rustling their new crinolines. They seem to hold their breath. I can tell they admire my dress, but it is my spirit, bordering on sassiness (womanishness), they secretly applaud.

5   "That girl's a little _mess_," they whisper to each other, pleased.

6   Naturally I say my speech without stammer or pause, unlike those who stutter, stammer, or, worst of all, forget. This is before the word "beautiful" exists in people's vocabulary, but "Oh, isn't she the _cutest_ thing!" frequently floats my way. "And got so much sense!" they gratefully add . . . for which thoughtful addition I thank them to this day.

7   _It was great fun being cute. But then, one day, it ended._

8   I am eight years old and a tomboy. I have a cowboy hat, cowboy boots, checkered shirt and pants, all red. My playmates are my brothers, two and four years older than I. Their colors are black and green, the only difference in the way we are dressed. On Saturday nights we all go to the picture show, even my mother; Westerns are her favorite kind of movie. Back home, "on the ranch," we pretend we are Tom Mix, Hopalong Cassidy, Lash LaRue (we've even named one of our dogs Lash LaRue); we chase each other for hours rustling cattle, being outlaws, delivering damsels from distress. Then my parents decide to buy my brothers guns. These are not "real" guns. They shoot "BBs," copper pellets my brothers say will kill birds. Because I am a girl, I do not get a gun. Instantly I am relegated to the position of Indian. Now there appears a great distance between us. They shoot and shoot at everything with their new guns. I try to keep up with my bow and arrows.

9   One day while I am standing on top of our makeshift "garage"—pieces of tin nailed across some poles—holding my bow and arrow and looking out toward the fields, I feel an incredible blow in my right eye. I look down just in time to see my brother lower his gun.

10   Both brothers rush to my side. My eye stings, and I cover it with my hand. "If you tell," they say, "we will get a whipping. You don't want that to happen, do you?" I do not. "Here's a piece of wire," says the older brother, picking it up from the roof;

"say you stepped on one end of it and the other flew up and hit you." The pain is beginning to start. "Yes," I say. "Yes, I will say that is what happened." If I do not say this is what happened, I know my brothers will find ways to make me wish I had. But now I will say anything that gets me to my mother.

11   Confronted by our parents we stick to the lie agreed upon. They place me on a bench on the porch and I close my left eye while they examine the right. There is a tree growing from underneath the porch that climbs past the railing to the roof. It is the last thing my right eye sees. I watch as its trunk, its branches, and then its leaves are blotted out by the rising blood.

12   I am in shock. First there is intense fever, which my father tries to break using lily leaves bound around my head. Then there are chills: my mother tries to get me to eat soup. Eventually, I do not know how, my parents learn what has happened. A week after the "accident" they take me to see a doctor. "Why did you wait so long to come?" he asks, looking into my eye and shaking his head. "Eyes are sympathetic," he says. "If one is blind, the other will likely become blind too."

13   This comment of the doctor's terrifies me. But it is really how I look that bothers me most. Where the BB pellet struck there is a glob of whitish scar tissue, a hideous cataract, on my eye. Now when I stare at people—a favorite pastime, up to now—they will stare back. Not at the "cute" little girl, but at her scar. For six years I do not stare at anyone, because I do not raise my head.

14   Years later, in the throes of a mid-life crisis, I ask my mother and sister whether I changed after the "accident." "No," they say, puzzled. "What do you mean?"

15   *What do I mean?*

16   I am eight, and, for the first time, doing poorly in school, where I have been something of a whiz since I was four. We have just moved to the place where the "accident" occurred. We do not know any of the people around us because this is a different county. The only time I see the friends I knew is when we go back to our old church. The new school is the former state penitentiary. It is a large stone building, cold and drafty, crammed to overflowing with boisterous, ill-disciplined children. On the third floor there is a huge circular imprint of some partition that has been torn out.

17   "What used to be here?" I ask a sullen girl next to me on our way past it to lunch.

18   "The electric chair," says she.

19   At night I have nightmares about the electric chair, and about all the people reputedly "fried" in it. I am afraid of the school, where all the students seem to be budding criminals.

20   "What's the matter with your eye?" they ask, critically.

21   When I don't answer (I cannot decide whether it was an "accident" or not), they shove me, insist on a fight.

22   My brother, the one who created the story about the wire, comes to my rescue. But then brags so much about "protecting" me, I become sick.

23   After months of torture at the school, my parents decide to send me back to our old community, to my old school. I live with my grandparents and the teacher they board. But there is no room for Phoebe, my cat. By the time my grandparents decide there *is* room, and I ask for my cat, she cannot be found. Miss Yarborough,

the boarding teacher, takes me under her wing, and begins to teach me to play the piano. But soon she marries an African—a "prince," she says—and is whisked away to his continent.

24   At my old school there is at least one teacher who loves me. She is the teacher who "knew me before I was born" and bought my first baby clothes. It is she who makes life bearable. It is her presence that finally helps me turn on the one child at the school who continually calls me "one-eyed bitch." One day I simply grab him by his coat and beat him until I am satisfied. It is my teacher who tells me my mother is ill.

25   My mother is lying in bed in the middle of the day, something I have never seen. She is in too much pain to speak. She has an abscess in her ear. I stand looking down on her, knowing that if she dies, I cannot live. She is being treated with warm oils and hot bricks held against her cheek. Finally a doctor comes. But I must go back to my grandparents' house. The weeks pass but I am hardly aware of it. All I know is that my mother might die, my father is not so jolly, my brothers still have their guns, and I am the one sent away from home.

26   "You did not change," they say.

27   *Did I imagine the anguish of never looking up?*

28   I am twelve. When relatives come to visit I hide in my room. My cousin Brenda, just my age, whose father works in the post office and whose mother is a nurse, comes to find me. "Hello," she says. And then she asks, looking at my recent school picture, which I did not want taken, and on which the "glob," as I think of it, is clearly visible. "You still can't see out of that eye?"

29   "No," I say, and flop back on the bed over my book.

30   That night, as I do almost every night, I abuse my eye. I rant and rave at it, in front of the mirror. I plead with it to clear up before morning. I tell it I hate and despise it. I do not pray for sight. I pray for beauty.

31   "You did not change," they say.

32   I am fourteen and baby-sitting for my brother Bill, who lives in Boston. He is my favorite brother and there is a strong bond between us. Understanding my feelings of shame and ugliness he and his wife take me to a local hospital, where the "glob" is removed by a doctor named O. Henry. There is still a small bluish crater where the scar tissue was, but the ugly white stuff is gone. Almost immediately I become a different person from the girl who does not raise her head. Or so I think. Now that I've raised my head I win the boyfriend of my dreams. Now that I've raised my head I have plenty of friends. Now that I've raised my head classwork comes from my lips as faultlessly as Easter speeches did, and I leave high school as valedictorian, most popular student, and *queen*, hardly believing my luck. Ironically, the girl who was voted most beautiful in our class (and was) was later shot twice through the chest by a male companion, using a "real" gun, while she was pregnant. But that's another story in itself. Or is it?

33   "You did not change," they say.

34   It is now thirty years since the "accident." A beautiful journalist comes to visit and to interview me. She is going to write a cover story for her magazine that focuses on my latest book. "Decide how you want to look on the cover," she says. "Glamorous, or whatever."

35   Never mind "glamorous," it is the "whatever" that I hear. Suddenly all I can think of is whether I will get enough sleep the night before the photography session: if I don't, my eye will be tired and wander, as blind eyes will.

36   At night in bed with my lover I think up reasons why I should not appear on the cover of a magazine. "My meanest critics will say I've sold out," I say. "My family will now realize I write scandalous books."

37   "But what's the real reason you don't want to do this?" he asks.

38   "Because in all probability," I say in a rush, "my eye won't be straight."

39   "It will be straight enough," he says. Then, "Besides, I thought you'd made your peace with that."

40   And I suddenly remember that I have.

41   *I remember:*

42   I am talking to my brother Jimmy, asking if he remembers anything unusual about the day I was shot. He does not know I consider that day the last time my father, with his sweet home remedy of cool lily leaves, chose me, and that I suffered and raged inside because of this. "Well," he says, "all I remember is standing by the side of the highway with Daddy, trying to flag down a car. A white man stopped, but when Daddy said he needed somebody to take his little girl to the doctor, he drove off."

43   *I remember:*

44   I am in the desert for the first time. I fall totally in love with it. I am so over-whelmed by its beauty, I confront for the first time, consciously, the meaning of the doctor's words years ago: "Eyes are sympathetic. If one is blind, the other will likely become blind too." I realize I have dashed about the world madly, looking at that, storing up images against the fading of the light. *But I might have missed seeing the desert!* The shock of that possibility—and gratitude for over twenty-five years of sight—sends me literally to my knees. Poem after poem comes—which is perhaps how poets pray.

On Sight

I am so thankful I have seen
The Desert
And the creatures in the desert
And the desert itself.

The desert has its own moon
Which I have seen
With my own eye.

There is no flag on it.

Trees of the desert have arms
All of which are always up
That is because the moon is up
The sun is up
Also the sky
The stars
Clouds
None with flags.

> If there *were* flags, I doubt
> the trees would point.
> Would you?

45 *But mostly, I remember this:*

46 I am twenty-seven, and my baby daughter is almost three. Since her birth, I have worried about her discovery that her mother's eyes are different from other people's. Will she be embarrassed? I think. What will she say? Every day she watches a television program called "Big Blue Marble." It begins with a picture of the earth as it appears from the moon. It is bluish, a little battered-looking, but full of light, with whitish clouds swirling around it. Every time I see it I weep with love, as if it is a picture of Grandma's house. One day when I am putting Rebecca down for her nap, she suddenly focuses on my eye. Something inside me cringes, gets ready to protect myself. All children are cruel about physical differences, I know from experience, and that they don't always mean to be is another matter. I assume Rebecca will be the same.

47 But no-o-o-o. She studies my face intently as we stand, her inside and me outside her crib. She even holds my face maternally between her dimpled little hands. Then, looking every bit as serious and lawyerlike as her father, she says, as if it may just possibly have slipped my attention: "Mommy, there's a *world* in your eye." (As in, "Don't be alarmed, or do anything crazy.") And then, gently, but with great interest: "Mommy, where did you *get* that world in your eye?"

48 For the most part, the pain left then. (So what, if my brothers grew up to buy even more powerful pellet guns for their sons and to carry real guns themselves. So what, if a young "Morehouse man" once nearly fell off the steps of Trevor Arnett Library because he thought my eyes were blue.) Crying and laughing I ran to the bathroom, while Rebecca mumbled and sang herself off to sleep. Yes indeed, I realized, looking into the mirror. There *was* a world in my eye. And I saw that it was possible to love it: that in fact, for all it had taught me of shame and anger and inner vision, I *did* love it. Even to see it drifting out of orbit in boredom, or rolling up out of fatigue, not to mention floating back at attention in excitement (bearing witness, a friend has called it), deeply suitable to my personality, and even characteristic of me.

49 That night I dream I am dancing to Stevie Wonder's song "Always" (the name of the song is really "As," but I hear it as "Always"). As I dance, whirling and joyous, happier than I've ever been in my life, another bright-faced dancer joins me. We dance and kiss each other and hold each other through the night. The other dancer has obviously come through all right, as I have done. She is beautiful, whole and free. And she is also me.

A Modest Proposal

Jonathan Swift

Born in 1667 in Ireland, Jonathan Swift was an Anglican priest who eventually became dean of St. Patrick's Cathedral in Dublin. He is best known for his satires, often addressing the English exploitation of the Irish, including his masterpiece *Gulliver's Travels*

(1726). This essay, originally a pamphlet written in 1729 during a terrible famine and at a time when the English were proposing a severe tax on the Irish, uses irony and satiric exaggeration to emphasize Ireland's desperation and England's greed.

For Preventing the Children of
Poor People in Ireland
from Being a Burden to Their Parents
or Country,
and for Making Them Beneficial to the Public

1   It is a melancholy object to those who walk through this great town or travel in the country, when they see the streets, the roads, and cabin doors, crowded with beggars of the female sex, followed by three, four, or six children, all in rags and importuning every passenger for an alms. These mothers, instead of being able to work for their honest livelihood, are forced to employ all their time in strolling to beg sustenance for their helpless infants, who, as they grow up, either turn thieves for want of work, or leave their dear native country to fight for the Pretender in Spain, or sell themselves to the Barbadoes.

2   I think it is agreed by all parties that this prodigious number of children in the arms, or on the backs, or at the heels of their mothers, and frequently of their fathers, is in the present deplorable state of the kingdom a very great additional grievance; and therefore whoever could find out a fair, cheap, and easy method of making these children sound, useful members of the commonwealth would deserve so well of the public as to have his statue set up for a preserver of the nation.

3   But my intention is very far from being confined to provide only for the children of professed beggars; it is of a much greater extent, and shall take in the whole number of infants at a certain age who are born of parents in effect as little able to support them as those who demand our charity in the streets.

4   As to my own part, having turned my thoughts for many years upon this important subject, and maturely weighed the several schemes of other projectors, I have always found them grossly mistaken in the computation. It is true, a child just dropped from its dam may be supported by her milk for a solar year, with little other nourishment; at most not above the value of two shillings, which the mother may certainly get, or the value in scraps, by her lawful occupation of begging; and it is exactly at one year old that I propose to provide for them in such a manner as instead of being a charge upon their parents or the parish, or wanting food and raiment for the rest of their lives, they shall on the contrary contribute to the feeding, and partly to the clothing, of many thousands.

5   There is likewise another great advantage in my scheme, that it will prevent those voluntary abortions, and that horrid practice of women murdering their bastard children, alas, too frequent among us, sacrificing the poor innocent babes I doubt, more to avoid the expense than the shame, which would move tears and pity in the most savage and inhuman breast.

6   The number of souls in this kingdom being usually reckoned one million and a half, of these I calculate there may be about two hundred thousand couples whose wives are breeders; from which number I subtract thirty thousand couples who are able to maintain their own children, although I apprehend there cannot be

so many under the present distress of the kingdom; but this being granted, there will remain an hundred and seventy thousand breeders. I again subtract fifty thousand for those women who miscarry, or whose children die by accident or disease within the year. There only remain an hundred and twenty thousand children of poor parents annually born. The question therefore is, how this number shall be reared and provided for, which, as I have already said, under the present situation of affairs, is utterly impossible by all the methods hitherto proposed. For we can neither employ them in handicraft nor agriculture; we neither build houses (I mean in the country) nor cultivate land. They can very seldom pick up a livelihood by stealing till they arrive at six years old, except where they are of towardly parts; although I confess they learn the rudiments much earlier, during which time they can however be looked upon only as probationers, as I have been informed by a principal gentleman in the county of Cavan, who protested to me that he never knew above one or two instances under the age of six, even in a part of the kingdom so renowned for the quickest proficiency in that art.

7   I am assured by our merchants that a boy or a girl before twelve years old is no salable commodity; and even when they come to this age, they will not yield above three pounds, or three pounds and half a crown at most on the Exchange; which cannot turn to account either to the parents or kingdom, the charge of nutriment and rags having been at least four times that value.

8   I shall now therefore humbly propose my own thoughts, which I hope will not be liable to the least objection.

9   I have been assured by a very knowing American of my acquaintance in London, that a young healthy child well nursed is at a year old a most delicious, nourishing, and wholesome food, whether stewed, roasted, baked, or boiled; and I make no doubt that it will equally serve in a fricassee or a ragout.

10   I do therefore humbly offer it to public consideration that of the hundred and twenty thousand children, already computed, twenty thousand may be reserved for breed, whereof only one fourth part to be males, which is more than we allow to sheep, black cattle, or swine; and my reason is that these children are seldom the fruits of marriage, a circumstance not much regarded by our savages, therefore one male will be sufficient to serve four females. That the remaining hundred thousand may at a year old be offered in sale to the persons of quality and fortune through the kingdom, always advising the mother to let them suck plentifully in the last month, so as to render them plump and fat for a good table. A child will make two dishes at an entertainment for friends; and when the family dines alone, the fore or hind quarter will make a reasonable dish, and seasoned with a little pepper or salt will be very good boiled on the fourth day, especially in winter.

11   I have reckoned upon a medium that a child just born will weigh twelve pounds, and in a solar year if tolerably nursed increaseth to twenty-eight pounds.

12   I grant this food will be somewhat dear, and therefore very proper for landlords, who, as they have already devoured most of the parents, seem to have the best title to the children.

13   Infant's flesh will be in season throughout the year, but more plentiful in March, and a little before and after. For we are told by a grave author, an eminent French physician, that fish being a prolific diet, there are more children born in Roman Catholic countries about nine months after Lent, than at any other season;

therefore, reckoning a year after Lent, the markets will be more glutted than usual, because the number of popish infants is at least three to one in this kingdom; and therefore it will have one other collateral advantage, by lessening the number of Papists among us.

14   I have already computed the charge of nursing a beggar's child (in which list I reckon all cottagers, laborers, and four-fifths of the farmers) to be about two shillings per annum, rags included; and I believe no gentleman would repine to give ten shillings for the carcass of a good fat child, which, as I have said, will make four dishes of excellent nutritive meat, when he hath only some particular friend or his own family to dine with him. Thus the squire will learn to be a good landlord, and grow popular among his tenants; the mother will have eight shillings net profit, and be fit for work till she produces another child.

15   Those who are more thrifty (as I must confess the times require) may flay the carcass; the skin of which artificially dressed will make admirable gloves for ladies, and summer boots for fine gentlemen.

16   As to our city of Dublin, shambles may be appointed for this purpose in the most convenient parts of it, and butchers we may be assured will not be wanting; although I rather recommend buying the children alive, and dressing them hot from the knife as we do roasting pigs.

17   A very worthy person, a true lover of his country, and whose virtues I highly esteem, was lately pleased in discoursing on this matter to offer a refinement upon my scheme. He said that many gentlemen of this kingdom, having of late destroyed their deer, he conceived that the want of venison might be well supplied by the bodies of young lads and maidens, not exceeding fourteen years of age nor under twelve, so great a number of both sexes in every country being now ready to starve for want of work and service; and these to be disposed of by their parents, if alive, or otherwise by their nearest relations. But with due deference to so excellent a friend and so deserving a patriot, I cannot be altogether in his sentiments; for as to the males, my American acquaintance assured me from frequent experience that their flesh was generally tough and lean, like that of our schoolboys, by continual exercise, and their taste disagreeable; and to fatten them would not answer the charge. Then as to the females, it would, I think with humble submission, be a loss to the public, because they soon would become breeders themselves; and besides, it is not improbable that some scrupulous people might be apt to censure such a practice (although indeed very unjustly) as a little bordering upon cruelty; which, I confess, hath always been with me the strongest objection against any project, how well soever intended.

18   But in order to justify my friend, he confessed that this expedient was put into his head by the famous Psalmanazar, a native of the island Formosa, who came from thence to London above twenty years ago, and in conversation told my friend that in his country when any young person happened to be put to death, the executioner sold the carcass to persons of quality as a prime dainty; and that in his time the body of a plump girl of fifteen, who was crucified for an attempt to poison the emperor, was sold to his Imperial Majesty's prime minister of state, and other great mandarins of the court, in joints from the gibbet, at four hundred crowns. Neither indeed can I deny that if the same use were made of several plump young girls in this town, who without one single groat to their fortunes cannot stir abroad

without a chair, and appear at the playhouse and assemblies in foreign fineries which they never will pay for, the kingdom would not be the worse.

19   Some persons of a desponding spirit are in great concern about that vast number of poor people who are aged, diseased, or maimed, and I have been desired to employ my thoughts what course may be taken to ease the nation of so grievous an encumbrance. But I am not in the least pain upon that matter, because it is very well known that they are every day dying and rotting by cold and famine, and filth and vermin, as fast as can be reasonably expected. And as to the young laborers, they are now in almost as hopeful a condition. They cannot get work, and consequently pine away for want of nourishment to a degree that if at any time they are accidentally hired to common labor, they have not strength to perform it; and thus the country and themselves are happily delivered from the evils to come.

20   I have too long digressed, and therefore shall return to my subject. I think the advantages by the proposal which I have made are obvious and many, as well as of the highest importance.

21   For first, as I have already observed, it would greatly lessen the number of Papists, with whom we are yearly overrun, being the principal breeders of the nation as well as our most dangerous enemies; and who stay at home on purpose to deliver the kingdom to the Pretender, hoping to take their advantage by the absence of so many good Protestants, who have chosen rather to leave their country than to stay at home and pay tithes against their conscience to an Episcopal curate.

22   Secondly, the poorer tenants will have something valuable of their own, which by law may be made liable to distress, and help to pay their landlord's rent, their corn and cattle being already seized and money a thing unknown.

23   Thirdly, whereas the maintenance of an hundred thousand children, from two years old and upwards, cannot be computed at less than ten shillings a piece per annum, the nation's stock will be thereby increased fifty thousand pounds per annum, besides the profit of a new dish introduced to the tables of all gentlemen of fortune in the kingdom who have any refinement in taste. And the money will circulate among ourselves, the goods being entirely of our own growth and manufacture.

24   Fourthly, the constant breeders, besides the gain of eight shillings sterling per annum by the sale of their children, will be rid of the charge for maintaining them after the first year.

25   Fifthly, this food would likewise bring great custom to taverns; where the vintners will certainly be so prudent as to procure the best receipts for dressing it to perfection, and consequently have their houses frequented by all the fine gentlemen, who justly value themselves upon their knowledge in good eating; and a skillful cook, who understands how to oblige his guests, will contrive to make it as expensive as they please.

26   Sixthly, this would be a great inducement to marriage, which all wise nations have either encouraged by rewards or enforced by laws and penalties. It would increase the care and tenderness of mothers toward their children, when they were sure of a settlement for life to the poor babes, provided in some sort by the public, to their annual profit instead of expense. We should see an honest emulation among the married women, which of them could bring the fattest child to the market. Men would become as fond of their wives during the time of their

pregnancy as they are now of their mares in foal, their cows in calf, or sows when they are ready to farrow; nor offer to beat or kick them (as is too frequent a practice) for fear of a miscarriage.

27   Many other advantages might be enumerated. For instance, the addition of some thousand carcasses in our exportation of barreled beef, the propagation of swine's flesh, and improvements in the art of making good bacon, so much wanted among us by the great destruction of pigs, too frequent at our tables, which are no way comparable in taste or magnificence to a well-grown, fat, yearling child, which roasted whole will make a considerable figure at a lord mayor's feast or any other public entertainment. But this and many others I omit, being studious of brevity.

28   Supposing that one thousand families in this city would be constant customers for infants' flesh, besides others who might have it at merry meetings, particularly weddings and christenings, I compute that Dublin would take off annually about twenty thousand carcasses, and the rest of the kingdom (where probably they will be sold somewhat cheaper) the remaining eighty thousand.

29   I can think of no one objection that will possibly be raised against this proposal, unless it should be urged that the number of people will be thereby much lessened in the kingdom. This I freely own, and it was indeed one principal design in offering it to the world. I desire the reader will observe, that I calculate my remedy for this one individual kingdom of Ireland and for no other that ever was, is, or I think ever can be upon earth. Therefore, let no man talk to me of other expedients: of taxing our absentees at five shillings a pound: of using neither clothes nor household furniture except what is of our own growth and manufacture: of utterly rejecting the materials and instruments that promote foreign luxury: of curing the expensiveness of pride, vanity, idleness, and gaming in our women: of introducing a vein of parsimony, prudence, and temperance: of learning to love our country, in the want of which we differ even from Laplanders and the inhabitants of Topinamboo: of quitting our animosities and factions, nor acting any longer like the Jews, who were murdering one another at the very moment their city was taken: of being a little cautious not to sell our country and conscience for nothing: of teaching our landlords to have at least one degree of mercy towards their tenants: lastly, of putting a spirit of honesty, industry, and skill into our shopkeepers; who, if a resolution could now be taken to buy only our native goods, would immediately unite to cheat and exact upon us in the price, the measure, and the goodness, nor could ever yet be brought to make one fair proposal of just dealing, though often and earnestly invited to it.

30   Therefore, I repeat, let no man talk to me of these and the like expedients, till he hath at least some glimpse of hope that there will ever be some hearty and sincere attempt to put them into practice.

31   But as to myself, having been wearied out for many years with offering vain, idle, visionary thoughts, and at length utterly despairing of success, I fortunately fell upon this proposal, which, as it is wholly new, so it hath something solid and real, of no expense and little trouble, full in our own power, and whereby we can incur no danger in disobliging England. For this kind of commodity will not bear exportation, the flesh being of too tender a consistence to admit a long continuance in salt, although perhaps I could name a country which would be glad to eat up our whole nation without it.

32   After all, I am not so violently bent upon my own opinion as to reject any offer proposed by wise men, which shall be found equally innocent, cheap, easy, and effectual. But before something of that kind shall be advanced in contradiction to my scheme, and offering a better, I desire the author or authors will be pleased maturely to consider two points. First, as things now stand, how they will be able to find food and raiment for an hundred thousand useless mouths and backs. And secondly, there being a round million of creatures in human figure throughout this kingdom, whose sole subsistence put into a common stock would leave them in debt two millions of pounds sterling, adding those who are beggars by profession to the bulk of farmers, cottagers, and laborers, with their wives and children who are beggars in effect; I desire those politicians who dislike my overture, and may perhaps be so bold as to attempt an answer, that they will first ask the parents of these mortals whether they would not at this day think it a great happiness to have been sold for food at a year old in this manner I prescribe, and thereby have avoided such a perpetual scene of misfortunes as they have since gone through by the oppression of landlords, the impossibility of paying rent without money or trade; the want of common sustenance, with neither house nor clothes to cover them from the inclemencies of the weather, and the most inevitable prospect of entailing the like or greater miseries upon their breed forever.

33   I profess, in the sincerity of my heart, that I have not the least personal interest in endeavoring to promote this necessary work, having no other motive than the public good of my country, by advancing our trade, providing for infants, relieving the poor, and giving some pleasure to the rich. I have no children by which I can propose to get a single penny; the youngest being nine years old, and my wife past childbearing.

CHAPTER 33

Literature

Perhaps the World Ends Here

Joy Harjo

Joy Harjo is a contemporary poet and musician who holds a Master of Fine Arts degree from the University of Iowa. Inspired by her Muscogee/Creek Native American heritage, Harjo often performs by combining poetry with an original blend of tribal music, jazz, and rock. A former professor at the University of New Mexico, she has published seven award-winning books of poetry, the most recent being *How We Became Human* (2002). This poem appears in *The Woman Who Fell from the Sky* (1994).

The world begins at a kitchen table. No matter what, we must eat to live.

The gifts of earth are brought and prepared, set on the table. So it has been since creation, and it will go on.

5 We chase chickens or dogs away from it. Babies teethe at the corners. They scrape their knees under it.

It is here that children are given instructions on what it means to be human. We make men at it, we make women.

At this table we gossip, recall enemies and the ghosts of lovers.

10 Our dreams drink coffee with us as they put their arms around our children. They laugh with us at our poor falling-down selves and as we put ourselves back together once again at the table.

This table has been a house in the rain, an umbrella in the sun.

Wars have begun and ended at this table. It is a place to hide in the
15　shadow of terror. A place to celebrate the terrible victory.

We have given birth on this table, and have prepared our parents for
burial here.

At this table we sing with joy, with sorrow. We pray of suffering
and remorse. We give thanks.

20　Perhaps the world will end at the kitchen table, while we are laughing
and crying, eating of the last sweet bite.

Ozymandias

Percy Bysshe Shelley

Percy Bysshe Shelley is considered one of the finest English poets and a major figure in the nineteenth-century Romantic movement. Born in 1792, Shelley was educated at Eton but was expelled from Oxford. He married Mary Wollstonecraft (later famous for her novel *Frankenstein*) and traveled in Europe, where he produced some of his best work, including "To a Skylark," "The Cloud," and "Ode to the West Wind." In 1822, at age 29, Shelley drowned in Italy. The sonnet presented here was written in 1818.

I met a traveler from an antique land
Who said: Two vast and trunkless legs of stone
Stand in the desert . . . Near them, on the sand,
Half sunk, a shattered visage lies, whose frown,
5　And wrinkled lip, and sneer of cold command,
Tell that its sculptor well those passions read
Which yet survive, stamped on these lifeless things,
The hand that mocked them, and the heart that fed:
And on the pedestal these words appear:
10　"My name is Ozymandias, king of kings:
Look on my works, ye Mighty, and despair!"
Nothing beside remains. Round the decay
Of that colossal wreck, boundless and bare
The lone and level sands stretch far away.

Poem for an Inked Daughter

Jane Wheeler

Jane Wheeler is a northern Colorado teacher and writer, whose prose and poetry have been published nationally in a variety of venues, from books to buses. This poem, written to her teenage daughter, was first published in *UU World* in 2006; since then it has been reprinted frequently and has been taught in both college and community writing courses.

I did it too you know, just differently.
Way back then
when I was angry young
I pierced my ears with a rusty ice pick,
5 and willfully wore dangly earrings
(and a smirk) to Christmas dinner.
My scandalized Mother
referred to me for days as
"my daughter, the dirty gypsy."
10 I let my ears jingle silver music, ultimately
dancing right over her Victorian disapproval
out of that house forever.

And now here you are,
fresh from a different kind of parlor,
15 with that defiant dragon
curling dark over your shoulder.
No, of course you know I don't like it.
Another gauntlet thrown down
in the ongoing Mother-Daughter Wars.

20 But hear this, my own gypsy girl:
I know something you don't.
That under that fierce fire-breathing dragon,
claws bared, ready for the next battle,
under the skin where the purple ink turns to blood,
25 your blood is my blood,
rushing red to red, flowing in a long bond
linking my heart to you no matter what,
like the swirling, twisting lines
of an intricate intimate tattoo,
30 invisible, indelible, forever permanent.

A Jury of Her Peers*

Susan Glaspell

Susan Glaspell was a novelist, playwright, and co-founder of the innovative Provincetown Playhouse. She published nine novels, over a dozen plays, and more than forty short stories; her play *Alison's House* won the Pulitzer Prize in 1931. As a young woman, Glaspell was a reporter in Iowa, where she covered the trial of Margaret Hossack, accused of murdering her husband. From that experience Glaspell wrote her play *Trifles* (1916), followed the next year by the short-story version reprinted here.

1   When Martha Hale opened the storm door and got a cut of the north wind, she ran back for her big woolen scarf. As she hurriedly wound that round her head her eye made a scandalized sweep of her kitchen. It was no ordinary thing that called her away—it was probably farther from ordinary than anything that had ever happened in Dickson County. But what her eye took in was that her kitchen was in no shape for leaving: her bread all ready for mixing, half the flour sifted and half unsifted.

2   She hated to see things half done; but she had been at that when the team from town stopped to get Mr. Hale, and then the sheriff came running in to say his wife wished Mrs. Hale would come too—adding, with a grin, that he guessed she was getting scarey and wanted another woman along. So she had dropped everything right where it was.

3   "Martha!" now came her husband's impatient voice. "Don't keep folks waiting out here in the cold."

4   She again opened the storm door, and this time joined the three men and the one woman waiting for her in the big two-seated buggy.

5   After she had the robes tucked around her she took another look at the woman who sat beside her on the back seat. She had met Mrs. Peters the year before at the county fair, and the thing she remembered about her was that she didn't seem like a sheriff's wife. She was small and thin and didn't have a strong voice. Mrs. Gorman, sheriff's wife before Gorman went out and Peters came in, had a voice that somehow seemed to be backing up the law with every word. But if Mrs. Peters didn't look like a sheriff's wife, Peters made it up in looking like a sheriff. He was to a dot the kind of man who could get himself elected sheriff—a heavy man with a big voice, who was particularly genial with the law-abiding, as if to make it plain that he knew the difference between criminals and non-criminals. And right there it came into Mrs. Hale's mind, with a stab, that this man who was so pleasant and lively with all of them was going to the Wrights' now as a sheriff.

6   "The country's not very pleasant this time of year," Mrs. Peters at last ventured, as if she felt they ought to be talking as well as the men.

7   Mrs. Hale scarcely finished her reply, for they had gone up a little hill and could see the Wright place now, and seeing it did not make her feel like talking. It looked very lonesome this cold March morning. It had always been a lonesome-looking

---

*Readers might see several ironies at work in Glaspell's choice of titles. Recall that at this time women in Iowa could neither serve on juries nor vote.

place. It was down in a hollow, and the poplar trees around it were lonesome-looking trees. The men were looking at it and talking about what had happened. The county attorney was bending to one side of the buggy, and kept looking steadily at the place as they drew up to it.

8   "I'm glad you came with me," Mrs. Peters said nervously, as the two women were about to follow the men in through the kitchen door.

9   Even after she had her foot on the doorstep, her hand on the knob, Martha Hale had a moment of feeling she could not cross the threshold. And the reason it seemed she couldn't cross it now was simply because she hadn't crossed it before. Time and time again it had been in her mind, "I ought to go over and see Minnie Foster"—she still thought of her as Minnie Foster, though for twenty years she had been Mrs. Wright. And then there was always something to do and Minnie Foster would go from her mind. But *now* she could come.

10   The men went over to the stove. The women stood close together by the door. Young Henderson, the county attorney, turned around and said, "Come up to the fire, ladies."

11   Mrs. Peters took a step forward, then stopped. "I'm not—cold," she said.

12   And so the two women stood by the door, at first not even so much as looking around the kitchen.

13   The men talked for a minute about what a good thing it was the sheriff sent his deputy out that morning to make a fire for them, and then Sheriff Peters stepped back from the stove, unbuttoned his outer coat, and leaned his hands on the kitchen table in a way that seemed to mark the beginning of official business. "Now, Mr. Hale," he said in a sort of semiofficial voice, "before we move things about, you tell Mr. Henderson just what it was you saw when you came here yesterday morning."

14   The county attorney was looking around the kitchen.

15   "By the way," he said, "has anything been moved?" He turned to the sheriff. "Are things just as you left them yesterday?"

16   Peters looked from cupboard to sink; from that to a small worn rocker a little to one side of the kitchen table.

17   "It's just the same."

18   "Somebody should have been left here yesterday," said the county attorney.

19   "Oh—yesterday," returned the sheriff, with a little gesture as of yesterday having been more than he could bear to think of. "When I had to send Frank to Morris Center for that man who went crazy—let me tell you, I had my hands full *yesterday*. I knew you could get back from Omaha by today, George, and as long as I went over everything here myself—"

20   "Well, Mr. Hale," said the county attorney, in a way of letting what was past and gone go, "tell just what happened when you came here yesterday morning."

21   Mrs. Hale, still leaning against the door, had that sinking feeling of the mother whose child is about to speak a piece. Lewis often wandered along and got things mixed up in a story. She hoped that he would tell this straight and plain, and not say unnecessary things that would just make things harder for Minnie Foster. He didn't begin at once, and she noticed that he looked queer—as if standing in that kitchen and having to tell what he had seen there yesterday morning made him almost sick.

22   "Yes, Mr. Hale?" the county attorney reminded.

23   "Harry and I had started to town with a load of potatoes," Mrs. Hale's husband began.

24   Harry was Mrs. Hale's oldest boy. He wasn't with them now, for the very good reason that those potatoes never got to town yesterday and he was taking them this morning, so he hadn't been home when the sheriff stopped to say he wanted Mr. Hale to come over to the Wright place and tell the county attorney his story there, where he could point it all out. With all Mrs. Hale's other emotions came the fear now that maybe Harry wasn't dressed warm enough—they hadn't any of them realized how that north wind did bite.

25   "We come along this road," Hale was going on, with a motion of his hand to the road over which they had just come, "and as we got in sight of the house I says to Harry, 'I'm goin' to see if I can't get John Wright to take a telephone.' You see," he explained to Henderson, "unless I can get somebody to go in with me they won't come out this branch road except for a price *I* can't pay. I'd spoke to Wright about it once before; but he put me off, saying folks talked too much anyway, and all he asked was peace and quiet—guess you know about how much he talked himself. But I thought maybe if I went to the house and talked about it before his wife, and said all the women-folks liked the telephones, and that in this lonesome stretch of road it would be a good thing—well, I said to Harry that that was what I was going to say—though I said at the same time that I didn't know as what his wife wanted made much difference to John—"

26   Now, there he was!—saying things he didn't need to say. Mrs. Hale tried to catch her husband's eye, but fortunately the county attorney interrupted with:

27   "Let's talk about that a little later, Mr. Hale. I do want to talk about that, but I'm anxious now to get along to just what happened when you got here."

28   When he began this time, it was very deliberately and carefully:

29   "I didn't see or hear anything. I knocked at the door. And still it was all quiet inside. I knew they must be up—it was past eight o'clock. So I knocked again, louder, and I thought I heard somebody say 'Come in.' I wasn't sure—I'm not sure yet. But I opened the door—this door," jerking a hand toward the door by which the two women stood, "and there, in that rocker"—pointing to it—"sat Mrs. Wright."

30   Every one in the kitchen looked at the rocker. It came into Mrs. Hale's mind that that rocker didn't look in the least like Minnie Foster—the Minnie Foster of twenty years before. It was a dingy red, with wooden rungs up the back, and the middle rung was gone, and the chair sagged to one side.

31   "How did she—look?" the county attorney was inquiring.

32   "Well," said Hale, "she looked—queer."

33   "How do you mean—queer?"

34   As he asked it he took out a notebook and pencil. Mrs. Hale did not like the sight of that pencil. She kept her eye fixed on her husband, as if to keep him from saying unnecessary things that would go into that notebook and make trouble.

35   Hale did speak guardedly, as if the pencil had affected him too.

36   "Well, as if she didn't know what she was going to do next. And kind of—done up."

37   "How did she seem to feel about your coming?"

38   "Why, I don't think she minded—one way or other. She didn't pay much attention. I said, 'Ho' do, Mrs. Wright? It's cold, ain't it?' And she said, 'Is it?'—and went
on plcatin' at her apron.

39   "Well, I was surprised. She didn't ask me to come up to the stove, or to sit down,
but just set there, not even lookin' at me. And so I said: 'I want to see John.'

40   "And then she—laughed. I guess you would call it a laugh.

41   "I thought of Harry and the team outside, so I said, a little sharp, 'Can I see John?'
'No,' says she—kind of dull like. 'Ain't he home?' says I. Then she looked at me.
'Yes,' says she, 'he's home.' 'Then why can't I see him?' I asked her, out of patience
with her now. "Cause he's dead,' says she, just as quiet and dull—and fell to pleatin'
her apron. 'Dead?' says I, like you do when you can't take in what you've heard.

42   "She just nodded her head, not getting a bit excited, but rockin' back and
forth.

43   "'Why—where is he?' says I, not knowing *what* to say.

44   "She just pointed upstairs—like this"—pointing to the room above.

45   "I got up, with the idea of going up there myself. By this time I—didn't know
what to do. I walked from there to here; then I says: 'Why, what did he die of?'

46   "'He died of a rope round his neck,' says she; and just went on pleatin' at her
apron."

47   Hale stopped speaking, and stood staring at the rocker, as if he were still seeing
the woman who had sat there the morning before. Nobody spoke; it was as if every
one were seeing the woman who had sat there the morning before.

48   "And what did you do then?" the county attorney at last broke the silence.

49   "I went out and called Harry. I thought I might—need help. I got Harry in, and
we went upstairs." His voice fell almost to a whisper. "There he was—lying over
the—"

50   "I think I'd rather have you go into that upstairs," the county attorney interrupted, "where you can point it all out. Just go on now with the rest of the story."

51   "Well, my first thought was to get that rope off. It looked—"

52   He stopped, his face twitching.

53   "But Harry, he went up to him, and he said, 'No, he's dead all right, and we'd
better not touch anything.' So we went downstairs.

54   "She was still sitting that same way. 'Has anybody been notified?' I asked. 'No,'
says she, unconcerned."

55   "'Who did this, Mrs. Wright?' said Harry. He said it businesslike, and she
stopped pleatin' at her apron. 'I don't know,' she says. 'You don't *know*?' says Harry.
'Weren't you sleepin' in the bed with him?' 'Yes,' says she, 'but I was on the inside.'
'Somebody slipped a rope round his neck and strangled him, and you didn't wake
up?' says Harry. 'I didn't wake up,' she said after him.

56   "We may have looked as if we didn't see how that could be, for after a minute
she said, 'I sleep sound.'

57   "Harry was going to ask her more questions, but I said maybe that weren't our
business; maybe we ought to let her tell her story first to the coroner or the sheriff. So Harry went fast as he could over to High Road—the Rivers's place, where
there's a telephone."

58   "And what did she do when she knew you had gone for the coroner?" The attorney got his pencil in his hand all ready for writing.

59   "She moved from that chair to this one over here"—Hale pointed to a small chair in the corner—"and just sat there with her hands held together and looking down. I got a feeling that I ought to make some conversation, so I said I had come in to see if John wanted to put in a telephone; and at that she started to laugh, and then she stopped and looked at me—scared."

60   At the sound of the moving pencil the man who was telling the story looked up.

61   "I dunno—maybe it wasn't scared," he hastened; "I wouldn't like to say it was. Soon Harry got back, and then Dr. Lloyd came, and you, Mr. Peters, and so I guess that's all I know that you don't."

62   He said that last with relief, and moved a little, as if relaxing. Every one moved a little. The county attorney walked toward the stair door.

63   "I guess we'll go upstairs first—then out to the barn and around there."

64   He paused and looked around the kitchen.

65   "You're convinced there was nothing important here?" he asked the sheriff. "Nothing that would—point to any motive?"

66   The sheriff too looked all around, as if to re-convince himself.

67   "Nothing here but kitchen things," he said, with a little laugh for the insignificance of kitchen things.

68   The county attorney was looking at the cupboard—a peculiar, ungainly structure, half closet and half cupboard, the upper part of it being built in the wall, and the lower part just the old-fashioned kitchen cupboard. As if its queerness attracted him, he got a chair and opened the upper part and looked in. After a moment he drew his hand away sticky.

69   "Here's a nice mess," he said resentfully.

70   The two women had drawn nearer, and now the sheriff's wife spoke.

71   "Oh—her fruit," she said, looking to Mrs. Hale for sympathetic understanding. She turned back to the county attorney and explained. "She worried about that when it turned so cold last night. She said the fire would go out and her jars might burst."

72   Mrs. Peters's husband broke into a laugh.

73   "Well, can you beat the women! Held for murder, and worrying about her preserves!"

74   The young attorney set his lips.

75   "I guess before we're through with her she may have something more serious than preserves to worry about."

76   "Oh, well," said Mrs. Hale's husband, with good-natured superiority, "women are used to worrying over trifles."

77   The two women moved a little closer together. Neither of them spoke. The county attorney seemed suddenly to remember his manners—and think of his future.

78   "And yet," said he, with the gallantry of a young politician, "for all their worries, what would we do without the ladies?"

79   The women did not speak, did not unbend. He went to the sink and began washing his hands. He turned to wipe them on the roller towel—whirled it for a cleaner place.

80   "Dirty towels! Not much of a housekeeper, would you say, ladies?"

81   He kicked his foot against some dirty pans under the sink.

82   "There's a great deal of work to be done on a farm," said Mrs. Hale stiffly.

83   "To be sure. And yet"—with a little bow to her—"I know there are some Dickson County farm-houses that do not have such roller towels." He gave it a pull to expose its full length again.

84   "Those towels get dirty awful quick. Men's hands aren't always as clean as they might be."

85   "Ah, loyal to your sex, I see," he laughed. He stopped and gave her a keen look. "But you and Mrs. Wright were neighbors. I suppose you were friends, too."

86   Martha Hale shook her head.

87   "I've seen little enough of her of late years. I've not been in this house—it's more than a year."

88   "And why was that? You didn't like her?"

89   "I liked her well enough," she replied with spirit. "Farmers' wives have their hands full, Mr. Henderson. And then—" She looked around the kitchen.

90   "Yes?" he encouraged.

91   "It never seemed a very cheerful place," said she, more to herself than to him.

92   "No," he agreed; "I don't think any one would call it cheerful. I shouldn't say she had the homemaking instinct."

93   "Well, I don't know as Wright had, either," she muttered.

94   "You mean they didn't get on very well?" he was very quick to ask.

95   "No; I don't mean anything," she answered, with decision. As she turned a little away from him, she added: "But I don't think a place would be any the cheerfuler for John Wright's bein' in it."

96   "I'd like to talk to you about that a little later, Mrs. Hale," he said. "I'm anxious to get the lay of things upstairs now."

97   He moved toward the stair door, followed by the two men.

98   "I suppose anything Mrs. Peters does'll be all right?" the sheriff inquired. "She was to take in some clothes for her, you know—and a few little things. We left in such a hurry yesterday."

99   The county attorney looked at the two women whom they were leaving alone there among the kitchen things.

100   "Yes—Mrs. Peters," he said, his glance resting on the woman who was not Mrs. Peters, the big farmer woman who stood behind the sheriff's wife. "Of course Mrs. Peters is one of us," he said, in a manner of entrusting responsibility. "And keep your eye out, Mrs. Peters, for anything that might be of use. No telling; you women might come upon a clue to the motive—and that's the thing we need."

101   Mr. Hale rubbed his face after the fashion of a show man getting ready for a pleasantry.

102   "But would the women know a clue if they did come upon it?" he said; and, having delivered himself of this, he followed the others through the stair door.

103   The women stood motionless and silent, listening to the footsteps, first upon the stairs, then in the room above them.

104   Then, as if releasing herself from something strange, Mrs. Hale began to arrange the dirty pans under the sink, which the county attorney's disdainful push of the foot had deranged.

105   "I'd hate to have men comin' into my kitchen," she said testily—"snoopin' round and criticizin.'"

106   "Of course it's no more than their duty," said the sheriff's wife, in her manner of timid acquiescence.

107   "Duty's all right," replied Mrs. Hale bluffly; "but I guess that deputy sheriff that come out to make the fire might have got a little of this on." She gave the roller towel a pull. "Wish I'd thought of that sooner! Seems mean to talk about her for not having things slicked up, when she had to come away in such a hurry."

108   She looked around the kitchen. Certainly it was not "slicked up." Her eye was held by a bucket of sugar on a low shelf. The cover was off the wooden bucket, and beside it was a paper bag—half full.

109   Mrs. Hale moved toward it.

110   "She was putting this in there," she said to herself—slowly.

111   She thought of the flour in her kitchen at home—half sifted, half not sifted. She had been interrupted, and had left things half done. What had interrupted Minnie Foster? Why had that work been left half done? She made a move as if to finish it,—unfinished things always bothered her,—and then she glanced around and saw that Mrs. Peters was watching her—and she didn't want Mrs. Peters to get that feeling she had got of work begun and then—for some reason—not finished.

112   "It's a shame about her fruit," she said, and walked toward the cupboard that the county attorney had opened, and got on the chair, murmuring: "I wonder if it's all gone."

113   It was a sorry enough looking sight, but "Here's one that's all right," she said at last. She held it toward the light. "This is cherries, too." She looked again. "I declare I believe that's the only one."

114   With a sigh, she got down from the chair, went to the sink, and wiped off the bottle.

115   "She'll feel awful bad, after all her hard work in the hot weather. I remember the afternoon I put up my cherries last summer."

116   She set the bottle on the table, and, with another sigh, started to sit down in the rocker. But she did not sit down. Something kept her from sitting down in that chair. She straightened—stepped back, and, half turned away, stood looking at it, seeing the woman who had sat there "pleatin' at her apron."

117   The thin voice of the sheriff's wife broke in upon her: "I must be getting those things from the front room closet." She opened the door into the other room, started in, stepped back. "You coming with me, Mrs. Hale?" she asked nervously. "You—you could help me get them."

118   They were soon back—the stark coldness of that shut-up room was not a thing to linger in.

119   "My!" said Mrs. Peters, dropping the things on the table and hurrying to the stove.

120   Mrs. Hale stood examining the clothes the woman who was being detained in town had said she wanted.

121   "Wright was close!" she exclaimed, holding up a shabby black skirt that bore the marks of much making over. "I think maybe that's why she kept so much to herself. I s'pose she felt she couldn't do her part; and then, you don't enjoy things when you feel shabby. She used to wear pretty clothes and be lively—when she was Minnie

Foster, one of the town girls, singing in the choir. But that—oh, that was twenty years ago."

122 With a carefulness in which there was something tender, she folded the shabby clothes and piled them at one corner of the table. She looked up at Mrs. Peters, and there was something in the other woman's look that irritated her.

123 "She don't care," she said to herself. "Much difference it makes to her whether Minnie Foster had pretty clothes when she was a girl."

124 Then she looked again, and she wasn't so sure; in fact, she hadn't at any time been perfectly sure about Mrs. Peters. She had that shrinking manner, and yet her eyes looked as if they could see a long way into things.

125 "This all you was to take in?" asked Mrs. Hale.

126 "No," said the sheriff's wife; "she said she wanted an apron. Funny thing to want," she ventured in her nervous little way, "for there's not much to get you dirty in jail, goodness knows. But I suppose just to make her feel more natural. If you're used to wearing an apron—. She said they were in the bottom drawer of this cupboard. Yes—here they are. And then her little shawl that always hung on the stair door."

127 She took the small gray shawl from behind the door leading upstairs, and stood a minute looking at it.

128 Suddenly Mrs. Hale took a quick step toward the other woman.

129 "Mrs. Peters!"

130 "Yes, Mrs. Hale?"

131 "Do you think she—did it?"

132 A frightened look blurred the other thing in Mrs. Peters's eyes.

133 "Oh, I don't know," she said, in a voice that seemed to shrink away from the subject.

134 "Well, I don't think she did," affirmed Mrs. Hale stoutly. "Asking for an apron, and her little shawl. Worryin' about her fruit."

135 "Mr. Peters says—." Footsteps were heard in the room above; she stopped, looked up, then went on in a lowered voice: "Mr. Peters says—it looks bad for her. Mr. Henderson is awful sarcastic in a speech, and he's going to make fun of her saying she didn't—wake up."

136 For a moment Mrs. Hale had no answer. Then, "Well, I guess John Wright didn't wake up—when they was slippin' that rope under his neck," she muttered.

137 "No, it's *strange*," breathed Mrs. Peters. "They think it was such a—funny way to kill a man."

138 She began to laugh; at sound of the laugh, abruptly stopped.

139 "That's just what Mr. Hale said," said Mrs. Hale, in a resolutely natural voice. "There was a gun in the house. He says that's what he can't understand."

140 "Mr. Henderson said, coming out, that what was needed for the case was a motive. Something to show anger—or sudden feeling."

141 "Well, I don't see any signs of anger around here," said Mrs. Hale. "I don't—"

142 She stopped. It was as if her mind tripped on something. Her eye was caught by a dish-towel in the middle of the kitchen table. Slowly she moved toward the table. One half of it was wiped clean, the other half messy. Her eyes made a slow, almost unwilling turn to the bucket of sugar and the half empty bag beside it. Things begun—and not finished.

143   After a moment she stepped back, and said, in that manner of releasing herself:

144   "Wonder how they're finding things upstairs? I hope she had it a little more red up there. You know,"—she paused, and feeling gathered,—"it seems kind of *sneaking*; locking her up in town and coming out here to get her own house to turn against her!"

145   "But, Mrs. Hale," said the sheriff's wife, "the law is the law."

146   "I s'pose 'tis," answered Mrs. Hale shortly.

147   She turned to the stove, saying something about that fire not being much to brag of. She worked with it a minute, and when she straightened up she said aggressively:

148   "The law is the law—and a bad stove is a bad stove. How'd you like to cook on this?"—pointing with a poker to the broken lining. She opened the oven door and started to express her opinion of the oven; but she was swept into her own thoughts, thinking of what it would mean, year after year, to have that stove to wrestle with. The thought of Minnie Foster trying to bake in that oven—and the thought of her never going over to see Minnie Foster—.

149   She was startled by hearing Mrs. Peters say: "A person gets discouraged—and loses heart."

150   The sheriff's wife had looked from the stove to the sink—to the pail of water which had been carried in from outside. The two women stood there silent, above them the footsteps of the men who were looking for evidence against the woman who had worked in that kitchen. That look of seeing into things, of seeing through a thing to something else, was in the eyes of the sheriff's wife now. When Mrs. Hale next spoke to her, it was gently:

151   "Better loosen up your things, Mrs. Peters. We'll not feel them when we go out."

152   Mrs. Peters went to the back of the room to hang up the fur tippet she was wearing. A moment later she exclaimed, "Why, she was piecing a quilt," and held up a large sewing basket piled high with quilt pieces.

153   Mrs. Hale spread some of the blocks on the table.

154   "It's log-cabin pattern," she said, putting several of them together. "Pretty, isn't it?"

155   They were so engaged with the quilt that they did not hear the footsteps on the stairs. Just as the stair door opened Mrs. Hale was saying:

156   "Do you suppose she was going to quilt it or just knot it?"

157   The sheriff threw up his hands.

158   "They wonder whether she was going to quilt it or just knot it!"

159   There was a laugh for the ways of women, a warming of hands over the stove, and then the county attorney said briskly:

160   "Well, let's go right out to the barn and get that cleared up."

161   "I don't see as there's anything so strange," Mrs. Hale said resentfully, after the outside door had closed on the three men—"our taking up our time with little things while we're waiting for them to get the evidence. I don't see as it's anything to laugh about."

162   "Of course they've got awful important things on their minds," said the sheriff's wife apologetically.

163   They returned to an inspection of the blocks for the quilt. Mrs. Hale was look-ing at the fine, even sewing, and preoccupied with thoughts of the woman who had done that sewing, when she heard the sheriff's wife say, in a queer tone:

164   "Why, look at this one."

165   She turned to take the block held out to her.

166   "The sewing," said Mrs. Peters, in a troubled way. "All the rest of them have been so nice and even—but—this one. Why, it looks as if she didn't know what she was about!"

167   Their eyes met—something flashed to life, passed between them; then, as if with an effort, they seemed to pull away from each other. A moment Mrs. Hale sat there, her hands folded over that sewing which was so unlike all the rest of the sew-ing. Then she had pulled a knot and drawn the threads.

168   "Oh, what are you doing, Mrs. Hale?" asked the sheriff's wife, startled.

169   "Just pulling out a stitch or two that's not sewed very good," said Mrs. Hale mildly.

170   "I don't think we ought to touch things," Mrs. Peters said, a little helplessly.

171   "I'll just finish up this end," answered Mrs. Hale, still in that mild, matter-of-fact faction.

172   She threaded a needle and started to replace bad sewing with good. For a little while she sewed in silence. Then, in that thin, timid voice, she heard:

173   "Mrs. Hale!"

174   "Yes, Mrs. Peters?"

175   "What do you suppose she was so—nervous about?"

176   "Oh, *I* don't know," said Mrs. Hale, as if dismissing a thing not important enough to spend much time on. "I don't know as she was—nervous. I sew awful queer sometimes when I'm just tired."

177   She cut a thread, and out of the corner of her eye looked up at Mrs. Peters. The small, lean face of the sheriff's wife seemed to have tightened up. Her eyes had that look of peering into something. But next moment she moved, and said in her thin, indecisive way:

178   "Well, I must get those clothes wrapped. They may be through sooner than we think. I wonder where I could find a piece of paper—and string."

179   "In that cupboard, maybe," suggested Mrs. Hale, after a glance around.

180   One piece of the crazy sewing remained unripped. Mrs. Peters's back turned, Martha Hale now scrutinized that piece, compared it with the dainty, accurate sewing of the other blocks. The difference was startling. Holding this block made her feel queer, as if the distracted thoughts of the woman who had perhaps turned to it to try and quiet herself were communicating themselves to her.

181   Mrs. Peters' voice roused her.

182   "Here's a bird-cage," she said. "Did she have a bird, Mrs. Hale?"

183   "Why, I don't know whether she did or not." She turned to look at the cage Mrs. Peter was holding up. "I've not been here in so long." She sighed. "There was a man round last year selling canaries cheap—but I don't know as she took one. Maybe she did. She used to sing real pretty herself."

184   Mrs. Peters looked around the kitchen.

185   "Seems kind of funny to think of a bird here." She half laughed—an attempt to put up a barrier. "But she must have had one—or why would she have a cage? I wonder what happened to it?"

186   "I suppose maybe the cat got it," suggested Mrs. Hale, resuming her sewing.

187   "No, she didn't have a cat. She's got that feeling some people have about cats—being afraid of them. When they brought her to our house yesterday, my cat got in the room, and she was real upset and asked me to take it out."

188   "My sister Bessie was like that," laughed Mrs. Hale.

189   The sheriff's wife did not reply. The silence made Mrs. Hale turn round. Mrs. Peters was examining the birdcage.

190   "Look at this door," she said slowly. "It's broke. One hinge has been pulled apart."

191   Mrs. Hale came nearer.

192   "Looks as if some one must have been—rough with it."

193   Again their eyes met—startled, questioning, apprehensive. For a moment neither spoke nor stirred. Then Mrs. Hale, turning away, said brusquely:

194   "If they're going to find any evidence, I wish they'd be about it. I don't like this place."

195   "But I'm awful glad you came with me, Mrs. Hale." Mrs. Peters put the birdcage on the table and sat down. "It would be lonesome for me—sitting here alone."

196   "Yes, it would, wouldn't it?" agreed Mrs. Hale, a certain determined naturalness in her voice. She had picked up the sewing, but now it dropped in her lap, and she murmured in a different voice: "But I tell you what I *do* wish, Mrs. Peters. I wish I had come over sometimes when she was here. I wish—I had."

197   "But of course you were awful busy, Mrs. Hale. Your house—and your children."

198   "I could've come," retorted Mrs. Hale shortly. "I stayed away because it weren't cheerful—and that's why I ought to have come. I"—she looked around—"I've never liked this place. Maybe because it's down in a hollow and you don't see the road. I don't know what it is, but it's a lonesome place, and always was. I wish I had come over to see Minnie Foster sometimes. I can see now—" She did not put it into words.

199   "Well, you mustn't reproach yourself," counseled Mrs. Peters. "Somehow, we just don't see how it is with other folks till—something comes up."

200   "Not having children makes less work," mused Mrs. Hale, after a silence, "but it makes a quiet house—and Wright out to work all day—and no company when he did come in. Did you know John Wright, Mrs. Peters?"

201   "Not to know him. I've seen him in town. They say he was a good man."

202   "Yes—good," conceded John Wright's neighbor grimly. "He didn't drink, and kept his word as well as most, I guess, and paid his debts. But he was a hard man, Mrs. Peters. Just to pass the time of day with him—." She stopped, shivered a little. "Like a raw wind that gets to the bone." Her eye fell upon the cage on the table before her, and she added, almost bitterly: "I should think she would've wanted a bird!"

203   Suddenly she leaned forward, looking intently at the cage. "But what do you s'pose went wrong with it?"

204   "I don't know," returned Mrs. Peters; "unless it got sick and died."

205   But after she said it she reached over and swung the broken door. Both women watched it as if somehow held by it.

206   "You didn't know—her?" Mrs. Hale asked, a gentler note in her voice.

207   "Not till they brought her yesterday," said the sheriff's wife.

208   "She—come to think of it, she was kind of like a bird herself. Real sweet and pretty, but kind of timid and—fluttery. How—she—did—change."

209   That held her for a long time. Finally, as if struck with a happy thought and relieved to get back to everyday things, she exclaimed:

210   "Tell you what, Mrs. Peters, why don't you take the quilt in with you? It might take up her mind."

211   "Why, I think that's a real nice idea, Mrs. Hale," agreed the sheriff's wife, as if she too were glad to come into the atmosphere of a simple kindness. "There couldn't possibly be any objection to that, could there? Now, just what will I take? I wonder if her patches are in here—and her things."

212   They turned to the sewing basket.

213   "Here's some red," said Mrs. Hale, bringing out a roll of cloth. Underneath that was a box. "Here, maybe her scissors are in here—and her things." She held it up. "What a pretty box! I'll warrant that was something she had a long time ago—when she was a girl."

214   She held it in her hand a moment, then, with a little sigh, opened it.

215   Instantly her hand went to her nose.

216   "Why—!"

217   Mrs. Peters drew nearer—then turned away.

218   "There's something wrapped up in this piece of silk," faltered Mrs. Hale.

219   "This isn't her scissors," said Mrs. Peters in a shrinking voice.

220   Her hand not steady, Mrs. Hale raised the piece of silk. "Oh, Mrs. Peters!" she cried. "It's—"

221   Mrs. Peters bent closer.

222   "It's the bird," she whispered.

223   "But, Mrs. Peters!" cried Mrs. Hale. "*Look* at it! Its neck—look at its neck! It's all—other side *to*."

224   She held the box away from her.

225   The sheriff's wife again bent closer.

226   "Somebody wrung its neck," said she, in a voice that was slow and deep.

227   And then again the eyes of the two women met—this time clung together in a look of dawning comprehension, of growing horror. Mrs. Peters looked from the dead bird to the broken door of the cage. Again their eyes met. And just then there was a sound at the outside door.

228   Mrs. Hale slipped the box under the quilt pieces in the basket, and sank into the chair before it. Mrs. Peters stood holding to the table. The county attorney and the sheriff came in from outside.

229   "Well, ladies," said the county attorney, as one turning from serious things to little pleasantries, "have you decided whether she was going to quilt it or knot it?"

230   "We think," began the sheriff's wife in a flurried voice, "that she was going to—knot it."

231   He was too preoccupied to notice the change that came in her voice on that last.

232   "Well, that's very interesting, I'm sure," he said tolerantly. He caught sight of the birdcage. "Has the bird flown?"

233   "We think the cat got it," said Mrs. Hale in a voice curiously even.

234   He was walking up and down, as if thinking something out.

235   "Is there a cat?" he asked absently.

236   Mrs. Hale shot a look up at the sheriff's wife.

237   "Well, not *now*," said Mrs. Peters. "They're superstitious, you know, they leave."

238   She sank into the chair.

239   The county attorney did not heed her. "No sign at all of any one having come in from the outside," he said to Peters, in the manner of continuing an interrupted conversation. "Their own rope. Now let's go upstairs again and go over it, piece by piece. It would have to have been some one who knew just the—"

240   The stair door closed behind them and their voices were lost.

241   The two women sat motionless, not looking at each other, but as if peering into something and at the same time holding back. When they spoke now it was as if they were afraid of what they were saying, but as if they could not help saying it.

242   "She liked the bird," said Martha Hale, low and slowly. "She was going to bury it in that pretty box."

243   "When I was a girl," said Mrs. Peters, under her breath, "my kitten—there was a boy took a hatchet, and before my eyes—before I could get there—" She covered her face an instant. "If they hadn't held me back I would have"—she caught herself, looked upstairs where footsteps were heard, and finished weakly—"hurt him."

244   Then they sat without speaking or moving.

245   "I wonder how it would seem," Mrs. Hale at last began, as if feeling her way over strange ground—"never to have had any children around?" Her eyes made a slow sweep of the kitchen, as if seeing what that kitchen had meant through all the years. "No, Wright wouldn't like the bird," she said after that—"a thing that sang. She used to sing. He killed that too." Her voice tightened.

246   Mrs. Peters moved uneasily.

247   "Of course we don't know who killed the bird."

248   "I knew John Wright," was Mrs. Hale's answer.

249   "It was an awful thing was done in this house that night, Mrs. Hale," said the sheriff's wife. "Killing a man while he slept—slipping a thing round his neck that choked the life out of him."

250   Mrs. Hale's hand went out to the birdcage.

251   "His neck. Choked the life out of him."

252   "We don't *know* who killed him," whispered Mrs. Peters wildly. "We don't *know*."

253   Mrs. Hale had not moved. "If there had been years and years of—nothing, then a bird to sing to you, it would be awful—still—after the bird was still."

254   It was as if something within her not herself had spoken, and it found in Mrs. Peters something she did not know as herself.

255   "I know what stillness is," she said, in a queer, monotonous voice. "When we homesteaded in Dakota, and my first baby died—after he was two years old—and me with no other then—"

256   Mrs. Hale stirred.

257   "How soon do you suppose they'll be through looking for the evidence?"

258 "I know what stillness is," repeated Mrs. Peters, in just that same way. Then she too pulled back. "The law has got to punish crime, Mrs. Hale," she said in her tight little way.

259 "I wish you'd seen Minnie Foster," was the answer, "when she wore a white dress with blue ribbons, and stood up there in the choir and sang."

260 The picture of that girl, the fact that she had lived neighbor to that girl for twenty years, and had let her die for lack of life, was suddenly more than she could bear.

261 "Oh, I *wish* I'd come over here once in a while!" she cried. "That was a crime! That was a crime! Who's going to punish that?"

262 "We mustn't take on," said Mrs. Peters, with a frightened look toward the stairs.

263 "I might 'a' *known* she needed help! I tell you, it's *queer*, Mrs. Peters. We live close together, and we live far apart. We all go through the same things—it's all just a different kind of the same thing! If it weren't—why do you and I *understand*? Why do we *know*—what we know this minute?"

264 She dashed her hand across her eyes. Then, seeing the jar of fruit on the table, she reached for it and choked out:

265 "If I was you I wouldn't *tell* her her fruit was gone! Tell her it *ain't*. Tell her it's all right—all of it. Here—take this in to prove it to her! She—she may never know whether it was broke or not."

266 She turned away.

267 Mrs. Peters reached out for the bottle of fruit as if she were glad to take it—as if touching a familiar thing, having something to do, could keep her from something else. She got up, looked about for something to wrap the fruit in, took a petticoat from the pile of clothes she had brought from the front room, and nervously started winding that round the bottle.

268 "My!" she began, in a high, false voice, "it's a good thing the men couldn't hear us! Getting all stirred up over a little thing like a—dead canary." She hurried over that. "As if that could have anything to do with—with—My, wouldn't they *laugh*?"

269 Footsteps were heard on the stairs.

270 "Maybe they would," muttered Mrs. Hale—"maybe they wouldn't."

271 "No, Peters," said the county attorney incisively; "it's all perfectly clear, except the reason for doing it. But you know juries when it comes to women. If there was some definite thing—something to show. Something to make a story about. A thing that would connect up with this clumsy way of doing it."

272 In a covert way Mrs. Hale looked at Mrs. Peters. Mrs. Peters was looking at her. Quickly they looked away from each other. The outer door opened and Mr. Hale came in.

273 "I've got the team round now," he said. "Pretty cold out there."

274 "I'm going to stay here awhile by myself," the county attorney suddenly announced. "You can send Frank out for me, can't you?" he asked the sheriff. "I want to go over everything. I'm not satisfied we can't do better."

275 Again, for one brief moment, the two women's eyes found one another.

276 The sheriff came up to the table.

277 "Did you want to see what Mrs. Peters was going to take in?"

278 The county attorney picked up the apron. He laughed.

279 "Oh, I guess they're not very dangerous things the ladies have picked out."

280   Mrs. Hale's hand was on the sewing basket in which the box was concealed. She felt that she ought to take her hand off the basket. She did not seem able to. He picked up one of the quilt blocks which she had piled on to cover the box. Her eyes felt like fire. She had a feeling that if he took up the basket she would snatch it from him.

281   But he did not take it up. With another little laugh, he turned away, saying:

282   "No; Mrs. Peters doesn't need supervising. For that matter, a sheriff's wife is married to the law. Ever think of it that way, Mrs. Peters?"

283   Mrs. Peters was standing beside the table. Mrs. Hale shot a look up at her, but she could not see her face. Mrs. Peters had turned away. When she spoke, her voice was muffled.

284   "Not—just that way," she said.

285   "Married to the law!" chuckled Mrs. Peters's husband. He moved toward the door into the front room, and said to the county attorney:

286   "I just want you to come in here a minute, George. We ought to take a look at these windows."

287   "Oh—windows," said the county attorney scoffingly.

288   "We'll be right out, Mr. Hale," said the sheriff to the farmer, who was still waiting by the door.

289   Hale went to look after the horses. The sheriff followed the county attorney into the other room. Again—for one final moment—the two women were alone in that kitchen.

290   Martha Hale sprang up, her hands tight together, looking at that other woman, with whom it rested. At first she could not see her eyes, for the sheriff's wife had not turned back since she turned away at that suggestion of being married to the law. But now Mrs. Hale made her turn back. Her eyes made her turn back. Slowly, unwillingly, Mrs. Peters turned her head until her eyes met the eyes of the other woman. There was a moment when they held each other in a steady, burning look in which there was no evasion nor flinching. Then Martha Hale's eyes pointed the way to the basket in which was hidden the thing that would make certain the conviction of the other woman—that woman who was not there and yet who had been there with them all through that hour.

291   For a moment Mrs. Peters did not move. And then she did it. With a rush forward, she threw back the quilt pieces, got the box, tried to put it in her handbag. It was too big. Desperately she opened it, started to take the bird out. But there she broke—she could not touch the bird. She stood there helpless, foolish.

292   There was the sound of a knob turning in the inner door. Martha Hale snatched the box from the sheriff's wife, and got it in the pocket of her big coat just as the sheriff and the county attorney came back into the kitchen.

293   "Well, Henry," said the county attorney facetiously, "at least we found out that she was not going to quilt it. She was going to—what is it you call it, ladies?"

294   Mrs. Hale's hand was against the pocket of her coat.

295   "We call it—knot it, Mr. Henderson."

CREDITS

This page constitutes an extension of the copyright page. We have made every effort to trace the ownership of all copyrighted material and to secure permission from copyright holders. In the event of any question arising as to the use of any material, we will be pleased to make the necessary corrections in future printings. Thanks are due to the following authors, publishers, and agents for permission to use the material indicated.

Readings

"The Ultimate in Diet Cults: Don't Eat Anything at All" from the Bay Area Institute. Reprinted with permission.

"A Bureaucrat's Guide to Chocolate Chip Cookies" by Susan E. Russ from the *Washington Post*, 1982.

"Our Youth Should Serve" by Steven Muller as appeared in *Newsweek*, July 10, 1978. Reprinted by permission of the author.

"Black Men in Public Space" first appeared in *Ms.* Magazine, 1986. Brent Staples writes editorials on politics and culture for *The New York Times* and is the author of the memoir *Parallel Time: Growing Up in Black and White*. Reprinted by permission of the author.

"Cinematic Riches in 'Millionaire'" by Ty Burr from the *Boston Globe*, November 21, 2008. Reprinted by permission.

"Designing an Effective Presentation." Reprinted by permission of the author.

"Four is not enough" by *USA Today* and "We like the 4-day week" by Gregory Schmidt from *USA Today*, November 17, 2008. Copyright © 2008. Reprinted with permission.

"Geraldo No Last Name" from *The House on Mango Street*. Copyright © 1984 by Sandra Cisneros. Published by Vintage Books, a division of Random House, Inc., and in hardcover by Alfred A. Knopf in 1994. Reprinted by permission of Susan Bergholz Literary Services, New York, NY and Lamy, NM. All rights reserved.

"Grant and Lee: A Study in Contrasts" by Bruce Catton. Copyright © U.S. Capitol Historical Society, all rights reserved. Reprinted with permission.

"Judging by the Cover" by Bonnie Gainley. Reprinted by permission.

"Perhaps the World Ends Here," from *The Woman Who Fell From the Sky*" by Joy Harjo. Copyright © 1994 by Joy Harjo. Used by permission of W. W. Norton & Company, Inc.

"Poem for an Inked Daughter" by Jane Wheeler. Reprinted by permission of the author.

"Salvation" from *The Big Sea* by Langston Hughes. Copyright © 1940 by Langston Hughes. Copyright renewed 1968 by Arna Bontemps and George Houston Bass. Reprinted by permission of Hill and Wang, a division of Farrar, Straus and Giroux, LLC.

"Shikata Ga Nai" from *Farewell to Manzanar* by James D. and Jeanne Wakatsuki Houston. Copyright © 1973 by James D. Houston. Reprinted by permission of Houghton Mifflin Harcourt Publishing Company. All rights reserved.

"So What's So Bad About Being So-So?" by Lisa Wilson Strick. First appeared in *Woman's Day* Magazine, April 14, 1984. Copyright © 1984 by Lisa Wilson Strick. Reprinted by permission of the author.

"Some Lessons from the Assembly Line" by Andrew Braaksma from *Newsweek*, My Turn, September 12, 2005, p. 17. All rights reserved. Reprinted by permission.

"Thank You" by Alex Haley from *Parade* Magazine, November 21, 1982. Copyright © 1982 Alex Haley. Initially published in Parade Magazine. All rights reserved.

"The Extendable Fork." Copyright © 1995 by Calvin Trillin. Reprinted by permission of Lescher & Lescher, Ltd. All rights reserved.

"The Myth of the Latin Woman: I Just Met a Girl Named Maria" by Judith Ortiz Cofer from *The Latin Deli: Prose and Poetry*. Reprinted by permission of The University of Georgia Press.

"The Picture of Health" by Kim Lute from *Newsweek*, December 1, 2008. Copyright © 2008. Reprinted by permission.

"The Road Not Taken" by Robert Frost © 1916, 1969 by Henry Holt and Company, Copyright 1944 by Robert Frost. Reprinted by permission of Henry Holt and Company, LLC.

"The Teacher Who Changed My Life" by Nicholas Gage from *Parade*, December 17, 1989. Reprinted with permission from Parade, Copyright © 1989, and permission from the author.

"To Bid the World Farewell" from *The American Way of Death* by Jessica Mitford. Reprinted by permission of The Estate of Jessica Mitford. Copyright © 1963, 1978 by Jessica Mitford, all rights reserved.

"Walking on the Moon" by David R. Scott from *National Geographic*, September 1973, Volume 144, No. 3.

"Cell Phones and Social Graces" by Charles Fisher. Used by permission of the author.

"Defining the SAT Downward" from *USA Today*, March 3, 2009, p. 8A. Reprinted by permission.

The Way to Rainy Mountain by N. Scott Momaday. Reprinted by permission of the University of New Mexico Press.

"Mystery!" by Nicholas Meyer as appeared in *TV Guide*, 1980. Reprinted by permission of the author.

Page 227 from Chapter 13 "The Horns of the Altar" from *Pilgrim At Tinker Creek* by Annie Dillard. Copyright © 1974 by Annie Dillard. Reprinted by permission of HarperCollins Publishers.

"What is Really in a Hot Dog?" from www .sixwise.com.

"38 Who Saw Murder and Didn't Call the Police" by Martin Gansberg from *The New York Times*, March 17, 1964. Copyright © 1964 The New York Times Co. Reprinted by permission.

"A Day at the Theme Park" by Bruce Cameron, published in the *Rocky Mountain News*, August 22, 1999, p. 15F. Reprinted with permission of the Rocky Mountain News.

"A Scientist: I Am the Enemy" by Ronald M. Kline, MD. Originally published in *Newsweek*, December 18, 1989. Dr. Kline is the Director of Pediatric Bone Marrow Transplantation. Reprinted by permission of the author.

"Beauty: When the Other Dancer is the Self" from *In Search of Our Mother's Gardens: Womanist Prose*, copyright © 1983 by Alice Walker, reprinted by permission of Harcourt, Inc. and David Hingham Associates.

"Crossing the Great Divide" by Peter Fish from *Sunset* Magazine, May 1998, pp. 24, 28. Reprinted by permission of Sunset Publishing Corp.

"Darkness at Noon" by Harold Krents from *The New York Times*, May 26, 1976. Copyright © 1976 The New York Times Co. Reprinted by permission.

"Don't Let Stereotypes Warp Your Judgments" by Robert L. Heilbroner, originally appeared in *Reader's Digest*. Robert Heilbroner is the author of many books, including his best known work, *The Worldly Philosophers*. Reprinted by permission of the author.

"I Have a Dream" by Martin Luther King, Jr. Reprinted by arrangement with the Estate of Martin Luther King, Jr., c/o Writers House as agent for the proprietor New York, NY. Copyright 1963 Dr. Martin Luther King Jr., copyright renewed 1991 Coretta Scott King.

"I Slalomly Swear" by Dave Barry as appeared in *San Diego Union Tribune*, February 4, 1989. Copyright © 1989. Reprinted by permission of Tribune Media Services.

"I'm Still Learning from My Mother" by Cliff Schneider from *Newsweek*, March 20, 2000. Copyright © 2000 Newsweek. All rights reserved. Reprinted by permission.

"Let's Celebrate Nerdiness" by Tom Rogers from *Newsweek*, December 11, 2000. Copyright © 2000 Newsweek. All rights reserved. Reprinted by permission.

"Mother Tongue" by Amy Tan. Copyright © 1990 by Amy Tan. First appeared in *Threepenny Review*. Reprinted by permission of the author and the Sandra Dijkstra Literary Agency.

"My Real Car" from *Mama Makes Up Her Mind and Other Dangers of Southern Living* by Bailey White, pp. 192–196. Copyright © 1993 by Bailey White. Reprinted by permission of Perseus Books Publishers, a member of Perseus Books, L.L.C.

"Once More to the Lake" from *One Man's Meat*, text copyright 1941 by E.B. White. Copyright renewed. Reprinted by permission of Tilbury House, Publishers, Gardiner, Maine and Allene White.

"Party Manners" by Richard Grossman, originally appeared in *Health* Magazine, June 1983. Copyright © 1983 by Richard Grossman. Reprinted by permission of the author.

"Preparing for the Job Interview: Know Thyself" by Katy Piotrowski. Reprinted by permission.

"The Jeaning of America" by Carin Quinn from *American Heritage*, April 1978. Copyright © 1978. Reprinted by permission of American Heritage.

"The Munchansen Mystery" by Don R. Lipsitt from *Psychology Today*, February 1983. Reprinted with permission from Psychology Today Magazine. Copyright © 1983 Sussex Publishers, Inc.

"The Plot Against the People" by Russell Baker from *The New York Times*, June 18, 1968. Copyright © 1968 The New York Times Co. Reprinted by permission.

"Those Winter Sundays". Copyright © 1966 by Robert Hayden, from *Collected Poems of Robert Hayden* by Robert Hayden, edited by Frederick Glaysher. Used by permission of Liveright Publishing Corporation.

"What Is Poverty?" by Jo Goodwin Parker in *America's Other Children: Public Schools Outside Suburbia* by George Henderson. Reprinted by permission of University of Oklahoma Press.

INDEX